MW01566820

MOSES

The Emancipator of Israel

**Bible Biography Series
Number Twelve**

John G. Butler

Copyright © 1996 by John G. Butler

Published by
LBC Publications
325 30th Avenue North
Clinton, Iowa 52732

Printed in the United States of America

ISBN 1-889773-12-3

First Printing 1996
Second Printing 1997
Third Printing 2000

INTRODUCTION

The Bible Biography Series is a series of twenty books written about Bible characters by John G. Butler. These books are expository studies of the Scripture. They are extensively organized and outlined, filled with Gospel lessons and practical applications of Scripture to every day life, written in easy to understand laymen's language, and theologically and morally they take a strong, old-fashioned, fundamentalist position which is increasingly unpopular but greatly needed in our day.

These books are very helpful to preachers in providing material for sermons and lessons on these Bible characters and texts. They will also be found to provide much instruction for the individual in his or her personal Bible study; and because of their organized structure, they are very adaptable to Sunday School classes and Bible study groups.

The twenty books of the Bible Biography Series consist of books on *Joseph, Jonah, Elijah, Elisha, Gideon, Samson, John the Baptist, Peter, Abraham, Lot, Paul, Moses, Joshua, Samuel, David, Nehemiah, Jacob, Hezekiah, Mordecai,* and *Ruth.*

The author, a native of Iowa, is a veteran, fundamentalist, Baptist preacher who has been teaching and preaching the Word of God for over forty years with nearly thirty-five years of pastoral experience in Ohio, Michigan, Illinois, and Iowa.

CONTENTS

PREFACE 11

I. SLAVERY IN EGYPT 13
(Exodus 1)
A. The Souls in Slavery
B. The Sovereign of Slavery
C. The Slaying in Slavery

II. SON OF DESTINY 36
(Exodus 2:1–10)
A. The Arrival of Moses
B. The Attitude About Moses
C. The Adoption of Moses

III. SEPARATION FROM PHARAOH 56
(Exodus 2:11–22, Hebrews 11:24–26, Acts 7:23–29)
A. The Refusals of Moses
B. The Reformation by Moses
C. The Refuge for Moses

IV. SHRUB ON FIRE...81
(Exodus 3:1–9)
A. The Manifestation of God
B. The Message From God

V. SUMMONED TO SERVICE 101
(Exodus 3:10–22)
A. The Command for Moses
B. The Concerns of Moses
C. The Communiqué for Moses

5

VI. SHRINKING FROM SERVICE..............................126
(Exodus 4:1–17)
A. The Skepticism of Moses
B. The Speech of Moses
C. The Substitute for Moses

VII. SUBMITTING TO SERVICE 147
(Exodus 4:18–31)
A. The Parting From Midian
B. The Problem of Neglect
C. The Pursuit of Duties

VIII. STIRRING UP PHARAOH 167
(Exodus 5)
A. The Request to Worship
B. The Reviling by Pharaoh
C. The Repining of Israel

IX. SUPPORT FROM GOD 189
(Exodus 6:1–13)
A. The Encouraging of Moses
B. The Expounding by Moses
C. The Exhorting for Moses

X. SNAKES AND RODS 211
(Exodus 6:14 – 7:13)
A. The Reviewing Before the Miracles
B. The Rendering of the Miracles
C. The Rejection of the Miracles

XI. SMITING OF EGYPT 231
(Exodus 7:14 – 10:29)
A. The Aim of the Plagues
B. The Analysis of the Plagues
C. The Artifice During the Plagues

XII.   SLAYING THE FIRSTBORN 290
(Exodus 11 – 12:36)
A. The Preliminaries to the Slaying
B. The Protection From the Slaying
C. The Products of the Slaying

XIII. STARTING TO CANAAN.....................................325
(Exodus 12:37 – 13:22)
A. The Moment of the Starting
B. The Multitude in the Starting
C. The Memorials in the Starting
D. The Movements in the Starting

XIV. SEA OF DELIVERANCE 348
(Exodus 14)
A. The Path to the Sea
B. The Peril at the Sea
C. The Pleas by the Sea
D. The Parting of the Sea

XV. SONG OF VICTORY...376
(Exodus 15:1–21)
A. The Prologue of the Song
B. The Praise in the Song
C. The Prophecies in the Song

XVI. SWEETENING BITTER WATER 392
(Exodus 15:22–27)
A. The Problems Before the Sweetening
B. The Particulars About the Sweetening
C. The Pathway After the Sweetening

XVII. SENDING THE MANNA 409
(Exodus 16)
A. The Murmuring About the Food
B. The Message About the Food

XVIII. SHORTAGE OF WATER 431
(Exodus 17:1–7)
A. The Occurrence of the Shortage
B. The Outrage Over the Shortage
C. The Overcoming of the Shortage

XIX. STRIFE WITH AMALEK 448
(Exodus 17:8–16)
A. The Making of the Strife
B. The Mastering of the Strife
C. The Memorials of the Strife

XX. SOJOURN OF JETHRO 468
(Exodus 18)
A. The Reunion of the Family
B. The Remonstrating About the Work

XXI. STATUTES FOR ISRAEL 490
(Exodus 19,20)
A. The Preparation for the Statutes
B. The Proclaiming of the Statutes

XXII. SANCTUARY OF GOD..517
(Exodus 25 – 31, 35 – 40)
A. The Plan for the Tabernacle
B. The Provisions for the Tabernacle
C. The Parts of the Tabernacle
D. The Priests for the Tabernacle

XXIII. SIN OF IDOLATRY 544
(Exodus 32)
A. The Character of the Sin
B. The Condemnation of the Sin
C. The Compassion for the Sinner

XXIV.   SPEAKING WITH GOD 566
        (Exodus 33)
        A. The Pronouncement in the Speaking
        B. The Place for the Speaking
        C. The Petitions in the Speaking

 XXV.   SECOND SINAI SESSION 593
        (Exodus 34)
        A. The Readying of Moses
        B. The Revelation for Moses
        C. The Repeating for Moses
        D. The Radiance of Moses

XXVI.   SERIES OF COMPLAINTS 621
        (Numbers 11)
        A. The Complaining by the Laggards
        B. The Complaining by the Lusters
        C. The Complaining by the Leader

XXVII. SHUTTING OUT MIRIAM....................................648
        (Numbers 12)
        A. The Criticism of Moses
        B. The Counsel From God
        C. The Curse on Sin

XXVIII. SPYING OF CANAAN 664
        (Numbers 13,14)
        A. The Record of the Spying
        B. The Report of the Spies
        C. The Response of the People
        D. The Reconciliation With God
        E. The Retribution From God
        F. The Revolt of the People

XXIX.   SEDITION OF KORAH..701
       (Numbers 16,17)
       A. The Confronting of Moses
       B. The Consuming by God
       C. The Confirming With Rods

XXX.   STRIKING THE ROCK 730
       (Numbers 20)
       A. The Shortage of Water
       B. The Supplying of Water
       C. The Sin About Water

XXXI. SERPENT OF BRASS 752
       (Numbers 21:4–9)
       A. The Conduct of the People
       B. The Curse on the People
       C. The Cure for the People

XXXII. SETTLEMENT OF GILEAD....................................768
       (Various texts)
       A. The Passing to Gilead
       B. The Possessing of Gilead
       C. The Protecting of Gilead
       D. The Partitioning of Gilead

XXXIII. SEPULCHER IN MOAB 797
       (Deuteronomy 34)
       A. The Showing for Moses
       B. The Succumbing of Moses
       C. The Successor for Moses
       D. The Superiority of Moses

QUOTATION SOURCES.......................................809

PREFACE

Moses, the great emancipator of Israel, is one of the most prominent character in the Old Testament. He is so prominent and important that the great contrast between the Testaments and between law and grace is often expressed in terms of Moses and Sinai and Christ and Calvary. This prominence of Moses in the Old Testament emphasizes that Moses was indeed a colossal figure, a great "man of God" (Deuteronomy 33:1). His obituary also bears out his greatness; for it says, "There arose not a prophet since in Israel like unto Moses, whom the LORD knew face to face" (Deuteronomy 34:10). His greatness is further emphasized by God Himself saying that Moses was a pattern for the coming Christ: "I will raise them up a Prophet [Christ] from among their brethren, *like unto thee*" (Deuteronomy 18:18).

Though a great giant in the faith, he was, however, a man like Elijah in that he "was a man subject to like passions as we are" (James 5:17). F. B. Meyer in emphasizing that truth said, "Moses was a man like other men; with great qualities that needed to be developed and improved; with flaws that veined the pure marble of his character; with deficiencies that had rendered him powerless but for the all-sufficient grace that he learned to appropriate." This truth about Moses is not stated to discredit Moses and water down his greatness. Rather, it is to encourage us that we, too, can by faith accomplish great things for God. Moses lived in our world and had the same struggles with the flesh as we do. But he won the victory. So can we.

Our study of Moses is limited mostly to the narrative of his life. There are some excursions into such things as the Tabernacle, the law, and some writings of Moses; but this is done only because of the significance they had to the narrative of Moses' life. These other subjects are so large and great that they form studies in themselves. Our study in this book, however, was to especially focus on the character of Moses; hence, the emphasis on the narrative of his life.

11

I.

SLAVERY IN EGYPT

EXODUS 1

THE GREAT NEED for the emancipating work of Moses is made very clear in the first chapter of Exodus. This chapter reports that Israel was under the bondage of an extremely cruel slavery in the land of Egypt. Their very existence was being threatened by the murderous oppression from the Egyptians. A deliverer was desperately needed. And as God always does, a deliverer was raised up by Him in due time to bring about the rescue of the children of Israel from their terrible slavery. That deliverer, the great emancipator of Israel, was Moses.

To help us appreciate the oppressive circumstances of Israel in Egypt and, therefore, their great need of deliverance, we will in this first chapter of our study on Moses look in detail at what the Bible says about Israel's condition in Egypt. It is not a pretty picture. Unfortunately, the picture is not unique. We can write chapters like Exodus 1 about every age of man. When man turns from God and serves his own base passions, he can become like a brute beast in his treatment of his fellow man. Though society be educated, sophisticated, and computerized, without God it can become a jungle in morals and manners.

In the study of this first chapter of Exodus, a chapter that serves as an introduction to the coming of Moses, we will consider the souls in slavery (vv. 1–7), the sovereign of slavery (vv. 8–14), and the slaying in slavery (vv. 15–22).

A. THE SOULS IN SLAVERY

Here we take a look at the Israelites, the people who will be emancipated by Moses. We learn of their presence, their productivity, and their pollution in Egypt.

1. Their Presence in Egypt

"Now these are the names of the children of Israel, who came into Egypt; every man and his household came with Jacob" (v. 1). We note three things about Israel's presence in Egypt: the reason for it, the region of it, and the ratification of it.

The reason for it. What is Israel doing in Egypt? Even a casual reader of the Bible knows the answer. The last quarter of the book of Genesis gives us the explanation for why Israel is in Egypt (for a detailed study of this section of Genesis, see the author's book on Joseph). Joseph, the favorite son of Jacob, was sold by his cruel brothers to slave traders. They took Joseph to Egypt and Joseph was sold into slavery there. He was the first of the Israelites to experience slavery in Egypt. But Joseph did not remain a slave. Though his slavery led to prison, one day he came out of the prison to be the number two ruler in Egypt and to save Egypt from being destroyed in a severe seven year famine. The famine brought Joseph's brothers to Egypt for food which eventually led to Jacob and all his family in Canaan moving to Egypt to be under the care of Joseph. What started out as a great tragedy ended up a great blessing. God is a Master at causing our dark circumstances to bring us great light.

The region of it. Joseph desired that his brethren dwell in Goshen, and he succeeded in obtaining orders from Pharaoh for his brethren to dwell there (Genesis 46:28 – 47:6). The region of Goshen was located on the eastern side of Egypt. It was a most fertile area of land, being watered by the delta of the Nile River. This made it a great place for Israel with all their flocks. It provided them land that was most helpful to their prospering and growing into a great nation. Israel settled there and remained in Egypt for some four hundred years before their emancipation under the leadership of Moses. God knows where to put us to provide for our specific needs at the time they are especially needed.

The ratification of it. Israel's presence in Egypt was under the approval of God (46:3). We need to make that clear, for generally a trip to Egypt by the patriarchs evidenced disobedience. Egypt spoke of the world. Full of paganism and materialism, its effect upon the character and spirituality of God's people was generally most negative. Egypt does not represent spiritual life but spiritual death. Abraham's trip to Egypt (Genesis 12:10–20), the first such trip by God's chosen people to Egypt, was an act of unbelief and resulted in lying and many other problems (such as the acquiring of Hagar, the Egyptian maid that plagued him all his life). Later in Israel's national history, their alliances with Egypt (Isaiah 30) and the emigration by some to Egypt (Jeremiah 43) evidenced their rejection of God and always cost them plenty. But there were exceptions when Israel's being in Egypt did not reflect disobedience. One case was that of Jacob and his family going to Egypt in Joseph's time. Another was when Joseph and Mary of the New Testament were ordered to take the Christ Child to Egypt for several years for protection from Herod (Matthew 2:13–15). Carnality would like to make the exception the rule, but spirituality knows better and does not go to Egypt unless there is a clear, unmistakable command from God. Such was the case in Jacob going to Egypt with his family and in Joseph taking Mary and the Christ Child to Egypt.

2. Their Productivity in Egypt

"And the children of Israel were fruitful, and increased abundantly, and multiplied, and waxed [became] exceedingly mighty; and the land was filled with them" (v. 7). The productivity of Israel in Egypt was the fulfillment of a promise which God had given Jacob when Jacob and his family were moving to Egypt. God promised Jacob, "I will *there* make of thee a great nation" (Genesis 46:3). The fulfillment of this promise gives us some good lessons about the fulfillment of all Divine promises.

15

We especially note the lessons concerning the place, problems, and patience involved in the fulfillment.

The place of fulfillment. "I will *there* make of thee a great nation" (Genesis 46:3). "There" was the place of fulfillment. "There" in Jacob's case meant Egypt. God's promise specified the place for its fulfillment. Had Jacob and his family not abode in Egypt as instructed, they would have missed the blessing of this fulfillment.

Not every place is the Divinely appointed place of blessing. It is, therefore, very important that we be in the particular place where God said the blessing would be if we expect to receive the promised blessing. We can see this truth in other incidences in Scripture as well as in the case of Jacob. As an example, the prophet Jeremiah was instructed to go to the potter's house to hear from God. Jeremiah was told, "*There* I will cause thee to hear my words" (Jeremiah 18:1). Had Jeremiah not gone to the potter's house as instructed, he would not have received the blessing of hearing God's Word.

Those who complain they are coming up short on the promised blessings of God are often those who are not careful about being "there" in the place of blessing. Promises are not apart from responsibilities. One of the great responsibilities is to be "there" in the appointed place of blessing. For those who have difficulty with knowing where "there" is (and many church people evidence they have much trouble here), we can give some help. As an example, "there" will be church on Sunday morning, not the beach or the lake or home watching TV or mowing the lawn.

"There" may not be where we necessarily want to go. But wherever God's "there" is, that is where the promised blessing will be; and it is, therefore, the best place for us to be. We need to be "there" no matter what our feelings.

The problems of fulfillment. As we noted at the start of this chapter, Exodus 1 records some of the great persecution problems which confronted Israel in Egypt which threatened to destroy them. Yet, in spite of these great persecution problems, the Israelites still grew and multiplied. God's promise proved, as always, to be stronger than man's problems. If God said He would make Israel a great nation in Egypt, He would do it in spite of the problems which slavery brought upon the Israelites. The devil really fights the promises of God, and at times the saints in viewing their current circumstances may wonder if God's promises will prevail. But have no fear. If God promised, God will fulfill! How encouraging this should be to God's people. If God can fulfill the promise of productivity for Israel amidst the opposition that abounded in Egypt, He can also fulfill His promises to us in spite of the opposition of our enemy who so discourages us at times by making our circumstances very negative.

The patience of fulfillment. This productivity of Israel did not occur overnight. It took several hundred years before they became a great people and nation. In fact, Israel was in Egypt for some four hundred years before they left the land as a nation. There were just seventy souls (v. 5) when they moved to Egypt—few compared to a nation. But year after year the number increased until finally they were a great people and nation.

The flesh is so impatient regarding God's promises. It wants total fulfillment of the promise moments after the promise is made. If the promise is not fulfilled quickly, it complains quickly. But the writer of Hebrews spoke the exhortation we so often need regarding God's promises. He said, "Ye have need of patience that, after ye have done the will of God, ye might receive the promise" (Hebrews 10:36). Having to wait for the fulfillment of the promise will test our faith, of course. But this gives us opportunity to strengthen our faith and to give greater proof of the sincerity of our faith. These are two things we indeed need a lot more of today. We need stronger faith in order to live more victoriously, to overcome temptation, and to serve faithfully. And we need greater proof of the sincerity of our faith

17

in order to have a better testimony to the world.

3. Their Pollution in Egypt

The Israelites did not maintain a strong stand in the faith in Egypt. Some, of course, stood true, such as the parents of Moses. But a great portion of Israel was polluted spiritually and morally. We learn of this pollution of the Israelites in Egypt by looking at several passages of Scripture outside of Exodus, specifically Joshua 24:14 and Ezekiel 20:6–8. In the Joshua text, Joshua told the Israelites after they had arrived in Canaan, "Put away the gods which your fathers served on the other side of the flood [the Euphrates], and in Egypt, and serve ye the LORD" (Joshua 24:14). The phrase, "and in Egypt," in this text reveals the fact that idolatry was practiced by the Israelites in Egypt. This fact is confirmed in the Ezekiel text in which God is reported as saying to Israel when they were about to leave Egypt, "Cast ye away every man the abominations of his eyes, and defile not yourselves with the idols of Egypt" (Ezekiel 20:7). Israel did not heed well what God said on that occasion, however; for the next verse in Ezekiel says, "But they rebelled against me, and would not hearken unto me; they did not every man cast away the abominations of their eyes, neither did they forsake the idols of Egypt" (Ezekiel 20:8). Israel's rebellion is hard to believe. You would think they would have been glad to do anything to get out of the hard bondage in Egypt, but sin had a grip on them. "The worship of the calf, the lusting of Kibroth-hataavah [Numbers 11:34], the outbreak of iniquity on the frontiers of Moab, all proved how deeply the taint of Egyptian idolatry and impurity had wrought" (F. B. Meyer). Israel not only needed to be taken out of Egypt, but Egypt needed to be taken out of Israel. Unfortunately, Israel was taken out of Egypt much easier and quicker than Egypt was taken out of Israel, though removing Israel from Egypt was no easy and quick task.

Egypt being a land of ease and luxury would encourage spiritual and moral decay in undisciplined souls. Goshen, which "is to this day considered the richest province of Egypt" (Edersheim), would especially provide ease and luxury, for the fertileness of the land and the warm climate prevailed there. "Beneath the seductive influences of the Egyptian climate . . . their character became greatly relaxed. The ideals of Abraham's monotheistic faith and strenuous hardihood grew dim and faint" (F. B. Meyer).

God had located Israel in a choice place in Egypt to make it conducive for them to prosper and grow. But like so many folk in every age, material advantages instead of being used to help one spiritually were used to degrade. In our land this condition prevails so obviously in our churches. Church members have nice houses, automobiles, clothes, many luxuries—all of which should give them more time and convenience and means for serving the Lord. But instead, these material advantages have often taken the members away from the Lord and His service. These folk are so busy spending their time and material gain on fleshly pleasures, that they have little time for God. This explains why many folk are off pleasure seeking on Sunday instead of being in church. It also explains why our churches are shot through with moral degradation. Divorce, children born out of wedlock, and moral scandals of numerous kinds permeate the membership of many churches. Material blessings and advantages are not wrong in themselves; but when they are used to pamper the flesh instead of promote the spirit, character will be destroyed. When this happens, God is forced to bring many and mighty afflictions upon folk in order to bring them back to Him even as He afflicted Israel in Egypt—which we will note much about in this chapter.

B. THE SOVEREIGN OF SLAVERY

"Now there arose a new king over Egypt" (v. 8). This statement indicates that more than just a different person became king; for the words "new king" indicate "a king who follows different principles of government from his predecessors" (Keil). Acts 7:18 speaks similarly when it describes the change as "another" king. "There are in the Greek two different words for 'another':

allos, which means 'another of the same kind'; *heteros*, which signifies 'another of a different kind.' It is the latter word which is used in Acts 7:18" (A. W. Pink). All of this tells us that this new king was not of the same dynasty that had ruled when Joseph was the number two ruler in Egypt. Some believe the new king was a foreigner who had conquered Egypt. But whoever he was or wherever he came from, the coming of this new king to the Egyptian throne signaled a big and hostile change in the policy of the Egyptian government towards Israel. We will examine this change of policy by noting the deficiency, deduction, and design of the sovereign.

1. The Deficiency of the Sovereign

The great deficiency of the new sovereign was in the fact that he "knew not Joseph" (v. 8). Though Joseph was such a great man, yet he was forgotten. How often mankind forgets the best and noblest of people and deeds. "Within seventeen years of Waterloo the Duke of Wellington [the victorious leader over Napoleon] was compelled to protect the windows of Apsley House with iron shutters" (F. B. Meyer). Solomon, in Ecclesiastes 9:14,15, also gives us an illustration of this failure of mankind. However, though man forgets noble deeds, those who serve the Lord can be comforted by the fact that "God is not unrighteous to forget your work and labor of love, which ye have shown toward his name" (Hebrews 6:10).

This deficiency of the king in not knowing about Joseph would bring about the ruin of Egypt. The king could know ten thousand other things, but it would not make up for his failure to know about Joseph. Where this king was raised and trained, the knowledge of Joseph was not honored or thought necessary to learn. This king was obviously trained in many ways about government or he would not be king. He knew how to gain control of a nation. He had political power. He would have respect by many. But his lack of knowing about Joseph would curse him and his nation.

This ignorance of the king about Joseph illustrates the peril of ignorance in spiritual matters. The prophet Hosea spoke of this peril when he said, "My people are destroyed for lack of knowledge" (Hosea 4:6). Israel lacked in spiritual knowledge in Hosea's day, and it ruined them. It ruined their character and brought Divine judgment upon them. They eventually went into captivity; and for several thousand years the Jews had no national status. All because they lacked in spiritual knowledge.

Times have not changed. The most important knowledge is spiritual. Specifically, we need to know Jesus Christ. As the failure to know Joseph resulted in the ruin of Egypt, so the failure to know Jesus Christ will result in the ruin of the soul which means eternal damnation for the soul in hell fire. You may be well learned in many areas; but if you do not know Jesus Christ, you will experience the worst fate a human can possibly experience. Yet, in spite of this fact, our land mocks and dishonors this spiritual knowledge today. You cannot teach about Jesus Christ and His Redemption in our public schools. You cannot teach from the Bible, the greatest book ever to come to mankind. You can learn many things in our public schools, but you will never learn the truth about Jesus Christ. And no ignorance is so great and so perilous. How deficient our education system is today because it will not teach about Christ and the Bible.

2. The Deduction of the Sovereign

"And he said unto his people, Behold, the people of the children of Israel are more and mightier than we. Come on, let us deal wisely with them, lest they multiply, and it come to pass, that, when war occurs, they join also unto our enemies, and fight against us, and so get them up out of the land" (vv. 9,10). Because the king knew not Joseph, he made some very unwarranted deductions concerning the Israelites. Summed up, he viewed Israel as a liability and not as an asset. He feared that in war they would side with the enemy (which would give the enemy an advantage in attacking Egypt), and he feared they were large enough in number to leave the land though Egypt opposed. But his fears not justified. His deduction that Israel

21

was "more and mightier than we" (v. 9) was hardly correct at this point in time. "The expression is no doubt an exaggerated one . . . the sort of exaggeration in which unprincipled persons indulge when they would justify themselves for taking an extreme and unusual course" (George Rawlinson).

This king is not the first nor the last ruler to view Israel in a negative way. A number of rulers and their nations have viewed Israel this way, and all have suffered as a result. God's promise concerning His people is, "I will bless them that bless thee, and curse him that curseth thee: and in thee shall all families of the earth be blessed" (Genesis 12:3). Beware of talk and national policy which is anti-Jew. It will destroy a nation. This does not mean, of course, that all that the Jews and the nation of Israel do is right. Rather, it exhorts an attitude towards the Jews that in national relationship is that of an ally, not an enemy; and in personal relationship is that of respect and honor, not ridicule and persecution. This attitude is mandated by God's Word.

When men do not know Jesus Christ, as the king did not know Joseph, they will have difficulty in discerning situations correctly and making proper deductions of them. What God calls good, they will call evil. What God condemns, they will commend and justify. What God forbids, they will require. And what God requires, they will forbid. Does not this explain the strange thinking that permeates our society. Our society forbids prayer in school but permits and encourages the favorable teaching of homosexuality to the students. Through environmental laws, we protect the eggs of animals; but at the same time we permit and promote abortion of humans. Furthermore, God's people, like Israel in Egypt, are being represented as dangerous to society. Liberals speak of conservative Christianity in terms of "dangerous" and "harmful." As Matthew Henry said, "It has been the policy of persecutors to represent God's Israel [God's people in general] as a dangerous people, hurtful to kings and provinces, not fit to be trusted, nay, not fit to be tolerated." Oh, how messed up the mind and judgment of man becomes when he is plagued by spiritual ignorance.

22

3. The Design of the Sovereign

"Let us deal wisely with them, lest they multiply, and it come to pass, that, when there falleth out any war, they join also unto our enemies, and fight against us, and so get them up out of the land. Therefore they did set over them taskmasters to afflict them with their burdens" (vv. 10,11). The design of the new king was to put Israel under such a severe slavery that it would keep them from multiplying and thus not be, as he feared, a threat to join up with Egypt's enemies or be strong enough in numbers to be able to leave the land though Egypt opposed it. We note the folly of the design, the foulness of the design, the failure in the design, and the feelings from the design.

The folly of the design. "Let us deal wisely with them" (v. 10) sounds so noble. But what the new king said and what he did were two different things. What he called "wisely" is called "subtilly" in Acts 7:19. "Subtilly" here means crafty. Dealing "craftily" is never true wisdom. But evil men are forever wrongly characterizing their evil actions as "wise" and "smart." As Matthew Henry said, "When men deal wickedly, it is common for them to imagine that they deal wisely." But the new king's actions were not wise. They were very foolish and stupid. They alienated the very people he ought to have sought as allies.

Men may think they are so smart to engage in some evil plan. They may think that through it they will gain much in possessions or prestige or power or pleasure. But when it violates the law of God, it will one day evidence itself as complete folly. Yet, men argue craftily against God's ways. Even professing believers become very clever in arguing against the will of God at times. With crafty arguments, they to try to justify divorcing their mates, decreasing their giving at church, skipping church services, cheating in business, and marrying the unsaved. But this is not wisdom. Rather, it is great folly; and time will prove it so. Their craftiness will turn on them and ruin them.

The foulness of the design. "They did set over them taskmasters to afflict them with their burdens" (v. 11). They made "the children of Israel to serve with rigor" (v. 13). The meaning of the word "rigor" in verse 13 summarizes the cruelness and purpose of the slavery. "The word translated 'rigor' is a very rare one. It is derived from a root which means 'to break in pieces, to crush.'" (Rawlinson). Israel's slavery was inhumane. They were treated in the same beastly manner as the war prisoners of the Nazis, communists, and other cruel peoples were treated. Under this cruel, forced labor, the Israelite slaves "built for Pharaoh treasure cities [storage cities for supplies for the army], Pithom and Raamses" (v. 11); and they worked "in all manner of service in the field" (v. 14). The work conditions were terrible, for "There is not such exhausting toil as that of working under the hot Egyptian sun . . . from sunrise to sunset, as forced laborers are generally required to do" (Rawlinson).

It is instructive to note that the slavery which was imposed upon the Israelites gives a good picture of the work of sin upon mankind. We see the work of sin in three ways here: sin enslaves, embitters, and extracts.

First, sin *enslaves*. The sin of the king of Egypt enslaved multitudes of Israelites. Sin ever enslaves. It does not bring freedom. Sin enslaves to evil and destructive habits. Sinners often think that godly people lack freedom to do as they please because the godly do not indulge in evil habits. But it is the sinner, not the godly, who lacks freedom.

Second, sin *embitters*. "They made their lives bitter" (v. 14). Sin does not make people happy. Sin advertises itself as that which brings great fun to one's life (beer advertisements especially emphasize this lie). It is true that sin does bring pleasure for a season (Hebrews 11:25). But that season is mighty short; and after it is over, bitterness sets in on a permanent basis unless one comes to Christ for cleansing from sin.

Third, sin *extracts*. When the taskmasters were done with the slaves each day, the slaves would have little strength left for anything else. Sin always takes the best from us. It extracts a great price. It bankrupts us morally and spiritually. It takes our energy, our time, our possessions, our character, our interests, our health, our happiness, and finally our soul. When church members allow sin to gain control of their lives, they no longer have much interest and time and energy and means by which to serve the Lord. Sin has extracted it all from them.

The failure in the design. "But the more they afflicted them, the more they multiplied and grew" (v. 12). Slavery failed to diminish the number of Israelites. Though the death rate among the Jews might increase through slavery, the birth rate increased even more. "The multiplication of Israel went on just in proportion to the amount of the oppression" (Keil). How this reflects the work of affliction. Affliction often looks to destroy us. But instead it builds us up. Afflictions are not pleasant experiences. They are bitter and painful. But God uses them to benefit us.

The affliction that came upon the Israelites through slavery in Egypt fulfilled another promise God made about His people in Egypt (Genesis 15:13). We noted earlier that God had promised that Israel would be fruitful and multiply to become a great people and nation in Egypt (Genesis 46:3). Now here we note God also promised them affliction in Egypt. We like the promises about fruitfulness, but we do not like the promises about affliction. But affliction and fruitfulness are not unrelated. Affliction brings fruitfulness; yea it is often necessary for fruitfulness. The Psalmist expresses some of the benefits of affliction when he says, "Before I was afflicted I went astray, but now have I kept thy word" (Psalm 119:67) and "It is good for me that I have been afflicted, that I might learn thy statues" (Psalm 119:71). How often God has to employ affliction as a disciplinary measure to cause people to finally turn from their wicked ways. All affliction is not chastisement for sin, of course; but a lot of it is. But whether it is for chastisement or not, it can benefit us much in our faith and character.

Israel's affliction would help them to improve in faith and character—something they greatly needed. We noted a bit earlier that Israel had become involved in heathen idolatry and its licentious practices while in Egypt. Affliction purifies and would, therefore, help Israel to clean up. It helped to get Egypt out of Israel as well as give Israel a desire to get out of Egypt. It would help them to turn to God. "In their affliction they will seek me early" (Hosea 5:15). Affliction would also toughen them for the rugged wilderness journey. Living in ease and luxury in Egypt would not fit them for the journey ahead. But affliction would correct that problem.

The feelings from the design. "And they were grieved because of the children of Israel" (v. 12). The Hebrew word translated "grieved" in our text means "to loathe, abhor, to be weary of; implying mingled chagrin and abhorrence" (William Wilson). These were most unhealthy feelings to have about the Jews. But when you mistreat anything, you will eventually come to abhor it. If you do not give God due honor, you will end up scorning God and loathing the things of God. If you do not honor your church, you will scorn it. This explains why many professing Christians have so little interest in church. Also, we would add here that when a husband and wife mistreat each other, they will discover their love for each other will diminish and their marriage will be imperiled. In our land we have mistreated so many things we ought to be honoring, and the results have been very ugly. We now loathe virtue, integrity, industry, religion, authority, and godliness because we have not honored these things. But on the other hand we give respect and honor to the vilest of practices because we refuse to take a strong stand against these evils.

C. THE SLAYING IN SLAVERY

Since the hard bondage which the Israelites had been put under had failed to stop their multiplication, the king of Egypt devised another murderous plan to eliminate the Jews—kill the male babies. He did not stop the savage slavery but simply added more cruelty to the slaves.

If the king of Egypt had his way, there would not have been

any people left for Moses to emancipate. But he was fighting God and would not win. You may be able to eliminate some other races, but you will never eliminate the Jews. God said through Jeremiah, "Though I make a full end of all nations to which I have scattered thee, yet will I not make a full end of thee" (Jeremiah 30:11). To emphasize the indestructibility of the Jews, God also gave through Jeremiah the impossible formula for eliminating the Jews: "Thus saith the LORD, who giveth the sun for a light by day, and the ordinances of the moon and of the stars for a light by night, who divideth the sea when its waves roar; The LORD of hosts is his name: If those ordinances depart from before me, saith the LORD, then the seed of Israel also shall cease from being a nation before me forever" (Jeremiah 31:35,36). The only way the king of Egypt will get rid of the Jews is to get rid of the universe—and that he cannot do! As Dean Inge of England said, "The Jew has stood at the graveside of every persecutor."

The plan to kill the male Jewish babies made infanticide the law of the land for the Jews. Does this not sound familiar? Yes, indeed. We do not call it infanticide; but we call it abortion or as the liberals prefer, "pro-choice." But it is no different—it is still murder, and God will judge it as murder. As did the king of Egypt, many countries today practice killing the innocent babe to control population. Abortion, not drowning, is the usual method of killing today. But like the drowning, abortion is so barbaric, so cruel, and so terribly unjust. We marvel that God's judgment has not descended in devastating ways on America already for our abortion practices. But it will! Egypt went many years before they suffered the Divine hand of judgment upon them. But it eventually came, and how heavy it was. If you think America will escape with light judgment, you have not read the Bible or history books.

In examining this slaying of the Jewish infants, we will note the orders for the slaying, the obstacles to the slaying, the obstinacy in the slaying, and the objectives in the slaying.

27

1. The Orders for the Slaying

"And the king of Egypt spoke to the Hebrew midwives . . . And he said, When ye do the office of a midwife to the Hebrew women, and see them upon the stools; if it be a son, then ye shall kill him: but if it be a daughter, then she shall live" (vv. 15,16). The order to slay the male Jewish babies involved betrayal and brutality.

Betrayal. The midwives' work was to assist women to have a successful birthing experience. Their work was to help preserve life. This was fundamental, basic. Yet, the Egyptian king ordered them to do just the opposite. Hence, the midwives were ordered to betray the trust that women had in them. The midwives were to pretend they were helping save life when, in fact, they were to trying to kill. How deplorable the orders—and they were government sanctioned.

Abortion is the same. It operates under gross deceit. First, the doctors who abort betray their medical oath to save life. They are suppose to be saving life, not killing it. However, abortion takes that which is living and kills it. That is completely contrary to the fundamental principle of being a physician. Second, women who come for abortion are told terrible lies. They are told that the abortion will not hurt physically, but how untrue! We have read testimony in which women have confessed that abortion hurt worse than the worst childbirth pain. Women are also told that abortion will not hurt them emotionally. That, too, is a great untruth. We have read testimony that informs us of the heavy guilt which comes upon the woman who has aborted her baby. It is a guilt which destroys all the joys of living. And the guilt hangs on forever. According to the testimony of those who have experienced an abortion, they have a tendency to size up the age of children who are in their presence and to especially focus on the child that is of the age their aborted one would have been if not aborted. Yes, abortion, like the infanticide in Egypt, is filled with great deceit.

Brutality. The cruelty of the proposed infanticide in Egypt is unthinkable to decent people. No one is so innocent as a new born child. Yet, without defense, the child is to be murdered. The midwife was to do whatever was necessary to kill the male child. Suffocation, unstopped bleeding, or a blow to the head could all be easily resorted to in order to quickly slay the child. And these things could be done in a manner that the mother would not know that the midwife was killing the child.

In our hardened day of abortion, many will not be repulsed in this brutal slaying of the new born Jewish boys. But sin is brutal whether the heart is hardened to it or not—and abortionists are indeed hardened to it. They are so hardened to their brutal, bloody, barbaric, and beastly practice that they can go on with their murdering day after day. However, if one of the abortionist people is shot down by a gun, suddenly the abortionist people become very compassionate and full of feeling and righteous indignation against the gunman's deed. But in this they are so grossly hypocritical! They are the last people in the world who have a right to complain about brutal death! Also, it needs to be noted that the gunman killed a murderer when he killed an abortionist, whereas the abortionists kill the innocent.

2. The Obstacles to the Slaying

"But the midwives . . . did not as the king of Egypt commanded them, but saved the men children alive" (v. 17). The king's carefully laid plans to slay the infants ran into a big obstacle—the midwives. We note the fear, failure, and favoring of the midwives.

Fear. The midwives "feared God" (v. 17). They may have also feared the cruel, wicked king. But they feared God more. The One they feared the most was the One who could kill the soul, not just the body (cp. Luke 12:4,5). And that fear purified their conduct! Because they "feared God," they "did not as the king of Egypt commanded them, but saved the men children alive" (v. 17). The fear of God will give man character, but the

29

fear of man will corrupt man. A big problem in the world today is that we have great fear of man but little fear of God. We are so concerned about what man thinks of us and what man will do to us that we adjust our conduct to try and please man even though that conduct may be grossly wicked. Those who fear God will adjust their conduct to please Him regardless of whether or not it pleases man.

Failure. When the king found out things were not going as he planned, he "called for the midwives, and said unto them, Why have ye done this thing, and have saved the men children alive? And the midwives said unto Pharaoh, Because the Hebrew women are not as the Egyptian women; for they are lively, and are delivered before the midwives come in unto them" (vv. 18,19). Though what the midwives said had some basis for truth, yet they lied, for their intention was to deceive the king. The midwives had refused to do what the king said to do; but when asked about it, they offered an excuse that was not true. The true reason why the male babies had not been killed was that the midwives had simply refused to kill them.

While the midwives refusal to obey the king's murderous decree is so very commendable, it does not justify their lying. Some may argue that if they had not lied, they would have lost their lives. Maybe so, but dishonest living is not better or more honorable than honest dying. Furthermore, do not discredit the results of telling the truth. Telling the king the truth may have so shamed the king that he would have changed his ways. And if the midwives had told the truth, what a great influence this would have had in promoting integrity in many people over the years.

We need to promote truth, not lying. Truth is not so weak that we must resort to lying at times to advance the cause of God. We have an obligation before God to be truthful. That obligation does not cease when our life is on the line. But, of course, it takes much spiritual strength to stand true at all times. The midwives were not as strong spiritually as they ought to have been. They, of course, did not have the spiritual advantages we do today. But that does not excuse their lying. It does, however, shame many saints of our day; for the midwives performed far better in the faith even with their failure than most saints perform today with all the spiritual advantages that are present in our land.

Favoring. "God dealt well with the midwives . . . And it came to pass, because the midwives feared God, that he made them houses" (vv. 20, 21). The midwives conduct brought them much favor from God. This favor was a faithful, family, and fitting reward for their not killing the Jewish male babies.

First, it was a *faithful* reward. God is faithful to always give due reward for our service to Him. Joseph Parker rightly said, "They who serve God serve a good Master . . . No honest man or woman can do a work for God without receiving a great reward." The midwives' failure regarding the truth did not prevent their reward. If God were to withhold reward until we were perfect, none would be rewarded. When the coach says, "Nice game," he is not justifying the player's mistakes. Later he will go over those mistakes. But the "nice game" compliment still stands. God never condones evil, but neither does He withhold due blessings. The blessing would have been greater, of course, had the midwives not lied.

Second, it was a *family* reward. The phrase "made them houses" (v. 21) means God gave them families. The blessing of families given the midwives was a great blessing, but it is would not be cherished much in our day, for families are not valued much in our time. But God values them, and the midwives valued them. Families are indeed choice blessings. They bring great strength to society, the nation, and the church. Weaken the family and you will weaken society, the nation, and the church.

Third, it was a *fitting* reward. The midwives being blessed with families reminds us that service done for God is often repaid in kind. These midwives had preserved families by their daring disobedience of the king's command, and God in turn gave them families. We sow and reap, and we reap what we sow not only in our evil conduct but also in our good conduct.

3. The Obstinacy in the Slaying

"And Pharaoh charged all his people, saying, Every son that is born ye shall cast into the river, and every daughter ye shall save alive" (v. 22). The king of Egypt is obstinate in wanting to kill off Israel. If one plan fails, he will adopt another. This new plan was a drowning, disheartening, and a demanding plan.

Drowning plan. Drowning the babies sounded so easy and efficient. Joseph Parker described it in a sanctified sarcastic way, as he is so skilled in doing, when he said, "Pharaoh did not charge the people to cut the sod, and lay the murdered children in the ground; the sight would have been unpleasant, the reminders would have been too numerous; he said, Throw the intruders into the river: there will be but a splash, a few bubbles on the surface, and the whole thing will be over. The river will carry no marks; will tell no stories; will sustain no tombstones; it will roll on as if its waters had never been divided by the hand of the murderer."

Abortionists are like this. While they do not throw their dead babies in the river, they do virtually the same thing when they throw them in trash containers lined with plastic bags. These bags are picked up by garbage trucks and then taken to landfills. There they are dumped in the deep ditches of the landfill and covered over with dirt. In due time the landfill is made like a green field. No tombstones, no markers. Just a nice green field. But God sees in the river, God sees under the surface of the landfill, God sees in the hearts, and God will judge! Men often think they can conceal their sins; but to the contrary, "Be sure your sin will find you out" (Numbers 32:23).

Disheartening plan. This plan had to be very disheartening to the Israelites. It made what normally would be a time of great rejoicing a time of great sorrow instead. How well this unhappy situation shows the vile work of evil. "The Divine gift [newborn child] becomes a trial through the wickedness of man. Sin turns blessings into curses, and joy into sorrow" (J. C. Gray). Few things are as delightful as the coming of a newborn into a family. Yet, in our society, many children are being born unwanted by their parents. Birth is unwelcomed; it brings no joy, only unhappiness. Abortion tries to solve the birth problem but only creates worse problems. Why this attitude about new babies? The answer is sin. Mankind cannot live a foul, immoral lifestyle and maintain the delights of childbirth.

Demanding plan. "And Pharaoh charged all his people" (v. 22). Drowning the male Jewish babies became the law of the land for all the people of Egypt, for they were commanded by the king to kill the innocent. How wicked an evil government can become. And, unfortunately, we are seeing this in our own nation today. When police officers are ordered to guard an abortion clinic so it can continue to operate, it is the government ordering men to help murder the innocent infants. The king of Egypt has nothing on our own government. Our government may be a bit more sophisticated in the way it kills the infants, but it does not change the vile character of the government or make the killing any less than brutal murder. In fact, abortion is more painful for the infant than a quick drowning in the Nile River. Any abortionist who is critical of the king of Egypt for ordering the drowning of babies is an extreme hypocrite.

When a nation stoops to ordering evil, it has stooped to a despicable and destructive low. And our nation is doing it more and more and in many ways. Abortion is not the only way our government forces citizens to do evil, to kill that which is good. Citizens are also forced to do evil by laws which favor homosexuality and gambling and alcohol and tobacco and atheists— laws that slay virtue. A nation either protects righteousness or evil. There is no middle ground. The laws of the land honor good or they honor evil. May God give us the courage to scorn and disobey all evil laws.

33

4. The Objectives in the Slaying

The immediate objective of the king of Egypt was to stop Israel from multiplying so they would not side with Egypt's enemy in fighting against Egypt and so they would not by their strength in numbers have the power to leave Egypt and head back to Canaan. In this objective, there are two primary objectives. These primary objectives are to stop the work of God and the Son of God.

Stopping the work of God. God had promised that Israel would go back to Canaan. Satan would endeavor to stop that plan. His business is to always oppose the work of God. He is often devious in doing it, however, so much so that the spiritually naïve frequently fail to see the devil working. But he is always masterminding the opposition to God's work. So it is when church troublemakers stir up trouble at church. The ultimate purpose of the troublemaking is to stop the work of God. But so many in the church are so spiritually undiscerning that they never catch on and see the real cause. They end up defending the troublemakers and condemning church officials who the troublemakers are attacking. These undiscerning folks never catch on that the reason the troublemakers are upset is that the work of God is being promoted by these church people and programs the troublemakers so ardently attack. All the complaints and fussings and threatenings are nothing but a smoke screen for the real goal of stopping God's work. The troublemakers may even disguise their complaints as concern for the work of God. But it is wolves in sheep's clothing.

Stopping the Son of God. Behind this attack upon the Jewish race, was the attack of Satan upon the Son of God. "It is not difficult to peer behind the scenes and behold one who was seeking to use Pharaoh as an instrument with which to accomplish his fiendish design. Surely we can discover here an outbreaking of the Serpent's enmity against the Seed of the woman. Suppose this effort had succeeded, what then? Why, the channel through which the promised Redeemer was to come had been destroyed. If all the male children of the Hebrews were destroyed there had been no David, and if no David, no David's son" (A. W. Pink).

We can follow this attack of Satan upon the Son of God all the way through the Scriptures. Satan tried to so corrupt the human race in Noah's time that Christ would not be able to come through the human race as promised. He tried to eliminate the Jewish race in Egypt. He tried to kill David through Saul to eliminate the line of David. He tried to kill Christ in Bethlehem through Herod's decree. In a number of incidences in the ministry of Christ, Satan tried to kill Christ before He reached the cross. Revelation 12 portrays it well when it tells of the great red dragon going after the male child born of the woman. But every attempt by Satan to eliminate the Son of God failed. God reigns supreme. The attack in Egypt will not succeed. The Jews will not be eliminated nor will the Son of God be stopped.

II.

SON OF DESTINY

EXODUS 2:1–10

NO ISRAELITE WHO was born in Egypt had a greater earthly destiny than did Moses. The birth of Moses began the life of the man whom God destined to lead the oppressed and enslaved Israelites out of bondage into the freedom of an independent nation. Moses' birth began the life of the man who was destined by God to bring about great destruction upon the land of Egypt. The land would be laid waste and Egypt's army and king would be destroyed. Significantly and incredibly all of this came about without a single military soldier lifting a sword or bow in attack upon Egypt. And this destruction of Egypt and the emancipation of Israel under Moses' leadership would put great fear in many nations for centuries. The birth of Moses also began the life of the man destined to be the greatest human spokesman for God that had ever been up to that time. The zenith of Moses' position as God's spokesman would occur at Sinai where God gave Moses so many significant revelations including the giving of the law. What a great destiny indeed was in store for the Jewish boy born amidst cruel oppression in Egypt.

To study the birth of Moses and the events surrounding it, we will consider the arrival of Moses (vv. 1,2), the attitude about Moses (vv. 3–9), and the adoption of Moses (vv. 6–10).

A. THE ARRIVAL OF MOSES

Though the Israelites did not know it at the time, the arrival of Moses on the scene in Egypt signaled that the days of Israel's emancipation were in sight. Their long oppression under Egyptian bondage was going to cease. God's promises were indeed going to be fulfilled. We will particularly note two aspects of his arrival: the time of his arrival and the tribe in his arrival.

1. The Time of His Arrival

Moses was born in a dangerous time but also in due time. The time that Moses was born is instructive and encouraging.

Dangerous time. When conditions had gotten to their very worst in Egypt for a Jewish boy to be born, "in which time [at that time] Moses was born" (Acts 7:20). After Scripture reports that the savage sovereign of Egypt had decreed that all male babies of the Israelites were to be thrown into the Nile River (1:22), it then begins the report of the birth of Moses. After painting the background as dark as could be, the Holy Spirit then focuses on the birth of Moses. After describing conditions that would make a successful birth of a Jewish boy more diffi- cult than ever before, Scripture then reports the successful birth of the great emancipator.

This timing of Moses' birth is so encouraging to our faith. It announces to us that God is still on the throne. It informs us that God is the Almighty, that He can defy the devil any time He pleases and succeed. It tells us that no circumstance is too great for God to overcome. It reminds us that we who would serve God, serve a great God!

The birth of Moses is not the only time in Scripture we wit- ness God defying the best that the devil has to offer. The most significant birth of all, the birth of Jesus Christ, also came at a most precarious time. It was when wicked Herod the Great ruled over Israel. He was a ruler who thought nothing of killing who- ever and whenever he desired. His decree to kill all the children two years and under in Bethlehem demonstrated his capricious and hellish brutality. Yet, it was "in the days of Herod the king" (Matthew 2:1) that Christ came to earth as a helpless infant in the care of two lowly peasants.

God loves to display His power when the enemy is at his

strongest. This demonstrates that God is all-powerful. When the enemy rages and becomes greater and greater in power, let us not lose faith. God has not lost control. He is simply waiting till the enemy reaches his peak of power, then God will move in and show how puny the enemies' strength is compared to God's power.

Due time. God had promised Abraham that Abraham's descendants would be afflicted for four hundred years (Genesis 15:13; Acts 7:6) in a land that was not their land, namely, Egypt. God does not fall asleep on the watch; He pays attention to what time it is. So at just the right time, Moses was born. Since Moses was eighty (Exodus 7:7) when he began his work as the emancipator of the Israelites from Egyptian bondage, God would bring Moses on the scene that amount of time before the emancipation began. We learn in the twelfth chapter of Exodus that the emancipation occurred "at the end of four hundred and thirty years, even [on] the selfsame day" (Exodus 12:41). God would not be one day tardy (the extra thirty years is easily accounted for in that it was not a time of affliction when the Israelites first came to Egypt).

The timing of the coming of Jesus Christ was also precisely the time appointed. "When the fulness of time was come, God sent forth his Son" (Galatians 4:4). The crucifixion of Christ likewise occurred at the appointed time, for "in due time Christ died for the ungodly" (Romans 5:6). The punctualness of Divine providence ought to inspire the punctualness of God's people. We expect and want God to be on time; therefore, we ought to act the same. It greatly dishonors God when we are tardy in performing our service for Him. It also promotes much trouble in our lives, for it delays and even forfeits many blessings. We need all the blessings we can obtain from God. To delay or forfeit them only spells problems for us.

2. The Tribe in His Arrival

"And there went a man of the house of Levi, and took to

wife a daughter of Levi. And the woman conceived, and bare a son" (vv. 1,2). We note two features about the tribe in which Moses was born. They are the obscurity and the odiousness of the tribe—both which Moses eventually changed.

Obscurity. Though the birth of Moses was more important than all the millions of births that had occurred among the Israelites in Egypt, his birth would attract little attention; for Moses was not born in a prominent family or tribe. And the obscurity is emphasized by the fact that the parents of Moses are not even named in our text. We learn later in Scripture (Exodus 6:20) that the father's name was Amram and the mother's name was Jochebed. We also learn later in Scripture (Ibid.) that Moses had an older brother named Aaron who was three years older than he (Exodus 7:7). Our text does reveals that Moses had a sister. Though she had an important part in our text, she, however, is not named until Exodus 15 and her exact age is never given in Scripture. But her actions in the text indicate she was at least twelve to fifteen at the time of Moses' birth.

The prominent tribes of the Israelites at this time were such tribes as Reuben, Judah, Joseph, and Benjamin. Reuben was the firstborn. The firstborn normally has considerable prominence in a family. Judah was a born leader. He was the mediator between his brothers and Joseph when the brothers finally learned of Joseph's identity in Egypt. Joseph was, of course, prominent because of the high position he had held in the Egyptian government. Benjamin would gain prominence from the standpoint of the special honor given him from Joseph. But Levi was just another tribe. However, obscurity is not a hindrance to being used of God. Gideon complained that he was "the least in my father's house" (Judges 6:15), but that did not stop God from using him. David was the last of eight sons and considered so insignificant that he was not even called to the gathering when Samuel came to look for a king among David's brothers. But anyone who reads Scripture at all knows how great David became. That which keeps us from effectively serving God is not our lack of fame, but our lack of faith. If God wants us to be known, He will take care of it in a very effective way (cp. Exodus 11:3; Joshua 3:7). We need not concern ourselves about our fame. Our concern needs to be about our faith. Take care of the faith part and God will take care of the fame part. God often causes obscure folk to be mighty in His service in order that He might better get the glory.

Odiousness. Moses was born in a tribe that until he came along was under a cloud. Ever since the shameful incident in Shechem at which time Jacob said to Levi (and also Simeon), "Ye have troubled me to make me to stink among the inhabitants of the land" (Genesis 34:30), the Levites were not a promising lot. When bestowing his patriarchal blessings upon his twelve sons before he died, Jacob only cursed Levi (again along with Simeon). "Instruments of cruelty are in their habitations. O my soul, come not thou into their secret; unto their assembly, mine honor, be not thou united . . . Cursed be their anger, for it was fierce; and their wrath, for it was cruel: I will divide them in Jacob, and scatter them in Israel" (Genesis 49:5–7). But the book of Exodus is about redemption, about emancipation from bondage—not just physical bondage, but also spiritual bondage. Therefore, it is only fitting that the great emancipator of Israel come from such a tribe. This pictures Jesus Christ, the greatest Deliverer of them all. He came to earth as a human and, therefore, was identified with sinful humanity in order to save them.

You may be from a family or situation that is branded with disgrace. Yet, you may be the one who through a gallant walk in the faith will remove that disgraceful brand and put a new brand upon the family or situation. Moses' life lifted the Levites from the curse of shame and disgrace to great honor. Has your life brought honor or shame to your family, your church, your neighborhood, and your country. It does one or the other.

B. THE ATTITUDE ABOUT MOSES
When the time came for Jochebed to give birth to her third

child, there would be great concern in the household about whether the new child would be a boy or girl. Pharaoh's murderous decree made any approaching birth among the Israelites a time of real soul searching. Unlike today, when we can know long before birth if the child is to be a boy or girl, they did not know what gender the child would be until it was born. When it was learned that the new baby was a boy, various attitudes revealed themselves. What was the attitude of Moses' parents about the new baby boy? Were they angry that he was a boy? Did they complain to God? Would they obey the king's command and throw the new baby boy in the Nile River to his death? Or would they endeavor to keep him alive?

The attitude which predominated with Moses' parents was faith. The writer of Hebrews leaves no doubt about this fact; for he says, "By faith Moses, when he was born, was hid three months of his parents" (Hebrews 11:23). Then after the three months when they "could not longer hide him" (Exodus 2:3), he was put in an "ark of bulrushes, and . . . laid . . . in the flags by the river's brink" (Ibid.) where he would be seen by the princess, the daughter of Pharaoh. The princess had compassion on him, hired Moses' mother to nurse him, and then received him into her royal house as her son. Through these actions, which came about because of the faith of Moses' parents, Moses' life was saved.

What great faith the parents of Moses had in God and His Word. This is the attitude which needs to govern all of us. It will help us meet great crises with victory instead of defeat. Faith is the greatest blessing and the greatest heritage we can give our children. So many think fame, fortune, and fun (we must get them into little league, take them frequently to circuses and zoos, and give them all sorts of toys, etc.) are the important things, but faith is the most important.

We want to examine the great faith of Moses' parents for our instruction. In doing so, we will note the presence, partnership, perception, priority, peace, protection, prudence, patience, and prize of their faith.

1. The Presence of Their Faith

Much of Israel in the land of Egypt was given up to idolatry as Ezekiel 20:6–8 reports. But not all Jews had apostatized. There were still some who walked "by faith." Among those who walked by faith were the parents of Moses. Though they were an obscure couple among the thousands of Israelites, yet they lived their faith steadfastly. Their personal circumstances did not cause them to give up hope. Though Amram would be one of those slaves who worked long, torturous hours everyday, yet he and Jochebed maintained their faith in God in such a good way that when a crisis confronted them, they conducted themselves most nobly.

It is possible to live the Christian life even though all others around you are living as pagans. It is possible to live the Christian life even though few others are living it. Away with the excuses men would offer to justify failure in the faith. You do not have to go along with the crowd. You can indeed live obediently for God in spite of a hostile environment. If Moses' parents could live "by faith" in the terrible situation they were in, how dare we excuse our failure to live by faith in our land. One of the lessons the Bible teaches plainly is that faith is not dependent upon favorable outward conditions. It depends upon the heart of the individual. You may try to excuse your failure in the faith by the fact that you had a bad bringing up or a bad religious background. Such an excuse is unacceptable, however. Others before you have had it a lot worse, yet they have grown greatly in the faith and have done mighty things for God. Lack of advantages does not excuse lack of faith nor limit achievements in faith. It is only your heart which will do that.

2. The Partnership of Their Faith

Both Amram and Jochebed lived "by faith." But because Amram is not reported in our text as helping save Moses, some writers talk about the faith of Moses' mother in such a way that it makes it appear that Moses' father was not walking by faith. But the book of Hebrews clears up any doubts about Moses'

42

father having faith when it speaks of the faith of "his parents" (Hebrews 11:23). Amram would not be able to do some of the things which are reported of Jochebed in our Exodus' text because he would be out working as a slave much of the time. But his faith was in concert with the faith of Jochebed. This marriage was one in the faith. It was not a mixed marriage. There was no conflict in their spiritual beliefs. They both followed Jehovah.

How much better would our homes be if there were always a partnership in the faith between husband and wife. Great works for God could be accomplished as was the case with Moses' parents in their care for Moses. But so many marriages are a mismatch in the faith. Couples often marry only for fleshly reasons. Few seem concerned about the faith. But nothing matters more in choosing a marriage partner. Choose a mate that knows the Lord and walks obediently with the Lord. Mixed marriages will curse. God forbids the marriage of a believer with an unbeliever (II Corinthians 6:14). Such a marriage will always have a division in the most important matter of life. It may not affect the material aspect of the believer's life, but it will greatly hinder the believer's service for God.

3. The Perception of Their Faith

"And when she [it is "they" in Hebrews 11:23] saw him that he was a goodly [beautiful] child, she ["his parents" in the Hebrews text] hid him three months" (v. 2). The account of Moses' birth as given in Acts illuminates on what was involved in perceiving this child as a "goodly" (or beautiful) child. Acts 7:20 says that when Moses was born, he was "exceeding fair." The Greek text states literally that he "was fair to God." This is something more than outward beauty. The eye of faith could see something special in Moses. Yes, he was obviously a cute baby outwardly, but there was more than human looks that made Moses special. There was the touch of God upon him. "God sometimes gives early earnests of his gifts, and manifests himself betimes in those for whom and by whom he designs to do great things. Thus he put an early strength into Samson (Judges 13:24,25), an early forwardness into Samuel (I Samuel 2:18), [and] wrought an early deliverance for David (I Samuel 17:37)" (Matthew Henry). Delitzsch said the very beauty of the child was "a peculiar token of divine approval, and a sign that God had some special design concerning him."

Faith can perceive much that the flesh will never perceive. Faith saw in Moses a very special child. The king of Egypt would only see someone to kill. Faith sees great and wonderful truths in the Word of God. The flesh thinks the Bible is a boring, antiquated book which has no application to our life. Faith sees the value of worship; flesh values pleasure above attendance at church. Faith sees the great importance of spiritual matters; the flesh thinks little of spiritual matters but mostly of material and physical matters. What a tragedy it would have been if Moses' parents had viewed Moses without the eye of faith.

4. The Priority of Their Faith

The parents of Moses had to make a choice when Moses was born. The decree of the king of Egypt said that Moses must die. The greatest Sovereign of them all had a different decree. Who would they obey? Scripture makes it plain whom they obeyed. They obeyed God. They ignored the command of the king of Egypt. Therefore, "Moses . . . was hid three months of [by] his parents" (Hebrews 11:23).

Hiding Moses demonstrated the priorities of Moses' parents. Faith decided the priority. The priority of faith is obedience to God. The greater the faith the greater the obedience. It would take great faith to defy the king of Egypt. Moses' parents were laying their lives on the line in hiding Moses. But faith counts obedience to God more important than life.

Faith makes the best citizens of a country, but that does not mean faith gives the laws of the land top priority. Peter made it clear whose laws are given the greatest priority by faith when he said, "We ought to obey God rather than man" (Acts 5:29). Not many saints in our day have demonstrated the priority of faith, however. Few would hide Moses today. These folk take no risky stand against evils in the land. They won't even fight sin in the church. They not only give priority to the laws of the land over God's laws, but they also give priority to material and physical interests over spiritual interests. Yet, they, unlike Moses' parents, have had tremendous spiritual advantages over the years that should have caused them to grow greatly in the faith and have better priorities.

5. The Peace of Their Faith

Moses' parents "were not afraid of the king's commandment" (Hebrews 11:23). Faith in God is a great remover of fear and, therefore, a great source of peace. The distraught and trembling soul will find peace when it walks by faith in God's Word. Peter was doing fine walking on the waters by faith; but when he ceased to walk by faith, his heart was filled by fear of his circumstances and he began to sink. Walking according to the way of God—which is what faith causes us to do—brings a tranquility that beats all the world can offer.

Many in Israel obeyed the king's commandment and "they cast out their young children, to the end they [the male babies] might not live" (Acts 7:19). Walking in heathen idolatry, they feared the king's command. This did not bring them peace but rather terror and tragedy and tears. They experienced the curses of idolatry rather than the calm which comes from faith in the true God. Many would mock Amram and Jochebed for their old-fashioned faith which most of the Israelites had forsaken in favor of Egyptian gods. But they could not mock or mimic the peace this dedicated couple had. Let the world scorn our faith, let them jeer in derision; but when you remember what you have through your faith, their sneers will not upset you. When the smoker, who is full of cancer and is coughing out every word, mocks folk for not smoking, hardly does the non-smoking person get upset who is in good health because he did not smoke. And heaven-bound saints should likewise not be upset when hell-bound sinners mock the faith.

6. The Protection of Their Faith

Faith gives great protection. Because of their faith, Moses' parents protected Moses from death. They hid him the first three months after his birth; then, as we shall see next, he was put in a water tight basket and placed in the Nile River where Pharaoh's daughter would see him and adopt him.

Faith not only protected the baby Moses, but even more important it is also the great protector of the soul. "By grace are ye saved [protected from eternal condemnation] through faith" (Ephesians 2:8). "Believe [faith] on the Lord Jesus Christ, and thou shalt be saved [protected from divine judgment]" (Acts 16:31). We spend a lot of money protecting ourselves physically and materially. This is not necessarily wrong although a good many folk spend far too much in these areas. But how few cultivate their faith in order to protect the most valuable blessings of life. The greatest protection we can give our children is faith in God and His Word. The greatest protection our nation can have is this same faith.

7. The Prudence of Their Faith

The man of faith is a wise man. Wisdom keeps company with true faith. Faith does not cause folk to play the fool in their daily lives. The unwise decisions and behavior of many saints evidences their lack of faith. Such conduct does not impress the world about our faith. Churches often do not evidence much wisdom either in their administration, buildings, finances, etc. The world sees this and is unimpressed with our faith.

The prudence of faith in the lives of Moses' parents is evident in everything they did regarding the baby Moses. We will especially note the wisdom of their faith in regards to the ark of bulrushes provided for Moses. We will see prudence in the plan for the ark, the placement of the ark, and the proffer by the ark.

The plan for the ark. "When she could not longer hide him, she took for him an ark of bulrushes" (v. 3). Children grow. After three months, a babe becomes more difficult to conceal than in the first few months after birth. So another crisis faced Moses' parents. But faith had the answer. The ark was the answer. We note the concept of the ark and the construction of the ark.

First, the *concept* of the ark. Male babies were to be thrown into the Nile River. Moses' parents would now conform to the order. However, the baby boy would be put in a basket when put in the Nile. That would thwart the intended purpose of the cruel king while still doing according to his law. It would still give priority to God's ways, not the king's way. The ark would keep the baby from immediately drowning and would provide opportunity for rescue. Faith is not naïve, stupid, or lacking in ingenuity. This concept, though simple, was still very clever; and it worked wonderfully.

Second, the *construction* of the ark. "She took for him an ark of bulrushes, and daubed it with slime and with pitch" (v. 3). The word translated "bulrushes" is "papyrus, the paper reed: a kind of rush which was very common in ancient Egypt, but has almost entirely disappeared . . . It had a triangular stalk about the thickness of a finger, which grew to the height of ten feet; and from this the lighter Nile boats were made, whilst the peeling of the plant was used for sails, mattresses, mats, sandals, and other articles, but chiefly for the preparation of paper" (Keil).

Moses' mother either purchased the basket or more likely made it herself. To make it, she would take the stalks of papyrus and weave them into a basket large enough for Moses. She also made a cover for it to keep the sun and bugs off of the baby Moses. Then to make it water tight, she covered it with slime and pitch. The word translated "slime" is also found in Genesis 11:3 and 14:10 and means "asphaltus, bitumen" (Wilson). The word translated "pitch" means "bitumen" (Ibid.). We would call both the slime and pitch by our word "tar." It would make excellence substance to waterproof the ark.

Covering the ark of bulrushes with slime and pitch reminds us of another ark (same word) which Noah made. It, too, was sealed both "within and without with pitch" (Genesis 6:14).

Both arks served to save people from death. In that work they are a picture of Christ, the Great Ark of safety, in Whom One finds eternal safety when he trusts in Him for salvation.

The placement of the ark. After building the ark, Moses' mother "Put the child therein; and she laid it in the flags by the river's brink [edge]" (v. 3). Wisdom is seen here in placing the ark where protection was and where the princess washed.

First, where *protection was.* The ark was placed among the "flags." The word "flags" is translated from a word which refers to "a smaller species of papyrus" (Edersheim). This was a smart place to place the ark, for the "flags" would protect the ark from drifting down stream with the current. It would keep the ark stationary in one place. It was such a simple act; but a very sagacious one, too. Faith is that way. We would like to see more of this common sense wisdom in our churches. The dumb actions seen in so many churches today reflect a great deficiency in faith.

Second, where the *princess washed.* As we will note in the next few verses, this location where the ark was placed meant the ark would catch the attention of the princess, the daughter of Pharaoh, when she came to wash in the river. Moses' parents knew where the princess came to bathe. They wanted her to see the ark and discover what was inside. They believed, and rightly so, that when she saw what was inside, she would have compassion. Faith used that knowledge to direct the place where the ark would be placed in the river. Again, the prudence of faith was great. Walking by faith enhances our wisdom.

The proffer by the ark. "And his sister stood afar off, to wit [know] what would be done to him . . . Then said his sister to Pharaoh's daughter, Shall I go and call to thee a nurse of the Hebrew women, that she may nurse the child for thee? And Pharaoh's daughter said to her, Go. And the maid went and called the child's mother" (vv. 4,7,8). The wisdom of faith shines forth brightly in the proffer of services Miriam made to the princess. We note her work in an inconspicuous watch and an instructed watch.

First, an *inconspicuous watch*. It was necessary that the watch be inconspicuous if the proffer was to be made with success. The watch was inconspicuous in two ways. First, it was inconspicuous in *who* stood the watch. Miriam was a much better choice than her mother. Young girls are not as significant in a situation like this as a mother would be. Here is a case which illustrates that obscurity can serve better at times than being well known. Second, it was inconspicuous in *where* the watch (Miriam) was located. Faith wisely had Miriam located at a good distance from the ark of bulrushes. She "stood afar off" (v. 4) from the ark. It would look much too suspicious if Miriam was standing right beside the ark. Her task was to watch that nothing went amiss with the ark and that it was indeed the princess and her group that would find the ark, not some other people. She could stand this watch at a discreet distance from the ark.

Second, an *instructed watch*. After the princess opened the ark and was moved deeply with womanly compassion for the babe, Miriam moved quickly to come to the princess and proffer her services to find a nurse. This proffer would be treated with respect for it was a great need of the princess. In those days they did not have milk formulas and bottles to feed babies. A babe must be nursed by a woman if they were going to survive their early years of life. Moses' mother, of course, would be very able to do that. Therefore, Miriam obviously was carefully instructed in what to say to the princess so that in the end Moses' mother would be obtained to nurse Moses. How wise was faith in its instructions to Miriam. Parents of faith will give wise instructions to their children.

8. The Patience of Their Faith

After Moses' mother had placed the ark in the river and set Miriam to stand watch, she left the scene and then waited. This had to be one of the hardest waiting times the mother of Moses ever experienced in her life. She could not stay to see the outcome, for that would ruin the plan. She must wait away from the scene, and she did.

There is the time between commitment and reward that really tests our faith. By faith Moses' mother committed that ark to the Nile River. Then she departed and waited. How the devil likes to visit us at this time. He sneers at our commitment and reminds us that we have given all but have nothing in return. However, faith is patient and believes that in due time the reward will be forthcoming. We demonstrate our faith in a great way when we continue to live obediently for God even though at the time we have not received the promises. The world wants everything right now. They cannot wait God's time. But they will never experience the blessed rescue from the Nile. They will not experience the dividends of completing the task. They will not know the rewards of virtue. They will miss all these blessings because of their fleshly impatience.

9. The Prize of Their Faith

"And the maid [Miriam] went and called the child's mother. And Pharaoh's daughter said unto her, Take this child away, and nurse it for me, and I will give thee thy wages. And the woman took the child, and nursed it" (vv. 8, 9). Scripture takes second place to no book in terms of exciting and dramatic plots and action. Though it is just a few sentences, our text relates action that is as stirring and thrilling as any you will find in other books. What an exciting plan and fulfillment. The mother of Moses is going to raise Moses for the next two or three years (the usual time before weaning)—and will be paid for it by the princess no less! The king's daughter will pay money from the king's treasury to defy his commandment! Incredible! But that is one of the great prizes the parents of Moses received for living by faith.

The rewards of faith are great and wonderful. Hebrews 11 lists a number of them. We will not collect all the prizes of faith in this life, of course; but we will collect enough of them in this life for them to be a good earnest for the great prizes of faith that we will collect in eternity.

C. THE ADOPTION OF MOSES

"And when she had opened it, she saw the child: and, behold, the babe wept. And she had compassion on him . . . And the child grew, and she brought him unto Pharaoh's daughter, and he became her son. And she called his name Moses: and she said, Because I drew him out of the water" (vv. 6,10). Moses became the adopted son of Pharaoh's daughter. We will note the passion for the adoption, the presumption in the adoption, the personalizing of the adoption, and the purpose of the adoption.

1. The Passion for the Adoption

"And when she had opened it [the ark], she saw the child: and, behold, the babe wept" (v. 6). The king of Egypt had ignored human compassion in his cruel edict to murder all the new born Jewish boys. But he could not control his daughter's innate, womanly compassion for a weeping infant. Pharaoh's daughter was no match for a beautiful baby greeting her with tears. "Frequently it pleases the Most High to magnify His providence by things which men despise, by feeble instruments, and this, that it may the more plainly appear the excellency of the power of Him" (Pink).

A weeping babe seems so helpless, yet this was so strong that it eventually resulted in bringing great destruction upon the evil land and the evil leadership of Egypt. The cruel Pharaohs of Egypt thought they were so smart, but God "taketh the wise in their own craftiness" (Job 5:13). Pharaoh's plan to destroy Israel boomeranged. It turned out to be the plan to do the very thing the king of Egypt was trying to keep from happening.

2. The Presumption in the Adoption

The adoption of Moses was not done like it is today. There was no permission obtained from the biological parents. Pharaoh's daughter simply took what she wanted. Yes, one could say the babe was forsaken because it was in the river. But knowing the king's cruel decree would make it obvious that the baby was not willfully forsaken. The princess simply presumed and took the child for her own. After all, who was going to stop her? She was the king's daughter, and the Hebrews would gain nothing by stopping her. Rather, trying to stop her could have brought death to the child.

Dictatorial power, however, has never been a problem for God. Christ put things in perspective in this matter when He was before Pilate. Pilate said to Christ, "Knowest thou not that I have power to crucify thee, and have power to release thee?" (John 19:10). Jesus answered, "Thou couldest have no power at all against me, except it were given thee from above" (John 19:11). Power is from God. Man often misuses it, but he never takes it away from God. The presumptive adoption by Pharaoh's daughter was all in the control of God. Therefore, it worked out well for God's people; for it saved the life of the one who was to be the great emancipator of the Jews. Furthermore, as we will see later, it also trained the great emancipator in the ways of the Egyptian government so he could deal with the government more effectively at the time of the exodus.

3. The Personalizing of the Adoption

"And she called his name Moses: and she said, Because I drew him out of the water" (v. 10). We name our own children. The princess personalizes her possession by giving the baby a name. While Moses' parents may have named him when he was born (we'd be surprised if they did not—tradition, according to Jamieson, says he was named Joachim), the name the princess gave him is the only name by which we know him. The name was a play on words, as the meaning given in Scripture indicates. It was a most appropriate name. Not only did it fit the circumstances in which she found Moses, but what the princess did not know and may never have known in her life time, was that "the person *drawn out* did become, in fact, the *drawer out*" (Kurtz quoted by Keil). God even controlled the naming of the child so that it is a fitting name for the work Moses did.

4. The Purpose of the Adoption

The purpose of the adoption was twofold. There was the human purpose and the heavenly purpose. One had to do with the princess and the other had to do with God.

Human purpose. The purpose of the adoption as far as the princess was concerned was to give her a son. "Philo [Judaeus Philo the Jewish philosopher of Alexandria of approximately 20 B.C. to 50 A.D.] reports, she, though long married, had no child of her own" (Matthew Poole). It has always been important for royalty to have children. Lack of children can mean the end of a dynasty. We are not told how close this adoption would make Moses to the throne, but it is easy to see that he was somewhere in line for the throne. Some believe he was indeed next in line for the throne. But whether he was next in line or a few down the list, he would be high up in royal rank. Quite a change from his lowly beginnings in an obscure slave family. Reminds us of Joseph going from slave to number two in the kingdom of Egypt some centuries before. God has no difficulty promoting His people though they may come from situations wholly lacking in promotion potential.

The princess certainly would not be disappointed in Moses (not until, of course, he at the age of forty forsook his Egyptian heritage); for not only was Moses a good looking child, but he also became "mighty in words and deeds" (Acts 7:20). If there had been any criticism of her adopting a Jewish boy, it would be effectively silenced by Moses' achievements. And achievements are exactly what the princess would want. All royalty wants their children to excel. But we will see next that the purpose of the princess in adopting Moses would become subservient to the purpose of God in Moses being in the royal household. God will have the final say.

Before we pass to the next point, we need to ponder the fact that Moses was a good steward of his opportunities. He did not let the royal privileges spoil him. He applied himself well to his studies and work. That is why he became "mighty in words and deeds." All the advantages in the world will not make up for lack of discipline. The poor performance of a good number is not because of lack of opportunity, but lack of discipline. Do not complain about lack of advantages; address your attention to dedication in using what advantages you have.

Heavenly purpose. God's purpose for having Moses in the royal household was to prepare Moses for future service for God. Being in the royal household, Moses received quite a training. "And Moses was learned in all the wisdom of the Egyptians" (Acts 7:22). Some of the wisdom of the Egyptians would be worthless, but not all of it. Moses would be trained in many practical things, such as the ways of Egyptian government, military strategy, and skills in communication. For a man who was going to later on deal much with the Egyptian government, lead Israel in battles against other nations, and write the first five books of the Bible, he needed to be trained and skilled in these important practical areas.

God is not in the habit of putting people in places of service without their being duly trained for the position. If the training is not something the person realizes is necessary or is something out of practical reach (such as Moses being trained in the palace), God will work out circumstances so the training is provided anyway. The most important training is spiritual, of course; and Moses received some of that in his own home before he went to the palace, and he received a lot more spiritual training later in the desert after his Egyptian training. But that does not negate the need of his Egyptian training. The spiritual training is simply more vital. However, there are those who would stop with the Egyptian training, and that will kill Christian service.

Preparation for service is so vital in God's work. Never underestimate it. We make a great mistake when we thrust brand new Christians into teaching in Sunday School or into other posts of service before they have much knowledge in the things of God. We also make a great mistake when we put people into important church offices for which they have little practical ability or sense in order to perform the duties of the office. Some church treasurers, as an example, have little knowledge or skill in the area of bookkeeping. And some of those employed as teachers in the Christian schools are wholly short on qualifications. No, we do not buy some of the worldly qualifications for teachers that are so objectionable to holy morals. What we are talking about here is the important and practical abilities to know how to teach, to know the subject, to know how to handle a classroom full of children. Preachers are often wholly unprepared, too. This especially shows up in the pulpit. Preachers seldom spend much time in preparing their messages, and this makes the pulpit very ineffective in instructing the congregation in spiritual matters. God, however, puts much emphasis on preparation for service. Therefore, we should do likewise.

III.

SEPARATION FROM PHARAOH

EXODUS 2:11–22; HEBREWS 11:24–26; ACTS 7:23–29

MOSES' DECISION TO separate from the house of Pharaoh would be stunning news in the land of Egypt. It reminds us of the time when King Edward of England stepped down from the throne although King Edward's decision certainly did not reflect the noble character and faith that was involved in Moses' case. Had Moses' day had our news media, the newspapers would have headlined this news in the boldest of print, and radio and TV would have made it the leading story for a number of days. People would have gasped in unbelief at Moses' decision. "The announcement would be, perhaps, met by bitter tears and hot indignation on the part of her to whom he owed so much . . . In how many circles it would be discussed, and what different interpretations would be placed on it! Some would attribute it to mortification or jealousy; others to the presence in his veins of base slave-blood; others to some scheme of ultimate self-aggrandizement. All would commiserate the princess, whose kindness seemed so rudely requited. But no one guessed the strength or purity of his hidden purpose, born of God, and nurtured by His Holy Spirit" (F. B. Meyer).

This separation from the house of Pharaoh was made when Moses was "forty years old" (Acts 7:23) and in the prime of his life. After being raised in his early years by his mother, he had been taken to the palace as the adopted son of Pharaoh's daughter. In the palace Moses excelled, as we noted in our previous chapter. He "was learned in all the wisdom of the Egyptians, and was mighty in words and in deeds" (Acts 7:22). He was well known and well respected. He brought much honor and esteem to the palace—something royalty craves and thrives upon. All of this only added to the shock, the incredibleness, and significance of the separation of Moses from the house of Pharaoh.

Did anyone besides Moses and God understand or appreciate the separation of Moses from Pharaoh's house? Heathenism could not comprehend the action of Moses—and the Egyptians and also many Israelites were given over to heathenism. If some did discern the wisdom of Moses' decision, they would be few in number; for few men even of the faith would have enough faith to do as Moses did. Natural man's thinking would have only encouraged Moses to stay in the palace and to use his influence there to help Israel. Natural man would think that "to abandon his high, honorable, and influential position, could only be regarded as the result of a misguided zeal which no sound judgment could approve . . . But faith thought differently; for nature and faith are always at issue. They cannot agree upon a single point. Nor is there anything, perhaps, in reference to which they differ so widely as what are commonly called 'openings of providence.' Nature will constantly regard such openings as warrants for self-indulgence; whereas faith will find in them opportunities for self-denial" (C. H. Mackintosh).

To examine the details of this instructive and inspiring separation of Moses from the house of Pharaoh, we will consider the refusals of Moses (Exodus 2:11; Hebrews 11:24–26), the reformation by Moses (Exodus 2:11–15; Acts 7:23–29), and the refuge for Moses (Exodus 2:15–22).

A. THE REFUSALS OF MOSES

"By faith Moses, when he was come to years, *refused* to be called the son of Pharaoh's daughter" (Hebrews 11:24). The separation of Moses from Pharaoh involved some very significant refusals on the part of Moses. To examine these refusals, we will look at the particulars of the refusals, the preferences in the refusals, and the prompting of the refusals.

1. The Particulars of the Refusals

Moses refused at least four significant things when he separated himself from the house of Pharaoh. He refused position, popularity, pleasures, and possessions.

He refused position. "Moses . . . refused to be called the son of Pharaoh's daughter" (Hebrews 11:24). To refuse to be any longer the son of Pharaoh's daughter was to refuse high position indeed in the land of Egypt. Some believe it even meant that Moses refused the throne. "Josephus tells us that Pharaoh had no other children, and that his daughter Thermutis [Moses' adopted mother], had no children of her own. So most probably Moses would have succeeded to the throne" (A. W. Pink). Whether he actually was in line to be the next Pharaoh or not, his position as the son of Pharaoh's daughter gave him very high position in the land; few if any would be above him. And his achievements would only enhance any position he had coming to him as the son of Pharaoh's daughter. But as high and mighty as the position was that was waiting for Moses, he refused it. He turned it down flat. He rejected it in total.

Worldly position is a very difficult gem to refuse. Men pay dearly to gain positions—and positions which are far inferior to that which Moses refused—for position has tremendous appeal to the flesh. But the nobility of Moses' character was very great. He could refuse the prized jewel of the flesh in the interest of the things of God. Few have been those who have done likewise. Offer them height and they throw character to the winds to obtain it. This explains why few men in high position have had much character.

He refused popularity. A man "mighty in words and deeds" (Acts 7:22) and having high position in the land will indeed be popular! Royalty and rulers bask in fame day and night. As an example, the royalty of England today, even though nothing more than national window dressing, is in the news so very frequently. They cannot go anywhere without reporters and photographers and a crowd following because they are most popular even if they behave poorly. The same is true of the rulers in our land. They are continually in the limelight. They are continually followed by the news media and by crowds. Add the great achievements of Moses to high position, and the popularity is even greater.

But Moses refused all of this. In doing this, he did something few would do. But his character was more noble than the character of most people. Popularity did not have priority with him. God did. He did not crave popularity with mankind, but he did want to find favor with God. Oh, that more men would be this way. Nothing will help character so much as having a greater desire for the favor and approval of God than of men.

He refused pleasures. "Choosing rather to suffer affliction with the people of God, than to enjoy the pleasures of sin for a season" (Hebrews 11:25). The palace in Egypt, as do all palaces and the White House and many other government headquarters and dwellings, provided unlimited fleshly pleasure. Much of the pleasures were licentious; but they were protected, of course, by the walls of the palace. So those in the palace could drink deeply of the pleasures of sin. Wine, women, and song were readily available in the palace anytime Moses wanted them. But he refused these illicit pleasures. Moses wisely saw that these pleasures, though great they may be, were only "for a season." And the season is short, especially when compared to eternity. Then when the season is over, the curse sets in. Moses was not spiritually and morally nearsighted. He could see beyond the temporal. He saw the future when sin's pleasures ceased to be pleasures but only pain.

How many in every age could wish they had the noble character and wisdom of Moses. They gave themselves to the pleasures of the flesh and drank deeply at the cistern of immoral passion. They did indeed find great delight in their pursuits—but only for a season. Then the curse destroyed them.

If you are ever going to amount to anything for God, you

will have to refuse much in the line of fleshly pleasure. The tempter will have licentious pleasure beckoning on every hand, and it will be accompanied by clever arguments and approval of those in high position (e.g. educators, government officials, etc.) which will encourage you to indulge to excess. But when you do, you will greatly limit or even completely eliminate your service for God. Moses would never have been the great emancipator he was had he not refused the pleasures of the palace. How many wrecks we see in society and in the church who have sacrificed Divine usefulness on the altar of worldly pleasure.

He refused possessions. "Esteeming the reproach of Christ greater riches than the treasures in Egypt" (Hebrews 11:26). Egypt's royalty was not poor. Every king would inherit his predecessor's wealth and would add to it during his reign by various means—mostly evil. "The treasures of Egypt" were waiting for Moses. These were great treasures. Even today archeologists continue to dig up evidences of the immense treasure the Egyptian royalty possessed. It was all waiting for Moses. But he refused it. He refused to weigh himself down with treasure that had a curse upon it, which was in great part obtained through oppression and evil, which would destroy the possessor of character, and which would have shorn him of blessings from God.

Wealth is not evil in itself. Some great Christians have been wealthy, such as Abraham. But not many have been wealthy. And few of the wealthy can say they gained their wealth in honest toil and business. So much wealth is gained evilly. And even if not gained evilly, it too often turns the heart to evil. Be careful about wealth. "Having food and raiment let us be therewith content. But they that will be rich fall into temptation and a snare, and into many foolish and hurtful lusts, which drown men in destruction and perdition" (I Timothy 6:8,9).

2. The Preferences in the Refusals

Here we look at the positives of Moses' refusals. We have noted four negatives of his refusals—worldly position, popularity, pleasures, and possessions. Now we note four positives of his refusal. They are the afflictions of righteousness, the association with God's people, the abuse of Christ, and the awards of heaven. He was making a choice between products. On one hand was the best Egypt had to offer, on the other hand was what God had to offer. To the natural eye, Egypt looked far better; but Moses wisely preferred God's products instead.

Afflictions of righteousness. "Choosing rather to suffer affliction with the people of God, than to enjoy the pleasures of sin for a season" (Hebrews 11:25). Moses preferred to do right and suffer as a result than to do wrong and experience much pleasure instead. Moses chose God, even though much pain would accompany the choice, rather than choosing Egypt with all its pleasures.

Most people understand that at times they must chose suffering if they are going to have the best of life. But they generally only see this in a physical and material sense, such as when an operation is required to improve one's health or much work is involved in getting worldly gain. Spiritually and morally the world just does not comprehend the need for suffering. Here they view pain to be evil and pleasure to always be good. But how foolish. What if Christ had not suffered on the cross for our sins? What great loss it would have been for the redeemed had He not endured pain. What pain have you preferred to pleasure? Your answer will reveal your character, and it will also reveal where you are spiritually.

Association with God's people. "Choosing rather to suffer affliction with the people of God" (Hebrews 11:25). Moses preferred to be with the Israelites than with the Egyptians no matter the cost. The reason for this was that the Israelites were the "people of God." They may not have been living like it, but the fact was they were God's chosen people, and Moses wanted to cast his lot with these people. Moses' race was obviously not concealed from him, for he knew they were "his brethren" (Exodus 2:11). And he was not ashamed of the fact that he was of the Jewish race, for they were the people of God.

We reveal what kind of character we have by the people we prefer to be with. Those who are truly God's people want to be identified with God's people. God's people may not be in a place of honor by the world, but that does not stop the godly from wanting to identify with God's people. They much prefer fellowship with the saints than with the world. Those who do not desire fellowship with the godly give away their true identity. Birds of a feather flock together. True saints seek the company of true saints, but hypocrites seek the company of the ungodly. The godly are not comfortable in fellowship with sinners. What company do you prefer?

Abuse of Christ. "Esteeming the reproach of Christ greater riches than the treasures of Egypt" (Hebrews 11:26). Moses knew about Christ. He did not know about Him as well as we do, of course; but He knew enough about Him to know he preferred Christ and His reproach to anything Egypt had to offer. "Reproach" in this text means verbal abuse, "insult" (R. Young), "defamation" (W. E. Vine), "contumely" (Strong). To follow Christ involves a great deal of reproach in any age. This is why few follow Him faithfully. We have plenty of fair-weather Christians who hold up the banner of Christ as long as reproach is not occurring. But as soon as the reproach shows up, the banner comes down, and they quit.

The fact that Christ is reproached by the world shows how sick the world is. Christ is very God, sinless, perfect, and the great Redeemer of mankind; yet, in every age, Christ and His followers are scorned and despised. How fatally foolish is the world. They adore that which curses, and they abuse and abhor that which blesses. Few have the noble wisdom of Moses to perceive that the reproach of Christ is better than any honor the world may give. And if the reproach of Christ is so blessed, how blessed will be the honor of Christ which one day will come to those Who follow Him.

Awards of heaven. "For he had respect unto the recompense of the reward" (Hebrews 11:26). Moses preferred God's rewards to anything man could give him. He "had respect" for the rewards of God, but he did not respect the rewards of man. He preferred to wait for spiritual rewards rather than have fleshly rewards now. What a noble perspective Moses had. How little of this we see in the world today. Even professing Christians evidence very little preference for spiritual blessings in contrast to physical and material blessings. Preach to them about the great spiritual awards waiting them in eternity for faithfully living for God, and they will yawn and tune out the message. But speak to them about physical and material awards in this life, and they are all ears. To increase their crowd, a number of churches have given themselves over to the material and physical emphasis in their preaching and program. But all this has done is fill the church with a carnal crowd—and that will not help any church do the work of God.

3. The Prompting of the Refusals

What was the fundamental motivation which prompted Moses' refusals? What was it that caused Moses to separate from Pharaoh? The answer is faith. "By *faith* Moses . . . refused" (Hebrews 11:24). Moses faith in God's Word was what prompted his refusals. We want to note the significance of one's motivation, the surprise of this motivation, and the superiority of this motivation in our considering what prompted these refusals by Moses.

The significance of one's motivation. It is very important to discover and know what prompted Moses to make the decisions he did, for it determines the character of his actions. That which motivates a man reveals his character. All of us are motivated by something in everything we do. Unfortunately, most people are motivated by base desires and appetites. Money, praise of man, earthly position, fleshly pleasure, and evil vengeance are some of the predominant motivations which control most people's actions. And these motivations reveal the greatness of the degradation that grips our society.

Motivation is especially important in determining how God assesses our actions. It determines Divine judgment or commendation. Some folk may outwardly appear to be serving the Lord, but God knows their heart's motivation and will judge accordingly regardless of how well they appear outwardly. What motivates you? If you want to pass muster with God, you had better be motivated by faith; for "without faith it is impossible to please him" (Hebrews 11:6).

The surprise of this motivation. One certainly would not expect a man who has been raised in the heathen palace of the Pharaoh of Egypt to be motivated by faith in the true God—and to be so strongly motivated by this faith that he would utterly forsake the palace and all its glitter and glory. That Moses possessed this faith, and that he possessed it in a great way tells us the importance of the home. In the few years in which Moses was in the presence of his mother while she was raising him for Pharaoh's daughter, Moses experienced the influence of a godly home. It left an imprint that the palace could not take away.

A godly home has a great impact upon people regarding the faith. The great lack of faith in our land today can be largely attributed to the decay of the home. No wonder Satan so attacks the home as is evident in the attack on the family in our society.

The superiority of this motivation. Faith is a much better motivation for our conduct than anything else. It will sustain us when other motivations will fail. Had Moses been prompted by a lesser motive such as pity, he would never have survived as Israel's emancipator. He would have given it up long before the task was completed.

The fact that many drop out of Christian service is indicative that many who enter Christian service are not being motivated primarily by faith. Some are moved by the emotion of the hour. Some by vain ideas of glory. Some are inspired to serve because their friends are serving. Some are moved by what they see as adventure in the service of the Lord. These motives get people pretty excited at times, and those around them may not detect readily that an inferior motive is moving these folk. But time will expose the inferior motive. However, if the motive is faith, you will see folk serving God in bad times as well as in good times. Faith is the superior motive. It submits to the Word of God and the will of God. It has much character which other motivations do not.

The motive of faith not only gives faithfulness in our lives, but it also is a great purifier of our conduct. Other motivations can and do corrupt. But faith fosters good character. Moses' refusals evidenced high character and holy wisdom. The world's motivations would not have made the decisions Moses made, for they do not encourage character.

B. THE REFORMATION BY MOSES

Separating from the house of Pharaoh and identifying himself with the Israelites involved more for Moses than just giving up royal privileges, advantages, and opportunities. It also involved his becoming the emancipator of Israel. And when the separation occurred, Moses attempted to commence the work of emancipation by trying to reform the conditions of the oppressed Israelites. But the attempted reform lasted only two days, and it accomplished little except to make it very plain that the time had not come for Moses to deliver the Israelites from Egypt.

In the study of this attempted reformation, we will note the revenging of the Egyptian, the rebuking of the Israelite, and the reacting of the king.

1. The Revenging of the Egyptian

The first act by Moses in this doomed reformation attempt was to attack and kill an Egyptian taskmaster who was smiting an Israelite slave. In the study of this unwarranted action, we will see both good and bad in the behavior of Moses as we note his compassion, calling, cruelty, and caution.

His compassion. "When Moses was grown . . . he went out unto his brethren, and looked on their burdens" (Exodus 2:11). There is something noble about the fact that Moses looked on the burdens of his people. Joseph Parker said, "Alas! Some of us can go up and down in society and never see the burdens which our brethren are called to bear." How true. We do not have compassion for those under heavy burdens. We are generally too self-centered and only see our own burdens and problems and needs. But Moses had his eyes on others—not in envy or for evil, but to alleviate their burdens.

As noble as this compassion of Moses was, it still was not justification enough for him to proceed in the emancipation attempt as he did. It is not difficult, however, for us to understand why the oppression of Israel would inspire Moses to his reformation attempt. Israel was under severe bondage, and anyone with any human compassion in him at all would be fired up in righteous indignation over Israel's condition. But *compassion* is not enough in God's work. One must also have a *command* from God to proceed before he acts. Moses had the compassion at this juncture in time, but he lacked the command from God to proceed. Moses had the *passion* to serve but not the *precept* to begin his service of emancipating the Israelites. The orders for that would not come until some forty more years had passed.

A number of folk, like Moses, have great difficulty in making passion subservient to the will of God. Normally we think of this problem of passion controlling us instead of the will of God as being associated with doing some evil deed such as being immoral. But this problem of passion is also seen in the service of the Lord. "If some touching tale is told, some piteous appeal made for help, or some crowded gathering swept by a wave of missionary enthusiasm, they are the first to yield to the impulse, to volunteer their service, to give their money, and fling themselves into the breach. But, after all, this is not the loftiest motive for Christian service, and it certainly is not the most permanent. After a little while it dies down, and leaves us stranded as by a receding tide" (F. B. Meyer).

His calling. Though the reformation attempt was not according to God's plan, Moses did indeed have a calling from God to be Israel's emancipator—and he knew it at the time of his attempted reformation. We learn of this fact in the account given in the book of Acts of this attempted reformation. "And when he was full forty years old, it came into his heart to visit his brethren the children of Israel" (Acts 7:23). B. H. Carroll asks, "The question now comes up: How did it come into Moses' heart to make that visit of inspection to his brethren?" The answer is found in Hebrews 11:24,25 where we are told that Moses acted by faith. Faith rests upon the Word of God. Therefore, "when he was forty years old, evidently a communication was made to him from God to this effect: 'You are to deliver this people Israel'" (Carroll).

Moses' problem in this reformation was not in lacking a call to be Israel's deliverer. He was not presumptuous in that he was trying to do something for which he was never called to do. His problem in this attempted emancipation of Israel from their burdens was in the area of timing, methods, and attitude. It was not God's time yet for the emancipation, the methods were not the strong arm methods Moses used, and the attitude he manifested was certainly not the right one either. We will see more on these problems shortly.

His cruelty. "And he spied an Egyptian smiting an Hebrew, one of his brethren. And he looked this way and that way, and when he saw that there was no man, he slew the Egyptian, and hid him in the sand" (Exodus 2:11,12). Moses saw injustice and responded, but he responded much too strongly. There is no question as to the injustice in the act he witnessed. We have been reading in Exodus of Israel's brutal slavery, a slavery that was intended to reduce the population of Israel. Taskmasters were terribly cruel and the "smiting" was unjustified. But Moses' response to this particular incident of injustice was still wrong. The punishment he inflicted upon the taskmaster was not in accordance with the taskmaster's crime. Death comes for murder. The taskmaster had not murdered the slave. Therefore, Moses' method of dealing with the injustice was wrong. As Joseph Parker said, "We applaud Moses, but it is his impulse rather than his method which is approved. Every man should burn with indignation when he sees oppression."

Methods are important. Those out of the will of God often use the wrong methods. In our churches we frequently endeavor to justify worldly methods on the basis of the objective. The worldly philosophy that the end justifies the means has no place in God's work, however; but many in our churches embrace this philosophy anyway. Moses was right in being upset about the unjust oppression. But he was wrong in killing the Egyptian. The same is true today about abortion. Some fanatics have shot and killed abortionists. It is true they have killed a murderer; and for those of us who are appalled at abortion, it is hard to be upset that a murderer has been eliminated from society. But that is not the method God gives us for eliminating abortionists.

His caution. "And he looked this way and that way, and when he saw that there was no man, he slew the Egyptian, and hid him in the sand" (Exodus 2:12). The cautious "looking this way and that way" before Moses took revenge and killed the Egyptian taskmaster reveals an attitude in Moses that definitely was not of faith. It is an attitude that is apprehensive of what man thinks. "Whenever we look around to shun a mortal's frown or catch his smile, we may rest assured there is something wrong; we are off the proper ground of divine service" (C. H. Mackintosh).

Frequently we are reminded of Moses' faulty attitude here in observing how Christians serve the Lord. They seem very anxious as to what man thinks. Often some pastors have their finger up in the air to see which way the wind of opinion at church is blowing before they take action lest they go against the will of the congregation. Others have their eyes so much on man that if they are not applauded or patted on the back enough or if they are criticized by others, they will quit serving. We will never do God's work well if we are looking this way and that way before we do anything. Those who truly serve God only look up to see if God approves.

2. The Rebuking of the Israelite

"And when he went out the second day, behold, two men of the Hebrews strove together; and he said to him that did the wrong, Wherefore smitest thou thy fellow? And he said, Who made thee a prince and a judge over us? Intendest thou to kill me, as thou didst kill the Egyptian? And Moses feared, and said, Surely this thing is known" (Exodus 2:13,14). What Moses did the second day of the two-day reformation attempt was lawful action. But it accomplished nothing in terms of a reformation. We will look at the scorning of his rebuking and the shock after his rebuking

The scorning of his rebuking. "And he said, Who made thee a prince and a judge over us? Intendest thou to kill me, as thou didst kill the Egyptian? (Exodus 2:13). The contempt expressed here by the wrong-doing Hebrew really condemns the wrong-doer—not Moses—though Moses' action the day before was out of order and wrong. "This forcible interference on behalf of his brethren could and should have aroused the thought in their minds that God would send them salvation through him. 'But they understood not' (Acts 7:25)" (Keil).

The reaction of the wrong-doer to his rebuke is typical of unrepenting sinners. Instead of receiving the rebuke humbly as he should have—for he was wrong—he railed on Moses. We note two ways in which he did this.

First, he challenged Moses' right to rebuke. One who will not acknowledge his wrong is ever doing this (which explains why church dissidents are ever challenging the pastor's authority). But "A man needs no great authority for the giving of a friendly reproof, it is an act of kindness; yet this man needs will interpret it an act of dominion, and represents his reprover as imperious and assuming" (Henry).

Second, the wrong-doer unjustifiably accused Moses of wanting to kill the wrong-doer. This is another typical reaction of an unrepenting sinner towards those who would rebuke or arrest him. He tries to make the rebuker as evil as possible and to focus on this supposed evil instead of on the evil of the criminal. This attitude is seen in our society in the attack in court by the criminals upon the arresting officer. Unfortunately, our society is so naïve morally and spiritually that they give honor to the criminal's attack.

All of this contempt for Moses revealed that Israel was not ready yet to be delivered from Egypt. They did not respect Moses; they did not want to forsake their own evils; and they did not view the evil of their oppression as serious enough. This is rather incredible, but we see attitudes like this all the time. The extermination of the Jews in Russia and Germany over the years did not bother a number of folk. In like manner, abortion is acceptable to many today. But man must be upset about evil if God is to do a great work on his behalf.

The shock after his rebuking. "And Moses feared, and said, Surely this thing is known" (Exodus 2:14). The shock Moses received after he had rebuked the wrong-doing Israelite was twofold. He had to be shocked about being rejected and about being revealed.

First, *the shock of being rejected.* Rejection would be a very shocking blow to Moses. "He had renounced his rights to the Egyptian throne because he was so convinced that his own people needed a deliverer, yet he was not recognized or received as their deliverer" (Theodore Epp). Moses "supposed his brethren would have understood how that God by his hand would deliver them; but they understood not" (Acts 7:25) and they treated him scornfully. Even when Moses came back to Israel forty years later in the will of God, his brethren still frequently despised him and complained bitterly about and at him at times.

This experience is not unique to Moses. No one experienced it more pronouncedly than Jesus Christ. And anyone who would serve Christ will also discover that the very ones he is trying to help will often despise him, intentionally misinterpret his actions, and rail on him. This shows how important it is that the servant of God act according to God's commands, not by whether or not people appreciate his service.

Second, *the shock of being revealed.* "Moses feared, and said, Surely this thing is known" (Exodus 2:14). Though he had "looked this way and that way" (Exodus 2:11) before he killed the Egyptian, Moses' deed was not concealed from all eyes. Moses had hoped no one would find out. But they did, and it was to Moses' shame that his deed was revealed.

How forcefully this shocking experience of Moses drives home the truth that "be sure your sin will find you out" (Numbers 32:23). We may try ever so hard to conceal the evil deed, but we will never conceal the evil from God, and if God knows, the whole world can be told.

3. The Reacting of the King

"Now when Pharaoh heard this thing, he sought to slay Moses. But Moses fled from the face of Pharaoh, and dwelt in the land of Midian" (Exodus 2:15). Moses' decision to separate from Pharaoh's house would stir up in Pharaoh much animosity towards Moses. However, the killing of the Egyptian taskmaster stirred up Pharaoh even more. It really enraged Pharaoh, for he wanted to kill Moses. It was not the murder, however, that upset Pharaoh so greatly. After all, murder was Pharaoh's business. What upset Pharaoh was that this action by Moses presented a threat to Pharaoh. For all Pharaoh knew, this action could instigate a great uprising among the Jews which would cause great trouble for Egypt and even threaten the stability of the throne. Matthew Poole said, "He sought to slay Moses; not out of zeal to punish a murderer, but to secure himself from so dangerous a person, probably supposing that this was the man foretold to be the scourge of Egypt, and the deliverer of Israel."

Years later when Moses was emancipating Israel according to God's will, the Pharaoh at that time was also most hostile towards Moses. But in contrast to this time, Moses stood un-flinching before him. But here Moses "fled from the face of Pharaoh" (Exodus 2:15). What a difference it makes when we are walking according to God's plan. It does not necessarily eliminate our enemies or their great animosity towards us, but it gives us boldness and Divine safety in the face of the evil.

C. THE REFUGE FOR MOSES

The failed reformation forced Moses to flee Egypt to find a re-fuge from Pharaoh's wrath. We will consider the country of the refuge, the chivalry in the refuge, the companions in the refuge, the charge in the refuge, and the compensations of the refuge.

1. The Country of the Refuge

"Moses fled from the face of Pharaoh, and dwelt in the land of Midian" (Exodus 2:15). In Moses' time the country of Midian was located generally to the south of Moab and down the east-ern side of the eastern gulf of the Red Sea. Later we will see Moses in the southern part of the Sinai peninsula, where Mount Horeb is, shepherding a flock belonging to the Midianites who became his in-laws. So the Midianite area also extended at that time into the southern part of the Sinai peninsula.

The location of Midian provided Moses much protection, for it was far enough away from Egypt in Moses' day to protect him from the king of Egypt. Furthermore, Pharaoh's anger and fears were probably alleviated by the knowledge that Moses was too far away to be of any effective influence upon the Israelites. Hence, Midian was an excellence refuge for Moses.

The Midianites were descendants of Abraham via Keturah (Genesis 25:2). Most references to the Midianites in Scripture are condemnatory of the Midianites' actions towards Israel. But this reference is an exception, for Moses found acceptance and a refuge with them. This encourages us that God can provide for His own in places and amongst people that natural men would think unlikely for the task. God provided food for Elijah by the unlikely means of ravens. Later He also provided for Elijah for several years through a poor widow. Christ provided money for the Temple tax in the unlikely way of the mouth of a fish that Peter caught. It is not the means of our supply that we need to focus on as much as it is the Master Who provides for us. Using unexpected means gives more glory to the Master Supplier.

2. The Chivalry in the Refuge

"Moses . . . sat down by a well. Now the priest of Midian had seven daughters; and they came and drew water, and filled the troughs to water their father's flock. And the shepherds came and drove them away; but Moses stood up and helped them, and watered their flock" (Exodus 2:15–17). Moses discovered in Midian, as all of us will in due time, that no matter where one goes there he will find injustice. On this side of heaven, there is no place where evil will not be found. Moses saw great injustice in Egypt, and now he sees injustice in Midian.

Moses' reaction to the injustice was to try to help those experiencing the injustice. He had done that in Egypt, howbeit unsuccessfully. But in Midian, he was most successful in helping those being treated unjustly. In his chivalry in Midian, we see in Moses the character to help, the convictions in helping, the consistency to help, the compulsion to help, the courage in helping, the capability to help, and the consequences of helping.

The character to help. "Moses stood up and helped them" (Exodus 2:17). The action here by Moses indicates that he was in character a helper, for he "helped" them. What a great person to have around. Many are not like that. When they show up on the scene, they hinder instead of help. They are obstructionists who impede progress rather than encourage it. They are takers, not givers. They are a burden, not a blessing. But Moses was a helper of those who were good. The church needs more helpers like that. We have too many of the other kind.

The convictions in helping. Moses "stood" and helped the shepherdesses. The word "stood" indicates more than the fact that Moses rose to his feet. It also indicates that Moses had convictions. He "stood" for fairness and kindness. Therefore, he stood against the evil shepherds who were being most unfair and unkind to the seven girls. These shepherds would wait until the seven girls had drawn enough water to fill the water troughs by the well, then they would drive away the girls' flock and let their own flocks drink of the water in the troughs. This meant the girls ended up drawing water for both their flock and the flocks of these rude shepherds. It was a dastardly deed by some mean men. But Moses had convictions about this evil and stood against it. We need more folk with holy convictions in our society if things are ever going to improve.

The consistency to help. After his attempted reformation failed in Egypt and after receiving such a despicable rebuff from his own brethren there, we would not have blamed Moses had he not intervened here to give help to the seven shepherdesses in watering their father's flock. Joseph Parker created an imagined bit of thinking that Moses would have been doing (that we all can easily identify with at times) if he had not been the gallant man that he was. "Never so long as I live will I interfere in another quarrel: I have had experience of two interpositions, and my heart is sad. When men are fighting again, I shall let them finish as they please; not one word will I say either on the one side or the other: from this day forth I shut my eyes in the presence of wrong, and hold my peace when righteousness is going to the wall." But Moses did not act that way. When he saw the injustice being done to the shepherdesses trying to water their flock, he "stood up and helped" (Exodus 2:17). The devil likes to discourage us as much as he can in our service for the Lord. But let us never quit because of being rejected in the past. We are obligated to duty regardless of how others respond to us.

The compulsion to help. The word "stood" in Exodus 2:17 means he "sprang to his feet" (Rawlinson). Moses was prompt to help. He had an inner compulsion that would not let him sit and watch injustice take place. Once he saw it, he immediately sprang into action. He came quickly to the aid of the girls. Had he been dilatory in helping, he would have given no help at all. But Moses was not a dilatory person. We will see this again and again in his life.

The courage in helping. Moses was outnumbered but this did not stop him from dealing with the shepherds who were being so cruel. These shepherds were bullies who knew they could push the girls around and get away with it. But Moses was a different story. They could not push him around. He boldly stood up against them. He was not timid. And his courage won the day.

In order to perform our duty successfully and serve the Lord faithfully, we will have to have much courage. Christianity is not a sissies' game. Joshua was told to "Be strong and of good courage" (Joshua 1:9). All saints must be this way if they are to live victoriously.

The capability to help. Moses had the ability to help the seven girls. After all he had been a man "mighty in words and in deeds" (Acts 7:22). Moses was not like some in church today who have the ability to help but will not. Some have money they could give which would greatly help the work of the church, but they refuse to give. Others have talents they could employ which would help the services, but they refuse to use them for God's glory. Others have cars with which they could provide rides for people to church, but they refuse to do so. Others have homes they could use to keep visiting speakers, but they prefer to live selfishly and to not be hospitable. Many churches today are filled with those who could help, but these churches still need much help because those who could help refuse to help. Moses, however, was of far better character. He had the ability and strength to help the shepherdesses, and he used that ability to stop the injustice. Beware if God has given you ability and you refuse to use it for His service.

The consequences of helping. Helping the girls eventually resulted in Moses being provided with both a job and a place to live—two things he greatly needed after leaving Egypt. This demonstrates that one of the best means for solving our own problems is to help other folk in their problems. Too often when problems come into our lives, we get so taken up with our own problems that we have little interest in anyone else's problems. That only makes matters worse, for selfishness never improves our situation or helps to solve our problems. But in our problems and trials let us endeavor to help others, and we will discover that it will be the best medicine to help our own problems. Joseph also illustrated this truth when he was in prison (Genesis 40). He had troubles a plenty from being terribly slandered and put in prison in Egypt where he had been sold as a slave. His troubles were enough to make a man sit down and continually mourn in self-pity. But Joseph did not do that. Instead, he endeavored to help the butler and baker who were in prison with him. This eventually led to is own release from prison and his subsequent elevation to high office in Egypt. Let us learn well from these unselfish actions of both Joseph and Moses.

3. The Companions in the Refuge

"And when they came to Reuel their father, he said, How is it that ye are come so soon today? And they said, An Egyptian delivered us out of the hand of the shepherds, and also drew water enough for us, and watered the flock. And he said unto his daughters, And where is he? Why is it that ye have left the man? Call him, that he may eat bread. And Moses was content to dwell with the man: and he gave Moses Zipporah his daughter. And she bare him a son, and he called his name Gershom; for he said, I have been stranger in a strange [foreign] land" (Exodus 2:18–22). As we just noted in the previous point, the episode at the well resulted in Moses being invited to dwell in the home of the father of the girls. Thus the people of this home became Moses' companions. Also a girl from this home became the wife of Moses, and our text reports the birth of their firstborn child.

76

The home was not a bad home to live in. It was not a heathen home full of idolatry. The name Reuel means "friend of God." This meaning along with his "priest of Midian" description and later incidences (Exodus 18 as an example) makes it evident that these folk were monotheistic ("el" at the end of the name Reuel means "Elohim" the generic name for God—such names as Bethel, Samuel, and Daniel end the same). The Hebrew name for Moses' father-in-law is translated "Reuel" in our Exodus' text but "Raguel" in Numbers 10:29. There is, however, no justification for two different renderings of this Hebrew word. Elsewhere, the KJV indicates that Moses' father-in-law was also called Jethro (Exodus 3 and 18). But the identity of Reuel with Jethro rests chiefly on the assumption that the Hebrew word translated "father-in-law," which is applied frequently to Jethro in Exodus 3 and 18, always means "father-in-law." However, the word simply means to be related to one by marriage. This word is translated "sons in law" in Genesis 19:14 and "husband" (applied to Moses) in Exodus 4:25 and 26. When the name Jethro is first mentioned (Exodus 3:1), it is forty years after Moses arrived in Midian in which time Moses' father-in-law would be much aged and probably dead. Jethro would then be the son who became the head of the family after his father died. But regardless of whether Jethro is a father-in-law or brother-in-law, the lessons from the text do not change. And it is the lessons that are the important things about the text. Critics may get excited at some uncertainties, but the uncertainties never have to do with important lessons and doctrine.

Moses would live with these people for some forty years before he would go back to Egypt to begin the work of emancipating the Israelites. Then he would still have some encounters with them as Exodus 18 and Numbers 10 indicates.

4. The Charge in the Refuge

Moses did not sit around twiddling his thumbs living off of welfare in Midian. He was given a charge, a job. He became employed as a shepherd (Exodus 3:1). He was put in charge of the flocks of his father-in-law. We will note in our next chapter that it was while he was shepherding the flock in Sinai in the vicinity of Mount Horeb that God came to him in the burning bush experience.

Moses being a shepherd shows him as a type of Christ. But this is not the only way in which Moses is a type of Christ. Hence, we will stop here and point out fifteen ways in which Moses has thus far in Scripture foreshadowed the Savior, Jesus Christ.

First, Moses was born in the Jewish race. Christ was also born in the Jewish race, for Mary was a Jew.

Second, Moses was born in a place of poverty. To emphasize the extent of the poverty, his parents were slaves. Christ was also born into a poor family. That they were poor is emphasized by the fact that when Joseph and Mary made the required offering in the Temple when Christ was circumcised, they offered two birds (Luke 2:24) instead of a lamb because the lamb was much more expensive. Leviticus says the offering was to be a lamb unless "she [the mother] be not able to bring a lamb, then she shall bring two turtles [turtledoves], or two young pigeons" (Leviticus 12:8).

Third, Moses was born during a time of oppression for Israel. Christ was born when Israel was under the iron hand of Roman oppression.

Fourth, Moses' birth gained the attention of the king of Egypt. This was accomplished through his daughter adopting Moses. Through the visit of the wise men, the birth of Christ gained the attention of Herod the king of Judea.

Fifth, Moses was subject to the murderous opposition of the king when he was born, for the command to drown all male babies was in force at the time of his birth. Christ came under the murderous decree of Herod the king when after learning of his birth, Herod ordered all children two years and under to be slain in Bethlehem where Christ was born.

Sixth, Moses was preserved in Egypt from the murderous decree of the king. Christ also was preserved in Egypt from the murderous decree of the king. He was taken to Egypt by Joseph and Mary under the command of God shortly after His birth to protect Him from wicked King Herod's murderous orders.

Seventh, Moses was adopted. Pharaoh's daughter adopted him shortly after he was born. When Christ was born, He also was adopted—by Joseph in His case.

Eighth, Moses had early knowledge of his mission long before the time came for him to fulfill it as is noted in Acts 7:23. Christ knew when He was young what His ministry was as is attested by His comments in Luke 2:49.

Ninth, Moses had compassion for his brethren as we have noted earlier in this chapter. Christ had compassion for His brethren which is expressed so well in Matthew 23:37.

Tenth, Moses became part of a royal family. Christ was born in the royal family of the line of David.

Eleventh, Moses was rejected by his brethren when he first tried to deliver them from their oppressors as we have noted already in this chapter. Christ was rejected by His brethren (John 1:11) in His first coming.

Twelfth, when Moses was rejected by his brethren, he took a Gentile bride—Zipporah the Midianite. When Christ was rejected by His brethren, He took a Gentile bride—the church.

Thirteenth, Moses was found sitting beside a well and there gave help to some women. Christ also was found sitting by a well (John 4) and there gave great help to a woman.

Fourteenth, Moses was a shepherd. Christ called Himself the "good shepherd" (John 10:14), and a whole chapter in the Bible (John 10) deals with the shepherd figure for Christ.

Fifteenth, Moses experienced a season of seclusion before he entered into his public ministry as Israel's deliverer. Christ lived a secluded life for some thirty years before He entered into His public ministry.

5. The Compensations of the Refuge

Moses' stay in Midian not only provided him protection, daily provisions, a place to live, a job, and a wife and family (all which we have noted earlier), but it also did much to ready Moses for being Israel's emancipator. The many years which Moses spent in Midian was not wasted time, though at the time Moses may have felt he was doing nothing but treading water. When Moses came to Midian, he had a Divine call to be Israel's emancipator, but he was not ready yet to deliver Israel when he came to Midian. However, the years at Midian accomplished much in preparing Moses for his great task. It helped to change his attitude. It gave him time to mature and to develop in grace and patience. The many years spent shepherding the flocks would do much to develop that superior meekness in Moses, and it would give him much quiet time to do some serious thinking and meditating and especially to do some communing with God. It would also help him to become well acquainted with the wilderness through which he must lead the Israelites for many years. Hence, the forty years at Midian was certainly not wasted time, but it was a time of valuable preparation for Moses for his task of emancipating Israel. We will note more on this in our next chapter.

We do not learn everything in a palace. Many great truths can be learned only in the pasture, in the obscure out-of-the-way places which the flesh so despises. God may stick you in a job or ministry in some forsaken and obscure desert place as Moses was stuck out in the desert of Sinai tending sheep, but do not complain. It will provide much training to serve Him if you will only let it.

IV.

SHRUB ON FIRE

EXODUS 3:1–9

WE NOW COME to the burning bush episode in the life of Moses. It is one of the most famous experiences of Moses. On this occasion the Sovereign of the universe reveals Himself in a most unusual way through a fire in a shrub in the Sinai desert. The burning bush episode signaled that the emancipation of the Israelites was now to begin.

The burning bush experience also marks a change in the character of the narrative in Exodus. "Hitherto the narrative has been studiously brief, stating only what was necessary to be known as preparatory to those events; but from this point Moses dwells minutely on the details" (F. C. Cook). These details relate some of the most significant history in the annals of the world. Yet, in spite of that fact, our public schools ignore it or give it little significance if they do make mention of it; or they ridicule it as nothing but fables. Such attitudes in our public schools regarding these extremely important Scriptural records only show how defective our public education system has become.

To examine this burning bush experience of Moses, we will consider the manifestation of God (vv. 1–4) and the message from God (vv. 5–9).

A. THE MANIFESTATION OF GOD

"And the angel of the LORD appeared unto him" (v. 2). How wonderful that God should manifest Himself so graciously to man. We will note six features that are involved in the manifestation of God here. They are the adjustments for the manifesta-

81

tion, the activity before the manifestation, the area for the manifestation, the angel in the manifestation, the agency for the manifestation, and the attentiveness to the manifestation.

1. The Adjustments for the Manifestation

The manifestation from God signaling that the emancipation of Israel was to begin came when the circumstances were ready for it. Prior to this time, circumstances were definitely not ready for the emancipation. The failed attempts by Moses to help the Israelites showed us that fact plainly. But things have changed during the forty years Moses was in Midian, and these changes permit the burning bush experience to take place. We will note three of the changes or adjustments that occurred in the forty years Moses was in Midian which paved the way for the deliverance of Israel from Egypt. They concern the monarch, the multitude, and Moses.

Monarch. "And it came to pass in the process of time, that the king of Egypt died" (2:23). The man who sought Moses' life was gone. "One of the obstacles in the way of Moses coming back to Egypt was removed" (Carroll). A new king was now on the throne. While the new king was still hostile towards Israel and, as we will see later, not very receptive to Moses, yet Moses could have an audience with him—something he could not have had with the previous king who sought to kill Moses (2:15). Those who would serve God can learn from this situation with the king. We may be anxious to serve in some area, but the time is not ready. People and situations which will greatly hinder our work have to be removed or changed. Hence, we need to seek the mind of God as to where and when our service is to occur so that circumstances are ready for our service.

We should not complain if we have to wait for circumstances to change before we can enter a place of service, for many others before us have had to wait. Even Christ had to wait several years in Egypt during the first few years of His incarnation until "Herod was dead" (Matthew 2:19). Then "the Lord

appeareth in a dream to Joseph [Mary's husband] in Egypt, Saying, Arise, and take the young child and his mother, and go into
the land of Israel: for they are dead which sought the young
child's [Christ] life" (Matthew 2:19,20). Instead of being upset
about waiting, we need to use the waiting period to better prepare ourselves for our coming service.

Multitude. The multitude we refer to is Israel. There had
been some most significant adjustments in their attitude which
made their emancipation from Egypt now feasible. In our last
chapter we noted how Israel was not ready for emancipation.
They rejected Moses as the emancipator and their general attitude about leaving Egypt was that they were not all that interested in leaving. But in the forty years Moses was in Midian, the
multitude of the Israelites had some great attitude changes. We
learn of this in the last few verses of Exodus 2. "And the children of Israel sighed by reason of the bondage, and they cried
[to God], and their cry came up unto God by reason of the
bondage" (v. 23, cp. Deuteronomy 26:6,7).

Until Israel began to earnestly cry out to God for deliverance, they were not ready for deliverance. Until the oppression
upset them enough to seek God's help, they were not ready for
His deliverance. You would think that they would have immediately cried out for help when the cruel slavery began and when
the murdering of the male babies began. But they did not. In
like manner, you would think the lost sinner would cry out to
God quickly because of the guilt and loss caused by sin. But this
is seldom the case. It often takes much time before the sinner
finally is overcome by the problems of sin and seeks deliverance
from his evil. And until the lost sinner cries out to God for
deliverance from his sins, he is not ready for salvation.

Moses. Great changes had also taken place in Moses. "After
forty years of monotonous pastoral life, affording abundant
opportunity for meditation and for spiritual communion with
God, and when he had attained to the great age of eighty years,

and the hot blood of youth had given place to the calm serenity of advanced life, God at last revealed Himself to Moses" (Rawlinson). Moses' attitude at eighty was far different than at forty. At forty he ventured out in the strength of his flesh to do a task that could never be done alone in the strength of the flesh but would require the great power of God to do. Now at eighty, after forty years in Midian, Moses no longer had confidence in his flesh. He sees himself as nothing, as a failure, helpless, and unworthy for God's service (we will see more about this attitude in our next chapter when we examine his objections to the call to emancipate Israel). But that is just where God wants him. He can now use him to do great things for God.

How often it is that God waits until we have come to the end of ourselves before He puts us into important places of service for Him. It is when we see ourselves as nothing that we are most serviceable to God. When we recognize the futility of our abilities and wisdom, then we will be of the mind to heed God's ways and orders as well as seek and rely upon His power and not our own. Many folk are of little use to God because they are not small enough. They think too highly of themselves and of their skills. They act as though God should to be glad and thankful they are available for His service. But it is when God has brought us down low to see that we are weak and nothing that we are ready for His service. It is when we wonder why God would even want to use us, that we are becoming fit for His service. Athletic coaches tell us that often it takes a humiliating defeat before some players will start heeding what the coaches have to say. This principle is true with many saints. It was certainly true with Moses. Before he was ready for God's service, he had to experience great defeat in Egypt, go through forty years of humble living in Midian, and come to the place where he felt he was most inadequate for God's service.

2. The Activity Before the Manifestation

"Now Moses kept the flock of Jethro his father in law, the priest of Midian" (v. 1). We note two aspects of Moses' activity when the manifestation came to him: the industriousness of his activity and the insignificance of his activity.

Industriousness. Moses was engaged in honorable work when the revelation from God came to him. He was not loafing or sitting around twiddling his thumbs in idleness. God "does not come with his revelations to day dreamers; they are left to build their castles in the air. They who despise common and daily work, on the pretext that they are fitted for something much better, will at last be thrown into the corner among the refuse" (D. Young). God's revelations "will encourage industry. The shepherds were keeping their flocks when they received the tidings of our Savior's birth. Satan loves to find us idle; God is well pleased when he finds us employed" (Matthew Henry).

Insignificance. Though Moses was commendably engaged in work, he was not in a position of fame or power when the revelation came from God. He was in the lowly position (in the world's eyes) of a shepherd of a flock—and it wasn't even his own flock which further emphasizes his lowly status. "His marriage [to Reuel's daughter] . . . and his long stay in the country do not seem to have brought him much external prosperity. He has not reached even the modest point of success in the eyes of a Midianite shepherd, viz. to have a flock of his own" (D. Young). This insignificance of Moses' job should encourage God's people, for it says you do not have to have some high and influential position in the world to be of service to God or to be called to some important work for God. Earthly position is not a qualification for God's service. But faith and character are. If you want to serve God, be more concerned about your faith and character than anything else.

3. The Area for the Manifestation

"He led the flock to the backside of the desert, and came to the mountain of God, even to Horeb" (v. 1). We will note the place, particulars, and prominence of Mount Horeb where

Moses received the revelation from God at the burning bush.

The place of Mount Horeb. The general area where Mount Horeb was located was the Sinai peninsula. The specific place on the Sinai peninsula where it was located was the southern end of the peninsula. In comparison to where Moses lived (in the home of his in-laws), it was called the "backside of the desert." To understand what is meant by the "backside," we need to know that in the Bible when directions are given, they are given with the understanding that a person is looking east. Therefore, in front or before a person is east, to the left of a person is north (cp. Genesis 14:15), to the right of a person is south, and in back of a person ("backside of the desert") is west. Therefore, the place where Moses was located (Mount Horeb) when this manifestation of God came to him was in the general direction of west from his Midianite dwelling place. This helps to explain why Moses, when he returned to Egypt from his father-in-law's home (where he had gone to bid farewell) shortly after this burning bush experience, passed through Horeb where he met up with Aaron who at the God's command had come from Egypt to meet Moses (Exodus 4:27).

The particulars of Mount Horeb. The Mount Horeb area was an especially good place to shepherd a flock at certain times of the year. Those of us raised in the rich farm lands of the fertile midwest think of the Sinai peninsula as a barren waste. But it was not all wilderness. Some parts of the peninsula, particularly the Mount Horeb area (Mount Horeb was the chain of mountains in the south, and Mount Sinai the main mountain of the chain), were good pasture lands. "In certain seasons of the year the best pasturage in the Sinaitic Peninsula is to be found on the slopes of the highest mountains" (Carroll). There "you will find the most fertile valleys, in which even fruit-trees grow. Water abounds in this district, consequently it is the resort of all the Bedouins when the lower countries are dried up" (Rosenmuller quoted by Keil). These facts about the Mount Horeb area help us not only to understand why Moses was shepherding his flock there, but also why a few years later Israel encamped there for some time. God knows where the best places for us are to provide for our needs. If we are careful to follow His leading, we will find that our needs will be adequately taken care of. Disobedience, on the other hand, will lead us into barren experiences even if the place is promising to the natural eye.

The prominence of Mount Horeb. This place has attained a prominence that few places in the world have attained. In our text, it is called in anticipation "the mountain of God." When Moses wrote this book, he would have already had the great spiritual experiences of this place and, therefore, the title "the mountain of God" was current, though it was not current when he met God in the burning bush. In this mount occurred some very significant events. There, of course, occurred the famous burning bush experience. There occurred the giving of the law, the most significant event in the history of Israel. There was revealed the details for building the Tabernacle which in so many ways foreshadowed Jesus Christ and man's redemption through Him. There is where the nation of Israel was given its constitution and was organized into an official nation by God. Also, Mount Horeb is where centuries later, a discouraged Elijah had a meeting with God and was renewed for service.

The true prominence and importance of any place will be found to be associated with spiritual events more than anything else. We have many places in this world that are quite famous today. Cities such as New York, Chicago, Washington D.C., Los Angeles, Moscow, London, Paris, and others are famous primarily because of worldly events and attractions—not because of spiritual events. But time will eventually obliterate worldly fame while spiritual fame rises to the top in prominence. Let us remember this truth in our own lives. So many things in life do not matter, but spiritual things always matter. May we not become so taken up with things that do not matter that we ignore that which matters the most.

4. The Angel in the Manifestation

"And the angel of the LORD appeared unto him" (v. 2). Many times "the angel of the LORD" manifestation of God occurs in the Old Testament. Some of those who experienced this manifestation are Hagar, Gideon, and Samson's parents. That these and others actually experienced a manifestation of God is evidenced by the fact that in verse 4 of our text "the angel of the LORD" is simply called "LORD." This word is the translation of the name we know as "Jehovah" which is the special name of God given Israel. Specifically the name refers to the second person of the Trinity, Jesus Christ; for the Jehovah of the Old Testament is the Jesus (the Savior) of the New Testament (see Isaiah 43:11).

How fitting that the orders to begin the emancipation of Israel should begin with a manifestation of the Redeemer. Delivering Israel from Egypt is in a number of ways a picture of the redemption of the sinner. It is Christ Who redeems, saves, and delivers from the bondage of sin. Any deliverance that does not include Jesus Christ is of secondary importance compared to the deliverance that He brings to mankind.

5. The Agency for the Manifestation

"The angel of the LORD appeared unto him in a flame of fire out of the midst of a bush" (v. 2). The agency for this Divine manifestation to Moses at Mount Horeb was twofold: the bush and the burning.

The bush. The word "bush" is translated from the Hebrew word "seneh." This word "is still the name of a thorny shrub, a species of acacia, common in the Sinaitic district" (Rawlinson). We note the character of the bush and the choosing of the bush.

First, the *character* of the bush. The bush was a thorny bush. The thorny character of the bush reminds us of three important facts.

It reminds us of the *curse* of sin. "Naturalists tell us that thorns are abortive branches, which if developed would bring forth leaves and fruit" (A. W. Pink). Sin curses mankind and leaves him fruitless in the area of good works. The curse of sin in Genesis fittingly includes "thorns, also and thistles [just another form of thorns]" (Genesis 3:18).

It reminds us of the *cry* of Israel and sinners in their bondage. Thorns hurt; and Israel's cries for help were because they hurt from the cruel, thorny treatment by the Egyptians. In like manner, the bondage of sin causes the sinner to eventually cry out in pain. Paul knew what this painful pricking of sin was all about; for when he met the Savior on the road to Damascus, Christ said to him, "It is hard for thee to kick against the pricks" (Acts 9:5).

It reminds us of the *crown* of Christ. In His crucifixion Christ had a crown of thorns put on His head (John 19:2) as He being our substitute experienced the painful pricking of the curse of sin.

Second, the *choosing* of the bush. God did not choose some majestic tree or other means by which He would manifest Himself to Moses; but He chose a lowly, thorny bush. Does this not speak to us of the incarnation of Jesus Christ which was necessary for the greatest deliverance of all? "This humble bush, which possessed neither beauty not comeliness, became, temporarily, the abode of Jehovah" (Pink). In like manner, in the Incarnation, Jesus Christ came to earth in the "likeness of man" (Philippians 2:7); and Isaiah said in prophesying this, "He hath no form nor comeliness; and when we shall see him, there is no beauty that we should desire him" (Isaiah 53:2).

God choosing a bush for a Divine manifestation can also instruct us that it is not how great we may be in the eyes of the world but how surrendered we are to God that determines our usefulness in His service. We may feel that we are nothing but a thorny and insignificant bush in the desert; but if we are surrendered to God, we can be used wonderfully by Him to show others about Him.

The burning. The bush was on fire. Two things can be said

about the fire and its meaning: the preservation in the fire and the revelation in the fire.

First, the *preservation* in the fire. The significance of the fire in the bush was that though it was on fire, "the bush was not consumed" (v. 2). There was preservation in the conflagration. This phenomena caused Moses to take note. "And Moses said, I will now turn aside, and see this great sight, why the bush is not burnt" (v. 3). There are many applications to this phenomena of preservation. We note a few here as follows:

It pictures Israel's preservation in Egypt. Burned with great affliction, yet Israel was not destroyed.

It pictures Israel in history. Often, like the three Hebrew children (Daniel 3), Israel has been in the furnace of persecution but never consumed.

It pictures the preservation of the saints in their daily trials. Paul described it well when he said, "We are troubled on every side, yet not distressed; we are perplexed, but not in despair; persecuted, but not forsaken; cast down, but not destroyed" (II Corinthians 4:8,9). God allows the fiery trials to come oftentimes; but though great the fire, He can keep us from being consumed in it.

It pictures Jesus Christ Who was put in the furnace of the crucifixion, but death did not consume Him, for He arose triumphantly from the grave!

It pictures the chastisement God often has to bring upon His own. Though the chastening looks to destroy us, it will not destroy us (Hebrews 12:11) but only help to burn out the dross of our disobedient lives.

It pictures the history of the Bible. How often it has been burned by men, but it has never been consumed, for "my words shall not pass away" (Mark 13:31).

The burning but not consuming also pictures the great Gospel truth that man, because of Jesus Christ, can come into contact with a holy God and not be destroyed in judgment. "Fire in Scripture is uniformly the emblem of Divine judgment, that is, of God's holiness in active opposition against evil. The final word on the subject is, 'Our God is a consuming fire' (Heb. 12:29). Here, then is the deeper mystery: How can God, who is 'a consuming fire'—burning up all that is contrary to His holy nature—reveal Himself without consuming? Or, to put it in another form: How can He who is 'of purer eyes than to behold evil and canst not look on iniquity' (Hab. 1:13) have to do with men, other than in judgment! Nothing but the Gospel contains any real solution to this problem" (Pink).

Second, the *revelation* in the fire. The fire spoke of the presence of God—which was the foundational purpose of the flame in the bush that day. "All nations have seen in fire something emblematic of the Divine nature" (Rawlinson). "Throughout Scripture, fire is the emblem of Deity. Even the rites of heathendom were based on the belief that the swift power and ruddy tongues of fire were symbols of Divine attributes. When God entered into covenant with Abram, His Presence was denoted by the lamp of fire that passed between the pieces. The pledge of God's leadership of Israel was the pillar which in the daylight seemed only a column of wavering smoke, but when darkness fell was shown to be composed of flame—a veritable fire-cloud . . . The mission of our Lord was a Baptism of Fire; and on the Day of Pentecost the Holy Spirit's chosen symbol was the fire that sat on each meekly bowed head. In the Apocalyptic Vision seven lamps of fire are seen burning perpetually before the Throne. . . . Therefore when this bush is said to have burned with fire . . . we are constrained to conclude that it was the symbol of Jehovah's Presence" (F. B. Meyer).

This fire representing the holiness, the presence, and the glory of God helped Moses to become better acquainted with God. This is a great prerequisite of service. The better we know God, the better we will serve God. Moses will not become Israel's emancipator while being ignorant of God!

6. The Attentiveness to the Manifestation

"And Moses said, I will now turn aside, and see this great sight, why the bush is not burnt" (v. 3). The response Moses gave to this Divine manifestation is a commendation of him and resulted in valuable compensation for him.

Commendation of him. How folk respond to Divine revelation reveals their heart. "God's revelations act as a moral test" (J. Orr). Moses' response to the burning bush really commends him, for he responded quickly and earnestly. When Moses saw the bush burn and yet not'be consumed, he knew he was witnessing something very special, something Divine which demanded his attention. He knew this was very important and said so when he described the phenomena as "great" (v. 3). "The burning bush was to Moses what both miracles and parables were to those who came into contact with Jesus. To some the miracles were mere wonders; to others they revealed an open door of communication with God. To some the parables were only aimless narratives, mere story telling. To others the Divine Teacher was able to say, 'It is given unto you to know the mysteries of the kingdom of heaven' . . . In a similar way, when Moses came suddenly upon the burning bush, there was also a sudden revelation of the state of his heart" (D. Young).

This turning aside to see the burning bush said much about Moses' interest in the things of God. It said Moses was willing to take time, even in the midst of his many duties, to concern himself with God and to learn more about God and His way. How this rebukes us today. Few people are interested enough in spiritual matters to turn aside and take notice at any time. They would not have viewed the burning bush as "great" in importance and would have ignored the burning bush and gone on their way. Others will not turn aside to attend to spiritual matters unless it is convenient. They would have been too busy with the things of the world to take time to turn aside to see the bush. These are the kind that are always too busy to read and study the Word of God and to attend the services at church. They profess to be Christian but their priorities are not Christian.

Compensation for him. "And when the LORD saw that he

turned aside to see, God called unto him out of the midst of the bush" (v. 4). Moses' good response to the Divine phenomena of the burning bush resulted in his being rewarded with greater revelation—he heard God speak. Of course, carnal men see little reward in hearing God speak; they do not prize the Word of God or the hearing of sermons from the Word. But wise men know that hearing God speak, having the Word of God in our hands, and hearing the Word of God preached is blessing supreme.

This great compensation Moses received for responding well to Divine revelation emphasizes an important truth. This truth is that when we respond well to Divine revelation, we will receive more revelation. God does not give more to those who have not treated well what He has already given them. He does not give out His choice blessings to just anybody but reserves them for those who respect them. Moses treated well the burning bush phenomena, so he is given more revelation. Many who complain that they are always coming up short in blessings from God will find their problem right here. They simply have not responded well to the opportunities they have already had for blessings. Moses would have missed the blessing of hearing God speak had he not paid good attention to the sign God gave him in the burning bush. It was "when the LORD saw that Moses turned aside to see" that God then blessed Moses with more blessings. Those complaining of lack of blessings have never gotten to the "turning aside" business.

Note also that Moses said, "I will *now* turn aside" (v. 3). He was not tardy or delinquent in responding to the revelation. If he had not turned aside "now," he would have missed the blessing. Put off reading the Bible, put off going to church, and put off praying and you will miss the opportunity for more blessing. Opportunities for receiving more from God are not always available and need to be heeded the moment we receive them.

B. THE MESSAGE FROM GOD

Here we examine the message God spoke to Moses which was the blessing Moses received for turning aside to see the burning bush. It was a wonderful message, and it became a great turning point in Moses' life. After this message, Moses' life would never be the same again. We will note the call, command, clarification, and compassion in the message.

1. The Call

"God called unto him out of the midst of the bush, and said, Moses, Moses. And he said, Here am I" (v. 4). This was a short exchange between God and Moses, but it said plenty. We will see this in noting the significance of the call and the submission to the call.

Significance of the call. The introductory words from God were simply the calling of Moses' name two times. But this repeating of the name is most significant. It emphasizes importance and urgency. Abraham (Genesis 22:11) and Samuel (I Samuel 3:10) of the Old Testament also received the double-name calls. And their calls, like the call to Moses, came at critical junctures in their lives. The double-name call needs to be responded to quickly and well. When God says something is important, we had better make it important in our life, or we will be in big trouble in a hurry. God does not have to say our name twice to make the call important and urgent, of course. The fact that He is the One Who makes the call is enough to make the call important and urgent.

Submission to the call. Moses' response to the call was a ready "Here am I." The phrase "Here am I" has two important meanings besides simply saying where one is. First, it says I am ready to listen; and, second, it says I am ready to serve. Such is the noble attitude we need to have when God addresses us. We need to be ready to listen attentively, and we need to be ready to serve earnestly. This requires that we adjust our priorities and make God first in our lives. A good many folk who claim to be Christians cannot answer, "Here am I" because they are too busy at the time to listen to God or serve God.

2. The Command

"And he said, Draw not nigh hither: put off thy shoes from off thy feet, for the place whereon thou standest is holy ground" (v. 5). The command was twofold: there was a restriction and a removal in the command.

The restriction. "Draw not nigh hither" was the restriction. This command is dispensationally Old Testament. "God, under the Old Covenant, impressed on man in a multitude of ways his unapproachableness" (Rawlinson). Hence, the forbidding of the Israelites from touching the mount. Hence, the veils in the Tabernacle and the Temple to keep prying eyes and people from intruding. The emphasis is that God is a holy God, and we are unholy which forbids us from Him. The only way we can come to God is through Jesus Christ. The Old Testament speaks of the law which condemns man and forbids him from drawing near to God. The New Testament speaks of Christ Who saves men and opens the way for man to draw near to God. Here at Mount Horeb with Moses, we are in an Old Testament situation; therefore, the command is "draw not nigh thither."

The removal. "Put off thy shoes from off thy feet, for the place whereon thou standest is holy ground." This command to remove the shoes (actually they were sandals in today's terminology) gives additional emphasis on the holiness of God. The reason the place was holy was because God was there. The practice of putting off the shoes "before entering a temple, a palace, or even a private apartment of a house, was, and is, universal in the East—the rationale of it being that the shoes or sandals have dust or dirt attaching to them" (Rawlinson). To put them off before going into a temple or other sanctuary was symbolic of the fact that we must remove all defilement before we can communicate with a Holy God. It also spoke of respect. "Putting off the shoe was then what putting off the hat is now, a token of respect and submission" (Matthew Henry).

All of this removal of the shoes exhorts reverence in our

approach to God. Joshua also experienced the same command some years later (Joshua 5:15). Keil rightly says, "Putting off the shoes was intended to express not merely respect for the place itself, but that reverence which the inward man . . . owes to the holy God." Our day certainly does not show much reverence towards God. Profane mouths and profane lifestyles reflect great disrespect of God. Sometimes even in our churches irreverence is rather pronounced in how flippantly and cheaply God is addressed and spoken to and of in our prayers and preaching.

3. The Clarification

"Moreover he said, I am the God of thy father, the God of Abraham, the God of Isaac, and the God of Jacob. And Moses hid his face; for he was afraid to look upon God" (v. 6). This verse makes it very clear Who is addressing Moses. We believe that Moses suspected a Divine manifestation here in the bush. Now the identity of the speaker is made very clear. Moses is told he is being addressed by the Almighty. We note the importance of this clarification and the influence of this clarification.

Importance. It was very important that Moses know with certainty the identity of the One speaking to him. It would make a big difference as to the validity of the message and his response to the message. If God is speaking, then it is the truth; and Moses must take heed and obey. We need to check the identity of the messages we hear today. Many messages are being proclaimed, but few are from "holy ground" or a "Holy God." Furthermore, because the Bible is the Word of a Holy God, we need to give more respect and submission to the Bible. If the Bible is God's Word, and it most certainly is, there is no message equal to it. It must have priority in our lives.

This passage is used by Jesus Christ as proof of the doctrine of the resurrection. "Now that the dead are raised, even Moses showed at the bush, when he calleth the Lord the God of Abraham, and the God of Isaac, and the God of Jacob. For he is not a God of the dead, but of the living" (Luke 20:37, 38). Not only did Christ give proof of the resurrection in using this text, but He also gave validation to the fact that Moses wrote the book of Exodus, for He said, "Moses showed." This is a valuable bit of authentication that does not help the credibility of the critics.

Influence. "And Moses hid his face; for he was afraid to look upon God" (v. 6). When a good man comes plainly face to face with God, he will be overcome by God's holiness. That Moses was so affected by the holiness of God is a tribute to the condition of Moses' heart. It is to the condemnation of so many men today that they can be confronted with the things of God and their response is nothing but scorn. They can use the name of God profanely without one bit of remorse and fear. God can reveal His power in mighty acts upon the earth, but this bunch goes on their ungodly ways without being influenced in the slightest in the area of respect for God. But Moses was different. His respect for the God was so great he could not look upon Him. No wonder God used Moses in such a great way.

Those who would serve God must have a great appreciation for His holiness—an appreciation which causes them to be like Moses who when God appeared to him was fearful of looking profanely upon God or like Isaiah who when he had a vision of God's holiness cried out, "Woe is me! for I am undone; because I am a man of unclean lips, and I dwell in the midst of a people of unclean lips" (Isaiah 6:5). Holiness is God's fundamental attribute. No one will know or serve God well who has not been greatly impressed and influenced by God's holiness.

4. The Compassion

"And the LORD said, I have surely seen the affliction of my people which are in Egypt . . . And I am come down to deliver them out of the hand of the Egyptians . . . the cry of the children of Israel is come unto me: and I have also seen the oppression wherewith the Egyptians oppress them" (vv. 7–9).

The message God gave Moses about the condition and future of the children of Israel evidences God's great concern and care for Israel—in short, God's great compassion for Israel. In this encounter which Moses had with God at the burning bush, the holiness of God was first, then came the grace of God—God's great compassion. Likewise, the Old Testament is first with the law which reveals the holiness of God and the sinfulness of man. Then comes the New Testament which emphasizes God's grace as it is given to man through Jesus Christ.

How great is God's compassion. But men are forever accusing God of being uncaring, unloving, and unkind. They blame wars, disasters, and diseases on Him, forgetting it is man's sin, not God, that causes these problems in the world. Sinful men simply will not give honor to God's compassion, to God's grace. But "No student of God's character in the Bible can doubt that he compassionates . . . His words declare it . . . His deeds attest it, and . . . the Cross demonstrates it" (J. Orr).

We note two evidences of God's compassion in what He said to Moses at the burning bush: the awareness of God and the action of God.

The awareness of God. "And the LORD said, I have surely seen the affliction of my people which are in Egypt . . . heard their cry . . . I know their sorrows . . . the cry of the children of Israel is come unto me: and I have also seen the oppression wherewith the Egyptians oppress them" (vv. 7,9). God's message towards Moses demonstrated that God is aware of what is going on in Egypt. God sees, hears, and knows all. And this awareness showed His compassion for the Israelites. He was reminding Moses that He did care. He was not uncognizant of Israel's needs, but paid attention to them.

How good it is to know that God sees, hears, and knows all about our every need. Christ emphasized this fact when He said, "Are not two sparrows sold for a farthing? and one of them shall not fall on the ground without your Father. . . . Fear ye not therefore, ye are of more value than many sparrows" (Matthew 10:29,31). In the Luke account of Christ's words here, it says regarding the sparrows, "Not one of them is forgotten before

God" (Luke 12:6). He is ever aware of our situation. This speaks of God's great care and concern and compassion. And it is a great antidote for our anxiety!

The action of God. God's compassion does more than just feel sorry for us. It provides a way to remedy our needy condition. "I am come down to deliver them out of the hand of the Egyptians, and to bring them up out of that land unto a good land and a large, unto a land flowing with milk and honey; unto the place of the Canaanites, and the Hittites, and the Amorites, and the Perizzites, and the Hivites, and the Jebusites" (v. 8). What God told Moses had to be great news to Moses. Moses had been very concerned about the condition of the Israelites. But his ill-designed and rejected efforts to free Israel had left him a fugitive from Egypt with little hope of being involved in any deliverance—if in fact it was going to come. But now God says the time has arrived. Deliverance is on the way.

We want to note the validation, incarnation, salvation, and location that are involved in this action being taken by God.

First, *validation.* True compassion always takes action. God now proves the validity of His compassion by taking action to deliver Israel from their Egyptian oppression. Sometimes folk tell us they really care, but they lack the evidence of action to show that they care. Some church members want us to believe they really have a compassion for the work of the church, for missions, and for souls. But they lack action to validate their talk of compassion. God demonstrates a better way. He is a God of great compassion and shows it by His actions on our behalf. And no action shows His compassion better than the giving of His Son, Jesus Christ, to be our Savior.

Second, *incarnation.* We get a foreshadowing of the incarnation of Jesus Christ in our text when God said, "I am come down to deliver" (v. 8). Christ had to come to earth to bring about the greatest emancipation of all—the redemption of man's soul. And note that the Deity of Christ is foreshadowed here also; for it is God speaking in our text when it says, "I" will come down. Yes, Jesus is God; and we see it plainly taught in both the New Testament and the Old Testament.

Third, *salvation*. A great truth about salvation is taught in the dual work of God regarding the Israelites. God said He was going to bring Israel "out" (v. 8) of Egypt and "unto" [into] (Ibid.) the promised land. Our salvation not only keeps us from going to an eternal hell, but it also sends us to an eternal heaven. We need both actions! In practical Christian living, we sometimes do not exemplify this truth. We separate from the things of the world but do not separate unto the things of God. We don't do this and we don't do that, but we do not have any positives. We are to separate "from" in order that we may separate "unto." Some things we do not do in order that we may do other things. Salvation is a two-way street—both "out" and "unto."

Fourth, *location*. God made it clear where Israel was going. It was "unto a land flowing with milk and honey; unto the place of the Canaanites, and the Hittites, and the Amorites, and the Perizzites, and the Hivites, and the Jebusites" (v. 8). It was a definite place, a delightful place, and a difficult place.

God was taking Israel to a *definite* place. God spells it out exactly where this place is—"unto the place of the Canaanites." God had promised Abraham's descendants this land, and God keeps His promises.

God was taking Israel to a *delightful* place—a place "flowing with milk and honey." While this was in a sense literally true, the phrase is, however, proverbial for a fruitful, prosperous place. Israel would find more blessings than just literal milk and honey in Canaan. Follow God and you will find your most delights in life.

God was taking them to a *difficult* place—a place where some cruel nations were who would engage Israel in many battles. God's blessings are not to make us lazy, soft, and undisciplined. In this life there are battles to be fought, victories to be won. His blessings are to help us gain the victory.

V.

SUMMONED TO SERVICE

THE DIVINE CALL of Moses as Israel's emancipator had occurred long before the burning bush experience. Forty years earlier "it came into his [Moses] heart" (Acts 7:23) to deliver Israel. But it was not God's time yet, and this was especially confirmed by the fact that Israel did not recognize his call then. "He supposed his brethren would have understood how that God by his [Moses] hand would deliver them: but [at that time] they understood not" (Acts 7:25). Moses knew he had the call, but Israel was not ready to believe it. Now forty years later, God informs Moses it is now time to begin the emancipation of Israel and, thus, to fulfill his calling. Moses had not lost his calling, as he surely must have concluded after forty years in seclusion as a shepherd in the obscurity of the Sinai peninsula. It had simply not been the time to begin his work during those years. But now the summons from God signals that the time has arrived for Moses to begin the work to which he had been called many years earlier.

To examine this summons given by God to Moses to inform him it is now time to start serving as Israel's emancipator, we will consider the command for Moses (v. 10), the concerns of Moses (vv. 11–15), and the communiqué for Moses (vv. 16–22).

A. THE COMMAND FOR MOSES

"Come now therefore, and I will send thee unto Pharaoh, that thou mayest bring forth my people the children of Israel out of Egypt" (v. 10). In studying this command, we will look at the

101

expectation, the earnestness, the encouragement, the extent, and the enlisted of it.

1. The Expectation of the Command

After Moses had experienced the marvelous burning bush manifestation of God, he certainly should not have been surprised to receive a command from God for duty; because revelation brings responsibility. Moses was not given the phenomena of the burning bush experience for mere entertainment to break up the monotony of his shepherding duties. The purpose of the revelation was to instruct and involve in service. This is always true. When God illuminates us, it is to influence our conduct. When God teaches us, what He says is to be applied to our lives. There are a number of folk who do not like this conclusion, however. They want to see the burst of God's glory in the flame, they want to experience the arresting miracle which adds spice to their dull life, they want the thrill of hearing a Divine voice, they want the emotion of taking off the shoes, they want to hear the exciting promises of deliverance and to know all about prophecy and the end times. But perish the thought that all of this should obligate them in service. They want the dramatic but not the duty. They want the prophecies but not the precepts. They want the spectacular but not the summons. They want the show but not the service. However, it does not work that way. When God reveals truths to us, we can expect Him also to reveal tasks for us. Moses had quite an experience at Mount Horeb with the burning bush. But it was all intended to start Moses on his way in leading Israel out of Egypt.

2. The Earnestness of the Command

The command said, "Come *now*." The time had arrived for the emancipation. There was to be no delay. God had specified in His promise to the patriarchs how many years Israel would be afflicted in Egypt (Genesis 15:13). God has a habit of always keeping His promises. Therefore, when the number of years is about to expire, He calls Moses to his work. There can be no delay if God is to keep His promise. Hence, the earnestness in the command.

When God calls any of us, it is with the same earnestness. When God says, "Now," He does not mean sometime when you get around to it. He does not mean that you are to think it over awhile before you respond. Rather, He means that you are to act immediately. We may not be as aware of some specific time involved as we are of Israel's time in Egypt. But that does not mean God is not running on a schedule. He always moves on a schedule. Therefore, for us to be delinquent in our response to God means we risk missing out on many blessings from God. One does not have to look around very hard to see lives that have been delinquent in responding to God's commands; and, as a result, they have suffered greatly. Do not take God's orders lightly. When God says something, pay attention. Treat it earnestly. You will never regret it.

3. The Encouragement of the Command

When God commanded Moses to begin the emancipation of Israel, He encouraged him by saying He would "bring forth my people the children of Israel out of Egypt." There would, of course, be many difficulties in the work. But a great encouragement to obey the command to start the work was that it would be successful. Moses would indeed lead the Israelites out of the land of Egypt.

God's commands are accompanied by God's encouragements. Somewhere in the orders God gives us, we will find that which will encourage us to obey. The flesh may not find encouragement, of course; for God's orders do not appeal to the flesh. All the flesh sees are difficulties. But the spirit will find encouragement, for it is always present.

We note here from Scripture some examples of this Divine encouragement. When God through Paul commanded us to "come out from among them, and be ye separate, saith the Lord, and touch not the unclean thing" (II Corinthians 6:17), the accompanying encouragement was, "I will receive you, and will be a Father unto you, and ye shall be my sons and daughters" (II Corinthians 2:17,18). When Christ told us to "lay not up for yourselves treasures upon earth . . . but lay up for yourselves treasures in heaven" (Matthew 6:19,20), the accompanying encouragement was that in heaven our treasures will not be corrupted by "moth nor rust" (Matthew 6:20) and there "thieves do not break through nor steal" (Ibid.). When Christ exhorted us to "enter in at the strait [narrow] gate" (Matthew 7:13), the accompanying encouragement was the strait gate "leadeth unto life" (Matthew 7:14). When Paul was told by the Lord at Corinth to "be not afraid, but speak, and hold not thy peace" (Acts 18:9), the accompanying encouragement was "for I am with thee, and no man shall set on thee to hurt thee; for I have much people in this city" (Acts 18:10). These are just a few examples of the encouragements that come with God's commands. We urge the reader in reading the Scripture to be alert to the many places where this encouragement truth is emphasized. It will be a great help in obeying God's commands.

4. The Extent of the Command

God told Moses that he was to "bring forth my people the children of Israel out of Egypt." Note it was only "out" not "unto." God had earlier promised that He, God, would "bring them up *out* of that land *unto* a good land" (Exodus 3:8), and He would later repeat this promise in verse 17. We noted in detail in our previous chapter the "out" and "unto" aspects of God's promise. Here we want to especially note that Moses was only to bring the children of Israel "out" of Egypt. Nothing is said about Moses bringing them "unto" Canaan, for the extent of Moses' command was limited to "out." Bible students are, of course, familiar with the fact that the limiting of Moses to only the "out" of God's promise was sealed when Moses some years later sinned in smiting the rock for water when he was only to speak to it (Numbers 20:7–12). This disobedience of Moses brought forth from God the specific command forbidding his entrance into the promised land.

104

In the limited extent of this command is an important doctrinal truth. Moses represents the law. The law cannot save us. It will not bring us into the heavenly land. It can take us out of the Egyptian way of life. Indeed, it can reform our lifestyle a good deal. But as good as that is, it will not save us. The one who would lead Israel into Canaan was Joshua. Fittingly, Joshua's name is the Hebrew equivalent of Jesus. All of this is a wonderful picture of salvation. It is Jesus (grace), not Moses (law), who brings us into the eternal promised land of heaven.

5. The Enlisted of the Command

Israel was in bondage and needed emancipation. God could have sent an angel to do the job or "had he so pleased He could have appeared before the Hebrews in person and brought them out of their house of bondage. But this was not His way. Instead, He appointed a human ministry to effect a Divine salvation. To Moses He said, 'I will send *thee*' . . . Human instrumentality is the means He most commonly employs in bringing sinners from bondage to liberty, from death to life" (A. W. Pink).

The fact that God uses human instruments is no cause for human pride, however. To the contrary, it is a manifestation of God's grace that He uses us. Therefore, we must view our opportunities to serve as great privileges. What a great blessing it is that God would allow us to be involved in His work. Service for God is a choice blessing indeed. This attitude, however, is certainly not embraced by those who try to get out of serving. They mistakenly view service as a burden not a blessing. But the true view of service should be that of blessing, of privilege. As such it ought to inspire dedicated performances. God does not need us to do His work, but we need to be involved in God's work to obtain blessing.

B. THE CONCERNS OF MOSES

Moses' response to God's summons was not what we might have predicted. "Considering the patriotic views that had formerly animated the breast of Moses, we might have anticipated that no mission could have been more welcome to his heart than to be employed in the national emancipation of Israel. But he evinced great reluctance to it" (Jamieson). Here we see that reluctance manifested in two concerns he voiced about his doing as God commanded. These two concerns are the beginning of a series of objections Moses raised about his doing the work God wanted him to do. These objections sometimes do not appear to be objections (especially the second concern we will examine from our text), for they are couched in terms of apparent noble concern. But the resistance to the summons is always present, and it becomes more pronounced and more obvious the more Moses speaks.

The two concerns of Moses expressed in our text are about the insignificance of Moses and the identification of God. They ask two questions: "Who am I?" and "Who are You?" God most adequately answered these two questions, as we will see in our study of them. But this did not stop Moses from raising more objections later (we will note three more objections in our next chapter), for Moses simply did not want to obey the summons.

1. The Insignificance of Moses

"And Moses said unto God, Who am I, that I should go unto Pharaoh, and that I should bring forth the children of Israel out of Egypt?" (v. 11). In examining this concern, we will note the character of the concern and the countering of the concern.

The character of the concern. This concern reflected both humbleness and stubbornness. Both good and bad are in the concern. It is a mixture of the spirit and the flesh.

First, *humbleness.* Humility is certainly evident in this concern. Moses is not bragging about how great he is. "Who am I?" is not the language of pride but of humility. Humility is essential for service for God. "It is when a man says I can do nothing, that he is fit for God to employ" (Henry). God cannot use us when we think we are somebody. Great men of God down through the ages have all confessed unworthiness for their God-appointed tasks. Paul saw himself as the "least of the apostles" (I Corinthians 15:9), "less than the least of all saints" (Ephesians 3:8), and "chief" of sinners (I Timothy 1:15). When Jeremiah received his call from God, he said, "Ah, Lord GOD! behold, I cannot speak; for I am a child" (Jeremiah 1:6). We are indeed nothing apart from God. We need to always remember that fact; or we will not serve God well, if at all.

As we noted in our previous chapter, Moses changed a great deal in forty years. His humility here reveals some of the big changes that occurred in his thinking from forty years earlier when he tried to deliver Israel on his own. Then he was full of self-confidence, now he is full of self-doubt. Then it was who I am, now it is who am I. Then he thought he was somebody; now he thinks he is nobody. Then he had all the answers; now all he has are questions. Then he was courageous; now he is timid. Then he was speeding; now he is stalling. Then he thought he could conquer; now he thinks he will be conquered. Then he was willing but not ready; now he is ready but not willing. Forty years in the desert as a shepherd had indeed changed the attitude of Moses. And many other men of God of every age will testify that before they could be effectively used by God, they also had to go through years of humbling experiences. Do not despise these experiences. They do much to equip you for service.

Second, *stubbornness*. While the concern reflected humbleness. Moses used that show of humbleness to resist God's summons to duty. "If we have reason to believe that any duty, great or small, is laid on us by God, it is wholesome that we should drive home to ourselves our own weakness, but not that we should try to shuffle out of the duty because we are weak" (Henry). There are a number of humble-sounding church members who beg off doing work at church on the basis that they feel they are not able to do it. They lament that they simply cannot teach, could not usher, have no ability to help on a workday, could not help in the nursery, could not possibly feed or keep a missionary guest in their home, and do not have the income to give any extra to the church. This sounds all so humble. But it is just false humility to disguise rebellion. God, however, is not fooled, He sees through it all. We need to be humble, but beware of using humility as an excuse for not serving God. Then the humility becomes arrogance, for it is arrogance that argues against God's will.

The countering of the concern. God wonderfully counters Moses' concern by making a twofold promise: "Certainly I will be with thee; and this shall be a token unto thee, that I have sent thee: When thou hast brought forth the people out of Egypt, ye shall serve God upon this mountain" (v. 12). The two promises God gave Moses to alleviate his concern of being insignificant and thus to encourage his submission to God's summons had to do with the presence of God and the providence of God.

First, the *presence of God.* "Certainly I will be with thee" is a tremendous promise. Hence, it was not Moses alone against Pharaoh, or Moses alone in dealing with the children of Israel; but it was Moses and God. The presence of God should alleviate the fears. As a small boy, I was afraid to go to a lot of different places. But if my father was with me, my fears disappeared. How much more should this be true when our Heavenly Father is with us. When Christ gave the great commission to His disciples, the great promise to encourage them to fulfill it was, "Lo, I am with you always, even unto the end of the world" (Matthew 28:20). Moses later showed his great appreciation for the presence of God when he said to God at Mount Sinai during some difficult times with the Israelites, "If thy presence go not with me, carry us not up hence" (Exodus 33:15). The value of God's presence is also emphasized in the life of Joseph when he was in Egypt. Three times in Genesis 39, we read that the Lord was with Joseph (Genesis 39:3,21,23). That helped Joseph to triumph over some very rugged experiences that would have otherwise destroyed him. Value the presence of God as you value no other one's presence. You need it more than the presence of anyone else. When it is promised to you, you have absolutely no excuse for not serving God as He has commanded.

Second, the *providence of God*. Though the promise of God's presence was enough to encourage Moses to obey, God still added another promise. He said, "This shall be a token unto thee, that I have sent thee: When thou hast brought forth the people out of Egypt, ye shall serve God upon this mountain." God promised that He would so direct providence that Moses would bring the Israelites to the very place where Moses and God were now conversing. It was a big promise, for it encompassed the deliverance of Israel from Egypt. It meant that Moses would be successful in bringing the Israelites out of Egypt. This should have greatly encouraged Moses, for we all like to be promised success. Of course, God did not promise Moses there would not be difficulties, but the success promise was a promise that Moses would overcome the difficulties.

As we noted in some detail earlier in this chapter, when God gives us orders, we will find encouraging promises with them. And these promises are to remove any hesitation we may have in obeying Him. Therefore, let us listen carefully to God's orders so we will not miss the encouragements.

2. The Identification of God

Moses first concern was "Who am I?" Now his second concern is "Who are You?" Moses is concerned here about God's name. "And Moses said unto God, Behold, when I come unto the children of Israel, and shall say unto them, The God of your fathers hath sent me unto you; and they shall say to me, What is his name? what shall I say unto them?" (v. 13). In studying this second concern, we will note the relevance of the concern, the resistance in the concern, and the revelation for the concern.

The relevance of the concern. Asking to know the name of God was a very important question; for knowing the name of God was important for knowing God, serving God, and honoring God. All of these things were very relevant to Moses' call.

First, it was important for *knowing God*. Requesting to know the name of God was a request to know about God, for the names of God declare the character of God. Many names we choose for people and places are chosen for nothing more than sentimental reasons or because we like the sound of the name. But the names of God are not given in that way. The names of God speak forth important truths about God. Truths that will encourage us to put our faith in God. Hence, the Psalmist said, "They that know thy name [God's name] will put their trust in thee" (Psalm 9:10). As we will see a bit later in God's answer about His name, the name God gave in response to Moses' question did indeed tell much about the character of God. It disclosed some very significant and fundamental truths about God. This would encourage both Israel and Moses to put their trust in God for the emancipation of Israel from Egypt.

Second, it was important for *serving God*. To know God aright is to enhance our service, for "the people that do know their God shall be strong, and do exploits" (Daniel 11:32). Knowing what sort of person God is will have a big effect upon how one serves God. Moses is about to embark on some great service for God. He needed to know God well if he is to serve well. Those who know God best will serve God best. A poor knowledge of God will result in poor service for God.

Third, it was important for *honoring God*. It was imperative when Moses went back to Egypt that he declare that the God of the Israelites was Someone much superior to the gods of the Egyptians. The name of God would aid him in doing this, for the names of God were very important in Moses' day. "The heathens generally gave names to their gods, and the Egyptians in particular plumed [prided] themselves on the invention of appropriate names to [for] the various idols they worshipped" (Jamieson). Moses would honor Israel's God above the Egyptian's gods, and so he needed to have a good name for God.

If any minister is to help people, he must honor God. But many ministers fail here. They dishonor God's Word by saying it is not true. They dishonor God's power by attacking the miracles in the Bible. And they dishonor God's Son by denying His Deity and His sinlessness. Such a God is no help to any man.

The resistance in the concern. Though the question is an important one as we have noted, the context bears out that the question was used to resist the command to serve God. It was just another subtle stalling tactic. The question was a most valid one, and it needs to be answered. But men can ask the best of questions with the wrong objective in mind. So it was with Moses. He was using the question to resist submitting to God's orders; for once it was answered, Moses did not submit but offered more resistance as we will see in our next chapter. Therefore, though the question was a good one and suggests some noble attitudes, it was not asked with the integrity we would have liked it asked.

Sometimes people in church are like this. They ask the pastor such noble sounding questions about spiritual things, but they have an ulterior motive when doing so, and it soon comes out. Sometimes people ask questions simply to try to impress people of their spirituality, for they soon give evidence they are not truly interested in the answers. Sometimes they ask questions in such situations as a Sunday School class in order to keep the teacher from getting on with the lesson or to avoid the bringing up of other subjects the questioner does not wish to discuss in class. So all good questions do not come with good motives. Moses had an excellent question, an excellent concern; but, unfortunately, it was with a tainted motive. He was using the question more to resist his call than to better fulfill it. God does not think kindly of such tactics, and when they are persisted in, He will bring judgment on the rebeller.

The revelation for the concern. God's answer to Moses' question concerning God's name was a wonderful revelation about God. Though Moses used the concern about God's name to resist his call, God graciously, as He had done with the first concern, answered the question about His name with a wonderful answer. God answered, "I AM THAT I AM" (v. 14). We note the equivalent, the explaining, the expansion, and the employment of this new name for God which God gave to Moses.

111

First, the *equivalent of the name*. It is very important to note that the words "I AM THAT I AM" come from the same root word as the word "Jehovah." Thus, "The word 'I AM' in Hebrew is equivalent in meaning to Jehovah, and differs from it very slightly in form" (Cook). This means that when God said His name was "I AM THAT I AM," He was simply instructing Moses about the meaning of the name Jehovah.

The name Jehovah (some render it Jahveh or Yahweh—without the vowel points it can also be rendered JHVH or YHWH) was the special name by which God revealed Himself to the Israelites. It was, therefore, an extremely important name, a name greatly and justifiably revered by Israel. It is found over 6,000 times (exactly 6,823 says Ryrie) in the Old Testament. However, the frequent use ("majestic repetition" says F. B. Meyer) and great significance of the name is unfortunately obscured in most English translations (the American Standard Version of 1901 being the most notable exception) by the way the name is translated. In the King James Version (which we use in our books), the word "Jehovah" is normally translated "LORD" (all capital letters). About 300 times it is also translated GOD (all capital letters). The actual name "Jehovah" only appears seven times in the KJV—four times alone (Exodus 6:3, Psalm 83:18, Isaiah 12:2 and 26:4) and three times in a name combination (Jehovah-jireh in Genesis 22:14, Jehovah-nissi in Exodus 17:15, and Jehovah-shalom in Judges 6:24).

The reason the word is rendered LORD (all caps) so many times is the influence of unwarranted Jewish tradition. The Jews, in their superstitious fear of using this name of God profanely, refused to pronounce the name when they came across it in the Scriptures. When reading Scripture aloud, they would substitute the Hebrew word "Adonai" for Jehovah. The English translators, unfortunately and unjustifiably, followed this habit of the Jews in translating the word. But since Adonai is properly translated "Lord," the English translators, to distinguish between Adonai and Jehovah, capitalized the word (LORD) when it referred to Jehovah. It is a clumsy form of translation that does not help but only hinders the learning of important spiritual truths. It shows how deeply an unwarranted tradition can influence men in adverse ways. The average reader of Scripture does not readily discern the difference between "Lord" and "LORD." Yet there is a most significant and instructive difference. The typical English translation, however, prefers to obscure that difference by persisting in this translation practice.

Second, the *explaining of the name*. The name "I AM THAT I AM" is such an awesome name because of what it means. "The idea expressed by the name is that of real, perfect, unconditioned, independent existence" (Rawlinson). As such, the name plainly and forcefully states that Jehovah is sovereign, self-existent, eternally existent, immutable, and all powerful. It means that there is no equal to Jehovah. He is above all. Thus this name sets Israel's God apart from all other gods. "This name precluded any comparison between the God of the Israelites and the deities of the Egyptians and other nations, and furnished Moses and his people with strong consolation in their affliction, and a powerful support to their confidence in the realization of His purposes of salvation [the emancipation from Egypt] as made known to the fathers" (Keil). When Moses asked for a name, God gave him a great name. The Psalmist could truly say of the name, "O LORD [the name Jehovah] our Lord, how excellent is thy name in all the earth!" (Psalm 8:1). The name ought to have shut Moses' mouth to any more objections to serving God as the emancipator of Israel.

This name, "I AM THAT I AM," should not only improve Moses' attitude about God, but it should also improve our attitude about God. How frequently God is viewed so disgracefully less than He really is. All of us certainly must hang our heads in shame at our lack of faith in God, for our lack of faith belittles the character of God. It dishonors His ability, His power, and His person. What a great person God is to be able to say, "I AM THAT I AM." We certainly cannot say that. Instead, we must say as one of the greatest of all saints said, "By the grace of God I am what I am" (I Corinthians 15:10). God can say, "I AM THAT

113

I AM"; but we can only say, "By the grace of God I am what I am." There is an infinite difference between these two statements, and we need ever to realize that there is an infinite difference between us and God. We can only bow low before Him in recognition of His extreme greatness.

Third, the *expansion of the name*. Christ is the great expansion of the "I AM" name. Bible students know that the Jehovah of the Old Testament is the Jesus of the New Testament. And they know that since Christ is the great manifestation of God, then the Jesus of the New Testament will greatly increase our knowledge of the Jehovah of the Old Testament. One of the ways in which Jesus Christ increases our knowledge of Jehovah God is in His significant association with the term "I AM" (an abbreviation of "I AM THAT I AM"—an abbreviation verified in the last part of verse 14). In His association with the "I AM" term, He wonderfully expands our knowledge of what is involved in the "I AM" name. This is especially and fittingly seen in the Gospel of John, the book of the four Gospels which especially emphasizes the Deity of Christ. However, this expansion of the "I AM" name in Christ is not readily perceived in our English translations; for the "I AM" association with Christ is unfortunately often obscured in our English translations. As the translators obscured the Jehovah emphasis in the Old Testament, so they have obscured the "I AM" emphasis concerning Christ in the New Testament. They have obscured the "I AM" relationship with Christ by doing such things as adding the word "he" and by ignoring the order of the Greek words in some of the texts. Some notable examples of this problem are as follows:

John 4:26. Here in Christ's experience with the woman at the well, He plainly identifies Himself as the "I AM" though the English translation obscures it. The woman made reference to the Messiah (John 4:25), and Jesus in response to her said that He was the Messiah (which, of course, is Jehovah). In the literal Greek, Jesus said to her, "I am who am speaking to you" (John 4:26). The KJV translates, "I that speak unto thee am *he*." The obscuring of the "I AM" emphasis here is done by inserting "he" and by an unwarranted separating of "I" from "am."

John 6:20. This verse is about Christ coming to the disciples in the midst of the Sea of Galilee during a storm. They did not know who He was and were afraid (John 6:19). But He calmed their fears by saying (in the literal Greek text), "I am; fear not." What a fantastic statement! The disciples missed the significance of it, but so do the English translators. They completely obscure the "I AM" reference by leaving out the "am" and translating, "It is I; be not afraid."

John 8:24. In this verse Jesus said, "If ye believe not that I am *he*, ye shall die in your sins." Again the adding of the "he" to the text by the translators obscures the significance of Christ's statement. He plainly said He is the "I AM" and that if you do not believe that fact, the consequences are eternal condemnation. It is a personal testimony of Christ's deity.

John 8:28. In this verse, like the one above, Christ also plainly states that He is the "I AM." He said, "When ye have lifted up the Son of man, then shall ye know that I am *he*." The "he" is in italics in the English translations and, therefore, does not belong in the text. Take out the "he" and the "I AM" emphasis is more clearly seen as it ought to be.

John 18:6. The most powerful demonstration of the "I AM" identity of Christ which is obscured by the translators is found in John 18 which describes the scene in the Garden of Gethsemane when Jesus was arrested. Christ asked the arresters "Whom seek ye?" (John 18:4); they answered Him, "Jesus of Nazareth" (John 18:5). Then our English versions say that Christ answered, "I am *he*." But the "he" is in italics. It is not in the Greek. To insert it obscures the identity and impact of the "I AM." This is especially noted in the next verse which says, "As soon then as he had said unto them, I am *he*, they went backward, and fell to the ground" (John 18:6). Take out the inserted and italicized "he" and you have the powerful effect of the Divine name "I AM." For when Christ said, "I am," all his arresters fell to the ground. But the arresters, so blind in their sin, got up off the ground and continued to arrest him. What a display of folly on the part of the arresters to continue the arresting after this evident display of Divine power. But those who are given up to sin "don't get it" no matter how plain the demonstration is. How greatly sin blinds.

This knowledge that Christ is the "I AM" of the Old Testament will give us added appreciation for and understanding of those great "I am" statements Christ made which are recorded in the Gospel of John that tell us what Christ is for mankind. They, as well as the other associations of Christ with "I AM," expand the meaning of the "I AM" name. These statements include "I am the bread of life" (John 6:35); "I am the light of the world" (John 8:12); "I am the door" (John 10:9); "I am the good shepherd" (John 10:11); "I am the resurrection, and the life" (John 11:25); "I am the way, the truth, and the life" (John 14:6); and "I am the true vine" (John 15:1). Truly, Jesus Christ greatly expands our knowledge of "I AM"—Jehovah God.

Fourth, the *employment of the name.* After revealing to Moses the great name, "I AM THAT I AM," God then tells Moses how to use the new name. He said to Moses, "Thus shalt thou say unto the children of Israel, I AM [an abbreviation of the full name] hath sent me unto you . . . Thus shalt thou say unto the children of Israel, The LORD [the word Jehovah which is from the same root word as I AM THAT I AM] God of your fathers, the God of Abraham, the God of Isaac, and the God of Jacob, hath sent me unto you: this is my name for ever, and this is my memorial to all generations" (vv. 14,15). Moses was to employ the name "I AM THAT I AM" with the name "Jehovah," a name Israel already knew. In these orders to Moses, God emphasizes that the "I AM" is the Jehovah Who is "the God of Abraham, the God of Isaac, and the God of Jacob." Thus, the "I AM" is not a new god. It is the same One that Israel's fathers worshipped. Israel had been much influenced by Egyptian paganism; and, therefore, it was needful to make clear that a new name did not constitute another new god as some would reason. It was only a further revelation as to the character of The One True God that was the God of Israel's fathers.

In the first message Moses was to speak to the Israelites, he would with the new name be, therefore, helping them to know more about God. How instructive this is. If we are going to deliver people from the bondage of sin, we need to instruct them about God! We need to improve the people's knowledge of God. This, however, is not being done well in our churches. And this failure breeds apostasy as few other things do.

C. THE COMMUNIQUÉ FOR MOSES

After answering Moses' first two concerns, God elaborates upon Moses' work and the outcome of it. This communiqué laid out significant information for Moses regarding his work. To examine this communiqué, we will look at the repeating of the summons, the reception by the elders, the request for Pharaoh, the reaction of Pharaoh, and the riches for Israel.

1. The Repeating of the Summons

"Go, and gather the elders of Israel together, and say unto them, The LORD God of your fathers, the God of Abraham, of Isaac, and of Jacob, appeared unto me, saying, I have surely visited you, and seen that which is done to you in Egypt. And I have said, I will bring you up out of the affliction of Egypt unto the land of the Canaanites, and the Hittites, and the Amorites, and the Perizzites, and the Hivites, and the Jebusites, unto a land flowing with milk and honey" (vv. 16,17). The hesitancy of Moses, revealed by his voiced concerns, necessitated a repeating of the summons. If some readers are still doubting that Moses was resisting the summons, the repeating of the summons should certainly help to take away that doubt; for we do not need our orders repeated if we are prompt in obeying them. The repeating of the summons can be divided into three parts: the mandate to serve, the men to see, and the message to speak.

The mandate to serve. "Go" (v. 16) is the command this time. It is substantially the same as "Come now" (v. 10) of the first summons, except one can justifiably see in the "Go" a more

117

earnest exhortation. Moses was stalling and God wanted to stop the stalling. The "Go" is a call to get moving. The time has come and Moses must not delay. Unfortunately, Moses will have to be prodded two more times to get going. "Now therefore go" (Exodus 4:12) and "Go, return unto Egypt" (Exodus 4:19) are the other two admonitory calls to get going. We will see more on these other two admonitory calls in the next two chapters of our book.

How slow the flesh is to respond to God's calls. How often we have to be prodded again and again to do what God has told us to do. And the longer we delay, the worse we make matters; for delay does not help our attitude nor our work. Furthermore, too many of these proddings and we will be out of His service. That explains why a number of professing believers are on the sideline. God will only prod you so long, then it is curtains for your service.

The men to see. "Gather the elders of Israel together, and say unto them" (v. 16). This aspect of his repeated summons gives some additional specifics that have not been stated before. However, it doubtless was implied with the first summons, as the order is most logical. If Moses is going to deliver the Israelites effectively, he needs to first meet with those who are the representative heads of the various tribes and groups. It is the way he could effectively communicate to the Israelites, for he did not have radio, TV, or newspapers to inform the people.

These elders were "equivalent to the sheiks of Arab tribes. These were recognized as the public representatives of the people" (Jamieson). Though Israel had been in Egypt many years and were under the oppression of slavery, they still maintained some organization. It was a good thing; for when Moses led the Israelites out of Egypt, organization was very essential. If you take a million or more people on a walking journey without some organization of the group, you will not go very far.

Some churches who do things so haphazardly could learn from the organization of the people of Israel. While organization is no substitute for the working of the Spirit, it is not an option in doing the Lord's work. God is organized and any work for Him that thrives will reflect some good organization. Paul's exhortation: "Let all things be done decently and in order" (I Corinthians 14:40) addresses the same matter.

How much more prudent is the approach Moses is to take this time in delivering the Israelites than what he took the first time. The first time he simply went out at random to deal with situations. Here, he is instructed to start with the elders. When God is in control, things are done more wisely.

The message to speak. "The LORD God of your fathers, the God of Abraham, of Isaac, and of Jacob, appeared unto me, saying, I have surely visited you, and seen that which is done to you in Egypt: And I have said, I will bring you up out of the affliction of Egypt unto the land of the Canaanites" (vv. 16,17). The message, which was stated (with a few variations) the first time in verse 15, was threefold. It spoke of the authority of Moses, the action of God, and the assurance of deliverance.

First, the *authority of Moses.* "The LORD God of your fathers, the God of Abraham, of Isaac, and of Jacob, appeared unto me [in verse 15 it is 'hath sent me unto you']" (v. 16). Moses needed to show the elders his credentials. The elders needed some evidence that Moses was the Divinely appointed emancipator. They needed to know his calling was of God and that he was not a renegade or self-appointed leader who would lead them down a dead-end road.

We need to stress in our day of psychoanalysis and other strange ways of seeking to know one's calling, that the call must originate with God. It was God that "visited" Moses; and God will let you know in a personal way His call for you, too. It may not be by a burning bush experience, but the call will be made in a way which will give you confidence that you have His will for your life. Be earnest in the study of the Word of God and in prayer, and you will know the will of God for your life.

Second, the *action of God.* "I have surely visited you, and

119

seen that which is done to you in Egypt" (v. 16). This statement becomes much more significant and meaningful when it is compared to Genesis 50:25 where Joseph is recorded as saying, "God will surely visit you." To the Israelites then, this statement of God's action would be a fulfillment of what Joseph predicted and would, therefore, carry much weight. Joseph's bones were with the Israelites (cp. Genesis 50:25 and Exodus 13:19) and were a constant testimony to his prediction.

God's faithfulness is being emphasized in this part of the message. Our messages should always speak of God as faithful. So many, even professing believers, are quick to blame God for failure. Our messages must counter this blasphemy of God's character. It is man that is unfaithful, "but the Lord is faithful" (II Thessalonians 3:3).

Third, the *assurance of deliverance.* "I have said, I will bring you up out of the affliction of Egypt unto the land of the Canaanites . . . a land flowing with milk and honey" (v. 17). The assurance here is based on both the Word of God and the power of God. The assurance from the Word of God is seen in "I have said." This statement is a reminder to Israel that God has not forgotten. This is assurance that God will keep His Word and bring deliverance. God's Word never fails. Hence, it is great assurance to the soul. The assurance from the power of God is seen in "I will." The One Who is the "I AM THAT I AM" can justifiably say, "I will" deliver. No one is as powerful as He. His power is another great assurance for the soul.

2. The Reception by the Elders

"And they shall hearken to thy voice" (v. 18). This surely had to be welcomed news to Moses, and it should have helped to put a damper on any further objections. Moses would not forget how his brethren had scornfully rejected him forty years earlier. He had quit the palace and thus given up much to identify with his people, but his people still rejected him with scorn. Rejection can stick in one's craw for a long time. For one to go back to the rejecters, one needs much encouragement that there will not be rejection again. Moses got that encouragement. But as we will see in our next chapter, it did not stop him from continuing to oppose the call.

Moses was not the only one that had changed greatly in the last forty years. Israel had also changed. In our last chapter, we noted that they finally began to call on the Lord for deliverance. Here we are told they would now also be more responsive to Moses. This reminds us of some of our experiences in the ministry. Some folk who were very hostile to the Gospel and to our visits did in time, through pressing circumstances, change their attitude greatly. Rather than being hostile to our visits, they requested them. And rather than being hostile to the Gospel, they became receptive to it. Ministers who have had these experiences know something of how Moses must have felt when God told him, "They shall hearken to thy voice."

3. The Request for Pharaoh

"And ye shall say unto him [Pharaoh], The LORD God of the Hebrews hath met with us: and now let us go, we beseech thee, three days' journey into the wilderness, that we may sacrifice to the LORD our God" (v. 18). This request does not seem to agree with the promised deliverance of the Israelites from Egypt unto their own land in Canaan. However, Jamieson gives a good answer to this puzzle. He said, "It may seem strange that God should instruct Moses to make such a request for a temporary absence when the real design was a total withdrawal from the country. But God was pleased to put it on the ground at first, in order that by the king's refusal of so small and so reasonable a request, the unyielding, tyrannical character of the Egyptian monarch might be the more strikingly displayed."

One important reason it was necessary to go three days' journey to worship Jehovah instead of worshipping Him right in the land is that "the Israelites could not offer their proper sacrificial animals in the presence of the Egyptians without the risk of provoking a burst of religious animosity, since among the animals would necessarily be some which all, or many of the

Egyptians regard as sacred, and under no circumstances to be killed. The fanaticism of the Egyptians on such occasions led to wars, tumults, and massacres" (Rawlinson). Exodus 8:26 records Moses' concern regarding this problem. In replying to Pharaoh when Pharaoh told him to sacrifice in the land, Moses said, "Shall we sacrifice the abomination of the Egyptians before their eyes, and will they not stone us?"

The Egyptians' unwarranted attitude towards animals is not unlike the sick thinking we are seeing today in the "animal rights" movement. It is the sick thinking that comes when men depart from the true God. Apostasy in a land always leads to strange philosophies. Leave out God and the mind will think weirdly. Today, in such lands as India where animals are considered sacred and people believe they are reincarnated after death into some beasts, some folk suffer from great hunger problems because they will not kill these animals for food. The Bible tells us a better way of life. After the flood, God instructed us to eat meat. "Every moving thing that liveth shall be meat for you; even as the green herb have I given you all things" (Genesis 9:3). God is not the author of the today's vegetarian philosophy!

4. The Reaction of Pharaoh

"And I am sure that the king of Egypt will not let you go, no, not by a mighty hand" (v. 19). We have entitled this point the "reaction" of Pharaoh, not the rejection by Pharaoh. The reason we have done this is that Pharaoh will not always reject the request for Israel to leave. God did not stop with verse 19 in describing Pharaoh's reaction to Moses' request for freedom. If He had stopped with verse 19, then it would have been just the rejection by Pharaoh, and Moses would have had a strong argument for objecting to his summons. Why go if the Israelites will not be delivered? But we cannot read verse 19 without reading verse 20 which says, "I will stretch out my hand, and smite Egypt with all my wonders which I will do in the midst thereof: and *after that* he will let you go." Pharaoh will not let them go at first, but eventually he will. And what causes him to change his mind? It is the destruction of Egypt which will cause him to change his mind. Rebellion against God resulted in retribution from God—"I will stretch out my hand and smite Egypt." But "after that he will let you go."

Pharaoh is like so many folk in every age in that after God tells them what to do, they rebel again and again. However, God in grace speaks to them time after time and urges them to repent and obey. But when they continue to rebel, finally God smites them. Destruction comes to the rebeller. God touches their life with judgment, and it is not a pretty situation. "Those will certainly be broken by the power of God's hand that will not bow to the power of his word" (Henry). After the judgment, they finally give in to God—but at what a cost. Oh, let this case of Pharaoh be a warning to any who are rebelling against the will of God. It can be a disastrous experience.

5. The Riches for Israel

"I will give this people favor in the sight of the Egyptians: and it shall come to pass, that, when ye go, ye shall not go empty; but every woman shall borrow of her neighbor, and of her that sojourneth in her house, jewels of silver, and jewels of gold, and raiment . . . and ye shall spoil the Egyptians" (vv. 21,22). Israel was going to be enriched before they left Egypt. We note the criticism of the riches, the compensation in the riches, the cooperation about the riches, and the contribution from the riches.

The criticism of the riches. There has been much criticism of this action by the Israelites. "The 'spoiling of the Egyptians' has called forth much bitter comment . . . It has been termed a combination of 'fraud, deception and theft'—'base deceit and nefarious fraud'—'glaring villainy,' and the like" (Rawlinson). However, the criticism of Israel's action here is not justified, for it is based on a poor translation. The word "borrow" in verse 22 is translated from a Hebrew word which means to ask, not to borrow. A different Hebrew word is translated "lent" in Exodus

12:36 (which refers to this action in our text), but that word "means to grant or give" (Keil), not to lend with the idea of getting paid back (the same is true of the word "lent" in I Samuel 1:28). If the word in our text did indeed mean "borrow," then the criticism would be just; for the Israelites had no intention of paying back the Egyptians. But the word does not mean borrow. It simply means to ask, to request. The Israelites were to ask the Egyptians to give them silver and gold and clothes.

How important it is that we know what the Word of God really says if we want to interpret it correctly. To know the Word of God correctly, we must spend a good deal more time in the Scriptures than just a few hurried minutes each day.

The compensation in the riches. It was only just and right that Israel should be given these riches of Egypt. These riches were compensation for the labor they had given the Egyptians as their slaves. "Divine justice sees this a rightful nemesis. Oppressed, wronged, downtrodden, miserably paid for their hard labor during centuries, the Israelites were to obtain at last something like a compensation for their ill-usage" (Rawlinson). For years Israel had been working in slave labor for the Egyptians without proper remuneration. Now God is balancing the account. Egypt will finally pay for the labor they forced from the Israelites. And they will pay dearly, for when Israel left Egypt, they literally stripped Egypt of her wealth. "Ye shall spoil the Egyptians" (v. 22, cp. Exodus 12:36).

God will see to it that eventually all accounts will be balanced. This is both a warning and an encouragement. It is a warning to those who cheat and defraud others, and it is an encouragement to those who have been wronged and short-changed. Church members need to take note here. They often pay their pastors miserably while they themselves live in plenty. But God sees all of this injustice, and He will judge!

The cooperation about the riches. "And I will give this people favor in the sight of the Egyptians" (v. 21). Without this explanation, we would really be puzzled as to why the Egyptians would want to give all these riches to the Israelites. But with this verse, we understand why they were so cooperative. God put the generous attitude in their heart. He made them receptive to the Israelites' request. Matthew Henry said regarding this truth, "God sometimes makes the enemies of his people not only to be at peace with them [Proverbs 16:7] but to be kind to them."

This promise that Egypt would give riches to the Israelites is a good lesson for God's people about asking and receiving. God told the Israelites to ask for the riches of the Egyptians, and He promised the Israelites in this text that when they asked they would receive. What a pity had they not asked. One wonders how many Israelites did not ask and as a result came up empty handed. If they were like a number of God's people in every age, doubtless some did not ask as they should have. Jesus said, "Ask, and it shall be given you" (Matthew 7:7). But for one reason or another, we often fail to ask. Therefore, as James said, "Ye have not, because ye ask not" (James 4:2).

The contribution from the riches. When God blesses us, we need to be alert as to how we are to use that blessing to honor Him. Israel was loaded down with much wealth when they left Egypt, but they soon learned that it was not just for their own carnal pleasures. It was also to be used to serve God. At Mount Sinai, God gave Moses the plans for the Tabernacle. It called for much gold and silver and other materials. These expensive materials were to be contributed by the people for the Tabernacle. With the riches of Egypt, the Israelites were more than able to contribute. God had made them able. So it is with us. God gives us talents, abilities, possessions, money, and many other things—not just for our own personal use, but also to be used for God's service. Let us endeavor, therefore, to be good stewards of God's blessings.

VI.

Shrinking from Service

Exodus 4:1–17

YOU WOULD THINK that after the gracious revelations and promises already given Moses, he would stop resisting the Divine summons given him. But not so. These revelations and promises were not enough to send Moses enthusiastically on his way. Though Moses witnessed the fire in the bush that did not consume the bush; heard the voice of God speak personally to him; was promised the presence of God in his work; was given the marvelous revelation of the name of God; was told that Israel would hearken to his voice; was informed that after Egypt was smitten by the Divine hand, Israel would be able to leave Egypt; and was assured that when Israel left Egypt, they would leave with the riches of Egypt; still Moses continued to object to his calling and make excuses for not obeying. "As fast as one difficulty is swept away, his fearful and fertile mind has another ready to take its place" (D. Young). But "man excusing himself from duty is a familiar picture . . . How inventive we are in finding excuses for not doing the will of God" (Joseph Parker).

These objections of Moses are progressively more obvious. At first, his objections were subtle and not easy to discern, as we noted in our previous chapter. But after awhile they become very pronounced and more evident until Moses finally comes right out and tells God to send someone else.

C. H. Mackintosh rightly said, "How hard it is to overcome the unbelief of the human heart. How difficult man ever finds it to trust God. How slow he is to venture upon the naked promise of Jehovah." That was the story of Moses when God summoned him to begin the emancipation of Israel; and, unfortunately, it is frequently the story of mankind in every age.

Moses made a total of five objections to his call to emancipate Israel. The first two objections, which we noted in our last chapter, concerned the significance of Moses (he thought he was too insignificant for the job) and the sovereign of Moses (he wanted a new name identity for God before he would obey the summons). In this chapter we will consider the final three objections—the skepticism of Moses (vv. 1–9), the speech of Moses (vv. 10–12), and the substitute for Moses (vv. 13–17). Moses does not believe Israel will believe him, he complains he does not have the ability to speak well, and finally he curtly tells God to get someone else for the task. Not a very noble performance by Moses to say the least.

Moses' objections are not new or obsolete. They have been used in every age. The excuses Moses makes to God sound like those the average church member makes to the pastor or other church official when the church member is asked to do some service around the church. The excuses may sound acceptable to the natural man, but they have never passed muster with God.

A. THE SKEPTICISM OF MOSES

"And Moses answered and said, But, behold, they will not believe me, nor hearken unto my voice; for they will say, The LORD hath not appeared unto thee" (v. 1). This objection, the first one of this study and the third one overall, concerns the unbelief of the Israelites. Moses is skeptical about Israel believing him. He felt the sting of their rejection forty years earlier, and he does not think they have changed. We will note the contradiction in his skepticism, the condition in his skepticism, and the combating of his skepticism.

1. The Contradiction in His Skepticism

What makes Moses' skepticism so bad is that it outright contradicted that which God had just said. God had just told Moses as an encouragement for him, "They shall hearken to thy

127

voice" (3:18). Moses then said they would not. "Attempts have been made to soften down this contradiction of God's words . . . and to represent Moses as merely saying, 'What if the people will not hearken . . . What shall I do then?' . . . But the phrase is really emphatic and peremptory" (Rawlinson). Moses simply refused to believe God and said so.

It is one thing to express your doubts to God. It is another thing if the doubts you express to God are a contradiction of what God has just plainly told you, for that calls God a liar. This is what Moses' skepticism did, and it is ever the habit of unbelief, for unbelief is continually saying that what God said is not so. This makes unbelief a very serious matter. To call God a liar is not a trivial misdeed. Our fellow man gets mighty upset when we call him a liar, how much more is God justified in getting upset when we call Him a liar—which is what unbelief does.

Unbelief always corrupts the tongue. Moses said a terrible thing about God because of the unbelief in his heart. We hear a lot of bad things said about God today—all the way from gross profanity by the men of the world to the denials of the great attributes of God by apostate ministers. It is all promoted by unbelief. Faith cleans up the tongue and helps it speak honorably about God. But unbelief does the opposite. Listen to what most men say today; and you will readily perceive that unbelief, not faith, predominates among men. The tongue says so.

2. The Condition in His Skepticism

Using his skepticism (about Israel believing him) as an excuse for rejecting God's summons, Moses was virtually saying that he conditioned his service for God on the basis of whether people would believe and accept him or not. This, however, should definitely not be the basis for our service for God. When God orders us to do something, we must obey regardless of the reaction of our fellow man. We must never base our compliance to God's orders on what man thinks. It only matters what God thinks. Therefore, we must not condition our service on the basis of popularity or results or success in men's eyes.

We must condition our service on the basis of God's orders.

When we condition our obedience to God on what God says, we will not be a quitter in God's service when things do not go well and people do not respond well to us. It was good that the prophet Isaiah had his eyes on the Lord instead of man, or he would have quit when God told him what to expect. "Then said I, Lord, how long [shall I serve]? And he answered, Until the cities be wasted without inhabitant, and the houses without man, and the land be utterly desolate, And the LORD have removed men far away, and there be a great forsaking in the midst of the land (Isaiah 6:11,12). To put it in present day vernacular, Isaiah was to keep preaching even though everyone in the church left. Noah also did not have the encouragement of a great response from man. But he did not quit; for he conditioned his service on what God said, not on what man said. Later on Moses will act that way, too; but here he certainly did not.

3. The Combating of His Skepticism

Even though Moses' skepticism was most dishonoring to God, God in grace continued to combat the skepticism by providing additional encouragements for Moses to obey. How gracious is God! He would have been most justified in smiting Moses right on the spot and leaving him nothing but a dried up corpse on the desert ground. But God gives man so many chances. It is this way with the salvation of our souls, too. Therefore, if man goes to hell, he has no one to blame but himself. Mankind has to fight past numerous acts of God's grace to go to hell. And Moses was also fighting against numerous acts of God's grace in his resistance to God's summons. Again and again God demonstrates unmerited grace to Moses. This time it is in God giving Moses the ability to perform three miracles (or signs as verses 8 and 9 call them) in order to authenticate his calling and to assure that Israel will accept him.

Significantly, giving Moses this miracle power made Moses the first worker of miracles in the Bible. Heretofore, the Bible does not record any man as working miracles. But beginning with Moses, we now will see various men down through the ages being given this power to work miracles.

The three miracles which Moses was given to perform before the Israelites to help them believe him had to do with (1) his rod and a snake, (2) his hand and leprosy, and (3) water from the Nile River and blood. These signs represented revolt, restoration, and retribution.

The rod and snake. "And the LORD said unto him, What is that in thine hand? And he said, A rod. And he said, Cast it on the ground. And he cast it on the ground, and it became a serpent; and Moses fled from before it. And the LORD said unto Moses, Put forth thine hand, and take it by the tail. And he put forth his hand, and caught it, and it became a rod in his hand. [This was to be done] That they may believe that the LORD God of their fathers . . . hath appeared unto thee" (vv. 2–5). There is more written about the rod and the snake miracle than there is about the other two signs, so we should not be surprised that we glean more lessons from the rod and snake miracle than from the other two miracles. A significant lesson in this miracle is the successful *revolt* by Israel against Egypt and their rule over Israel. But there are also other lessons for us here in this miracle; and we want to pursue them, too. To study these lessons from this rod and snake miracle, we will note the inquiry about the rod, the instructions about the rod, and the intent of the rod.

First, the *inquiry about the rod.* "What is that in thine hand?" is such an arresting question. It was not asked, of course, to give God information He did not have; for God is omniscient and knew what was in Moses' hand. The question was asked instead to direct Moses' attention to what he had in his hand. In this question there is an appeal, an appraisal, and an admonition.

An *appeal.* When God asks you about something you have, it is often an appeal from God to use it in His service. If God is going to further His work through Moses, He must have what is in Moses' hand to do it. If God is going to show a miracle to

Moses, He must have Moses' rod. If we are going to do anything for God, we must be willing to give to God what is in our
hand. If we are stingy and unwilling, we will hinder God's work
and hinder our own faith. It is so sad that many church members
are this way. They will not give God what is in their hand. Then
they wonder why their life always seems so unfulfilled.

An *appraisal*. When God asked Moses what was in his
hand, Moses answered simply, "A rod." This was Moses' shepherd crook or staff which was normally about three to six feet
long. It certainly was nothing special to look at, and Moses saw
nothing special in it. But God did. When it was yielded to God,
it would do much for God; and it would be given the most honorable and significant name, "the rod of God" (Exodus 4:20,
17:9). The first thing it would be used for was to perform a miracle involving snakes as we will note shortly. Later it would be
used in the great plagues upon Egypt (Exodus 9:23, 10:13—it is
sometimes called Aaron's rod in a number of these plagues, but
it was properly Moses' rod which was placed in Aaron's hands
inasmuch as Aaron was acting on behalf of Moses). Then it
would be used to open the Red Sea for the Israelites (Exodus
14:16); to bring water from a rock (Exodus 17:5,6); and to give
victory over Amalek (Exodus 17:8–13).

What is in our hand is generally appraised lower by us than
it is by God. "Men imagine that splendid ends can only be
reached by splendid means, but such is not God's way" (C. H.
Mackintosh). God's use of Moses' rod demonstrates that He can
use insignificant things to do great work for Him if they are
yielded to His control. Ehud had a single dagger in his hand, but
it was used to give Israel freedom. Shamgar had an oxgoad, but
he used it to give God's people relief from oppression. Gideon
and his men had a pitcher, lamp, and a trumpet in their hands—
hardly impressive weapons to rout the Midianites—but they did
just that. David had but a sling shot and a stone in his hand, but
he slew the Philistine giant with them. The widow had only two
mites in her hand, but she has inspired consecration in millions
down through the ages. The key is not how impressive an object

131

is which we have in our hand, but what we do with it. Yielded to God, our talents and gifts, though small in the eyes of man, can accomplish great things for God. Not yielded to God, the most impressive possessions and abilities will do nothing for Him.

An *admonition*. The question "What is that in thine hand?" can also be asked in an admonitory way. Do you have something in your hand that you should not have? Do you have something in your hand that will defile you, hurt you, cause trouble for yourself or others, and dishonor God? Do you have a magazine or book in your hand that is unholy? Do you have in your hand the hand of a man or woman whose hand you should not be holding? Do you have in your hand lottery tickets or other things pertaining to gambling? Do you have in your hand that which smokes or a bottle full of hellish drink? "What is that in thine hand?" is a two-way question. It not only seeks dedication of what you have for God's service, but it can also ask in an admonitory way what you have in your hand that you should not have. Moses could give a good answer, can you?

Second, the *instructions about the rod*. God told Moses to do two things with the rod in regards to this miracle. God told Moses to "Cast it on the ground" (v. 3); then he was to "take it by the tail" (v. 4). The character of the Egypt's government and the conquering of the Egypt's government are seen in these instructions regarding the rod.

The *character of the Egypt's government*. In the Bible the rod often speaks of government. And like this rod, when government has been given to man, it has often been cast down and become serpentine in character and then has turned on men (Moses had to flee the serpent) rather than helped them. The Egyptian government was certainly serpentine in character, and the snake on the ground before Moses certainly reflected the Egyptian government. But what makes the snake miracle here even more applicable to the Egyptian government is that in Egypt the "serpent was the symbol of royal and divine power [and its image was] on the diadem of every Pharaoh" (Edersheim). Evil sometimes portrays itself better than it realizes.

The *conquering of the Egypt's government*. The successful conquering of Egypt's government is suggested in Moses picking up the stick and having it cease to become a threat to him. Moses would indeed lead Israel in a successful revolt against the Egyptian government which would cause it to cease being a threat to God's people. The conquering would require courage, however. God was not giving Moses an easy job. The need of courage is demonstrated here in the way Moses was to pick up the snake. Moses was instructed to pick it up by the tail, which is the most dangerous way to pick up a snake (snake charmers pick up snakes by the neck so the snake cannot bite the charmer). This pictured the danger into which Moses would enter in confronting Pharaoh and the courage he would need to do his work. But he was successful in picking up the snake here because God was with him. And because God would also be with Moses in Egypt, Moses would be successful in his battle with Pharaoh even though Moses was in a very precarious position when dealing with Pharaoh.

In passing, we note that two stages of Moses' life are pictured here in Moses' fleeing from the snake and then in his picking it up. Forty years earlier, Moses fled from the serpentine Pharaoh of Egypt. But now he will go back to Pharaoh and deal with him face to face. And he will go back courageously as the picking up of the snake indicates. We always need courage to do as God says. But that which bolsters our courage is that God is with us and will give us the victory.

Third, the *intent of the rod*. "That they may believe that the LORD God of their fathers . . . hath appeared unto thee" (v. 5). The main intent of this miracle and also the other two miracles was to encourage the Israelites to believe that Moses was indeed sent from God. These miracles were credentials and strong proofs that Moses was God's man. "From this sign the people of Israel would necessarily perceive, that Jehovah had not only called Moses to be the leader of Israel, but had endowed him with the power to overcome the serpent-like cunning and might of Egypt; in other words, they would believe that Jehovah, the

God of the fathers, had appeared to him" (Keil).

God still accompanies His servants with proof of their calling. It may not be the same proofs that accompanied Moses, but it will be proofs fitting for each person's calling. Wise men will recognize these proofs, and the person called will also be cognizant of them. And these proofs will not need a microscope to be discovered, for they will be very obvious. Some who profess to have a calling do not have the proof of it in their lives. This is because they are either presuming a call or they are disobedient to a call. Woe be they who presume a calling that is not their calling. But also woe be they who refuse to obey their calling. Either situation will bring God's judgment.

The hand and leprosy. "And the LORD said furthermore unto him, Put now thine hand into thy bosom. And he put his hand into his bosom; and when he took it out, behold, his hand was leprous as snow. And he said, Put thine hand into thy bosom again. And he put his hand into his bosom again; and plucked it out of his bosom, and, behold, it was turned again [restored] as his other flesh" (vv. 6,7). The theme in this miracle is *restoration.* And it was a restoration done by the power of God. The leprosy here is described as white as "snow." That is the worst kind of leprosy. People considered that only God could heal leprosy. Therefore, when Moses' hand was healed of the worst kind leprosy, they would be greatly encouraged to recognize that God's great power was involved.

It is important to observe here that in this and the first miracle, nothing happened until Moses obeyed God (the third miracle will reflect this truth also, however, it was not performed at Mount Horeb but was performed later in Egypt). If we do not perceive God doing much in our life, perhaps this is the problem—we have not obeyed His orders. His orders are not always easy to obey (such as picking up the snake by the tail); but until we obey, we will not experience the blessings. And that obedience must be complete obedience. Partial obedience will not satisfy. If we only obey the first part of the command then cease obeying, we will be left with a snake on the ground and leprosy of the hand. Not good situations at all! Only complete obedience is satisfactory; anything less is perilous.

We note three areas of restoration which this miracle can speak of: the restoration of the nation, the restoration of the emancipator, and the restoration of the faith.

First, the *restoration of the nation*. Israel had lost much of its national distinction in its slavery in Egypt. But the emancipation of Israel under the leadership of Moses would restore to Israel her national position and esteem. Israel will no longer be viewed as slaves of another nation but will be esteemed as an individual nation in themselves. Israel will no longer be a leper as a nation but will be restored to honorable national status.

Second, *the restoration of the emancipator*. One can also see a symbolic application here regarding Moses' attempts in emancipating Israel. His first attempt was like the first time he put his hand into his bosom—it came out leprous. Moses' first attempt to emancipate Israel turned out very ugly; and, like a leper, he had to leave the country and be separated from his people. But here he is being restored as the emancipator. His second attempt will turn out better. The second time he put his hand into his bosom, it resulted in the complete healing of his hand of leprosy. So it will be in Moses' second attempt to emancipate Israel. He will succeed completely in freeing Israel from their Egyptian bondage.

Third, the *restoration of the faith*. Israel had drifted far from God in the land of Egypt. Many were given up to idolatry and living iniquitous lives which idolatry fosters. But Israel will not only be delivered from the country of Egypt but also from the corruption of Egypt. They will once more become a people who worship the true God in contrast to the heathen nations around them. They will no longer be leprous spiritually as the heathen nations are, but they will worship Jehovah.

The water and blood. "And it shall come to pass, if they will not believe also these two signs, neither hearken unto thy voice, that thou shalt take of the water of the river [Nile], and pour it upon the dry land; and the water which thou takest out of the river shall become blood upon the dry land" (v. 9). The message this miracle proclaimed was one of Divine judgment. It spoke of *retribution* just as the previous two miracles spoke of revolt and restoration respectively. We note the confirmation of judgment and the certainty of judgment in this miracle.

First, the *confirmation* of judgment. That this miracle teaches judgment is confirmed by the fact that of the three miracles, this one does not return anything back to its original, acceptable state. The snake was turned back into a harmless rod. The leprous hand was turned back into a good hand. But the blood is not turned back into water. That is not a blessing but a curse. Hence, the message here is judgment—in this case judgment for unbelief of the first two signs. Later this sign will also be used (Exodus 7:14–22) with a few variations to bring judgment (the first of ten plagues) upon Egypt for their unbelief. Unbelief does not bless; it only brings judgment.

Second, the *certainty* of judgment. If unbelief is persisted upon, it will indeed experience judgment. This sign warns Israel about not believing Moses. The certainty of judgment is emphasized by the two words "shall become" in verse 9. The "water which thou takest out of the river *shall become* blood upon the dry land." The Hebrew from which "shall become" is translated can be rendered "shall be, even shall be, i.e. it shall assuredly be so" (Matthew Poole). Going along with this rendering, the King James Version had in the margin of its original edition, "Shall be and shall be." Yes, judgment is certain when man persists in unbelief. We have a number today who want to water down the idea of God's judgment and pave the way for everybody to go to heaven. But that is not the message of God's Word. Unbelief will result in judgment—most assuredly.

B. THE SPEECH OF MOSES

As great as the three signs were and as encouraging as they should have been to Moses, he still raises another objection to his call. "And Moses said unto the LORD, O my Lord, I am not eloquent, neither heretofore, nor since thou hast spoken unto thy servant; but I am slow of speech, and of a slow tongue" (v. 10). Here Moses attempts to get out of his calling by claiming he cannot speak well enough to fulfill the calling God is giving him. We note the inexcusable prevarication, the inconsequential qualification, and the instructive exhortation from this fourth objection (the second of this study) and God's response to it.

1. The Inexcusable Prevarication

Moses made a shameful statement to God when he claimed he could not speak well. We learn in Acts 7:22 that he was a man "mighty in words and in deeds." Being a man "mighty in words" is hardly a description of one who cannot speak well. We are amazed at how many commentaries and writers try to gloss over that fact. Many of them want to agree with Moses in his claim that he could not speak well. Some even go so far as to twist the meaning of Acts 7:22 so it does not disagree with Moses' excuse. But such efforts to tone down Moses' rebellion are unscholarly, unjustified, vain, and unnecessary. A man who could so quickly contradict God regarding the fact that Israel would believe him is not going to hesitate to fabricate about his speech. He, like some people in our churches, simply denied he was capable of doing something that he could do—and do very well. It was not an uncommon excuse.

In the middle of this excuse is a phrase added by Moses in an attempt to strengthen his speech deficiency claim: "neither heretofore, nor since thou hast spoken unto thy servant" (v. 10). By this phrase he claimed he had never been a fluent speaker (which was a bold denial of the truth seen in Acts 7:22), nor had he become one by Divine gift since God had been speaking to him here at the burning bush. This was very bad talk by Moses. But when we do not speak the truth, we get worse and worse in our untruthfulness. When we lie, we then try to support it with another lie. All this does is make fools of ourselves and gets us deeper and deeper into trouble with God and man.

2. The Inconsequential Qualification

Moses' excuse put an unjustified emphasis on the need of eloquence in order to have success in the Lord's work. Joseph Parker said regarding this excuse of Moses, "'I am not eloquent, and therefore this mission cannot succeed in my hand,' is equivalent to saying, 'I am an eloquent man, and, therefore, this undertaking must be crowned with signal success.'" While God does not put a premium on sloppy speech, and it is not justified here, we do not need oratory to get the message across. Paul emphasized this truth when he said to the Corinthians, "And I, brethren, when I came to you, came not with excellency of speech" (I Corinthians 2:1), and "Though I be rude [not discourteous, but unskilled and untrained in eloquence] in speech, yet not in knowledge" (II Corinthians 11:6). Paul was not an orator, but spoke in common language. That does not mean his speech was crude, vulgar, or unintelligible. It means it was simple, plain, everyday common words. He did not "butcher the King's English" as we would say today. Paul's comments about his speech are no excuse for that sort of inexcusable hillbilly haranguing. Paul simply spoke clearly and sensibly, but not with oratorical skills that would impress an audience by his speech regardless of what he was saying. Moses especially did not need to be an eloquent orator in order to do the work he was called to do. So his trying to excuse himself from the call because he was not eloquent was not a sufficient excuse even if his claim of poor speech was valid.

Eloquence is not wrong in itself—Isaiah the great prophet of the Old Testament was certainly eloquent (we lose that fact in translating the Hebrew into the English, but it certainly is there in the Hebrew). But the point is, God's work does not depend on your being a skilled orator. Rhetorical skills, in fact, have been used more to hinder the work of God than to help it. How often error is propagated this way. The skilled rhetoric of the apostates deceives many people. Folk are taken in with the fair speech of these emissaries of Satan. The eloquence of these evil men so impresses people that they do not pay proper attention to what the evil speaker is saying, but just go along with him thinking he must be right because he speaks so nicely and impressively. We need to be alert to this practice of Satan. Paul warned his followers about this peril of clever words: "This I say, lest any man should beguile you with enticing words" (Colossians 2:4); for "by good words and fair speeches [they] deceive the hearts of the simple [innocent]" (Romans 16:18).

3. The Instructive Exhortation

"And the LORD said unto him, Who hath made man's mouth? or who maketh the dumb, or deaf, or the seeing, or the blind? have not I the LORD? Now therefore go, and I will be with thy mouth, and teach thee what thou shalt say" (vv. 11,12). God said much in His short answer to Moses' fourth objection to the summons. To study the answer, we will divide it into three parts: the creation of man, the command for Moses, and the capacity for service.

The creation of man. The questions in verse 11 with their implied answers underscore Who is the Creator of man. Moses needed a review of the fact that God is the Creator and that He can, therefore, make man what He wants to make him. Moses' excuse argued against that fact. He acted as though his alleged inability to speak well could not be corrected. Jehovah reminds Moses that Jehovah is the Creator and can do what He wants with His creation.

We always get in trouble in our thinking when we ignore the truth about creation. Leaving God out of the creation (which evolution delights to do) does not help man think well. It only confuses his mind and causes him to draw wrong conclusions about the most important matters of life. Recognizing that God is the Creator is not just something to emphasize in the science classroom, but it is something to remember in our everyday life. It influences so many things that we think, say, and do. When we acknowledge the fact that God created us, we acknowledge a Sovereign in our life and see Divine purpose in everything. Evolution does none of this. It makes anarchists of man, acknowledges no sovereign but man, sees no Divine purpose in life, and, therefore, defiles men's lifestyles. When we look at our defiled society, it is not difficult to see that evolution is prevailing in the thinking of man. And with the emphasis on the environment today and the fact that some of the environmentalists who are evolutionists have accused creationists of being a problem for the environment (a ludicrous accusation but one that shows the hatred of evolutionists for creationists), we would add that evolution thinking does not help man to understand the environment and its problems either. Genesis 19 will shed more light on the cause of environmental problems and how to correct them than all the EPA people put together will ever do.

The command for Moses. "Now therefore go" (v. 12). In God's response to Moses' fourth objection, He gives Moses another command to fulfill his calling. This is the third time God has told Moses to begin his work of emancipating the Israelites. The previous two times were recorded in Exodus 3:10 and 3:16. As we noted in our previous chapter, when God has to repeat His commands to us, it is an indication that we are being delinquent in obeying. God does not have to repeat his orders to those who are busy doing them.

In this third command, as in the first, the "now" aspect of God's orders is emphasized. It stresses the urgency to obey. Moses does not have time to waste. He needs to get busy and get on his way. Delinquency in God's work is never productive in God's work. It only hinders—it never helps.

The capacity for service. "I will be with thy mouth, and teach thee what thou shalt say" (v. 12). The repeated commission is accompanied with a great encouragement about Moses' capacity to serve. The encouragement dealt with the area that Moses had just cited as a problem, namely, his speech. Moses was given two significant promises by God here. The first one had to do with the ability to speak, and the second one had to do with the message to speak.

First, the *ability to speak*. Moses had complained that he was not eloquent. God did not promise to make Moses eloquent, but He did promise to "be with thy mouth" which meant Moses would not have difficulty in speaking well enough for his job. What this says is that when God calls, God enables! How encouraging this truth should be to every servant of God. Our tasks often look bigger than our abilities. But if God has called us, He will provide the necessary abilities to do the task. No task is bigger than God.

Second, the *message to speak*. Speaking for God involves more than just the ability to speak, it involves what you say. The world does not care about the message as much as the ability. But God's servants had better put much emphasis on what is said. If the message is not a worthy message, there is no use to speak. We get our message from God. In today's application, that means we get our message from God's Word. If you want to speak for God, you must get your message from God. Many preachers have strayed from the proper source of the message. They are listening to philosophers of the world and taking their messages from them rather than from the Word of God. This is especially seen in the so-called Christian psychologists who try to mix the fraud of Freudian psychology with the faith.

Note that God said He would "teach thee what thou shalt say." The idea of teaching involves discipline in learning. This means you must study the Word of God diligently if you are going to have a message worth speaking and listening to. Lazy preachers who will not study the Scriptures are shortchanging their congregations in the messages they preach to them. "Teach" does not mean God hands you your message on a silver platter. "Teach" means you must do some earnest studying in the Word to obtain your message. God helps us but not in a way that will make us lazy and unindustrious.

C. THE SUBSTITUTE FOR MOSES
"And he said, O my Lord, send, I pray thee, by the hand of him

whom thou wilt send" (v. 13). Incredibly, after all the gracious encouragement from God, Moses still will not submit to the Divine summons to go back to Egypt and to begin the emancipation of the Israelites. In this fifth objection (the third in this study), we note an unmasked stubbornness, an unhappy Sovereign, an undesirable substitute, and an unchanged strategy.

1. Unmasked Stubbornness

The mask is off. Moses no longer disguises his rebellious attitude under various excuses. He now plainly tells God to get someone else. His excuses had became progressively more evident that he did not want to do as God says. But this statement in verse 13 takes away any doubt as to Moses' rebellious attitude. It confirms that all the questions and excuses given previously were indeed given from a heart that simply did not want to do God's will. This statement of Moses proves that his claim of insignificance, his question as to the name of God, his complaint that Israel would not believe, and his claim of deficiency of speech were simply cover-ups for the rebellion in his heart to God's will.

This rebellious statement of Moses is in the Hebrew "curt and ungracious; much curter in the original than in our version" (Rawlinson). He not only comes right out and says to get someone else to do the job, but he also says it in an unkind and disrespectful way. This is typical of rebellion, however; for rebellion never shows due respect for God. Furthermore, when a person rebels against God, he will also demonstrate disrespect for a lot of people he ought to be respecting. When you see a young person being continually disrespectful of his elders, you are seeing a young person who is not walking in the will of God. When you see a church member continually disrespectful of their pastor, you are seeing a church member who is not walking in the will of God. Disrespect is a symptom of rebellion to the will of God. With so much disrespect for people and things we ought to respect today, we have a pretty sad commentary on the rebellion to God that prevails in our society.

2. Unhappy Sovereign

"And the anger of the LORD was kindled against Moses" (v. 14). We have mentioned in the previous chapter that God was not pleased with Moses and that there was in the language of God a warning sternness. Now that the rebellion of Moses is unmasked, so is the anger of God. This statement regarding the anger of the Lord is not a mild statement. "The expression used is a strong one" (Rawlinson). It says God is very upset with Moses.

God is justified in being upset with Moses. God is always justified whenever He gets angry with mankind. However, the world is not so sure. But the world seldom reads the context of this text or the context of the lives of those people God is angry with, for they are so intent on defending evil. The context of this text shows that God was so very gracious and patient with Moses, yet Moses was very guileful and rebellious. After reading the context, the question isn't "Why did God get angry?" but rather, "Why didn't God get angry sooner?"

One of our big problems today is that we do not get upset about getting God upset. We only worry about upsetting our worldly peers and friends. But if we are going to be wise, we will be more concerned about God's reaction to our conduct than anyone else's reaction. As we will see next, when God gets angry with us, we will pay a big price!

3. Undesirable Substitute

"And the anger of the LORD was kindled against Moses, and he said, Is not Aaron the Levite thy brother? I know that he can speak well. And also, behold, he cometh forth to meet thee; and when he seeth thee, he will be glad in his heart. And thou shalt speak unto him, and put words in his mouth; and I will be with thy mouth, and with his mouth, and will teach you what ye shall do. And he shall be thy spokesman unto the people; and he shall be, even he shall be to thee instead of a mouth, and thou shalt be to him instead of God" (vv. 14–16). Beware of second best. When God gets angry and accommodates your wishes, you

143

will soon wish you had never had those wishes. God is going to send Aaron to assist Moses. He will be Moses' substitute to do the speaking and to perform many of the miracles. This may appeal to Moses now, but it is really not good news for him.

This arrangement God brought upon Moses because of his rebellion will lower Moses from the position he was to originally to have. "God inflicts on him a sort of punishment— degrades him, as it were—deposes him from the position of sole leader, and associates Aaron with him in such sort that Aaron must have appeared, both to the Israelites and to the Pharaoh, as the chief leader rather than Moses" (Rawlinson). Look out when God amends His orders to accommodate your stubborn will, you will regret it all your life. "Let us all beware. If you refuse to use your powers, they will atrophy. If you will not step up to the opportunity which God offers, you will not only miss it, but will live to see it filled by an inferior man to yourself, through whom you may have to suffer many sorrows" (F. B. Meyer).

To examine this action of God regarding Aaron and Moses, we will look at the description of the substitute and the directives regarding the substitute.

The description of the substitute. Three things are said about Aaron in our text. First, he is a *good speaker.* God said, "I know that he can speak well" (v. 14). But being a good speaker does not mean Aaron is a good man. Moses was putting too much emphasis on eloquence. He will learn in time that it is often more of a liability than an asset. Second, he was a *glad brother.* "Behold, he cometh forth to meet thee; and when he seeth thee, he will be glad in his heart" (Ibid.). Aaron had not seen Moses in some time. It will be good for him to see Moses again and to know that Moses is returning to Egypt (when Aaron sees him, Moses will by then, of course, have submitted to God's orders). But he will not always be a glad brother and Moses will not always be glad to have Aaron around. Third, he was a *guileful assistant.* Aaron was a problem for Moses. Aaron caused a really great problem in the camp at Sinai. Aaron was a people pleaser and as a result helped the people in their golden calf episode which brought the wrath of God upon them and terribly upset Moses. Later Aaron, along with Miriam, criticized Moses; and they questioned if the "LORD indeed [had] spoken only by Moses" (Numbers 12:2). This resulted in Divine judgment in which Miriam had a bout with leprosy which stopped the Israelites from traveling for a week and caused Aaron to plead earnestly with Moses to heal Miriam.

The directives regarding the substitute. The directives from God regarding Aaron and his service concerned the speaking of Aaron, the teaching of Moses, and the delegating of authority.

First, the *speaking of Aaron.* "Thou shalt speak unto him, and put words in his mouth" (v. 15). God would not speak to Aaron, but Moses would. Moses would pass it on to Aaron. This was just more bureaucracy. It was cumbersome. It did not need to be that way, but Moses brought it on by his rebellion.

Second, the *teaching of Moses.* "I . . . will teach you what ye shall do" (v. 15). This part is not disciplinary; it is always needed. Earlier we learned that God would "teach thee what thou shalt say" (v. 12). Here God will "teach you what ye shall do." Times have not changed. God is still teaching us what to do. Our problem is that we do not pay any attention to what He teaches us. That explains so many of our problems.

Third, the *delegating of authority.* Moses and Aaron were not equals. "He [Aaron] shall be thy spokesman . . . he shall be to thee instead of a mouth, and thou [Moses] shalt be to him instead of God" (v. 16). The relationship here dictates that Moses is the one in charge. He has rank over Aaron. Any organization must have various ranks. The church is no different. If the pastor is not in charge, the church is in trouble. Many rebel against the idea of authority in the home, in society, and in the church. They want everyone to have the same authority. But God does not so order things, and we better not either. Aaron rebelled at times against Moses' authority but never successfully and never without causing trouble.

145

4. Unchanged Strategy

"And thou shalt take this rod in thine hand, wherewith thou shalt do signs" (v. 17). God's plans have not changed, therefore Moses is to take the rod along with him. God still intends that Moses perform the signs God had just showed him. Moses' rod, of course, is not going to make points with the Egyptians; for shepherds are an abomination to them (Genesis 46:34); and so, of course, the rod will be scorned; for it will be the rod of a shepherd, not the rod of those who are in Egypt. The word "rod" is a generic term and can mean anything from a shepherd's crook to a king's scepter. We must examine the context to know what sort of rod it is. The Egyptian magicians are also said to have rods (Exodus 7:12), but their rods would not be shepherds' rods. They would be likely to be gilded and decorated while the shepherd's rod was plain and ugly in comparison.

God tells us to take along a lot of things and to do a lot of things that the world will not esteem. We may have to dress differently, carry a Bible, and carry convictions with us that the world will scorn. The flesh does not like to travel with the things God tells us to take along, for it does not like the reproach of the world. The flesh does not want to "put on the whole armor of God" (Ephesians 6:11) as we are told to do, but we must wear it if we are to succeed in life where it counts the most. Do not make the mistake of leaving behind what God says to take along on your journey through life! It will handicap you more than you realize. Moses takes his rod or he will be without that with which God will do "signs." There is a hymn in our hymnals which is entitled, "Take the name of Jesus with you." It has a great message and gives the same message we have been addressing here regarding Moses taking the rod with him to Egypt.

VII.

SUBMITTING TO SERVICE

EXODUS 4:18–31

AFTER ARGUING AT length with God at the burning bush about being the man to emancipate Israel from Egypt, Moses finally gave in to the Divine summons and submitted to the service God decreed for him. God had silenced all of Moses' objections, as God will always do when we oppose Him; and so Moses wisely quit resisting the call and began to embark on the greatest work of his life.

This embarking on the great work of emancipating Israel begins the third and final period of Moses' life. Moses lived 120 years before he died (Deuteronomy 34:7). Those 120 years can be divided into three periods of 40 years each. The first 40 years he spent in Egypt in royalty as the adopted son of Pharaoh's daughter. The first 40 years ended when Moses tried on his own to deliver Israel but was summarily rejected by his own brethren and his life hunted by the Egyptians. The second 40 year period was spend in Midian where Moses lived in obscurity and quietness as a shepherd—a great contrast indeed to the first 40 years of his life. During those second 40 years, Moses' hopes for Israel's deliverance had so dimmed and his enthusiasm to be their deliverer had so diminished that at eighty (Exodus 7:7), he objected repeatedly to being Israel's emancipator. But God prevailed and Moses submitted to the call. However, Moses' first steps in following God's call were not without some stumbling. Moses did not hit the ground running. The flesh is never easily conquered. But God met him at the place of each difficulty and helped him overcome them all.

To examine this period in Moses' life in which he begins to fulfill his calling to deliver Israel from Egypt, we will consider the parting from Midian (vv. 18–23), the problem of neglect (vv. 24–26), and the pursuit of duties (vv. 27–31).

A. THE PARTING FROM MIDIAN

To study the parting of Moses from Midian, we will note the permission for leaving, the procrastinating in leaving, the possessions for leaving, and the precepts in leaving.

1. The Permission for Leaving

Though Moses had a Divine call, he did seek permission from his earthly overseer to leave Midian to return to Egypt. Moses' request to leave and Jethro's (his earthly overseer) response to the request are both instructive.

The request. "And Moses went and returned to Jethro his father in law, and said unto him, Let me go, I pray thee, and return unto my brethren which are in Egypt, and see whether they be yet alive" (v. 18). Moses did not drop his present duties irresponsibly and head for Egypt. No, he sought permission from Jethro. Submitting to God's summons was not contingent on Jethro's permission, of course, but requesting the permission was an act of courtesy which Moses owed to Jethro. "Jethro had taken him in while a fugitive from Egypt, had given him his daughter to wife, and had provided him with a home for forty years. Moreover Moses had charge of his flock . . . It would, then, have been grossly discourteous and the height of ingratitude had Moses gone down to Egypt without first notifying his father-in-law. This request of Moses manifested his thoughtfulness of others, and his appreciation of favors received. Let writer and reader take this to heart. Spiritual activities never absolve us from the common amenities and responsibilities of life. No believer who is not a gentleman or a lady is a true Christian in the full sense of the word. To be a Christian is to practice Christliness, and Christ ever thought of others" (Pink).

While the request was an honorable action by Moses, the words he spoke did not entirely reflect good character. The request to return to his brethren in Egypt was not faulty. It was the reason he stated for returning to his brethren that was faulty. He said he wanted to "see whether they be yet alive" (v. 18). That was not the reason! The reason he was returning to Egypt was to deliver the Israelites from the hand of Pharaoh.

Some want to excuse Moses' subterfuge here on the basis that it is prudent not to speak publicly about some of our spiritual experiences which the world may not understand, which reflects spiritual pride in the telling about them, and which would only provoke scorn by others and, hence, the discouragement of our faith. Though it may be true we should be careful about disclosing all our personal spiritual experiences, it certainly does not justify untruths and misleading statements. Moses did not need to tell Jethro all about the fire and the bush and the signs. But Moses could have told Jethro of his Divine call. Moses' failure here reminds us that, as we have noted above, the flesh does not die quickly. Even in the most spiritual of men, the flesh intrudes into their actions at times. It warns us to keep a constant vigilance on our life in order to keep the flesh subdued.

The response. "Jethro said to Moses, Go in peace" (v. 18). Jethro granted Moses' request without protest. One reason for this good response by Jethro was that Moses had performed well during the forty years in Jethro's home. While a good performance is not always reciprocated well by others, it nevertheless needs to be practiced in order to encourage a favorable reciprocation. If you want an extra day off or some other special privilege, you had better be a good hard worker and do your job right at all times. Your boss is more likely to grant your requests if your conduct is good on the job than if it is mediocre or bad. But whether or not he grants your special requests, do not let his rejection of your requests be because you have been a poor worker, irresponsible, lazy, and disrespectful. Some want their rejection by others to always be because they are a Christian when in truth the rejection is because they have not lived a very exemplary life. They have not conducted themselves in a good Christian manner.

2. The Procrastination in Leaving

Again we have more evidence in Moses' life that the flesh does not give up quickly. It fights to the very last minute of the game. Even though Moses had now gone to Jethro and obtained his blessings for leaving Midian, Moses delayed his leaving. We note the admonishing and the assuring regarding this procrastination on the part of Moses.

The admonishing. "And the LORD said unto Moses in Midian, Go, return into Egypt" (v. 19). This is the fourth time God has told Moses to go to Egypt. The first time God commanded Moses to go to Egypt to emancipate the Israelites is recorded in Exodus 3:10. Then repeated commands came in Exodus 3:16, 4:12, and here in our text. As we have said in the previous repeated commands, God does not generally repeat His commands to us if we are doing what He has told us to do. It is when we are delaying our obedience that He has to repeat His command. Abraham had to have his orders repeated when he got sidetracked in Haran (cp. Acts 7:3,4 with Genesis 11:32 and 12:1). Peter had to be told three times to take care of God's flock (John 21:15,16,17). Jonah had to have his commission repeated a second time before he obeyed (Jonah 3:1). And many are the saints of God in every age who will testify that they, too, had to be repeatedly prodded by God before they surrendered to His will. Though all of this prodding demonstrates the grace of God, let not the grace of God in these many instances encourage you to procrastinate in doing God's will. One who does that will soon discover the judgment of God. We gain nothing by delay, but we risk everything.

The assuring. "And the LORD said . . . all the men are dead which sought thy life" (v. 19). Here we learn that Moses had another reason for objecting to his call. He feared revenge by those Egyptians who would be seeking his life for his killing of the cruel Egyptian taskmaster. Moses did not voice this concern to God at the bush, but it was in his heart and God knew it. That this was indeed a concern of Moses is evident by the fact that God does address it. When God gives a word of encouragement regarding some particular problem, it is because that problem is present. As an example, when God told Paul, "Be of good cheer, Paul; for as thou hast testified of me in Jerusalem, so must thou bear witness also at Rome" (Acts 23:11), it was because Paul was not of good cheer and was not confident he was ever going to get to Rome to preach the Gospel there. He had been arrested several days before and was in the custody of some Roman soldiers. Hence, he needed that encouragement from God. So it was here with Moses. He feared for his life. Therefore, God assured Moses about his safety in Egypt by informing him that those seeking his life were dead. The Pharaoh who ruled when Moses killed the Egyptian was one of those who wanted to kill Moses. But he had died and according to Jamieson, his death "took off his proscription of Moses, if it had been publicly issued." Today we would say the the statue of limitations had expired on Moses' crime. This would take off any legal claims of others who might seek to kill Moses in revenge for the death of the Egyptian. But whether the decree was issued or had expired or not, the men who wanted to kill Moses were dead; and this made it safe for Moses to return to Egypt.

Again we have God giving an encouragement to obey His commands. We saw this several times in our last chapter and noted how frequently in Scripture this truth is emphasized. How gracious of God to encourage us where we need it to obey His orders. Look for those encouragements and park on them rather than on the difficulties you see. And remember these encouragements take away our excuses for not obeying.

3. The Possessions for Leaving

Those who are going to move to another area must gather

together all those things they wish to take with them. Suitcases must be packed and arrangements be made to move furniture and other household effects. Scripture does not tell us much about all that Moses had to move to Egypt, but it does tell us about two distinct things he took along with him on his trip back to Egypt. They were very important things. He "took" his family and he "took" his rod.

The family. "And Moses took his wife and his sons, and set them upon an ass, and he returned [started on his return] to the land of Egypt" (v. 20). This is the proper family order in the Lord's work. Moses the husband and father leads the way. In present day application, this means Moses would take his family to church—not just send them as many delinquent husbands and fathers do today. So many wives in church are not accompanied by a husband but come on their own. Also, many children come without either parent. We are glad that the wives come and the children come even though they are not accompanied by a husband or a parent. But it is an indication of the sad state of affairs in spiritual matters in society that fathers are not doing well in leading the family spiritually today. It does not help build strong churches either. Women and children are certainly part of God's church; but without godly men, no church will do well; for God has ordained that men should lead in the church as well as in the home and society. God has endowed men with leadership ability. He did not give that same ability to women or children. When men fail, it puts women and children in a very difficult position. And many men are failing today.

While Moses demonstrates good leadership in the family here, we will note a bit later that he did not do well in some other matters. And his failure caused some serious problems. Husbands and fathers must be diligent in all matters regarding the family, or failure will result. To Moses' credit, an early failure was corrected; and then his wife and family followed him well. How important it is to have the family in order. Today's situation where the family unit is mostly in chaos is so tragic and only causes trouble for the work of God.

The rod. "And Moses took the rod of God in his hand" (v. 20). God had earlier instructed Moses to "take this rod in thine hand" (v. 17) when he went to Egypt in order to do the signs that God had ordered to be done in Egypt. Moses' rod was his shepherd's crook which was a humble rod that would not be esteemed in Egypt, as we noted in our last chapter. But Moses was to take it anyway because God so ordered. Hence, this statement in Scripture noting that he took it commends Moses.

Note that Moses' rod is called the "rod of God" here which among other things tells us that the things which the world despises are often highly esteemed by God. In our society today, such things as honesty and purity are scorned by many folk, but God holds them in very high esteem. Especially is Jesus Christ and the Bible, both of which God really holds in high esteem, scorned by the world. The literal "rod" of correction is also something God values that our world certainly is devaluing today. Spanking is being attacked in our day as though it was a very bad thing. But God thinks highly of that "rod"; for His Word says, "He that spareth his rod hateth his son" (Proverbs 13:24) and "Foolishness is bound in the heart of a child; but the rod of correction shall drive it far from him" (Proverbs 22:15). Moses' rod can represent many things today that God wants us to take along on our life's journey. Though the world despises them, we must take them with us anyway if we want to live a victorious life for God.

4. The Precepts in Leaving

God gave Moses some more orders and instructions as Moses' was leaving Midian. Some of the precepts were review while some were new. These instructions concerned the miracles he was to do and the message he was to speak. The miracles were a review, but the message was a new revelation.

The miracles to do. God's instructions regarding the mira-

153

cles were twofold: they spoke of the responsibility of Moses and of the rejection by Pharaoh.

First, the *responsibility* of Moses. "And the LORD said unto Moses . . . see that thou do all those wonders before Pharaoh, which I have put in thine hand" (v. 21). The language here indicated there could be some reluctance in performing these miracles. We can understand why. Picking up snakes by the tail is not easy, neither would it appeal to Moses to have his hand all covered with leprosy. Pouring out water from the Nile and making it blood may not be as difficult to do, but it could provoke the Egyptians who attached sacredness to the river.

We are often told to do things for God that we do not especially like to do. Yet, we must do them. Anyone who is looking for a calling that does not involve any detestable tasks is looking for a calling that does not exist. In fact, it is safe to say that no job, secular or sacred is without undesirable duties. But if you are going to serve well, be it for God or man, you must do those unliked duties with as much care as you do the tasks that you like to do.

Second, the *rejection* by Pharaoh. "I will harden his heart, that he shall not let the people go" (v. 21). God had informed Moses earlier at the burning bush that Pharaoh was not going to be very receptive to Moses: "I am sure that the king of Egypt will not let you go, no not by a mighty hand" (Exodus 3:19). Here He again tells Moses that Pharaoh will reject him. It may seem redundant for God to again tell of Pharaoh's rejection. But we do need to be reminded periodically that in our work for the Lord we will experience rejection by many. "We must not think it strange if we meet with those who will not be wrought upon by the strongest arguments and fairest reasonings" (Matthew Henry). Being aware of this fact will keep us from being greatly discouraged when the rejection comes. Rejection is a big discourager in service; but if we know it is coming, we will be better prepared to react wisely to it than if we had no idea it was coming. We will not quit when some turn away from us.

The expression "I will harden his heart" is recorded here for the first time in Scripture. But we will see it a number of times again especially from chapters 7 through 14 in the book of Exodus. The term here in verse 7 bothers some, for they see it as God being mean and unjust to Pharaoh. But that is not the case at all. God is justified in this judgment. God is only doing to Pharaoh what Pharaoh has already done to himself and will continue to do to himself. Pharaoh had hardened his heart to the cruel slavery of the Israelites and allowed it to continue. Now God simply comes along and hardens Pharaoh's heart in justified punishment upon Pharaoh for his evil of hardening his heart to Israel's condition. This practice of God is illustrated in the New Testament as well as the Old Testament. As an example, in Romans 1 we are given some illustrations of this justified practice of God. It tells us that when men "glorified him [God] not as God, neither were thankful; but became vain in their imaginations . . . And changed the glory of the uncorruptible God into an image made like corruptible man, and birds, and fourfooted beasts, and creeping things . . . God also gave them up to uncleanness through the lusts of their own hearts, to dishonor their own bodies" (vv. 21,23,24). It reports that when men "changed the truth of God into a lie, and worshipped and served the creature more than the Creator . . . God gave them up unto vile affections" (vv. 25,26); and this first chapter of Romans says that when men "did not like to retain God in their knowledge, God gave them over to a reprobate mind" (v. 28). George Rawlinson summed it up well when he said, "Among the natural punishments which God has attached to sin . . . [is] the hardening of the entire nature of the man who sins."

Therefore, don't blame God for Pharaoh's hard heart. The hardening of Pharaoh's heart was a result of Pharaoh's poor behavior. As Keil says, "As the earthly sun produces different effects upon the earth, according to the nature of the soil upon which it shines, so the influence of the divine sun of grace manifests itself in different ways upon the human heart, according to its moral condition." Sun melts ice but causes clay to harden. Sun causes garbage to rot and put forth a foul odor, but it makes the flowers bloom and give forth a beautiful fragrance. The sun is not to blame for the detestable; neither is God to blame for Pharaoh's hardened heart.

It is of interest to note that eighteen times in Exodus, Pharaoh's heart is said to be hardened. Sometimes God is said to have hardened it, sometimes the Bible says Pharaoh hardened his own heart, and sometimes Scripture simply states that Pharaoh's heart was hardened. Three different Hebrew words are translated as "hard" or "hardened." These words speak of a heart that is firmly set against surrender to God's way; of a heart that is so evil it cannot make sense of good sense such as good advice or Divine revelation; and of a heart that is cruel, harsh, obstinate, and unfeeling. The "hard" heart is an awful condition for the heart to be in, but many souls through their rejection of God and His Word end up with a heart like that. And that assures them of spending eternity in hell fire.

The message to speak. God had promised Moses earlier that He would teach Moses what to say (v. 12). Here is some of that teaching. To study the message Moses is to speak, we will look at the source of the message, the son in the message, the service in the message, and the slaying in the message.

First, the *source* of the message. "Thou shalt say unto Pharaoh, Thus saith the LORD" (v. 22). The source of the message is "Thus saith the LORD." So the source of the message is God's Word. Moses, therefore, will have a good message, a valid message, a message of truth. In our last chapter we mentioned this lesson about where we are to get our message. Preachers especially need to pay attention here. We are to get our message from God's Word. We are to preach God's Word! Paul has exhorted us to do this with his "Preach the Word" (II Timothy 4:2). In order to preach the Word, we must, however, get into the Word in diligent study. This is where many preachers fail. They are so busy running here and there, attending this meeting and that meeting, and conducting weddings and funerals that they have little time to study God's Word. What a tragedy. Preachers do the congregation little good if they do not have a good substantial Bible message. There needs to be a lot more emphasis put on quality preaching today. Churches need to put more emphasis on the preaching part of the church's ministry. Churches without good preaching are not good churches!

The significant phrase "Thus saith the LORD" appears for the first time in the Bible in this verse. Hereafter, it will appear hundreds of times throughout the Word of God. Whenever we see "Thus saith the LORD," we need to take heed and pay attention. What God has to say is more important than what anyone else says. Men, however, often seem more interested in and spend more time on such things as "thus saith the lying, perverted news report" (newspapers and news magazines) and "thus saith the imagination" (fiction books). Eternity will be hard on such people.

Second, the *son* in the message. "Israel is my son, even my firstborn: And I say unto thee, Let my son go, that he may serve me" (vv. 22,23). The main theme of the message is the son, God's son. How evangelical is the connotation here to speak about the emancipation of man with the main theme of the message being about God's son; for the Gospel message about the emancipation of man from the bondage of sin has as its main theme God's Son, Jesus Christ. "Neither is there salvation in any other; for there is none other name under heaven given among men, whereby we must be saved" (Acts 4:12). Israel's deliverance from Egypt is a great picture of the redemption of the sinner—especially will this be seen in Exodus 12. And Christ, the Son of God, will be most conspicuous in type throughout Israel's emancipation from Egypt just as He is most conspicuous in person in the matter of our soul's salvation.

Third, the *service* in the message. There is a very important truth in this message about serving God. God told Pharaoh to "Let my son go, *that* he may serve me" (v. 23). Emancipation freedom is for the purpose of service. Israel is delivered from Egypt so they can serve God. After salvation is service. There are many professing believers in our churches today who need this truth emphasized in their life. They profess to be saved, but they have no interest in service. They do not want to go to hell, but they do not want to serve the One Who saved them from hell. The message of the Word of God, however, is that after one is saved, he is to serve. We will see this lesson repeatedly in the emancipation of Israel from Egypt.

Fourth, the *slaying* in the message. "If thou refuse to let him go, behold, I will slay thy son, even thy firstborn" (v. 23). Judgment (slaying) is also a part of the message. Many like to leave out the judgment part, but judgment is as essential as any part of the message.

Three things are said about judgment in this message. They are the certainty of judgment, the criteria of judgment, and the character of judgment. (1) The *certainty of judgment* is emphasized in the words "Behold, I will." You cannot ignore God's orders without consequences. You cannot sin without impunity. If Pharaoh refuses to let Israel go, he will be judged! Exodus 12 records the fulfillment of this warning given Pharaoh. (2) The *criteria of judgment* is on how Pharaoh treats God's son ("Let my son go" [v. 23]). How evangelical that message is! Whether a man goes to heaven or hell is determined solely on what he does with Jesus Christ, God's Son. Receive Christ as Savior and it is heaven for eternity. Reject Christ and it is hell fire for eternity. Whether a person goes to heaven or hell is not based on money, popularity, or achievements in business, politics, education, sports, or other things. What determines your eternal destiny is based solely upon what you have done with God's Son. (3) The *character of judgment* reminds us that you will often be judged in the coin in which you have sinned. If Pharaoh does not let God's firstborn son go free, then Pharaoh (and all Egypt) will lose their firstborn sons. God's chastening of His own people is often that way, too. He punishes you where you have sinned. That certainly makes Divine judgment fair and just.

B. THE PROBLEM OF NEGLECT
A sobering experience occurred shortly after Moses began his

trip from Midian to Egypt. It nearly cost Moses his life. The experience concerned the failure of Moses to have one of his sons circumcised. To study this experience, we will look at the character of the neglect, the chastening for the neglect, the correcting of the neglect, and the contempt in the neglect.

1. The Character of the Neglect

"Zipporah took a sharp stone, and cut off the foreskin of her son" (v. 25). Moses had neglected to take care of a very important matter in his family. One of his sons, Eliezer, the youngest of Moses' two sons, had not been circumcised. Circumcision was not a trivial act for the Jews. God gave circumcision to Abraham as a sign of the covenant (Genesis 17:9–14). This act was so important that failure to be circumcised would result in the uncircumcised being cut off from God's people: "And the uncircumcised man child whose flesh of his foreskin is not circumcised, that soul shall be cut off from his people; he hath broken my covenant" (Genesis 17:14).

So Moses had neglected to do a very important duty. Hence, it would be very inconsistent for Moses to lead in the fulfilling of God's part of the covenant when Moses had neglected fulfilling his own part of the covenant in his own family. "If Moses was to carry out the divine commission with success, he must first of all prove himself to be a faithful servant of Jehovah in his own house" (Keil). Therefore, God dealt with the matter.

We who preach the Word of God ought to live the Word of God. How inconsistent for us to encourage folk to follow the Lord if we are not faithfully following the Lord ourselves. Also let those who are critical of churches who have strict standards for their Sunday School teachers and church officers ponder this text. Sunday School teachers should live what they teach just as preachers should live what they preach. Church officers need to lead an exemplary life if they are to lead the church to do the same. It is not unreasonable to have high standards for Sunday School teachers and church officers. It is only consistent with the position they hold.

2. The Chastening for the Neglect

"And it came to pass by the way in the inn, that the LORD met him, and sought to kill him" (v. 24). We will note the severity of the chastisement and the support for the chastisement.

The severity of the chastisement. This chastisement was no light slap on the wrist. It nearly killed Moses. Exactly what God did to bring Moses near to death's door we are not told. Some speculate sickness, others think he had a death-threatening encounter with an angel similar to Balaam's experience (Numbers 22:22–33). But whatever it was, we do know that it disabled Moses from circumcising the boy; for when Moses was prodded by chastisement to order the circumcision of his boy, he did not do it himself as fathers normally did. Zipporah his wife did it (v. 25). This was very unusual and says that Moses was not able to do it. His chastisement had disabled him.

The support for the chastisement. Some think the chastisement was wholly disproportionate to the evil committed. But there are two factors about the evil which make the chastening justified: the magnitude of the evil and the man doing the evil.

First, the *magnitude of the evil.* As we noted earlier, circumcision was a very important sign of the covenant. Failure to circumcise a male would cut the uncircumcised off from the people of God. Failure to circumcise was rejection of the covenant. Therefore, we are not talking here about a trivial sin as some want to make it. This was a major failure. In New Testament language it was comparable to rejecting Jesus Christ. As rejecting circumcision cut one off from being part of God's earthy people, so rejecting Christ will cut one off from God's heavenly people.

Second, the *man doing the evil.* Moses was the one who neglected to do his duty of circumcising his son. Moses was not just an ordinary person. Rather, he had been appointed the chief leader of Israel. He had an extremely important position in God's service. And "the more responsibility an individual has, the more God expects of him" (Epp). The higher a person's position in God's work, the more sternly God will deal with him when he fails. F. B. Meyer speaks the same when he says, "The more dear we are to God, the more care will He expend on us. The more fruit-bearing qualities we possess, the more thoroughly shall we be pruned. The finest, rarest, metals are exposed to the whitest heat. And it was because Moses was to be so eminently used, that he came into God's most searching discipline." The surgeon going into the operating room will be required to be much cleaner and exact in regulations than the average man going about his mundane duties. There are some places in life where tolerances are extremely small. In the electrical part of a computer, tolerances are reduced to microscopic allowances. So it is spiritually. God's people who have been given much light and much responsibility will be given far less tolerance for their neglect and failures than will the young Christian who has little light and understanding in the faith and little position in service.

3. The Correcting of the Neglect

"Then Zipporah took a sharp stone, and cut off the foreskin of her son" (v. 25). When God chastens, the right way to respond is to correct the fault. Moses had neglected to circumcise his son. When God smote Moses in a death-threatening smite, the only right thing to do was to circumcise the son. "When God discovers to us what is amiss in our lives, we must give all diligence to amend it speedily, and particularly return to the duties we have neglected . . . The putting away of our sins is indispensably necessary to the removal of God's judgment" (Matthew Henry). Another speaks likewise when he said, "True repentance includes reparation for wrong, and where that is possible, performance of neglected duties" (J. Orr). We have many in society and in our churches that want to be forgiven but do not want to correct anything or make restitution anywhere. That is not true repentance. Moses must have his son circumcised or the matter will not be solved. And he did have his son circumcised. Though the chastening was stern, the corrective (circum-

161

cision) was successful in removing the chastening hand of God as "So he [God] let him [Moses] go" (v. 26) indicates.

4. The Contempt in the Neglect

"Zipporah . . . cast it [the foreskin of Eliezer] at his [Moses] feet, and said, Surely a bloody husband art thou to me" (v. 25). This was not a compliment from Zipporah. "The words are clearly a reproach, and the gist of the reproach seems to be that Moses was a husband who cost her dear, causing the blood of her sons to be shed in order to keep up a national usage which she regarded as barbarous" (Rawlinson). Zipporah reminds us of several other wives in the Bible who did not have the spiritual dedication their husbands had and, as a result, spoke scornful words about spiritual things. Job's wife told Job after he had been afflicted, "Curse God, and die" (Job 2:9). Job wisely responded, "Thou speakest as one of the foolish women speaketh" (Job 2:10). David's first wife Michal "despised him in her heart" (II Samuel 6:16) because of his great enthusiasm for the ark of God when it was being brought to Jerusalem. Then she told David in scornful exaggeration, "How glorious was the king of Israel today, who uncovered himself today in the eyes of the handmaids of his servants, as one of the vain fellows shamelessly uncovereth himself" (II Samuel 6:20). But David gave her a good answer when he said, "It was before the LORD . . . And I will yet be more vile [a sarcastic retort, in describing his dedication, to correspond to her exaggerated accusation] than thus, and will be base in mine own sight" (II Samuel 6:21,22).

Being a Midianite, Zipporah did not have appreciation for the covenant which God had made with Abraham and his seed. Thus she was not very compatible to Moses spiritually and would, as a result, have a negative influence on Moses in such matters as circumcision. This doubtless contributed to the neglect of this very important act for their son. This is a great warning about letting those around us, who do not have the zeal and interest in spiritual matters as we do, diminish our dedication to the things of the Lord. These folk may be friends or members of our close family whom we love much. But if their spiritual dedication is not what ours is, they can influence us in a bad way if we are not careful. This situation also exhorts those contemplating marriage not to marry one whose spiritual interest, dedication, and doctrine is not compatible. Spiritual capability is the most important thing to consider in marriage. Other things are important and have their place. But spiritual compatibility covers the most important areas of our life. Not being careful in this matter invites marriage disaster or spiritual disaster or both. And there are many wrecks from these disasters littered over the landscape of society.

Zipporah's contempt for a very important spiritual matter is obviously the reason she and the boys were sent back to Midian temporarily. They did not continue on with Moses as he journeyed back to Egypt, for Exodus 18:2 said, "He had sent her back." But Exodus 18:5 tells of their reunion with Moses after he had led the Israelites out to Mount Horeb. Some people, like Zipporah, are not spiritually capable of being on the front lines in the battle for God. Moses had some real battles in Egypt. Zipporah was not ready yet for those battles. Let us not be of the kind that are so spiritually weak that we have to be taken to the rear when the battle gets hot. Let us be so spiritually strong and dedicated that God can use us on the front lines without fear that we will lose heart and give up during the extreme intensity of the battle that occurs on the front lines.

C. THE PURSUIT OF DUTIES
With the neglect problem out of the way, Moses can begin to move on in the pursuit of his initial duties of leading Israel out of Egypt. In our text, this pursuit will involve the partner in the work and the persuading of the people.

1. The Partner in the Work
God had told Moses at the burning bush that Aaron would be his partner in the work (v. 14). While this was a result of Moses' rebellion, we still can see some encouraging lessons

here regarding Aaron and Moses. We will note these lessons as we look at the meeting of Aaron and the message for Aaron.

The meeting of Aaron. "And the LORD said to Aaron, Go into the wilderness to meet Moses. And he went, and met him in the mount of God, and kissed him" (v. 27). Moses needed to meet with Aaron in order to show him God's plan. God made the arrangements so the meeting would take place in a good spot—Mount Horeb. As Moses was making his way to Egypt, Aaron was making his way to see Moses—and they met at Mount Horeb.

Divine providence is most evident here. God speaks at both ends of the line. If Moses does what God tells him to do and Aaron does likewise, they will meet and in a place conducive for going over God's plan. Both men did obey God's orders here. Aaron went into the wilderness as instructed by God, and Moses headed for Egypt as instructed by God. Then they met at Mount Horeb. God rewards obedience. Things will "work together" (Romans 8:28) for those in the will of God. Do what God says, and you will meet the right people at the right time and in the right place. How many times, however, we miss these blessed providential workings together because we have not been concerned about doing the will of God.

The message for Aaron. "And Moses told Aaron all the words of the LORD who had sent him, and all the signs which he had commanded him" (v. 28). Moses did a good job of instructing Aaron. He told Aaron "all" the words which God had told Moses and about "all" the signs. Aaron needed to know these things if he was going to be the spokesman and if he was going to do the signs.

Moses' action in fully informing Aaron was just good plain common sense. If you want someone to do a job for you, give him adequate instructions. We have much lack of this wise practice in our churches, and it causes many church troubles. This is especially seen regarding the pastor's duties. Few people in the

church know what the pastor's duties are. Few pulpit commit-
tees ever know enough about the pastor's duties to spell out to
the candidates they interview what they expect of the pastor.
Some years ago when being interviewed by a pulpit committee,
I sensed quickly that the committee had very little knowledge of
what a pastor's calling was. So I said to the committee, "I know
my calling, do you?" Of course, they did not like that question;
but the question was needed to help them recognize their great
shortcomings. Many a pastor would escape much unjust criticism if his congregation knew what the duty of a pastor was. On
another occasion in one of my pastorates, an arrogant and ignorant dissident was railing on me for not getting something done
that he thought should be done. I told the dissident that I worked
nearly twice as many hours as he did at his job but got paid a
whole lot less than he did; and, therefore, he ought to quit complaining if I did not get everything done that he wanted me to
do; for the church was getting more than their money's worth.
Moses and Aaron would not have that problem, for Moses knew
what Aaron was to do and told Aaron "all" that he needed to do
so there would be no ignorance about Aaron's job.

2. The Persuading of the People

"And Moses and Aaron went and gathered together all the
elders of the children of Israel. And Aaron spake all the words
which the LORD had spoken unto Moses, and did the signs in
the sight of the people" (vv. 29,30). Upon arriving in Egypt,
Moses and Aaron proceeded with their duties of speaking the
message of God and doing the signs. The response of the people
was excellent. They believed and they worshipped.

They believed. "And the people believed" (v. 31). God had
told Moses they would believe (3:18), but Moses was a skeptic
(4:1). However, as always, time proved God right. The people
rejected Moses the first time. But this is forty years later and
things have changed. They are of a different mind than before.
When Aaron spoke "all the words which the LORD had spoken

165

unto Moses" (v. 30) and when he "did the signs in the sight of the people" (Ibid.), faith was the reaction of the Israelites.

Note that Aaron did the signs "in the sight of the people." When a work is genuine, it does not have to be done under the table or with slight of hand or with slick props to conceal the fraud that is in the work. Unfortunately, many popular religious programs today cannot do as Aaron because they are not real. But if a ministry is truly of God, it does not have to hide or conceal anything. It does not have to fear inspection by the people.

They worshipped. "Then they bowed their heads and worshipped" (v. 31). There are two factors which would cause Israel to worship here. One is faith and the other is gratitude.

First, *faith* caused the worship. Israel believed God's message. Therefore, they would worship; for faith leads one to worship. Belief bows before God. Unbelief does not, of course. We have a lot of folk who claim to have the faith, but they do not worship well. We seldom see them at church. Faith, however will be in church to worship. When a person is truly saved, his church attending habits will noticeably change especially if he was not in the habit of attending church prior to his salvation.

Second, *gratitude* also caused the worship. People who are truly thankful to God will worship God. "Worship [is] the proper outcome of thankfulness. Israel, down-trodden, oppressed, crushed beneath an intolerable tyranny, no sooner hears the promise of deliverance, than it displays its gratitude by 'bowing the head and worshipping.' Many Christians talk of being thankful for God's blessings vouchsafed to them, but never think of showing forth their thankfulness by any extra act of worship, or even any increased intensity in that portion of their ordinary worship which consists in thanksgiving . . . Time was when each national success was at once celebrated by a *Te Deum* [praise to God], and when each blessing granted to an individual drew forth a special offering. The thankfulness that does not show itself in some such overt act must be a very poor thankfulness" (Rawlinson).

166

VIII.

STIRRING UP PHARAOH

EXODUS 5

THE FIRST CHAPTER of Exodus focuses on the cruel slavery Israel was experiencing in Egypt. The next three chapters (two through four) focus on Moses, the man chosen by God to be the emancipator of Israel. Then the next ten chapters of Exodus (five through fourteen) focus on the great contest between Moses and Pharaoh, that traumatic ordeal of a year or so which was a battle of wits, words, and wonders, and which culminated in Israel's exodus from Egypt. In this chapter of our book, we commence the study of that ordeal. We will look specifically at how it all began with the stirring up of Pharaoh by the first of a number of visits of Moses and Aaron to him. That first visit was only a request for Israel to worship; but though the request was a simple one, it threw down the gauntlet in the battle with Pharaoh to free Israel from Egyptian bondage and boundaries.

The beginning of this conflict with Pharaoh was an especially trying time for Moses because of the problem of scorn which he faced. What made the scorning so bad is that he was not only scorned by the Egyptians, but he was also scorned by the Israelites. But those who serve God should not be surprised about this scorning Moses received by both friend and foe; for even Jesus Christ, the Greatest Servant of them all, experienced this cruel and wholly unmerited scorning. His enemies scorned Him His entire ministry, and in the end His closest friends forsook Him. If Christ and Moses suffered scorn for faithfully serving God, we, who are so very inferior to them, certainly should not complain if we suffer scorn in God's service.

In this study of the stirring up of Pharaoh which began the great conflict with Pharaoh over Israel's freedom, we will consider the request to worship (vv. 1,3), the reviling by Pharaoh (vv. 2,4–14), and the repining of Israel (vv. 15–23).

A. THE REQUEST TO WORSHIP

"And afterward Moses and Aaron went in, and told Pharaoh, Thus saith the LORD God of Israel, Let my people go, that they may hold a feast unto me in the wilderness (v. 1). To examine this request which so stirred up Pharaoh, we note the ramifications of the request, the reasonableness of the request, the repeating of the request, the requirements in the request, and the revealing by the request.

1. The Ramifications of the Request

Pharaoh would receive many requests every day from various people in his kingdom. But no request he received had more ramifications than this one from Moses and Aaron. It was a request that was going to affect the welfare of all the Egyptians. It, more than any other request, would determine the future of Egypt and reveal the wretched character of Pharaoh. But little did anyone in Pharaoh's palace realize the significance of this request and that Pharaoh's answer would make or break Egypt and himself. Little did anyone realize that when Moses and Aaron walked into Pharaoh's presence, it would greatly stir up Pharaoh and would be the beginning of the greatest assault upon Egypt that Egypt had ever experienced. In the coming months, the halls of the palace would echo again and again with devastating news. First the news of the great destruction of the plagues would reverberate throughout the palace repeatedly as each plague worked havoc on the land. Then would come the extremely bitter news that Pharaoh's first born son and all the firstborn sons of the Egyptians had died in the same night from the terrifying visit of the death angel. Finally, the shocking news that Pharaoh and the entire Egyptian army had been destroyed at the Red Sea would fill the palace with overwhelming defeat and dejection. Egypt had terribly mistreated Israel, and judgment time had come. But no Egyptian saw the harbinger of judgment in that initial visit of Moses and Aaron. No Egyptian saw in the request to worship the great ramifications involved. But when mankind rebels against God for a long time, suddenly without warning judgment comes.

2. The Reasonableness of the Request

There was nothing about this request that was not reasonable. Pharaoh could not reject it as being too demanding, too unusual, too strange, or too outlandish. We especially look here at three important ways in which the request should have been considered reasonable by Pharaoh. It was reasonable because of the practice of the day, because of the place for the worship, and because of the Person behind the request.

The practice of the day. The idea of worshipping a god of some sort was very acceptable in Moses' day. Atheism, unlike in our land today, did not influence the government to view worship as questionable. Rather, worship was very important. Pharaoh was not a non-religious person. In fact, he perceived himself as a god and paid tribute to all the other pagan deities in Egypt. Keil said, "When we consider that every nation presented sacrifices to its deities, and celebrated festivals in their honor, and that they had all their own modes of worship, which were supposed to be appointed by the gods themselves . . . the demand presented to Pharaoh on the part of the God of the Israelites appears so natural and reasonable." Our land, with all its boasted education, isn't as smart as the pagans in regards to believing religion is important in a person's life.

The place for the worship. Some might say that while it was reasonable for Moses and Aaron to request that Israel have a special time to worship God, it was unreasonable to request that they have this special occasion "in the wilderness" (v. 1) away from Egypt. But even this request should not have seemed unreasonable to Pharaoh. We note two reasons why—the attitude about location and the attitude about livestock.

First, the attitude about *location*. It was universally recognized among the heathen that their gods "could not be worshipped acceptably in every place" (Keil). Their gods had to be worshipped in specified places (note in John 4:20 the comment to Jesus by the woman at Jacob's well reflecting this belief). Hence, for Moses and Aaron to ask to go to a certain place to worship should certainly not have seemed an unusual or strange request to Pharaoh, but one he should have understood very well. It is true, of course, that we can worship the true God anywhere. But the point here is that the request to go to the desert to worship would not be an unreasonable request at all in the thinking of an Egyptian.

Second, the attitude about *livestock*. One important reason it was necessary for Israel to get out of Egypt to worship was the belief that the Egyptians had about animals. In their worship, Israel was to make sacrifices of animals—such as sheep, oxen, cows, etc. As we noted in a previous chapter of our book, these animals were held as sacred with the Egyptians; therefore, to sacrifice them in Egypt in front of the Egyptians would cause many problems indeed. Some weeks later, Moses argued this point with Pharaoh when Pharaoh wanted Israel to worship in Egypt. "And Moses said, It is not meet so to do; for we shall sacrifice the abomination of the Egyptians to the LORD our God; lo, shall we sacrifice the abomination of the Egyptians before their eyes, and will they not stone us?" (Exodus 8:26). As we noted in a previous chapter, Rawlinson said, "The fanaticism of the Egyptians on such occasions led to wars, tumults, and massacres." So the part of the request to go three days into the desert to worship should have seemed very reasonable to Pharaoh. He could not justifiably argue it otherwise.

The Person behind the request. Moses and Aaron made it plain that the request to worship came from their God. "The LORD God of Israel" (v. 1) was the source of the request. The idea of God commanding people to worship was very current in Pharaoh's day. Thus, the Person behind the request would also make the request reasonable. Pharaoh could understand very well the idea of a god requesting people to worship him at stated times and in stated places. So here is another reason that should have made the request to worship very reasonable to Pharaoh.

This reasonableness of the request to worship reflects the character of all of God's requests which He makes of us. Man, of course, does not think most of them are reasonable, and often complains. But no complaint is justified; for God is the Creator, and that gives Him the right to request anything of us. Paul spoke of the reasonableness of God's requests when he said, "I beseech you therefore, brethren, by the mercies of God, that ye present your bodies a living sacrifice, holy, acceptable unto God, which is your *reasonable* service" (Romans 12:1). Carnality will never call that "reasonable" service, however; for like Pharaoh, any request from the true God is too much for the flesh.

3. The Repeating of the Request

After the initial request was quickly and scornfully refused (v. 2) which we will note more about later, Moses and Aaron repeated their request. We note the determination and the decorum in the repeating of the request.

The determination. "And they said, The God of the Hebrews hath met with us; let us go, we pray thee, three days' journey into the desert [same word that is translated 'wilderness' in verse 1], and sacrifice unto the LORD our God; lest he fall upon us with pestilence, or with the sword" (v. 3). Moses and Aaron did not let the scornful refusal of their first request defeat them. But they repeated their request. They were "not abashed by a single refusal. They expostulate and urge fresh reasons why Pharaoh should accede to their request" (Rawlinson). Moses and Aaron were a determined duo that were not going to be easily turned aside by Pharaoh. Not only in this visit will they evidence their determination, but their continued contending with

Pharaoh over the coming months will also show it as well.

In the Lord's work determination is a very important factor if we are to serve Him acceptably. If we lack determination, we will wilt at the first difficulty, run away from our post when the first shot is fired at us, put up the white flag of surrender when the enemy first comes into view, and quit when the first criticism is heard. Moses will face many a set-back and disappointment in his dealing with Pharaoh. Without determination, he would never have made it past the first day.

We see determination in many different ways. Conviction is belief with determination. Faithfulness is determination to always do right. Courage is determination in times of perilous situations. A lot of people have determination in the things of the world but not in the things of God. Let God's people pray for more determination to serve Him well.

The decorum. "Let us go, we pray thee" (v. 3). "We pray thee" is not the language of disrespect but of good decorum. In the repeating of the request, Moses and Aaron exercised most respectable manners towards Pharaoh. They cannot be faulted for behaving themselves unbecomingly. Pharaoh may not like their message, but he certainly cannot criticize their conduct.

Unfortunately, the world often sees different behavior from God's people. Church officials, in dealing with the world, often reflect the arrogant, disrespectful attitude of the world that airs its complaints uncharitably. Church business meetings are seldom an example of good decorum. In one of our churches, a deacon in a deacons' meeting came off his chair in anger with a doubled-up fist to punch another deacon for no justified reason at all. This is generally the behavior of those who are in the wrong. When one is in the right, it is much easier to behave with proper decorum. And proper decorum is necessary if we are to reflect Christ in our conduct.

4. The Requirements in the Request

Here we look at what the request required of Israel. The

request not only required Pharaoh to let the people go, but very importantly, it required some specific things of the Israelites. We will examine the particulars of the requirements and the priority of the requirements.

The particulars of the requirements. The worship requirements for Israel involved three specific things: jubilation (the feast), oblation (the sacrifice), and separation (the three days into the wilderness).

First, *jubilation.* "Let my people go, that they may hold a feast unto me in the wilderness" (v. 1). The word "feast" does not speak of sorrow but of joy. William Wilson in his *Old Testament Word Studies* said the word means "a festival or occasion of great joy." Israel would indeed have great joy. It is always great joy to be liberated from bondage. In type, this feast represents the greatest joy of all. It is the joy of being redeemed. There is no greater joy, for there is no greater deliverance or blessing.

Worship should be a joyous occasion for the redeemed. But the carnal often skips out of the worship services to enjoy the pleasures of the world instead. Such folk do not know what real joy and the greatest joy is all about. Paul said, "Rejoice in the Lord always; and again I say, Rejoice" (Philippians 4:4). It is strange that we have to be told to rejoice in the Lord, but the flesh is so strong in us that we must have the exhortation given us at times.

Second, *oblation.* Israel was instructed to go into the wilderness to "sacrifice unto the LORD our God" (v. 3). There is both a theological lesson and a practical lesson in the requirement to sacrifice.

The *theological lesson* is that the true worship of God will revolve around Jesus Christ, The Great Sacrifice, which all the animal sacrifices represented in type. The shedding of blood for man's sin is the message of these blood sacrifices. "Without shedding of blood is no remission" (Hebrews 9:22) of sin. These sacrifices sent forth a message that is just as appropriate today as it was then. The message, in New Testament terminology, is that "the blood of Jesus Christ his Son cleanseth us from all sin" (I John 1:7). If that is not front and center in your worship, you are not worshipping correctly, your theology is no good, and you are not better than the pagans in your worship.

The *practical lesson* is that true worship involves sacrifice. In order for us to serve God we will find it necessary to sacrifice. We will have to sacrifice time, energy, money, and any number of other things in order to worship. This lesson has not gotten through to many professing believers in our modern age. As an example, many of these folk want a nice church building to worship in but do not want to give financially to make the building possible.

Third, *separation*. Israel was to go "into the wilderness . . . three days' journey" (vv. 1,3) to sacrifice. Earlier we looked at the practical problem of their worshipping in Egypt because of the animal sacrifices. Here we note another practical lesson regarding the separation. It is about the truth that when we worship the Lord, we are to separate from Egypt and what it represents. We cannot worship with the world without corrupting our worship. We cannot worship in a church that denies the great doctrines of the faith. We cannot join hands with modernists in church meetings without compromising our doctrine. Biblical separation in our worship is not a favorite or respected belief of most people, but it is taught in Scripture. Separatists in worship are often viewed as legalists and "holier-than-thou" people, but that does not negate the wisdom of separation in worship.

The priority of the requirements. How important was it that Israel worship God? It was extremely important. Israel was to worship God "lest he [God] fall upon us with pestilence, or with the sword" (v. 3). It is worship or judgment. It is still thus. Men either bow down in worship or they will fall down in judgment. A number of folk need a reminder of the priority of worship. They attend church rather infrequently. Their worship habits are spasmodic. They have no fear of God about being unfaithful in worship. But God is to be worshipped! The church worship services are not optional occasions. However, our nation is not doing well in worshipping God; and, as a result, judgment has been pressing on us more and more. Will we as a nation change our worship habits before it is too late and judgment destroys us? The trend of the times certainly does not encourage a favorable answer.

This judgment warning ought to have helped Pharaoh to give priority to Israel's worship request from the standpoint that if Israel was smitten for failing to worship, Pharaoh would lose a great host of laborers for his nation. But Pharaoh missed the warning as he would miss many warnings given later. His sin so hardened his heart that he was no longer perceptive of Divine warnings. It is a terrible condition to be in, but it is what happens when we persist in our sin.

5. The Revealing by the Request

This first encounter with Pharaoh was to reveal Pharaoh. It was to expose his heart. Especially would it reveal his attitude about his possessions and his honor. It would challenge Pharaoh to see if he considered his possessions (the Israelite slaves) just his or in truth that they belonged primarily to God, and it would challenge Pharaoh to see if he placed his own honor above God's honor. Unfortunately, Pharaoh failed these challenges miserably and revealed quickly the wretchedness of his heart regarding personal possessions and honor.

These challenges which involve a man's possessions and honor will touch man in his most tender spots and will quickly reveal where man stands regarding God. This truth is often observed in church. Let the pastor preach on giving and people will often complain. Of course, they can go out and spend their money liberally on many wasteful things and not be bothered. But let the pastor put God's claim on their possessions and they immediately react adversely. Also, how quickly do people in church get upset if they are not duly recognized and honored. I learned early in my ministry that to even leave out of the Sunday bulletin a name of a person who poured kool-aid at Vacation Bible School could get the pastor in trouble with some of his parishioners. Why? Because it had to do with honor. Even failing to give the slightest of honors upsets some.

Before anyone will be used much by God, they will have to deal with this matter of possessions and honor. They will have to take a loose hold of their possessions so God can take a stronger hold, and they will have to learn humility. But we should not complain. Jesus Christ had to meet those challenges successfully to become our Redeemer. In regards to possessions, "though he was rich, yet for your sakes he became poor, that ye through his poverty might be rich" (II Corinthians 8:9). In regards to honor, he "made himself of no reputation, and took upon him the form of a servant" (Philippians 2:7). Pharaoh destroyed his kingdom and himself because he failed in the tests concerning possessions and honor. Unfortunately, he is not the only one to do the same. The world is filled with wrecks of kingdoms and lives because of failures in the matter of one's possessions and honors.

B. THE REVILING BY PHARAOH

Pharaoh's response to the request for Israel to worship was full of scorn. His scorn for Moses and for Israel and their welfare and their God knew no bounds. To examine his reviling action, we will note his confession of ignorance, his charge of idleness, his cruelty to Israel, his contempt for instructions, and his comrades in iniquity.

1. His Confession of Ignorance

"And Pharaoh said, Who is the LORD, that I should obey his voice to let Israel go? I know not the LORD, neither will I let Israel go" (v. 2). We need to understand that what Pharaoh really said here was, "Who is Jehovah?" not "Who is the Lord?"; for "Lord was a common name applied to objects of worship; but Jehovah was a name the king of Egypt had never heard of" (Jamieson). Pharaoh knew well about the idol gods, but he did not know about Jehovah God Who is the Almighty God, and he unashamedly confesses his ignorance of Him in our text. It is one thing to be ignorant, but it is another to be arrogantly ignorant as was Pharaoh. A year from this time, however, his proud defiance and ignorance would be completely gone. He would not be speaking this way anymore, for he would be suffering greatly in hades for his rejection of Jehovah God.

Pharaoh's confession had two significant parts to it which are always related. We call them the "Who" and "do" parts. He did not know Israel's God (the "Who" part) and so he would not obey what Israel's God said to do (the "do" part). The important lesson here is that we must know the "Who" if the "do" is to occur. The Apostle Paul asked two questions when he was converted, and these questions spoke this same truth. First, he asked the "Who" question—"Who art thou, Lord?" (Acts 9:5); then he asked the "do" question—"What wilt thou have me to do?" (Acts 9:6). Paul certainly became well acquainted with the "Who" part, and that accounts for why he was so excellent in the "do" part.

The "Who" and "do" issue is the reason for Christ's judgment on man, for Scripture says when He returns "in flaming fire . . . [He will take] vengeance on them that know not God, and that obey not the Gospel of our Lord Jesus Christ" (II Thessalonians 1:8). Judgment comes upon those who did not know the "Who" and as a result did not "do" what He commanded them to do.

Our churches need to be more earnest about teaching the "Who" if they are going to get people to live the "do." But our churches are not doing a good job teaching about God. They seem to avoid any substantial teaching about Him. Any teaching they do is shallow and only a repeating of common place terms which say very little concerning the person and work of the Almighty. But "do" is always based on the "Who." If we have not taught well the "Who," we will not see the "do" performed well. Pharaoh was extremely deficient in the "Who," and this made the "do" likewise.

2. His Charge of Idleness

"And the king of Egypt said unto them, Wherefore do ye, Moses and Aaron, let the people from their works? get you unto your burdens . . . ye make them rest from their burdens . . . they be idle . . . Ye are idle, ye are idle" (vv. 4,5,8,17). Pharaoh had no basis for this scornful charge. To the contrary, evidence was everywhere showing the great labor the Israelites had done for the Egyptians. "They built for Pharaoh treasure cities, Pithom and Raamses" (Exodus 1:11) and made many bricks and served "in all manner of service in the field . . . with rigor" (Exodus 1:14). But wicked men do not need facts in order to accuse. They say whatever they need to say to support their cause or contention regardless of whether it is true or not.

Note in this charge the subtle scorn Pharaoh heaped on Moses as well as on Aaron. He said to them, "Get you unto your burdens" (v. 4). Pharaoh would not give any respect to Moses and Aaron as being the chief representatives of Israel. No, he would treat them as nothing but lowly slaves. But as we noted earlier, those who would serve God need not be surprised if they are given little honor by the world. But they will get honor from God, and honor from God is what matters.

This charge of idleness shows how evil people view true worship. They view it as only something to do if there is nothing else to do. "Men who choose not to obey the calls of God will always revile those who do. They will impute their zeal to hypocrisy, or idleness, or conceit, and vanity" (Charles Simeon). These evil folk view true worship as a hindrance to progress and a productive way of life. So today Sundays are big business days for the stores and big days for the entertainment field. Many church members reflect this spirit of the world by their spasmodic church attendance. They, too, indicate by their poor church attendance that worship is only when you have nothing else to do and when it does not interfere with other matters in life. Sunday work now is hardly protested, but the day will come when those who went off to work on Sunday will loathe their lack of dedication to worship.

178

3. His Cruelty to Israel

Pharaoh did not stop with reviling words, but resorted to reviling deeds. His response to Moses and Aaron's request to worship was to heap more cruel treatment upon the Israelites. We note the particulars of the cruelty, the purpose of the cruelty, and the promptness of the cruelty.

The particulars of the cruelty. Pharaoh's cruel reaction to the request to worship consisted in his ordering the taskmasters to "no more give the people [the Israelites] straw to make brick, as heretofore; let them go and gather straw for themselves. And the tale [number quota] of the bricks, which they did make heretofore, ye shall lay upon them; ye shall not diminish ought thereof" (vv. 7,8). Straw did for the brick here what our reinforcing rods do for concrete. The straw was chopped into small stems and mixed in the clay that was made into brick. Some of the very ancient buildings of Egypt bear out the fact that straw was indeed mixed with the brick to strengthen the brick. Heretofore, the straw had been furnished by the Egyptians for the Israelite brick makers. But now the Israelites are required to get the straw themselves. This would, of course, really add to their workload and make it impossible for them to keep up the quota of bricks. And to make matters worse, the Egyptian taskmasters had no sympathy for this problem; for when the Israelites failed to keep up the quota of bricks because they had to spend so much time gathering straw for the bricks, "the officers of the children of Israel, which Pharaoh's taskmasters had set over them, were beaten" (v. 14).

Pharaoh's cruelty was despicable. It was so unjust. His reaction to the request to worship was barbarous. But such cruelty reflects one's contempt for God. Matthew Henry correctly said, "Ignorance and contempt of God are at the bottom of all the wickedness that is in the world." The more men reject God, the more cruelty will be seen in society. History abundantly bears out this fact. Nations ruled by godless rulers have been characterized by terrible atrocities. Stalin, Hitler, and Mao are some recent examples of this truth. Abortion demonstrates the great increase of the rejection of God in our land today. So does the increase in crime. Our jails and prisons are not filled with God-fearing criminals, but with God-scorning criminals.

The purpose of the cruelty. The purpose for this cruelty was twofold. First, Pharaoh would put *fear in their heart.* By this cruel, additional workload, he would endeavor to frighten the Israelites away from making anymore requests to worship. He would want them to think that anymore such requests would result in even more punishment. This would certainly check the extent of one's dedication to worship. Second, Pharaoh would put *fullness in their hours.* By this cruel, additional workload, he would endeavor to fill their lives so full that they would not have time to worship or even think about worship. This is a typical practice of Satan. We need to be wise here and watch our own schedule lest we fall into this snare of the Satan.

The promptness of the cruelty. Pharaoh's cruel orders were given "the same day" (v. 6) that Moses and Aaron spoke to Pharaoh requesting time to worship. Pharaoh did not waste anytime in giving his cruel orders. This is a great rebuke to the saints for their slow response in their service for God. If trouble begins to brew in the church, the members are very slow in doing anything about it. Hence, the troublemakers do a lot of damage, often irreparable damage, before the good members finally decide to do something about it. The same is true in the individual lives of believers. Temptation comes along and they are slow to react. But if they "the same day" begin to fight it, they would not be suffering so many defeats. Evil is energetic and does not delay; God's people need to be the same way in their consecration.

4. His Contempt for Instructions

"Vain words" (v. 9) was how Pharaoh characterized the instructive words of God regarding worship spoken by Moses and Aaron. Pharaoh's attitudes about the things of God certainly do not reflect good judgment or intelligence. But it has been the habitual habit of the high and mighty in the world to be void of wisdom in the most important matters of life. "They have ever been the most forward to write folly and vanity upon the divine testimonies" (Mackintosh). If you want to get a stupid and ridiculous answer about God, about Jesus Christ and salvation, and about the Word of God just ask the president of our country or some important figure in the halls of our Congress or some judge in a high federal court. They may know their way around politics and other matters of life, but when it comes to the most important matters of life, they are not any better than a half-wit. Calling God's Word "vain" is ludicrous. It was Pharaoh's words that were vain, not God's Word.

5. His Comrades in Iniquity

"And the taskmasters of the people went out, and their officers, and they spake to the people, saying, Thus saith Pharaoh, I will not give you straw. Go ye, get you straw where ye can find it; yet not ought of your work shall be diminished . . . And the taskmasters hasted them, saying, Fulfill your works, your daily tasks, as when there was straw" (vv. 10,11,13). As grossly inequitable as the orders of Pharaoh were, he had no difficulty finding those who would go along with him and enthusiastically enforce his orders. This is ever the case with evil. Wicked men have no difficulty in finding comrades to assist them in their evil. Unfortunately, this is not true when it comes to good causes. Especially is this not true in the work of the Lord. As an example, many godly pastors will have difficulty getting church members to help serve in the ministry of the church. But let some dissident come along and stir up trouble in the church, and that dissident will quickly gather a following to help him stir up more trouble.

One of the reasons people so readily follow an evil person is that they have no convictions or moral backbone. Let the boss decree that all clerks must sell lottery tickets and every clerk falls in line, even those who claim to be Christian. If the professing Christians had convictions, they would not do this. They would give up their job before they cooperated with evil. But Christendom today lacks good convictions. They may talk big when the opposition is not around, but when evil shows up and starts giving orders, they fall in line.

C. THE REPINING OF ISRAEL

The repining reaction of Israel to all of this mistreatment is seen in a threefold way: the cry to Pharaoh, the condemnation of Moses, and the complaint to God. It was not a good performance by anyone in Israel. They did not react to their problem well at all. But it is a performance that most of us are guilty of repeating all too often ourselves when troubles beset us.

1. The Cry to Pharaoh

"Then the officers of the children of Israel came and cried unto Pharaoh, saying, Wherefore dealest thou thus with thy servants? . . . behold, thy servants are beaten; but the fault is in thine own people" (vv. 15,16). Rawlinson said, "The shrill 'cry' of Orientals when making complaint has often been noticed by travellers, and is probably here alluded to." Though what the officers said to Pharaoh was indeed true, the cry of the officers to Pharaoh was a faulty cry. We see this in two ways: whom they cried to and what they cried about.

Whom they cried to. The fault of the Israelite officers in whom they cried to about their problem was that they did not cry to God. They only cried to Pharaoh, and it was a futile effort in solving their problems. While it was not necessarily wrong for the Israelites to go to Pharaoh, nor is it necessarily wrong for people to go to government leaders of our day, it is an effort that is often greatly over-valued as to its effectiveness; and it is no substitute for going to God for help. But as Pink said when commenting on this text, "How true to human nature is this! Instead of crying unto the Lord, these leaders of the Israelites turned unto Pharaoh for relief. Doubtless they hoped to appeal to his pity or to his sense of justice. Surely [in their thinking] they could show him that his demands were unreasonable and impossible of fulfillment. Alas, the natural man ever prefers to lean upon an arm of flesh than be supported by Him who is invisible."

There is a great increase in emphasis today in our churches on petitions to government officials, on protest meetings, and on picketing. These are not evil in themselves, but what often causes them to be an indictment upon the churches is the fact that we seldom see the same zeal and enthusiasm in seeking God for the correction of an evil or for having meetings to call church members to repentance of their sins in order to remedy some of their problems. You can often get a multitude of church members to petition the government that you cannot get out to any special prayer meeting at church or even the regular prayer meeting. Furthermore, those who evidence so much zeal for picketing places of iniquity and attending protest meetings in the community seem to have very little zeal for doctrinal correctness, for they stand side by side with modernists and apostates in the picketing and protesting endeavors. They seem oblivious to the fact that poor doctrine is what is at the bottom of all the evil in the land.

What they cried about. The officers of the people complained to Pharaoh about their work situations, not about their worship situation. That betrays their poor priorities. In contrast, when Moses and Aaron went into Pharaoh, they did not mention the unjust work conditions. They mentioned the lack of worship opportunities, for to them the worship situation had a priority over the work situation.

The priority problem of the officers is not unique. We see this in our own lives all too often. Ask for prayer requests in a church prayer meeting and the great portion of the requests have to do with material and physical needs, not spiritual needs. It is not wrong to bring our material and physical needs to God—we ought to, in fact, do this. But there is something wrong with us when there is a much greater emphasis on the material and physical than on the spiritual. The officers of Israel as well as anyone else will learn that when we put our spiritual needs above our physical and material needs, we will have much more success in meeting our material and physical needs than if we give them more priority than our spiritual needs. "Seek ye first the kingdom of God, and his righteousness; and all these things shall be added unto you" (Matthew 6:33) confirms that fact.

2. The Condemnation of Moses

That the Israelite officers were not of good character in going to Pharaoh is confirmed by the unkind way they treated Moses (and also Aaron). "And they met Moses and Aaron, who stood in the way, as they came forth from Pharaoh. And they said unto them, The LORD look upon you, and judge; because ye have made our savour to be abhorred in the eyes of Pharaoh, and in the eyes of his servants, to put a sword in their hand to slay us" (vv. 20,21). Moses and Aaron were waiting for the officers to come back from their meeting from Pharaoh. That is what "Who stood in the way" (v. 20) means. This meeting "was not [an] accident but design that had brought the two brothers to the spot. They were as anxious as the officers to know what course Pharaoh would take—whether he would relax the burdens of the people or no—whether he would have compassion or the contrary" (Rawlinson). Moses and Aaron would not be happy with what Pharaoh said. Neither would they be happy with the condemnation the Israelite officers heaped upon them for their problems.

Blaming Moses and Aaron for the problems evidenced very plainly that these officers of Israel were unable to analyze their problems correctly. They never saw the root cause or the foundational reason for their conflicts. They were shallow in discernment and only saw the surface of their situation. So it is with many people. Take government welfare as an example. All the government money in the world is not going to solve the problems of those on welfare because the welfare people have greater problems than lack of money or a job. But how many people in society are savvy enough to recognize that welfare is caused by poor morals, poor behavior, alcohol, gambling, etc. and that if you do not address these problems, you have no remedy whatever. In the church we also see many who have little ability to analyze problems well. They look at the scoreboard (the attendance board); and if the attendance goes up, the pastor is okay. If the attendance goes down, the pastor is bad and needs to be dismissed. They have no more sense than that as to why attendance goes up and down. When it goes down, they never perceive the rebellion of sinful natures as a cause; they only see the pastor as the cause though he warns against rebelling against God. They never see worldliness as a cause; they only see the pastor as the cause though the pastor warns against worldliness more than anyone else in the church.

But if all you are going to listen to is Pharaoh, you will not analyze your problems well. If you spend more time listening to the perverted news media than you do to the Word of God, you will not perceive well the causes of evil and the needs of the church and of your own life. You will think Moses is the culprit when it is Pharaoh. You will castigate those who are your friends and honor your enemies. You will vote for those you should vote against.

3. The Complaint to God

"And Moses returned unto the LORD, and said, Lord, wherefore hast thou so evil entreated this people? why is it that thou hast sent me? For since I came to Pharaoh to speak in thy name, he hath done evil to this people; neither hast thou delivered thy people at all" (vv. 22,23). We note five features about this complaint. They are the commendation, the charge, the challenge, the censure, and the charity in the complaint.

The commendation in the complaint. "And Moses returned unto the LORD" (v. 22). While Moses' comments to God were

185

not good ones, what is to be commended about Moses' action here is that he took his troubles to God. When the officers of Israel showered him with scorn and Pharaoh's actions got worse, he simply went to God in prayer. And as we will see in our next chapter, he did not seek God in vain. Even though his attitude was deficient, God still honored him for coming to Him.

The world and carnal saints do not go to the Lord as readily as Moses did. They prefer to go to the world for help as did the officers of Israel. They ignore God and seek help from those who have little use for God. Counselors, psychiatrists, psychologists, newspaper columnists, and other people of the world are besieged for help; but few seek God. As the officers of Israel discovered in seeing Pharaoh, those who seek the world in exclusion of God will only increase their problems, not decrease them. Leave God out of the picture, and you will never get much help for your problems, but you will see your troubles increase.

The charge in the complaint. "Wherefore hast thou so evil entreated this people?" (v. 22). Moses did in his complaint what so many people do in every age—they blame God for the evil in the world. Later in the complaint, Moses correctly said that Pharaoh "hath done evil to this people" (v. 23). But here he blames God for the evil. When will mankind ever learn that God is not to blame for evil? But typical of man, he will blame God quicker for problems than he will blame anyone else. Frequently we hear folk ask, "Why does God allow all the suffering and wars and diseases to plague the world?" But that is not the right question. There are better questions than that one to ask. We need to ask, "Why do men disobey God and ignore His warnings and thus bring upon themselves so much trouble?" We need to ask, "Why do men hate and steal and kill and thus bring so much sorrow and suffering upon the earth?" It is not God that brings evil upon mankind! If a doctor tells you what to do to become healed of your infirmity and you fail to do that, is it the doctor's fault that you are still sick or that you die? Of

186

course not. Neither is it God's fault when you rebel against His ways and as a result bring much trouble into your life.

The challenge in the complaint. "Why is it that thou hast sent me? For since I came to Pharaoh to speak in thy name, he hath done evil to this people" (vv. 22,23). Moses challenges God about the value of his calling. Since he did not see good results right away, he questions the wisdom of God in calling him to emancipate Israel. Moses' reaction to adversity in service is not unusual though it is wrong. Anyone who has tried to serve the Lord knows this feeling. But "We must never suppose that the difficulties which confront us indicate that we are not on God's path, and doing his work" (F. B. Meyer). The Apostle Paul had good perspective in this matter when he said, "For a great door and effectual is opened unto me, and there are many adversaries" (I Corinthians 16:9). James Smith of *Handfuls on Purpose* said, "Who has ever achieved great things for Him without having overcome bitter and desperate conditions?" Our calling is not determined by quick success or even success in the eyes of men but by the will of God.

The censure in the complaint. "Neither hast thou delivered thy people at all" (v. 23). Moses censures God for failure to deliver Israel. But the accusation of failure was totally unjust. In this censure, Moses ignored the promise of God. God had not promised deliverance right away. Moses had been duly instructed that Pharaoh would not immediately let Israel go, but that it would only be after God had smitten Pharaoh that he would finally let Israel go (Exodus 3:19,20; 4:21). Moses has no reason at all to accuse God of failure. Moses simply did not have the patience for the fulfillment of the promise.

This is a hard lesson to learn. We are instantly saved the moment we trust Christ as Savior, but most other blessings do not come instantly. Salvation needs to come instantly because of eternal safety, but other blessings come over a period of time to teach us character. So when we plant seed in the ground, it is months before harvest comes. We become sick and go to a doctor and are given medicine; but it may be weeks, even months, before we are fully recovered. A good work, a good healing will not always come overnight. We rejoice when they do; but when they take time, it helps us to learn patience and wisdom. It takes time to correct the problems of government, too. People make a mistake if they think we can undo in a few weeks what the government has been doing in the last fifty years. Those in countries which have recently overthrown communism are disappointed in capitalism because it does not make them like the United States overnight. But they need to understand that the benefits of capitalism in the United States did not come overnight and neither will they enjoy the results of capitalism overnight.

People are so unfair with God in this complaint. They take their jolly good time in coming around in dedication and in doing His orders, but they want God to do things right now when they make their request.

The charity in the complaint. You will note in this prayer of complaint to God that Moses does not mention the cruel castigation he received from his own brethren. After what the officers of Israel said to Moses, we would have thought Moses would have gone to God and spent nearly his entire prayer on these ungrateful Israelites and their unjust accusations of him. That he did not pray that way was a mark of charity in a prayer that otherwise lacked charity. It was a bit of fresh air in the midst of the foul air of the complaint Moses made to God. It was a glimpse of the meekness of Moses' character that was so commendable. And it exhorts us to be more charitable towards those who are upset and experiencing severe troubles who may in the midst of their troubles speak out harshly to us.

IX.

SUPPORT FROM GOD

EXODUS 6:1–13

IN THIS STUDY we give special attention to the great support that God gave Moses during the early days of his emancipation work in Egypt. It was a critical time for Moses. Things seemed to be going from bad to worse. The initial request made by Moses to Pharaoh to give Israel some time to worship only resulted in more trouble for Israel from Pharaoh. This caused even the Israelites to turn against Moses. As we noted at the end of our last chapter, this turn of events had put Moses in such despair that he was questioning his call to be Israel's emancipator. But in his despair, there was One Who did not forsake him. God did not forsake him but stood by Moses and gave Moses much support for his work. When it seemed like everybody and every circumstance were against him, "Then" (v. 1) Moses found that God was still for him. When we do the will of God faithfully, we will always find that God is for us even though everyone and everything else seems to be against us. We may lack the support of people and circumstances; but if we have God's support, we will have enough support to get the victory.

To further study this great support God gave Moses in this critical juncture in Moses' work as Israel's emancipator, we will consider the encouraging of Moses (vv. 1–8), the expounding by Moses (v. 9), and the exhorting for Moses (vv. 10–13).

A. THE ENCOURAGING OF MOSES

Greatly discouraged by the worsening of Israel's situation, Moses is given some great encouragement from God to lift his

189

spirits and keep him going in God's service. These encouragements were fourfold: the power of God, the person of God, the performance of God, and the promises of God.

1. The Power of God

"Then [after Moses had prayed] the LORD said unto Moses, Now shalt thou see what I will do to Pharaoh; for with a strong hand shall he let them go, and with a strong hand shall he drive them out of his land" (v. 1). This statement had to be tremendously encouraging to Moses. It indicated two important things about God's power: the moment of God's power and the magnitude of God's power.

The moment of God's power. "*Now* shalt thou see what I will do to Pharaoh" says the wait is over. "Now" Moses would start seeing the power of God displayed against Pharaoh, that evil tyrant who had so mercilessly added to Israel's cruel bondage after Moses made the request for Israel to worship. The curtain was being raised on the stage of Divine revenge and the intervention of God was to begin. The long wait was over. "Now" Moses would see things happen. Though Pharaoh would not let Israel go right away, Moses would, however, start seeing the signs and wonders of God's power as never before. That in itself would encourage him and would compensate for the immediate lack of deliverance of the Israelites from Egypt.

Our hearts can certainly be encouraged in this "now" aspect of God's power in our text. It shows us that the moment of God's power is when the enemy seems to have his greatest power and we are weaker than ever before. The moment of God's power is when from the natural standpoint we look the least likely to overcome the enemy. God often waits until things are their worst before He steps in. This gives Him opportunity to show how great His power really is. And the greater we behold His power, the greater our faith can be encouraged.

The magnitude of God's power. The display of God's power

would take second place to no other display of power. Pharaoh had been a man of great power, but he would be overwhelmed by God's power. He would to be rendered helpless by the power of God. Though strong Pharaoh may be in the eyes of man, God's power is so great that Pharaoh will be laid low and forced to do as God desires. Pharaoh will not be able to keep Israel in Egypt. "For with a strong hand shall he let them go, and with a strong hand shall he drive them out of his land" (v. 1).

We need to clarify the meaning of this verse lest it be misunderstood as it easily can be. The "strong hand" in the verse is God's hand, not Pharaoh's hand. A more understandable rendering of the verse is this: "Because of the strong hand of God, Pharaoh will let them go; and because of the strong hand of God, Pharaoh will drive them out of the land." God's power will so overcome Pharaoh that Pharaoh will end up urging and forcing Israel to do the very thing that Pharaoh had been fighting against for so long. The climax of this action is seen in Exodus 12 which tells us that when all the firstborn of the Egyptians were slain, "Pharaoh rose up in the night . . . And he called for Moses and Aaron by night, and said, Rise up, and get you forth from among my people, both ye and the children of Israel" (Exodus 12:30,31). Pharaoh ordered the Israelites to leave; he drove them out of the land because of the force of God's hand to change Pharaoh's mind.

How wonderful is God's power. It can cause the enemy to do the very thing the enemy adamantly opposes. It can cause Pharaoh to insist on action he had heretofore strongly opposed. It can cause Haman to give honor to Mordecai though he utterly despised Mordecai and sought his destruction. God's power can cause our most adverse circumstances, which threaten our destruction, to become circumstances that promote our well being. God's power can make the wrath of man to praise Him (Psalm 76:10). In our dark hours, let us be encouraged by this knowledge of God's power. We often limit God to circumstances; that is, if they are easy then God can help us; but if they are difficult, then we assume God is helpless, and so we give up.

No circumstances were more discouraging than what Moses faced. Yet, within a year or so he would see amazing changes because of God's power.

2. The Person of God

The next encouragement for Moses was to have reiterated to him the character of the person of God. "And God spake unto Moses, and said unto him, I am the LORD: And I appeared unto Abraham, unto Isaac, and unto Jacob, by the name of God Almighty, but by my name JEHOVAH was I not known to them" (vv. 2,3). Here again we wish the translators had used the word "JEHOVAH" consistently instead of replacing it in verse 2 with the word "LORD." Using the word "LORD" in verse 2 obscures the significance of the statements about the name of God in that verse and fails to show its relationship with the "JEHOVAH" statement in the next verse as well as in the previous chapters. Using the word "LORD" in verse 2 and "JEHOVAH" in verse 3 does not make good sense. It is confusing and illogical and obscures important Divine truth.

What God is telling Moses here is related to what He told Moses in the wilderness about His name. The message is that from now on, God will be known primarily to Israel by the name of Jehovah. While Abraham, Isaac, and Jacob knew the name Jehovah as one of the names of God, that name was not a prominent name to them. It was not the primary name by which they knew God. But now it will be. And we need to be aware of that fact and understand it well if we are going to understand other Scripture well. As an example, the issue at Mount Carmel was who was God? Jehovah or Baal. It was not Almighty God or Baal, but Jehovah or Baal. Jehovah was Almighty God to the faithful; Baal was evil's Almighty God.

While the flesh sees little encouragement in knowing the name of God, Scripture, as we learned in an earlier chapter, tells us otherwise—"They that know thy name will put their trust in thee" (Psalm 9:10), and "the people that do know their God shall be strong, and do exploits" (Daniel 11:32). In an earlier

192

chapter, we learned that the names of God indicate the character of God. The meaning of the name Jehovah (amplified in the "I AM THAT I AM") underscores His greatness, His power, His self-existence, and thus His superiority. Since it is Jehovah, not some lesser person, Who is making these great promises to Moses, this will provide much encouragement for Moses. Hence, the emphasis on the person of God in these two verses is a very significant encouragement for Moses.

In our day of shallow sermons and shallow knowledge of God, let us learn from this Scripture the importance of really knowing God and Who He is. The better we know God, the better our faith, and, therefore, the greater our encouragement in difficult times.

We would note in passing that the statement, "I am the LORD" (v. 2) is repeated twice more (verses 6 and 8) in this chapter, and in each case it underscores the Deity of Christ. The reason it declares the Deity of Christ is that it is plainly stated in our text that God is speaking, and it is plainly stated that God said He was "Jehovah." Knowing that the Jehovah of the Old Testament is the Jesus of the New Testament, we have here, then, an emphatic declaration of the Deity of Jesus Christ. But every time the word "LORD" is used instead of "Jehovah," this fact is obscured.

3. The Performance of God

"And I have also established my covenant with them, to give them the land of Canaan, the land of their pilgrimage, wherein they were strangers. And I have also heard the groaning of the children of Israel, whom the Egyptians keep in bondage; and I have remembered my covenant" (vv. 4,5). Here the encouragement Moses is being given from God is a review of some of the things God has already done on Israel's behalf. The past performance of God will greatly encourage one's faith regarding God's future performance. It will give much encouragement in those times when adverse circumstances threaten to overcome us. The performances of God in the past, which God

193

is reminding Moses about in our text, can be divided into three distinct acts each beginning with "I have." They speak of the covenant with Israel, the compassion for Israel, and the commitment to Israel.

The covenant with Israel. "I have also established my covenant with them, to give them the land of Canaan" (v. 4). This was an encouraging reminder to Moses that Egypt is not the permanent dwelling place of Israel, but the land of Canaan is to be their permanent land. Israel had been in Egypt over four hundred years at the time of our text, and this would cause the flesh to have difficulty perceiving Israel was going to do anything but stay in Egypt forever. With Pharaoh's opposition to Israel's leaving Egypt being so strong and with the ill feelings of the Israelites towards Moses being so bad, leaving Egypt and going to Canaan looked like nothing more than a mere pipe dream that could never possibly come to pass. But God reminds Moses that the land of Canaan is something more than a pipe dream. It is, in fact, part of a covenant He has established with Israel. In the covenant God promised Israel a particular land of their own, and that land was not in Egypt.

We need to go back to the Word of God often and review the promises of God to find encouragement. We need those promises in difficult circumstances, and we need to remember that they were "established" by God. As Matthew Henry said, "The covenants [and we can include all of God's promises here] God makes he establishes; they are made as firm as the power and truth of God can make them."

The compassion for Israel. "I have also heard the groaning of the children of Israel, whom the Egyptians keep in bondage" (v. 5). Moses had heard earlier at the burning bush about God's compassion for Israel. There God said, "I have surely seen the affliction of my people which are in Egypt, and have heard their cry by reason of their taskmasters; for I know their sorrows" (Exodus 3:7). Now God reminds him again that God cares.

194

We have a need to be reminded frequently that God cares, for we are so prone to accuse God of not caring. Though God cares for us far greater and more faithfully than anyone else, we still are likely to accuse Him more quickly of not caring than we accuse anyone else. Hence, the continued reminders of God's care are necessary. If we are faithful in reading the Bible, we will be reminded frequently of God's care, and that His compassion is great. Our every care is noted by God. To emphasize this compassion and care, Christ told men that "even the very hairs of your head are all numbered" (Luke 12:7). The Psalmist, in noting the care of God, spoke of God keeping track of our tears: "Thou tellest my wanderings; put thou my tears into thy bottle; are they not in [recorded in] thy book?" (Psalm 56:8).

God's compassion for us is such a great encouragement especially in difficult times. But it is also a great rebuke to us. Too often we complain of God's lack of care when the problem is never God's failure in this area but ours. We are the ones who lack compassion for the things of God. It is a good thing God does not care for us like we care for Him!

The commitment to Israel. "I have remembered my covenant" (v. 5). The third "I have" underscores God's faithful, everlasting commitment to Israel. He has not forgotten the covenant. Therefore, it will be fulfilled. God is committed to fulfilling His part to the last jot and tittle of the covenant. Moses and Israel may think God has forgotten after four hundred years of Egyptian bondage, but God has not forgotten. God never forgets; it is man that forgets. One of the indictments upon Israel years later was that they kept forgetting God. "They soon forgat his works" (Psalm 106:13); "They forgat God, their savior" (Psalm 106:21). Forgetting here is not a mental problem but a spiritual problem. It plagues many people even today.

The faithfulness of God is that upon which we can find much encouragement in any circumstance. We are often discouraged by the unfaithfulness of man in time of need. But God will never let us down. We can count on Him. If He has promised, He will fulfill. When He makes a commitment, it will never be forsaken. Let this encourage us to strive to be faithful in our commitment to serving God.

4. The Promises of God

God gave Moses seven great "I will" promises about what He was going to do for Israel. These promises made it clear that Israel was going to be delivered from Egypt and given their own land. These promises also said great judgment would come upon the land of Egypt where Israel had been so cruelly treated for so many years. The stating of one promise after another in this series of seven promises would certainly provide great encouragement to Moses.

Note that these promises are sandwiched between two identical statements that speak of the "Jehovah" identity of God. "I am the LORD [JEHOVAH]" (v. 6) precedes the giving of the promises, and "I am the LORD [JEHOVAH]" (v. 8) immediately follows the last of the seven promises. The repetition of the "Jehovah" name of God and the surrounding of the promises with the "Jehovah" name emphasizes that Jehovah is the name God is making prominent in the emancipation. And the seven times God says, "I will" in prefacing the promises fits the meaning of the Jehovah name which is "I AM THAT I AM." Only the "I AM THAT I AM" could make such great promises.

While these promises speak of deliverance of the Israelites from Egypt, there is also in the promises a great picture of the work of soul salvation in mankind which we especially want to emphasize here. The deliverance of Israel from the bondage of Egypt certainly shows in many ways and at many times the greater deliverance of the soul of man from the bondage of sin—and here is one case in point. And we need to note that with the deliverance of Israel from Egypt picturing so well the redemption of the soul, the name Jehovah now appropriately becomes the main name for God. With Jehovah of the Old Testament being the Jesus of the New Testament, the association of Jesus Christ with redemption here in Exodus is very evident, appropriate, and significant. We do not have to wait until we get to the New Testament before we can see Christ and redemption, for we have many wonderful pictures of the redemptive work of Jesus Christ throughout the Old Testament, and none of these Old Testament pictures are so full and so clear as the redemption of Israel from their Egyptian bondage.

The seven promises stated here are the promises of rest, rescue, redemption, reception, recognition, relocation, and riches.

Rest. "I will bring you out from under the burdens of the Egyptians" (v. 6). The burdens of Egypt were extremely heavy. The burden of labor provided Israel with little time for rest. And with the recent added task of collecting straw, Israel would have difficulty finding any time to rest.

One of the curses of sin is the lack of rest for the soul. "The wicked are like the troubled sea, when it cannot rest" (Isaiah 57:20). But Christ Who is the great Emancipator of the soul said, "Come unto me, all ye that labor and are heavy laden, and I will give you rest" (Matthew 11:28). The load of sin is too great a burden to carry. But when a sinner comes to Christ, that terrible load is removed and rest is given. The fourth chapter of Hebrews especially speaks of salvation in terms of "rest." Nine times in the first eleven verses the word "rest" is found. The message in summary is that "There remaineth therefore a rest to the people of God" (Hebrews 4:9). Israel will find rest when they have the heavy burden of Egyptian slavery removed. Sinners will find rest when they have the heavy burden of sin removed. And in each case the rest will come through Jesus Christ.

Rescue. "I will rid you out of their bondage" (v. 6). The word "rid" is translated from a Hebrew word which means "to pluck out of the hands of an oppressor or enemy" (William Wilson), "to snatch . . . from danger" (Gesenius). Hence, it means to rescue, to free, to give liberty to that which was bound and in bondage. Israel was going to soon be free from their Egyptian bondage. They were going to be rescued from their slavery, from the murderous decrees, and from terrible oppression.

So it is in soul salvation, man is rescued from the enslavement of sin and from the second death—eternity in hell fire. Christ has come to "set at liberty" (Luke 4:18) the sin-shackled soul. As the hymn says, the work of the Gospel is to "rescue the perishing . . . snatch them in pity from sin and the grave."

Redemption. "I will redeem you with a stretched out arm, and with great judgments" (v. 6). God speaks of Israel's deliverance from Egypt in different ways to show the many blessings of the deliverance. First, we saw it in terms of rest, then in the term of release. Now we see it in the term of "redeem," and how instructive all of this is regarding the Gospel. Three aspects of our salvation are spoken of in this text about redemption. We have the price of salvation, the power of salvation, and the punishment to bring about salvation.

First, the *price* of salvation. To redeem something means to purchase something. Therefore, a price is involved. This is expressly stated regarding soul salvation when Paul says to the Corinthians, "Ye are brought with a price" (I Corinthians 6:20). And that price was a great price, just as it was in the case of Israel's deliverance. But, significantly, both in soul salvation and in Israel's deliverance, the price was not paid by the one being delivered, but by another. Egypt was the one that paid for Israel's redemption. They paid for it in the plagues, in the loss of the firstborn, and in the riches they gave to the Israelites. In salvation, the price is paid by Jesus Christ Who gave His life on Calvary that we might be saved. While salvation is free to the sinner, it costs more than anything else. But the sinner does not pay for his salvation. God takes care of the payment. This, of course, rules out works for salvation; for salvation is all of God because He alone paid the entire price for our redemption.

Second, the *power* of salvation. Our text says, God would "redeem you with a stretched out arm." The figure of the stretched out arm speaks of power. "The figure is common and quite intelligible; it may have struck Moses and the people the more forcibly since they were familiar with the hieroglyphic which represents might by two outstretched arms" (F. C. Cook). In the plagues that brought great destruction to the country of Egypt, God displayed His great power in redeeming Israel from the Egyptian oppression. The last plague—the death of the first-born—especially demonstrated God's power, and it devastated the Egyptians. The redemption of the soul also requires the great power of God. Paul speaks of this power when he says, "For I am not ashamed of the gospel of Christ; for it is the power of God unto salvation" (Romans 1:16).

Third, the *punishment* to bring about salvation. "I will redeem you . . . with great judgments" (v. 6). Before Israel was redeemed from the Egyptian oppression, great judgment had to take place upon evil. Egypt had to be punished. The judgment brought great destruction upon Egypt and left it powerless to keep Israel in bondage. How wonderfully is salvation pictured in this truth of judgment being necessary for the redemption of Israel from Egypt. In order for salvation to become a reality for the sinner, judgment must occur upon sin. That judgment came not upon the ones to be redeemed but upon Jesus Christ at Calvary. Calvary, therefore, was absolutely essential for our soul's salvation. It was the place where judgment came in order for salvation to become a reality. As Israel did not experience the judgment that came on the land of Egypt for their redemption, so the sinner does not experience the judgment that comes for the redemption of his soul. The judgment came upon Egypt in Israel's case and it came upon Christ in the sinner's case. Truly we have a wonderful salvation.

Reception. "I will take you to me for a people" (v. 7). Despised and enslaved Israel was going to be received by God as His people. What a glorious promise this was. In Egypt, Israel was downtrodden and rejected. No one esteemed them. But God did; and they, not the Egyptians, were going to be the people of God. The receiving of Israel by God was certainly of grace. Israel had drifted far from God while in Egypt. Yet, God in mercy would bring them back to Him.

This receiving of Israel by God is another picture of soul salvation. Through salvation we are received by God as His people. "I will . . . receive you unto myself" (John 14:3) states the blessed truth well. And as Israel was received by grace, so the sinner is received by grace in salvation. We did not deserve salvation; for we, like Israel, had turned away from God. But God in grace saved us and then received us. "You, that were sometime alienated and enemies in your mind by wicked works, yet now hath he reconciled" (Colossians 1:21).

It is a wonderful thing to be accepted of God. It is a wonderful promise that when we come to heaven's door, we will be received and welcomed warmly into heaven. Foolish man ever strives to be accepted by man and often throws character to the winds in order to gain acceptance by man. But the acceptance of man is not nearly as important as acceptance by God. Let man reject you, but make sure God does not reject you but instead receives you.

Recognition. "I will be to you a God; and ye shall know that I am the LORD your God, which bringeth you out from under the burdens of the Egyptians" (v. 7). Israel's deliverance was to be accompanied by an increase in the knowledge of God. They would recognize ("know") God. He had been a stranger to most of them, but the emancipation will result in vastly improved knowledge of God. In the wilderness, they will learn so much about God. Through the statues and the Tabernacle, Israel will be instructed about God and come to know God as they never knew Him before.

Soul salvation also greatly increases the knowledge of God in the redeemed. The mind darkened by sin is illuminated by the light of God in salvation, and so the saved greatly increase in the knowledge of the things of God. When we are saved, we "put on the new man, which is renewed in knowledge after the image of him that created him" (Colossians 3:10).

Relocation. "I will bring you in unto the land, concerning the which I did swear to give it to Abraham, to Isaac, and to Jacob" (v. 8). We note two things about this relocation: the land of the relocation and the leading to the relocation.

First, the *land.* The land was that which was promised to Abraham, Isaac, and Jacob in the covenant which God had referred to earlier (v. 4). Hence, it was the land of Canaan. Israel's move was not to a different place in Egypt but to a different country. Egypt at its best was no match for Canaan, the land promised to the patriarchs. In salvation, the soul is also promised a different location. That location is not some improved earthly situation. No, that location is heaven. Christ said, "I go to prepare a place for you" (John 14:2). Jehovah provided Israel with a new location. Jesus provides the saints with a new location.

Second, the *leading.* "I will bring you in unto the land" is a most encouraging statement about God's guidance. He will show the way to the land. We will see later in our studies how God led Israel with the pillar of fire by night and the pillar of cloud by day (Exodus 13:21,22). God would guide the Israelites through the wilderness to the new land. In like manner, God will guide the redeemed soul through the pathways of life till we arrive in heaven. We need Divine guidance, and it is one of the blessings of salvation. God shows us through His Word and through the promptings of the Holy Spirit the pathway we should take.

Riches. "I will give it you for an heritage" (v. 8). Israel was in poverty in Egypt. The Jews did not possess the land but the land possessed them. In Canaan it will be indeed different. They will possess a good land, "a land flowing with milk and honey" (Exodus 3:8). Israel's redemption resulted in their being given a great heritage. Hence, it resulted in their gaining great riches. The same is true regarding salvation. The redeemed are "heirs of God, and joint heirs with Christ" (Romans 8:17). To be an heir of a wealthy man on this earth would impress most of us.

201

But to be an heir of God is beyond our comprehension. His riches know no bounds. His wealth is so great; it is untold. And we are heirs of all of that. We already have the "earnest of our inheritance" (Ephesians 1:14) in the sealing with the Holy Spirit (Ephesians 1:13). What a glorious inheritance the redeemed can look forward to because of our redemption in Jesus Christ.

B. THE EXPOUNDING BY MOSES

After Moses had been with God, he went back to speak with the people. In his discouragement Moses had gone to the Lord; and, as a result, he had found great encouragement to keep going. If we want to stay in God's service, we need to be often with God in prayer and in His Word.

To examine this expounding by Moses to the Israelites, we will note the declaration in the expounding and the disinterest in the expounding.

1. The Declaration in the Expounding.

"And Moses spake so unto the children of Israel" (v. 9). From the word "so" in our text we can see the contents of the message Moses expounded and the character of the messenger who is Moses.

Contents of the message. The word "so" in our text tells us that Moses told the children of Israel exactly what God had just told him. God had just given Moses a message and Moses went to Israel and "spake so"; that is, he spoke what God had spoken to him. It was a great message. It declared the power of God, the person of God, the performance of God, and the promises of God—all of which we noted in detail above. Moses did not go to the people empty handed like so many preachers go into the pulpit. Moses had a wonderful message about God for the people. It was a message with great substance. It was not a shallow message filled with a lot of stories to entertain the people instead of edify them, which is too often the character of the messages we hear in pulpits today.

The reason Moses had a great message was because Moses had spent some time with the Lord. We noted in an earlier chapter that preachers need to quit doing so much running around hither and yond and spend more time alone with God; then they will have something worthwhile to say on Sunday! Preachers are to fill the pulpit. But many sermons are like Mother Hubbard's cupboard—empty of food.

Character of the messenger. "So" not only tells us what Moses spoke, but it also tells us that Moses was faithful in declaring Divine truth. He gave Israel the right message. He did not water it down or change it to suit the occasion. He simply told them what God had told him. Ministers who are faithful like Moses was here in proclaiming Divine truth are few and far between. The world is filled with those who are greatly lacking in integrity regarding the Divine message. God does not look lightly on that lack of faithfulness, and He will judge in due time. Let all those who have been Divinely called to be God's messenger be absolutely faithful regarding the message. The message will oftentimes not be popular, and it may even provoke personal peril at times. But do not waver from telling it the way God told it to you.

2. The Disinterest in the Expounding

"But they hearkened not unto Moses for anguish of spirit, and for cruel bondage" (v. 9). Israel did not respond well to Moses' great message. They were not interested in it at all. We note the commonness of the disinterest and the cause of the disinterest.

The commonness of the disinterest. The reaction of the people had to be very disappointing to Moses. He had heard from God, and it had greatly revived and encouraged him in his work. Then he hastened to tell the people (who were also discouraged) the wonderful news. But when he told the people, they were not revived or encouraged at all. That which had so enthused Moses did nothing for the people.

It is not uncommon for God's ministers to experience this disinterest by their listeners. That which has so interested and rejoiced the heart of God's man seems often to have no effect on the people to whom he preaches. What God's man is so excited about, the people often have no enthusiasm about at all. God's preacher gets into the Word of God during the week and discovers great truths that greatly inspire his heart. However, when he delivers the message on Sunday, the people often yawn and show little interest and pay even less attention. It can be very disconcerting to the preacher. But the fact that the great message does not inspire or excite the people does not mean it is not a great message. Rather, it reflects negatively upon the heart of the people. Mankind often rejects the best that God gives them. The naïve think that means what God has given is not good. However, that is not the case. The problem is the rejecters' hearts. It is the people, not the preaching, that is bad.

The cause of the disinterest. Israel's rejection of this great message was a result of the "anguish of spirit" and the "cruel bondage" which they were experiencing. While we certainly do not want to play down the seriousness of the troubles the Israelites were experiencing, for they were extremely great, we are, however, warned here by Israel's disinterest. The warning is about the peril of letting our troubles so dominate us that we pay no attention to what God says. We must not let our troubles drive us away from God, but only to God. Matthew Henry said, "Disconsolate spirits often put from them the comforts they are entitled to, and stand in their own light . . . By indulging ourselves in discontent and fretfulness, we deprive ourselves of the comfort we might have both from God's word and from his providence, and must thank ourselves if we go comfortless." Arthur Pink spoke likewise when he said, "We defeat ourselves by being occupied with the difficulties of the way." Satan delights to heap troubles upon us to get us away from God, to distract our attention from God's Word. But let us take this warning to heart. When troubles mount, give God even more attention, not less. When problems burden you and threaten to hinder your service for God, purpose in your heart to be even more dedicated and faithful in your service than before.

C. THE EXHORTING FOR MOSES

After Moses had spoken to the people and witnessed their great disinterest, the "LORD spake unto Moses" (v. 10) again and exhorted him on to further service. We will note the command in the exhortation, the complaint about the exhortation, and the charge in the exhortation.

1. The Command in the Exhortation

"Go in, speak unto Pharaoh king of Egypt, that he let the children of Israel go out of his land" (v. 11). Moses may not have been received very well by the Israelites, but God is the One Who controls the speaking engagements, and He has another very important one for Moses. This time it will be before Pharaoh. God commanded Moses to go to Pharaoh and give him a short message. We note three facts about the message: it was a changed message, a gracious message, and a difficult message.

A changed message. The message given Pharaoh told him to "let the children of Israel go out of his [Pharaoh's] land." This is a different message than what God had Moses give Pharaoh earlier. The earlier message asked for a temporary leave to go three days' journey into the wilderness to hold a feast unto the Lord (Exodus 5:1,3). Now this message goes much farther. It says to let the Israelites leave permanently. It is the message of emancipation.

The first message was a test for Pharaoh, and he failed it miserably. Now God is going to go farther in His demand. Since Pharaoh would not submit to the small demand, he is now being given a bigger demand. This is often the way God works with mankind. If we respond to a trial by complaining and fussing and slacking off in our devotion to God, God's reaction is often to send us a greater trial as chastisement for our poor response to the lesser trial. "If God lays a light burden upon us and we refuse it, we may expect him to exchange our light burden for a heavier one. [Therefore] We had better accept the first cross he offers" (Rawlinson).

A gracious message. God could have brought down judgment upon Pharaoh for his scornful and cruel rejection of the first request given to him by Moses. But God did not do that. God is giving Pharaoh ample opportunity to yield to God's demand. Pharaoh would not be punished until he had repeatedly rejected the requests to let Israel go. Matthew Henry describes this act of God's grace well when he says, "God repeats his precepts before he begins his punishments." Before Pharaoh will be punished with the signs and wonders, God will graciously give him precepts by which he could escape the punishment. As we see often throughout Scripture, we see the message of the grace of God in our text. And it tells us that no man who experiences the judgment of God can complain, for God's grace gives man sufficient opportunities to turn from his sin and to obey God's command before He brings judgment upon the sinner.

A difficult message. The message is going to be a difficult one for Moses to give to Pharaoh. If the message was only the repeating of the first request to go three days' journey into the wilderness to worship, it would still be a difficult message to deliver because of Pharaoh's scornful, cruel rejection of that request. But with the increased demand, it makes the task of going to Pharaoh much more difficult indeed. Moses could justifiably fear for his safety in going back to Pharaoh, for Pharaoh had reacted very hostilely and cruelly when approached about Israel's situation first by Moses and Aaron and then by the officers of Israel. If Moses could carry a conciliatory message, it might be easier. But the message he is to carry now is even more demanding than before. It is indeed a difficult message to proclaim. It makes the assignment a really tough one.

God's assignments are not always what we would prefer. We like to speak before nice, large, sympathetic crowds that will "Amen" our message and then after the service pat us on the back for good preaching. But to be asked to speak to a hostile crowd is something else. And besides being a perilous situation, it is not going to give us any exciting decisions to brag about at the next preachers' meeting. But it is God's command; and, therefore, we must obey it.

2. The Complaint About the Exhortation

"And Moses spake before the LORD, saying, Behold, the children of Israel have not hearkened unto me; how then shall Pharaoh hear me, who am of uncircumcised lips?" (v. 12). We are disappointed to see this reaction by Moses to God's command, but noting his previous complaints about his call, we probably should not surprised at the response. Furthermore, very few, if any, of us would have responded much better considering the circumstances. The response, of course, is not justified. But after the poor response of the Israelites, the flesh is not going to think encouragingly about going to Pharaoh.

Moses falls back on two of his previous objections in this verse. They concern his skepticism and his speech.

His skepticism. "Behold, the children of Israel have not hearkened unto me; how then shall Pharaoh hear me." Moses had some good logic here. If God's people do not heed God's message, how can we expect the world to believe. But Moses' skepticism, though it has some logic to it, is to be condemned because he is using it to try and withdraw from his call. He does not want to continue on as God's man. He is using the unbelief of his audience as a reason to not do as God commanded. But Pharaoh's not hearkening to Moses has nothing to do with Moses' calling. We noted in an earlier chapter when Moses first used skepticism of others (in that case it was the skepticism about Israel believing him) as an excuse for not serving God, that our service must not be conditioned on how folk respond to our message. We are to do what God says whether people believe God's message or do not believe it. God sent Moses back to Pharaoh again and again even though Pharaoh never believed. Our calling is simply not dependent on whether people believe or not. It is dependent upon God's commands.

His speech. "How then shall Pharaoh hear me, who am of uncircumcised lips?" Moses again tries to use his so-called speech problem as an excuse for no longer continuing his calling. To be of "uncircumcised lips" means to be of lips that do not speak well just as "uncircumcised ears" in Scripture means ears that do not hear or hearken well, and as an "uncircumcised heart" is a heart that does not believe well.

Moses' excuse, of course, is not valid. It is not rhetoric that is the key to converting people. People, however, often think that if they had more oratorical powers, they could convince more people about the Gospel. While God does not approve of sloppy and crude speech, yet a man of God does not need to have great skills in rhetoric to be a great preacher. He needs to be more concerned about the substance of his message and about living a holy life so that the Spirit of God can work through him when he preaches. The power of the Spirit of God is what turns people's hearts to God, not the oratorical skills of the messenger of God.

3. The Charge in the Exhortation

"And the LORD spake unto Moses and unto Aaron, and gave them a charge unto the children of Israel, and unto Pharaoh king of Egypt, to bring the children of Israel out of the land of Egypt" (v. 13). Some Hebrew scholars believe this verse begins a new paragraph and is a brief summary of the emancipation orders which is recorded here to introduce the genealogy of Moses and Aaron which follows. This is not fanciful thinking, for it is characteristic of Hebrew writers of Scripture to do this very thing. The last few verses of chapter six and the first seven verses of chapter seven (the chapter division could be improved regarding where chapter seven begins) reflect another habit of Hebrew writers, namely, the habit of giving a capsule review at the end of a section. The last few verses of chapter six and the first seven verses of chapter seven recapitulate that which has gone before and help to close the paragraph concerning the genealogy of Moses and Aaron, a paragraph which is of parenthetical character. All of this reminds us that Scripture is not a hodgepodge of stories and sayings thrown together without rhyme or reason. Rather, it is a great (the greatest of all, in fact) literary piece that reflects skilled literary practices of the writers—writers who, we need to note, wrote under the inspiration of the Holy Spirit.

From verse 13 we will especially note two lessons. They have to do with the repeating of the orders and the responsibility regarding the orders.

The repeating of the orders. It makes no difference whether this verse is a summary of what God has already said or whether it is a new statement; either way it is another repeating of the orders for the emancipation of Israel. The lesson we learn from this fact is that God has left no doubt about His orders regarding the emancipation. No one can complain that God did not make it clear about Israel's deliverance. Opposition to Israel's emancipation had no excuse.

This same truth is seen in the Gospel. God has repeatedly stated in His Word the necessity of man's salvation if he wants to escape the judgment of hell and gain heaven as his eternal dwelling place. Man cannot complain that God has not sufficiently informed him about his duties, his call, his orders.

The responsibility regarding the orders. "Charge . . . the children of Israel, and . . . Pharaoh king of Egypt, to bring the children of Israel out of the land of Egypt." The charge not only makes Moses and Aaron responsible for the emancipation of Israel; but the way it is stated, it also makes the emancipation the responsibility of the children of Israel and Pharaoh. No one in Egypt can stand by as a disinterested third party and claim they are not responsible regarding the emancipation. Moses must lead the emancipation, but Israel and Pharaoh must cooperate. Therefore, rebellion in any area will be punished. If Moses fails, God will deal with him. If Israel does not cooperate, they can expect God's judgment. And if Pharaoh will not cooperate, he can also expect Divine retribution. Throughout the next chapters we will see Moses doing as instructed and the Israelites doing as instructed. But Pharaoh is the stubborn one, and his stubbornness will be judged of God in devastating ways.

The extension of Moses' charge to others is a reminder to us that we are more responsible in the Lord's work than we often think we are. It is not just the pastor or the missionary who is responsible for their ministry. It is also others who are responsible, such as church members who have the responsibility to financially aid the pastor and aid the missionary and others in their work for God. We cannot stand by as idle bystanders and pass off the responsibility to a few select servants of God.

X.

SNAKES AND RODS

EXODUS 6:14 – 7:13

THE PRELIMINARIES ARE over. The initial request to worship has been made and rejected, and the fallout from the rejection has taken place. Now, as God had promised Moses in His most recent communiqué to Moses, the signs and wonders are going to start occurring. Israel's emancipation has not been stopped by Pharaoh's increased oppression and cruelty to them. The battle is not over as Pharaoh and the Israelites and Moses may have thought because of the circumstances. No, the battle is simply going to become more heated. Pharaoh is now going to be confronted with more than words; he will now have to deal with the mighty acts of God's miracle power.

The first demonstration of God's power in the miracle world will be two miracles involving snakes and rods. Moses worked some miracles before the Israelites earlier, but until now no miracle had been performed by Moses before Pharaoh. That is going to change immediately.

In this study of the first miracles Moses performed before Pharaoh, we will consider the reviewing before the miracles (6:14 – 7:7), the rendering of the miracles (7:8–12), and the rejection of the miracles (7:13).

A. THE REVIEWING BEFORE THE MIRACLES

We noted in our last chapter the literary technique of the Hebrew writers in the Scripture to summarize and review to begin and end sections and divisions in their writings. Here we will take time to look at such a passage that is a summary

211

review of some things that have occurred thus far in the record of Moses and the emancipation and also of some things which are going to happen in the next weeks and months. While some of this review repeats much of what we have already covered in previous chapters, we will find it profitable to review this information. When God repeats in Scripture like this, it is not because He is senile or forgetful but because it is important. Hence, the information in this review passage is important—it is important to know in order to help us to appreciate, understand, and be instructed by that which we will next read in the infallible Word of God.

In the study of this review section, we will note the representatives of Israel, the resistance in service, the ranking of men, the request for Pharaoh, and the retribution upon Egypt.

1. The Representatives of Israel

Moses and Aaron are the representatives of Israel who will deal with Pharaoh. Scripture pauses to give some details about them. We note their family ancestors, their faithfulness in assignments, and their fullness of age.

Their family ancestors. Genealogies are not the most interesting and edifying reading in the Scriptures. But some of them are more interesting, important, and instructive than others, especially those which show the line of Christ from David. While the one before us is not involved in the line of Christ, it is, however, more important and edifying than a number of genealogies; for it gives us some pertinent facts about Moses' family. First, we learn that he comes from the tribe of Levi (6:16,20). Then we learn that his father's name is Amram (6:20) and his mother's name is Jochebed (Ibid.). The genealogy also confirms that Aaron is Moses' brother. Some details of Aaron's family are recorded to substantiate the high priest position of Eleazar, Aaron's successor, and Phinehas, Eleazar's successor. While that may mean little to us today, we must remember it was very important to the Jews in Moses' day. Genealogies were proof for claims of office and privileges and property. Today we have legal papers, titles, and deeds to give proof for position and proof of ownership of property.

The matter of proof is very important in spiritual matters and must not be disrespected and ignored. God is careful to substantiate His work in many ways in order to encourage our faith and to manifest the integrity of His work. Hence, the work of Moses and Aaron is substantiated by the genealogy. Likewise when Christ came to earth, His claims of being the Messiah could easily be attested by the examination of His genealogy. Through both Joseph and Mary (whose respective genealogies are carefully given in Matthew and Luke), the lineage of Christ back to David is stated very plainly. Had the critics of Christ's day examined the genealogies as they ought to have done, they would have had to confess that Christ was indeed the promised Messiah. The resurrection also comes with many proofs: "To whom also he showed himself alive after his passion by many infallible proofs" (Acts 1:3). Unbelief is not interested in proof or in the confirmation of claims or in the substantiation of Biblical teaching. But faith is. Fraud does not want to address the matter of proof, but truth certainly does. One important lesson this genealogy teaches us is that God's work is built on a solid foundation of facts. Our faith is not resting on thin ice. It can be investigated without fear of being exposed as fraud. It is a different story, however, with the fraudulent religions and philosophies of the world.

Their faithfulness in assignments. "And Moses and Aaron did as the LORD commanded them, so did they" (7:6). One of the things we are told about in this review section is the faithfulness of Moses and Aaron in fulfilling their God-given assignments. It is worthy to note that from here on through the exodus of Israel from Egypt, the obedience of Moses and Aaron was impeccable. No longer is there any resistance (we will review Moses' past resistance in our next point) on their part to God's orders. They did indeed do "as the LORD commanded them."

213

Faithfulness is the prime criteria by which God judges our service. We frequently forget that truth because of the influence of the world's philosophies upon us. Therefore, when we judge one's success, we often look at how much money one makes, or at how big a house or car or how many vehicles and boats one has. When we determine if one is successful or not, we generally look at how high up one is in position in the world, how large a church a pastor has, how many games a coach's team wins, and how popular one is. But faithfulness to God is seldom used to judge much of anything. Faithfulness is so little esteemed today, that few lower their judgment of people even when they have been unfaithful to their wedding vows. But God judges people on their faithfulness, especially their faithfulness to Him. "Moreover it is required in stewards, that a man be found faithful" (I Corinthians 4:2). If you want God's approval rating of you to be high, be faithful to Him in all matters. You may not gain much approval in the world, but what does the world know about good judgment—they crucified the Greatest of them all, Jesus Christ, as a criminal. You may be very successful in life but still be looked upon as a failure by the world.

Their fullness of age. "And Moses was fourscore years old, and Aaron fourscore and three years old, when they spake unto Pharaoh" (7:7). While men often lived longer in Moses' day than they do today, so that eighty would not seem as old to people in Moses' day as it does in our day, nevertheless, it is significant that Moses did not begin his greatest work until he was eighty. He would die forty years later at 120, but even then he still had good health and eyesight (Deuteronomy 34:7). When Moses was objecting to his call, one objection he did not raise was his age. He certainly could have raised that as an objection even in his day when men lived generally longer than we do. But commendably, he did not bring up the age issue. Too many in our churches do, however, and even when they are far from an age that would limit their service. It is true that when we get older and our physical body weakens because of age, we cannot

214

do some things we used to do in our younger days. But it is a pitiful shame to see so many church members gathering along the sidelines out of the game when they still could be doing much for God in the work of the church.

It is a rebuke to this attitude of retiring early to note the great achievements some have had in old age. Michelangelo did the great work of painting the ceiling of the Sistine Chapel lying on his back on a scaffold when he was almost 90. Tennyson wrote the famous poem, "Crossing the Bar," when he was 83. John Wesley was preaching everyday when he was 88. Ignace Paderewski, Rudolph Serkin, and Artur Rubinstein, some of the greatest pianists in classical music, were still giving great concerts in their late seventies and into their eighties. Ronald Reagan was in his seventies when he was president of the United States. Some years ago a survey was done of 400 famous men, each one who had some great achievements in their life. It was most instructive that 35 percent of the group's greatest achievements were done in their sixties, 23 percent in their seventies, and 8 percent in their eighties. This meant that of these 400 great men, 66 percent of their greatest achievements had come after sixty years of age. We are not criticizing folk retiring from some of their jobs—what we are criticizing is their retiring to an easy life of laying around, taking frequent vacations hither and yond, spending more time at play rather than at work, and withdrawing themselves from service at church. Let the age of Moses and Aaron at the outset of the emancipation of Israel rebuke that selfish, slothful spirit.

2. The Resistance in Service

Again we read in Scripture of Moses' resistance to his call to service. What we read in verses 28 to 30 of chapter 6 is generally a repeat of what immediately preceded the genealogy. It tells of God ordering Moses to speak to Pharaoh and then of Moses' complaining, "Behold, I am of uncircumcised lips, and how shall Pharaoh hearken unto me?" (6:30). This, then, is the third time in a few chapters that we are told about Moses claiming he could not speak well enough to be God's emancipator. God would emphasize in all of this repeating of Moses' speech complaint that rhetoric and oratorical skills are not as important in God's work as we would think. As we noted in a previous chapter, this does not give license to be crude, vulgar, sloppy, and slangy in our speech in God's work. But it does say we do not have to be a spellbinding orator to preach the Word. We need to be more concerned about preaching with substance and in the power of the Holy Spirit. It is said that when Jonathan Edwards preached his famous sermon, "Sinners in the hands of an angry God," he read the sermon holding the manuscript so close to his face that the audience could not see his face, and that he read it in a monotone voice. Obviously something more than oratorical skills did the job that day, and we should be more interested in that than in oratorical abilities.

3. The Ranking of Men

"And the LORD said unto Moses, See, I have made thee a god to Pharaoh: and Aaron thy brother shall be thy prophet" (7:1). This verse instructs us plainly that God does not rank men as mankind does. To the human eye, Pharaoh held the supreme rank in Egypt. After all, he was the "king of Egypt" (6:27,29). Egypt was a powerful nation in the world in those days which added stature to his position in man's eyes. Therefore, mankind would bow low before Pharaoh and give him much adulation. But Moses would not be given such respect, for he had been nothing but a shepherd in the obscure wilderness of Sinai for the last forty years. But how differently God thought. Of the three men—Moses, Aaron, and Pharaoh—Pharaoh was the lowest in rank in God's ranking system.

There are a lot of people in this world who in God's eyes are of much higher rank and esteem than the world gives them. And in eternity, if not before, that rank will be made very evident. God's people need to learn what God ranks high and give due respect to that whether the world gives respect to it or not. This ranking not only includes mankind, but it also includes a lot of other things such as our values. The world's value system is despicable and too many professing Christians reflect the world more than they do God in this matter. The world's poor values are demonstrated in many ways. As an example, society does not value learning the Word of God. Rather, it puts great value and emphasis on studying the strange and corrupt and worthless philosophies of evil men. Students staying home from church to study their school assignments, which involve learning what the world says is important instead of what God says is important, are aping the world's value system and not God's. Great loss in the things that matter the most will be the result of following this worldly practice.

4. The Request for Pharaoh

"Thou shalt speak all that I command thee: Aaron thy brother shall speak unto Pharaoh, that he send the children of Israel out of his land" (7:2). We note two things about this message that requests Pharaoh to let Israel leave Egypt. They are the source of the message and the stewardship of the message.

The source of the message. The source of the message that Moses and Aaron were to proclaim was God. "I" in our text is Jehovah God and He is the One who determines what Moses and Aaron are to say. So again we have an emphasis in the story of Moses on the importance of having the right message when we speak to mankind. Moses and Aaron were to declare God's Word. They were not to invent their own message. God's Word provided all the message they needed.

The true preacher will be a man of the Word. When he stands behind the pulpit, he will be holding God's Word in his hand and declaring it with his mouth. Woe be the preacher who goes to the pulpit to declare other than God's matchless Word. How blessed is every church whose pastor goes to the pulpit and opens the Bible and reads and expounds therefrom. It is one of the choicest blessings a church can have. They may not have numbers or a fancy building or a lot of various programs that

217

churches seem to think are so necessary today; but if they have a pastor who goes to the pulpit with God's Word and preaches it, they have what they dearly need.

The stewardship of the message. God said to speak "all" that He commanded. This reminds us of the Apostle Paul who stated to the Ephesian elders, "I have not shunned to declare unto you all the counsel of God" (Acts 20:27). Preaching "all" the counsel of God does not mean we must preach from every verse of Scripture before we pass from this life, but it means we must be faithful to preach all the message God gives to us to preach. We are to be good stewards of the message God gives us. We are not to alter the message. The "all" in the charge given Moses and Aaron spoke of their faithfulness in saying what God told them to say. Going to Pharaoh and giving him the message they did was not going to be easy as we noted in our previous chapter. Pharaoh had already rejected with cruelty the previous message which was even less demanding of him than the current message. But Moses and Aaron were to declare it "all" anyway. Preachers are often tempted to alter the message by leaving out some things in their messages so they do not offend or upset some folk in the congregation. This is a cowardly practice and is the opposite of faithfulness. But many preachers do it in order to curry favor with men.

5. The Retribution Upon Egypt

God promised Moses that great judgments would fall upon Egypt for their cruel treatment of the Israelites and for their refusal to let Israel leave. We look at some details and designs of the retribution.

The details of the retribution. "I will harden Pharaoh's heart, and multiply my signs and my wonders in the land of Egypt" (7:3). There are two details of this Divine retribution upon Egypt which we want to note. They are the hardening of the heart and the multiplying of the miracles.

First, the *hardening of the heart*. "I will harden Pharaoh's heart." In our earlier examination of this judgment of God upon Pharaoh, we emphasized that this action was not cruelty and injustice on the part of God. Pharaoh was just getting what he asked for. He had hardened his heart regarding the unjust situation of the Israelites; and now in justified Divine judgment, God gives him what he preferred. But within a year, more or less, Pharaoh will wish that he had never wanted a hard heart, for he will perish in the Red Sea because of it. Few forms of judgment in this life are as severe upon mankind as the judgment in which God lets you have your sinful way. If you want a hard heart and persist in a hard heart, God will see to it that your request is granted. If you insist upon doing something or getting something which God forbids, God in judgment may just let you do it or obtain it. But it will not be long before you will loath the day you wanted to do it or obtain it.

Second, the *multiplying of the miracles*. "I will . . . multiply my signs and my wonders in the land of Egypt." In a few words, the destruction of Egypt is predicted. Those signs and wonders spoke of the devastating plagues that would come upon Egypt over the next year or so and bring great destruction upon the land. One blow after another from God would make short work of Egypt. When men refuse to repent when hit with a plague, God simply brings another plague. How often this happens in the world with individuals and with nations. They seem never to learn. They rebel against God and live wicked lives. God sends judgment upon the nation in the form of storms or diseases or wars. Does the nation learn? Seldom. Rather, they get up off the ground, where God's blow has laid them, and go right on sinning more.

The designs of the retribution. The designs of God's judgment upon Egypt had many purposes, for God always has many reasons and objectives in mind when He does something. We note here from our text two of the most obvious designs of this retribution from God upon the land of Egypt: the deliverance of

Israel and the discernment about God.

First, the *deliverance of Israel*. "That I may lay my hand upon Egypt, and bring forth mine armies, and my people the children of Israel, out of the land of Egypt by great judgments" (7:4). Egypt had for many years oppressed the Israelites. God had spoken to them through Moses to let the people go. But they paid no attention to the Word of God. Therefore, God will resort to His judgment to cause Egypt to let Israel go.

It is easy for us to see the folly of Egypt's stubborn rebellion, but it is not so easy for us to see the same within ourselves. However, it is often there in our heart. God speaks to us to do something, but we ignore His gentle voice speaking to us. Then God speaks more earnestly and strongly. Yet, we continue to ignore Him. Finally God comes upon us with the strong arm of His judgments and smites us. And sometimes He must smite us again and again before we obey. Let us be diligent to heed God when He first speaks to us so that we do not have to be smitten before we obey Him. Being smitten by God extracts a cost we cannot afford to pay.

Second, the *discernment about God*. Another reason for the judgment upon Egypt is that "the Egyptians shall know that I am the LORD, when I stretch forth mine hand upon Egypt, and bring out the children of Israel from among them" (7:5). We learned in the previous chapter of our book that Israel would come to know Jehovah God much better because of their deliverance from Egypt (6:7). Here we learn that the Egyptians will also have their knowledge of Jehovah God increased. However, Egypt's learning about Jehovah God will be through judgment, not through emancipation.

How much better to learn of God in redemption than in judgment. When we are redeemed, our hearts and minds are illuminated regarding the knowledge of God. The Word of God ceases to be a closed book, and God opens our mind to perceive much about the things of God. This learning of God is a great blessing to our souls. But when men reject God, it is a different story. They will still eventually learn about God, but not in a way that will rejoice their hearts. They will learn the hard way. They will find out at the judgment throne of God many truths about God, but it will all be to their sorrow. Which way will you learn about God?

B. THE RENDERING OF THE MIRACLES

With the introductory review completed, our text returns to the action at hand. Moses and Aaron now go to Pharaoh the second time, and they carry the changed message which demands more than a time to worship in the desert but a demand for total freedom from Egypt. The demand is accompanied this time by the rendering of two miracles involving snakes and rods. To study these miracles, we will look at three significant features involved in them: the snake, the simulation, and the swallowing.

1. The Snake

"And the LORD spake unto Moses and unto Aaron, saying, When Pharaoh shall speak unto you, saying, Show a miracle for you; then thou shalt say unto Aaron, Take thy rod, and cast it before Pharaoh, and it shall become a serpent. And Moses and Aaron went in unto Pharaoh, and they did so as the LORD had commanded; and Aaron cast down his rod before Pharaoh, and before his servants, and it became a serpent" (7:8–10). The first miracle of turning a rod into a snake gave proof of the Divine calling of Moses and Aaron, and it also demonstrated the power for the calling that is essential in anyone's calling if they are to serve God effectively.

The proof of the calling. It was not unexpected that Pharaoh should demand some evidence that Moses and Aaron represented the Divine being they claimed to be speaking for in making the requests to Pharaoh. After all, there are always in every age plenty of frauds in society who want to pass as representatives for God in order to obtain personal gain and aggrandizement. While Pharaoh should have let the Israelites have freedom from their oppression just from a humanitarian standpoint,

221

Moses and Aaron did claim to speak for Jehovah God, and this made it legitimate for Pharaoh to ask them for evidence of their professed calling.

When Pharaoh asked for their credentials, for the proof of their calling, the proof was readily shown: Aaron cast down his rod and immediately "it became a serpent" (7:10). When one is truly called of God, the evidence will always be readily seen. If one is called to preach, the call will be evidenced with obvious ability to preach. When one is called to teach, teaching ability will be evident. When one is called to a musical ministry, the obvious musical talent will be present. Every calling evidences itself. Those who out of pride or greed or rebellion presume a calling will lack the true evidences of their calling though they may be able to deceive the general public who often is not very discerning. Saints of God need to get into the Word of God so that they are able to discern the evidences of the truly called and are able to expose the falseness of those not called but who presume a calling.

The power for the calling. "Aaron cast down his rod before Pharaoh, and before his servants, and it became a serpent" (7:10). The power of God was most evident in this miracle. We note the essentialness, encouragement, and enlisting of this power in the service of God.

First, the *essentialness* of this power. Without Divine power assisting Aaron's performance, Aaron would have been a flop, in fact, a laughing flop. When he threw the rod down, it would simply have rattled on the floor or ground of the palace; and everyone observing Aaron's performance would have laughed greatly at his ineptness. But the power of God was present and transformed the simple act of casting down the rod into the miracle of it becoming a writhing snake.

All of this demonstrates the truth that we cannot serve successfully without the power of God. What we can do without Divine power is extremely little. All Aaron could do was cast the rod down on the ground. The big part of the miracle was left up to God. We must have God's power or we are helpless. "Except the LORD build the house, they labor in vain that build it; except the LORD keep the city, the watchman waketh but in vain" (Psalm 127:1).

Our churches often forget the essentialness of God's power in the work of the church. They include everything else, from Hollywood glitz to Madison Avenue advertising and salesmanship techniques. But we had better seek to have the power of God if we want to do a real work. We may be without all the props the world thinks are essential and still do a great work for God because we have the power of God working for us.

Second, the *encouragement* of this power. The great work of the power of God in Aaron's miracle is a great encouragement to serving God. So many tasks look utterly impossible for us to do in ourselves. Our abilities and our assets are no match for the task assigned. We cannot possibly change sticks into snakes or do a host of other things our service for God demands. But with God's power accompanying us, the task can be done with excellence. Aaron only cast down his rod, God did the rest. Moses will only strike the rock, but God's power will bring forth the water (Exodus 17:17). The priests carrying the ark could not part the waters of the Jordan. They could walk into the waters— not much of a task compared to parting the waters. But when the power of God accompanied them, the waters parted when they put their feet into the waters (Joshua 3:15,16). When the widow in Elisha's day poured the oil out of her cruet, though it was so little in amount, yet with the power of God accompanying her, the oil filled vessel after vessel (II Kings 4:1–6). How encouraging to see what man can do when the power of God is involved.

Third, the *enlisting* of this power. It is very important that we observe how this power is obtained. It comes through obedience. When Aaron obeyed the Divine command given to Moses, then the power of God came upon the scene. Let us remember this truth well. So much power is lost through disobedience. When we disobey, it is like pulling the plug from the socket. We simply lose contact with the power and nothing happens. We become like Samson after he got his haircut on the lap of the harlot. Obedience to simple commands may seem unimportant, but it is the key to great power. Practice obedience to God and you will experience the wonderful power of God in service and in gaining victory over those strong and mighty temptations that threaten to overwhelm you.

2. The Simulation

"Now the magicians of Egypt, they also did in like manner with their enchantments. For they cast down every man his rod, and they became serpents" (7:11,12). Satan likes to simulate, to duplicate, to imitate Divine deeds and works. He does this in the spiritual realm in order to deceive mankind into rejecting the truth and embracing error. Here it was done to keep Pharaoh from believing God, and Pharaoh took the bait and embraced unbelief as we will see more about shortly.

Satan's counterfeiting of God's work is repeatedly seen and warned about in the Scriptures and in experience. The Apostle Paul speaks of this simulating work of Satan in his epistles. To the Corinthians he wrote, "For such are false apostles, deceitful workers, transforming themselves into the apostles of Christ. And no marvel; for Satan himself is transformed into an angel of light. Therefore, it is no great thing if his ministers also be transformed as ministers of righteousness" (II Corinthians 11:13–15). To the Thessalonians Paul wrote that the antichrist will come with "power and signs and lying wonders" (II Thess. 2:9). Christ warned of "false Christs, and false prophets . . . [who] shall show great signs and wonders; insomuch that, if it were possible, they shall deceive the very elect" (Matthew 24:24). In the days of the early church, apocryphal gospels were written and placed alongside the true Gospels. In our day we have the Book of Morman, the Koran, and other religious writings of the cults and isms which Satan places alongside the Bible in an effort to discredit the Bible and to try to show it does not have any special authority over man. And we also are plagued with a number of Satan's counterfeits in the ministry who have fleeced the fortunes and faith of multitudes.

The ability of Satan to simulate the work of God is often played down and doubted. Most commentators lean towards the explanation that the magicians simply cast down snakes that were charmed into rod-like appearance. Then when these snakes hit the ground, they were startled out of their stiffness. It is true that they could have done that, for this trick was not unknown. But the Scriptural language simply does not allow for such an explanation. Scripture says the magicians "cast down every man his *rod*" (7:12), not charmed snakes. And, furthermore, it says that "Aaron's rod swallowed up their *rods*" (Ibid.), not their charmed snakes that looked like rods. The commentators are justifiably very critical of those who would explain away the miracles of God as nothing more than natural phenomena, but they commit the same sin of the Bible critics when they try to explain away this simulating work of Satan. Satan has a lot of power. We must recognize that fact or we will not deal well with him. Satan had the power to do a lot of damage to Job and his possessions; he is able through his demon helpers to indwell humans and animals and control their actions; he was able to take Christ to Jerusalem and sit Him on a pinnacle of the Temple (Matthew 4:5) and to take Christ up to "an exceeding high mountain, and showeth him all the kingdoms of the world, and the glory of them" (Matthew 4:8); and he will, as we noted above, work great signs and wonders through the antichrist. Therefore, he certainly should not have any difficulty changing a few rods into snakes.

But in spite of the evidences in Scripture that Satan has miracle working power, many simply cannot accept the fact. However, he does have the power. So where did he get the power? Well, of course, he got the power from God. All power comes from God. But Satan misuses the power just as men today misuse their God-given abilities to do evil instead of to do good. Satan will meet his doom someday for his terrible evil, and all those who have perverted their gifts to practice and promote evil will likewise meet their doom unless they repent. How are you using your gifts?

3. The Swallowing

"But Aaron's rod swallowed up their rods" (7:12). In this second miracle of the snakes and rods, the superiority of Jehovah God over the gods of Egypt and the superiority of God over Satan is demonstrated in a very forceful way by Aaron's rod (in snake form) swallowing up the rods (also in snake form) of the magicians of Pharaoh. This superiority of Jehovah God over the Egyptian gods would establish His authority over them. It would declare that Pharaoh must let the Israelites go, for a higher authority than he is or his gods are insists that the Israelites be set free.

The swallowing of the rods of the magicians had to be embarrassing to the magicians. When Aaron picked up the serpent and it turned back into his rod, there would only be one rod, the magicians' rods would have disappeared completely. No trace of them would be anywhere. The magicians were outdone and really outdone. That was not their usual experience, but here they were dealing with the true God, and He is superior to any evil spirit or slight of hand.

It is most encouraging to our faith to know that when God so pleases, He can swallow up any of His enemies. The enemies of God may put on quite a show and deceive many. But God can take care of the best the enemy has to offer. Egypt oppressed Israel mercilessly, but the day came when God "stretchedst out thy right hand, [and] the earth *swallowed* them" (Exodus 15:12). Korah raised rebellion against Moses, but his rebellion ended when through Divine intervention, "the earth opened her mouth, and *swallowed* them up, and their houses, and all the men that appertained unto Korah, and all their goods" (Numbers 16:32). And those who are redeemed by Jesus Christ have the wonderful promise in Scripture that "Death is *swallowed* up in victory" (I Corinthians 15:54) an3d "that mortality might be *swallowed* up of life" (II Corinthians 5:4).

C. THE REJECTION OF THE MIRACLES

"And he hardened Pharaoh's heart, that he hearkened not unto them; as the LORD had said" (7:13). Pharaoh completely rejected the message of the miracles done with Aaron's rod. We note three things concerning this rejection: the opportunity for unbelief, the obduracy of heart, and the oracle of truth.

1. The Opportunity for Unbelief

When Aaron performed the miracle of turning the rod into a snake, Pharaoh called his magicians; and they duplicated the miracle (7:11,12). The reason Pharaoh called the magicians was to hopefully obtain from them a reason for rejecting the message the miracle of Aaron's rod gave. If Pharaoh can obtain an equal or superior miracle from his magicians, who represent the gods of Egypt, then he does not have to give respect to Moses and Aaron or to the God they claimed sent them—which would mean Pharaoh would not have to grant their request to worship or to leave. The magicians, of course, were able to provide some encouragement for Pharaoh's unbelief; for they, too, could make their rods into snakes. If nothing else would have happened in Pharaoh's court, then he would have had cause for concluding that Jehovah God merited no more respect than Egypt's gods. But more did happen. Aaron's rod swallowed up the other rods. This demonstrated unequivocally that the God of Moses and Aaron was superior to the gods of Egypt.

This most evident proof of superiority did not register with Pharaoh, however. Pharaoh had found opportunity to disbelieve and he did. He did not need overwhelming proof to reject Jehovah God. Unbelief never does. Just give them a fragment of doubt, a difficult verse in Scripture, or an apparent "loophole" or "exception" text and they embrace unbelief with tenacity. This bunch can be given an abundance of evidence to believe God, but they will not believe as long as they can find something that appears to teach the opposite of what God plainly says. This is the way people are with salvation as an example. The Word plainly teaches that salvation is by grace alone with absolutely no works involved. But unbelief looks for some text that might at least appear on the surface to teach works for salvation, such as adding baptism for salvation. If they can find such a text, they will ignore all the multitude of plain texts to the contrary and cling to the doubtful text. Divorced people are especially addicted to this practice. The Bible has enough very plain texts on divorce to nail it and remarriage to the wall. But most divorced people diligently search the Scriptures to find "exception" texts that would give them something to justify their divorce and remarriage.

This practice of rejecting the obvious and clinging to that which is not obvious reveals a rebellious heart. Those with this kind of heart do not want to believe the obvious texts though they may say they believe the Bible. Therefore, when they do not like something in Scripture, they look diligently for some text that can be twisted to justify their rejection of the plain text. And those texts can be found, for opportunity for unbelief is provided by God. That is, God tests mankind by providing them with some difficult and vague passages in Scripture which can be twisted to teach something opposite to the many clear passages of Scripture (that is just one purpose of those passages, another purpose is to provide special blessings for those who will earnestly dig into these passages to find wonderful lessons in them). What men do with these texts really reveals their faith. Those anxious to junk the many plain texts for a twisted interpretation of a difficult passage reveal their rebellion against God. Their eagerness to turn away from the obvious to embrace the doubtful manifests their disobedient heart. God permitted the magicians to work a miracle, but He also showed His superiority in having Aaron's rod swallow up the magicians' rods. The evidence was very plain as to Who was superior. But Pharaoh had found his text, and he clung to it while ignoring the plain text (the swallowing miracle) that showed God's superiority.

2. The Obduracy of Heart

"And he hardened Pharaoh's heart, that he hearkened not

228

unto them" (7:13). In the Hebrew the first "he" is not in the text in the way the KJV translators have rendered it. The Hebrew simply says that Pharaoh's heart was hard or grew hard. In other places in Scripture, it is correctly stated that God hardened Pharaoh's heart. But in this text, the "he" is not supported by the Hebrew. "The verb employed is not active, but neuter; and 'his heart' is not the accusative, but the nominative. Pharaoh's heart was too hard for the sign [miracles] to make much impression on it" (Rawlinson). The emphasis here is that the obduracy of Pharaoh's heart kept him from letting the miracles with the snakes and rods influence him positively. Pharaoh's heart had become hard because of sin. And a hard heart will not be receptive to God's revelations but will rebel against Divine decrees.

The hard heart explains a lot of attitudes and actions in every age. The hard heart, as an example, was why Moses permitted divorce (Matthew 19:8) and is why people get divorced today. The hard heart is why so much brutal crime is committed, why murders occur, why terrorists around the world blow up buildings, planes, trains, and buses. The hard heart is why people gamble, have abortions, and live immorally. The hard heart is simply not responsive to God. And it will send its owner into the eternal lake of fire.

3. The Oracle of Truth

Pharaoh's rejection of the sign of authority was "as the LORD had said" (7:13). God had predicted repeatedly to Moses (Exodus 3:19; 4:21; 7:4) that Pharaoh would refuse to let Israel go. Now twice this prediction has been proven true. Our text emphasizes the veracity of God's prediction.

This emphasizing of a fulfilled prediction should encourage our hearts. It tells us we can even find encouragement for our faith in bad circumstances as well as in good circumstances. While it is discouraging that Pharaoh would not accept the message in the miracles of the snakes and rods—it is encouraging to note that Pharaoh's reactions were exactly what God said they would be. The Word of God is proven true in his behavior.

Pharaoh may rant and rave against God, but in all his evil he only vindicates the Word of God. Likewise, in our day wickedness may rant and rave and abound more and more, but we do not have to wring our hands and think that God has lost control. Rather, we can rejoice that God's Word is true, for the Scriptures says of our day, "This know also, that in the last days perilous times shall come" (II Timothy 3:1). All the wickedness of mankind will not dethrone God. It will simply confirm the greatness of God. Evil only vindicates God's Word. "Surely the wrath of man shall praise thee" (Psalm 76:10) speaks the message of Divine victory. You cannot fight against God and win. Pharaoh proved that to be true.

XI.

SMITING OF EGYPT

EXODUS 7:14 – 10:29

GOD HAD PROMISED Moses at the burning bush that "I will stretch out my hand, and smite Egypt with all my wonders" (Exodus 3:20). This chapter will cover much of that smiting of Egypt promised by God. Thus far in our study of Moses, we have only seen the Israelites suffer, not the Egyptians (except the Egyptian Moses killed). The Israelites were victims of a most cruel slavery. And when Moses requested of Pharaoh that they be given some time off to worship, the oppression of the Israelites was made even worse by the Egyptians. So Israel suffered much while Egypt did not suffer. But that will now change! God will now smite the land of Egypt. Moses will now witness the fulfillment of the promise of God about the smiting of Egypt, and he will be very involved and very prominent in all that goes on regarding this justified judgment on Egypt.

The smiting of the land of Egypt came in the form of ten plagues. In this chapter of our book, we will look at the first nine plagues and leave the tenth plague, which is a tremendous event in itself, for our next chapter. We will divide this chapter's study as follows: the aim of the plagues, the analysis of the plagues, and the artifice during the plagues.

A. THE AIM OF THE PLAGUES

God never does anything without good and noble reasons. Here we will examine the three main reasons or aims of these plagues. We have touched on these reasons in previous chapters but not all at the same time or as extensively. Here we will

231

examine them together and more extensively to enhance our study of these plagues. The three great aims for the plagues had to do with God, Egypt, and Israel. They were the glorification of God, the mortification of Egypt, and the emancipation of Israel.

1. The Glorification of God

Everything that God does is to glorify Himself. This is only right; for "Thou art worthy, O Lord, to receive glory and honor and power; for thou hast created all things, and for thy pleasure they are and were created" (Revelation 4:11). Therefore, one of the aims of smiting Egypt with the plagues would be to glorify Jehovah God. This would, in fact, be the primary aim God would have in these plagues. There are other important purposes for the plagues, which we will note in our study; but the purpose of bringing glory to God is the primary reason for the plagues. To glorify God should also to be the main reason for all our actions (I Corinthians 10:31). But mankind too often thinks only of glorifying himself, not God.

There are especially two areas in which the plagues would glorify God. They are the power of God and the pre-eminence of God.

The power of God. The ten plagues would be a great demonstration of Divine power. They would show that God has the power to do with the creation what He so pleases and when He so pleases. Even centuries later, the plagues were still a testimony of the power of God. The Philistines gave this testimony four centuries later when they said, "Woe unto us! who shall deliver us out of the hand of these mighty Gods? these are the Gods that smote the Egyptians with all the plagues in the wilderness" (I Samuel 4:8). The plagues demonstrated that Jehovah God had the power to control nature (the water turned to blood plague), the animal kingdom (the frogs, lice, flies, and locust plagues), diseases (the murrain and boils plagues), the weather (the hail plague), light and darkness (the darkness plague), and life and death (the slaying of firstborn plague).

When the plagues were over, the evidence was overwhelming that God had power to control all of creation.

We need to notice here that God demonstrated His power against a very dark background. God especially delights to do this, for it shows God's power better than demonstrating it with an amiable background. It is when things get really bad with His people that God steps in to show His power. It is when the enemy seems to have an insurmountable powerful grip on God's people that God enters the scene and shows His power. God's people can encourage themselves in this great truth; for when our situation seems impossible to overcome, it is then that God especially delights to step in and show us His great power on our behalf.

The pre-eminence of God. The plagues would also show that God was above all the pagan gods of Egypt. God told Moses, "Against all the gods of Egypt I will execute judgment" (Exodus 12:12); and later Moses wrote similarly when he said, "Upon their [Egypt's] gods also the LORD executed judgments" (Numbers 33:4). "By entering into the spheres which were ruled by the gods of Egypt, and by overruling them; by predicting exactly what would happen, and by causing the prediction to come to pass; by leaving the magicians, with all their arts, outdistanced and ashamed; Jehovah . . . gave incontestable proof that He was God of gods" (F. B. Meyer). When visiting Moses after the emancipation had taken place, Jethro confessed this fact about the superiority of Jehovah God. After Moses had "told his father in law all that the LORD had done unto Pharaoh and to the Egyptians" (Exodus 18:8), Jethro said, "Now I know that the LORD is greater than all gods; for in the thing wherein they dealt proudly he was above them" (Exodus 18:11). Rivals to God may have their day, but the time will come when He will display His pre-eminence at their expense. May we ever keep God the pre-eminent One in our lives lest the time come when He will have to display His pre-eminence through judgment upon us.

2. The Mortification of Egypt

As we noted in the introduction of this chapter, the plagues were to "smite" Egypt (Exodus 3:20). Egypt verily deserved to be smitten and for two significant reasons—mistreatment of humanity and mistreatment of Hebrews.

Mistreatment of humanity. The cruel way Egypt treated their fellow man was most evil. They took away from the Israelites their freedom, and they ground them into the ground under the heavy foot of slavery. No nation or peoples have a right to do that sort of thing to God's creation. After Cain had slain Abel and God had asked Cain where Abel was, Cain scornfully asked, "Am I my brother's keeper?" (Genesis 4:9). The answer to Cain's question is "Yes." We are our brother's keeper. That is, we are obligated to treat our brother with due respect. Christ summed up the tables of the law into two great commandments. The first was to love God and the second was to love our neighbor (Matthew 22:37–40). Man has trouble with both of them. And the reason we have trouble with the second commandment is that we do not do well regarding the first commandment. When we do not love God as we ought, we will not love man as we ought. Egypt did not love the true God. Pharaoh admitted he did not even know Him. All that Pharaoh and Egypt knew were pagan gods, the invention of evil minds. They did not know the One True God and, therefore, did not love Him. Hence, they were cruel to their neighbors, to their fellow man, and dealt most evilly with Israel. God does not think kindly of that sort of behavior and punishes it in due time. As a result, Egypt was smitten by God with these ten plagues.

Mistreatment of Hebrews. God gave a special promise to Abraham and his descendants which said, "I will bless them that bless thee, and curse him that curseth thee" (Genesis 12:3). It is a promise that every age proves true. Attack the Jews and you are doomed. Egypt found out that Genesis 12:3 was no joke. They had for years and years persecuted God's chosen people, but in time the wrath of God came upon them and smote them with the judgment of the ten plagues which made Egypt an also-ran among the nations of the world. The most notable attack on the Jews in our time was that of the German persecution of the Jews under Adolph Hitler. When the persecution began, Germany was rising to great power under Hitler. But within a decade or so, Germany lay in utter ruins and has never risen to much power since. Germany and Egypt are not alone in experiencing this curse, for many other nations over the centuries have also experienced destruction because they attacked the Jews.

Our day needs more emphasis on the peril of mistreating the Jews. In our country today we are hearing more and more anti-Jew talk, and we watch our government cease to be the strong ally it used to be to Israel. These are ominous sounds of coming judgment if we do not repent of our evil regarding Israel.

3. The Emancipation of Israel

When God promised Moses that He would "smite Egypt" (Exodus 3:20), He said, "After that he [Pharaoh] will let you go" (Ibid.). So here we learn of another aim of the plagues which smote Egypt, namely, the emancipation of Israel from their Egyptian bondage. There are two lessons here in the fact that judgment provided freedom for the Israelites. They concern the warning about stubbornness and the way of salvation.

The warning about stubbornness. The message to Pharaoh was "Let my people go" (Exodus 5:1). But the response of Pharaoh was a stubborn refusal to let them go. He would not grant them freedom. This, of course, did not go over well with God. Therefore, God smote Egypt with the great plagues that brought untold destruction upon the land of Egypt. This caused Pharaoh to let Israel go—just as God promised it would (Exodus 3:20). God still deals in like manner with stubbornness to His demands. Refusal to submit to His will eventually results in great loss. You never gain by resisting God's way. Sooner or later He will stretch out His hand and smite you. Let us learn from this sinful stubbornness of Pharaoh. Let us not resist God's will. Resisting God's will is a costly experience.

The way of salvation. Judgment coming upon sin before Israel could be free certainly reminds us of the Gospel of Jesus Christ. Before the sinner who is bound in the bondage of sin can be free, judgment must come also upon sin. And like Israel in Egypt, the sinner does not experience the judgment. Egypt bore the judgment in Israel's case and Jesus Christ bears the judgment in the sinners' case. Christ bore our sins on Calvary that we might be free from the penalty of sin. Without that judgment upon sin, the sinner cannot be free. God must bring judgment upon sin or He is not a holy God. But in grace He provided His Son Jesus Christ to die on Calvary in our place. When we receive Christ as our Savior, we gain the greatest freedom of all.

B. THE ANALYSIS OF THE PLAGUES

The ten plagues which God employed to smite the land of Egypt were (1) the turning of water into blood, (2) the frogs, (3) the lice, (4) the flies, (5) the murrain, (6) the boils, (7) the storm, (8) the locusts, (9) the darkness, and (10) the death of the firstborn. These ten plagues are arranged in three groups of three with the tenth plague standing alone. In each group of three, a warning is given in the first two plagues of the group but not in the third plague of the group.

When dividing the plagues into pairs in which the number of the pairs equals 11, there is a close relationship of the two plagues. Plagues 1 and 10 mention the blood. Plagues 2 and 9 are associated with darkness (frogs and the plague of darkness). Plagues 3 and 8 both have a confession associated with them. The magicians in the third plague confessed, "This is the finger of God" (8:19); and Pharaoh in the eighth plague confessed, "I have sinned" (10:16). In plagues 4 and 7 it is specifically mentioned that Goshen had been exempted from the plagues. And in plagues 5 and 6 animals are prominent in the plagues.

We mention these various and interesting groupings of the

plagues to again emphasize, as we did in a previous chapter, that the Word of God is not some jumbled up mess of myths thrown together at random by some simpletons. Rather, it is a Divinely authored book put together intricately in a demonstration of literary excellence and spiritual inspiration. Failure to see the excellency of the Word of God is not the fault of the Word of God. It is the fault of the individual. One will never see the excellency of the Word if he does not believe the Word of God and does not diligently and faithfully study the Word.

We will now examine each plague separately to learn some of the many lessons God has for us in this great smiting of the land of Egypt.

1. The Plague of Blood (7:14–25)

The first plague consisted of turning the water of the Nile and its associated streams and canals and reservoirs into blood. We will consider the reproving before the plague, the revelation in the plague, the ruin from the plague, the reaping in the plague, the religion in the plague, the repeating of the plague, and the rejection of the plague.

The reproving before the plague. Before the first plague came about, Pharaoh was duly reproved by Moses. Moses said, "The LORD God of the Hebrews hath sent me unto thee, saying, Let my people go, that they may serve me in the wilderness; and, behold, hitherto thou wouldest not hear" (7:16). Pharaoh had already twice rejected the order to let Israel go. And it looked like his scornful rejection would be uncontested. But now he is to find out that he can no longer reject God's demand for Israel's freedom without incurring Divine judgment. Sin brings judgment, and that judgment is to begin in Egypt. Matthew Henry said, "God warns before He wounds." Pharaoh had been warned adequately about letting Israel go. But since he rejected the warning, the wounding will now begin. Oh, how much wounding we could escape if we only heeded His commands promptly.

The revelation in the plague. "Thus saith the LORD, In this thou shalt know that I am the LORD" (7:17). When Moses and Aaron first appealed to Pharaoh in the name of Jehovah to let the Israelites go, Pharaoh scornfully told Moses and Aaron, "I know not the LORD [Jehovah]" (Exodus 5:2). That is going to change. God is going to give Pharaoh a crash course on the knowledge of Jehovah God. It will begin with the first plague, as our text states, and will continue through each of the plagues. In a very pungent fashion, Pharaoh will learn about the true God. He will learn that God is holy, all powerful, and is superior by far to any gods Pharaoh has ever known.

Pharaoh's increase in the knowledge of Jehovah God as a result of the plagues is part of the first reason for the plagues which we cited earlier, namely, to praise God. The better men know God the better they will praise Him. Israel (Exodus 6:7) and Egypt (Exodus 7:5) as well as Pharaoh are all said in the Scripture to come to know God better through this smiting of Egypt.

In everything God does, He does it to reveal Himself to mankind. God is not performing these miracles of the ten plagues just to entertain. God is doing them to enlighten men in the most important truths of life. Would that our churches would emphasize the enlightening work more in their ministries. Many churches, however, seem to be in the entertainment business instead. Their services do very little to enlighten people about God and His Word. They may be very entertaining, but it is very evident they do not instruct well in the Word of God. But God is not that way. When He does something, it is to enlighten our knowledge of Him. If churches are interested in doing a true work for God, they will be careful to do the same.

The ruin from the plague. "And all the waters that were in the river were turned to blood. And the fish that was in the river died; and the river stank, and the Egyptians could not drink of the water of the river; and there was blood throughout all the land of Egypt" (7:20,21). This plague brought considerable ruin in at least three major areas of Egypt. It brought ruin to their eating, their ecology, and their economy.

It ruined their *eating*. This plague polluted their drinking water supplies and killed many fish, one of the main items of their food (Numbers 11:5). Had they not been able to find some water by digging wells (7:24), Egypt would have perished quickly. Their fish supply, however, would take a long time to recover; for when the Nile went back to water, fish would not grow overnight. So this plague was a major blow to their eating.

It ruined their *ecology*. With the river turned to blood and the fish in the river all dead, no wonder the Scripture says, "The river stank" (7:21). The air would be putrid. The river would be a foul mess. It would give Egypt some major ecology problems. This underscores the fact that a great many of the ecology problems of our day are a result of sin. But you will never get the environmental people to recognize that truth. The wickedness of Sodom and her sister cities also brought havoc to the ecology of the land. We have "Earth Day" and "Save the Earth" programs in our times that are mostly worthless endeavors because they never attack the biggest ecology problem of all—sin.

It ruined their *economy*. Fishing, a big business in Egypt, would really be hurt by this plague. This would cause many other businesses to also be adversely affected, for businesses are so interrelated in economical well-being. It would not be business as usual with this huge problem in the land. The economy would take a big blow in Egypt. Like the ecology problems, the economy problems also have their roots in sin. What a great loss our society suffers everyday because of such sins as drunkenness, immorality, dishonesty, greed, and other evils.

The reaping in the plague. This plague of turning water into blood caused Egypt to reap what they had sown. It punished Egypt in the coin in which the nation had sinned. Egypt had stained the river with the blood of the Jewish male babies. What a gruesome carnage must have existed day after day as Jewish baby boys were thrown into the river at the command of the king of Egypt. Crocodiles, which invested the river, would feast on the babies, and that would make the blood flow in the river. Now chickens come home to roost. Egypt was not bothered by the blood they put in the river, but they are certainly bothered by the blood God puts in the river. You cannot sow without reaping in this matter of sin. And it is only fitting that you reap the same seed that you have sown.

The religion in the plague. We noted earlier in this chapter of our book that the plagues would attack the pagan gods of Egypt and show God's superiority over them. This plague of the water of the Nile turning into blood attacked Egypt's river god. "The Nile was worshipped as a beneficent deity, in whose honor hymns were chanted by the priests. The papyri furnish the very words of those ancient odes" (F. B. Meyer). Others tell us a temple was built in most cities to honor this god, and that the god was pictured as a man with his mouth open and water issuing from it as the Egyptians did not know the source of the river. The glory of the river god would be greatly diminished with this plague. This plague made it clear that the river god was much inferior to Jehovah God, for it could not overcome the power of Jehovah God.

Sooner or later all the things we trust in and honor above God will fail us as God judges us for our disloyalty to Him. The judgment upon Egypt's river god gives us at least three instructive principles about letting other things become more important to us than God.

First, it tells us that anything which becomes an idol with us will one day become a plague to us. Someone has written a wise exhortation regarding this principle: "The dearest idol I have known, whate'er that idol be; help me to tear it from Thy throne, and worship only Thee."

Second, it tells us that anything which tasted sweet in sin will someday become unpalatable. In their sin, the Egyptians had enjoyed the Nile, but "the Egyptians could not drink of the water of the river" (7:21) after it turned to blood.

240

Third, it tells us that blessings misused become curses. The river, a great source of blessing to Egypt, had been misused by worshipping it and by killing the Jewish babies in it. Let the wise take heed regarding the lessons of this judgment.

The repeating of the plague. "And the magicians of Egypt did so with their enchantments" (7:22). Two things can be said about this work of the magicians. It was a smaller work than that of Moses and Aaron, and it was a stupid work.

First, it was *a smaller work.* The magicians would not have much water left to turn into blood. To turn water into blood, they would have to get their water from the wells that the Egyptians had dug for water after all the other water had turned to blood. Therefore, though they could duplicate the miracle, they were no match for Moses and Aaron who did a much greater miracle. God is never second best. Would that we always gave Him first best.

Second, it was *a stupid work.* Why did not the magicians change the blood back into water? That would have alleviated Egypt's distress. Changing the water into blood only aggravated the situation for the Egyptians. There was not much good water around and the magicians made it even less. How dumb! What mercies Egypt had, they would take even those away. All of this tells us the devil cannot remove judgment, he can only add to it. Likewise when people come up with clever arguments to reject God's will and way, they do not improve their situation but only make it worse. They do not bless society by encouraging others with their clever arguments to disobey God; they only curse it.

The rejection of the plague. "Pharaoh's heart was hardened, neither did he hearken unto them [Moses and Aaron]" (7:22). We note three things about Pharaoh's rejection: a cause for the rejection, a curse from the rejection, and a copy of the rejection.

First, a *cause* for the rejection. It is right after Scripture reports the magicians repeating the plague with their enchantments that we are told, "Pharaoh's heart was hardened, neither

241

did he hearken unto them [Moses and Aaron]." The magicians' performance "was accepted by Pharaoh as an equivalent to what had been effected by the Israelites chiefs, but which must have fallen far short of it. [However] Pharaoh would not be a severe critic [of the magicians lesser performance]" (Rawlinson). As we noted in the miracle of the rod and snakes, Pharaoh was provided with a small exception or loophole text by the magicians' work, and he clung to it in spite of the overwhelming evidence to the contrary.

Rawlinson made an interesting and instructive comment when he said in the above statement, "Pharaoh would not be a severe critic [of the magicians]." Error never gets inspected by unbelief like the truth does. Evil philosophies are accepted without proof while the Bible must be continually examined by the critics to see if it is true. The wicked liberal press of our day glosses over the great evils of the liberal politicians, but it examines the conservatives with high powered microscopes. In the church the pastor's every more is scrutinized by the congregation to see if he shows enough love and patience, but dissidents can live shoddy lives and be outright disrespectful to the pastor and other officers at church, yet most of the congregation will defend the dissidents. Yes, evil is most tolerant of evil but not of good. Pharaoh could accept an inferior performance by the magicians but the great work of Moses and Aaron is found unconvincing to his heart. It is a terrible state to get into. We must pray frequently that we discern correctly in the important matters of life.

Second, a *curse* from the rejection. "And all the Egyptians digged round about the river for water to drink; for they could not drink of the water of the river" (7:24). Thanks to a government that rejected God, the citizens were cursed to extra duty and deprived of a great convenience. The spiritual poverty of political leaders is a burden to the citizens of the land. Oh, the great hardships that have been brought on lands because of wicked rulers. Unless we see a spiritual revival in our government, our land will be likewise cursed in more and more ways.

242

Third, a *copy* of the rejection. The actions of Pharaoh describe our day. Great and mighty wonders are present, but the message they send us is rejected. God can send devastating storms and earthquakes and diseases; but many people today, like Pharaoh in his day, harden their hearts to the truth. So we end up toiling in digging instead of enjoying Divine blessings. Instead of repenting of our sins, we are trying to invent better shovels for digging. Instead of turning from our vile morals, we get out the shovels and dig for better condoms and medicine to combat venereal diseases caused by immorality. Our age acts no better than Pharaoh.

2. The Plague of Frogs (8:1–15)

The second plague consisted of a great invasion of frogs into the land of Egypt. We will note the mediation before the plague, the infiltration of the plague, the aggravation of the plague, the multiplication of the plague, the supplication about the plague, the imploration to end the plague, and the putrification of the plague.

The mediation before the plague. "And the LORD spake unto Moses, Go unto Pharaoh, and say unto him, Thus saith the LORD, Let my people go, that they may serve me. And if thou refuse to let them go, behold, I will smite all thy borders with frogs" (8:1, 2). The second plague provides Pharaoh an opportunity to repent and escape its coming as did the first plague. Divine mercy is manifested in Moses' mediation prior to the second plague. How gracious is God. Pharaoh had been so evil in his conduct. He had rejected the reasonable request for Israel to worship. He had rejected the snakes and rods' sign. He had rejected the plague of water turning into blood. Yet, through Moses' mediation, God still offers Pharaoh opportunity to escape from further judgment. Pharaoh, however, rejected that offer of mercy as the frog plague was eventually ordered by God (8:5). Mankind cannot always reject Divine mercy without judgment coming upon him.

243

The infiltration of the plague. The frogs infiltrated every area of the land. "And the river shall bring forth frogs abundantly, which shall go up, and come into thine house, and into thy bedchamber, and upon thy bed, and into the house of thy servants, and upon thy people, and into thine ovens, and into thy kneadingtroughs; And the frogs shall come up both on thee, and upon thy people, and upon all thy servants" (8:3,4). This infiltration of the land by the frogs symbolizes the infiltration of sin into the lives of mankind. The frogs were in their beds—sin stops rest. The frogs were in the food—how much sin is found in what we put in our mouths from booze to poisonous pills. The frogs filled their ears with their incessant croaking sound (Rawlinson said the particular kind of frog of this plague "has the scientific name of *Rana Mosaica* . . . and croaks perpetually")—sin does not produce pleasant sounds as rock music attests. The frogs were "upon the people" (8:4)—sin destroys beauty, corrupts, contaminates, makes ugly, and ages the body. Yes, the frogs were everywhere just as sin is everywhere. As the Bible reports, "All have sinned" (Romans 3:23), and "From the sole of the foot even unto the head there is no soundness in it; but wounds, and bruises, and putrefying sores" (Isaiah 1:6). If God were to let the frogs loose today to show us where we are sinning, the frogs would indeed fill every nook and cranny of our land and lives. Sin is everywhere—in the mouths, in the minds, and in the manners of people.

The aggravation of the plague. What really aggravated the plague of frogs was the Egyptians' attitudes towards the frogs. We note three aggravating attitudes. They are the veneration, the imputation, and the preservation attitudes.

First, the *veneration* attitude. The Egyptians worshipped the frog. The frog was one of their gods. Therefore, we learn in this plague what we learned in the first plague, namely, that what becomes an idol to us will someday become a plague to us. Anything that gets between us and God will eventually curse us. God does not tolerate competition. Our idols must go. He will make them a real problem to us if we do not forsake them.

Second, the *imputation* attitude. The Egyptians imputed to the frog god the powers of fertility. So again, as in the first plague, God is punishing Egypt in the coin in which it sinned. It worshipped the frog as a god of fertility; now in the plague, the frog's fertility will run wild and produce abundantly. They "covered the land of Egypt" (8:6), but it was a curse to the land of Egypt.

Third, the *preservation* attitude. Egypt's religion forbid the killing of the frog. Thus, though the frogs became a terrible nuisance to the land; they could not be killed. What a predicament Egypt got into because of their pagan theology. It made them indefensible to evil in their land.

Sin always makes us indefensible. Today, we have the same preservation troubles. Environmentalists and animal rights people have gotten ridiculous laws passed that protect all sorts of animals to the extent that humans lose their jobs, cannot develop and farm some lands, cannot get rid of nuisance animals, and cannot build houses and other structures on their land. It is all so sick and reflects a pagan mentality. Also, in our land, we have made a number of laws that protect the criminal. Crime plagues the land, but our godless laws prohibit us from doing much about it. That is a result of sin! Evil men make evil laws which curse the land.

The multiplication of the plague. "And the magicians did so with their enchantments" (8:7). Again, as in the first plague, the magicians only made matters worse. Why didn't they try to remove the frogs? The reason is that all anyone who turns from the true God can do is make matters worse. As we noted in the first plague, those who try to explain away the work of God as the work of others (which the magicians were trying to do) only cause more trouble for society. Clever arguments to keep men from repenting of their sin (the magicians' work encouraged Pharaoh's unbelief and, hence, his disinterest in repentance) only increases the problems of mankind.

The supplication about the plague. "Then Pharaoh called for Moses and Aaron, and said, Entreat the LORD, that he may take away the frogs from me, and from my people; and I will let the people go, that they may do sacrifice unto the LORD" (8:8). The plague got to Pharaoh. For the first time in Moses' encounters with Pharaoh, Pharaoh backs down. He requests Moses to have the plague removed; then he, Pharaoh, will let the people go. This request looks good on the surface, but there are four major problems with it. They have to do with the priority, procrastination, prerequisite, and pretentiousness of the request.

First, the *priority* of the request. The order of the prayer shows the selfish priority of Pharaoh. He mentioned himself first. He asked that the frogs be taken away "from me" and then he adds "from my people." Typical of most rulers, he was looking out for himself first. His personal interests were above the interest of his country. We will see more of this later.

Second, the *procrastination* of the request. Moses asked Pharaoh to be specific as to when he wanted the frogs removed (8:9). Pharaoh's answer was "Tomorrow" (8:10). This was an insane answer. Why not "now"? Pharaoh would have to sleep another night with the frogs. But sin is ever stupidly procrastinating. Many with life imperiling habits put off stopping the habit. Many without Christ put off salvation to a more convenient time (cp. Acts 24:25). Sin never makes us smarter; it destroys good sense. It only prolongs the suffering.

Third, the *prerequisite* of the request. "Entreat . . . and I will let the people go" (8:8). Pharaoh put a condition on letting the people go. The condition was that the frogs had to be removed first. The condition, however, is not noble. Pharaoh should let the people go because God demanded him to do so. Bargaining with God is the habit of man, but it is bad habit. It would make God's commands subservient to our conditions. God in grace condescends to us in this oftentimes, but it does not justify bargaining. True faith does what God demands regardless.

Fourth, the *pretentiousness* of the request. The insincerity of the request is seen when the frogs were removed. "But when

Pharaoh saw that there was respite, he hardened his heart, and hearkened not unto them" (8:15). Pharaoh prayed like many do in every age. When in trouble they promise God all sorts of things if God will get them out of trouble. But once out of trouble, they renege on their promise and go back to their old ways.

The imploration to end the plague. "And Moses cried unto the LORD because of the frogs which he had brought against Pharaoh" (8:12). Here we find the first of some of Moses' noble prayers to God. Hitherto, Moses has prayed some not so noble prayers. But this one like some that follow is most noble. His earnestness here is especially noteworthy. Rawlinson says, "The expression [cried] is a strong one, and seems to imply special earnestness in prayer." Moses' earnestness is a rebuke to us for our lack of earnestness in praying for lost sinners. Moses was especially good at praying for the deliverance of the undeserving. As an example, he did it at Mount Sinai regarding the Israelites (Exodus 32:31,32), and he also did it for Miriam in the wilderness (Numbers 12:13). Would that all of us would learn to plead for the salvation of sinners as earnestly as Moses prayed for the removal of the frogs.

The putrification of the plague. "And they gathered them together upon heaps; and the land stank" (8:14). This is the third time in the first two plagues that we are told of the awful smell the plagues caused in Egypt (the other two times are in 7:17 and 7:21). Sin causes an unholy stench to permeate a land and an individual (smokers illustrate this fact). And we learn here that even after we have turned from our sin, restoration takes awhile. Forgiveness occurs immediately, but restoration does not. When Pharaoh recanted, the frog plague was stopped; but the cleanup took awhile. You may be forgiven of your sin, but the stench of your sins will hang on for a long time. Therefore, do not be critical when people do not quickly restore you to their confidence and to positions of service in the church after some major sin. They are simply waiting for the smell to leave.

3. The Plague of Lice (8:16–19)

The third plague consisted of "a species of gnats, so small as to be hardly visible to the eye, but with a sting which . . . causes a most painful irritation of the skin. They even creep into the eyes and nose" (Keil). There was no warning about the plague, no worship during the plague, no witchcraft in the plague, and no wisdom in rejecting the plague's message.

No warning about the plague. "And the LORD said unto Moses, Say unto Aaron, Stretch out thy rod, and smite the dust of the land, that it may become lice throughout all the land of Egypt" (8:16). Unlike the first two plagues, this plague came upon the land without warning. This will occur again in the future. Pharaoh had broken his promise to let Israel go if the frog plague was ended. It served him justice to receive no warning about this plague.

God still uses this principle with wicked men. "He that being often reproved hardeneth his neck, shall suddenly be destroyed, and that without remedy [without warning or mercy]" (Proverbs 29:1). Do not ignore the warnings of God. Do not play the fool and think that since no recent warning has come that no judgment will come. You will miss many warnings by not reading the Word of God and not hearing it preached and taught. But that does not stop the coming of judgment. It just stops you from receiving a warning that could save you from the judgment.

No worship during the plague. The effect of this plague on the bodies stopped the Egyptians from worshipping because it stopped the priests from shaving their heads and bodies. The priests did this shaving every few days or so in order to not have any vermin or other impurities on them in the exercise of their duties. But with these small insects coming "upon" (8:18) the bodies and causing itching, numerous sores, and infection, it made it impossible to keep up the ritual shaving and preparation for worship. Hence, there would be a stopping of the Egyptians' worship. In this particular problem from the plague, we learn that God's judgment is fitting but man's judgment is faulty.

First, God's *judgment is fitting*. Once again in these plagues we can see God judging Egypt in the coin in which Egypt had sinned. Egypt would not let Israel worship, now this plague will not let Egypt worship. Chickens are again coming home to roost for the Egyptians. We do well to examine our own problems to see if they do not at times reflect this reciprocal judgment of God upon us. If we are miserly with God, we should not be surprised if God is miserly with us. If we are slow at paying bills, we should not be surprised if others are slow in paying us our dues. If we are dishonest with others, we should not be surprised if others are dishonest with us.

Second, man's *judgment is faulty*. The Egyptians judged one's cleanliness by their physical body, not spiritual. The priests' shaving habits reflected this attitude. Our day also has this problem. We put a great emphasis on the outward cleanliness of a person but not on the inward. So today, when we go to a drug or grocery store, we see the food and drugs all controlled and guarded by stringent laws to insure purity of the product for the physical body. But go to the check-out and you will see racks of lewd literature. Great care is taken in these stores to protect the physical body from defilement; but dirty books and magazines thrive in the same places unguarded, uncensored, and unworried about.

No witchcraft in the plague. "And the magicians did so with their enchantments to bring forth lice, but they could not" (8:18). The magicians, as before, played the fool here; for they tried to add to the misery of the people rather than trying to relieve them of their misery. They are like our government in its welfare program—they are not helping the people on welfare; they are only making it worse for them by giving them all the money and food stamps.

The magicians being stopped demonstrated Who was running the show. Jehovah God can allow Satanic forces to work.

249

But when He wants to stop them, He will. And the magicians admitted He was running the show, for when the magicians could not duplicate the lice plague, they said to Pharaoh, "This is the finger of God" (8:19). They are beginning to catch on! God had told Moses that He would "stretch out my hand and smite Egypt" (3:20), now the magicians see part of that hand. Since they were not monotheistic in their religion, they doubtless thought "God" was just another God who was superior to the ones they knew. And indeed He was superior whether their pagan gods were real or invented deities.

The acknowledgement of the magicians of God's supremacy is something all men will do sooner or later. Paul tells us in Philippians 2:10 and 11 that every knee will bow in acknowledgment of Christ as the Lord, and every tongue will likewise confess Christ as Lord. But not all acknowledgements will result in blessing upon the one confessing the supremeness of Christ. Many will only confess the supremeness of Christ in judgment, as did the magicians.

No wisdom in rejecting the plague's message. "Pharaoh's heart was hardened, and he hearkened not unto them" (8:19). Pharaoh rejected the message of the plague, and he also rejected his revered magicians' message about the plague. When a man is set on a course of sin, all testimony and warning to the contrary will avail nothing. Sin deadens the soul and makes it a fool in conduct. Pharaoh had no reason to reject the plague's message. Previously he thought he had the work of the magicians to give him an excuse for rejecting the messages of the plagues. But he does not even have that fraudulent excuse anymore, for the magicians now acknowledge the message of the plagues and tell Pharaoh so. But he will not listen to the magicians now. Like many who only listen to you if you say what they want you to say, Pharaoh did not like their message; so he rejected it. There was no wisdom whatever in his action. But those who reject the truth about God will lose all wisdom concerning God and will play the fool to their own destruction.

4. The Plague of Flies (8:20–32)

The fourth plague, which started the second triad of plagues, consisted of a "grievous swarm" (8:24) of some sort or sorts of flying insects. The King James Version calls the swarm "flies" but places the word in italics as the translators added the word— it was not in the Hebrew. Psalm 78:45 speaks of it as "divers [various] sorts of flies." Not being certain of what particular type or types of insects were involved really makes no difference. It is the damage that is significant, for the plague was one of judgment; and, as we will see shortly, Scripture is clear about the great damage the insects did.

To examine this plague and the events involved with it, we will note the dedication before the plague, the decision about the plague, the division during the plague, the devastation from the plague, the denunciation in the plague, and the deliverance from the plague.

The dedication before the plague. "And the LORD said unto Moses, Rise up early in the morning, and stand before Pharaoh; lo, he cometh forth to the water; and say unto him, Thus saith the LORD, Let my people go, that they may serve me; Else, if thou wilt not let my people go, behold I will send swarms of flies" (8:20,21). One cannot serve God well without dedication to God. While Moses argued earlier with God at the burning bush when given the summons to be the emancipator of Israel, he, however, evidenced great dedication once he got into the work of the plagues. Three aspects of his great dedication are addressed in the verses quoted above. We look at them under the headings of the morning, the mandate, and the message.

First, the *morning.* God instructed Moses to "Rise up early in the morning" (v. 20) to get started on his work. "Early in the morning" means Moses will have to show some real dedication if he is going to do his duty here. Those who lounge lazily in bed when they ought to be getting up and working will never amount to much in God's work or in any other work. Furthermore, those who want to serve God need to remember that the

251

world gets up early to do their business. Moses had to get up early so he could meet Pharaoh at the river. That means Pharaoh got up early, too. We will never defeat evil if our dedication does not exceed that of evil men.

Second, the *mandate*. God ordered Moses to "stand before Pharaoh" (v. 20). Moses was not given an easy assignment. Moses' mandate was to "stand" before a vile, brutal man who hated Jehovah. It is easy to stand before those who sympathize with our beliefs, but it is not easy to stand before those who viciously oppose our faith. Peter was outspoken in his stand for Christ when he was before the other disciples in the Upper Room. But not many hours later, he denied Christ when he was before those who were hostile towards Christ. Many in every age are like that. However, if we are truly dedicated to the Lord, we will "stand" regardless of our situation.

Third, the *message*. As it has been so many times before, Moses' message was, "Thus saith the LORD" (v. 20). Here is another place where dedication is tested. Moses, as most ministers can easily understand, would have preferred to give Pharaoh a different message—a message that would not upset Pharaoh. But Moses was to declare God's Word. Preaching God's Word may mean preaching what is unpopular. But dedication will preach God's Word in every situation.

The decision about the plague. "Let my people go, that they may serve me. Else, if thou wilt not let my people go, behold, I will send swarms of flies" (vv. 20, 21). Again God graciously gives Pharaoh an opportunity to escape Divine judgment. The previous plague did not afford Pharaoh that opportunity. But this one does as did the first and the second plagues. This means Pharaoh has a decision to make. He must decide whether he will let the Israelites go or let Egypt experience a plague of Divine judgment. He either obeys or "Else" (v. 21).

The "else" reminds us of the warning which was given several churches in the book of Revelation. The church in Ephesus was told to "repent . . . or else" (Revelation 2:5). Also, the

252

church at Pergamos was told to "repent. . . . or else" (Revelation 2:16). The world does not like the "or else" message, and many preachers do not preach it. But with God it is either do what He says "or else" judgment. There is no middle road. The decision is yours. How tragic that so many make the decision to choose the "or else" option as did Pharaoh regarding this plague. If you end up in hell, you have no one to blame but yourself. God gave you opportunities for salvation but you refused them.

The division during the plague. "And I will sever in that day the land of Goshen, in which my people dwell, that no swarms of flies shall be there; to the end thou mayest know that I am the LORD in the midst of the earth. And I will put a division between my people and thy people" (vv. 22,23). Here we are distinctly told that Israel will not experience this plague that will come upon Egypt.

Our text states the reason why the division occurred. We would normally expect that the reason would be to protect Israel from suffering. It is true that separation keeps God's people from many problems and this division did protect Israel from suffering. But our text notes another important purpose in the separation instead. It is to promote the testimony of God. The message to Pharaoh was that the division would help "thou [Pharaoh] . . . know that I am the LORD in the midst of the earth" (v. 22). So many professing Christians think we need to be like the world in order to reach the world with the truth about God. But our text will not support that carnal thinking. Separation, not mixing, is what helps the world to know about God. The separated church will have the best testimony in town.

The devastation from the plague. This plague was another very devastating plague. Scripture says, "There came a grievous swarm of flies into the house of Pharaoh, and into his servants' houses, and into all the land of Egypt; the land was corrupted by reason of the swarm of flies" (v. 24). The word "corruption" in our text sums up the devastation of the plague. This word is

253

translated from a Hebrew word which means "to destroy, to ruin, to lay in ruins . . . to mar, to spoil, to make good for nothing" (William Wilson). That meaning does not leave much respite in the plague. This plague was no slap on the wrist. It left the land devastated. Today, when catastrophes occur in society, we generally hear a dollar figure as to the amount of destruction that occurred. If we were to give a dollar figure to the Egyptian destruction in this plague, it would be enormous. And to think that this was only the fourth plague. Egypt recovered somewhat from the plague as later plagues found crops, etc. to destroy. But that does not lessen the great destruction of this plague. It left Egypt in ruins for awhile. Oh, the great destructive work of sin. We see many folk today who are heading for eternal devastation because they, like Pharaoh, persistently reject God. And no devastation is worse than hell fire.

The denunciation in the plague. "Let not Pharaoh deal deceitfully any more in not letting the people go to sacrifice to the LORD" (v. 29). Moses denounced Pharaoh for his deceitfulness when Pharaoh requested the plague to end. Pharaoh had "called for Moses and for Aaron" (v. 25) after the plague had worked havoc on the land, and he proposed several compromises. We will note all the compromises Pharaoh offered during the plagues in our last main point of this chapter. Here we simply note that after Moses rejected both compromises and after he agreed to call off the plague, he denounced Pharaoh for the way he had reneged on his past promise. Pharaoh had promised during the frog plague that he would let Israel go (8:8). But when the plague ended, he reneged on his promise. He had only made the promise to get rid of the frogs. Moses was not fooled by Pharaoh's actions. He knew Pharaoh was dishonest, a crafty deceiver; so he rebuked him. Pharaoh needed to be rebuked, so do all deceivers. They may not repent as a result of the rebuke, but the innocent will learn deception is unacceptable no matter who you are.

Pharaoh's deception is not unique. Many still do it today

when in tough times. They promise God a list of things they will do if God will get them out of trouble. But when they are relieved of their troubles, they pay no more attention to their promises than Pharaoh did. Deceivers like this will deceive their hearts to personal destruction.

The deliverance from the plague. "And Moses said . . . I will entreat the LORD that the swarms of flies may depart . . . tomorrow . . . And the LORD did according to the word of Moses; and he removed the swarms of flies . . . there remained not one. And Pharaoh hardened his heart at this time also, neither would he let the people go" (vv. 29–32). The deliverance from the swarms of flies was delayed, decisive, and defied.

First, it was *delayed.* Moses said he would get rid of the flies "tomorrow" (v. 29). Pharaoh could not complain about the delay, for he asked for the same delay regarding the frogs (8:10). This delay reminds us that the consequences of our evil are not necessarily removed quickly. We've seen this truth before in this study of the plagues, and it is a sobering truth that ought to hasten our repentance of evil.

Second, it was *decisive.* "There remained not one" (v. 31). The removal of the plague was absolute and amazing. "The complete disappearance was as abnormal as the sudden coming" (Rawlinson). Here is a good Gospel picture. When we come to Christ for salvation, every single sin is washed away by the blood of the Lamb. Not one sin will remain to keep us out of heaven. No one cleanses like God cleanses. "The blood of Jesus Christ his Son cleanseth us from *all* sin" (I John 1:7).

Third, it was *defied.* After the plague was removed, Pharaoh again hardened his heart and refused to let the Israelites leave (v. 32). God intends that His goodness encourage men to repent (Romans 2:4). But many are like Pharaoh and pervert their blessings to encourage sinning instead of repentance. Many interpret reprieve and escape from troubles as a sign that their evil was not so bad after all; and, as a result, they pursue their evil again. We need to pray earnestly that our hearts will not be so hardened by defiance to God that we twist and pervert the good things of God to promote evil. It is a terrible state of mind to be in and one that brings great judgment upon a person.

5. The Plague of Murrain (9:1–7)

The fifth plague consisted of a disease which afflicted the livestock of Egypt. To examine this plague, we will note the commission in the plague, the clemency before the plague, the carnage from the plague, the care in the plague, and the contempt after the plague.

The commission in the plague. "Then the LORD said unto Moses, Go in unto Pharaoh, and tell him, Thus saith the LORD God of the Hebrews, Let my people go, that they may serve me" (9:1). The commission given Moses is substantially the same one that has been given him repeatedly before (cp. Exodus 5:1; 7:16; 8:1; 8:20). We note some key features of it: the confrontation, the claim, the consecration, and the compliance.

First, the *confrontation.* Moses was again directed to confront Pharaoh. Confronting sinners is often the work of God's servants. God has a contention with man concerning their sin and God's servants will be asked to do the confronting for God. Note the language of "Go . . . and tell" in this commission. It reminds us of the "Go . . . and teach" (Matthew 28:19) and of the "Go . . . and preach" (Mark 16:15) of the Great Commission. God tells us where to go and what to say when He employs us in His service. Those who would serve successfully and faithfully will be careful to obey both the where and what.

Second, the *claim.* God demands that Pharaoh let "my" people go. We have seen this issue of possessions before, but we note it here again. God is only asking Pharaoh for what belongs to God. This applies to all of us. Whatever God asks of us only belongs to Him anyway. To withhold from God is therefore robbery (cp. Malachi 3:8). The idea that this is my own life and I will do with it what I please is not a Biblical concept.

Third, the *consecration.* The primary reason Israel was to be set free was "that they may serve me." This truth is repeated a number of times in the emancipation record. It reminds us that our freedoms, our blessings, our abilities, etc. are given us to primarily enhance our service for God. But the flesh ignores this truth and wants to use these things for selfish reasons. We need to examine our hearts as to our attitudes about our blessings. Do we pray for health so we can serve God better or so we can pursue carnal pleasures better? Do we pray for freedom from poverty so we can give more to God's work or so we can spend more on our own carnal interests? If we want to serve God well, we must use our blessings primarily for His service. But this is not a truth many understand well or want to understand well.

Fourth, the *compliance*. Though it is not specifically stated, it certainly is implied and obvious that Moses complied again to God's commissions. As we noted before, though Moses balked at the beginning regarding his call, once the judgment time came for Egypt, Moses served with excellence. Each time God ordered him to confront Pharaoh, Moses obliged though the task was dangerous and did not meet with Pharaoh's yielding to God's demand. Moses needed courage and consistency to serve God well. Mankind still needs these two ingredients to be successful in God's work.

The clemency before the plague. "And the LORD appointed a set time, saying, Tomorrow the LORD shall do this thing in the land" (9:5). Again God gives grace to Pharaoh. After warning Pharaoh that "if thou refuse to let them go, and wilt hold them still, behold, the hand of the LORD is upon thy cattle which is in the field, upon the horses, and upon the asses, upon the camels, upon the oxen, and upon the sheep; there shall be a very grievous murrain" (9:2,3), God gave him the day (9:5) to think about the warning of the next plague. Pharaoh, therefore, had time to escape Divine judgment. He had until tomorrow to act.

This is the third time the word "tomorrow" (previous mentions in 8:10 and 8:29) is associated with Pharaoh. But in each case he misused his "tomorrow." He is not alone in that habit.

257

Many are those in every age who misuse their tomorrows. God gives them time to escape Divine judgment, but they spurn His gracious tomorrows and suffer judgment instead.

The carnage from the plague. After each plague we think things could not get worse, but they do. The previous plagues have been very destructive. But the carnage from this one is not to be outdone by what has gone before. This plague was a "very grievous murrain" that destroyed the livestock. Specifically "all the cattle of Egypt died" (9:6). The carnage of this plague demonstrated how adversely the plague affected their religion and their resources.

First, *religion.* Egypt held many animals as sacred (cp. Exodus 8:26). With all the cattle and other livestock dying, the Egyptians would be greatly hindered in their worship. As we noted before in the other plagues when they hindered worship, this was chickens coming home to roost. Egypt would not let Israel worship; now they are not able to worship. We reap and we sow; and we reap *what* we sow.

Second, *resources.* This plague would be a devastating blow to their resources. Besides losing all the cattle, they lost the oxen who did the plowing, the camels who brought merchandise, the horses who were vital for the military, and the sheep who were an important source of wealth. This great lost of resources would ruin the economy. And, unlike the previous plagues, there was no calling off of the plague, for there was no need to call it off. The disease finished off all the livestock and that ended the plague. It is the worst way for a plague to end.

The care in the plague. "The LORD shall sever between the cattle of Israel and the cattle of Egypt; and there shall nothing die of all that is the children's of Israel . . . all the cattle of Egypt died; but the cattle of the children of Israel died not one" (9:4,6). This is the second plague in which Israel's exemption is specifically mentioned. That it was prophesied before it happened would emphasize the power of Jehovah God.

In the last plague we noted that when the plague was ended "there remained not one" fly. The "not one" illustrated the Gospel truth that when God removes sin, He cleanses away all sin. In the protection of Israel's livestock in this plague, we have two similar phrases which also give us a good Gospel lesson—"Nothing die" (9:4) and "not one" (9:6). They remind us of the security of the believer. Jesus said, "I give unto them eternal life; and they shall never perish, neither shall any man pluck them out of my hand" (John 10:28). No saved person, "not one," will perish in his sins.

The contempt after the plague. "Pharaoh was hardened, and he did not let the people go" (9:7). This statement was made after the Scripture said, "Pharaoh sent, and, behold, there was not one of the cattle of the Israelites dead" (Ibid.). Pharaoh checked out the word of Moses about Israel's cattle. But even though the facts proved Moses right, Pharaoh would not recant. This is typical of unbelief. They have contempt for the facts. You can show this kind of unbelief the best possible facts. But they turn away as though you gave them no evidence at all. Christ gave an abundance of evidences that He was indeed the Son of God and Israel's Messiah. But unbelief demonstrated a great contempt for the facts and crucified Christ. Do not be surprised when you preach or teach the Word of God that many listening to you will still reject the facts though they are as plain as day. Even though the Bible states the truth plainly, there are those who will deny it anyway. Unbelief creates a great contempt for facts in the spiritual arena.

6. The Plague of Boils (9:8–12)

The sixth plague consisted of an attack of boils upon the bodies of the people and of the beasts of Egypt. These boils progressed into pussy, ulcerous sores. To study this plague, we will consider the pre-eminence, the place, the publicity, the pitilessness, the punishment, the perverters, and the promise in the plague.

The pre-eminence in the plague. "And the LORD said unto Moses and unto Aaron, Take to you handfuls of ashes of the furnace, and let Moses sprinkle it toward the heaven in the sight of Pharaoh" (9:8). There is a lesson about position in service here that we do well to note. Moses was to sprinkle the ashes in the air; Aaron was only to hold the ashes. Prior to this, Aaron did the glory work. He cast down his rod before Pharaoh in the snake and rod miracle (7:10). He stretched out the rod in the plague that turned water to blood (7:19), in the frogs' plague (8:5), and in the lice plague (8:16). But here he only holds the ashes because Moses has the pre-eminence. Many would have been to proud to do this lowly task of holding the ashes.

Position in the Lord's work causes more problems that just about anything else. Few people can take a back seat when necessary and hold ashes, but that is a most needed task. So many people in church want the high seats. If they do not get them, they will not perform. Let us be willing to work in the background when God so requires it.

The place in the plague. The plague commenced at a "furnace" (9:8). The ashes (Rawlinson says the Hebrew word means "soot") to be sprinkled in the air to start the plague were to be taken from a "furnace." The Hebrew word translated furnace, means "brick-kiln" (Rawlinson). Those furnaces were part of Israel's agony in making bricks—one of their slave jobs. The slaves were still working there, of course; and Pharaoh is evidently out checking on things as the ashes were to be thrown in the air in his presence.

This site of the plague's beginning is a lesson in sowing and reaping. The Egyptians had used these furnaces to make the Israelites suffer, now God will use these same furnaces to make the Egyptians suffer. This lesson on sowing and reaping is repeated again and again in the plagues. Let the emphasis in the plagues on this important truth prompt us to live better lives.

The publicity in the plague. The ashes were to be sprinkled in the air "in the sight of Pharaoh" (9:8). It would have been easier to sprinkle the ashes in the air before anyone else than Pharaoh. But as we saw in a previous plague where God told Moses to "stand before Pharaoh" (8:20), so we also see here the truth that we must profess our faith in hard places as well as easy places. Many are good at giving their testimony before believers in church, but they do poorly before the ungodly in the world who will respond hostilely to their testimony.

The pitilessness in the plague. There was no warning with this plague. Like the third plague, the sixth plague happened without Pharaoh having any warning that it was coming and, thus, without any opportunity to escape. The lesson here is the same as it was in the third plague; that is, God will not always show grace. Continue to reject grace, and you will be hit with sudden judgment with no chance of escape.

The punishment in the plague. "And it shall become small dust in all the land of Egypt, and shall be a boil breaking forth with blains [ulcerous sores] upon man, and upon beast throughout all the land of Egypt" (9:9). This plague especially attacked the bodies of the Egyptians. The Egyptians were very concerned about the purity of their body but not about the purity of their behavior. We noted in the third plague that this inconsistency is very evident in our day also. We fight earnestly the germs that can harm us physically, but we allow all sorts of germs to exist that can harm us morally and spiritually. We are much more concerned about physical sickness than moral or spiritual sickness. While all physical problems are not punishment from God for some sin, it is very evident that a great many of our physical problems would be eliminated if we put more emphasis on our moral and spiritual health.

The perverters in the plague. "And the magicians could not stand before Moses because of the boils; for the boil was upon the magicians, and upon all the Egyptians" (9:11). At the end of the first triad of plagues, the magicians were no longer able to reproduce the plagues and confessed that the "finger of God" (8:19) was doing this work. Now at the end of the second triad, we read of another stopping of these perverters—they could no longer stand in the presence of Moses because they were so bothered with the boils. Moses may be despised and his work may be mimicked for awhile; but he is God's man; and, before it is over, none of the enemies will be standing. We have a number of theological magicians in society who can juggle Scripture to give approval of evil ways. But their days are numbered, and in the end only the true men of God will be standing.

The promise in the plague. "And the LORD hardened the heart of Pharaoh, and he hearkened not unto them; as the LORD had spoken unto Moses" (9:12). God had promised Moses that He would harden Pharaoh's heart (4:21), and He is doing it here just as He promised He would. Elsewhere God promises the same punishment for all who insist on persistently rejecting Him (Romans 1:28). If we persist in hardening our heart regarding spiritual things, God will come along and help harden it for us. And when God hardens the heart, the heart will be permanently hardened. "If men shut their eyes against the light, it is just with God to close their eyes. Let us dread this as the sorest judgment a man can be under on this side of hell" (Matthew Henry).

7. The Plague of Hail (9:13–35)

The seventh plague consisted of a terrible hail storm that came upon the land of Egypt. It was accompanied by rain, great thunderings, and severe lightening. We will examine this plague by noting the demand before the plague, the declaration before the plague, the denunciation before the plague, the deliverance from the plague, the destruction from the plague, and the duplicity in the plague.

The demand before the plague. "Let my people go, that they may serve me" (9:13). This is at least the sixth time God has demanded of Pharaoh that he let Israel go (see Exodus 5:1, 7:16, 8:1, 8:20, and 9:1 for the previous five times). The repetition of the demand emphasizes two facts. First, it emphasizes the greatness of Pharaoh's rebellion. How hard his heart was to repeatedly reject God's demand even after the great destruction from the previous plagues. The great hardness of people's hearts today is likewise evident in their continued rebellion in spite of the destructive storms, earthquakes, floods, diseases, and other disasters God has brought upon the world. Second, the repetition of the demand emphasizes the greatness of God's grace. In spite of rejection, God continued to give Pharaoh opportunity to do right. God has done this for all of us, and it is a good thing, for how many of us responded the first time God called us to salvation or service? Had it not been for repeated calls, few would be saved or serving. But continually spurn God's grace, as Pharaoh did, and God will cease calling and commanding.

The declaration before the plague. After making the sixth demand to Pharaoh to let Israel go, Moses declared to Pharaoh a message about future plagues. The message was about the place, power, purpose, and provoker of the future plagues. This declaration ought to have caused Pharaoh to fear and tremble.

First, the *place* of the future plagues. "For I will at this time send all my plagues upon thine heart, and upon thy servants, and upon thy people" (9:14). The place of destruction has some added dimensions. The heart, the servants, and the people are now included as targets of the plagues. True, the people had suffered some physically from the previous plagues. But now they were going to suffer greatly—many would even die. Furthermore, the plagues would go to the heart of Pharaoh. He would have wrestlings in his heart and would agonize in heart as never before. He would make confessions and concessions he had heretofore scorned. But, in spite of that, his heart would also grow harder than before. God would stricken Pharaoh's heart with a hardness that could not truly repent but that could only lead him to destruction.

263

Second, the *power* of the future plagues. "For now I will stretch out my hand, that I may smite thee and thy people with pestilence; and thou shalt be cut off from the earth" (9:15). As with the past plagues, so with the future plagues—God's power will be seen to be great. God has the power to smite Egypt whenever and however He wants. He also has the power to "cut off" Pharaoh. Pharaoh thought he was the man of power. He had for a time appeared to indeed have that power over mankind. But these plagues will show him how powerless he really is compared to God's power.

Third, the *purpose* of the future plagues. "That thou mayest know that there is none like me in all the earth . . . thou shalt be cut off from the earth . . . for to show in thee my power; and that my name may be declared throughout all the earth" (9:14–16). The purpose of the future plagues corresponds to the purpose of the past plagues. They will instruct and give testimony about God, for people "throughout all the earth" will learn about God because of these plagues. And the plagues will bring judgment upon evil men, for Pharaoh will be "cut off from the earth" as a result of the plagues.

Fourth, the *provoker* of the plagues. "For this cause have I raised thee up . . . that my name may be declared throughout all the earth" (v. 16). Pharaoh was the provoker of the plagues. But God used Pharaoh's evil to glorify Himself. "Surely the wrath of man shall praise thee" (Psalm 76:10). We will all glorify God; even Pharaoh will glorify God. But some will glorify God in obedience while some will glorify God in disobedience. Those who glorify God in disobedience will do so through the judgment they receive for their disobedience. This was how Pharaoh glorified God. As such, Pharaoh received no blessing for glorifying God; for only obedience is blessed for glorifying God.

The denunciation before the plague. "As yet exaltest thou thyself against my people, that thou wilt not let them go?" (9:17). Moses denounced pride here (instead of dignifying it as the world often does). Pharaoh's problem was pride. We have seen this before, but it is worthy to note again, for pride is such a problem with man. It was the cause of Satan's downfall (Isaiah 14:12–15), it was involved in the fall of man, and it is a big problem everywhere in every age. The church is continually hindered by the pride of its members. It is often the root cause of many church problems.

The deliverance from the plague. "Send therefore now, and gather thy cattle, and all that thou hast in the field; for upon every man and beast which shall be found in the field, and shall not be brought home, the hail shall come down upon them, and they shall die. He that feared the word of the LORD among the servants of Pharaoh made his servants and his cattle flee into the houses; And he that regarded not the word of the LORD left his servants and his cattle in the field" (9:19–21). The grace of God is again seen in the judgment of God. Divine clemency is offered to Pharaoh. The clemency is not in an opportunity to stop the plague as before, but is a warning on how to avoid the effects of the plague. Pharaoh is told that the people and the beasts can be spared if they will stay under shelter. All of this is a good picture of soul salvation in that (1) the way of escape was given in ample time to flee judgment—they had until "tomorrow" (9:18) to get ready, (2) it was unmerited, (3) it was a simple way of escape that all could understand, (4) it was given to all, and (5) it was according to the Word of God.

Many did not escape from the plague, however; for they rejected the warning. This was so foolish; for (1) they rejected the fact that every prediction by Moses had proven true, (2) they had nothing to lose by putting themselves and their beasts in shelter, and (3) they "regarded not the word of the LORD" (9:21). The key is that they had no respect for God's Word. The great separator of mankind for time and eternity is one's attitude towards God's Word—both the Written and Incarnate Word.

The destruction from the plague. We note the extent of the destruction and the exemption from the destruction.

First, the *extent*. The destruction was devastating to the land. Egypt had recovered some from the previous plagues. But this plague wiped out the recovery; and the judgment reached into areas hitherto unreached, e.g. killing of people. Besides killing all the beasts in the field, it also killed all the people out in the open. And it must have been extremely frightening to the rest of the people with the "grievous hail" (9:18) accompanied by "mighty thunderings" (9:28), rain, and the extreme lightening that was so great that "the fire ran along upon the ground" (9:23). We have seen farm crops that have been completely destroyed by hail storms. But such storms would pale into insignificance compared to the storm that hit Egypt.

Second, the *exemption*. "Only in the land of Goshen, where the children of Israel were, was there no hail" (9:26). Again Scripture reports that God's people were exempted from the judgment. This exemption would be discovered quickly by the Egyptians and would show that Jehovah God was superior in power to the Egyptians' gods. This exemption pictures, as previous exemptions have, the blessed safety of those who have trusted in Jesus Christ for salvation. They are eternally exempted from soul judgment.

The duplicity in the plague. Here we look at Pharaoh's behavior regarding this plague. It can all be put under the heading of duplicity. He was a rascal and did not know how to be honest with God. To examine this duplicity of Pharaoh in his dealing with Moses and God, we will note the repentance of Pharaoh, the request of Pharaoh, the response of Moses, the rebuke by Moses, the removal of the plague by Moses, and the recanting by Pharaoh.

First, the *repentance*. "And Pharaoh sent, and called for Moses and Aaron, and said unto them, I have sinned this time: the LORD is righteous, and I and my people are wicked" (9:27). This repentance sounds really good. He admits to sinning; he admits that God is righteous; he admits that both he and his people are wicked. We would not argue with anything he said here.

266

But the problem is, he does not really mean it. Pharaoh is in a jam and needs reprieve from his troubles. Like many, he will confess to anything to get out of the troubles. Hence, duplicity reeks in this repentance as is confirmed in his later recanting of his promise to free Israel.

Second, the *request*. "Entreat the LORD (for it is enough) that there be no more mighty thunderings and hail; and I will let you go, and ye shall stay no longer" (9:28). The request is faulty because it says Pharaoh will not let the people go until the storm is stopped. That is not faith. In fact, it is disobedience. Pharaoh should let the people go regardless of the storm because God has commanded him to free the people. If he had been honest, he would have let the people go and trusted God to stop the storm as a result. Many pray like Pharaoh, however. And all such praying is suspect praying. To pray, "Lord, if you will get me well, then I will serve you" is sinful praying. It adds a condition we have no right to add. If God has commanded, we are to obey regardless. Adding conditions is a clever form of disobedience.

Third, the *response*. "And Moses said unto him, As soon as I am gone out of the city, I will spread abroad my hands unto the LORD; and the thunder shall cease, neither shall there be any more hail; that thou mayest know how that the earth is the LORD'S" (9:29). Grace was the response. How typical this is of the grace of God. The Psalmist said, "Thou, Lord, art good, and ready to forgive" (Psalm 86:5). God is most anxious to forgive sinners. Let them simply begin to think about turning to Him, and He is right there ready to forgive. God is, in fact, more ready to forgive than we are to repent. Let every sin-burdened person, who wonders if God will forgive, ponder this blessed truth that God is "ready to forgive." Moses' Divinely ordered actions towards Pharaoh here reflect that truth well.

Fourth, the *rebuke*. "But as for thee and thy servants, I know that ye will not yet fear the LORD God" (9:30). Moses was not fooled by Pharaoh's duplicity. "Little credit is to be given to confessions upon the rack" (Matthew Henry). Though Moses

267

acted as Pharaoh had spoken—he took Pharaoh at his words—
he saw through this eloquent confession of Pharaoh and told
Pharaoh so. We must admire the forthrightness of Moses' language and actions here. He did not let grace take away from
truth as many do.

Fifth, the *removal*. "And Moses went out of the city from
Pharaoh, and spread abroad his hands unto the LORD; and the
thunders and hail ceased, and the rain was not poured upon the
earth" (9:33). Moses kept his word which he promised Pharaoh
(9:29). Pharaoh, however, will not keep his word as we will note
next (9:34,35). There are two aspects of this removal worth noting. (1) The *purpose* of the removal was "that thou mayest
know how that the earth is the LORD'S" (9:29). This is similar
to the purpose stated in an earlier plague. The removal was to
instruct Pharaoh regarding God. Would that all the work we did
in church was to help people learn more about God. But the
church programs are filled with so much of the flesh today that
though people attend church regularly, they will learn very little
about God. But the actions of Moses were different. He would
act in a way that would instruct mankind about God. (2) The
place where Moses prayed for the removal was not in Pharaoh's
palace but "out of the city [away] from Pharaoh" (9:33). That
demonstrated that Moses was protected from the storm when he
walked through the city to the place of prayer. This ought to
have curbed Pharaoh's duplicity; but, of course, it did not.

Sixth, the *recanting*. "And when Pharaoh saw that the rain
and the hail and the thunders were ceased, he sinned yet more,
and hardened his heart, he and his servants . . . neither would he
let the children of Israel go" (9:34,35). Pharaoh's duplicity now
comes out in plain sight. And note that when Pharaoh hardens
his heart this time, his servants do the same. Pharaoh was leading others to destruction by his rebellion. How often evil men in
high places have helped to harden the heart of others against the
Lord. Many professors in college, many rulers in government,
and many ministers in religion have all done as Pharaoh—they
have helped to harden the hearts of others against God. This is a

great warning to all mankind about being careful as to whom we follow in our life.

8. The Plague of Locusts (10:1–20)

The eighth plague consisted of a great invasion of locusts into the land of Egypt which devoured every thing on the land that the previous plagues had left or that had recovered from the previous plagues. In examining this plague we will note the duty, design, declaration, defending, destruction, and deceit in the plague.

The duty in the plague. "And the LORD said unto Moses, Go in unto Pharaoh; for I have hardened his heart, and the heart of his servants" (10:1). All duty is not delightful or easy. Much duty, like the duty of Moses in repeatedly confronting Pharaoh, is very difficult. Those who would serve God faithfully need to be aware that duty will involve many difficulties, hardships, problems, and nasty people. God did not promise Moses success in converting Pharaoh, but told Moses to see Pharaoh anyway. However, whether Pharaoh is converted or not, the glory of God can still be seen in Moses doing his duty. We must not throw our hands up in despair if our preaching of the Gospel does not result in a host of people coming to Christ. If God has commanded us to preach the Gospel, we need to preach it regardless of the response of men; for the preaching of the Gospel glorifies God whether men receive the Gospel or not. And the bottom line in all our service is that God be glorified.

Note here that God not only says He will harden Pharaoh's heart, but that He will also harden the heart of Pharaoh's servants. We saw at the end of the last plague that Pharaoh's servants were hardening their hearts along with Pharaoh. Now we are told here that they will suffer the same judgment as Pharaoh does for hardening his heart—God will help to harden their hearts. It is a severe judgment that we need to avoid at all costs.

The design in the plague. The word "that" appears three

times in verses 1 and 2. This points out a threefold design of the plagues which came upon Egypt as a result of Pharaoh's hard heart. The designs are to show the power of God, give opportunity for telling about God, and provide instruction in the knowledge of God. We have seen these designs before but note them again because they are in the text and because it is good to be often reminded about the designs of God in the troubles of man.

First, the *power of God.* "That I might show these my signs before him" (10:1). The signs (plagues) really displayed the power of God. Pharaoh, and all Egypt, were getting a real demonstration of God's power in the plagues. It demonstrated that God was more powerful than any god they worshipped. Mankind needs to know about God's power if they are going to honor Him properly. And sometimes it is only through our troubles that we can learn well about God's power.

Second, the *telling about God.* "That thou mayest tell in the ears of thy son, and of thy son's son, what things I have wrought in Egypt, and my signs which I have done among them" (10:2). These plagues would give the Israelite parents an opportunity to tell their children about God. This design of the plagues emphasizes the parents' responsibility to tell their children about the Lord. Parents have the first and foremost responsibility to tell their children about the Lord. Israel was later instructed repeatedly and in detail about this vital task (Exodus 12:26,27; 13:8,14; Deuteronomy 4:9; 6:7; 11:19). Sunday Schools and Christian day schools have their place. But they are not to be a substitute for the parents. A good number of parents today are trying to pass off to other people their responsibility of training their child spiritually. The results are not good to say the least.

Third, the *knowledge of God.* "That ye may know how that I am the LORD" (10:2). The plagues were to increase people's knowledge about God. Trials in life are not wasted experiences when we look at them from the standpoint that they can instruct us in the knowledge of God. The Psalmist said, "It is good for me that I have been afflicted; that I might learn thy statutes" (Psalm 119:71). Our knowledge of God is never completed. We can always learn more about God. Troubles often help us learn things about God which we would not learn otherwise. And the more we know about God, the more we can tell to others about God; for knowledge of God is so essential for telling about God.

The declaration in the plague. Moses and Aaron visited Pharaoh again and declared unto him some very important truth. This declaration consisted of the condemning of Pharaoh, the commanding of Pharaoh, and the cautioning of Pharaoh. This was not an easy message to deliver to Pharaoh. Many modern day preachers would, therefore, never have addressed Pharaoh this way because they simply do not want to condemn sin, nor do they want to risk their jobs or lives to be true to God. Folk so often get velvet on their lips when they are speaking in the palace before important people. But Moses and Aaron were faithful to the Lord and proclaimed the truth regardless of the place where they were.

First, the *condemning* of Pharaoh. "How long wilt thou refuse to humble thyself before me?" (10:3). This is the second time Pharaoh is spoken to about his pride. The first time was just before the last plague (9:17). Pharaoh's big problem, as we noted in the last plague, was pride. If not repented of, pride will bring plague after plague upon a person.

Second, the *commanding* of Pharaoh. "Let my people go, that they may serve me" (10:3). This is the seventh time God has specifically commanded Pharaoh to "Let my people go, that they may serve me." It is a great command. It shows the ownership of God—the people belong to God, not Pharaoh. It shows the purpose of freedom—to serve God. It shows the authority of God—He is over Pharaoh. And, as we noted earlier, the repetition of the command shows the greatness of Pharaoh's rebellion and also the greatness of God's grace.

Third, the *cautioning* of Pharaoh. "Else, if thou refuse to let my people go, behold, tomorrow will I bring the locusts into thy coast" (10:4). While the message which Moses and Aaron gave Pharaoh condemned and commanded, it also offered grace.

Pharaoh was warned of impending judgment. He was given time (until "tomorrow") to change his ways. So once again Divine grace is extended to Pharaoh. But Pharaoh will be a poor steward of this grace as he has been in the past. When grace has been given him, he has always wasted it and, therefore, judgment came. How tragic are the lives of those who waste grace.

The defending in the plague. "And Pharaoh's servants said unto him, How long shall this man be a snare unto us? let the men go, that they may serve the LORD their God; knowest thou not yet that Egypt is destroyed?" (10:7). This is the one bright spot in the performance of Pharaoh's servants. They had previously hardened their hearts along with Pharaoh at the close of the plague of hail, and Moses was told by God that their hearts would continue to harden. But here is a respite from that hardening of their hearts. They defend the request of Moses for Israel to leave. They base their defending of the request on the fact that Egypt is destroyed. They make a backhanded insult of Pharaoh when they ask, "Knowest thou not yet that Egypt is destroyed?" The way Pharaoh was acting, he did not evidence that he knew the obvious. Many cruel dictators are like this. When being defeated, they seem totally unaware of the situation.

The defending of Moses and Aaron by Pharaoh's servants resulted in the two being brought back into Pharaoh's presence again (10:8). However, in this second visit regarding this plague of locusts, Pharaoh, instead of recanting of his evil, tried to compromise the conditions of letting Israel go. Moses rejected the compromise as we will note more about later. Pharaoh simply would not submit completely to God. Pharaoh's reaction to his rejected compromise offer was to have Moses and Aaron "driven out from Pharaoh's presence" (10:11). But when you drive out that which you need you will pay a big price. And the time will come when you will want them back, but it will be too late to advert great loss.

We need more people who will, like Pharaoh's servants, reason with folks after the sermon has been preached and urge them to heed the sermon. We have too many who after the sermon is preached only criticize the preacher and the sermon.

The destruction in the plague. "And the locusts went up over all the land of Egypt, and rested in all the coasts of Egypt; very grievous were they; before them there were no such locusts as they, neither after them shall be such. For they covered the face of the whole earth, so that the land was darkened; and they did eat every herb of the land, and all the fruit of the trees which the hail had left; and there remained not any green thing in the trees, through all the land of Egypt" (10:14,15). Locusts are well known for their devastating work. But our text says the hordes that came upon Egypt in this plague had no equal before or since in destruction. They simply stripped Egypt bare of vegetation. Their coming upon Egypt demonstrates that sin will extract more and more from us. The cost is ever rising in the sin business. Society is filled with those who continue to lose more and more because they will not stop sinning. Sin causes people to lose their morals, health, family, virtue, character, money, and other valuables. Sin really costs!

The deceit in the plague. Pharaoh's deceitfulness shows itself pronouncedly in this plague as it has in some of the other plagues. To examine his deceit here, we will look at the repentance of Pharaoh, the removal for Pharaoh, and the reneging by Pharaoh.

First, the *repentance* of Pharaoh. "Then Pharaoh called for Moses and Aaron in haste; and he said, I have sinned against the LORD your God, and against you. Now therefore forgive, I pray thee, my sin only this once, and entreat the LORD your God, that he may take away from me this death only" (10:16,17). This is another "battlefield" repentance by Pharaoh (cp. 8:8, 8:25–28, and 9:27). Under the duress of the plague, he backs down and confesses he has sinned. However, time verifies that such confessions are seldom real. The confessions are flawed and instead of submission to God they dictate conditions for

God. Pharaoh's confession here was impressive, but it was very insincere. He only wanted the plague stopped. He was not about to let the Israelites leave. He would say anything that would get the plague removed. Pharaoh is like the people who come to church seeking money who will make a profession of faith if necessary to get the money. They don't mean a thing by going through the motions to be saved, they only want the handout.

Second, the *removal* for Pharaoh. "And he [Moses] went out from Pharaoh, and entreated the LORD . . . there remained not one locust in all the coasts of Egypt" (10:18,19). Moses and God were not deceitful. They fulfilled their side of the agreement. The locusts were removed and right to the final locust ("there remained not one"). That is how we are to fulfill our agreements—right to the last locust. But many folk are not interested in keeping their word. Star athletes sign multi-million dollar contracts; and then long before the contract time expires, they want to break the contracts. Couples marry "until death do us part"; but long before that happens, they want to break their marriage vows.

Third, the *reneging* by Pharaoh. "But the LORD hardened Pharaoh's heart, so that he would not let the children of Israel go" (10:20). Pharaoh's deceit was helped by God. This, of course, did not sully God's character in any way. God's hardening of Pharaoh's heart was simply a form of judgment upon Pharaoh which we have noted repeatedly. Persist in evil and God will make permanent your evil pursuit. It is a terrible judgment, but many receive it.

9. The Plague of Darkness (10:21–29)

This ninth plague consisted of three consecutive days of extreme darkness in Egypt described as a darkness "which may be felt" (v. 21) and "a thick darkness" (v. 22). To study this plague we will note the disadvantage in the plague, the dynamics of the plague, the demotion in the plague, the deprivation from the plague, the division in the plague, and the decisions in the plague.

The disadvantage in the plague. "And the LORD said unto Moses, Stretch out thine hand toward heaven, that there may be darkness over the land of Egypt, even darkness which may be felt. And Moses stretched forth his hand toward heaven; and there was a thick darkness in all the land of Egypt" (10:21,22). The disadvantage in this plague as far as Pharaoh is concerned is that he received no warning of its coming. As in the third plague of the last two triads of plagues, God gives no warning to Pharaoh. Moses is not directed to give Pharaoh time to repent to avoid the plague. Therefore, as we have learned before in these plagues, grace continually rejected becomes grace eventually removed. God gives us opportunities; but when we disregard them, they will be taken away. God said, "My spirit shall not always strive with man" (Genesis 6:3). When He ceases striving with man, judgment is the next experience for man.

The dynamics of the plague. Some years back, the *Reader's Digest* magazine had an article which attempted to attribute every plague to some natural phenomenon. It was a study in unbelief of God's Word. Furthermore, their explanations were so far fetched that it was a whole lot easier to believe what the Bible said about the plagues than what the *Reader's Digest* said. We expect the world to offer such explanations for the plagues. But what is surprising is to read similar explanations in the writings of some reliable and respected Bible scholars in regards to the cause of the plagues. Just as the world does, they leave out the Divine dynamic in the plagues. As an example, the cause of this darkness is suggested to be a result of "a well known natural phenomenon . . . Wind of the Desert" (Rawlinson). Even venerable F. B. Meyer mentions this as a possible cause. But attempts to attribute the plagues to some natural phenomenon is time wasted. The plagues described in Scripture require a miracle to adequately explain what is said of them. No wind is mentioned in this plague—wind was mentioned in the locust plague, but not here. A supernatural darkness came here in Egypt for three days just as it did for three hours in Jerusalem when Christ was on the cross. With the power of our God, we do not need the unsteady crutch of natural phenomenon to explain these plagues. Do not leave out the Divine dynamic in these plagues.

The demotion in the plague. One of the Egyptians' gods was the sun god whose name was Ra. Some believe the name of the sun god became part of the title Pharaoh. With the thick darkness embracing the land with a vice-like grip, it was evident that Jehovah God had more power than the sun god. The sun god was eclipsed and could not be worshiped in the thick darkness. Again, as we have noted before in these plagues, Jehovah God is demonstrated as superior to the Egyptian gods. The Egyptian gods are demoted to worthless deities by the plagues.

As in previous plagues, Egypt is again reaping what she sowed. Egypt would not let Israel worship; now Egypt cannot worship either. The sowing and reaping lesson is very prominent in these plagues. It is a lesson we cannot learn too well.

The deprivation from the plague. For "three days" (10:22) the Egyptians "saw not one another, neither rose any from his place for three days" (10:23). Everything came to a halt with the Egyptians for three days. They did nothing. They did not even rise from their beds. The darkness really restricted their activity and their lifestyle. It deprived them of a good life.

The world ever mocks Christians by claiming they have so many restrictions in life for being a believer that they are deprived of having any fun in life. That, of course, is a lie from Satan and is, in fact, just the opposite of what the situation really is in life. It is not the Christian that is deprived, but it is the unbeliever that is deprived of good times in life. As the Egyptians were very deprived in this plague of darkness, so the sinner is very deprived because of his sin. He becomes shackled by many evil habits and is sometimes incarcerated in prison by his criminal conduct. The believer on the other hand enjoys the freedom of a righteous life unbound by the shackles of sin that destroys all that is good and blessed in life.

The division in the plague. "But all the children of Israel had light in their dwellings" (10:23). It is different with God's people than it is with the ungodly as we have noted in some of the previous plagues. Here the message is the universal truth applicable to all ages that God's people walk in the light. Jesus spoke this truth plainly when He said, "I am the light of the world; he that followeth me shall not walk in darkness, but shall have the light of life" (John 8:12). God's people walk in the light regarding matters that are the most important in life. The world may understand things that pertain only to this life, but God's people are given understanding by the Holy Spirit regarding the next life. The world may understand its books; but God's people are given light to understand His Book, the Bible, the greatest book of all.

The decisions in the plague. "Pharaoh called unto Moses, and said, Go ye, serve the LORD; only let your flocks and your herds be stayed . . . And Moses said . . . there shall not an hoof be left behind . . . Pharaoh said unto him, Get thee from me, take heed to thyself, see my face no more; for in that day thou seest my face thou shalt die" (10:24–26,28). Both bad and good decisions are made in this text. The decisions came about because of the oppressiveness of the plague. The darkness was very upsetting to Pharaoh. He who had earlier ordered that Moses and Aaron be "driven out from Pharaoh's presence" (10:11) was so upset by the darkness that he made the decision to call for Moses in the dark. But Pharaoh's change of heart was not sincere, for he made a decision to seek a compromise (we will see more of that later in our last main point of this chapter). Moses' decision regarding the compromise was firm, however. He would have none of the compromise. Pharaoh then made the decision to order Moses from his presence, and he threatened Moses with death if Moses should ever venture into Pharaoh's presence again.

Our decisions certainly manifest our heart. Pharaoh's decisions reflected a wicked man indeed. Moses' decision reflected a

277

very noble character. Yet, it is the noble character that is often driven out by the ruler of the land. Such is frequently the case in every age. Governments generally want little to do with men whose decisions reflect holy character.

C. THE ARTIFICE DURING THE PLAGUES

The crafty dealings of Pharaoh were most evident during the plagues. His artifice was especially seen in the four compromises he offered Moses during the smiting of Egypt by the plagues. The first two compromise offers came during the fourth plague, the plague of flies. The third compromise was offered in an attempt to ward off the eighth plague, the plague of locusts. The fourth compromise was proposed to Moses during the ninth plague, the plague of darkness.

The devil ever employs compromise in his efforts to defile mankind. Before we look in detail at each of the four compromises offered by Pharaoh, it will be of value to note that there are at least three significant reasons why the devil uses compromise frequently. They are the appeal of compromise, the acceptableness of compromise, and the assault by compromise.

First, the *appeal of compromise*. Compromise appeals because it seems to offer you your desire quickly. It often provides a shortcut to your goal. But, of course, the shortcut is not without your sacrificing some part of your goal. The compromise would argue that it is better to have part of your desire than not any. But what this actually does is give you part now instead of all later. It cheats you. It short-changes you. And in the area of character and spirituality, that is a tragedy.

Second, the *acceptableness of compromise*. Compromise is the rule of the land today. It is sometimes called consensus. If you are unwilling to compromise, you are considered unreasonable, stubborn, and inconsiderate. Compromise may be acceptable in some situations, but it is never acceptable when right and wrong are involved.

Third, the *assault by compromise*. Compromise assaults obedience. Disobedience is Satan's goal with man. Compromise with God's orders assaults obedience by advocating partial obedience which is simply another form of disobedience. Compromise opposes complete obedience. It says God is not Lord but we have some say, too. It sanctions negotiation with God's orders, not submission to them. All of this is a subtle assault on obedience to God.

Now as we look in detail at the four compromise offers of Pharaoh to Moses, we will note that they had to do with the place of worship, the passion to worship, the people in worship, and the possessions for worship.

1. The Place of Worship (8:25–27)

The first compromise offer by Pharaoh involved the place where Israel would worship God. We note the defiance in the compromise, the defilement in the compromise, the danger in the compromise, and the defeat of the compromise.

The defiance in the compromise. "And Pharaoh called for Moses and for Aaron, and said, Go ye, sacrifice to your God in the land" (8:25). This compromise proposal defied submission to God's Word. The compromise may sound conciliatory, but it is disguised defiance just the same. God had ordered that Israel should go "three days' journey" into the wilderness (Exodus 5:3) and there worship God. God had made it plain where Israel was to worship. Pharaoh's compromise was a direct attack upon God's orders about the place. He opposed doing as the Word of God said to do. He would allow Israel to worship—which was an improvement upon his past attitude—but he would not allow them to go into the wilderness to worship. Hence, he was advocating partial obedience—which we noted in our introduction of this section was one of the tactics of compromise. But partial obedience is not acceptable with God. It will not bring the fullness of blessing which we need. Partial obedience incorporates defiance of God's Word. There is nothing good about that.

The defilement in the compromise. To worship in the land

279

meant that Israel would not be able to separate from the Egyptians when they worshipped. This would defile them; for if Israel worships in Egypt, they will end up compromising even more to avoid the derision and the danger which will come from worshipping in Egypt. One compromise leads to another. Compromise promotes defilement. Scripture says we should "Come out from among them, and be ye separate, saith the Lord, and touch not the unclean thing" (II Corinthians 6:17). But separation is not popular with most people. They want to mix with the world and be like the world—ignoring the fact that then you will with the world be condemned by God.

The danger in the compromise. "And Moses said, It is not meet so to do; for we shall sacrifice the abomination of the Egyptians to the LORD our God; lo, shall we sacrifice the abomination of the Egyptians before their eyes, and will they not stone us?" (8:26). There was a very great danger physically for Israel if they were to worship in the land. The danger came chiefly from the fact that Israel would be sacrificing many animals which were held sacred by the Egyptians. The Egyptians reaction to killing a sacred animal was very pronounced. "Death was the legal penalty for willfully killing any sacred animal in Egypt . . . On one occasion even a Roman ambassador was put to death for accidentally killing a cat" (Rawlinson). We noted this peril earlier in our book. Moses had a very legitimate concern about the compromise because of this danger alone.

True worship always provokes animosity from some quarter. It is an indictment upon the world that true worship is often most unacceptable by the world. But this is the case in many places in the world even in our own land. In our land the worship of God is being ordered out of this place and that place by court rulings. Unless God intervenes, this animosity to worship will continue to increase, not decrease. We will find true worship restricted more and more in our land. But woe be to the land that is hostile to true worship. They will, as did Egypt, experience much Divine judgment.

The defeat of the compromise. "We will go three days' journey into the wilderness, and sacrifice to the LORD our God, as
he shall command us" (8:27). Moses stands so gallantly against
Pharaoh's compromise offers. Here, his answer is a beauty. He
was firm in his word and faithful to God's word.

First, Moses was *firm in his word*. One cannot read this
verse without easily seeing the firmness of Moses' word. He did
not show one bit of weakness. There was no backing down.
There was great resoluteness in his statement. It made crystal
clear where he stood and that the compromise was totally unacceptable. This is the only way to answer evil. Our "No" to temptation must be firm or we will never defeat temptation. Our
answers to evil must not be weak and wishy-washy. They must
be straightforward. Evil looks for weakness. If our answer is not
firm, we give evil an opportunity to gain ground with us. Slam
the door against evil—don't shut it gently. If you don't slam the
door, you may not get it shut.

Second, Moses was *faithful to God's Word*. "As he shall
command us" was such a great answer. This said that the final
authority for Moses was God's Word. Moses would guide his
conduct by God's orders. He would be faithful to God's Word.
Our churches need to get back to God's Word for their final
authority. Individually, people need to get back to God's Word
for their final authority. We have let the world's philosophy dictate too much of our ways. And compromise with the world
instead of going all the way with God's Word is the way to
defeat, not the way to victory.

2. The Passion to Worship (8:28, 29)

The second compromise offer by Pharaoh involved the matter of passion in regards to worship. When Moses refused the
first compromise offer and argued about Israel's safety, Pharaoh
said, "I will let you go . . . only ye shall not go very far away"
(8:28). This second compromise was like the first in that it, too,
tried to compromise on the place. But we will look at it from the
standpoint of passion, for we covered the "place" in the previ-

ous point. To study this second compromise, we will note the substance, selfishness, and scorning of the proposal.

The substance of the proposal. Telling Moses to "not go very far away" says, a number of things which we hear frequently today. It says to cool your passion in spiritual matters, do not get too excited and enthused about spiritual things, do not read your Bible or pray too much (as if you could do those things too much), and do not attend all the services at church.

To hear some folk talk, there is great peril in getting overly involved and excited about the things of the Lord. But we notice that those who are so worried about overdoing it spiritually are not concerned about overdoing it in temporal matters. If a boy must get up at four in the morning to deliver newspapers, he is called a real go-getter by these folks. But if the church required him to do the same for the Lord, they would accuse the church of being radical, outlandish, and demanding much too much of the boy. If a person buys an expensive automobile and has to make sizeable payments for the next five years or so, these people admire his auto, conclude he must be doing well, and congratulate him on his new purchase. But if he makes equally large and regular payments for the Lord's work, they will criticize him and question his intelligence. If a man works an extra day each week for overtime pay, these folk think he is smart to grab all the extra money he can. But if a man spends an extra day a week at church helping out, they think he is some religious fanatic. Yes, Satan's philosophy exhorts us to not go too far in spiritual matters. And many practice this philosophy. Even professing believers sing this tune all too often.

The selfishness of the proposal. "Entreat for me" (8:28). Selfishness is a kinfolk of compromise. Pharaoh's compromises were all self-serving. Here the compromise is specifically aimed at stopping the plague. He was not all that concerned about Israel's worship; he was chiefly concerned about getting the plague stopped. His compromise would sacrifice much for Israel in order that he might gain.

All the devil's compromises are this way. They do not have your best interests at heart. They are disguises to promote Satan's program, not God's program. Compromise never helps God's work; it only hinders it. But it sure helps Satan's work. Beware of the selfishness of compromise.

The scorning of the proposal. Moses did not give a direct answer to Pharaoh regarding this proposal, but he gave it an indirect and justifiably scornful answer when he said, "Let not Pharaoh deal deceitfully any more in not letting the people go to sacrifice to the LORD" (8:29). After Pharaoh had asked Moses to stop the plague, Moses complied. This, however, did not mean he was accepting Pharaoh's last compromise about going too far. Proof of that is in Moses describing Pharaoh's conduct as deceitful. Moses saw through the compromises of Pharaoh. He saw the duplicity, the cheating, the selfishness, and the ulterior motives in Pharaoh's actions and words. Pharaoh had been deceitful in the past in dealing with Moses and the plagues. He had not changed, and Moses told him so. Moses did not accept the compromise. Had Israel been let go then, Moses doubtless would have led Israel as far into the desert as God instructed. Moses was not giving Pharaoh's proposals any honor. He would do as God ordered.

3. The People in Worship (10:8–11)

Pharaoh asked Moses "Who are they that shall go [to worship]?" (10:8). When Moses emphasized that the children would be going as well as the others, Pharaoh objected and said, "I will let you go, and [but] your little ones; look to it; for evil is before you. Not so: go now ye that are men, and serve the LORD" (10:10,11). Pharaoh's third compromise would limit the number of people involved in worship. Satan is always trying to limit the number of people who worship God—and he appears to be succeeding well by the looks of the small crowds in many churches. Pharaoh tried here to stop the children, women, and elderly from worshipping. Since the children are given the main attention in this compromise, we will likewise give them the main attention in noting some lessons from this compromise. To examine this compromise and the lessons involved in it regarding the children, we will note the protecting, parenting, preventing, and participating of the children.

The protecting of the children. Pharaoh tried to convince Moses that the children should not go because "Your little ones; look to it; for evil is before you" (10:10). That is, the wilderness trip would be a dangerous trip. It would be too hard for the children. Pharaoh wants Moses to believe the children are just too small and helpless to survive such a rugged ordeal.

The principle of this argument is heard even in our day. It says we do not want our children to experience any tough situations in life. We do not want them to go without or to have any hardships in their life. We would make it as easy as possible for them. No discipline, no duties, no deprivings. But how foolish. It is those things which put backbone into one's life. If you raise your children on the soft and easy road, they will not have the toughness to face difficulties in life. Interestingly, when Israel did get to the wilderness, the rigors of the wilderness were harder on the adults than on the children; for the children made it to the promised land; but the adults did not. The adults could not survive the grueling discipline that was required, and so they rebelled and were not permitted to enter the promised land. But the children made it to the promised land.

The parenting of the children. If the children are left behind as Pharaoh desires, then someone besides the parents will be required to take care of them. This, too, is the devil's plan. God's plan is that the parents are to take care of the children. After all, He gave the children to the parents—not to the day care center or baby sitter. When God gives you something, He expects that you should take care of whatever He gives you. But the devil convinces man that God's way is wrong.

It is a shameful thing today to have so much parenting of the children passed off to day care centers and baby sitters. It is equally shameful that fundamental Bible believing churches set up day care centers in their churches. That only encourages what they should be opposing.

The preventing of the children. Pharaoh's proposal would prevent the children from attending the worship services. It is a proposal that is still advocated today. Churches have their worship services so divided up today that hardly any family member attends together. Yes, we understand by personal experience the problem of unruly children in the church services and the distraction this problem is to the services. Many children are often present whose parents are not. This presents a problem that necessitates taking a number of children out of the services. But that does not mean all children should be taken out of the services. Parents who do come, especially church members, ought to be instructed to teach their children to behave so they can sit quietly in a worship service. Running the children off to gym time or some other substitute for worship is only a compromise. Of course, some argue that children do not understand much of the service. But they understand more than we think. This is apparent by the comments children make about a lot of situations in which they are allowed to be with their parents.

In the book of Acts, there is a beautiful picture of the family being together in a spiritual meeting. In describing Paul's departure from Tyre, the Scripture says, "And they all brought us on our way, with the wives and children, till we were out of the city; and we kneeled down on the shore, and prayed" (Acts 21:5). Note that the children were present. They were not sent to a nursery or gym time or some other place. They had a great experience of being where the action was. What a shame had they missed this experience. But the way our churches are organized today, they would not have been within gun shot of the scene. We want our children to be in everything today, but the worship service is an exception. One of the earliest memories of

285

my life is as a two year old boy watching my father help my six year old brother down the aisle of the church during the invitation time of a service because my brother wanted to be saved (it was a special service in the 1930s with Charles Fuller of the Old Fashioned Revival Hour speaking). That was an invaluable experience and is still an inspiring memory. Why wasn't I in the nursery? The answer is that I had been trained to behave. We could sure use a great deal more of that kind of training today!

The participating of the children. Moses did not yield to this compromise offer. Again with a firm answer, he announced to Pharaoh "We will go with our young . . . with our sons and with our daughters" (10:9). Note that the participation of the children depended on the participation of the parents. "We will go" precedes the children going. Too many send their children to church instead of take them. The Israelite parents will take them. They will lead the way. There will be a lot less drop outs in the spiritual realm when parents take their children to church instead of sending them to church with others. When children are sent by their parents instead of taken, they get the message that parents do not need to go to church. So they wait for the day when they are old enough to ditch worship. Therefore, the right way is for parents to take the children to church and lead them in worship.

4. The Possessions for Worship (10:26)
The fourth and final compromise proposal by Pharaoh had to do with Israel's possessions being taken with them to worship. It was made to Moses during the plague of darkness. Pharaoh gave ground a little bit more in this compromise; that is, he allowed the children to go. But he did not want Israel to take their possessions, especially their flocks and herds. This compromise would greatly affect Israel's service to the Lord. To study this compromise we will note the disabling of service, the delight in service, the discontinuing of service, the dedication for service, and the directives for service.

The disabling of service. "And Pharaoh called unto Moses, and said, Go ye, serve the LORD; only let your flocks and your herds be stayed [left behind]" (10:24). Here is another practice of Satan; namely, allow people to worship but convince them to not give of their possessions in worship. This, however, disables one in service. If the Israelites do not take the animals, they cannot offer sacrifices unto the Lord. Hence, they will be greatly disabled in their worship and service.

We have a number in our churches who have readily gone along with Pharaoh's compromise attitude. They will come to church, but they will not give much to the church. If everyone was like that, there would be no church buildings and no worship services. Preach to these folks about giving, and they quickly complain that the church is always talking about money. That is not true, of course. What is true is that they are always thinking about money in terms of themselves. Also, what is true is that the church needs money to provide for its ministry.

When you refuse to give to God, you limit your service in a great way. No stingy, tightwad person has ever been used much by God in His service. Those who are willing to give of their possessions will be used much by God.

The delight in service. God instructed the Israelites to have a "feast" (Exodus 5:1) in the wilderness. The feast spoke of joy, of delight. But if they leave their flocks and herds behind, there will not be a feast—that's for sure. Hence, there will not be any delight in their worship experience. That explains why a lot of folk have little joy in coming to church to worship and why they have little joy in their Christian walk. Stingy people who refuse to sacrifice for the cause of the Lord will know little about the joy of the Lord or as the song says, "The joy of serving Jesus." Sacrifice is necessary for joy in both worship and service.

The discontinuing of service. If the Israelites go into the wilderness to worship and do not take their flocks and herds, they will soon be back in Egypt. Pharaoh knew that, and it would be one reason why he would propose such a compromise. As Rawlinson said, "This will be, he considers, a sufficient security for their return; since without cattle they would be unable to support life for many days in the wilderness." The principle here is that when we do not sacrifice for the Lord's work, we will soon discontinue our involvement in it. Lack of sacrifice reveals lack of interest. People who quit at church are not those who are sacrificing much for the Lord's work. The quitters are those who do not give much. There may be exceptions to this, for there are always some who give with the wrong motive. But usually the quitters are the poor givers while the faithful members are the good givers.

The dedication for service. Again Moses responds gallantly to Pharaoh's compromise proposal. He said, "There shall not an hoof be left behind" (10:26). That is such an inspiring answer. Moses was dedicated completely. Everything was on the line for the Lord. He would withhold nothing. He was not like Ananias and Sapphira who kept back a part (Acts 5:2). Moses would give it all, everything, not a hoof would he keep back. You cannot beat that sort of dedication. Furthermore, it is the only dedication that is really acceptable to God.

The directives for service. Moses made an important statement regarding service that we do not want to overlook. He said to Pharaoh, "We know not with what we must serve the LORD, until we come thither" (10:26). He told Pharaoh they must take everything they had with them, for they would not know until they got into the wilderness what all the Lord required. There are two lessons here we want to emphasize: preparation in service and revelation in service.

First, *preparation* in service. Taking everything into the wilderness said Moses wanted to be adequately prepared to serve the Lord well. He did not want to be found wanting when God gave His orders. Today we think of preparation for God's service as going to some college or seminary or both. This is often involved, but not always. But what must always be involved, if we are going to be adequately prepared to serve God, is our commitment of all that we have to God. We must be willing to give God whatever He asks whenever He asks for it. The rich man that came to Jesus did not serve because he was not ready to give all that God commanded him to give. Do not crimp your service by unwillingness to yield everything you possess to God.

Second, *revelation* in service. "Until we come thither" indicated that the will of God regarding Israel's service would be revealed when they got in the wilderness. God had revealed to Israel that they must go into the wilderness to worship. Once they did that, they would then be further instructed as to what they were to do. This is the usual way God works. It means, therefore, that if we want to know more about God's will, we must obey every step of the way. Do today what God tells you to do, and you will be told tomorrow what you are to do tomorrow. But if you do not do today what you are suppose to do, you will discover that you will be in the dark about tomorrow's directives. Many saints are floundering around talking much about the will of God but not knowing what God's will is for them because they have not been diligent to obey each step of the way.

XII.

SLAYING THE FIRSTBORN

EXODUS 11 – 12:36

THE BATTLE BETWEEN Pharaoh and Jehovah God over Israel leaving Egypt is about to end. "One plague more" (11:1) is to come upon Egypt. Then it will be over. Jehovah God will triumph gloriously over Pharaoh, for Pharaoh will not only let the Israelites leave, he will also "thrust" (Ibid.) them out.

This last plague, which is the tenth one in the series, will be by far the worst plague of them all. It will take the life of "all the firstborn in the land of Egypt . . . from the firstborn of Pharaoh that sitteth upon his throne, even unto the firstborn of the maidservant that is behind the mill; and all the firstborn of beasts" (11:5). This loss of life will bring the greatest sorrow upon the land of Egypt that ever was or will be (11:6).

There is more written in the Bible about this plague than about any of the other nine plagues. And unlike the other plagues, most of what is written about this plague concerns the protection from the plague. The reason for this feature of the Scripture record is obvious—this plague brings to us the greatest Gospel illustration in the entire Old Testament. One does not have to wait until he gets to the New Testament before he can see the Gospel. It is foreshadowed throughout the Old Testament, and no passage in the Old Testament does it better than this passage concerning the tenth plague.

To study this plague about the slaying of the firstborn, we will consider the preliminaries to the slaying (11:1 – 12:2), the protection from the slaying (12:3–28), and products of the slaying (12:29–36).

290

A. THE PRELIMINARIES TO THE SLAYING

Here we will look at some matters Scripture addresses which are introductory to the the tenth plague. They are the promises for Moses, the precept for Israel, the prominence of Moses, the proclamation for Pharaoh, the practice of the past, and the programming of the calendar. The emancipation of Israel is about to occur and God is getting things ready for it to take place.

1. The Promises for Moses

"And the LORD said unto Moses, Yet will I bring one plague more upon Pharaoh, and upon Egypt; afterwards he will let you go hence; when he shall let you go, he shall surely thrust you out hence altogether" (11:1). The record of the tenth plague in Scripture begins with some promises given to Moses by God. We will enumerate the promises, learn the essentialness of the promises, and note the encouragement from the promises.

The enumeration of the promises. The promises which God gave Moses greatly enlightened Moses concerning the ending of the battle between God and Pharaoh. The promises were three in number.

First, God promised that this tenth plague would be the last "one." This plague would end the siege of plagues upon Egypt.

Second, God promised that as a result of this tenth plague, Pharaoh now "will let you go." Pharaoh would not change his mind this time about letting Israel go as he had done before in previous plagues. This time he would actually let Israel leave.

Third, God promised that Pharaoh would not only let Israel go, but he would also "thrust" them out of Egypt. The word "thrust" is translated from a Hebrew word which means "to drive, to cast out, to expel" (Wilson). It is strong language. Pharaoh would literally order the Israelites to leave. This fact manifests the great power of God to accomplish His purposes as He desires even though men earnestly oppose Him. God can make man do with great zeal what man has opposed doing for a long time. Pharaoh really opposed letting Israel go. But in the end, he actually drives them out of the land. How foolish for man to fight against the will of God. It is a no-win situation.

The essentialness of the promises. The promises concerning Pharaoh's reaction to the last plague, especially his reaction of driving out the Israelites, was essential for Moses to know so he could more adequately prepare the Israelites for the exodus from Egypt. Later we will learn much more about the preparations Israel was to make for the exodus. Here we are simply given information that will help the Israelites to be earnest and prompt in making the preparations. The exodus was going to occur quickly. Therefore, they needed to be ready the moment the order came to leave Egypt. They did not have time to spare once the order came to leave.

As Israel was to be ready for the exodus from Egypt, so we need to be ready for our exodus from this life and also for the second coming of Christ. Each of us needs to have our soul prepared so that we are ready at any moment for these events to occur. When the trump of God sounds and Christ returns, we do not have time to get things together spiritually. We must already be prepared for the coming of Christ. The same is true with death. It could come at any moment, too, which means we cannot afford to procrastinate getting ready for it. God gives us ample warning about getting ready. Let us heed the warning so we will be ready for either the end of our earthly life or for the coming of Christ—whichever comes first.

The encouragement from the promises. What great encouragement it had to be to Moses to hear God say that only one more plague was necessary before the emancipation would occur. Though God had fully informed Moses that Pharaoh's heart would be hardened so that plague after plague would occur, it still had to be frustrating and often discouraging to Moses to have Pharaoh continually refuse to let Israel go. Moses had to keep those earlier promises of God continually in his heart in order to buoy up his faith in the difficult trials of the nine plagues. But now God says the end is very near.

This encouragement would be a real help to Moses to carry out the many details regarding the last plague. Never in the previous plagues was he required to do so much regarding the plague. But the tenth plague is different. God gave Moses many orders regarding the plague—especially regarding protection from the plague for Israel. It was not an easy task. But typical of God when He gives us a difficult assignment, He often encourages us in the doing of the assignment by giving us some special promise or promises which He did with Moses here. Look for those promises in the Word of God when you have a difficult duty to perform for God. They will encourage you to be faithful.

2. The Precept for Israel

God gave Israel a precept to enlarge their wealth. "Speak now in the ears of the people, and let every man borrow of his neighbor, and every woman of her neighbor, jewels of silver, and jewels of gold. And the LORD gave the people favor in the sight of the Egyptians" (11:2,3). This is the second time Scripture speaks of Israel's enrichment from the wealth of the Egyptians. The first time this was mentioned was in Exodus 3:21,22 when God was speaking with Moses at the burning bush. In Exodus 12 this action will be mentioned one more time. There we will comment extensively on the action. Here we will only note that this precept reminds us that God can supply His people their needs through means we would normally consider impossible. That the Egyptians would supply Israel all these riches is amazing. This ought to encourage every saint of God who is in need and cannot see any normal means by which his needs will be met. The God Who can sustain Elijah by a poor widow, bring water out of a rock, and cause the Egyptians, of all people, to be liberal givers to the Israelites, can supply our needs, too.

3. The Prominence of Moses

"Moreover the man Moses was very great in the land of Egypt, in the sight of Pharaoh's servants, and in the sight of the people" (11:3). In spite of the way things had gone, it was Moses who was being elevated in stature in the eyes of men, not Pharaoh. Pharaoh was still powerful enough among men to keep the nation of Israel under his slavish rule, but he was not powerful enough to keep even his own servants from greatly admiring the man Moses. "Those that honor God he will honor . . . how meanly soever they may pass through this world, there is a day coming when they will look great, very great, in the eyes of all the world" (Matthew Henry). Evil men often capture the limelight in the world and are accorded the respect and esteem and awards of greatness. But such greatness is a fleeting experience and will not last. Time will destroy it and expose it as empty of substance. The truly great, however, are those who live faithfully for God. Time will increase their greatness. All eternity will exalt them. Moses not only rose to greatness in Egypt in his lifetime; but today, some three millennia later, he is greater than ever in the eyes of men. Pharaoh, however, has been scorned by every generation since his time. Let these truths encourage the heart of the faithful to continue their faithfulness to God.

4. The Proclamation for Pharaoh

Before the tenth and final plague came upon Egypt, Moses paid a visit to Pharaoh and told him about the final plague and some matters related to it. We will look at the character of the proclamation and the contents of the proclamation.

The character of the proclamation. Here we note the display of courage, the demonstration of grace, and the demeanor of anger which are evident in Moses in his making this proclamation to Pharaoh.

First, the *display of courage.* Pharaoh had decreed that Moses should not see Pharaoh's face again without being put to death (10:28). Moses acknowledged that decree (10:29). But sometime after the plague of darkness had ended, we find Moses again before Pharaoh informing him of the tenth plague that was to come upon Egypt (11:4–8). Why would Moses go in to see

Pharaoh again after the death decree had been given? Obviously because God ordered him to see Pharaoh. The Bible does not specifically inform us that God commanded Moses to go see Pharaoh again, but it is most evident that Moses did not venture in to see Pharaoh again without a Divine order to do so. Moses was conducting himself throughout these plagues according as God ordered him, and seeing Pharaoh again in view of the death decree certainly had to be a result of God's orders.

To obey these orders after Pharaoh had decreed Moses' death if Moses saw Pharaoh again, would require much courage. When one guides his life by God's orders, it will sometimes require much courage to do as told. There are always some who fail to see this, however. They aspire to serve God because they like the glitter and the glamour of the service. They see servants of God spotlighted in church meetings and covet their fame. But such people are only being moved in the flesh and have little conception of what the servant of God must go through in order to be faithful to God's orders. They have little idea of the great courage that is continually necessary to do God's work. It is not easy serving God. It requires much dedication. One must be willing to lay his life on the line at times, and that will certainly separate the men from the boys in service.

Second, the *demonstration of grace.* "And Moses said, Thus saith the LORD, About midnight will I go out into the midst of Egypt; And all the firstborn of the land of Egypt shall die" (11:4,5). Though undeserving as he was, Pharaoh is still given advanced notice of the tenth plague. The advanced notice, of course, gave him opportunity to avoid the plague by repenting and letting Israel go free. This meant that Pharaoh was once again experiencing the grace of God in his life. In seven of the ten plagues, Pharaoh was warned in advance. Besides that, he was given several opportunities to free Israel at the beginning of the contest before any of the plagues occurred. How very long-suffering is God's grace! But as we have noted repeatedly in the plagues, the day of grace will eventually come to an end. Grace cannot be forever rejected without judgment eventually replacing grace. This extending of grace to Pharaoh will be the last time God acts in grace towards him. It is Pharaoh's last chance, his last opportunity to repent. But unfortunately, he rejected this offer of grace as he had done again and again before. It resulted in the terrible destruction of the slaying of the firstborn and led to his death and the death of all his army in the Red Sea.

Third, the *demeanor of anger*. "And he [Moses] went out from Pharaoh in a great anger" (11:8). Some people will insist a Christian should never get angry. If you disagree with these folks, they will often get angry at you which shows their hypocrisy as well as their ignorance. While it is true Scripture says, "Let all bitterness, and wrath, and anger, and clamor . . . be put away from you" (Ephesians 4:31) and "put off all these, anger, wrath, malice" (Colossians 3:8); yet Scripture also says, "Be ye angry, and sin not" (Ephesians 4:26). Therefore, there is indeed such a thing as righteous anger. That was the anger which Moses expressed here. He was angry at sin. And "To be angry at nothing but sin is the way not to sin in anger" (Matthew Henry).

Moses had good reasons to be angry at sin here. He could be angry at Pharaoh for perpetuating the cruel slavery of the Israelites. He could be angry at Pharaoh for all his past rejections of God's orders to let Israel go. He could be angry at Pharaoh for allowing the Egyptians to suffer greatly by his obstinate disobedience to God's orders. And he could be angry at Pharaoh for being unmoved by the announcement of this last plague. There was indeed plenty in the situation Moses was in to stir up righteous indignation.

We need to be angry with sin. We need to be upset about evil. However, our churches have been lulled into a passive stupor about evil by the watered down messages of disobedient ministers. Hence, when a person speaks out vehemently against evil, church people protest and say that person is not showing much love or compassion. They are wrong, of course; for the person with holy anger is showing great love and compassion for that which is right and true and holy and pure.

The contents of the proclamation. The contents were three-fold. They concerned the particulars of the tenth plague, the protection in the plague, and the plea after the plague.

First, the *particulars of the plague.* "About midnight will I go out into the midst of Egypt; And all the firstborn in the land of Egypt shall die, from the firstborn of Pharaoh that sitteth upon his throne, even unto the firstborn of the maidservant that is behind the mill; and all the firstborn of beasts. And there shall be a great cry throughout all the land of Egypt, such as there was none like it, nor shall be like it any more" (11:4–6). We will look in more detail concerning the particulars of the plague when we come to our last main point in this chapter which is about the products of the slaying. It is sufficient to note here that Moses told Pharaoh about the slaying of all the firstborn and about the sorrow that would result from the slaying. This information should have caused Pharaoh to fall on his knees in repentance and in earnest petition to stop the plague. But sin-hardened people never catch on; and so the proclamation concerning the plague, though it would be horribly alarming to a normal person, did not move Pharaoh.

Second, the *protection in the plague.* The proclamation Moses gave Pharaoh made a point of noting that "the LORD doth put a difference between the Egyptians and Israel" (11:7) in regards to the plague. God had previously made a division between Egypt and Israel in the past plagues. Now in this tenth plague, God will again make a definite distinction between Israel and Egypt. Israel, unlike the Egyptians, will be protected from the plague (the means of protection is detailed in Exodus 12, which we will study shortly). To emphasize the great extent of the protection provided for Israel, God said though Moses, "But against any of the children of Israel shall not [even] a dog move his tongue" (Ibid.). This was a proverbial expression declaring that absolutely nothing would harm the Israelites.

The security of God's people is great. The security of Israel physically is an illustration of an even greater security that comes to the soul who is protected by the blood of Jesus Christ.

Paul spoke of the greatness of this protection when he said, "I am persuaded, that neither death, nor life, nor angels, nor principalities, nor powers, nor things present, nor things to come, Nor height, nor depth, nor any other creature, shall be able to separate us from the love of God, which is in Christ Jesus our Lord" (Romans 8:38, 39).

Third, the *plea after the plague.* "And all these thy servants shall come down unto me, and bow down themselves unto me, saying, Get thee out, and all the people that follow thee" (11:8). Not only is Pharaoh going to want Israel to leave, but so are his servants. But notice how the servants will express their desire for Israel to leave. They will "bow down" to Moses and plead with him to leave. They have learned something which Pharaoh has not learned. They have learned who and what should be respected! Unfortunately, they learned it too late to avoid devastating judgment. Many are like that in every age.

5. The Practice of the Past

We have several verses at the end of Exodus 11 which are summary verses. We noted in an earlier chapter of our book that the Hebrew writers would sometimes end or begin a new section with a summary. This appears to be the case here in verses 9 and 10 of Exodus 11. Three matters are reviewed here: the failure of Pharaoh, the faithfulness of Moses and Aaron, and the fate of Pharaoh.

The failure of Pharaoh. "And the LORD said unto Moses, Pharaoh shall not hearken unto you; that my wonders may be multiplied in the land of Egypt" (11:9). Pharaoh was a great man in the world. But before God, he was a despicable creature. Many in our world are like that. They are hailed by the world as great successes, but in God's eyes they are great failures.

This statement about Pharaoh speaks of both the knowledge of God and the power of God. The *knowledge of God* is seen in His knowing that Pharaoh would harden his heart. God knows our behavior before we even do it. We can keep nothing from

God. Such knowledge ought to drive us low before God in repentance (cp. Psalm 139:1–6). The *power of God* is seen in that God is not defeated by the defiance of man. Pharaoh may rebel against God, but God will use that rebellion to glorify Himself through the plagues which came upon Egypt. We have seen repeatedly in these plagues that "Surely the wrath of man shall praise thee" (Psalm 76:10). It is an encouragement to the saint who sees the wrath of men appear to destroy all that is good around him.

The faithfulness of Moses and Aaron. "And Moses and Aaron did all these wonders before Pharaoh" (11:10). What a contrast are the comments of God in Scripture about Pharaoh and about Israel's two leaders. Pharaoh is unfaithful; Moses and Aaron are faithful. Pharaoh rejects God; Moses and Aaron accept God. Pharaoh scorns God; Moses and Aaron respect God. Pharaoh disobeys God; Moses and Aaron obey God. When Moses and Aaron came on the scene to deliver Israel, Pharaoh had superior position and the power. But when it was all over, those who were faithful to God had superior position and power. It always works that way. If we do not see it happen in this life, we will witness it emphatically in the next life.

Note the extent of the faithfulness of Moses and Aaron. They did "all" that God commanded them to do before Pharaoh. Doing "all" is the kind of faithfulness that is acceptable to God. It is the kind of faithfulness we must ever strive for in life. Never be satisfied with partial obedience; it is only another form of disobedience. Faithfulness is doing "all," not part.

The fate of Pharaoh. "And the LORD hardened Pharaoh's heart" (11:10). Again we see those tragic words regarding God and Pharaoh's heart. Pharaoh had repeatedly hardened his own heart against the demands of God before and during the plagues. His judgment for so doing was to have his heart hardened even more by God. This is the fate of every person who continues to rebel against God's will. One more time Scripture will report

God hardening Pharaoh's heart (Exodus 14:4), and that will be to cause Pharaoh to pursue the Israelites to the Red Sea and then to experience drowning in the Red Sea. Hard hearts lead to destruction. Beware that you do not cultivate a hard heart by continued disobedience and then, as a result, have God come along and further harden it.

6. The Programming of the Calendar

"And the LORD spake unto Moses and Aaron in the land of Egypt, saying, This month shall be unto you the beginning of months; it shall be the first month of the year to you" (12:1,2). The emancipation from Egypt was to change Israel's calendar. From now on Israel was to start their new year at the time the emancipation began. Israel would from that point on date their time and history in reference to the exodus from Egypt. The approximate first month of their new year according to our calendars is the month of April.

This calendar change is applicable to the Gospel. Since this plague so wonderfully illustrates the Gospel in the salvation of souls through the blood of Jesus Christ, it is fitting that the deliverance of Israel from Egypt should begin a new year. To be born physically is when one begins numbering the days of his or her life on earth. But when a person is saved through the blood of the Lamb, he has a new beginning; for he is said to be "born again." This begins the person's spiritual life which will survive the earth and live eternally in heaven. It is the greatest beginning of all, for life really never begins until one is saved.

We are going to see later on in this study of the tenth plague that other dates and times of the plague point to the crucifixion of Jesus Christ. All of this about the dates simply manifests again what a wonderful book the Bible is. It is truly a Divine book with no equal. Again and again mankind is forced to recognize the literary greatness of the Word of God. Everything is so intricately tied together in the Word as only God Himself could connect the writing which took place over some sixteen hundred years and employed some forty different writers.

B. THE PROTECTION FROM THE SLAYING

In our introduction to this chapter, we stated that most of what is written about the tenth plague has to do with how to be protected from it. We now come to the Scripture which speaks about the protection. The protection from the plague will come through a lamb. With protection from Divine judgment being provided in a lamb, we will in a prominent way see in this study wonderful Gospel pictures of Jesus Christ, The Lamb of God.

To examine the Scriptures about the lamb and the protection it gives from the slaying of the firstborn, we will note the provision of the lamb, the character of the lamb, the killing of the lamb, the blood of the lamb, and the eating of the lamb.

1. The Provision of the Lamb

"Speak ye unto all the congregation of Israel, saying, In the tenth day of this month they shall take to them every man a lamb, according to the house of their fathers, a lamb for an house. And if the household be too little for the lamb, let him and his neighbor next unto his house take it according to the number of the souls" (12:3,4). From these verses concerning the provision of the lamb for protection from the slaying of the first born, we will note the appointment, the application, and the availability of the lamb. Gospel lessons will be readily seen in each of these instructions about the lamb.

The appointment of the lamb. The lamb was a Divine appointment. It was not man's idea but God's idea. And the lamb was the only way of escape. God did not appoint a number of ways to escape but only appointed the lamb as the way of escape. If Moses had told Israel they could be saved through other means, Moses would have led multitudes to their death just as apostate preachers lead multitudes to hell through preaching another Gospel than the Gospel of Jesus Christ. For there is only one way of salvation. "Neither is there salvation in any other; for there is none other name under heaven given among men, whereby we must be saved" (Acts 4:12).

301

Throughout Scripture, the lamb is found as that which God has appointed to protect men from the judgment of God. In Genesis 22, the chapter that records Abraham offering up Isaac, it was the lamb that saved Isaac from death on the altar. When Abraham and Isaac got to the place for the sacrifice, Isaac asked, "Where is the lamb for a burnt offering?" (Genesis 22:7). Abraham's answer was filled with the Gospel overtones when he said, "God will provide himself a lamb for a burnt offering" (Genesis 22:8). God did provide the lamb, and "Abraham . . . offered him up for a burnt offering in the stead of his son" (Genesis 22:13) in a beautiful picture of Calvary.

The provision of the lamb for the salvation of man continues on in notable ways in other texts such as our text (Exodus 12) and in Isaiah 53. When we come to the New Testament, John's Gospel plainly describes Jesus Christ as the Lamb of God in "Behold the Lamb of God, which taketh away the sin of the world" (John 1:29, cp. John 1:36). In the epistles we read of "the precious blood of Christ, as of a lamb without blemish and without spot" (I Peter 1:19) as that which provides our deliverance from judgment. Finally, in the last book of the Bible, Christ is spoken of as a Lamb some twenty-eight times. It begins with the Lamb that was slain (Revelation 5:6) and ends with the Lamb on the throne (Revelation 22:1,3). So from Genesis to Revelation, we learn that God appointed the Lamb, Jesus Christ, to provide salvation for mankind.

The application of the lamb. "They shall take to them every man a lamb" (12:3). The provision of the lamb was for everyone. "Every" man must take a lamb for his household for protection from the slaying of the firstborn. None were exempted. The requirement of a lamb applied to all households. If the lamb was not used for protection, the firstborn in that house would die. In like manner, every soul needs the Lamb, Jesus Christ, for their soul's protection or they will perish in their sins. It makes no difference who the person is, what his social status is, where he is from, what his race or nationality is, how much money he has, or what position in society he occupies—what matters is whether his soul is protected by the Lamb of God, Jesus Christ. As there was no distinction in Israel—all families needed the lamb—so it is in soul salvation.

The availability of the lamb. "If the household be too little for the lamb, let him and his neighbor next unto his house take it according to the number of the souls; every man according to his eating shall make your count for the lamb" (12:4). Since the lamb was to be eaten by the people (we will see more on that later), it was understandable that a small household would not need a whole lamb to eat. Hence, the practical instructions about sharing the lamb.

The sharing of the lamb in the case of small households emphasizes that the lamb was available for everyone. No one would have to die because they could not find or could not afford a lamb. All were provided for in the instructions God gave Moses. Every situation was covered. So it is in the matter of salvation. Christ is most available. He is as near as a whispered prayer. God had made provision for all to be saved. The fact that many do not get saved is not a result of a lack in Divine provision but a lack in heeding God's plan of salvation.

2. The Character of the Lamb

"Your lamb shall be without blemish, a male of the first year" (12:5). The character qualifications for the lamb were threefold, and they speak of three important aspects of Christ. They are the sinlessness, sonship, and strength of Christ.

The sinlessness of Christ. The lamb was to be "without blemish." It could not have any physical flaw if it was to be acceptable to protect the Israelites from the plague. This speaks of the sinlessness of Christ. As the lamb for Israel's physical protection could not have any physical blemishes, so Christ the Lamb for our soul's protection cannot have any character blemishes if He is going to protect souls from judgment. If you are going to die in someone's place for their crime, you cannot be guilty of that crime, or you will have to suffer for it for yourself. So Jesus Christ could not be guilty of sin if He was going to die for our sin and protect us from eternal condemnation. Scripture repeatedly emphasizes the sinlessness of Christ. Peter said, "Christ [is] . . . a lamb without blemish and without spot" (I Peter 1:19). Paul said, "For such an high priest became us, who is holy, harmless, undefiled, separate from sinners" (Hebrews 7:26); and "He [God] hath made him [Christ] to be sin for us, who knew no sin; that we might be made the righteousness of God in him" (II Corinthians 5:21). Pilate testified three times of Christ's guiltlessness when he said of Christ, "I find in him no fault" (John 18:38, cp. John 19:4 and 19:6). Christ's sinlessness is also emphasized in the testimony of some at the cross at the time of the crucifixion. One of the thieves crucified with Christ said of Christ, "This man hath done nothing amiss" (Luke 23:41). And the centurion in charge of the soldiers at the cross said, "Certainly this was a righteous man" (Luke 23:47). If Christ was not sinless, He could not save us; and, furthermore, He would be one of the biggest prevaricators ever to set foot on the earth! But Scripture says otherwise and emphatically.

The sonship of Christ. The lamb was to be "a male." It could not be a female, for God specified a male.This also speaks of Christ. He is the "Son" of God, not the daughter or mother of God. The unisex emphasis of our day needs to take note of what Scripture says and not change it to suit its perverted philosophies and practices. When Christ was born, the Bible says, "She [Mary] brought forth her firstborn *son*, and wrapped *him* in swaddling clothes, and laid *him* in a manger" (Luke 2:7). "Son" and "him" are male, not female. Changing hymnbooks and messages and creeds to unisex is just another form of rejecting the true Lamb of God. If the lamb is not a male, it cannot save; for God appointed a male lamb to protect from the judgment of the tenth plague; and He appointed His "Son" be the One to save sinners from the eternal condemnation of sin.

The strength of Christ. The lamb was to be "of the first year." This meant the lamb was to be in the prime of life, not old or worn out and ready to die. The Psalmist speaks prophetically of Christ dying in "the midst of my days" (Psalm 102:24), that is, while still in the prime of life. Christ was only in His thirties when He was crucified. So once again the type holds forth accurately in this Old Testament passage. Christ is pictured in detail in the Lamb.

3. The Killing of the Lamb

"In the tenth day of this month they shall take to them every man a lamb . . . And ye shall keep it up until the fourteenth day of the same month; and the whole assembly of the congregation of Israel shall kill it in the evening . . . neither shall ye break a bone thereof" (12:3,6,46). We note the orders regarding the date of the killing, the doers of the killing, and disallowing in the killing of the lamb. Christ will be seen well in each order.

The date of the killing. Scripture states that the lamb was to be slain on "the fourteenth day" (12:6). The date of the slaying of the lamb in Egypt was incorporated into the Passover celebration (Leviticus 23:5). Christ, of course, was the fulfillment of the paschal lamb. "Study the closing chapters of each of the Gospels [and] it will be seen that the Lamb of God died at the very time that the paschal lambs were being slain in the temple" (Arthur Pink). The veil of the Temple being rent in twain and the slaying of the paschal lambs at the time of Christ's death doubtless were a great influencing factor in why "a great company of the priests were obedient to the faith" (Acts 6:7) later on after Pentecost.

It is instructive to note that the day of Christ's death is specified in Scripture but not the day of His birth. Yet we celebrate His birth on the same day every year while we celebrate His death on a host of different dates. How typical this is of human nature. What God makes certain, we make uncertain. But what God makes uncertain, we make certain.

The doers of the killing. Significantly, the Bible says "the whole assembly of the congregation of Israel shall kill it in the evening [of the fourteenth day]" (12:6). This, of course, is a general statement; for not every single individual actually took the knife and killed the lamb—only the head of the households would normally do it. But the heads of the households represented the entire assembly of Israel, and so Scripture says the "whole assembly of the congregation of Israel" killed the lamb.

The fact that Scripture associates all the Israelites with the killing of the lamb is important, for it makes accurate the foreshadowing message here about Christ. All Israel was indicted for the crucifixion of Christ (Acts 2:23). But it does not stop there. In the Gospel message, it is not Israel alone but all mankind that is guilty of crucifying Christ. It was our sins that put Him on the cross. We all are guilty. None of us can claim exemption from having a hand in the crucifixion of Christ.

The disallowing in the killing. "Neither shall ye break a bone thereof" (12:46). The fact that the lamb of Exodus 12 speaks of Christ is further proven by the mention of this disallowing of the breaking of any bone in the killing of the lamb. The Psalmist in prophesying of Christ said, "He keepeth all his bones; not one of them is broken" (Psalm 34:20). At the crucifixion it looked like this prophecy would not be fulfilled. Satan did his best to try and defeat the Word of God, but the Word of God shall stand every assault of the evil one. The account in John 19 reports this fact when it says, "The Jews therefore, because it was the preparation, that the bodies should not remain upon the cross on the sabbath day (for that sabbath day was an high day), besought Pilate that their legs might be broken . . . Then came the soldiers, and brake the legs of the first, and of the other which was crucified with him. But when they came to Jesus, and saw that he was dead already, they brake not his legs" (John 19:31–33). No bone was broken. Scripture was fulfilled to the detail in spite of the adverse circumstances. We can depend on the Word of God. It will never fail.

4. The Blood of the Lamb

In considering the blood of the lamb, we will note the prominence of the blood, the place for the blood, the putting on of the blood, and the power in the blood.

The prominence of the blood. "When I see the blood, I will pass over you" (12:13). "When he seeth the blood . . . the LORD will pass over the door, and will not suffer the destroyer to come in unto your houses to smite you" (12:23). The prominent thing that God was looking for in the deliverance of Israel was the blood. Nothing mattered so much as the blood of the lamb. If God did not see the blood, judgment would fall. The killing of the lamb would have done no good for any one in Israel if the instructions regarding the lamb's blood were disregarded, for the blood was absolutely essential in protecting the firstborn.

The blood is also absolutely essential in soul salvation, for "without shedding of blood is no remission" (Hebrews 9:22). However, in every age there has always been those who have opposed the importance of the blood. Some have gone so far as to mockingly call the emphasis on the blood a "slaughter house religion." But it is the lack of attention to the blood that slaughters. It would have been a "slaughter house" experience in Israel if the blood had not been applied on the houses, for without the blood there would have been a slaughter of the firstborn. It was the blood that prevented the slaughter! And it is the blood that protects the soul from spiritual slaughter in Divine judgment. Let preachers make the message of the blood prominent in their preaching. Otherwise they will end up preaching a bogus Gospel which slaughters the souls of men.

The place for the blood. The blood of the lamb was to be placed "on the two side posts and on the upper door post of the houses . . . ye shall take a bunch of hyssop, and dip it in the blood that is in the basin, and strike the lintel and the two side posts with the blood that is in the basin" (12:7,22). The various locations of the blood on Israel's houses point to Christ on the

307

cross. The blood on the lintel (the upper part of the door) pictures the blood from the thorn-crowned head of Christ. The blood on the two side posts of the door pictures the blood from the hands of Christ nailed to the cross. You will notice, however, that blood was not put on the threshold which would speak of the feet of Christ on the cross. This was so the blood would not be trampled underfoot in gross disrespect (cp. Hebrews 10:29). The blood need only be on "the lintel, and on the two side posts [and then] the LORD will pass over the door" (12:23). Would that mankind would so respect the blood today, but the theology of many tramples it underfoot in scorn.

The putting on of the blood. "Ye shall take a bunch of hyssop, and dip it in the blood that is in the basin, and strike the lintel and the two side posts with the blood" (12:22). Hyssop was a small plant with stiff branches and hairy like leaves which would make it a good brush applicator of the blood. It was to be used to put the blood on the door. It is mentioned in connection with some offerings (Leviticus 14:2–7; 14:49–52; Numbers 19:2–6; Hebrews 9:19) where it is implied it was used to make some application of the blood. It is also spoken of by David when he says, "Purge me with hyssop [obviously implying that the sacrificial blood was being applied by the hyssop], and I shall be clean; wash me, and I shall be whiter than snow" (Psalm 51:7).

With the hyssop being a small plant, it speaks of humility (cp. I Kings 4:33). With it being used to apply the blood, it speaks of faith. Both humility and faith are vital in the applying of the blood in the salvation of our souls. In humility we must recognize our sinfulness. By faith we receive Christ as Savior and thereby appropriate the blood of Christ as the cleansing needed for our sins.

The power of the blood. There was great power in the blood. It had power to protect the firstborn from death. It had power to stop the judgment of God. We have a song in our hymnbooks entitled, "Power in the Blood." It is a good song, but unfortunately some would exclude it from their hymnbooks, for they reject the prominence of the blood in God's plan of redemption. But the power of the blood needs more emphasis today in our churches, not less emphasis.

Before we pass from the subject of the blood of the lamb in the protection from the tenth plague, we want to emphasize the power of the blood. To do that we note some great blessings which the blood provides in regards to soul salvation as typified in the blessings the blood was to Israel in Egypt.

First, the blood provides *life*. "For the life of the flesh is in the blood; and I have given it to you upon the altar to make an atonement for your souls; for it is the blood that maketh an atonement for the soul" (Leviticus 17:11). Blood gives life to us physically. But this text instructs us that it can also give life to us spiritually. Atonement speaks of soul salvation. When our soul is saved, we are given new life! And it is all possible because of the blood of the Lamb. Israel's firstborn were given life through the blood of the lamb in Egypt as souls are given life through the blood of the Lamb, Jesus Christ.

Second, the blood provides *redemption*. "Thou wast slain, and hast redeemed us to God by thy blood" (Revelation 5:9). Israel's emancipation from Egypt is sometimes described as redemption (Exodus 6:6) just as soul salvation is, and in both cases the blood made redemption possible. To redeem means to purchase, to buy. It cost plenty to purchase our salvation. The price was so high that Peter said man cannot be redeemed with "silver and gold" (I Peter 1:18), and Christ stated that the wealth of the entire world cannot save us (Mark 8:36). But the blood of Christ can! Therefore, the blood of Christ has to be extremely valuable! No wonder Peter calls it "precious blood" (I Peter 1:19). The word "precious" means costly. Indeed, it is costly. It is worth more than all the riches of the world put together.

Third, the blood provides *justification*. "Being now justified by his blood, we shall be saved from wrath through him" (Romans 5:9). Israel, like the justified soul, was saved from

Divine wrath by the blood. Justification means to declare righteous. If we are not righteous, we will not get into heaven. But the blood of Jesus Christ will make us righteous. Great power has to be in the blood to make sinners righteous.

Fourth, the blood provides *cleansing*. "The blood of Jesus Christ his Son cleanseth us from all sin" (I John 1:7). Sin defiles. There is no soap, no cleanser that man can devise that can wash away our sin. But the blood of Jesus Christ has no difficulty washing away our sins. It is the most powerful detergent known to mankind, for it can wash away the most defiling stains. Israel was a defiled people in Egypt as we noted in some earlier chapters of our book. Hence, true to the type, before they could be brought out of Egypt, they must come in contact with the blood which represents the blood of Christ which cleanses from sin.

Fifth, the blood provides *restoration*. "But now in Christ Jesus ye who sometimes were far off are made nigh by the blood of Christ" (Ephesians 2:13). The blood restored Israel to God's promised land just as it restores the sinner into fellowship with God. Our belief in the blood of the Lamb drives many away from us theologically, but it does not drive away God! Instead it brings God near to us. Sin drove us away from God. But the blood restores our fellowship with Him.

Sixth, the blood provides *boldness*. "Having therefore, brethren, boldness to enter into the holiest by the blood of Jesus" (Hebrews 10:19). The word "boldness" here means confidence and assurance. When we have confidence and assurance we do indeed have the courage and boldness to act. Those of the Israelites whose house had the blood applied on the door would have confidence and assurance of heart and mind, This would not be the case with the Egyptians, however. Many have false assurance, of course. But it is never as great as true assurance, and only the blood of Christ can give true assurance.

Seventh, the blood provides *sanctification*. "Wherefore Jesus also, that he might sanctify the people with his own blood, suffered without the gate" (Hebrews 13:12). The word "sanctify" means to set apart, specifically to set apart for God's use, for God's service. Therefore, until you have been cleansed by the blood of the Lamb, you cannot serve God. Pharaoh was repeatedly commanded by God to "Let my people go, that they may serve me." But, significantly, before the Israelites could be freed to leave Egypt and to serve God, they must first be put under the blood.

Eighth, the blood provides *peace*. "Having made peace through the blood of his cross" (Colossians 1:20). The blood of Christ gives us peace with God, gives us peace in our hearts, and gives us a peaceful place (heaven) to live in for all eternity. Nothing brings peace to man like the blood of Jesus Christ. Egypt was in great despair—the opposite of peace—after the plague which killed the firstborn. But Israel knew peace after the plague because they applied the blood.

5. The Eating of the Lamb

The slaying of the Lamb and the applying of the blood of the Lamb on the door was not the end of the instructions about the Lamb. Israel was also to eat the lamb. We note the meal for the eating and the manner of the eating.

The meal for the eating. Four things are said about the meal centered around the lamb. They can be summed up under the headings of the flesh, the fire, the foods, and the forbidden.

First, the *flesh*. "They shall eat the flesh in that night" (12:8). The blood of the lamb saved, but the body of the lamb would provide strength. The eating of the lamb did not protect from the death of the firstborn—it was the blood that did this. Eating the lamb was not for security but for strength for the journey ahead.

As the lamb of Exodus 12 provided for both salvation and strength, so the Lamb of God, Jesus Christ, provides for both the salvation of the soul and for strength for service. We have already looked at the salvation part which is centered around the blood. Here we see the great truth that Christ is the One Who also strengthens us for our daily walk. Paul spoke of this when he said, "I can do all things through Christ which strengtheneth me" (Philippians 4:13). Christ also spoke on this subject of feasting on Him (John 6:48–58). Christ's words, however, have been greatly perverted and misunderstood by the Romanists who have made them into the doctrine of transubstantiation. But we do not eat of the literal body of Christ. We partake of His Word, and that feeds our soul.

Second, the *fire*. "Roast [the lamb] with fire" (12:8). Roasting with fire speaks of judgment. In type this represents the judgment Christ suffered in dying in our place for our sin. Christ's suffering the fire of Divine judgment is what is behind "I thirst" (John 19:28). It is what dried Him up. It was foreshadowed in the words of the Psalmist when he said, "For day and night thy hand was heavy upon me; my moisture is turned into the drought of summer" (Psalm 32:4).

Third, the *foods*. The lamb was to be eaten with two other foods: "unleavened bread; and with bitter herbs" (12:8). Leaven speaks of pollution, sin, and unrighteousness. Unless we are separated (unleavened bread symbolizes separation) from what Divine holiness abhors, we will not feast much on Christ. Sin takes away our taste for and fellowship with the Lamb. The bitter herbs speak of remorse and hatred of sin. Christ will be sweet when sin becomes bitter.

Fourth, the *forbidden*. Three things were forbidden regarding eating the lamb. (1) "Eat not of it raw" (12:9). Raw meat is unprepared meat. Time was not taken to prepare it properly for eating. It is thus unappetizing and unhealthy. The same is true regarding our study of Jesus Christ. We must take time to learn about Christ. The less time we take the less we will be interested in Christ. Study the Scriptures thoroughly about Jesus Christ and you will find Him to be very satisfying. Fail to study the Scriptures properly and you will not be impressed with Christ and will have little interest in Him. (2) "Nor sodden at all with water" (12:9). Boiling things in water takes away many vital nutrients oftentimes. Much theology is boiled in the waters of

312

human reasoning and is not Scriptural. It takes away a good deal which belongs to Christ such as His Deity, His virgin birth, His sinlessness, etc. When we water down the message of the Gospel, we dilute the truth, cool off the message, and put out the fire of judgment upon sin. (3) "Ye shall let nothing of it remain until the morning; and that which remaineth of it until the morning ye shall burn with fire" (12:10). "This was afterwards a general law of sacrifices; at once preventing all possibility of profanity [profane use of the lamb by man or beast], and of superstitious abuse, such as was practiced among some ancient heathens, who were wont to reserve a portion of their sacrifices" (F. C. Cook). Also this injunction prevented the lamb from putrefying (they had no refrigeration then) which would generate revulsion. The lamb was to be given utmost respect in every detail. Jesus Christ must be likewise respected. In our attitudes and in our teaching and preaching, Christ must be accorded great respect. This, of course, is something the unbelieving world does not do. Rather, they seem to love to putrefy His character. As an example, John Lennon of the vile and blasphemous Beatles singing group greatly putrefied Christ by calling him "a garlic eating, stinking, little, yellow, greasy, fascist . . . Catholic Spaniard." Hollywood movies have made films that also greatly putrefy Christ by picturing Him as immoral and even as a homosexual. Apostate ministers are little improvement. But beware of such disrespect for Christ. It will curse one greatly for all eternity.

The manner of the eating. Israel was instructed in how they were to eat as well as in what they were to eat. The manner of eating addressed skirts, shoes, staff, and speed.

First, the *skirts.* "And thus shall ye eat it; with your loins girded" (12:11). When the Israelites were eating, they were to be in the state of readiness for leaving Egypt. Thus they were to have their skirts belted so they would not be in the way. Loose apparel would make it difficult for a person to move quickly. The message to leave was imminent, and they must reflect it in

313

their apparel. In like manner, believers ought to reflect their faith in their apparel—something many are not doing today.

Second, the *shoes*. "Your shoes on your feet" (12:11). They also needed their shoes (sandals) on in readiness for the long trip God wanted them to make to serve Him. Without the shoes, they would not have been able go far in doing God's bidding. In the New Testament, shoes also speak of readiness, of preparation for doing God's will and fighting God's battles—"your feet shod with the preparation of the gospel of peace" (Ephesians 6:15). Without proper spiritual preparation, you will not go far in serving God, you will not last long in His service.

Third, the *staff*. "Your staff in your hand" (12:11). Again readiness is urged. The staff is something taken with a person when traveling. It was to be "in hand" not off in some corner or closet. When the summons came to leave, the Israelites would not have time to look around for their staff. Lack of readiness reflects a lack of dedication and will result in poor service.

Fourth, the *speed*. "Ye shall eat it in haste" (12:11). On the surface, this does not sound like good advice. We are always being told to stop eating so fast. But the message here is not a warning about gulping down your food too hurriedly. Rather, it speaks of eating in the posture of readiness. If they tarried in eating, they would not have eaten the meal before the summons came and would not have the strength they needed for the journey. This order for Israel attacks the problem of procrastination. Mankind is prone to procrastinate more in spiritual matters than in any other matter. Procrastination greatly imperils. Therefore, Israel was to eat in haste.

C. THE PRODUCTS OF THE SLAYING

Pharaoh had been warned in detail concerning the tenth plague. The warning went unheeded just as the warnings about the previous plagues had gone unheeded. Therefore, at the appointed time (midnight of the fourteenth of the month), the death angel passed through the country; and the tenth plague occurred.

We are going to look here at the products of the tenth

plague. They are the death of the firstborn, the despair of the people, the deliverance of the Israelites, and the despoiling of the Egyptians.

1. The Death of the Firstborn

"And it came to pass, that at midnight the LORD smote all the firstborn in the land of Egypt, from the firstborn of Pharaoh that sat on his throne unto the firstborn of the captive that was in the dungeon; and all the firstborn of cattle" (12:29). We note the specifics and the suitableness of this judgment.

The specifics of this judgment. The tenth plague resulted in the slaying of the firstborn of both man and beast (our text above just mentions the cattle, but Exodus 11:5 also includes the firstborn of all beasts). No family was exempted. "There was not a house where there was not one dead" (12:30). Both the high and lowly in the land were affected. "From the firstborn of Pharaoh that sat on his throne unto the firstborn of the captive that was in the dungeon" (12:29) and to the firstborn "of the maidservant that is behind the mill" (11:5).

The lost of the firstborn among mankind would be extremely tragic to the Egyptians. Scripture speaks of it as losing "the chief of all their strength" (Psalm 105:36). "The law of primogeniture prevailed in Egypt, as among most of the nations of antiquity. The monarchy . . . was hereditary, and the eldest son was known as *erpa suten sa* or 'hereditary Crown Prince.' Estates descended to the eldest son, and in many cases high dignities also. No severer blow could have been sent on the nation, if it were not to be annihilated, than the loss in each house of the hope of the family—the parents' stay, the other children's guardian and protector" (Rawlinson). The tenth plague was truly a devastating plague. It was the worst one of all. But the more you sin the worse the judgment.

The suitableness of this judgment. When God spoke to Moses at the burning bush, one of the ways in which He described Israel was as "my firstborn" (Exodus 4:22). There at the burning bush, God instructed Moses to tell Pharaoh, "Let my son go, that he may serve me; and if thou refuse to let him go, behold, I will slay thy son, even thy firstborn" (Exodus 4:23). Pharaoh refused to let God's firstborn people go. Now God has dealt with Pharaoh by slaying the firstborn in Egypt. The slaying of the firstborn is, therefore, a most suitable judgment upon Pharaoh and Egypt in that it punished them in the coin in which they sinned. They had over the years caused the death of many Israelites (God's firstborn) through the cruel, barbaric slavery they imposed on Israel; now God has punished Egypt in the death of their firstborn.

Throughout the plagues we have seen this important truth of reaping what we have sown and being punished in the coin in which we have sinned. God purposely and wisely punishes folk in the very place they have sinned, for such punishment is most suitable. It is suitable for it often hurts the sinner where he has hurt others. It is also suitable in that it helps the sinner to see why he is suffering the judgment, for it points to the sin that is being judged. So for killing the Israelites, God's firstborn, Pharaoh and Egypt are judged by having their firstborn killed. We must realize that if we sow weed seeds in our yards, we will get weeds in our yards—not beautiful grass. We only deceive ourselves if we think we can live our life in rejection of God without experiencing rejection by God.

2. The Despair of the People

"And Pharaoh rose up in the night, he, and all his servants, and all the Egyptians, and there was a great cry in Egypt; for there was not a house where there was not one dead" (12:30). We note the exhortation about the despair and the extent of the despair.

The exhortation about the despair. Unlike any of the previous plagues, a forewarning was given of the great sorrow that would come upon the Egyptians in the tenth plague. Moses told

316

Pharaoh, "There shall be a great cry throughout all the land of Egypt, such as there was none like it, nor shall be like it any more" (11:6). This warning was a strong exhortation to Pharaoh to repent of his evil, but Pharaoh ignored the exhortation.

God likewise warns sinners concerning the terrible sorrow that will come upon them for rejecting Christ. "Weeping and gnashing of teeth" (Matthew 8:12, 22:13, 24:51, and 25:30) is the repeated expression in the warning that ought to send sinners quickly to the feet of Christ for salvation. To warn people of this terrible sorrow, however, is not popular preaching. To tell folk of the terrors of hell is considered by a great majority of churches as unwanted and unwise scare tactics. But how foolish to mock such a warning. Jesus Christ Himself warned more about the sorrows and terrors of hell than anyone else. With such a terrible experience ahead for those who rebel against God, it is a great crime to not warn people of the judgment.

The extent of the despair. Exodus 12:30 describes the despair as "a great cry." That is bad enough, but Exodus 11:6 adds to the despair by stating that "there was none like it, nor shall be like it any more"—that is, the sorrow experienced as a result of this tenth plague would be so great in the land of Egypt that no previous sorrow or future sorrow in the Egypt would equal it. God was going to touch Egypt where they would hurt the most when He killed the firstborn. But Egypt had sinned greatly and sorrow will sooner or later overwhelm the sinner.

Helping to make this the worst sorrow of all in Egypt was the fact that the slaying of the firstborn happened at "midnight" (12:29). Tragedies in the darkness of the night only amplify the pain of the tragedies. God caused everything in this plague to work to the maximizing of the sorrow of the Egyptians. This is the future for all those who continually rebel against God.

Describing this sorrow from the tenth plague as the greatest sorrow ever to come to the land of Egypt reminds us of the greatest of all sorrows that can come to man. It is the sorrow of the lost soul in hell. We noted above that Christ repeatedly

317

described it as "weeping and gnashing of teeth" (Matthew 8:12, 22:13, 24:51, and 25:30). Other descriptions in Scripture about hell also make the sorrow greater than any other sorrow. Such descriptions as "furnace of fire" (Matthew 13:42,50), "outer darkness" (Matthew 22:13), "everlasting fire" (Matthew 25:41), "Where their worm dieth not, and the fire is not quenched" (Mark 9:44,46,48), and "I am tormented in this flame" (Luke 16:24) describe a situation that will produce a sorrow and suffering for the lost soul which is so great that our finite minds cannot fully comprehend it. Thankfully, we can escape this greatest of all sorrows. We can do so the same way Israel escaped the sorrow Egypt experienced—through the blood of the Lamb.

3. The Deliverance of the Israelites

The slaying of the firstborn broke the chain of bondage for the Israelites and gave them their freedom from Egypt. We especially want to note here the demand for the deliverance which was given by Pharaoh and the desire in the deliverance which was expressed by Pharaoh.

The demand for the deliverance. "And Pharaoh rose up in the night . . . And he called for Moses and Aaron by night, and said, Rise up, and get you forth from among my people, both ye and the children of Israel; and go, serve the LORD, as ye have said. Also take your flocks and your herds, as ye have said, and be gone . . . And the Egyptians were urgent upon the people, that they might send them out of the land in haste; for they said, We be all dead men" (12:30,31,33). The plague got to Pharaoh. It aroused him to action as nothing had before in the conflict over Israel's deliverance. It caused Pharaoh to do what he had hitherto not consented to do, namely, let Israel go. And Pharaoh not only decided to let Israel leave, but he demanded that they leave. He told Moses, "Rise up, and get you forth from among my people" (12:31). And so the Israelites were "thrust out of Egypt, and could not tarry" (12:39).

To further study Pharaoh's demand for Israel's deliverance, we will examine the control of the demand, the compliance in the demand, and the cooperation with the demand for Israel's deliverance.

First, the *control* of the demand. Before the start of the plagues when God was giving Moses some encouraging words, God had predicted Pharaoh would eventually "drive them out of his land" (Exodus 6:1). The promise would seem incredible to Moses at the time it was given, for Pharaoh was vehemently and successfully opposing the deliverance of Israel. To be forced to give up Israel is one thing, but to drive them out of the land is another thing. However, God is in control; and He is all powerful. He can so manage our circumstances that they will not only permit God's will, but will insist on it. This truth should be a great encouragement to every discouraged saint.

Second, the *compliance* in the demand. When Pharaoh told Moses and Aaron to leave, he twice said, "As ye have said" (12:31,32) regarding their past requests. This indicated he was complying completely with their requests to leave—no compromises were involved here. Therefore, Pharaoh included all the Israelites in the deliverance ("both ye and the children of Israel" [12:31]) which meant no excluding of the children or women or elderly (cp. 10:8–11). Also, he did not put any restriction on distance (cp. 8:25,28). And he told them to "take your flocks and your herds," (12:32) which he had refused to give up earlier (10:24). Yes, Pharaoh complied to every demand God made upon him. But he did it too late to receive any blessing for obedience. His delay cost him all the blessings.

Delayed obedience extracts a tremendous cost, and many folk in every age have learned this truth the hard way. They know what is right to do, but they put off doing it. However, the longer they put it off, the greater will be the cost. The longer a smoker puts off quitting his tobacco habit, the worse will be the results down the road in his health. When the tempted person puts off dealing with temptation, the tempter will get such a hold on him that he can only yield to temptation and, therefore, will pay the great cost of so doing. A number of folk have put off serving Jesus Christ until their opportunities have been squandered and their life shattered by chastisements. Comply quickly to God's demands or you will experience the "great cry" (12:30) of the Egyptians which no comforter can remedy.

Third, the *cooperation* with the demand. "And the Egyptians were urgent upon the people, that they might send them out of the land in haste; for they said, We be all dead men" (12:33). In proclaiming the coming of this tenth plague, Moses predicted to Pharaoh that other Egyptians would likewise demand that the Israelites leave. "All these thy servants shall come down unto me, and bow down themselves unto me, saying, Get thee out, and all the people that follow thee" (11:8). The prediction was fulfilled after the firstborn was slain, for then the Egyptians readily cooperated with Pharaoh in urging the Israelites to leave Egypt. Pharaoh had previously had cooperation from the Egyptians in furthering his cruelty upon the Israelites (Exodus 5:10–14). But now the Egyptians, like their ruler Pharaoh, realize the truth. Israel needed to be freed, not enslaved. But as we noted above, they learned the lesson too late.

The desire in the deliverance. "And bless me also" (12:32). Pharaoh desired the blessing but despised the conditions for obtaining the blessing. The world is full of folks like that. They think they can have the blessing without meeting the conditions for the blessing. But such thinking is vain. Pharaoh had waited too long to free Israel to obtain any blessing. Esau also wanted the blessing apart from the condition for blessing, for he wanted the blessing but not the birthright (Genesis 27:34–38). Blessings, however, do not come without the birthright—which speaks of Christ. We have many in the church who think in spite of the fact they have lived shoddy lives, they can still be treated the same as those who have lived upright lives. Divorced people are especially of this mind. They get very upset if we follow the Biblical injunction about church officers and, therefore, rule out divorced people for being pastors or deacons. They want the blessing without meeting the condition for the blessing. Another application of this truth is seen in one of Paul's epistles. He said, "If any would not work, neither should he eat" (II Thessalonians 3:10). If we followed this Biblical truth, we would not have the plague of welfare handouts that produces a disgusting drain of taxpayers' money. But, of course, some still try to tell us that meeting the conditions is not necessary to obtain the blessing. As an example, Economist John Kenneth Galbraith stated, "Those who dislike working should not be forced to work nor should they be penalized by depriving them of the benefits of our society." This ludicrous thinking of Galbraith is like the thinking of Pharaoh and Esau and many others. But God does not think that way. If you want the blessings of obeying God, then you will have to obey God. Disobedience will not gain the blessings. Rationalizing away your obligation to obedience will not change matters either. It will just cause you to say in vain as did Pharaoh, "Bless me also."

4. The Despoiling of the Egyptians

"And the children of Israel did according to the word of Moses; and they borrowed of the Egyptians jewels of silver, and jewels of gold, and raiment . . . And they spoiled [despoiled] the Egyptians" (12:35,36)). We want to look at the rightness of the despoiling, the retribution in the despoiling, the recompense in the despoiling, the receptiveness to the despoiling, the responsibility in the despoiling, and the requirements from the despoiling of the Egyptians.

The rightness of the despoiling. The word "borrow" in verse 35 is a misleading translation of the Hebrew word. We noted this problem before in Exodus 3:22, and it is also present in Exodus 11:2. When one borrows, it is with the understanding he will return what he has borrowed. But Israel did not return these riches to Egypt. The word "borrow," however, makes it look like a return was involved; and, therefore, Israel, under the orders of God reneged on their promise to return the riches. But the word translated "borrow" simply means to ask, to request. Hence, the Israelites were not borrowing at all. They were simply asking the Egyptians to give them these things. God never commands us to do evil.

The retribution in the despoiling. "And they spoiled the Egyptians" (12:36). The Egyptians lost their riches when they gave them to Israel. But they had no justification for complaint. They had gained these riches through the forced labor of the Israelites. You cannot gain riches evilly without paying a bigger price than what you gained. You will not enjoy those riches for long. They will either grow wings and fly away, or you will have other problems that will keep you from enjoying your riches even though you may still possess them. Those who win at gambling are gaining riches that will someday haunt them. Those who connive and cheat in business will gain riches that will curse them. Those who greedily go to court to sue in order to gain great riches will discover that what they gained will someday be viewed a bigger loss than their gain. Divine judgment comes upon those who gain riches in an evil way. Egypt certainly experienced that judgment.

The recompense in the despoiling. Israel had been treated as slaves in Egypt. Hence, they had not been paid properly but had been cruelly deprived of their due wages as we noted above. This command to ask for the riches of the Egyptians will, however, help to correct some of that mistreatment for the Israelites. It will compensate the Israelites for the lack of proper pay.

God's people often come up short in remuneration in this life. This is especially true with preachers and missionaries. Missionaries often sacrifice much materially in order to take the Gospel to far off lands. Pastors are often given meager salaries by their congregations and yet are expected and demanded to put in more hours on their job than anyone else in the congregation. It can all be pretty discouraging to God's servants if they do not keep their eye on the Word of God where God promises and illustrates that He has a way of balancing the scales. The day will come when His servants will be duly compensated. We have not served in vain when we serve God. If we are not fully compensated in this life, we most certainly will be in the next life where compensations are always better. Be faithful in serving Him and He will in due time recompense you for your service—and God pays the best wages of anyone.

The receptiveness to the despoiling. "And the LORD gave the people favor in the sight of the Egyptians, so that they lent [means to give, just as the corresponding word 'borrow' means to ask] unto them such things as they required" (12:36). This statement helps to explain why Israel was so successful in obtaining the riches of Egypt. Normally we would think that the Egyptians would utterly refuse to give Israel much of anything. But they did not refuse. Rather, they gave willingly and liberally to the Israelites because "the LORD gave the people favor in the sight of the Egyptians" (Ibid.).

Sometimes our duties look impossible to accomplish. But if God has assigned the duties, He will give the power to accomplish them. The duty of obtaining the riches of Egypt looked like an impossible task indeed. But God worked in the Egyptians' hearts, and the duty was performed well. We may be ministering to hard hearts and think they will never change. But if God can make the Egyptians liberal in giving to the despised Israelites, He can change anyone's heart.

The responsibility in the despoiling. Israel was instructed by God through Moses to ask for the Egyptians' riches. Had they not asked, they would have left Egypt empty handed. We noted above that God made the Egyptians' receptive. That is His responsibility. The Israelites' responsibility was to ask.

In like manner, we are told to "Ask" (Matthew 7:7) in prayer. And with the command to "Ask" we are given the promise that "it shall be given you" (Ibid.). But as we noted in an earlier chapter, many do not ask; therefore, "ye have not, because ye ask not" (James 4:2). Of course, some complain that they ask but do not obtain. James has an answer for that one, too. He says, "Ye ask, and receive not, because ye ask amiss, that ye may consume it upon your lusts" (James 4:3). The Israelites asked for what God told them to ask. We would do much better in the receiving department if we asked for those things God told us in His Word to ask for.

The requirements from the despoiling. Later in the wilderness, God required some of these riches for the material for the tabernacle. When He asked for the material for the tabernacle, the Israelites were well able to supply it; and they did. In fact, they gave more than was needed (Exodus 36:5–7). With their despoiling bounty, they were more than able to pay the cost.

When God blesses us we need to remember that the first reason for the blessing is to enable us to serve Him. Let us not be so eager to spend our blessings on ourselves but be attentive to the needs of God's work. We have many churches that are floundering because they do not have enough to enable them to do their work well. But the congregations generally have more than enough to help—they simply will not give it. Such miserly giving hurts the work of the Lord and invites the judgment of God upon the misers.

It is instructive to note that before God asked for the riches to build the Tabernacle, the devil was asking for donations. While Moses was in the mount conversing with God, the Israelites got impatient; and before long they were taking up an offering for Aaron to make the golden calf to worship (Exodus 32:1–4). We need to get our priorities right about our blessings lest we give them to the wrong places and for the wrong things. The flesh and the devil do not take long before they are soliciting our blessings. The devil would endeavor to deplete us of our blessings so we cannot help the work of the Lord.

XIII.

STARTING TO CANAAN

EXODUS 12:37 – 13:22

DURING VERY TRAUMATIC hours in Egypt, Moses gathered Israel together and started them on the long awaited journey to Canaan. Tragedy and turmoil reigned among the Egyptians because of the death of the firstborn, and Pharaoh had hastily ordered Israel's departure. Thousands of people—both Egyptians and Israelites—would be hurrying hither and yon in Egypt in the darkness of that memorable night. But what a difference in feelings would exist between the Egyptians and Israelites and also between the leaders of the two nations—Pharaoh and Moses. Pharaoh and the Egyptians would be in turmoil and suffering great sorrow over the loss of the firstborn, but Moses and the Israelites would be filled with great excitement and joy over the fact that they were now a free people. At last they could evacuate the land of Goshen where they had dwelt for four centuries and head for the promised land where they could be a free nation. What was death for the Egyptians was life for the Israelites. What was shame and disgrace and defeat for Pharaoh was glory and honor and victory for Moses. A similar great contrast exists between the lost and the saved. That which will be a time of rejoicing for the redeemed will be a time of great horror and suffering for those without Christ. That which is a time of honor for the saved will be a time of terrible shame for the lost. When the saved come into their greatest blessing, the lost will come into their greatest curse.

To examine the starting of the Israelites' journey to Canaan, we will consider the moment of the starting, the multitude in the starting, the memorials in the starting and the movements in the starting.

A. THE MOMENT OF THE STARTING

Two significant things are said in Scripture about the moment of the starting of the Israelites to Canaan. It was a promised moment and it was a prominent moment.

1. A Promised Moment

God had promised Abraham that "thy seed shall be a stranger in a land that is not theirs, and shall serve them; and they shall afflict them four hundred years; And also that nation, whom they shall serve, will I judge; and afterward shall they come out" (Genesis 15:13,14). The fulfillment of that promise of deliverance from Egypt after four hundred years is now occurring. "Now the sojourning of the children of Israel, who dwelt in Egypt, was four hundred and thirty years. And it came to pass at the end of the four hundred and thirty years, even the selfsame day it came to pass, that all the hosts of the LORD went out from the land of Egypt" (12:40,41). We note two things about this promised moment: the certainty of God's promise and the consistency of God's promise.

The certainty of God's promise. Pointing out that the deliverance of the Israelites from Egypt was on "the selfsame day" (12:41 and 12:51), that is, the exact day the four hundred and thirty years were completed, underscores the certainty of God's promise. When God promises, God performs! And He does it right on time and right to the letter. Furthermore, He does it regardless of the circumstances, which ought to really encourage us; for often our circumstances, like the Israelites' circumstances in Egypt, seem to argue against God's promises. Right up to the last few days, it looked like Israel was not going to get free of Egypt on time or even at any time. Pharaoh stubbornly held the Israelites even after the nine plagues. But God is God, and He never fails to keep a promise. His Word is absolutely certain, we can always count on it. Would that our own word was also as certain. A great mark of character is being a man of your word. The character of God is surely exalted in how He keeps His Word. Can we say the same about ourselves?

The consistency of God's promise. Bible critics are quick to point out that some Scripture texts speak of the Egyptian sojourn as being four hundred years (Genesis 15:13,14 and Acts 7:6) while other Scripture describes it as being four hundred and thirty years (Exodus 12:40,41). The critics use the difference in number of years to accuse the Bible of not being consistent. However, the critics seem unwilling to acknowledge that sometimes Scripture rounds off its numbers instead of giving an exact number—a universal custom among men in every age (Scripture sometimes even indicates it is rounding off numbers by using the term "about" as in Genesis 38:24, Exodus 32:28, Joshua 7:3, John 11:18, and Acts 4:4 to cite a few of many texts). In our Exodus text it is obvious that the number is not rounded off; for emphasis is laid on "the selfsame day." Rounding off numbers here would hinder us from seeing the exactness of the fulfill-ment. But Abraham would not need exact dates. A rounded-off number would be sufficient for him. So he was given the rounded-off figure of four hundred years.

Some other explanations have been given to account for the thirty years of the four hundred thirty year figure, such as, Israel was not under bondage the first thirty years but only the last four hundred years—the figure God spoke of in the Genesis text. However, the thirty years of freedom does not match up at all with the latter part of Genesis and would make the slavery begin while Joseph was in his seventies—he lived to be one hundred and ten years old—making the explanation most unsat-isfactory. The best and most logical understanding of the differ-ences is that some texts have rounded off the number of years while others are exact. We must not let the critics of God's Word cause us to doubt the consistency and fidelity of the Scripture nor cause us to devise strange and unusual interpretations of

Scripture to answer their every charge. It is totally unnecessary as it is here.

2. A Prominent Moment

God instructed Israel to "Remember this day" (Exodus 13:3); for "It is a night to be much observed unto the LORD . . . of all the children of Israel in their generations" (12:42). Instructions will be given later about the special observance of this deliverance by an annual event called the "Passover." The special event would help the Israelites to remember this moment of deliverance from Egypt.

It was very important for Israel to remember this occasion. If they did not, it would be a factor in causing them to depart from the Lord. When Israel did decline spiritually, Scripture sometimes points out that it was accompanied by forgetfulness of the important occasions in their history. The Psalmist, as an example, notes this in several places: "They soon forgot his works . . . They forgot God, their Savior, who had done great things in Egypt, wonderful works in the land of Ham, and awesome things by the Red Sea" (Psalm 106:13,21,22). God had warned Israel not to "forget the LORD thy God, which brought thee forth out of the land of Egypt, from the house of bondage" (Deuteronomy 8:14), and the annual Passover event was to help them remember this most significant moment in their history in which God did such a tremendous work for them.

There are some moments in everyone's life that are more significant than other moments and, therefore, should be duly honored and remembered. To forget those prominent moments in life can foster decline in the area of character. We need to remember the times which have been hallmarks in our spiritual life. This will help to encourage our devotion to the Lord. The day of our marriage is another time we ought to give much more attention than we do especially with all the divorce going on all about us. Church dedications and anniversaries are important days, for they can remind us of the great doctrines of the faith upon which the church was founded. Significant moments in the

328

history of our country also need to be duly honored. Armistice Day, Pearl Harbor, V-E Day, V-J Day, and other significant dates in history need to be kept prominent in the history books. However, in recent years the liberals have been taking many of these prominent dates and occasions out of the history texts used in schools. This in turn has resulted in students becoming ignorant of the great issues at stake which these prominent dates in history represent, and it will cause future generations to fall into the same mistakes which cost our nation so dearly in the past.

B. THE MULTITUDE IN THE STARTING

It was quite a crowd that departed from Egypt under the leadership of Moses. We note the count, composition, and condition of the multitude.

1. The Count of the Multitude

"And the children of Israel journeyed from Rameses to Succoth, about six hundred thousand on foot that were men, besides children" (12:37). When numbering people, Scripture usually counts only the men (women's libbers will not like that). Hence, the actual number of people in the multitude leaving Egypt was considerably more than the six hundred thousand. Conservative estimates range all the way to two million or more.

The number involved in the exodus makes the journey to Canaan a miracle in the daily care and control of the people. Feeding the people would require great supplies and, hence, great miracles—we will note more about that when we consider the manna miracle. And controlling the people, especially in hard times, would also (and did many times) need God's miracle help. But when God called Moses to lead Israel out of Egypt, He gave Moses the power to do it—as is most evident throughout the Scripture.

2. The Composition of the Multitude

"And a mixed multitude went up also with them" (Exodus 12:38). The mixed multitude was a diverse group from Egypt composed of rabble, nomads, foreigners, and others. Some of this group joined the exodus because they were intermarried with the Israelites (Leviticus 24:10). Others joined because it looked like an exciting venture. Still others of the mixed multitude would want to leave Egypt because the plagues had devastated the land and caused much dislike for the government. Then there were those who simply jumped on the band wagon. This kind always has their finger in the air testing the direction of the wind. If it blows favorably for Egypt, then they want to be Egyptians. If it blows favorably for the Israelites, then they want to be Israelites. Many are like that in every age. They have few, if any, convictions and even less character.

All in all, the mixed multitude did not attach themselves to Israel for spiritual reasons but for fleshly reasons. Hence, the group was a source of trouble. The mixed multitude joining up with Israel "was a wily move of the Enemy. Scripture presents him in two chief characters—as the roaring lion and as the cunning serpent. The former was exemplified by the cruel oppressions of Pharaoh; the latter, is what is here before us. Satan tried hard to keep some . . . of the Israelites in Egypt; failing in this, he now sends some of the Egyptians to accompany Israel to Canaan. But it was not long before this 'mixed multitude' proved a thorn in the side of Israel" (Pink). Some of their "thorn in the side" conduct involved their protest about the manna. "And the mixed multitude that was among them fell a lusting; and the children of Israel also wept again, and said, Who shall give us flesh to eat?" (Numbers 11:4). The mixed multitude got tired of the manna—which represents the Word of God. Their fleshly appetites wanted something else. It caused a big problem in the camp and resulted in many people dying, for "the LORD smote the people with a very great plague" (Numbers 11:33).

We still have trouble with this bunch. They are an especially big problem in our churches today. And what aggravates this problem is the churches' many fleshly promotional schemes for increasing attendance. This only encourages more and more of the mixed multitude to join up with the church. The mixed multitude goes through the motions in making professions of faith, but then they start causing trouble. Give them a diet of the Word of God service after service, and they will complain and cause even the true converts to complain. While we may never get rid of all the mixed multitude in our churches, we at least need to stop soliciting them by fleshly programs. We need to make it hard to join the church and easy to be removed from it. This would stop much of the mixed multitude from getting in the church. Unfortunately, however, most churches make it easy to join the church but difficult to be removed from its membership.

3. The Condition of the Multitude

Various verses in the Scriptures enlighten us regarding the condition of the multitude that left Egypt. We note three significant aspects of their condition: they were robust, regimented, and rich.

Robust. We learn this aspect of their condition not from our Exodus text but from a text in the book of Psalms which says, "There was not one feeble person among their tribes" (Psalm 105:37). Of course they were not feeble—they had been feeding on the lamb! The spiritual significance must not be missed here. When we feed upon the Word of God (which is how you feast upon Jesus Christ, THE Lamb of God) as Israel feasted upon the lamb, we will not be weak spiritually. We will be robust for service for God. We will be robust enough to overcome temptation, to survive our trials, and to live victoriously for Him. The weak condition of professing believers today is a result of a lean diet upon the Word of God. They do not study the Scriptures, and they do not get much but crumbs at church.

Regimented. Israel was not a disorganized mob shuffling out of the land of Egypt in confusion and chaos. Rather, they were a highly organized group. We learn this especially from the words "armies" and "harnessed" used in some verses in Exodus to describe the organized character of the Israelite multitude.

331

The Hebrew word translated "armies" is found five times in Scripture in relation to the multitude that headed for Egypt (6:26, 7:4, 12:17, 12:41 [translated "hosts" instead of "armies"], and 12:51). It means "an army, a host, a body of men marshalled, set in array, properly disposed, where everyone is appointed to his proper station and duty, and obliged to attend upon it" (William Wilson).

The Hebrew word translated "harnessed" (13:18) stresses the orderly way in which the people were placed in their march out of Egypt. The original King James Version had "by five in a rank" in the margin regarding the meaning of this word, and this helps us understand the idea of the word better.

To be regimented such as the Israelites were does not come automatically. Moses obviously did considerable work in instructing Israel along this line. Exodus 6:26 implies the ordering of this training. "The LORD said, Bring out the children of Israel from the land of Egypt according to their armies." In order to bring them out "according to their armies," Moses would have to work much with the Israelites in the organization and regimentation of the people.

The organizing of the flock by Moses is not a unique situation. God's men everywhere must organize their churches if they are going to lead them well. Of course, the church must cooperate regarding the organizing; or all the organizing efforts of the pastor will avail little for the church. We also need to be organized in our individual lives if we are to serve the Lord well. Paul exhorted the Corinthians, "Let all things be done decently [properly] and in order" (I Corinthians 14:40). It is a needed injunction amongst many of God's people. So many folk live a haphazard life without plan or purpose for their days. Such folk do not accomplish much, are always complaining about a lack of time and money, cannot be counted on to be faithful, and when you walk into their homes you see the disarray literally before your eyes. God is a God of order, and a life lived in accordance with the will of God will have order to it.

Rich. When Israel left Egypt, it was not a poverty march. They were wealthy. God had told Moses at the burning bush that when Israel left Egypt, they "shall not go empty" (3:21). And they certainly did not go empty when they left Egypt. They went loaded! God had also told Abraham that when Israel left Egypt they would "come out with great substance" (Genesis 15:14). Note it was not just substance but "great" substance. The Psalmist confirms it by saying, "He brought them forth also with silver and gold" (Psalm 105:37).

We have learned earlier how Israel was enriched. God ordered them to simply ask of the Egyptians for their jewels, etc. They were so successful in this that Scripture says, "They spoiled [despoiled] the Egyptians" (12:36). Israel had been in poverty in Egypt because of the slavery. But slavery did not stop God from fulfilling His promise even if the taking of Israel from poverty to great wealth had to happen in only a few hours or days. God is able to transform our situation with great speed if He so desires. Circumstances are no problem with Him.

Israel's enrichment in their emancipation speaks of an even greater enrichment which comes with the emancipation of the soul. This enrichment is in the spiritual area. The lost are paupers spiritually, but when they become saved, they become rich in Christ Jesus. "For ye know the grace of our Lord Jesus Christ, that, though he was rich, yet for your sakes he became poor, that ye through his poverty might be rich" (II Corinthians 8:9). This wealth exceeds the wealth of any earthling. The extreme greatness of this wealth is intimated when Paul says we are "joint-heirs with Christ" (Romans 8:17). It is a wealth we will never lose, inflation will never devalue it, and it will never be subject to the taxes of this world! Believers need not envy the wealthy of the world, for the rich men of the world are paupers in comparison to the lowest saint.

C. THE MEMORIALS IN THE STARTING

Included in the record in Scripture of the start of the Israelites to Canaan is the report of three memorials relating to Israel. Moses was prominently involved in all three. The three memorials are the observance of the Passover, the ownership of the firstborn, and the orders about Joseph's bones.

1. The Observance of the Passover

We have already noted that Israel was instructed by God through Moses to "Remember this day" (13:3) of their deliverance from Egypt. Here we want to take time to examine some of the instructions God gave Israel through Moses regarding the special festival for remembering their emancipation. It is called the "ordinance of the passover" (12:43) and repeats some of the actions of the Israelites the night of their emancipation. We note the permanence of the ordinance, the particulars of the ordinance, the perplexity about the ordinance, and the people for the ordinance.

The permanence of the ordinance. "Ye shall observe this thing for an ordinance to thee and to thy sons forever" (12:24, cp. 12:42), "from year to year" (13:10). The ordinance of the Passover was to be observed every year from that time on in Israel's history. Israel, however, did not always do a good job of keeping the Passover. But they did observe the Passover on the first anniversary of their emancipation (Numbers 9:1–5). And Scripture reports they also observed it shortly after they crossed the Jordan River to enter Canaan (Joshua 5:10). Later in Israel's history, they had some special observances of the Passover during times of revival. Two such occasions are recorded in the Scripture. One occasion was during the reign of King Hezekiah (II Chronicles 30) and the other was during the reign of King Josiah (II Chronicles 35). At the time of Christ in the New Testament, Israel, in contrast to their previous history, seemed to be very punctilious about observing the Passover. But for too many, the observance was only a fair show in the flesh; for they could crucify Christ in the midst of the occasion.

The particulars of the ordinance. We have seen most of the particulars about the ordinance as we studied the first Passover held in Egypt which preceded Israel's emancipation. Here we simply review. The festival involved the slaying of the lamb on the fourteenth of the first month. It also involved seven days of observance which were begun and finished with a special sabbath. Unleavened bread was to be eaten instead of leavened bread during that time. Everything involved in the ordinance was intended to remind Israel of the details of their deliverance and, of course, would foreshadow the coming of the Lord Jesus Christ, The Lamb of God, to die on Calvary. As we pointed out earlier, the Passover was being observed when Christ was crucified. He was fulfilling the type which the lamb had been over the years, but most of the Jews missed it all. They were taken up with the outward aspects of the observance but not the inward aspects. Like many folk in our churches today, they went through the motions but never saw the message or applied it to their heart. They had "a form of godliness, but denying the power thereof" (II Timothy 3:5). The carnal and unbelieving heart always has trouble going beyond the outward ceremony to see the spiritual application the ceremony represents.

The perplexity about the ordinance. "And it shall come to pass, when your children shall say unto you, What mean ye by this service? That ye shall say, It is the sacrifice of the LORD'S passover, who passed over the houses of the children of Israel in Egypt, when he smote the Egyptians, and delivered our houses" (12:26,27, cp. 13:8). Anyone who has had anything to do with children knows that they are generally full of questions. While their frequent asking of questions may get on the nerves of the parents or others caring for the children, the questions provide excellent opportunities to instruct the child. This was especially to be the case regarding the Passover. When the parents went about preparing for the Passover, the children would, of course, ask a host of questions. They would be perplexed about all the proceedings. The questions were to be duly attended to by the parents. And our text shows that God even provided answers for

335

the parents for these questions (some parents doubtless wish God would write a book with answers to all the questions children ask). The children's perplexity was an opportunity for spiritual instruction.

There is a lesson here regarding parental conduct. If the parents are not engaged in spiritual activity or exercise of any kind, the children will not have much opportunity to question the activity and thus learn about it. The instruction of the children in spiritual matters in Israel depended on the faithful observance of spiritual duties by the parents. It is still that way today. We do not have the Passover observance to keep, but we have many other spiritual duties that will provide opportunities to give the children needed instruction regarding the things of the Lord. But parents who are delinquent in spiritual duties will do a poor job of instructing their children in spiritual matters.

The people for the ordinance. Moses was instructed that not everyone could observe the Passover. Three particular classes of people were barred from eating the Passover. They were the stranger, the hired servant, and the uncircumcised. First, "There shall no stranger eat thereof" (12:43) because he was not part of the deliverance. It was only the children of Abraham who were protected by the Lamb and emancipated as a result. In like manner, an unsaved person cannot commemorate and rejoice in the work of redemption; for he has never been redeemed. Second, "An hired servant shall not eat thereof" (12:45) because "An 'hired servant' is an outsider; he is actuated by self-interest. He works for pay. But no such principle can find a place in that which speaks of redemption: 'To him that worketh not but believeth on Him that justifieth the ungodly, his faith is counted for righteousness Rom. 4:5'" (Arthur Pink). Third, "No uncircumcised person shall eat thereof" (12:48) because circumcision was a sign of the covenant and not being circumcised excluded one from the covenant—the covenant which included Israel's deliverance from Egypt.

There were, however, some strangers and servants who

could participate in the Passover. But these exceptions occurred when the stranger became qualified by being circumcised (which is a type of the Gentiles being included in the offer of the Gospel) and when the servant was "brought for money, [and] when thou hast circumcised him, then shall he eat" (12:44). The exceptions supported the rule. The rule emphasized that only God's people can celebrate redemption. Those outside the fold must be made part of the fold if they are going to be able to celebrate the occasion. A number of folk today do not like God's rules which exclude the unredeemed. But salvation through Jesus Christ, the Lamb of God, is the only way one can gain heaven eternally.

2. The Ownership of the Firstborn

The second observance that was mentioned in Scripture when Israel started to Canaan was the ownership of the firstborn. "And the LORD spake unto Moses, saying, Sanctify unto me all the firstborn, whatsoever openeth the womb among the children of Israel, both of man and of beast; it is mine" (13:1,2). We note the claim of the Lord and the curiosity of the children in regards to this ownership of the firstborn.

The claim of the Lord. The claim is stated succinctly—"It is mine" (13:2). God had spared the firstborn of the Israelites by providing them protection when He killed the firstborn of the Egyptians. Now God justifiably puts a claim upon the firstborn; for whom God saves, God has a claim upon. "If God acts in grace toward His people, He thereby establishes claims upon them, and it is these claims [of the firstborn] that are unfolded" (Edward Dennett). "A redeemed people become the property of the Redeemer" (Pink); for, as Scripture says of the redeemed, "Ye are not your own . . . for ye are brought with a price" (I Corinthians 6:19,20).

Later on the firstborn claim was adjusted to include all the Levites instead of the firstborn of every family in Israel. This adjustment did not change the principle involved. It only made for a more practical working out of the principle in Israel's case.

God's claim upon us for delivering us from the bondage of sin justly demands our devotion to Him. Arthur W. Pink says, "Personal devotedness is the first thing which God has a right to look for from His blood-brought people." But a great many in our churches today do not abide by this principle at all. Their attendance, their giving, and their performance in service represents very little dedication to the One Who saved them. They seem to resent any claim the Lord has upon them. But failure in service is a great affront to Christ, for He gave His all that we might be saved. How terribly ungrateful are those who will not serve Him steadfastly.

The curiosity of the children. "And it shall be when thy son asketh thee in time to come, saying, What is this? that thou shalt say unto him, By strength of hand the LORD brought us out from Egypt, from the house of bondage. And it came to pass, when Pharaoh would hardly let us go, that the LORD slew all the firstborn in the land of Egypt, both the firstborn of man, and the firstborn of beast: therefore I sacrifice to the LORD all that openeth the matrix [womb]" (13:14,15). As it was with the observance of the Passover, so it is with the observance of the firstborn dedication—it provided a great opportunity to instruct the children in spiritual matters. And as we noted in instructing the children about the Passover, so it is in instructing the children about the firstborn—the parent will not be able to instruct the children well if the parent does not fulfill his or her spiritual obligations. The parent has to be able to say, "I [not just they] sacrifice to the LORD all that openeth the matrix" (13:15) if he is going to do much of a job instructing his children. Children will not be instructed well in spiritual matters by parents who are delinquent in these matters. This parental delinquency explains why many children are ignorant of spiritual truths. Parents have a great responsibility to instruct their children in spiritual truths, but they must be dedicated in living them if they are going to excel in teaching them.

3. The Orders About Joseph's Bones

"And Moses took the bones of Joseph with him; for he [Joseph] had straitly sworn the children of Israel, saying, God will surely visit you; and ye shall carry up my bones away hence with you" (13:19). This lone verse about Joseph's bones is more significant than some may realize. It is a great testimony of faith in God's Word. We especially note this fact in the counsel of Joseph and in the compliance by Moses.

The counsel of Joseph. The last chapter of Genesis records the counsel of Joseph regarding his bones. "And Joseph said unto his brethren, I die: and God will surely visit you, and bring you out of this land unto the land which he sware to Abraham, to Isaac, and to Jacob. And Joseph took an oath of the children of Israel, saying, God will surely visit you, and ye shall carry up my bones from hence" (Genesis 50:24,25). An extensive study on this counsel of Joseph can be found in our book on Joseph. Here we briefly look at his counsel by noting the publicness, persuasiveness, patience, practice, promise and perspective of Joseph's faith.

First, the *publicness* of his faith. "Joseph said to his brethren." Joseph's faith was not concealed. He went public with it. He confessed his faith openly to his brethren. Sometimes confessing our faith to our kinfolk is the hardest place of all to the confess it, but it needs to be confessed there first.

Second, the *persuasiveness* of his faith. Joseph did not have weak faith. He was firmly persuaded in his heart about God's promises. Twice in these two verses in Genesis he evidenced his strong faith in God's promises by saying that God "will surely visit you." He did not doubt God. "Surely" is emphatic, strong, dogmatic. Many think we cannot have a "surely" faith, but any other kind is most unsatisfactory. If there is any place we need to be sure about things, it is in spiritual matters.

Third, the *patience* of his faith. The promise of God's visiting the Israelites and delivering them was in the distant future; for Joseph told them to take his bones, not his body, with them.

That meant that much time would expire in order for the body to decay and disintegrate. But the long time involved did not discourage Joseph's faith. Neither should it hinder ours. Just because God does not do something for us in a day or week or month does not mean we should give up our faith in Him. We need to remember that God's wisdom guides the exercising of God's power.

Fourth, the *practice* of his faith. Giving orders to take his bones to Canaan indicated that Joseph's faith affected the way he lived. He practiced what he professed. Some claim to have faith, but you never see it influencing the way they live. Such people do not have faith; it is simply talk. But Joseph's faith was real; it showed up in his walk.

Fifth, the *promise* of his faith. Joseph's counsel to his brethren about taking his bones to Canaan was a most promising prospect for his brethren. Over the years in Egypt, the Israelites would be encouraged in beholding Joseph's "coffin" (Genesis 50:26, a mummy case). It would encourage them that someday they would go back to the promised land. Real faith is encouraging to others. It promises blessings from trusting the Lord. Those, however, who do not walk in faith are no encouragement to mankind; for their life does not promise blessings at all.

Sixth, the *perspective* of his faith. Joseph's orders to take his bones to Canaan put perspective on the land of Egypt. It was not the permanent place for Israel. They had a better place to live which was in Canaan. True faith puts perspective on this old world (which Egypt typifies). It tells us that this world is only a temporary place for us. We must not get our roots down too deep or let our affections for this old world become too strong. We are only passing through the earth. Our lasting home is heaven.

The compliance of Moses. Moses complied to Joseph's request to take Joseph's bones with them when Israel left Egypt. This compliance confirmed Joseph's faith, commended Joseph's faith, and continued Joseph's faith in others.

First, the *confirmation* of Joseph's faith. The carrying of the bones of Joseph to Canaan confirmed that Joseph's faith in God's promises was most valid. Time always validates our trust in God's Word. Time always honors faith. "Whosoever believeth on him shall not be ashamed" (Romans 9:33; 10:11).

Second, the *commendation* of Joseph's faith. Joseph's orders given to his brethren four centuries earlier represented great faith in God's Word. In taking the bones with him, Moses gave honor to that great faith. Unlike much of our world, Moses did not scorn great faith in God's Word. He would give it much honor. That reflects well on Moses' character, for that which we honor and commend reveals much about our character.

Third, the *continuation* of Joseph's faith in others. Moses' compliance encouraged the continuation of Joseph's faith in others in Israel. This is seen in that Joseph's bones were eventually buried by the Israelites in Canaan. "And the bones of Joseph . . . buried they in Shechem" (Joshua 24:32). Our conduct either encourages or discourages others to have faith. Moses encouraged faith by his conduct. May we always do likewise.

D. THE MOVEMENTS IN THE STARTING

Scripture records some instructive details regarding the movements of Israel under Moses' leadership as they started on their way to Canaan. To study these details, we will note the pathway of the journey and the pillar for the journey.

1. The Pathway of the Journey

Three places are mentioned in regards to the early part of the trip to Canaan. They can be described as the bitter place, the battle place, and the barren place.

The bitter place. "And the children of Israel journeyed from Rameses to Succoth" (12:37). The city of Rameses was the starting point of the exodus from Egypt for the Israelites. It was where a general rendezvous of Israelites occurred to commence the journey after they were ordered out of the land by Pharaoh.

Succoth was fifteen to twenty miles or so south and east of Rameses and was the first stopping point on the journey. Some estimate it was probably reached after the first day of travel from Rameses.

The name "Rameses" is associated with at least thirteen Pharaohs with some of them reigning when Israel was in slavery in Egypt. The relationship of the city Rameses, from which the exodus commenced, to the children of Israel would be a bitter one. For Rameses was one of the two cities the Israelites built for Egypt after Egypt had put them in slavery—"Therefore they did set over them taskmasters to afflict them with their burdens. And they built for Pharaoh treasure cities, Pithom and Raamses [spelled 'Rameses' with one 'a' in all other texts]" (Exodus 1:11). But the exodus would remove Israel from that bitter place. That fact pictures the salvation of the soul. Sin brings the greatest bitterness of all, but salvation—deliverance from the bondage of sin—brings liberation from that bitterness.

The battle place. "And it came to pass, when Pharaoh had let the people go, that God led them not through the way of the land of the Philistines, although that was near; for God said, Lest peradventure the people repent when they see war, and they return to Egypt" (13:17). Later Israel would be engaged in much warfare. They will fight the Amalekites (Exodus 17) in their first battle after leaving Egypt, and they will have much more warfare before reaching Canaan and also in conquering Canaan. But when Israel left Egypt, they were not yet ready for war. They had not been duly prepared to battle. Until they are ready to fight, God will keep them from such situations.

God adjusts our trials to our strength. Mackintosh rightly says of this leading of God, "The Lord, in His condescending grace, so orders things for His people that they do not, at their first setting out, encounter heavy trials, which might have the effect of discouraging their hearts and driving them back." This principle was also seen in Abraham's life. His first trial was not the offering up of Isaac. That trial was given only after Abraham had grown much in the faith. God gives us time to prepare for our battles. Our problem is that we do not use that time to adequately prepare.

The barren place. "God led the people about, through the way of the wilderness of the Red sea . . . And they took their journey from Succoth, and encamped in Etham, in the edge of the wilderness" (13:18,20). Israel's path to Canaan would be a lengthy path through the barrenness of the wilderness of the Sinai peninsula. The flesh does not like the wilderness route. It prefers a short and quick route to get to the blessings of Canaan. But God seldom leads that way, and for some very good reasons. We cite three reasons.

First, Israel was to *sacrifice* unto God. Moses was instructed by God to ask Pharaoh to let Israel go "three days' journey into the wilderness, that we may sacrifice to the Lord our God" (Exodus 3:18). The wilderness was the most suitable place to sacrifice. As we noted in earlier studies, sacrificing in Egypt would be prohibitive because of the Egyptians' attitudes about animals. Sacrificing would also be impossible on the Philistine path because it was a place of warfare.

Sacrificing here speaks of worship. And the place where Israel was to worship reminds us that we must worship in the place of God's choosing. A wilderness church may not be popular with the world, for it will lack much that appeals to the flesh. But it is often the best place to worship. And you will find some mighty good preachers and teachers in such places—Moses in the wilderness of Sinai and John the Baptist in the wilderness of Judea (Matthew 3:3) to name a couple.

Second, Israel was to *serve* God. God had instructed Moses at the burning bush that Israel would "serve God upon this mountain" (Exodus 3:12). That mountain was Mount Horeb which was located in the southern tip of the Sinai peninsula. To get there, Israel must traverse through the wilderness. How often God tests our desire to serve Him by making it necessary for us to go through the struggle of a wilderness experience before we are given a place of service for Him.

Third, Israel was to be *schooled* of God. Israel needed to be schooled in the ways of God. They needed to be taught God's law and they needed to be organized into a nation. These things could not be done on the short way, the way which the flesh would have preferred in going to Canaan. Israel needed to be taken aside into the solitude of the wilderness to be edified, prepared, instructed, and readied to go to Canaan. The wilderness would provide good circumstances for this schooling.

The wilderness route is not an unprofitable route. The flesh does not like it, of course. But it is one where we will learn much and where our soul will be strengthened and prepared by God for the tasks ahead.

2. The Pillar for the Journey

Scripture makes it clear concerning Israel's journey to Canaan that "God led them" (13:17). The special means which He used to lead them was a pillar of cloud and fire: "And the LORD went before them by day in a pillar of a cloud, to lead them the way; and by night in a pillar of fire, to give them light; to go by day and night. He took not away the pillar of the cloud by day, nor the pillar of fire by night, from before the people" (13:21,22). To glean lessons from God's provision of this pillar for Israel, we will note the leading of the pillar and the likeness of the pillar.

The leading of the pillar. This method of leading Israel by the pillar was an unique way for leading people, but it still embodied some basic and significant principles by which God leads men in every age. We note this in the style, scope, and supremeness of its leading.

First, the *style* of its leading. The pillar led them step by step. It did not show them their journey a year ahead. But it simply went "before them" (13:21) to "lead [show] them the way" (Ibid.). Israel needed to only be concerned where the pillar was at the present time and moment. If they were always where the pillar was at the present, they would be assured of being where the pillar would be in the future. So many folk talk about the will of God down the road a ways but seem little concerned about the will of God today. However, not being concerned about the will of God today is a good way to miss the will of God for tomorrow.

Second, the *scope* of its leading. Not only did the pillar lead step by step, but it led every step of the way; for the pillar ordered both Israel's starts and stops. "And when the cloud was taken up from the tabernacle, then after that the children of Israel journeyed; and in the place where the cloud abode, there the children of Israel pitched their tents" (Numbers 9:17). People sometimes only talk about the will of God when they are at church involved in church business. But the will of God is very relevant to every facet of our life. God not only leads us in spiritual matters; He also leads us in material matters. He not only tells us when to move on, but He also tells us when to stay put. You cannot exempt the will of God from any place in your life.

Third, the *supremeness* of its leading. "At the commandment of the LORD the children of Israel journeyed, and at the commandment of the LORD they pitched . . . According to the commandment of the LORD they abode in their tents, and according to the commandment of the LORD they journeyed . . . At the commandment of the LORD they rested in the tents, and at the commandment of the LORD they journeyed; they kept the charge of the LORD, at the commandment of the LORD by the hand of Moses" (Numbers 9:18,20,23). The supremeness of the pillar in leading Israel is emphasized by the fact that the phrase "commandment of the LORD" is used seven times and the phrase "the charge of the LORD" is used once in these three verses to speak of the pillar. These are very authoritative phrases and make it clear that the pillar was the supreme authority where Israel was to go. God's leading is always so. No authority is equal or above His. If we are going to do His will, we must submit to His will above everything else.

The likeness of the pillar. It is not difficult to see the Holy Spirit in the work of the pillar. We note six ways in which the likeness of the Holy Spirit is seen in the pillar.

First, the *provision* of the pillar. Both the moment and the manner in which the pillar was provided for Israel speak of the Holy Spirit. The *moment* the pillar was provided was after Israel was freed from Egypt. In like manner, the Holy Spirit is provided for the soul after that person has been saved, not before (Ephesians 1:13). The *manner* in which the pillar was provided was as a gift from God. In like manner, the Holy Spirit is a gift from God. "I will pray the Father, and He shall give you another Comforter" (John 14:16).

Second, the *purpose* of the pillar. The pillar was given Israel to "lead them" (13:21). So it is with the Holy Spirit. He leads the believers: "As many as are led by the Spirit of God, they are the sons of God" (Romans 8:14), and "When he, the Spirit of truth, is come, he will guide you into all truth" (John 16:13). The Spirit of God leads us by the Word of God and this is typified well in the pillar when the Psalmist says, "He [God] *spake* unto them in the cloudy pillar" (Psalm 99:7). The Spirit does not lead us in contradiction to the Scripture. Some in our churches are doing questionable things which they claim the Spirit led them to do. But those things are contrary to the Word of God, which means these people are not truly being led by the Spirit as they claim.

Third, the *protection* in the pillar. The pillar not only provided leadership, but it also protected. The Psalmist tells us "He [God] spread a cloud [pillar] for a covering" (Psalm 105:39). Israel needed protection from the hot sun of the wilderness. The pillar also protected from the cold at night (the fire at night would protect from the cold which comes in the wilderness at night), from the perils of darkness at night, and, as we will see next, from Pharaoh's army. The Holy Spirit protects the believer. This is readily seen in the sealing by the Spirit "unto the day of redemption" (Ephesians 4:30). This assures the believer he will not lose his salvation.

Fourth, the *perplexity* about the pillar. At the Red Sea the pillar "came between the camp of the Egyptians and the camp of Israel; and it was a cloud and darkness to them . . . the LORD looked unto the host of the Egyptians through the pillar of fire and of the cloud, and troubled the host of the Egyptians" (Exodus 14:20,24). The pillar was a blessing to Israel but it certainly was not a blessing to Egypt. It protected Israel from the Egyptian army. But the pillar was a troubling perplexity to Egypt. So it is with the world and the Holy Spirit. "The natural man receiveth not the things of the Spirit of God; for they are foolishness unto him, neither can he know them, because they are spiritually discerned" (I Corinthians 2:14).

Fifth, the *permanence* of the pillar. "He took not away the pillar of the cloud by day, nor the pillar of fire by night, from before the people" (13:22). "The pillar of the cloud departed not from them by day, to lead them in the way; neither the pillar of fire by night, to show them light, and the way wherein they should go" (Nehemiah 9:19). Israel always had the pillar with them until their journey to the promised land was completed. It is the same with the Holy Spirit and the believer. "And I will pray the Father, and he shall give you another Comforter, that he may abide with you for ever" (John 14:16).

Sixth, the *place* of the pillar. "And he reared up the court round about the tabernacle . . . Then a cloud [the pillar] covered the tent of the congregation, and the glory of the LORD filled the tabernacle" (Exodus 40:33,34). When Moses finished setting up the Tabernacle and it, therefore, was then ready for service, the pillar descended upon the Tabernacle. The Tabernacle is, of course, a great type of Jesus Christ. As the pillar came upon the Tabernacle in the wilderness when the Tabernacle was ready to commence its service, so the Holy Spirit came upon Christ as He was ready to begin His public ministry. "And Jesus, when he was baptized, went up straightway out of the water; and, lo, the heavens were opened unto him, and he saw the Spirit of God descending like a dove, and lighting upon him" (Matthew 3:16).

347

XIV.

SEA OF DELIVERANCE

EXODUS 14

THE MIRACULOUS DIVIDING of the waters of the Red Sea to deliver Israel and to destroy Pharaoh and his army was one of the most significant miracles in the history of the nation of Israel. Arthur Pink said, "The miracle of the Red Sea occupies a similar place in the Old Testament scriptures as the resurrection of the Lord Jesus does in the New; it is appealed to as a standard of measurement, as the supreme demonstration of God's power." As an example, centuries later Isaiah appealed to the Red Sea miracle when he said, "Art thou not it [the One] which hath dried the sea, the waters of the great deep; that hath made the depths of the sea a way for the ransomed to pass over?" (Isaiah 51:10). The miracle not only left a great impression upon the Israelites, but it left a profound impression upon the heathen. As an example, Rahab of Jericho told the spies, "We have heard how the LORD dried up the water of the Red sea for you, when ye came out of Egypt . . . And as soon as we had heard these things, our hearts did melt, neither did there remain any more courage in any man, because of you" (Joshua 2:10,11).

But though Israel and her enemy nations were so impressed by the Red Sea miracle for so many centuries, the skeptics of our day are not so sure. Some like to call the Red Sea the Reed Sea and tell us that Moses simply guided the Israelites across the shallow part of the sea. But I like the story of the boy's response to a minister who tried to teach some children this view in order to get them to believe that there was no miracle at the Red Sea. The boy replied that a miracle still had to occur in

348

order for all the army of Egypt to be drowned in such shallow water. The boy's answer emphasizes that the explanations of unbelief always create more problems than they solve.

In our study of this momentous occasion in the experience of Moses and the Israelites, we will consider the path to the sea (vv. 1–4), the peril at the sea (vv. 3–9), the pleas by the sea (vv. 10–14), and the parting of the sea (vv. 15–31).

A. THE PATH TO THE SEA

"And the LORD spake unto Moses, saying, Speak unto the children of Israel, that they turn and encamp before Pi-hahiroth, between Migdol and the sea, over against Baal-zephon: before it shall ye encamp by the sea" (vv. 1, 2). Israel's journey commenced at Rameses (12:37). From there they went to Succoth (Ibid.) and then to "Etham, in the edge of the wilderness" (13:20). Now in our text God orders their path to turn away from the edge of the wilderness and to head for Pi-hahiroth. We note four aspects of this path to the sea: the perplexity of it, the precept for it, the proving by it, and the purpose in it.

1. The Perplexity of the Path

Canaan was Israel's eventual destination, but first they must go to the wilderness to sacrifice unto God (Exodus 3:18; 5:3). Going on a path from Rameses to Succoth to Etham seemed most logical. The next step would seem to be to continue on into the wilderness and set up camp there so Israel could worship. God had told Moses that Israel would "serve God upon this mountain [Mt. Horeb in the southern part of the Sinai peninsula]" (Exodus 3:12), and that was the direction Israel was headed when they stopped at Etham. But when God ordered them to head for Pi-hahiroth which was on the west side of the Red Sea, it seemed a very strange move indeed. This path led Israel down the west side of the Red Sea when they needed to be on the east side of the Red Sea if they were going to go to Horeb and then to Canaan. Going down the west side would only lead them farther into Africa. It would not take them to the wilderness or to Canaan—so human thinking would reason.

God's will—and this was God's will as we will see next—sometimes does lead us in ways that natural reasoning thinks strange. He is a rare saint who has not found himself in God-directed circumstances that seem for a time to not make any sense at all. And during those times God's people should not be surprised if the world laughs at them. The world's values and vices do not appreciate and cannot understand God's ways. When we are in such situations, we must, therefore, encourage ourselves by the knowledge that we are in the will of God and that the wisdom of God does not make any mistakes.

2. The Precept for the Path

As we just noted, this perplexing path was indeed the will of God. Our text tells us very plainly that it was God who ordered Moses to lead Israel on this unexpected path. "The LORD spake unto Moses" (v. 1) and gave him the precept to lead the Israelites from Etham to "encamp before Pi-hahiroth" (v. 2). Furthermore, not only did Moses have a specific precept to take this seemingly strange path, but the cloud also led Israel that way. It confirmed the precept. So both the command and the cloud of God led on this puzzling path. Hence, the path Moses was to take was made very evident.

This most evident leading of God here is instructive. It tells us that when God orders us to do things which to human reasoning seems downright strange and unwise, He will give us very plain and obvious orders to do these things. We will not have to guess at where to go and what to do. What we need to know to take the strange course of action will not be vague but very clearly revealed to us. Scripture will not have to be interpreted in an unusual way to justify our conduct.

This truth is much needed today, for there are some who are making strange decisions and exhibiting strange conduct who cannot justify their actions with the plain teaching of the Scripture. When you ask them to give proof of God's leading them into these strange ways, they give unintelligent answers and generally twist some verse or two of Scripture completely out of context to support their ways. This invalidates their claim of doing strange things, for God does not send us on strange missions without most evident orders. The stranger the mission (to natural reasoning), the more obvious will be the orders He will give for it. We may not understand the *why* of the orders, but we will have no trouble understanding the *what* of the orders. Do not leave Etham and go to Pi-hahiroth until the command of God and the cloud of God make it plain to do so, or you will cause the Israelites to perish in disgrace. Do not jump off the cliff until you have ample instructions and Scriptural principles to guide your way, or you will end up like Humpty Dumpty when he fell off the wall and will make a fool of yourself and greatly dishonor Christ and Christianity.

3. The Proving by the Path

God continually tests us just as teachers test their students in school. God tested Israel many times in their wilderness travels "that I may prove them, whether they will walk in my law, or no" (Exodus 16:4). Here, though the orders were very plain to take the path to Pi-hahiroth, the perplexity of the path would be a great test of faith for both Moses and the multitude.

A test for Moses. Moses was supposed to be the leader of the people, but it appears here to natural thinking that he is a very poor leader, for it looks like he is making a great mistake in leading the Israelites down the wrong side of the Red Sea. Not only is he not headed for the wilderness anymore, but he is headed the opposite way of Canaan. "The most inexperienced eyes in the whole multitude must have seen the apparent absurdity of the movement; and loud and deep must have been the murmurs and protestations of the people. 'Is this the way to Canaan? We know better! How dare you presume to lead us, when your very first tactics prove you to be wholly untrustworthy?'" (F. B. Meyer).

It is not easy to lead people on a path that seems contrary to

351

human reasoning, but any man who would lead people spiritually will sooner or later find himself having to do this. It is easy to lead people in the way they think is right. But it is very difficult to lead people contrary to their thinking even though the leading is according to God's will. Pastors who try to lead the church according to the Word of God run into this problem all the time with people who would run the church according to the way the world does things.

A test for the multitude. The Israelites had been instructed that the cloud was the Divine guide for their journey. When they began their journey and the cloud led them in the way they thought they should go, they followed without protest. Now, however, they are tested in following the cloud when it leads them contrary to their reasoning. It is a test which at times comes to every child of God to see if he is really earnest about following the revealed will of God or if he follows only when it is convenient.

4. The Purpose in the Path

God disclosed to Moses two purposes for leading Israel on this path. They were the enticing of Pharaoh and the exalting of God. Knowing these purposes would not clear up all the perplexity of the path, but it would help to console in the perplexity.

The enticing of Pharaoh. "For Pharaoh will say of the children of Israel, They are entangled in the land, the wilderness hath shut them in. And I will harden Pharaoh's heart, that he shall follow after them" (vv. 3,4). One of the important purposes for this path was to lure Pharaoh into pursuing the Israelites which would then result in his death and in the destruction of his great army in the Red Sea. This would consummate the judgment upon Pharaoh and Egypt for their cruel conduct towards the Israelites and for their obstinate, wicked rebellion against Jehovah God. Also, it would effectively end any threat Egypt would be to the freedom of Israel. With Pharaoh dead and his army drowned in the Red Sea, the leadership and ability of Egypt to attack Israel would no longer exist. Before Egypt could build up into a formidable foe again, Israel will be a dynamic power destroying the Canaanites left and right. Egypt will have no appetite to take on this dynamic force then.

The exalting of God. The destruction of Pharaoh and his army would not only enhance Israel's freedom, but it would also mean that God would "be honored upon Pharaoh, and upon all his host; that the Egyptians may know that I am the LORD" (v. 4). As with the plagues, this judgment upon Pharaoh and his armies was to exalt God. Though they had greatly dishonored God by their rebellion to His orders, in the end they will honor God through their judgment. All men will honor God. Some do it by obedience; others, such as the Egyptians, will only honor God through judgment upon their disobedience.

The glory of God is the supreme purpose of this path, for the glory of God is always the supreme purpose of any action by God. It should also be the supreme purpose of any action by mankind. "Whatsoever ye do, do all to the glory of God" (I Corinthians 10:31). Men, however, are not very interested in God's glory. They are concerned chiefly about their own glory. And they go to great efforts to honor themselves before other men. Even many preachers have this problem, sorry to say.

B. THE PERIL AT THE SEA

Pi-hahiroth by the Red Sea was not only a perplexing place (to human thinking) for Moses and Israel to be, but it also became a very perilous place for them to be. That which caused them such great peril was that Pharaoh and his armies pursued Israel there. We will note the motivation creating the peril, the men causing the peril, and the moment commencing the peril.

1. The Motivation Creating the Peril

God informed Moses about what would motivate Pharaoh to pursue Israel at Pi-hahiroth. Pharaoh had a twofold motivation to pursue the Israelites—the report of Israel's location and the regretting of Israel's liberty. That which helped make these two things motivations to pursue Israel and thus create great peril for the Israelites was that Pharaoh's heart was hardened by God. God told Moses that "I will harden Pharaoh's heart, that he shall follow after them" (v. 4). A good heart would not have been motivated by these two things. But evil hearts are motivated much differently than good hearts.

The report of Israel's location. "For Pharaoh will say of the children of Israel, They are entangled in the land, the wilderness hath shut them in" (v. 3). Through assigned agents or other means, Pharaoh was given reports regarding Israel's whereabouts after Israel was granted their freedom. When it was reported to him that Israel had gone to Pi-hahiroth by the Red Sea, he quickly concluded two things—they were confused ("entangled") and they were cornered ("shut . . . in").

First, he concluded they were *confused.* The word translated "entangled" means to be confused, "to be perplexed, to wander about in perplexity" (Wilson). We have already noted the perplexity to natural thinking of the path to Pi-hahiroth. Hence, it would be easy for Pharaoh to conclude that Israel did not know where they were going and that they were confused as to their directions. What Pharaoh, of course, did not realize was that this was all of God to lure Pharaoh into his fatal pursuit of Israel.

Second, he concluded they were *cornered.* Knowing the geography of the area of Pi-hahiroth where Israel was located, Pharaoh knew Israel was trapped if he pursued them there. They had walked themselves into a corner. "The Attakah range on their right, and the sea on their left, and the mountain heights of Abu-Deraj . . . in front; so that, with the Egyptians behind them, extrication from the cul-de-sac was by natural egress impossible" (Jamieson). One, of course, could pass through the mountains, but the passage would be very difficult and slow as mountainous passages are. This meant that the mountains would be a barrier to Israel as far as a means of escape from a pursuing army. Pharaoh could see that Israel's only natural escape was by the way they came into the Pi-hahiroth area. And that way could be blocked by Pharaoh's armies.

With his heart hardened to evil, Israel's situation would really motivate Pharaoh to attack them. His bloodthirsty heart would see Israel as a helpless victim of his pursuing army. He could see a quick slaughter of many and the taking of others captive so they could be returned to "serving us" (v. 5). Also he could see much spoil in all the animals and riches of Israel. Exodus 15:9 describes this attitude of Pharaoh and the pursuers well: "The enemy said, I will pursue, I will overtake, I will divide the spoil; my lust shall be satisfied upon them; I will draw my sword, my hand shall destroy them." It did indeed look like the enemy had God's people cornered. But when we have been cornered by His leading, He will deliver us wonderfully.

The regretting of Israel's liberty. "And it was told the king of Egypt that the people fled; and the heart of Pharaoh and of his servants was turned against the people, and they said, Why have we done this, that we have let Israel go from serving us? And he made ready his chariot, and took his people with him" (vv. 5,6). Matthew Henry rightly said, "The liberty of God's people is a heavy grievance to their enemies." So it did not take long for Pharaoh to regret giving liberty to Israel, and this regret became his second motivation to pursue Israel to Israel's peril.

It may seem incredible to us that Pharaoh would so quickly change his mind again. How could he possibly regret letting the Israelites go? Keeping them had caused all the destructive plagues, and the death of the firstborn was so painful that Pharaoh not only let Israel leave but ordered them to leave. Yet, in spite of all of that, he once again changes his mind and openly greatly regrets his action of letting Israel go free. And he was not alone. His servants also had a change of heart. The painful experiences of God's judgment were quickly forgotten by them, too.

Though this change of mind by Pharaoh may seem absolutely incredible to us, we should not have any trouble identifying with it; for we can see this happening repeatedly all around us. Furthermore, if we are honest, we will admit that we have the same problem all too often in our own lives. Sin makes us so stupid and blind. "It not only overpowers conscience, but it makes a man forget for a time all the sufferings under which he positively writhed before. It obliterates all the lessons of past experience, sets aside even the operations of the understanding, and hurries the sinner on with rapid steps to his own destruction" (George Wagner). When a man gets hopelessly drunk one night and then wakes up the next morning very sick, in his suffering, he will vow never to touch alcohol again. But give him a few days and he will repent of his vow and go back to his booze. "It is happened unto them according to the true proverb, The dog is turned to his own vomit again; and the sow that was washed to her wallowing in the mire" (II Peter 2:22). Though God judges us again and again for our sin, yet we often continue to go back to the same mud hole of iniquity. Therefore, we need to pray daily and earnestly for God to help us walk faithfully in His way. Unless that occurs, we will be just like Pharaoh. Our evil may not be as pronounced as his, but it will reflect his habit of returning again and again to his sin.

2. The Men Causing the Peril

"And he made ready his chariot, and took his people with him. And he took six hundred chosen chariots, and all the chariots of Egypt, and captains over every one of them . . . the Egyptians pursued after them, all the horses and chariots of Pharaoh, and his horsemen, and his army" (vv. 6,7,9). Pharaoh took the *best* and the *rest* of his army in this pursuit which put the Israelites in great peril. The *best* consisted of the "six hundred chosen chariots" (v. 7). "These 'chosen' chariots contained the flower and chivalry of Egypt . . . were most probably the royal guard, which according to Herodotus . . . consisted of 2,000 men, selected by turns every year from the entire army" (Jamieson). The *rest* included "all the chariots of Egypt, and captains over every one of them . . . all the horses and chariots of Pharaoh, and his horsemen, and his army" (vv. 7,9).

It is important to detail all that Pharaoh took in this pursuit, for it helps us to better appreciate the extent of the judgment that took place upon Egypt at the Red Sea—Pharaoh and the best and the rest of his military were destroyed at the Red Sea. God "destroyed the most potent armed force in the whole world" (Rawlinson). Some believe that not all the military was destroyed at the Red Sea, for throughout Egypt various watches and guards were generally posted. That may be so, but that would not save much of the army. So do not water down the destruction upon Egypt as some do. Read the text slowly so you do not miss all that went with Pharaoh. God's judgment upon Egypt at the Red Sea was devastating.

The total destruction of Pharaoh and his army after the great destruction upon the land in the ten plagues demonstrates how sin really amasses a great destruction upon mankind. Allow sin to continue anywhere and it will bring great destruction and send multitudes to hell for all eternity. Let us remember this when we want to be tolerant towards sin. Let people remember this when they become critical of the preacher preaching force-fully against sin. Let churches remember this when they are reluctant to take action against dissidents in the church. Let parents remember this in regards to the disobedience of their children. Let our courts remember this when giving out sentences for evil conduct. Our problem today in dealing with sin is not being too strict but being too lenient.

3. The Moment Commencing the Peril

"And the children of Israel went out with an high hand. But the Egyptians pursued after them" (vv. 8,9). On the surface it seems strange that Scripture would insert here that "Israel went out with an high hand." That sentence seems to belong back in Exodus 12 or 13 which reported the condition of Israel as they started on their trip from Egypt to Canaan. But inserting that statement here is no mistake. By its insertion God would teach us an important lesson as to the moment when Satan attacks the believer. It is when we are rejoicing in Divine blessing and walking encouragingly in our Christian faith that the enemy attacks. "Went out with an high hand" means to go out with confidence, courage, and triumphantly. And note that Numbers 33:3 says, "Israel went out with an high hand *in the sight of all the Egyptians.*" They walked in victory in front of their enemy. How Satan hates this. Therefore, he will soon attack.

The new convert knows what this experience is all about. He comes to Christ and with sins forgiven rejoices in his new found liberty and faith. He walks differently now in front of his unbelieving acquaintances, and he lives victoriously over sin and temptation. But soon the devil pursues him with "all the horses and chariots" (v. 9). The new convert is not alone in this experience. Let any blessing come to a believer which causes him to walk with lighter foot and to have increased joy and blessing in the Lord, and soon the evil one will pursue with troubles and temptations. But to be forewarned is to be fore-armed so the enemies' attack will not make us forlorn.

C. THE PLEAS BY THE SEA

"Pharaoh . . . and his army . . . overtook them [Israel] encamping by the sea, beside Pi-hahiroth, before Baal-zephon. And when Pharaoh drew nigh, the children of Israel lifted up their eyes, and, behold, the Egyptians marched after them; and they were sore afraid; and the children of Israel cried out unto the LORD. And [also] . . . unto Moses" (vv. 9–11). The pursuit by Pharaoh and his army resulted in Israel making an earnest plea both to God and to Moses.

1. The Plea to God

"The children of Israel cried out unto the LORD" (v. 10). The behavior of the Israelites which came about because of Pharaoh's pursuing them was mostly not good. But some of their behavior was commendable. Particularly can we commend their crying to God in prayer. When they saw Pharaoh's army

358

come into view and perceived their cul-de-sac situation at Pi-hahiroth, it is not surprising that "they were sore afraid" (v. 10). They understood all too well what Pharaoh's intentions were, and they were defenseless before him. They quickly concluded that a blood bath could easily occur, and it would be their blood. This caused them to lift up their voice in earnest prayer to God. As Matthew Henry said, "Their fear set them a praying, and that was a good effect of it." It is too bad their behavior did not continue to be this good.

When circumstances go sour—and they often do—we are wise to take the situation to the Lord in earnest prayer. There may be other wise things to also do, but wisdom will always go to the Lord in prayer in time of trouble. And note that we should not tarry about going to prayer. When Israel saw their situation, they immediately cried out to the Lord. We gain nothing by delay in seeking God's help. We only lose. So when troubles pursue us, let us quickly take them to the Lord for His help.

2. The Plea to Moses

"And they said unto Moses, Because there were no graves in Egypt, hast thou taken us away to die in the wilderness? wherefore hast thou dealt thus with us, to carry us forth out of Egypt? Is not this the word that we did tell thee in Egypt, saying, Let us alone, that we may serve the Egyptians? For it had been better for us to serve the Egyptians, than that we should die in the wilderness" (vv. 11,12). The reaction of Israel to their dire circumstances was first a flicker of faith (their plea to God) but then a great flame of flesh (their plea to Moses). That, unfortunately, is how many of us act so often amidst our troubles. The evidence of faith in our troubles is very slight, but the evidence of flesh is very significant—so much so that one wonders if we have any faith at all.

To examine this plea by the Israelites to Moses, we note the rascality of the plea and the response to the plea.

The rascality of their plea. The rascality of the plea is seen

359

in a threefold way—in the blaming of Moses for their troubles, in the boasting of their past prediction, and in the belittling of their present circumstances.

First, the *blaming* of Moses. "Hast thou taken us away to die in the wilderness? wherefore hast thou dealt thus with us, to carry us forth out of Egypt" (v. 11). Sizing up their situation as the natural eye saw it, they concluded that death was imminent via Pharaoh's army. Then they looked around for someone to blame for this situation—and Moses is the one they blame. After all, they would reason, he is our leader and has led us to this perilous situation. But their thinking was all in the flesh, for there was no consideration of the fact that Moses was leading them according as God instructed.

Blaming Moses reflects the typical action of church members when things do not go right at church. Every pastor who has pastored for any length of time knows what it is to be blamed for every problem at church and even for problems in the church members' families. Few church members want to blame Pharaoh or the devil or the world for causing the church trouble. It has to always be the pastor they blame. As an example, TV can destroy the character of many members. But when the members go bad, it is the pastor's fault according to many church members even though the pastor may have warned earnestly and faithfully about the evil of the TV programs. All that this blaming does is to reveal how little faith is in the members who blame the pastor.

Second, the *boasting* of their past prediction. It is bad enough that the Israelites should rail on Moses, but what makes it worse is that they boast to Moses about their own pessimistic, unbelief-filled prediction. "Is not this the word that we did tell thee in Egypt, saying, Let us alone, that we may serve the Egyptians?" (v. 12). How arrogant the flesh is. But in truth it only causes one to play the fool. If the Israelites were so smart, why did they follow Moses? Why did not they chart their own course if they knew so much better than Moses? Furthermore, what about all the predictions Moses made concerning the plagues and especially the protecting of the firstborn which came to pass? How poorly the flesh speaks when troubles come.

Third, the *belittling* of their present circumstances. "It had been better for us to serve the Egyptians than . . . die in the wilderness" (v. 12). This sick statement of the Israelites made to Moses is like those made by compromisers when communism was so dominate. They would say, "I'd rather be red than dead." But the true patriot says just the opposite. He says, "I'd rather be dead than red." This is the language of Patrick Henry who said, "Give me liberty or give me death."

This statement of the Israelites is so shortsighted. They had forgotten so quickly the cruelty of their bondage in Egypt where they were slaves, where they continually felt the deadly taskmaster's whip, and where they had to drown their male babies in the Nile. But when trials come, the vision of the flesh often becomes very poor. Only faith can see well in the darkness. George Wagner said, "It is the property of unbelief to make the heart think any other circumstances preferable to its own." How often we, like Israel, misjudge our circumstances. Israel was in a circumstance that would display mightily the power of God and give Israel one of the greatest moments in their history. Yet, when they first saw the circumstances, they thought the circumstances so bad that Egypt and slavery were better. Faith puts God in the circumstances, however; and that makes all the difference in the world how we view our circumstances.

The response to the plea. The nobility of Moses shines forth so brightly in how he responds to the Israelites here. "Never perhaps, was the fortitude of a man so severely tried as that of the Hebrew leader in this crisis, exposed as he was to various and inevitable dangers, the most formidable of which was the vengeance of a seditious and desperate multitude; but his meek, unruffled, magnanimous composure presents one of the sublimest examples of moral courage to be found in history" (Jamieson). Moses gave the Israelites a short but inspiring message that would comfort and encourage. "Instead of chiding them, he comforts them, and with an admirable presence and composure of mind, not disheartened either by the threatenings of Egypt or the tremblings of Israel, stills their murmuring, with the assurance of a speedy and complete deliverance" (Matthew Henry). We see this well in the precepts and promises Moses gave Israel.

First, the *precepts*. "Fear ye not, stand still . . . hold your peace" (vv. 13,14). The precepts were basically twofold. They had to do with peace and with patience. The precepts (which reflected the will of God, not just Moses' orders) would not be easy to do, for God's commands are seldom easy to do. But God's commands are always the right thing to do, and they can always be done. Furthermore, they must be done if we want the victory; for doing them is the key to victory.

The first precept had to do with *peace*. "Fear ye not" (v. 13). Matthew Henry wisely says, "It is our duty and interest, when we cannot get out of our troubles, yet to get above our fears, so that they may only serve to quicken our prayers and endeavors, but may not prevail to silence our faith and hope." That removing fear has to do with peace is seen in Judges 6:23: "And the LORD said unto him, Peace be unto thee; fear not." Without peace in our heart, we will not perform well. How necessary then is the message "fear not." Often in Scripture we see this message. God told Abraham, "Fear not, Abram; I am thy shield, and thy exceeding great reward" (Genesis 15:1). After the shocking defeat at Ai, God told Joshua, "Fear not, neither be thou dismayed; take all the people of war with thee" (Joshua 8:1). Gideon (Judges 6:23), Isaiah (Isaiah 35:4), and Daniel (Daniel 10:12) were also all acquainted with this great message. And when the angels announced the birth of Christ to the shepherds, their first words were, "Fear not" (Luke 2:10).

When God tells us we do not need to fear, we do not need to fear even though our circumstances would insist on the opposite. The world also tells us not to fear, but their message is a bogus one that imperils the souls of men. It is a false peace that slays. The world says we should not fear hell and the consequences of sin. It says we need not fear God and the failure to obey Him. But when it comes to the matter of fear, get your message from God, or you will discover what lasting fear is.

The second precept had to do with *patience*. "Stand still . . . hold your peace" (vv. 13,14). The flesh wants to be constantly doing something. It cannot wait for God's orders. It cannot wait for God to work. But Israel needed to "stand still" for awhile at Pi-hahiroth until God worked to divide the Red Sea. Had Israel got all excited and run hither and thither they would have become very confused and disorganized and, as a result, an orderly and efficient passing through the parted Red Sea would not have occurred. Patience is so essential in living successfully for God. Patience waits for God's orders, for God's time, and for God's choices—something the flesh will not do.

Second, the *promises*. "The salvation of the LORD, which he will show to you today; for the Egyptians whom ye have seen today, ye shall see them again no more for ever. The LORD shall fight for you" (vv. 13,14). The precepts of God came with promises. This is always the case with God. If a promise is not specifically stated with a precept, we still know that His precepts always in the end promise us blessings if we obey them. There were two promises in Moses' message to the Israelites— deliverance for the Israelites and destruction for the Egyptians.

The first promise spoke of *deliverance* for the Israelites. "See the salvation of the LORD . . . The LORD shall fight for you" (vv. 13,14). What an encouragement this promise was. Israel would be saved! Pharaoh's army would not slay them. God was on Israel's side. Israel had come to this situation in Pi-hahiroth because of God's orders; and when we come to Pi-hahiroth because of God's orders, you can be sure that God will fight for you when Pharaoh attacks you there. God does not forsake His own and leave them to be destroyed by the enemy when His own have followed Him! There are big benefits in following God's leading. One of them is "The LORD shall fight for you" (v. 14).

The second promise spoke of *destruction* for the Egyptians.

"The Egyptians whom ye have seen today, ye shall see them again no more for ever" (v. 13). Moses did not tell them how this would happen—it wasn't necessary to know how it would happen, and at that time Moses did not know how it would happen either. But he knew the promises of God, and we must cling to them whether we know or not the manner in which they will be fulfilled.

This promise was gloriously fulfilled in the destruction of Pharaoh and his army in the Red Sea. The Red Sea was the last place Israel saw them. Their actual last glimpse of any of the Egyptians was of the dead soldiers that floated to the shores.

D. THE PARTING OF THE SEA

To the natural eye, Israel had no way of escape. Pharaoh and his army were behind them, the mountains were to their right and in front of them, and the Red Sea was on their left. As is sometimes the case, God's people "may be in the way of our duty, following God and hastening towards heaven, and yet may be in great straits, troubled on every side, II Cor. 4:8" (Matthew Henry). But God is faithful and will make a way of escape for His people. The way of escape for Israel was through the parting of the Red Sea. But the way of escape for Israel was the way of entrapment for the Egyptians. What was a blessing to Israel was a curse to Egypt. What was life to Israel was death to Egypt (we will see this opposite effect of situations on Israel and Egypt again when we note the work of the cloud at the Red Sea).

1. The Escape of the Israelites

The miraculous dividing of the Red Sea to bring about Israel's escape from the peril of Pharaoh and his army should "encourage God's people in all ages to trust in him in the greatest straits. What cannot he do who did this. What will not he do for those that fear and love him who did this for these murmuring, unbelieving Israelites" (Matthew Henry). We want to note six aspects of this miraculous escape of the Israelites. They have to do with rebuking, commanding, lifting, blowing, drying, and walking. Moses was rebuked by the Lord, he was to command the people to go forward, he was to lift his rod to effect the parting of the sea, a great wind blew all night to part the sea, the sea bed was dried for the crossing, and Israel walked across the sea bed to safety.

The rebuking of Moses. "Wherefore criest thou unto me? speak unto the children of Israel, that they go forward" (v. 15). This text informs us indirectly that Moses had gone to God in prayer concerning the predicament Israel was in. Scripture, however, does not record the contents of Moses' prayer. Moses doubtless is glad that God did not have him record it; for by the way God spoke to him, the prayer had some fault to it. "While Moses presented an appearance of unbroken fortitude towards the people, rearing himself among them like a rock, before God he bent like a broken reed, crying to Him" (F. B. Meyer).

One fault in Moses' prayer which we can detect from Scripture was that it was too long, for God told Moses it was time to quit praying and start acting. Now this is a most unusual rebuke. The usual problem is that we do not pray enough. But this rebuke reminds us that "There is a time to act as well as a time to pray . . . It is wrong to act without deliberation and prayer; but it is also wrong to be deliberating when we ought to be acting. It is sin to 'go forward' without prayer; it is scarcely less so to be 'crying to God,' like the trembling paralyzed Israelites, when they ought to be going forward" (Wagner).

Prayer is to help our action, not stop it. Some, however, do indeed by an emphasis on prayer camouflage their disobedience to act. When we know what to do, we do not need to keep praying about what to do—we need to act. Insisting that we need to pray some more about it is nothing but a clever form of disobedience, and it does not fool God.

The commanding of Israel. God told Moses, "Speak unto the children of Israel, that they go forward" (v. 15). What a great command are the words "Go forward." Israel was not to retreat,

365

give up, surrender, or recant. They were to continue going on in their journey away from Egypt.

The command, however, seemed to mock common sense because Israel could not go forward. They were hemmed in on all sides. But when God commands, He will enable; and this situation certainly underscores that truth. God would part the Red Sea so Israel could go forward. Therefore, let God's people be ever in the attitude of going forward so when the door opens they will waste no time going through it. But, alas, our churches are often not of this mind. God wants the church to "go forward" and make progress in His work. However, the members often do not want to go forward. They want status quo and argue that it is not possible to go forward. They haven't realized that once they get in the attitude of willingness to go forward, they will be able to do so. Churches need to "go forward" in evangelism in their community, in missions, in building programs, and in schools. It may take a parting of some Red Sea obstacle to make it possible, but the biggest obstacle to going forward is seldom some Red Sea standing in the way—it is generally the stubborn attitude of the members who do not want to go forward. That explains why so many churches continually sit in shameful stagnation.

The lifting of the rod. God also told Moses to "lift thou up thy rod, and stretch out thine hand over the sea, and divide it" (v. 16). Lifting up the rod and holding it over the sea to bring about the dividing of the sea will to natural reasoning seem an utterly useless thing to do. But the lifting up of the rod was very important action. We note three reasons why it was important: it confessed faith, it certified leadership, and it confirmed the miraculous.

First, it *confessed faith.* When Moses lifted up his rod at the edge of the sea, he said by this action that he believed God. Often in the Scriptures when God is working miracles, He orders the person who is involved in working the miracle to do some seemingly small task or action. The task or action is unnecessary, of course, for God to work. But it gives opportunity for man to show his faith. And where there is faith, that is where God is pleased to work. That is what Hebrews 11 is all about. So it is here at the Red Sea. Before God works, faith must be demonstrated. And Moses demonstrated that faith in lifting the rod. Unbelief would have laughed at the command. It would have argued that lifting the rod was stupid and would not do a thing to help Israel or divide the sea. But faith knows better.

Second, it *certified leadership*. Moses' leadership was being challenged by the Israelites in their complaint about him leading them into a situation which seemed to be certain death. Indeed, as we noted earlier in the perplexity of going to Pi-hahiroth, natural reasoning would seriously question the wisdom of the direction taken. Now with Pharaoh pursuing them, the situation became even more unwise to the thinking of the flesh. So God goes to bat for Moses and gives him a task which will show Israel that Moses is still the certified leader of Israel. He is still the approved and appointed man in charge.

God will provide His servants with whatever they need to enable them to lead the people. He will verify their calling as he did for Moses here, and He will even provide for their reputation if they need that as did Joseph after he was released from many years of imprisonment.

Third, it *confirmed the miraculous*. With the Red Sea parting when Moses held up the rod, it was evident that Divine power was at work. Something more than Moses' rod was obviously at work. Mankind is so prone to look for a natural explanation for a miracle instead of recognizing that it was God Who did it. Therefore, we are not surprised to read often in Scripture that when God worked a miracle, what man did in regard to it being done is of such nature that it could not be used as an explanation for the miracle instead of God's power.

The blowing of the wind. "The LORD caused the sea to go back by a strong east wind all that night, and made the sea dry land, and the waters were divided" (v. 21). We note the blowing of the wind in order to refute the idea that a miracle really did not happen. The blowing of the wind does not take away the miraculous as some who want to deny the miraculous in the parting of the Red Sea would like it to do. Rather, the blowing of the wind emphasizes the miraculous; for no ordinary wind could do what that wind did. God had to be in it in a miraculous way for the wind to accomplish what it did. This was a miraculous wind, for it produced miraculous results which stayed that way until Moses "stretched forth his hand over the sea, and the sea returned" (v. 27). Furthermore, do not overlook the timing of the blowing of the wind in terms of a miracle. The wind was not only miraculous in how it blew but also in when it blew. It blew at just the right time to provide Israel with a way to escape from the Egyptians.

The drying of the sea bed. "Israel shall go on dry ground through the midst of the sea" (v. 16). Five times in Exodus (14:16,21,22,29 and 15:19) and once in Nehemiah 9:11, Psalm 66:6, and Hebrews 11:29 the dry ground fact is repeated. This emphasis on the dry ground is an emphasis on the miraculous. Whenever a river, creek, or lake dries up, the water bed takes a long time to become dry. So not only was it a miracle that the Red Sea was parted, but the drying was a miracle, too. Had the ground not been dry, it would have quickly become a muddy quagmire making it impossible for man or beast to travel on it successfully. Yet, at least two million Israelites and all their thousands and thousands of cattle and other beasts made it across the bed of the parted Red Sea without any difficulty whatsoever. The ground was rock-hard dry to say the least. Exodus 15:8 emphasizes that fact when it says, "The depths were congealed in the heart of the sea." The dry and hard sea bed truly underscores the greatness of the miracle.

The dry ground also takes away any natural explanation about the water parting. Earthquakes and other natural phenomena have caused rivers and lakes to make sudden changes temporarily. But to dry the ground is another story. The same is true about the crossing of the Jordan forty years later. Those who despise miracles insist it wasn't a miracle but that some event like a landslide on the narrow, curving Jordan temporarily caused the water to stop so Israel could cross. But such an explanation is no explanation at all, for it does not provide for the drying of the ground which is an absolute necessity if the crossing is to be successful. Elijah and Elisha also are said in Scripture to have crossed the Jordan "on dry ground" (II Kings 2:8) when Elijah parted the waters with his mantle. Don't miss the emphasis on the dry ground in all these crossings, for it amplifies the greatness of the miracle and refutes natural explanations.

The walking across the sea bed. "The children of Israel walked upon dry land" (v. 29). The writer of Hebrews tells us it was "by faith" (Hebrews 11:29) that the Israelites went across the Red Sea. It is indeed not difficult to see that it was by faith. With the water stacked up as "a wall unto them on their right hand, and on their left" (v. 22), it would take much faith to walk down to the sea bed and start walking across the sea. Anyone could quickly size up the situation and see that if those walls of water were to suddenly collapse, there would be no escape as the Egyptians discovered later. But Israel ventured down the bank of the Red Sea onto the sea bed trusting God to keep the water back as they traversed the sea bed.

Arthur Pink pointed out an instructive lesson when he said that the "walking" and not running demonstrated the confidence the Israelites had in God. "He that believeth shall not make haste" (Isaiah 28:16), a text many would like to use pervertedly to justify their sluggishness in doing God's work, applies here in the walking.

2. The Entrapment of the Egyptians

The divided sea, though it was salvation for the Israelites, was a snare for the Egyptians. It trapped Pharaoh and his army, and it trapped them permanently. To examine this entrapment, we will note the darkness before the entrapment, the driving into the entrapment, the disturbance in the entrapment, and the drowning by the entrapment.

The darkness before the entrapment. "And the angel of God, which went before the camp of Israel, removed and went behind them; and the pillar of the cloud went from before their face, and stood behind them; And it came between the camp of the Egyptians and the camp of Israel; and it was a cloud and darkness to them, but it gave light by night to these; so that the one came not near the other all the night" (vv. 19,20). God worked marvelously in that at the same time in which He used "the pillar of the cloud" to help the Israelites, He used it to also hinder Pharaoh and the Egyptian army. This movement of the cloud was to "prevent them [the Egyptians] from stirring till near daybreak . . . to secure their inaction, the pillar was made to overshadow them with a deep and preternatural darkness, so that it became almost impossible for them to advance. Meanwhile, on the side which was turned towards the Israelites, the pillar presented the appearance of a bright flame, lighting up the whole encampment, and rendering it as easy to make ready for the march as it would have been by day" (Rawlinson).

"It is at once most solemn and interesting to note the double aspect of the 'pillar' in this chapter. 'It was a cloud and darkness' to the Egyptians, but 'it gave light by night' to Israel. How like the cross of our Lord Jesus Christ! Truly, that cross has a double aspect likewise. It forms the foundation of the believer's peace, and, at the same time, seals the condemnation of a guilty world. The self-same blood which purges the believer's conscience and gives him perfect peace, stains this earth and consummates its guilt. The very mission of the Son of God which strips the world of its cloak, and leaves it wholly without excuse, clothes the Church with a fair mantle of righteousness, and fills her mouth with ceaseless praise. The very same Lamb who will terrify, by His unmitigated wrath, all tribes and classes of earth, will lead, by His gentle hand, His blood-bought flock through the green pastures and besides the still waters forever"

(Mackintosh). Alexander Maclaren describes similar contrasts which the cloud pictures. He said, "The ark which slew the Philistines and flung Dagon prone on his own threshold, brought blessings to the house of Obed-edom. The Child who was to be 'set for the fall,' was also for 'the rising of many.' The stone laid in Zion is 'a sure foundation,' and 'a stone of stumbling.' The Gospel is the savour of life unto life, or of death unto death (II Corinthians 2:16). The same fire melts wax and hardens clay. The same Christ is salvation and destruction. God is to each of us either our joy or our dread." May we so live our lives that Divine manifestations will be a blessing to us and not a curse. May our spiritual opportunities and advantages be used in such a way that they will multiply our blessings instead of increase our condemnation. They will do one or the other. It all depends on how we use them.

The driving into the entrapment. "I will harden the hearts of the Egyptians, and they shall follow them . . . And the Egyptians pursued, and went in after them to the midst of the sea, even all Pharaoh's horses, his chariots, and his horsemen" (vv. 17,23). When the cloud lifted so the Egyptians could see, they without caution pursued the Israelites through the path made in the sea for the Israelites' escape. Matthew Poole describes the Egyptians' actions very succinctly and accurately with two words: "Prodigious stupidity!" They paid no attention to the precariousness of their situation nor did they give any thought to the fact that being a Divine miracle, they were fighting against Jehovah God and would obviously risk being drowned in the sea. No, they were hardened and, hence, blinded by sin. "God hardened them to their ruin, and hid from their eyes the things that belonged to their peace and safety" (Matthew Henry).

The driving by the Egyptians into an obvious entrapment is not an unique experience for sinners. The writer of Proverbs describes the man going after an adulteress in the same fashion. He said, "He goeth after her straightway . . . as a bird hasteth to the snare, and knoweth not that it is for his life" (Proverbs

7:22, 23). Hardened sinners, like the Egyptians, become blind to their perilous situation. They no longer can see or hear warnings. They miss the obvious, and so in glee and earnestness run into the snare that will destroy them. All of this says we must fight sin in the bud if we want to escape the snare of sin.

The disturbance in the entrapment. "And it came to pass, that in the morning watch the LORD looked unto the host of the Egyptians through the pillar of fire and of the cloud, and troubled the host of the Egyptians, And took off their chariot wheels, that they drave them heavily; so that the Egyptians said, Let us flee from the face of Israel; for the LORD fighteth for them against the Egyptians" (vv. 24, 25). God disturbed the Egyptians in three major areas. He disturbed their hearts, their headway (progress), and their heading (direction).

First, God disturbed their *hearts*. Our text says God "looked unto the host of the Egyptians through the pillar of fire and of the cloud, and troubled the host of the Egyptians" (v. 24). The word translated "troubled" means "to agitate, to put to rout [confusion], to discomfort" (Wilson). We can all identify with the great effect of just a look from someone. It can rejoice and bless or it can put untold fear into one's heart. Maclaren said, "There is something very terrible in . . . that phrase 'the LORD looked . . . through the pillar.' It curdles the blood as no minuteness of narrative would do."

At the Red Sea, God took away Israel's fear by telling them to "fear ye not" (v. 13). But at the Red Sea, God, with this disturbing look, did just the opposite for the Egyptians by giving them great fear. The difference is that the Israelites were under the blood, the Egyptians were not. So it is in life. When the saint comes to the end of life, he finds peace in the Lord. But when the sinner comes to the end of his life, it is terrible horror.

Second, God disturbed their *headway*. "And took off their chariot wheels, that they drave them heavily" (v. 25). On the ground that Israel passed over so successfully, the Egyptians ran into some big trouble. Their chariot wheels began to come off.

We are told in the Psalms that during this time the "clouds poured out water; the skies sent out a sound; thine arrows also went abroad. The voice of thy thunder was in the heaven; the lightnings lightened the world; the earth trembled and shook" (Psalm 77:17,18). With such a storm descending on the Egyptians, the dry sea bed would quickly become a quagmire of mud. This would cause the chariot wheels to become clogged and mired down in the mud and to come off their axles. The soldiers could not move well in this quagmire either. God, of course, was in control of all of this. He slowed down greatly the headway of the Egyptians so they could not catch up to the Israelites.

Third, God disturbed their *heading*. With all the disturbance of heart and headway, the Egyptians' heading also became disturbed. "The Egyptians said, Let us flee from the face of Israel; for the LORD fighteth for them against the Egyptians" (v. 25). The Egyptians decided it was time to reverse their heading; for they rightly concluded that God was fighting for Israel, and Egypt could not win in such circumstances. Moses had told the Israelites that "The LORD shall fight for you" (v. 14), and now the Egyptians testify that this was so. We need to live so that God will fight for us as He did for the Israelites, and not against us as He did against the Egyptians.

The Egyptians, of course, had waited too long to change their direction. But this is the fate of the hardened sinner. He embraces his sin and will not let go, therefore, he becomes hardened and blind to his peril. Only when he can no longer escape does he suddenly have his eyes opened to see his peril. What a bad time to begin to see.

The drowning by the entrapment. "And the LORD said unto Moses, Stretch out thine hand over the sea, that the waters may come again upon the Egyptians . . . And Moses stretched forth his hand over the sea . . . And the waters returned, and covered the chariots, and the horsemen, and all the host of Pharaoh . . . there remained not so much as one of them" (vv. 26–28). This judgment was fatal, fitting, and fearful.

First, it was *fatal*. When the waters returned to their place in the Red Sea, they "covered" (v. 28) the Egyptians. The violently cascading waters quickly submerged the pursuing Egyptians. The Egyptians soldiers "sank into the bottom as a stone . . . [and] sank as lead in the mighty waters . . . the earth swallowed them [that is, the bodies sank into the sands of the sea bed]" (Exodus 15:5,10,12). Helping them to sink so speedily was the fact that many of the soldiers were weighted down with heavy military armament. As an example, "The warriors who fought in chariots commonly wore coats of mail, composed of bronze plates sewn on to a linen base, and overlapping one another. The coats covered the arms to the elbow, and descended nearly to the knee. They must have been exceedingly heavy; and the warrior who wore one must have sunk at once, without a struggle, like a stone or a lump of lead" (Rawlinson).

Scripture emphasizes that this fatal judgment of drowning included everyone that came from Egypt to attack the Israelites. "There remained not so much as one of them" (v. 28). It not only killed Pharaoh, but it destroyed his elite military men as well as the rest of his army. Israel no longer had to be concerned about any Egyptian attack in the wilderness. "The death of Pharaoh, and the entire loss of the chariotry and cavalry accounts for the undisturbed retreat [journey] of the Israelites through a district then subject to Egypt and easily accessible to their forces" (F. C. Cook).

In view of the description of the drowning of the Egyptians, we are surprised to read that some do not believe that Pharaoh was included in this drowning. But other Scripture plainly refutes that idea. Psalm 136:15 states that God "overthrew Pharaoh and his host in the Red sea." Pharaoh would be leading the troops, for this was customary. "The station of the king was in the vanguard: on every monument the Pharaoh is represented as the leader of the army" (F. C. Cook). Had Pharaoh not been killed, Israel would have experienced more attacks; for no judgment of God that left Pharaoh alive ever finally stopped Pharaoh from pursuing Israel. Exodus 15:19 states that "the horse of

Pharaoh went in" which would also indicate Pharaoh was drowned. But the Hebrew word translated "horse" in this verse is plural, not singular which makes verse 19 parallel to verse 23 of chapter 14. But the word "horse" being plural does not mean Pharaoh was not drowned with the rest of the troops.

Second, it was *fitting*. In the Egyptian bondage, one of the Pharaohs had decreed that Israel must drown all their male children. This was going on when Moses was born. Now the Egyptians in the loss of Pharaoh and his military through drowning fittingly reap the drowning seed that was sown in their land. We reap what we sow. This lesson has been seen time and time again in our study of Israel and their Egyptian bondage and the plagues upon Egypt. Let us not take this truth lightly. When God repeats something, it is because it is important. With God repeating this truth again and again in our study of Moses, it should prod us to earnestly examine our own life to see what seeds we are sowing and to make sure we are sowing only good seeds.

Third, it was *fearful*. "And Israel saw the Egyptians dead upon the sea shore. And Israel saw that great work which the LORD did upon the Egyptians; and the people feared the LORD, and believed the LORD, and his servant Moses" (vv. 30,31). The judgment upon the Egyptians had a very positive effect upon the Israelites. It produced godly *fear* in them. This fear promoted their *faith* in God and helped them to *follow* Moses better. Would that all calamities in our lives would improve our belief in God and our behavior towards mankind.

XV.

SONG OF VICTORY

EXODUS 15:1–21

EMANCIPATION BROUGHT JUBILATION for Israel. Freed from Egypt after the death of the firstborn, Israel's freedom appeared to be short-lived when Pharaoh decided to pursue them at Pihahiroth by the Red Sea. But God parted the sea for the escape of the Israelites and then closed it for the end of Pharaoh and his army. This great deliverance at the Red Sea sealed Israel's freedom, and it inspired the Israelites to lift up their voices in a song of victory to celebrate the fact that "the LORD . . . hath triumphed gloriously" (v. 1) in the combat with Pharaoh.

Moses was very much involved in this singing. He not only led the singing—"Then sang Moses and the children of Israel" (v. 1)—but he was, in fact, also the author of the song that was sung as we will see shortly. This song which he composed was a great song and poem. And it has lived on for some three millenniums inspiring people to lofty creeds and deeds.

To study this song of victory, we will consider the prologue to the song (v. 1), the praise in the song (vv. 1–13,19–21), and the prophecies in the song (vv. 13–18).

A. THE PROLOGUE TO THE SONG

As a prologue or an introduction to this song of victory, we will note the author, antiquity, antecedent, arrangement, affirmation, and accompanists of the song.

1. The Author of the Song

"Then sang Moses" (v. 1). As we noted above, Moses is the

author of this song sung on the eastern shores of the Red Sea. Scripture does not statedly say that Moses is the author. But "It is in accordance with the general modesty of Moses, that he says nothing of the composition of the 'song.' No serious doubt of his authorship has ever been entertained; but the general belief rests on the improbability of there having been among the Israelites a second literary genius of the highest order, without any mention being made of him" (Rawlinson). We know from Moses' authorship of the Pentateuch that he could write prose with excellence. From his song here and his song in Deuteronomy 32:1–43 and also his writing of Psalm 90, we learn that Moses not only had literary excellence in writing prose, but he could also write poetry with excellence.

Moses was a very gifted man. He had great leadership abilities, could devise military strategy with the best of them, was superb in the work of government, counseled with great sagacity, was one of the greatest religious leaders in the history of mankind, was a man "mighty in words" (Acts 7:22), and, as we can see in this song, being "mighty in words" was not in speech only, but also in pen; for Moses wrote with brilliance.

With his gifts and abilities, one can understand why God got upset with him at the burning bush when Moses tried through various excuses to exempt himself from the Divine summons to be Israel's emancipator. But after Moses surrendered to God's call, he employed all his talents to the fulfillment of his calling in a most exemplary way. God gives us talents primarily for use in His service. However, a good many folk have not learned that truth yet or in rebellion will not submit to that truth.

2. The Antiquity of the Song

This song of victory is the first song and poem in the Scriptures. It is also one of the earliest songs and poems we have in antiquity. Some believe it to be the oldest. Jamieson said, "This song is by some hundred years the oldest poem in the world"; and W. M. Taylor said, "It is presumably the oldest poem in the world." Whether it is the oldest poem and song or not, it certainly is a song of excellence. Too bad all the songs of men that followed Moses' song did not follow its example in character and contents. The trash that passes for songs today has no relationship whatsoever to the song sung by the banks of the Red Sea. And this trash includes much that goes under the heading of music in our church services, too. The song at the Red Sea was one of victory over evil. But by the sound of that which passes for music in many of our churches today, many songs are songs of victory over good instead.

The antiquity of the song gives significant evidence that the contents of the song are from Divine inspiration. W. M. Taylor says in this regards, "Long before the ballads of Homer were sung through the streets of the Grecian cities, or the foundation of the Seven-hilled metropolis [Rome] of the ancient world was laid by the banks of the Tiber, this matchless ode . . . was chanted by the leader of the emancipated Hebrews on the Red Sea shore; and yet we have in it no polytheism, no foolish mythological story concerning gods and goddesses, no gilding of immorality, no glorification of mere force; but instead, the firmest recognition of the personality, the supremacy, the holiness, the retributive rectitude of God. How shall we account for all of this? If we admit the Divine legation [mission] and inspiration of Moses, all is plain." Moses did not write from the inspiration of the culture and society of ancient Egypt. If he had, he would never have written such wonderful creed as is in this song. Truly Moses wrote under the inspiration of Almighty God.

3. The Antecedent of the Song

We learn the antecedent of this song in the word "Then" of verse 1. It was not until "Then" that Moses and the Israelites sang in jubilation. What does the "Then" refer to? It, of course, refers to the deliverance of the Red Sea. When Israel was delivered at the Red Sea, "Then" they could sing. "Up to this moment, we have not heard so much as a single note of praise. We have heard their cry of deep sorrow as they toiled amid the brick-kilns of Egypt . . . [and] their cry of unbelief when surrounded by what they deemed insuperable difficulties, but, until now, we have heard no song of praise. It was not until, as saved people, they found themselves surrounded by the fruits of God's salvation, that the triumphal hymn burst forth from the whole redeemed assembly" (Mackintosh). Arthur Pink spoke likewise when he said, "What a contrast is this [song] from what was before us in the earlier chapters! While in the house of bondage, no joyful strains were upon the lips of the Hebrews. Instead, we read that they *'sighed* by reason of the bondage, and they *cried* and God heard their *groaning'* [Exodus 2:24, 25]. But now their sighing gives place to singing; their groans to praising."

God's deliverance inspired Israel's hearts and voices to sing. It is always so. God's salvation of man has produced the finest music in the world. No inspiration is greater for great music than this. George Felix Handel's great oratorio, the Messiah, is an example of this truth. It is performed year after year at the Christmas season to large audiences. Why does it live on more than other music? Because it is about redemption and the Great Redeemer. While many sing its lyrics without much understanding of its message, that does not distract from the reason the music lives on. The antecedent for the oratorio was the same as for Moses' song—the message of redemption. Take out all the great music of the world that has to do with God's deliverance of man, and you will not have much good music left.

4. The Arrangement of the Song

This song of victory is capable of being divided into many and sundry parts. Basically the song has two parts. In our study of this song, we have called the first part praise and the second part prophecy. Rawlinson calls them retrospective and prospective. The first part looks back at what God did at the Red Sea. The second part looks ahead at what God is going to do in the future—if He can do what He did at the Red Sea, it predicts that He will do many more great works in the future. Past victory encourages future victory. Some divide the first part into three subdivisions each beginning with a description of the working of God at the Red Sea with it climaxing in the destruction of the Egyptians. Thus subdivision one ends, "they sank into the bottom as a stone" (v. 5), subdivision two ends "they sank as lead in the mighty waters" (v. 10), and subdivision three ends "the earth swallowed them" (v. 12). The second main division may also be divided into three subdivisions with the first subdivision being predictions about the heathen nations, the second subdivision being predictions about Israel, and the third subdivision being a prediction about the reigning of Jehovah.

These notations about the arrangement of the song are given to encourage the reader to study the song thoroughly and to make his own outlines and divisions of the song. Many outlines and divisions are possible and can be made according to the many different features of the song. The one thing we see in all of these analytical possibilities of the song is that this song evidences that Scripture is not a literary junk pile as the critics like to say it is. Rather the song evidences that Scripture need not take a back seat to any other literature of mankind. The Bible is the greatest piece of literature ever given to man. Reading and studying it only verifies that fact over and over again.

5. The Affirmation of the Song

"The LORD is *my* strength and song, and he is become *my* salvation; he is *my* God, and *I* will prepare him an habitation; *my* father's God, and *I* will exalt him" (v. 2). This song of victory affirms the faith of Moses and the singers. They believe God. They claim Jehovah God as their God. We have italicized each "my" and "I" in this verse to emphasize that this song is indeed speaking of personal faith in Jehovah God.

The Psalmist verifies that this song declared the faith of the singers when he said, "And the waters covered their enemies; there was not one of them left. Then believed they his words; and sang his praise" (Psalm 106:11,12). "Then" in this text in Psalms corresponds to the "Then" of our text in Exodus 15:1. The same truth is seen in "I believed, therefore have I spoken" (Psalm 116:10) with the "therefore" of that verse corresponding

380

to the "Then" of Exodus 15:1 and Psalm 106:12. The principle in these verses in Psalms and in our Exodus text is that faith opens the mouth in jubilation—it causes the heart to *rejoice* in God, in veneration—it causes the heart to *reverence* God, and in proclamation—it causes the heart to *report* about God. Let us elaborate a bit on each of these three truths.

First, faith promotes *jubilation*. Faith says, "He is my God" (v. 2). The Psalmist enlightens us as to what this does to the heart. He says, "Happy is that people, whose God is the LORD" (Psalm 144:15) and "Happy is he that hath the God of Jacob for his help, whose hope is in the LORD his God" (Psalm 146:5). Every one of us who are redeemed knows about the joy that comes with salvation when we put our trust in Jesus Christ and He becomes *my* Savior. The world mocks the need of God; but the world misses real joy, too.

Second, faith promotes *veneration*. Without faith we cannot and will not truly worship God. "Not only is worship impossible for those yet dead in trespasses and sins, but intelligent worship cannot be rendered by professing Christians who are in doubt as to their standing before God . . . Praise and joy are essential elements of worship; but how can those who question their acceptance in the Beloved, who are not certain whether they would go to Heaven or Hell should they die this moment—how could such be joyful and thankful? Impossible!" (Pink).

Third, faith promotes *proclamation*. Without faith one has no message of faith to proclaim. The apostates' message reflects their unbelief in God's Word, and the de-emphasis on the message in our churches reveals a deficiency of faith in God's Word.

6. The Accompanists of the Song

"And Miriam the prophetess, the sister of Aaron [she is also the sister of Moses], took a timbrel in her hand; and all the women went out after her with timbrels and with dances. And Miriam answered them, Sing ye to the LORD, for he hath triumphed gloriously; the horse and his rider hath he thrown into the sea" (vv. 20,21). The women give accompaniment to the song of victory with their timbrels and their voices. "Famous victories were wont to be applauded by the daughters of Israel (I Samuel 19:6,7), so was this" (Matthew Henry).

On the surface of the text, several problems present themselves regarding Miriam's choir of women. They are the problem of dominion and the problem of dancing.

First, the problem of *dominion*. Pink said, "Some persons have experienced a difficulty here in that Miriam also *led* in this Song of Victory. It seems to clash with the teaching of the New Testament, which enjoins the subordination of women to the men in the assembly. But the difficulty is self-created. There is nothing here which in anywise conflicts with I Corinthians 14:34 . . . [for] it was *only* women (v. 20) whom Miriam led in song! . . . Thus Divine order was preserved." And so Miriam's leading the women in singing does not give an example that would encourage women to be song leaders in a church service or that would encourage women to perform other functions in church which belong solely to man.

Second, the problem of *dancing*. The apostate church today is bringing the dance into their worship service. To us Bible-believing fundamentalists, this is utterly repugnant, immoral, and blasphemous. But in view of our position, what do we say about the fact that Scripture says Miriam led the women "with dances" (v. 20). Does that put her and the other women in the same category as the apostates of our day? Does that justify dance in our worship services? No, we most certainly do not believe that it does. Rawlinson gives a good explanation to this problem when he says, "In the nature of things, there is clearly nothing unfitting or indecorous in a dedication to religion of what has been called 'the poetry of gesture.' But human infirmity [depravity] has connected such terrible abuses with the practice that the purer religions have . . . denied it admission into their ceremonial." What we call dancing today was certainly not what Miriam and her choir was doing. But the vulgar and unholy of our day refuse to acknowledge the difference and would bring into the worship of God the vilest of conduct.

B. THE PRAISE IN THE SONG

The underlying theme of this song of victory is praise for Jehovah God. What a great theme! It should be the theme of our life. He is the One we need to be more concerned about honoring than anyone else. The world, however, is not honoring God; rather, it dishonors Him. But this song honors God. It makes honoring God its major theme. Right at the beginning of the song, we are told the song's main purpose—"I will exalt him" (v. 2). This truth is also stated in the sentence, "I will prepare him an habitation" (Ibid.). That this sentence also speaks of exalting God is learned from the fact that it is better translated "I will glorify him." This better translation of the Hebrew makes it a logical poetic parallel to the "I will exalt him" sentence. All in all, the emphasis is praise for Jehovah.

The emphasis on the exalting of Jehovah is also found in the fact that the name Jehovah (LORD in our English translations) occurs fourteen times in the twenty-one verses of our text of the song. Furthermore, the pronouns "he," "him," "thy," "thou," and "thee" which refer to Jehovah are found over thirty times in the song which means God is spoken of between forty and fifty times in the twenty-one verses in the Scripture text about this song. Truly, this is obviously not a song of the world; for God is so prominent throughout this song. Would that we had more songs like that. But in our day, men are pushing God out of their lives—and the music that is heard so much in the world reflects this fact very pronouncedly.

We will note five specific areas in which Jehovah's praises are sung in the song. They include the successes of God, the strength of God, the salvation by God, the sanctity of God, and the superiority of God. These are very important truths concerning God. They give us a creed upon which we can build our faith—a creed that is second to none.

1. The Successes of God

The song of victory speaks of a number of ways in which God was successful in His combat with Pharaoh. First it summarizes the successes by saying, "He hath triumphed gloriously" (v. 2). Then it continues by saying, "He is become my salvation" (Ibid.) which says God was successful in delivering Israel from Pharaoh. Success over Pharaoh is also cited in "Pharaoh's chariots and his host hath he cast into the sea; his chosen captains also are drowned in the Red sea. The depths have covered them; they sank into the bottom as a stone" (vv. 4,5). The continuing of the saga of success in combating Pharaoh and his armies is seen in "Dashed in pieces the enemy . . . overthrown them . . . consumed them" (vv. 6,7). Other success statements include "Thou didst blow with thy wind, the sea covered them; they sank as lead in the mighty waters . . . Thou stretchedst out thy right hand, the earth swallowed them" (vv. 10,12). Jehovah battled with Pharaoh, and it was all Jehovah. Pharaoh lost everything in the battle. Jehovah was the grand victor. Jehovah is not like the gods of the heathen who are often defeated in battle. Jehovah is never defeated. He is always successful.

Things have not changed. God is still successful in whatever He attempts to do. The devil and wicked man will not defeat God! It may look at times to human eyes that Satan is winning. But he is not; for when the battle is over, he will be a most defeated foe. God and His Word shall prevail! "So shall my word be that goeth forth out of my mouth; it shall not return unto me void, but it shall accomplish that which I please, and it shall prosper in the thing whereto I sent it" (Isaiah 55:11) is Isaiah's testimony regarding the success of God and His Word. That text ought to thrill the heart of every saint of God. The world would try to picture the saint as a loser. But the saint is on the side of success where it counts the most. On the other hand, beware of rebelling against God. You will never be successful in such a foolish endeavor.

2. The Strength of God

The great omnipotence of God is extolled repeatedly by Moses in this song—"The horse and his rider hath he thrown into the sea" (v. 1), "Pharaoh's chariots and his host hath he cast into the sea" (v. 4), "Thy right hand, O LORD, is become glorious in power" (v. 6), "Thy right hand, O LORD, hath dashed in pieces the enemy" (Ibid.), "Thou hast overthrown them that rose up against thee" (v. 7), "With the blast of thy nostrils the waters were gathered together [God is so powerful that just blowing His nose can destroy Pharaoh and his army!]" (v. 8), "Thou didst blow with thy wind, the sea covered them" (v. 10), "doing wonders" (v. 11), and "Thou stretchedst out thy right hand, the earth swallowed them" (v. 12).

All these references to God's power show that His power had been abundantly proven. He had just overthrown and destroyed the powerful Egyptian army and marvelously divided the Red Sea. God's power can overcome the greatest forces of man; and, as the song confirms, God also has power over the creation as well. Like the success of God, the strength of God should also encourage our faith in Him and discourage our rebellion against Him.

It is instructive for us to take note here about the term "thy right hand" which is used three times in this song (verse 6 twice, and verse 12 once). This is the first of many times this anthropomorphism is used of God in Scripture. The term speaks of power inasmuch as the right hand is the predominant hand in most people and, therefore, the strongest hand. The use of this figure regarding God demonstrates the greatness of His power. His power (His right hand) is unsurpassed. Nothing can overcome the power of God.

3. The Salvation by God

This entire song is about how Jehovah God saved His people. "He is become my salvation" (v. 2) is the testimony of the song. Israel's deliverance at the Red Sea certainly illustrates the Gospel. Therefore, we want to note here six aspects of the deliverance at the Red Sea which illustrate the salvation of the soul.

First, the *greatness* of salvation. The greatness of the salvation at the Red Sea is seen in its completeness. It made Israel's deliverance from Egypt complete. The enemy was totally destroyed. Never again would Pharaoh be a threat to the Israelites. God completely destroyed them in the Red Sea. So it is with soul salvation. When God saves us, we are forever delivered from the enemy of our soul. No longer is eternal damnation a threat to the soul. No wonder the writer of Hebrews calls it "so great salvation" (Hebrews 2:3).

Second, the *grace* in salvation. Wherever you find salvation by God, you will find the grace of God. So we are not surprised to read, "Thy mercy hast led forth the people which thou hast redeemed" (v. 13). Indeed it was mercy. Israel was stubborn, slow to believe God, and murmuring and complaining at the Red Sea. But God still delivered them. Israel had nothing in which they can boast about in their salvation. God did not deliver them because of their merit but because of His mercy.

Third, the *gaining* of salvation. Israel's salvation from the Egyptian tyranny is spoken of in terms of "the people which thou hast redeemed" (v. 13) and "the people . . . which thou hast purchased" (v. 16). We gain our salvation through redemption. Redemption involves a price and purchasing. God paid the price, and thus He purchased us in salvation. That says plenty in terms of practical application. Paul states it well when he says, "Ye are not your own . . . Ye are bought with a price; therefore glorify God in your body, and in your spirit, which are God's" (I Corinthians 6:19,20). In soul salvation the price is more than any man could possibly pay. Yet, God paid it willingly. That indeed obligates us to Him! Let us not shirk our service. Let us not turn from His will for our life. We have no right to do that! We belong to Him and must be absolutely subject to Him. Many folk rejoice in what God does for us in redemption, but they fail miserably to see what redemption means *we* must do. They like the privileges of redemption but not the responsibilities.

Fourth, the *gladness* of salvation. As we have noted before, salvation brought jubilation. This whole song bespeaks a glad heart. What great rejoicing must have gone on after this great deliverance at the Red Sea. And what great joy soul salvation brings to a person, too. Hence, the hymn "O, Happy Day" which speaks of the day of our salvation.

Fifth, the *guide* after salvation. It is significant that after the deliverance of the Israelites, this song of deliverance speaks of being "guided . . . unto thy holy habitation" (v. 13). This is in accord with soul salvation. After salvation we obtain a guide in the Holy Spirit. "For as many as are led by the Spirit of God, they are the sons of God" (Romans 8:14).

Sixth, the *glorifying* from salvation. After the deliverance at the Red Sea, Israel's prestige rose greatly in the eyes of other nations. Before their deliverance they would be viewed as just a bunch of despised slaves. But after the deliverance, Israel's honor suddenly shot upward. We will note more about this later. Suffice it to note here that because of this salvation for Israel, "The people [other nations] shall hear, and be afraid" (v. 14). This is true in soul salvation, too. Salvation takes those that are in the bondage (slavery) of sin and glorifies them in Christ. "Whom he justified, them he also glorified" (Romans 8:30). That is the theme of the hymn, "O, That Will Be Glory for Me" which Charles M. Alexander, the famed song leader of years past, called, "The glory song."

4. The Sanctity of God

God's holiness permeates this song. It is summed up in that great phrase, "glorious in holiness" (v. 11). The holiness of God is the fundamental attribute of God. Take it away and all the other attributes take on a much different and lesser light. But God is holy. Therefore, His hatred of sin is sanctified as well as sure. To evil "The Lord is a man of war" (v. 3) because of His holiness. His holiness causes Him to "sentest forth thy wrath" (v. 7) upon wicked Pharaoh and his army. Because He is holy, He is "fearful in praises" (v. 11) to the wicked. Indeed, when the wicked hear His holiness extolled, it will cause them to shake and tremble. This is what Scripture is speaking of when it says, "And the kings of the earth, and the great men, and the rich men, and the chief captains, and the mighty men, and every bondman, and every free man, hid themselves in the dens and in the rocks of the mountains; And said to the mountains and rocks, Fall on us, and hide us from the face of him that sitteth on the throne, and from the wrath of the Lamb; For the great day of his wrath is come; and who shall be able to stand?" (Revelation 6:15–17).

Arthur W. Pink said regarding the fact that God is holy and "a man of war" (v. 3) and sends "forth his wrath" (v. 7) upon evil that "This brings before us an aspect of the Divine character which is very largely ignored today . . . because He is holy, He hates sin; because He is righteous He must punish it. This is something for which the believer should rejoice; if he does not, something is wrong with him. It is only the sickly sentimentality of the flesh which shrinks from believing and meditating upon these Divine perfections. Far different was it here with Israel at the Red Sea. They praised God because He dealt in judgment with those who so stoutly defied Him."

5. The Superiority of God

In this song, Moses speaks of the superiority of God over other gods. The song asks, "Who is like unto thee, O Lord, among the gods? who is like thee, glorious in holiness, fearful in praises, doing wonders?" (v. 11). Egypt had a multitude of gods, but the song said Jehovah was superior all of them! "It was one great object of the whole series of miraculous visitations whereof Egypt had been the scene, that the true God, Jehovah, should be exalted far above all the gods of the earth" (Rawlinson). The plagues occurred so that "The Egyptians shall know that I am the LORD, when I stretch forth mine hand upon Egypt" (7:5). Also the Red Sea deliverance occurred so "that the Egyptians may know that I am the LORD" (14:4). F. C. Cook said, "A Hebrew just leaving the land in which Polytheism attained it highest development, with gigantic statues and temples of incomparable grandeur, might well on such an occasion dwell upon this consummation of the long series of triumphs by which the 'greatness beyond compare' of Jehovah was once for all established."

Today, though we may not have pagan gods to compete with the true God, we still allow circumstances and situations to be greater than God. Thus we make our trials and troubles a god who can overcome The God. Shame on us! Our little faith is no little dishonor for God! But God is superior to all. Let us pray that we will let this truth grip us with a vise-like grip that we might triumph in all our circumstances for the glory of our Great and Superior God.

C. THE PROPHECIES IN THE SONG

As we noted earlier, after seeing how great God was at the Red Sea, it is logical to predict He will be great in the future. The prophecies logically follow the praise. Matthew Henry said, "Our experiences of God's power and favor should be improved for the support of our expectations. 'Thou *hast*, therefore, not only thou *canst*, but we trust thou *wilt*,' is good arguing." We note the three major areas of prophecies in this song Moses wrote. They are the prophecies concerning the consternation for nations, the country for Israel, and the crown for Jehovah.

1. The Consternation for Nations

"The people shall hear, and be afraid; sorrow shall take hold of the inhabitants of Palestina. Then the dukes of Edom shall be amazed; the mighty men of Moab, trembling shall take hold upon them; all the inhabitants of Canaan shall melt away. Fear and dread shall fall upon them" (vv. 14–16). This particular prophecy of Moses in the song was certainly proven true in Israel's immediate history. Scripture reports that much consternation and much trepidation came to the nations in the area concerning Israel. "Esau [Edom] . . . they shall be afraid of you" (Deuteronomy 2:4). "Moab was sore afraid of the people" (Numbers 22:3), and Balak their king tried to get Balaam to curse Israel (Numbers 22–24). The fear of the people in Canaan is expressed by Rahab of Jericho when she said, "I know that the LORD hath given you the land, and that your terror is fallen upon us, and that all the inhabitants of the land faint because of you. For we have heard how the LORD dried up the water of the Red sea for you, when ye came out of Egypt; and what ye did unto the two kings of the Amorites, that were on the other side Jordan, Sihon and Og, whom ye utterly destroyed. And as soon as we had heard these things, our hearts did melt, neither did there remain any more courage in any man, because of you" (Joshua 2:9–11).

God is still working today and providing much evidence for the world of Who He is and what He can do. The evidence of Divine power is so substantial that it ought to create in every man a holy fear of the Almighty. Man has no excuse for rejecting God, for the evidence is too great. On every hand we can see the working of God mightily. As an example, "The heavens declare the glory of God; and the firmament showeth his handiwork" (Psalm 19:1). But many choose to ignore this evidence. They explain it away as chance or natural powers. But woe be to the people who ignore the evidence of Divine manifestations. They ignore God to their eternal judgment.

2. The Country for Israel

In this song, Moses prophesied the possessing of a country—the promised land—for Israel. "Thou shalt bring them in, and plant them in the mountain of thine inheritance, in the place, O LORD, which thou hast made for thee to dwell in, in the Sanctuary, O LORD, which thy hands have established" (v. 17). God had brought them "*out* of the hand of the Egyptians" (Exodus 3:8) to "bring them *in*" (v. 17) to the promised land. The fact that God had brought them "out" with such a great display of power encourages the prediction by Moses in this song that the bringing "in" will also occur. This is the language of Apostle Paul to the Philippians concerning their spiritual lives. He said, "Being confident of this very thing, that he which hath begun a good work in you will perform it until the day of Jesus Christ" (Philippians 1:6). It took the power of God to do a work of grace in the heart of the Philippians, and that encourages Paul to have confidence that God will be able to finish the work in them. It is a great text concerning the security of the believer.

3. The Crown for Jehovah

"The LORD shall reign for ever and ever" (v. 18). God's great performance at the Red Sea causes Moses to predict that God shall rule forever, for no god of the heathen could overcome Jehovah God. Rawlinson says, "In terms most simple yet most grand, often imitated . . . but never surpassed, the poet gives the final result of all God's providential and temporary arrangements, to wit, the eternal establishment of his most glorious kingdom."

Men may join together to fight the cause of God, and as Pharaoh appeared to be succeeding, so may men and nations in our day appear to be succeeding in their ungodly ways. But God's rule is not in jeopardy. The Psalmist stated this situation well when he said, "The kings of the earth set themselves, and the rulers take counsel together, against the LORD, and against his anointed, saying, Let us break their bands asunder, and cast away their cords from us. [But] He that sitteth in the heavens shall laugh; the Lord shall have them in derision. Then shall he speak unto them in his wrath, and vex them in his sore displeasure . . . Thou shalt break them with a rod of iron; thou shalt dash them in pieces like a potter's vessel" (Psalm 2:2–5,9). In a world gone mad, it is most encouraging to know that God is still on the throne and will always be. Matthew Henry sums it up well when he says, "It is the unspeakable comfort of all God's faithful subjects, not only that he does reign universally and with an incontestable sovereignty, but that he will reign eternally, and there shall be no end of his dominion." Let us exhibit our faith in that eternal rule of God by giving Him uncontestable rule in our everyday life.

XVI.

SWEETENING BITTER WATER

EXODUS 15:22–27

AFTER THE CELEBRATION of the Red Sea deliverance, "Moses brought Israel from the Red sea, and they went out into the wilderness of Shur" (v. 22). The Red Sea victory was a wonderful event, but it must not stop Israel from moving on in their journey. We must not be so taken up with the laurels and celebration of a victory that we forget there are more areas to conquer and more victories to be won. Victory is to help us on with our journey, not to hinder us. And so the pillar of cloud soon began to move forward, and Moses wisely got Israel back on the road again pursuing their journey to the land of Canaan.

The direction that the journey was now taking was towards the southern tip of the Sinai peninsula where Mount Horeb was located. Mount Horeb would be visited—as God had promised Moses at the burning bush (Exodus 3:12)—before the Israelites would turn northward and head for Canaan. To go to Mount Horeb, Moses and the Israelites headed "out into the wilderness of Shur" (v. 22) which is located in the northwestern area of the Sinai peninsula where the Israelites were located after they crossed the Red Sea. The Bible record of the journeys of the Israelites lists five of these "wilderness" areas of the Sinai peninsula. They are the *wilderness of Shur* (also called the wilderness of Etham in Numbers 33:8) where Israel commenced their journey from the Red Sea, the *wilderness of Sin* which is farther south towards Mount Horeb ("between Elim and Sinai" [Exodus 16:1]), the *wilderness of Sinai* which takes in the Mount Horeb area, the *wilderness of Paran* ("that great and terrible wilderness" [Deuteronomy 1:19; 8:15]) which is east and north of the Mount Horeb area, and the *wilderness of Zin* which is north of the wilderness of Paran and extends to the southern edge of Canaan and to the western edge of Edom. These wilderness areas became very familiar to the Israelites, for they spent some forty years in them before they finally entered Canaan.

These wilderness areas were, of course, difficult places to journey and live as are all wilderness areas. Israel soon experienced that fact when they left the Red Sea area and started into the wilderness of Shur, for they immediately faced a crisis regarding their water supply. This was the first of several crisis regarding water in their wilderness travels. We will study the other occasions in later chapters. Suffice it to note here that one of those later water crisis was instrumental in keeping Moses from entering the promised land.

This first water crisis ended as a result of and is especially known for the miracle which changed bitter water to sweet water. To further study this water crisis and the miracle involved with it, we will consider the problems before the sweetening (vv. 22–24), the particulars about the sweetening (vv. 25,26), and the pathway after the sweetening (v. 27).

A. THE PROBLEMS BEFORE THE SWEETENING
Three major problems faced Moses before the occurrence of the life-saving miracle that changed bitter water into sweet water. These problems were the deficiency of water, the defilement of water, and the disgruntlement about water.

1. The Deficiency of Water
"So Moses brought Israel from the Red sea, and they went out into the wilderness of Shur; and they went three days in the wilderness, and found no water" (v. 22). The first three days of travel from the Red Sea into the hot wilderness was through an area where there was no water whatever to replenish their supplies. We note the magnitude and moment of this problem.

393

The magnitude of the problem. The deficiency of water would create a very serious problem for the Israelites. Lacking water is never a trivial problem with anyone, but the size of Israel's camp and the multitude of the livestock traveling with them would increase the magnitude of the problem considerably. Yes, Israel would be carrying some water with them in their waterskins. But they could not carry a great deal of water in these waterskins. They could carry enough for the people for perhaps a day or so, but they certainly could not carry enough water for their livestock. New supplies would be needed each day for the livestock. Water is more critical than food. Men and beast can go much longer without food than without water. And with several million people and a great host of livestock in a hot climate and in a mostly hostile environment, water would be a continuous, great, and paramount need for the Israelite travelers. So the water problem was a big one indeed.

Problems and trials of considerable magnitude were permitted in the lives of the Israelites and are also permitted in our lives in order to reveal the magnitude of God's help. "He had permitted their trial to be great, in order that he might the more abundantly magnify his own power and mercy in their deliverance" (Simeon). If our trials are always small, we will not have opportunity to see God do a mighty work which can cause our faith to become much greater. The flesh does not want big trials, but without big trials we will miss seeing many big things from God and will not grow much in spiritual strength.

The moment of the problem. It is instructive to note when the problem of the water shortage came. To do this we will note the proximity and the pathway of the moment.

First, the *proximity* of the moment. In only "three days" (v. 22) of travel from the Red Sea, the water problem became acute. Thus, it did not take long to go from the problem of the Red Sea crisis to the problem of the lack of water. Before the Israelites had hardly finished celebrating their victory over one trial, they faced another trial. Life is often that way. As long as we walk on this earth—which is a wilderness in spiritual character—trial will be our portion. Each day has its problems.

This bit of news that problems and trials are a frequent experience in our life is not to make us pessimistic and despondent. Rather, it is to cause us to strengthen our faith and be prepared for trials that we might live in victory and not defeat. Besides that, as we have just noted, we need trials to grow in the faith. "The discipline of the wilderness [trials] is needful, not to furnish us with a title to Canaan, but to make us acquainted with God and with our own hearts . . . to enlarge our capacity for the enjoyment of Canaan when we actually get there . . . The wilderness ministers to our experience of what God is. It is a school in which we learn His patient grace and ample resources" (Mackintosh). We must experience many and heavy problems if we are going to grow strong in the Lord just as the weight lifter must lift increasingly heavier weights many times if he is going to increase his strength.

Second, the *pathway* of the moment. It is important and instructive to note that Israel experienced this great water problem when they were on the path of obedience. They were following the pillar, and Moses was leading them in the way which God was directing. But obedience is no exemption from trial. "Many are the afflictions *of the righteous*" (Psalm 34:19). "History has again and again shown us that the field of duty has been the field of danger, and that the way which has conducted directly from earth to heaven has been beset by temptations and difficulties too great for human strength. You may be right, even when the heaviest trial is oppressing you. You may be losing your property, your health may be sinking, your prospects may be clouded, and your friends may be leaving you one by one, yet in the midst of such disasters your heart may be steadfast in faithfulness to God" (Joseph Parker).

So just because we are experiencing problems does not mean we are out of the will of God. Yes, we need to examine our heart and lives to see that our troubles are not chastisements for disobedience. But many troubles come to the godly, as we noted above, to help them grow strong in the Lord. Furthermore, we must not forget that the devil will also see to it that the righteous will be troubled on the path of obedience. But continue to obey anyway, for it is the best path of all. Better to be on the path of obedience with troubles than on the path of disobedience without troubles. For when eternity comes, the obedient will no longer have problems, but the disobedient will have worse problems than ever—and they will never end!

While the pathway of obedience does not exempt us from problems and trials and difficulties, it does give us great advantage in meeting these troubles with victory instead of defeat. As we will see later, you can count on God coming to the aid of His obedient ones in time of trouble. Obedience secures His help and solaces the heart in the rough places of life. But disobedience is a far different story indeed.

2. The Defilement of Water

"And when they came to Marah, they could not drink of the waters of Marah, for they were bitter; therefore the name of it was called Marah" (v. 23). Having gone some time without finding water, the Israelites' spirits would soar when they spotted Marah. Water at last! F. B. Meyer pictured the scene well when he said, "How buoyant their hearts, how ready their expressions of confidence in Moses! Their fatigues and complaints and privations were all forgotten, as with quickened pace they made for the margin of the wells." But, alas, when they took their first drink of the water, they could drink no more. The water was defiled. It was bitter, much too bitter to drink. How extremely great was their disappointment. It was bad enough to be without water, but to find water and then discover it was unfit to drink only multiplied the pain of their trial. "It would evidently have been much less trying to them not to have discovered water at all. Nothing so thoroughly sifts the heart as disappointment—bright and lofty anticipations suddenly cast to the ground" (Wagner). The bitterness was so great that they named the place "Marah" which means bitterness (cp. Ruth 1:20).

While Israel, as we noted above, experienced this bitterness on the path of obedience, a lesson can still be gleaned here about the bitterness sin brings where pleasure had been anticipated instead. Sin, like the bitter waters of Marah, seems so promising. To the flesh it promises many pleasures; but once the cup of sinful pleasure is tasted, bitterness becomes the dominant and unwanted taste. "God can embitter that to us from which we promise ourselves most satisfaction." (Matthew Henry). That marriage outside the will of God looks so attractive to the disobedient, but bitterness will be the end result. That lucrative job offer, which, however, takes one out of church, looks very attractive; but bitterness will be the experience sooner or later. That high position in evil politics seems filled with great prestige, but bitterness will be the final reward.

3. The Disgruntlement About Water

"And the people murmured [grumbled, complained] against Moses, saying, What shall we drink?" (v. 24). Moses' problems are increasing. First was the problem of the deficiency of water, then the defilement of the water, now it is a disgruntled people who are murmuring about the water problems. We note the reason, repetition, rapidity, and reviling of this murmuring.

The reason for it. The reason for the murmuring was that Israel took their eyes off of God and focused them chiefly on their circumstances. That will always cause one to murmur sooner or later, for circumstances in this life are not reliable inspirers of rejoicing. The Apostle Paul did not exhort the Philippians to rejoice in their circumstances but to "Rejoice in the Lord always" (Philippians 4:4). And note that he said to "always" rejoice in the Lord, for we can always find cause to rejoice in the Lord, but that is definitely not the case with our circumstances. There are too many Marahs in our circumstances to always rejoice in them. Focus on the circumstances and you will soon be murmuring and complaining as Israel did on their journey from Egypt and Canaan.

The repetition of it. "Murmuring was the common mode in which they [the Israelites] vented their spleen when anything went ill with them" (Rawlinson). We have seen in our previous studies this habit of the Israelites to murmur. In our next chapter, we will see them again repeating this murmuring conduct, and we will deal extensively with it there. It was indeed common for them to murmur. And, unfortunately, they are not alone in this exercise; for "This picture is characteristic of God's people in all ages" (Stevens). We sound pretty fair in good situations, but trial soon sets us to complaining.

The rapidity of it. This murmuring came so soon after the Red Sea deliverance. That may surprise a lot of folk. But Charles Simeon has good perspective on the rapidity of the murmuring. He said, "Who that had heard the devout songs of Israel at the Red Sea, would have thought that in three days they could so totally forget their mercies, and indulge such a rebellious spirit? But look within; and see whether after an occasional exercise of religious affections, you have not, within a still shorter space of time, been hurried into the indulgence of the most unhallowed tempers, and the gratification of a spirit that is earthly, sensual, and devilish." Faith is so weak in so many of us that we can complain right on the heels of great blessing. It matters not how great the help from God has been in the past, the next trial sees us complaining like we never had any previous help from God.

This certainly admonishes and exhorts us to be frequent and faithful in our study of the Word of God and also in our praying. We cannot go long without spiritual refreshment and nourishment or our faith will quickly decline. A serious runner knows that if he stops training, his physical conditioning will fall off very rapidly in just a week or two. So it is spiritually. Therefore, we cannot afford to miss church or skip our Bible reading and prayer times. Failure in these spiritual exercises causes us to quickly forget spiritual axioms and blessings and thus weakens us spiritually which makes us easy prey for the devil.

The reviling in it. Note that the Scripture does not just say that the people murmured, but rather it says they murmured "against Moses." The Israelites cruelly reviled Moses. But he was not the reason for their problem here—instead he was a key to finding a remedy for it. That the murmuring was cruel will be seen more clearly in a later case of murmuring where it put Moses in the peril of being stoned (Exodus 17:3,4). Murmurers do not have a clue as to how to deal with their problems. They blame cures instead of causes, view symptoms as causes and not effects, and even blame God for their troubles (Exodus 16:7,8).

This murmuring against Moses reminds us that "The men who serve a nation best are during their lifetime least appreciated" (Rawlinson). F. B. Meyer said, "Benefactors must not count on gratitude. The mob broke the windows of Apsley House, the residence of the Duke of Wellington, though he had won Waterloo for them." Most preachers know what this is all about, for they experience it frequently. How often it is that after a pastor has gone to great lengths to help some person over a period of time (as Moses did the Israelites), that person will turn against the pastor. A pastor will win a person to the Lord, help him grow spiritually, see him through many difficulties only to have that person one day be the ringleader in running off the pastor. But the worst case of mistreatment of a benefactor is the way mankind treats Jesus Christ. Christ gave His life that we might be saved from eternal damnation. Yet we forsake Him in unfaithfulness, rebel against His commands, and blame Him for many of our problems. Hell will be filled with those who were against Christ, the greatest of all Benefactors for man.

B. THE PARTICULARS ABOUT THE SWEETENING

As we noted in our introduction, Israel's first water crisis ended as a result of a Divine miracle. God came on the scene and the bitter waters of Marah "were made sweet" (v. 25). We want to look at six things associated with this miracle sweetening of the bitter waters of Marah. They are supplication, revelation, application, examination, proclamation, and identification.

1. Supplication

"And he cried unto the LORD; and the LORD showed him a tree, which when he had cast into the waters, the waters were made sweet" (v. 25). Moses' response to the bitter water and murmuring problem was excellent. He "cried unto the LORD." This is the right way to meet troubles. It will help you conquer instead of being conquered by your troubles. As at Marah, it can help remove a lot of bitterness from your life.

The children of Israel ought to have cried unto God, too, instead of murmuring against Moses; but they didn't. Their attitude would have been much better had they prayed instead of murmured. That is the message of the words of that grand old hymn "What a Friend We Have in Jesus" which says, "O what peace we often forfeit, O what needless pain we bear, All because we do not carry, everything to God in prayer." Lehman Strauss said, "Anyone can murmur, but the trusting child of God will turn to his heavenly Father in prayer."

Moses' response to this problem emphasizes the great character of the man. His response to the various problems he faced as Israel's emancipator often underscored the fact that he was a man of exceptional faith and courage and compassion. How often in time of trouble he prostrated himself before the Lord. No wonder he was so successful in his work. Today, with all our technological advances, we think we are too smart and sophisticated to resort to prayer to solve difficulties. But such thinking is folly of the greatest kind. We may learn a lot of things in life that impresses man, but if we want to impress God and do things for God, we need to learn to pray.

2. Revelation

"And the LORD showed him a tree, which when he had cast into the waters, the waters were made sweet" (v. 25). Moses' supplication was rewarded with Divine revelation. What a great reward in any day! The revelation consisted of showing Moses a particular tree that could make the bitter waters sweet. To further examine this revelation, we will note the perceiving of the tree, the place of the tree, the power in the tree, the plan for the tree, and the portrayal by the tree.

The perceiving of the tree. God answered Moses' prayer by showing Moses the remedy and telling him how to use it. "God is to be acknowledged not only in the creating of things useful for man, but [also] in discovering their usefulness" (Matthew Henry). In our day of modernity with all its many inventions and discoveries that benefit life so much, we forget that it is God Who has given us the mind to perceive these discoveries and inventions. Our computers and space age technology do not rule out God but are a result of God enlightening our minds. The unbelieving world, however, does not want to admit that fact.

How dependent we are on God to help us see. The tree was near by, but Moses did not know that fact until God showed him. And he did not know about the properties and value of the tree, either, until God showed him. Hagar was in the wilderness ready to die when God revealed to her a well (Genesis 21:19). The well had been there all the time, but she had not seen it. Sometimes in our troubles we do not see a way out and so conclude there is no way out. How foolish is such thinking, for God knows the way out and can show us the way quickly. Do not discredit God because your vision is poor. When you cannot see, ask God to help you see.

The place of the tree. The tree was near at hand. Moses did not have to send someone on a long journey to find the tree. "In nature the antidote grows near the poison, the dock-leaf beside the nettle" (F. B. Meyer). How well this speaks to us of help from God. The Psalmist said that God is "a very present help in trouble" (46:1). His help is as near as prayer. His help is as near as the Bible. Our problem today is that with people so taken up with psychology and other like philosophies of the world, prayer and the Scriptures are not esteemed by people as much of a problem solver. But, in fact, they are the best problem solvers of all. And they are so near us ready to help us at a moment's

401

notice. Let us avail ourselves of them.

The power in the tree. When the tree was "cast into the waters, the waters were made sweet." The way Scripture is written, it appears that the tree had the power to heal the waters before Moses saw it. This would then make the miracle to be the revealing of the tree to Moses who heretofore knew nothing about the tree's healing powers. However, God could just have easily have given the tree power to heal the waters at that moment. Either way, the power of God is evident. All creation is a result of His power. And this tree manifests that God can give power to any of His creatures to do what He wants them to do. This should encourage those who feel so incompetent and weak to fulfill their calling. If God calls you to a task, He will endow you with the abilities to fulfill your task just as He did the tree.

The plan for the tree. In order to do any good, the tree had to be "cast into the waters" (v. 25). Here is another lesson about service. Before the tree could serve and be a blessing, God's plan for the tree was that it had to be cut down from its comfortable situation and cast into a bitter situation. It would be a painful and humbling experience for the tree to be cut down and cast into the bitter water. But all these things were necessary for the tree to serve God and be a blessing to mankind.

Many folks' idea of service is much different than the plan for this tree. They want comfort, convenience, and compliments. But the requirements for service are self-denial, sacrifice, and humility instead. Christ certainly knew the experience of this tree, and He instructed in this Divine plan for service when He said, "If any man will come after me, let him deny himself, and take up his cross, and follow me" (Matthew 16:24).

The portrayal by the tree. One cannot help but think of the cross of Christ when a "tree" is spoken of as giving life where death threatened; for in the Bible the cross is sometimes spoken of as a tree—"The God of our fathers raised up Jesus, whom ye slew and hanged on a *tree*" (Acts 5:30), "whom they slew and hanged on a *tree*" (Acts 10:39), "they took him down from the *tree*, and laid him in a sepulcher" (Acts 13:29), "Christ hath redeemed us from the curse of the law, being made a curse for us; for it is written, Cursed is every one that hangeth on a *tree*" (Galatians 3:13), and "Who his own self bare our sins in his own body on the *tree*" (I Peter 2:24). Like this tree at Marah, the tree at Calvary can remove bitterness and give sweetness instead. It can take away the great bitterness of sin and bring the wonderful sweetness of life in Christ Jesus.

3. Application

"Which when he had cast into the waters, the waters were made sweet" (v. 25). Divine revelation is for application to our lives. This miracle at Marah emphasizes this fact, for when God revealed the tree to Moses, Moses had to make a personal application of this revelation to his life. And that application was to cast the tree into the waters. It is one thing to know that the tree will heal. It is another thing to use the tree to heal. Many folk delight in revelation, but they do not do well in making personal application. Divine revelation is not just to tickle our ears and entertain our minds. It is to be applied to our everyday life! Without application there will be no blessing. Beware of Bible teachers and preachers who do not make personal application of their lessons and messages to their listeners' lives. Of course, not making personal application means that the teacher or preacher will not step on anybody's toes or hurt anybody's feeling. But without personal application, the message is a waste.

4. Examination

"There he proved them" (v. 25). The word "proved" in this verse means to put something to the test. God examines us; He tests us with trials to reveal the strength, the depth, and the sincerity of our faith in Him. Israel experienced tests repeatedly in the wilderness travels. And the tests continually revealed that their faith was not very strong. They talked a good line at times, but they certainly did not walk their faith well. Here at Marah their behavior was despicable. They murmured against Moses which was in truth murmuring against God, for it was God Who really led the Israelites to Marah.

Not many of us can throw stones at the Israelites, for we do not do well either when God tests us. When trials come, we often reveal that our faith is not very good. When temptations come, we reveal how weak we are spiritually. But like a poor grade on a test in school, a poor grade in a test from God should causes us to put forth more earnest efforts to improve our scores. It should drive us to our knees in prayer for Divine help, and it should inspire us to be more faithful and earnest in study the Word of God.

5. Proclamation

"There he made for them a statute and an ordinance . . . And said, If thou wilt diligently hearken to the voice of the LORD thy God, and wilt do that which is right in his sight, and wilt give ear to his commandments, and keep all his statues, I will put none of these diseases upon thee, which I have brought upon the Egyptians" (vv. 25, 26). The blessing of sweetening the waters came with a proclamation from God which told the Israelites they had some responsibilities as well as privileges. "They had hitherto dwelt only on their privileges without at all considering their duties: they thought of what God was to be to them; but not of what they were to be to God" (Simeon). In summary, the proclamation from God said that if Israel wanted continued blessing from God, they must be obedient to God. "This principle runs throughout the Scriptures and applies to every dispensation: blessing is dependent upon obedience" (Pink).

Our day is plagued by the "rights" movements and emphasis. Everyone is looking out primarily for himself and his own rights. Such an attitude does not encourage much emphasis on duty and responsibility. But we had better get back to duty, to responsibilities, and to obligations, and stop the emphasis on our rights. The best way for us to obtain and enjoy privileges is to be most attentive to our responsibilities.

The specific area of blessing mentioned in this proclamation was health. Israel was promised exemption from the diseases of Egypt if they would "diligently hearken" to the Word of God. A good many diseases today would be eliminated if mankind "diligently hearkened" to the Word of God. As an example, there would be no such thing as AIDS. The world may laugh and scorn the Bible, but they have no valid remedy for the AIDS problem while the Bible does.

6. Identification

"I am the LORD that healeth thee" (v. 26). God identifies Himself to Israel with another new name during this healing of the waters of Marah. It is a combination name of Jehovah which discloses more about the character of God. The combination is "Jehovah" with the word "rapha" and is written Jehovah-rapha. "The word *rapha* appears about sixty times in the Hebrew Old Testament, and it means to cure, to heal, to restore. The use of the word is not limited to the healing of the physical body, but to moral and spiritual healing as well" (Lehmen Strauss). It is a most fitting name revelation for the Marah experience.

This is one of the nine combination names of Jehovah given in the Old Testament. The King James Version only translates three of these names in a combination way. They are "Jehovah-jireh" (Genesis 22:14) which means Jehovah will provide; "Jehovah-nissi" (Exodus 17:15) which means Jehovah is our banner; and "Jehovah-shalom" (Judges 6:24) which means Jehovah is our peace. The other six are written out similar to the one in our text which is "The LORD that healeth thee" instead of Jehovah-rapha. As we noted in an earlier chapter, the names of God are most instructive as to the character of God. Also, as we noted in a previous chapter, our lament is that apart from a few versions (the most notable being the old American Standard Version of 1901), our English Bibles, except in just a few cases in the Scripture text, do not translate the name as "Jehovah" but insist on translating it as "LORD" (all caps) or "GOD" (all caps) instead. This conceals the instructive emphasis on the important name of Jehovah.

C. THE PATHWAY AFTER THE SWEETENING

"And they came to Elim, where were twelve wells [translated 'fountains' in Numbers 33:9] of water, and threescore and ten palm trees; and they encamped there by the waters" (v. 27). From Marah, Moses and the Israelites journeyed southward to Elim. We will look at Elim under the headings of commissary, comfort, camp, and comparison.

1. Commissary

Elim was truly an oasis in the desert. It was a commissary for Israel's basic needs. Our text states two particular features about it: it had twelve wells and seventy palm trees. The twelve wells, by far Elim's most important asset, would provide Israel with a sufficient supply of water for both the people and their flocks. The palm trees "were both pleasant for their shade and refreshing for their sweet fruit" (Poole). Jamieson said, "The shade of one of the remaining palm trees in Wady Ghurundel [where Elim was believed to be located] was found by measurement to be 180 feet in circumference." Of course, there were some two million people in Israel's camp, hence, the seventy palm trees would be for Israel more like a park in the midst of a large city than an area that would shade the entire camp. But even such a park offered relief for some of the people.

Providing abundantly for Israel's water needs in the wilderness reminds us that God can provide for the needs of His people anywhere. We may be in a wilderness situation which threatens to leave us desolate, but God is not limited by circumstances. He can supply adequately for us anywhere. He can provide Elims in the middle of the wilderness if necessary.

2. Comfort

Elim was a welcome relief from the rigors of the wilderness

travels and the trying time at Marah. The Israelites would be glad to see the cloud stop over Elim so they could rest and take comfort in the situation. It had been a tough and trying trip thus far from the Red Sea. Elim offered a welcomed respite.

God has a way of balancing our comforts with our discomforts. He balances our Marahs of disappointment with our Elims of encouragement. He balances our pain with pleasures, our heartaches with happiness, our groaning with glory. This was the case in the experiences of our Lord, too. As an example, after the devil left off tempting Christ, Scripture says, "Behold, angels came and ministered unto him" (Matthew 4:11). The angels were an Elim for Christ. We need Elims after our Marahs during our wilderness travels, and God graciously provides them for us. When trial besets you, be encouraged to know that God has an Elim down the road for you.

3. Camp

"Israel encamped there" (v. 27); that is, they did not take up permanent residence there but dwelt there only for a time. While Elims are nice places to be, and we rejoice in them; yet our journey is not finished at Elim. We only camp at Elim, we do not settle down for a long stay there. Someone said that Elim was like sleep. Sleep is good for us, but we are not to sleep all our life away. Elims are good for us, but that is not where we are to stay permanently. We have work to do, wars to fight, land to conquer. The proper perspective of our Elims is that they provide both healing from past wounds and help for our future battles. See to it that you treat your Elims accordingly.

4. Comparison

It is interesting and instructive to note that in the New Testament the number twelve (springs) and the number seventy (palm trees) show up associated together again. This association involved service for Christ. Luke 9 and 10 especially show us the association. Luke 9 speaks of twelve, and Luke 10 speaks of seventy. In Luke 9 we read, "Then he [Christ] called his *twelve* disciples together, and gave them power and authority over all devils, and to cure diseases. And he sent them to preach the kingdom of God, and to heal the sick" (Luke 9:1,2). In Luke 10 we read, "After these things the Lord appointed other *seventy* also, and sent them two and two before his face into every city and place, whether he himself would come" (Luke 10:1). The twelve springs and seventy palm trees certainly provided good service. Likewise the "twelve disciples" and the "other seventy" also provided good service. Allegory and typology in Scripture studies have often been abused. But we do not abuse Scripture when in comparing the association of these two numbers we make the application to be an emphasis on excellence in service. Service not only involves providing the water of life (the Gospel) for people, but it also involves providing shade (comfort and encouragement) for people. These are simple truths and lessons, but also much needed truths and lessons.

XVII.

SENDING THE MANNA

EXODUS 16

AFTER A REFRESHING stay of a week or two at Elim, Moses and "the children of Israel came unto the wilderness of Sin, which is between Elim and Sinai, on the fifteenth day of the second month after their departing out of the land of Egypt" (v. 1). Numbers 33 lists in detail the itinerary of Israel's travels from Egypt to Canaan and states that when Israel left Elim, they first "encamped by the Red sea" (Numbers 33:10) before "they removed . . . and encamped in the wilderness of Sin" (Numbers 33:11). So some of their early traveling on the way to Mount Horeb was done near the friendly coastline of the Red Sea which gave them some reprieve from the hostile wilderness.

Turning in from the Red Sea to the wilderness of Sin, Israel encountered another crisis; and Moses again came under attack. This crisis had to do with food, and it was on this occasion that God began sending the manna to the Israelites to sustain them through their wilderness journeys. Our text indicates that this crisis occurred just one month after the traumatic exodus from Egypt (the exodus began the fifteenth day of the first month [Numbers 33:3], and they arrived in the wilderness of Sin the fifteen day of the second month [Exodus 16:1]). It had indeed been a most memorable month of tragedy, triumph, and trials. It began with tragedy (the death of all the firstborn of the Egyptians), followed with the triumph of the exodus from Egypt, and then continued on with the trials of the Red Sea, the bitter water, and now the problem of food.

To study this latest trial in which God began sending the

manna to the Israelites, we will consider the murmuring about the food, and the message about the food.

A. THE MURMURING ABOUT THE FOOD

"And the whole congregation of the children of Israel murmured against Moses and Aaron in the wilderness . . . for ye have brought us forth into this wilderness, to kill this whole assembly with hunger" (vv. 2,3). Israel had experienced a shortage of water a few weeks earlier; now they think they are going to experience a shortage of food. As they had done with the water problem, so they did with the food problem—they murmured.

We promised in our last chapter that we would deal more extensively in this chapter with the problem of Israel's murmuring, and we will do so here. Murmuring is very prominent in this food crisis. We will note thirteen "ness" features about their murmuring in the wilder*ness* of Sin.

1. The Habitualness of Their Murmuring

In our last chapter we stated that "Murmuring was the common mode in which they [the Israelites] vented their spleen when anything went ill with them" (Rawlinson). The Israelites were addicted to murmuring. When a trial or trouble arose or when some crisis was encountered, Israel habitually murmured during their wilderness travels. They murmured when at the Red Sea (the word "murmured" or "murmur" etc. is not used in the text about the Red Sea, but murmuring conduct is certainly described and present there), they murmured when they experienced their first water supply problem, and now they murmur when they experience their first food supply concern. This habit was a bad one and only increased the pain of their trial. This is always true with murmuring. It is a habit that needs to be broken if we want joy and peace in life, and if we want to overcome our troubles instead of being overcome by them.

2. The Contagiousness of Their Murmuring

Murmuring is one of the most contagious character diseases

410

known to man. The murmuring in Israel's camp spread quickly until "the whole congregation" (v. 2) got to murmuring. Let a grumbler enter a scene, and soon that person will get many others grumbling. Judas criticized Mary's noble anointing of Christ (John 12:4,6) and got the other disciples to doing the same (Matthew 26:8,9). One murmuring church member can quickly get many in the church murmuring. Vaccinate yourself against this contagious disease with daily injections of the Word of God. Otherwise you will be easily infected and become a sour, complaining, disagreeable, and unhappy person and church member.

3. The Quickness of Their Murmuring

Murmuring does not take long to get started in the hearts of people. It does not wait until a problem has been around for a long time before it complains, rather it gets started practically before the problem has even begun. The food crisis had just suggested itself here, but the Israelites immediately got into a full-fledged murmuring mode. If things do not go exactly the way the murmurer wants or expects, he quickly murmurs. Just one month has passed since the glorious exodus from Egypt. Yet, Israel is now engaged in murmuring for the third time. Would that we would be as speedy to thank and praise God for His blessings as Israel was to murmur about their problems. Also, would that we were as speedy to pray when trials come as Israel was to murmur when trials came.

4. The Inexcusableness of Their Murmuring

Israel had no excuse to complain as they did. The idea that Moses and Aaron were bringing Israel into the wilderness "to kill this whole assembly with hunger" (v. 3) was preposterous. Israel had so many evidences in the recent past of God's care for them that it was totally unjustified for them to murmur. The ten great plagues that smote Egypt, the deliverance at the Red Sea, and the sweetening of bitter water at Marah all should have silenced Israel's murmuring forever. They had plenty of evidence that God would take care of them in any situation. God's past blessings and deliverances were very great, and the greatness of them made their murmuring even more inexcusable.

How often our complaining is likewise inexcusable. George Wagner made a wise observation about the inexcusableness of murmuring when he said, "Whenever we are tempted to murmur, there are always two things at least that we forget. First, we forget what we deserve at the hands of God—nothing but punishment; and then we forget all the mercy and love which He has shown us in His acts and His promises." Israel not only forgot the past blessings, but they also ignored the fact that they did not deserve those blessings. There is nothing justified about their or our murmuring. Both are totally inexcusable.

5. The Meanness of Their Murmuring

In great meanness the Israelites in their murmuring accused Moses (and Aaron, too) of murderous motives for bringing the Israelites into the wilderness. "Ye have brought us forth into this wilderness, to kill this whole assembly with hunger" (v. 3). How unkind were these sharp tongued accusations. But as Matthew Henry said of this treatment of Moses, "It is no new thing for the greatest kindnesses to be misinterpreted and basely represented as the greatest injuries. The worst colors are sometimes put upon the best action." We noted in the last chapter that pastors especially know about these accusations. The pastor's great sacrificing and long hours of work and care for the church will not stop the people from saying he lacks love and care for the church. Murmurers are always complaining (but unjustifiably) about being wounded by others and about others being mean to them. But when it comes to wounding others and being mean to others, few people can keep up with the murmurers.

6. The Untruthfulness in Their Murmuring

To make their present situation look bad, the murmurers painted a very false picture of their life in Egypt. They said that in Egypt "we sat by the flesh pots . . . and . . . we did eat bread to the full" (v. 3). Who were they kidding? "It is . . . evident that

412

in their hot-headed insubordination they lied, for as slaves of the merciless Egyptians, there is no ground whatever for us to suppose that they 'sat by the flesh-pots' or 'ate bread to the full'" (Pink). Egypt was not the nice place the murmurers said it was! There they were slaves. There they continually suffered cruel, barbaric treatment. There they were commanded to throw their male babies in the Nile River. There they were commanded to produce an impossible quota of bricks and then beaten by the taskmasters for failing to produce the quota. But since their exodus from Egypt, they have been free from tyranny, have seen God work marvelously on their behalf, and have enjoyed life as they never did before. "But discontent magnifies what is past, and vilifies what is present without regard to truth or reason. None talk more absurdly than murmurers" (Matthew Henry). If you exaggerate the advantages and ignore the disadvantages of a bad situation and then ignore the advantages and magnify the disadvantages of a good situation, you can make a bad situation sound good and a good situation sound bad. Church dissidents are skilled at doing that. So are evil politicians and the liberal new media people.

7. The Carnalness of Their Murmuring

The murmuring of the Israelites said they preferred Egypt with its idolatrous environment and wicked society to the company of *God's prophet* (Moses), being led by *God's pillar,* and supplied by *God's power.* Matthew Henry calls this grossly carnal attitude "Prodigious madness!" Murmurers are not known for having a priority on spiritual things. They may sound pious (the Israelites used the name of Jehovah in their murmuring speech to Moses [v. 3]), but underneath it all is their fleshly appetites which they are chiefly concerned about, not their spiritual needs. Murmuring is not a spiritual deed but a carnal deed.

8. The Fruitlessness of Their Murmuring

Murmurers have no solution to their problems except some bizarre, impractical, and ridiculous solution such as returning to

Egypt (cp. Numbers 14:4). They do not even suggest here to pray and seek God's help. Murmuring is fruitless in solving problems. Murmuring only multiplies problems; it does not mitigate them. It does not advance good plans to correct a problem or improve the situation. Lamenting that they wish they had stayed in Egypt (v. 3) does nothing to help their situation in Sinai. So church dissidents, who are the murmuring crowd at church, are mostly negative. Their solutions to church problems are lacking. They are mostly *against*, seldom *for* anything.

9. The Stubbornness of Their Murmuring

The root meaning of the Hebrew word translated murmur (also murmured or murmurings) in our text is "to show oneself obstinate, to be stubborn" (Wilson). Murmuring is, therefore, a symptom of rebellion. Numbers 14 records a serious murmuring problem (cp. 14:2) which brings out the rebellion aspect of murmuring very clearly. There the Israelites rebelled against the command to enter Canaan and wanted instead someone to replace Moses to lead them back to Egypt (Numbers 14:4). This rebellious spirit is also behind the murmurings of church dissidents. They do not want to submit to God's plan or God's man at church. They make it sound like many other things than rebellion, but it is still stubborn rebellion against God.

10. The Faithlessness of Their Murmuring

The murmuring of the Israelites reflected a serious case of unbelief. Murmuring does not evidence faith! God had done so much for the Israelites in the past year—such as the plagues upon Egypt, the Red Sea miracle, and the miracle at Marah. Yet, the Israelites do not believe He will continue to take care of them and meet their need of food. So they murmur and worry about being killed. "It argues great distrust of God, and of his power and goodness, in every distress and appearance of danger to despair of life, and to talk of nothing but being speedily killed" (Matthew Henry).

Not many of us are any better that the murmuring Israelites.

Though God blesses us again and again and supplies need after need, our current need seems to always cause us to fuss and worry about how our need will be supplied as though God had never helped us in the past. That is not faith. That is unbelief!

11. The Selfishness of Their Murmuring

Murmuring sees only self. The Israelites were concerned only about their own needs, their own cares. They did not care if they hurt Moses and Aaron with their words. They did not care if they gave God any honor or not. They were only focused on self. Murmuring may sometimes appear to be concerned about others and even God's work, but it is a smoke screen to cover up the real selfish attitude that is behind all their murmuring.

12. The Profaneness of Their Murmuring

"He heareth your murmurings against the LORD . . . which ye murmur against him . . . your murmurings are not against us, but against the LORD" (vv. 7, 8). While outwardly, Israel made it appear they were against Moses, the truth of the matter is they were chiefly against God. But because Moses was God's man, he would receive the brunt of their murmuring attack. God's men need to realize that. Much animosity against a pastor is simply animosity against God and His way.

That Israel's murmuring was chiefly against God has been seen in both the stubbornness and faithlessness aspect of their murmuring, but we wanted to give special emphasis of the truth here. Scripture tells us three times (twice in verse 7 and once in verse 8) that the murmuring was against God. Israel did not like the way God was directing the journey to Canaan. They did not like the way God's pillar of cloud and fire was leading them. They did not like God's arrangements at all. Being against God makes the murmuring really bad. It is a great dishonor to God. And this fact will condemn a lot of our complaining. As an example, when we complain about the weather, we really are complaining about the way God does things; for after all, He is the One Who determines the weather.

13. The Witness of Their Murmuring

Four times (verses 7,8,9, and 12) Scripture states that God heard the murmuring of the Israelites. This repeated reminder of God's omniscience will make wise men oppose every temptation to murmur. God not only hears the murmuring, but He also knows the evil motivation behind the murmuring. One of the greatest helps in controlling our conduct is to remember that nothing is hid from God. We may hide many things from man (although we do not hide things as well as we think), but we will never hide anything from God. He knows our every thought, word, and deed. That should drive us to our knees in repentance. He is the Almighty Witness. If we do not come to Him in confession of our sin, He will one day open His mouth and talk about what He knows of us. And it will be bad news for us indeed, for He will talk at Heaven's court, and what He says can condemn us to eternal judgment.

B. THE MESSAGE ABOUT THE FOOD

To examine the message about the manna, we will consider the compassion with the manna, the clarification in the manna, the character of the manna, the cooking before the manna, the collecting of the manna, the container of the manna, and the comparisons to the manna—there is a wonderful comparison of the manna with the Son of God and the Word of God.

1. The Compassion With the Manna

One of the salient features of chapter 16 of Exodus, which we can rightly call the manna chapter, is the grace of God. Whenever you think of the manna, think of the greatness of God's grace, for grace was so prominent in the giving of the manna. Israel's murmuring was so sinful, yet instead of raining fire and brimstone upon them (which they deserved) God said, "I will rain bread from heaven for you" (v. 4). That is grace indeed! And it is a great illustration of Romans 5:20 which says, "But where sin abounded, grace did much more abound." How great and wonderful is God's compassion for sinners.

From our text we note three workings of God's grace in the giving of the manna which are also seen in the giving of soul salvation. First is *preservation*. As the manna in grace saved the Israelites from physical death, so soul salvation in grace saves the sinner from spiritual death. Second is *reconciliation*. The Israelites were bidden to "Come near . . . the LORD" (v. 9). Sin drives us away from God, but the Gospel of grace invites us to come near Him. "Now in Christ Jesus ye who sometimes were far off are made nigh by the blood of Christ" (Ephesians 2:13). Third is *glorification*. God was greatly glorified in His gracious giving of the manna (vv. 7,10). God is also greatly glorified in His gracious giving of soul salvation. As an example, when Christ came to earth and was announced as the "Savior" (Luke 2:11) of men, Scripture says "The glory of the Lord shone round about them [the shepherds who were given the angelic announcement]" (Luke 2:9), and the angels were "praising God, and saying, Glory to God in the highest" (Luke 2:13,14).

2. The Clarification in the Manna

"Ye shall know that the LORD hath brought you out from the land of Egypt . . . ye shall know that I am the LORD your God" (vv. 6,12). Israel needed some clarification about God. In their murmuring, Israel had blamed Moses and Aaron for leading them into a bad situation. They said, "Ye have brought us forth into this wilderness, to kill this whole assembly with hunger" (v. 3). The giving of the manna would correct that sort of thinking. It would let them know that it was Jehovah God, not Moses and Aaron, Who "hath brought you out from the land of Egypt" (v. 6). True, Moses was God's servant to lead Israel; but the Great Shepherd was Jehovah, not Moses or Aaron. Moses led Israel to follow as God directed. Israel needed to get that clarified in their thinking. They needed to correct their theology. They did not know Jehovah God very well, or they would not have needed the clarification.

How fouled up our thinking becomes when we do not know God well. We will not rightly understand much of anything worthwhile. Because men do not know God, they do not understand how to govern nations, run churches, lead a family, or conduct themselves properly. They do not know right from wrong or wise from foolish. They may be esteemed as very successful by the world; but in eternity, it will be revealed they did not know the score in the most important matters of life.

3. The Character of the Manna

Here we look at the description of the manna. Several verses give some particulars about it. "Behold, upon the face of the wilderness there lay a small round thing, as small as the hoar frost on the ground. And when the children of Israel saw it, they said one to another, It is manna; for they wist not what it was. And Moses said unto them, This is the bread which the LORD hath given you to eat . . . it was like coriander seed, white; and the taste of it was like wafers made with honey" (vv. 14,15,31). From these verses we discover the name, size, color, taste, composition, and nutrition of the manna.

First, the *name*. This food has been given three names in Scripture. They are "manna" (vv. 15,31,33,35), "bread" (vv. 4,8,15,22,29,32), and "angel's food" (Psalm 78:25). The name *manna* means "what is it?" and speaks of the ignorance of the human mind about Divine workings. The name *bread* speaks of the value of the food. It supplied the basic food need of the Israelites. The name *angel's food* speaks of its heavenly source. Blessings come from above. "Every good gift and every perfect gift is from above, and cometh down from the Father" (James 1:17). We need to remember that truth so we will give more praise and thanksgiving to God.

Second, the *size*. The manna is said in Scripture to be like "a small round thing, as small as hoar frost on the ground" (v. 14) and "like coriander seed" (v. 31, cp. Numbers 11:7). A small pea in our culture comes about as close as anything to describing the size of manna. The size reminds us that things do not have to be big and large to be of great value.

Third, the *color*. It was "white" (v. 31). Numbers 11:7 says

418

it was the "color of bdellium" which thus means bdellium is also white in color. Being white helps us understand why it was compared to "hoar frost" (v. 14). Being white also would help it to be seen. It was a practical color. God is practical.

Fourth, the *taste*. We are told "the taste of it was like wafers made with honey" (v. 31). Numbers 11:8 adds that it also had the taste of "oil." This does not contradict our Exodus text, for wafers were made with oil. Whatever the taste of the oil was, we know that there was a sweet taste to manna because of its comparison to honey. It also had the taste of a roll or waffle or pancake for it is compared to wafers. The people used some ingenuity in preparing it which doubtless enhanced the taste— God expects us to enhance our blessings by wise use of them. "And the people went about, and gathered it, and ground it in mills, or beat it in a mortar, and baked it in pans, and made cakes of it" (Ibid.). So the taste was not blah. God is not against all pleasure, only sinful pleasure. Regardless of what the devil says, God does indeed furnish His own with plenty of pleasure.

Fifth, the *composition*. "When the sun waxed hot, it melted" (v. 21). In this character aspect of the manna, it was not like bread, for bread does not melt in the sun. It simply becomes harder. As we will see shortly, this composition of the manna would inspire the Israelites to make haste about collecting their manna each day. Delay would mean a deficient amount collected. God's gifts never promote sloth.

Sixth, the *nutrition*. That it was referred to as "bread"—a staple of life—and that the Israelites subsisted on this food for forty years (v. 35) meant that manna was indeed a nutritious food. Junk food does not come from God's kitchen. God provided a food that would provide the needed nutrients that the physical bodies of the Israelites would need. When God provides, it will be first class. This fact is especially evident in His provision of spiritual food, namely, the Word of God.

4. The Cooking Before the Manna

"The LORD shall give you in the evening flesh to eat . . . At

419

even ye shall eat flesh . . . And it came to pass, that at even the quails came up, and covered the camp" (vv. 8,12,13). The giving of the quails for a meal is easy to miss in this chapter, for the chapter speaks mostly of manna. But we note here that before the manna first came, the Israelites were given an evening meal of quail. Unlike the manna, the quail did not continue to come every day thereafter. Only once again are the Israelites recorded as eating quail in the wilderness, and that was a disastrous experience. "The wrath of the LORD was kindled against the people" (Numbers 11:33) because of their fleshly lusts at that time and many people died and "they buried the people that lusted" (Numbers 11:34, cp. Psalm 78:27–31).

The meal of quail here was not judgment upon Israel. It, like the giving of the manna, demonstrated the grace of God and also the power of God. God was demonstrating that He could indeed provide whatever the Israelites needed wherever the Israelites were. Israel's murmuring had questioned God's ability to care adequately for His people. But God rebuked their faithlessness by showing them His ability to provide for them.

5. The Collecting of the Manna

God gave Moses some rules about the collecting of the manna. These rules take up a large portion of Exodus 16. The rules had to do with four things: the duty of collecting the manna, the amount to be collected, the use of the collected manna, and the time for collecting the manna.

The duty of collecting manna. "The people shall go out and gather a certain rate every day . . . Gather of it every man" (vv. 4,16). Unlike the welfare program of our government, God's handout of food was operated in a very wise way. It did not promote sloth and make it easy to live a sordid life as the government welfare programs do. To the contrary, God's program promoted industry. Every man had to gather food. They did not shuffle down to the welfare office or to the post office to pick up their welfare check once a month. No, they had to work to get their food. The requirement of working for one's food was reiterated by the Apostle Paul when he said, "If any would not work, neither should he eat" (II Thessalonians 3:10).

The amount to be collected. "Gather of it every man according to his eating, an omer [estimated today as about two quarts] for every man" (v. 16). The rule would strike down both greed and gluttony. *Greed* was ruled out, for you were only to gather what you needed. You were not to hoard it. If you did hoard it and, therefore, did not use it right away, it would breed worms and stink (v. 20). Greed causes a lot of things to stink, especially the character of the greedy one. *Gluttony* was ruled out, too. Hence, the rule would strike down obesity for one thing. While all obesity is not caused by consuming large amounts of food, a great portion of it is a testimony to undisciplined appetites. But gluttony would not be a problem with manna.

The use of the collected manna. "Moses said, Let no man leave of it till the morning" (v. 19). God so ordered that Israel would have to collect the manna every day (except the Sabbath). This would promote faith in God. It would cause the people to have to trust God from day to day for a new and needed supply of food. The flesh does not like to do that. It likes to have material security for years to come. But when we walk the path of faith in obedience to God's commands, we will often find that material security, as the world likes it, will not be part of our life. We will not have great stores of riches in reserve, but may have our needs supplied day by day. It is not necessarily wrong to have a reserve, but generally those who serve God will know much about looking to Him daily for the supply of their needs.

Some of the Israelites disobeyed this rule. "Some of them left of it until the morning, and it bred worms, and stank; and Moses was wroth with them" (v. 20). Unbelief (as did greed which we noted above) sooner or later creates a repulsion and a foul smell of some kind. Moses being angry with the Israelites' failure here is a compliment. Today's crowd in church would not think highly of Moses for being angry, but today's crowd at church does not get very upset about sin either. Moses did, however; and it reflected his great spiritual character—something few members in church possess.

The time for collecting manna. Three different rules about time were involved in the collecting of the manna. They were the everyday rule, the early rule, and the exception rule.

First, the *everyday* rule. God told Moses, "The people shall go out and gather . . . every day" (v. 4). "Every day" meant six days a week—"Six days ye shall gather it" (v. 26). Gathering it daily for six days would promote industry and faithfulness. Since the food would not last to a second day except on the Sabbath, the Israelites could not sit around and loaf but had to daily arouse themselves to the task of gathering food.

Second, the *early* rule. The manna was gathered "every morning" (v. 21). Nothing specifically is said in the Bible that ordered Israel to gather the manna in the morning. But what would create the rule even if it was not specifically stated was the fact that "when the sun waxed hot, it melted" (Ibid.) thus making it impossible to collect it. The necessity of collecting the manna early promoted industry and attacked laziness. You did not lie in bed late in the morning if you wanted to have food to eat that day. Anyone who has ever amounted to anything in terms of character has practiced the "early" rule one way or another. "Remember now thy Creator in the days of thy youth" (Ecclesiastes 12:1) is the "early" rule for seeking God in our life. Failure here diminishes greatly your opportunity for salvation and service. We noted in previous chapters of this book that Moses frequently got up "early" to serve the Lord. In the book of Joshua, we will see Joshua doing the same. Staying in bed till late in the morning is not the mark of an achiever.

Third, the *exception* rule. More is written about the exception rule than any other rule. The exception rule stated that the manna was not to be collected on the Sabbath. "Six days ye shall gather it; but on the seventh day, which is the sabbath, in it there shall be none . . . abide ye every man in his place, let no man go out of his place on the seventh day" (vv. 26,29). It is significant and instructive that though the giving of the law had not yet occurred (this occasion was before Israel got to Mount Sinai where the law was given), yet the Sabbath principle still existed. One day in seven to rest and worship is still a valid principle. But the current use of Sunday by many totally ignores the one day in seven principle that we learn about in Scripture. Ball games and business dominate our Sundays. History will demonstrate that the more degraded a civilization becomes, the less they practice the seventh day principle.

Israel broke this exception rule (they would be right at home with our society's use of Sunday today). "It came to pass, that there went out some of the people on the seventh day for to gather, and they found none" (v. 27). These people discovered in an embarrassing way that God's Word is true. That is not the best way to learn that truth, however; for God gets unhappy when you distrust His Word. "And the LORD said unto Moses, How long refuse ye to keep my commandments and my laws?" (v. 28). "Though Moses is addressed, it is the people who are blamed. Hence the plural verb [in the Hebrew] 'refuse ye'" (Rawlinson). We noted above that Moses was upset about the breaking of the "use" rule; now we learn that God is upset about breaking one of the rules, too. The attitude of benevolence in our churches and society towards disobeying God is not shared by either Moses or God. And the consequences of disobeying God greatly favor the attitude of Moses and God!

6. The Container of the Manna

"And Moses said, This is the thing which the LORD commandeth, Fill an omer of it to be kept for your generations; that they may see the bread wherewith I have fed you in the wilderness, when I brought you forth from the land of Egypt. And Moses said unto Aaron, Take a pot, and put an omer full of manna therein, and lay it up before the LORD, to be kept for your generations. As the LORD commanded Moses, so Aaron laid it up before the Testimony, to be kept" (vv. 32–34). Keeping a sample of the manna in a container (the preservation of the sample was miraculous) was a good way of continually reminding Israel of one of their great blessings in the wilderness. It would be a constant testimony of God's daily care of Israel. As Matthew Henry said, "Eaten bread must not be forgotten. God's miracles and mercies are to be had in everlasting remembrance for our encouragement to trust in him at all times."

Hebrews 9:4 says that a "golden pot" of manna was put in the ark in the Tabernacle along with the tables of the law and the rod of Aaron's that budded (Numbers 17). Here in our text, it is just said to be "laid up before the Testimony" (v. 34). "The Testimony is not the Ark of the covenant, which is never so called, but the Covenant itself . . . the two tables of stone engraved by the finger of God, which are termed 'the testimony' in Exodus 25:16" (Rawlinson). So comparing the two texts, we learn that the manna was put in the ark by the two tables of the law.

It will help our learning to note that when the ark was put in Solomon's Temple, Scripture says, "There was nothing in the ark save the two tables which Moses put therein at Horeb, when the LORD made a covenant with the children of Israel, when they came out of Egypt" (II Chronicles 5:10). The manna and Aaron's rod that budded were gone. Solomon's Temple in some ways speaks of apostasy (as an example, small windows were made to let light in where the shekinah glory provided the only light in the Tabernacle). The contents of the ark certainly go along with that. The rod that budded spoke of the resurrection of Christ and the manna speaks of both the Son of God and the Word of God (which we will see shortly). Apostasy is characterized by an absence of belief in the resurrection of Christ and also in Christ Himself and in the Word of God.

7. The Comparisons to the Manna

The manna speaks very clearly of both the Son of God and the Word of God. As we finish up this chapter on the manna, we want to especially note some significant ways in which the manna speaks of the God's Son and God's Word. We will note ten ways in both cases.

Manna and the Son of God. We have no doubt about the manna speaking of the Son of God, for Christ Himself verifies this fact in John 6:32 and 33. The ten words we will use to compare Christ with the manna are present, place, people, praise, provider, purity, preservation, power, protestation, and proving.

First, *present.* Manna was a present, a gift from God to the Israelites. "This is the bread which the LORD hath *given* you to eat" (v. 15). Israel did not pay for it; all they had to do was accept it. Jesus Christ was also a gift. "For God so loved the world, that he *gave* his only begotten Son" (John 3:16).

Second, *place.* The place where the manna came to was the wilderness of Sin. It is a fitting name for the condition of the people. Christ also came to a place of sin. He came from heaven's glory to this old world, a place of great sin.

Third, *people.* The people to whom the manna came were the Israelites. Christ likewise came to the Israelites; for in His first coming to earth, Scripture says, "He came unto his own [the Israelites]" (John 1:11).

Fourth, *praise.* The Israelites were speaking against God God (vv. 7,8) prior to the coming of the manna. But the coming of the manna honored God. It gave praise to God, for "the glory" of God is associated with the coming of the manna. Twice we read of this "glory" in the giving of the manna: Israel "shall see the glory of the LORD" (v. 7) and "They looked . . . and, behold, the glory of the LORD appeared" (v. 10). When Christ came to earth, the glory of God was also manifested. As an example, we read twice of this "glory" in regards to the announcement of His birth to the shepherds. "The glory of the Lord shone round about them" (Luke 2:9); and the angels' message proclaimed, "Glory to God in the highest" (Luke 2:14).

Fifth, *provider.* Scripture speaks of manna coming from heaven. "Then said the LORD unto Moses, Behold, I will rain bread from heaven for you" (v. 4). Christ said of Himself in comparison to the manna, "My Father giveth you the true bread from heaven. For the bread of God is he which cometh down from heaven, and giveth life unto the world . . . I came down from heaven" (John 6:32,33,38). God is the One Who provided both the manna and the Master (Jesus Christ) from "heaven."

Sixth, *purity*. Scripture says that the manna was white in color (v. 31). White speaks of purity. The purity of Christ is spoken of throughout Scripture. He "knew no sin" (II Corinthians 5:21), He was "without sin" (Hebrews 4:15), and He "did no sin" (I Peter 2:22) are just a few texts that emphasize the whiteness of Christ's character.

Seventh, *preservation*. Manna gave life to the Israelites. It preserved them in the desert. Without it they would have died. Likewise Christ also gives life. But He gives more than physical life, He gives eternal life as well. He said, "I am that bread of *life*" (John 6:48), "the way, the truth, and the *life*" (John 14:6), and "the resurrection, and the *life*" (John 11:25). And He also said, "I am come that they [we] might have *life*, and that they might have it more abundantly" (John 10:10). Christ is the great Preserver of the soul.

Eighth, *power*. The manna not only gave the Israelites life, but it also provided them the power to live those forty years in the wilderness. It gave them strength to serve God. Christ does the same for us. He not only gives us life, but He also gives us strength to live our lives and to serve God. Hence, Paul said, "I can do all things through Christ which strengtheneth me" (Philippians 4:13).

Ninth, *protestation*. Israel came to a time in their wilderness travels where they protested having to eat the manna. "The mixed multitude that was among them fell a lusting, and the children of Israel also wept again, and said, Who shall give us flesh to eat? . . . our soul is dried away; there is nothing at all, beside this manna" (Numbers 11:4,6). Though it was a most nutritious food and kept them alive in the wilderness, they still despised and rejected it. Christ was even more despised and rejected than the manna. He was so "despised and rejected of men" (Isaiah 53:3) that He was crucified on the cross.

Tenth, *proving*. When God gave the manna, He told Moses it was done "that I may prove them, whether they will walk in my law, or no" (v. 4). The manna examined the Israelites and revealed their heart. Christ also examines mankind. He is the great test for man. The key test question is "What think ye of Christ?" (Matthew 22:42). You answer that question right or you will go to hell! God examines every man regarding Christ. Where you stand with Christ determines your eternal destiny.

Manna and the Word of God. As we used ten words to show how the manna spoke of the Son of God, so we will also use ten words—ten "tion" words—to show how the manna compares to the Word of God. These words are inspiration, location, assimilation, valuation, coloration, detestation, examination, delectation, nation, and revelation.

First, *inspiration*. The inspiration for the manna came from God. He was the Originator of the food. Men gathered it together, but it was God's idea, and He created it. The Scripture is no different. Man is the human instrument by which the Scripture was written and gathered together, but "All scripture is given by inspiration of God" (II Timothy 3:16).

Second, *location*. Manna came to the people where they were. So the Scriptures came to the people where they were. Paul said, "The word is nigh thee, even in thy mouth, and in thy heart" (Romans 10:8). Those in our part of the earth especially must acknowledge the nearness of the Word of God. In some places in the world, the Word is not near because they have thrust it far from them. That is their fault, not God's fault. The Scripture is translated into hundreds of languages which helps to make it near the people of the earth. Being near and accessible, of course, increases our responsibility. We either use it or we trample it under foot in criminal neglect.

Third, *assimilation*. The manna was to be gathered by the people to be eaten. It was not something to just look at or to set on shelves to admire or made a collection of—it was to be

427

assimilated in the body for daily sustenance. The Bible is to be used the same way. Some gather Bibles as a collection like antiques. Some buy a Bible to lay their hand on for some ceremony. Some buy Bibles for decorative pieces on tables and shelves. But the Bible is to be read, mediated upon, and lived!

Note that the manna was to be gathered in the morning—let us practice that in regards to the Word of God. Early in the morning let us in reading and studying God's Word gather spiritual manna to be assimilated by our souls.

Fourth, *valuation*. The value of the manna was extremely great, for Israel needed the manna in order to stay alive. Without it they would have perished. It was extremely essential for them. The Scripture is even more valuable for us. It is "More to be desired . . . than gold, yea, than much fine gold" (Psalm 19:10) and "The law of thy mouth is better unto me than thousands of gold and silver" (Psalm 119:72). The church programs of many churches today certainly do not reflect this value of the Word, however. These churches put more value and emphasis on entertainment, suppers, recreation, and a host of other fleshly appealing programs. But a church that rightly values the Word of God will have the Word front and center in its program. Without the Word, the program is worthless.

Fifth, *coloration*. The color of manna was white (v. 31) which speaks of purity (which we noted when comparing the manna with Christ). As the color spoke of the purity of the Son of God, so it also speaks of the purity of the Word of God. "The words of the LORD are pure words" (Psalm 12:6), "Thy word is very pure" (Palm 119:140), and "Every word of God is pure" (Proverbs 30:5) are a few texts which emphasize this great character feature of the Scriptures. The Word of God is without fault. And its pureness not only speaks of its faultlessness, but it also speaks of the wholesome effect it has on people. No book has so improved the character of mankind as the Bible.

Sixth, *detestation*. As we noted in comparing Christ to the manna, the manna was despised (Numbers 11:6). The mixed multitude led the way and soon had many of the other Israelites complaining about the manna and that it was all they had to eat. Sounds like folk in our churches who are not happy with a church program that emphasizes and concentrates on the Word. The church must be a religious country club or they will not come. The idea that the Word of God is enough is foreign to their thinking. But you can take out all the church programs that have little to do with the preaching and teaching of the Word, and you will not hurt the church one bit spiritually! It may cut the crowd, but it will not hurt the church spiritually.

Seventh, *examination*. As we also noted earlier in comparing the manna to Christ, the manna would "prove" (v. 4) the people. It would examine the people's dedication to Jehovah. It would test the people to reveal just where they were spiritually. So it is with the Word of God. It tests mankind in many ways.

It is a test of the *multitude* as to where they stand spiritually. Preach the Word faithfully and regularly and you will find out where the congregation of a church stands. God's people will respond well to the preaching of the Word. But phony saints will not. John 6 is a good illustration of how people revealed themselves when the Word was taught.

It is a test of the *minister*. Listen to his preaching and compare it to the Word. Are his sermons in accordance with the Word of God or do they reflect the thinking of the world?

It is a test of the *mind*. We have many philosophies of life out there in the world that have come from the minds of men, and they need to be examined by the Word of God lest we get our lives fouled up following some of these philosophies. If these philosophies are not in accordance with the precepts and principles of the Scripture, they are wrong and need to be shunned. The attitudes one reads about and hears about today in the news media, in schools, in our courts, and in society in general certainly are not those of the Word of God.

It is a test of *manners*. The Word of God has plenty to say about how we conduct ourselves, how we behave, how we act. If you want to know whether you are conducting yourself properly, check the Word of God. Much of what today's society says is acceptable is not acceptable with the Scriptures. Many in our churches echo the sentiments of society in many matters of conduct rather than reflecting the Word of God.

Eighth, *delectation*. The manna was sweet to the taste. "It was like wafers made with honey" (v. 31). The Word of God is also sweet to the taste. The Psalmist said it was "sweeter also than honey and the honeycomb" (Psalm 19:10). He also said, "How sweet are thy words unto my taste! Yea, sweeter than honey to my mouth" (Psalm 119:103). Of course, all mankind does not think the Word tastes that way. But sin can so foul up your taste that tobacco will taste good but good food will taste bad. The Word is sweet whether all people think so or not.

Ninth, *nation*. The manna was given to the nation of Israel. The same is true of the Scriptures. The Jews had the great privilege of having the Scriptures in their hands before the rest of the nations of the world did; and with the possible exception of Luke, God used Jews to be His agents in writing the Word. This blessing of having the Scriptures prompted Paul's statement in Romans which said, "What advantage then hath the Jews? . . . chiefly, because that unto them were committed the oracles of God" (Romans 3:1, 2).

Tenth, *revelation*. The giving of the manna was that which helped increase the Israelites' knowledge of God. "Ye shall know that the LORD hath brought you out from the land of Egypt" (v. 6) and "Ye shall know that I am the LORD you God" (v. 12) was to be an important effect of the manna on the people. How true this also is of the Word of God. It is through the Word of God that we learn about God. Jesus said, "Search the scriptures . . . they are they which testify of me" (John 5:39). And the day of the resurrection, when Christ spoke with the two on the road to Emmaus, "Beginning at Moses and all the prophets, he expounded unto them in all the scriptures the things concerning himself" (Luke 24:27).

XVIII.

SHORTAGE OF WATER

EXODUS 17:1–7

THE WILDERNESS TRAVELS recorded in our text take Moses and the Israelites closer to their predicted (Exodus 3:12) sojourn at Mount Horeb. "And all the congregation of the children of Israel journeyed from the wilderness of Sin, after their journeys, according to the commandment of the LORD, and pitched in Rephidim" (v. 1). Leaving the wilderness of Sin, the Israelites marched towards and into the mountain range in the southern part of the Sinai peninsula and camped at Rephidim. Rephidim is located in this mountain range area a few hours away from Mount Horeb (Mount Horeb and Mount Sinai are used interchangeably at times in Scripture). The scenery of this area Israel was now traveling "is described as inexpressibly grand. On each side of the narrow passes rise peaks and precipices of every form and color. Grey, red, brown, green, chalk-white, and raven-black are the hues of those entrance-gates of the most august temple of the world" (F. B. Meyer).

The detailed listing of the wilderness journeys given in Numbers 33 lists two stops for the Israelites between the giving of the manna and the arrival in Rephidim which Exodus does not list (but can be included in "after their journeys" [v. 1] which words in the Hebrew imply several stages and stops). These stops are Dophkah and Alush (Numbers 33:12,13). These two stops, like many of Israel's stops in their forty-year wilderness journey, were without any significant events; hence, nothing is recorded about them. But the stay at Rephidim was a different story. Two significant events occurred at Rephidim.

431

The first event had to do with a serious crisis regarding a shortage of water. The second event had to do with the war with Amalek. In this chapter we will focus on the water shortage crisis. In our next chapter we will look at the war with Amalek.

This water shortage crisis is the second crisis regarding water which Israel encountered in the wilderness. The first water crisis, which we studied several chapters back, happened only a few weeks prior to this second one. It occurred shortly after the triumphant Red Sea crossing and ended with the miraculous turning of bitter water into sweet water at Marah.

This second water crisis is particularly known for the smiting of a rock which produced an abundance of water for the Israelites. It was the first of two times that Moses smote a rock and brought forth water for the camp. The other time that Moses smote a rock to obtain water occurred towards the end of the forty years' journey in the wilderness. Unlike this first smiting, the second smiting was contrary to God's orders and resulted in Moses being excluded from the promised land.

In our study of the crisis regarding the shortage of water at Rephidim, we will consider the occurrence of the shortage (vv. 1,3), the outrage over the shortage (vv. 2–4), and the overcoming of the shortage (vv. 4–7).

A. THE OCCURRENCE OF THE SHORTAGE

"Israel journeyed . . . according to the commandment of the LORD, and pitched in Rephidim; and there was no water for the people to drink . . . and the people thirsted there for water" (vv. 1,3). We note the pain, purpose, and place of this occurrence of a water shortage.

1. The Pain of the Occurrence

"The people thirsted there for water" (v. 3). This water shortage was a very painful trial, for it was a trial that involved thirst. We noted in the first water crisis that thirst is one of the most painful of trials. "There is probably no physical affliction comparable to intense thirst" (Rawlinson). To emphasize this fact, thirst was the only physical suffering that Christ ever acknowledged in His earthly sojourn. That acknowledgement came on the cross when He said, "I thirst." (John 19:28). And that thirst represents the worst thirst problem of all—the thirst that lost souls will have in hell fire (cp. Luke 16:24).

Adding to the trial of thirst for the people was the problem of the Israelites' livestock also thirsting. The Israelites in their complaint to Moses mentioned their "cattle" (v. 3) being threatened with death by this shortage of water. Anyone who has had anything to do with farming knows that when cattle want water, they make a lot of noise. If the water tank runs dry or if in the winter time the tank freezes over, the cattle will let you know with much loud bawling of their water problem. So the situation in the camp of Israel was not a pleasant one. The people were experiencing the pain of thirst and their livestock would be bawling continuously for lack of water.

As the leader of Israel, Moses was confronted with a big problem at Rephidim with this shortage of water. And so once again we are reminded from Moses' life that while Divine callings have their blessings, they most certainly have their burdens, too. This means it takes considerable dedication to fulfill one's calling. Serving the Lord is not easy; but it still is worth it, however. Those who serve the Lord must not let the burdens and trials and troubles of their calling keep them from fulfilling their calling; for when the battle is over, the blessings will far exceed the burdens.

2. The Purpose of the Occurrence

The text does not state any specific purpose for this trial, but that does not mean the trial was purposeless. God never sends a trial without good reasons. They are all necessary. "Water is a necessity, and when Jehovah takes His people where there is no water to drink, it must be under the compulsion of a still higher necessity" (D. Young). Our physical needs are important but our spiritual needs are far more important. God's primary interest with men is helping them spiritually. To do this, He often has to inflict us physically. "Not that he delights in inflicting [physical] pain; but pain is often needful to teach great lessons" (Ibid.).

Israel had some real spiritual problems. These problems have been made most evident in the wilderness travels. Among their more prominent problems was their unholy reaction to troublous situations and their questioning of God's faithfulness and power to care for them in the wilderness. God sent trials to the Israelites in their wilderness journeys to help correct their spiritual problems. It takes many trials for God's people to grow and develop properly in the Lord. One trial will not correct all our spiritual problems, and it certainly did not do so with Israel. Hence, trial after trial occurred in order to correct their spiritual problems and to help them grow in the faith.

The fact that trials have noble Divine purposes should encourage us greatly when we experience trial. It is difficult in the midst of trial to perceive anything but the pain and loss in the trial. But there are noble purposes involved. This gives great value to our trials. And the knowledge of this fact can help us to view our trials in a more positive way. This in turn will help us deal better with our trials. "Suffering seen through the prism of the cross is reckoned as a part of the divine economy which is ordered for our good and for His glory" (Stevens).

3. The Place of the Occurrence

As it was with Israel's previous trials on their journey from Egypt, this trial also occurred in the place of obedience. This fact is plainly stated in Scripture: "the children of Israel journeyed . . . *according to the commandment of the LORD*, and pitched in Rephidim; and there was no water for the people to drink" (v. 1). As Matthew Henry said, "We may be in the way of our duty, and yet may meet with troubles." In previous chapters we have already emphasized this feature about the trials that came upon Israel in their wilderness travels. But we emphasize it again here in this trial because this fact about the trials needs repeated emphasis and for several reasons—our delusions about God's way and our departures from God's way.

First, the fact that trials come on the path of obedience needs repeated emphasis because of our *delusions* about God's way. So many seem to have the idea that if you are obeying God in your walk, your life will be peaches and cream. Many folk feel that obedience guarantees material wealth and prosperity, physical health, promotion on the job, and even winning in sports. When folk venture out in service for God, they often expect good results to come quickly and automatically without hard, discouraging difficulties to hinder their way. But all of that thinking lacks Biblical support. Furthermore, we can be glad, believe it or not, that life is not all on a smooth road; for if the path of the obedience was exempt from trial, it would also be exempt from those many blessings which come from trials.

Second, the fact that trials come on the path of obedience needs repeated emphasis because of our *departures* from God's way. Satan loves to use trials to get us to depart from God's path. His argument to the tried person is why obey if you are going to suffer so much? He does not tell the tried person about the blessings that come from the trials, he only looks at the temporary disadvantages. Therefore, we need to be frequently reminded that trials comes on the path of obedience so that trials will not cause us to depart from obedience.

B. THE OUTRAGE OVER THE SHORTAGE

"The people did chide [the Hebrew means to strive, to contend] with Moses . . . and the people murmured against Moses . . . And Moses cried unto the LORD, saying, What shall I do unto this people? they be almost ready to stone me" (vv. 2–4). We note the repetition of the outrage, the revelation in the outrage, the rigorousness of the outrage, and the reaction to the outrage.

1. The Repetition of the Outrage

The outrage of the Israelites in this trial was nothing new. They habitually reacted this way to their trials from the time that Moses returned to Egypt from Midian right through all their years of traveling in the wilderness. Whenever they got in some difficulty, they blamed Moses for it, often accusing him of bringing about a situation that would "kill us and our children" (v. 3, cp. Exodus 5:21, 14:12, and 16:3).

The Israelites' continual blaming of Moses for their troubles reflects a favorite habit of human nature. "To lay the blame of the situation on another is a huge satisfaction to the ordinary human mind, which shrinks from responsibility, and would fain shift the burden on someone else" (Rawlinson). How much like our day is this shifting of responsibility onto someone else! To hear folk talk today, no one is to blame for any of their own troubles. And this blaming of others becomes as ridiculous as the Israelites' blaming of Moses. Today, psychologists and other weird thinkers have folk blaming the strangest things for their troubles, such as the repeated dreams of a relative. Of course, none of this will solve any problems. Rather, it only aggravates the situation as did the blaming of Moses by the Israelites.

2. The Revelation in the Outrage

This outrage against Moses at Rephidim revealed very pungently that Israel had failed to learn their lessons well from their previous trials. They should have known better than to immediately attack Moses and blame him for this latest problem. Trial after trial was showing them that God would deliver them and care for them in any situation. But they failed to pay attention. And failing to pay good attention to the lessons of their trials can explain why they had so many trials. If we do not listen to God when He is teaching us a lesson, He has to teach us the same lesson over—and that will not be a pleasant repeating of the course. If we do not pay attention to a trial, God often sends a more difficult trial in order to get our attention. So pay attention in your trials to the lessons God wants to teach you from the trials. It can help eliminate some future trials.

3. The Rigorousness of the Outrage

"They be almost ready to stone me" (v. 4). The outrage was very rigorous. This is seen in how the Israelites attacked Moses.

The attack was not just a few sharp words. It involved the threat of murder, too; for the people were ready to stone Moses.

Those who lead people for God should not be surprised if they experience severe attacks from the people they are trying to lead, as we have noted in previous chapters. Many missionaries have been murdered or cruelly beaten by the very people they were trying to win to the Lord. And many are the men of God who have faithfully performed their duties as God's man in the church who have had as a reward from the congregation their being cruelly treated and forced out of the pastorate.

As Moses' experience here evidences, it is not easy to lead people in God's way. Moses had the pillar of cloud and fire to support his leading, but it did not stop a life-threatening attack upon him. Moses remained faithful to God, however; and missionaries and pastors also need to be faithful like Moses and stick with God's way regardless. Being faithful may not necessarily preserve one's job and life as Moses experienced, but it may cost one his job or life. God, however, will reward any loss one incurs for faithfulness to Him with eternal rewards which will more than compensate the loss!

4. The Reaction to the Outrage

The reaction of Moses to the outrage was most excellent. He did two things. First, he remonstrated with the people; and second, he requested help from God.

He remonstrated with the people. "And Moses said unto them, Why chide ye with me? wherefore do ye tempt the LORD?" (v. 2). Moses spoke wisely to the Israelites—at least someone in the camp was talking sense. He courageously and kindly told them that their striving with him and blaming him for the situation was actually attacking God. On the surface it sounded like the Israelites were only attacking Moses, but the truth of the matter was they were also attacking God. "It is usually in this indirect way that murmuring against God and rebellion against his will are carried out" (Orr). Moses' remonstrating here encourages us to reason with people and point out the error of their ways. They may not accept our reasoning, but grace inspires hope that some might be reconciled by the reasoning.

It is instructive to note how Moses described this attack against God. He said to the Israelites, "Ye *tempt* the Lord" (v. 2). What does tempting God involve? Verse 7 of our text will help answer this question; for it says that this tempting of God represented distrust in God. "They tempted the LORD, saying, Is the LORD among us, or not?" This distrust of God was about both His presence and power, and it was totally inexcusable, for the Israelites had already received many significant evidences of His presence with them and of His power for them. The plagues in Israel, the Red Sea crossing, the bitter water made sweet at Marah, and the daily supply of manna were all great evidences of God's presence and power which should have prevented the Israelites' outrage. But in spite of all these evidences, they still wanted more evidences. Therefore, to tempt God is "prescribing to him conditions of action, compliance or non-compliance with which to settle the question of his continued right to our trust and obedience . . . It is, as in the gospels (Matt. 16:1, etc.) the sign-seeking spirit, which, not satisfied with the ordinary evidences, demands exceptional ones, and lays down conditions on which belief in the revealed word is to be made to depend . . . It is, in short, the spirit which requires from God proofs of his faithfulness and love other than those which he has been pleased to give us, and which even presumes to dictate to him what these proofs shall be" (Orr).

Satan demonstrated this unbelieving attitude in his tempting of Christ. We note it here particularly in the temptation in which Christ used the word "tempt" in rebuking the devil. It was the temptation in which the devil took Christ to "the holy city, and setteth him on a pinnacle of the temple, And saith unto him, If thou be the Son of God, cast thyself down; for it is written, He shall give his angels charge concerning thee; and in their hands they shall bear thee up, lest at any time thou dash they foot against a stone" (Matthew 4:5,6). Satan was prescribing to

Christ how Christ should prove the Scriptures true, how He should prove the care of God the Father for Him, and how He should prove that He was indeed the Son of God. But these were not legitimate tests; and, furthermore, more proofs were not needed. Therefore, "Jesus said unto him, It is written again, Thou shalt not tempt the Lord thy God" (Matthew 4:7).

Many people, even a good number of professing Christians, need help in this area. They demand that God take action as they dictate, that He answer prayer as they insist, and that He remove them from their troubles all to prove that God is powerful, loving, and caring. God's power, love, and care are not in doubt, however. Proof of these attributes of God are so great that He does not have to do one more thing to prove them. As an example, Paul said, "But God commendeth his love toward us, in that, while we were yet sinners, Christ died for us" (Romans 5:8). The word "commendeth" is translated from a Greek word which means here "to prove, demonstrate" (Thayer). Hence, the verse says that God demonstrated and proved His love for us at Calvary. Yet, folk still tell God to prove His love. They will tell God that if He loves them then He should get them a job, or a house, or He should heal them. But God does not have to do those things to prove His love for them. He has already proven His love abundantly, beyond all doubt, at Calvary. To present another "proving" situation is to "tempt" God. It is simply unbelief. And that was indeed Israel's problem—they did not need more proof that God was with them and that He had the power to care for them. To question His presence and power was simply to demonstrate their great lack of faith.

He requested help from God. "What shall I do unto this people? they be almost ready to stone me" (v. 4). After remonstrating with the people, Moses wisely took his troubles to God in prayer. Matthew Henry said, "When men unjustly censure us and quarrel with us, it will be a great relief to us to go to God, and by prayer lay the case before him and leave it with him; if men will not hear us, God will; if their bad conduct towards us

439

ruffles our spirits, God's consolations will compose them."
Going to prayer in time of trouble was a common practice of
Moses (cp. Exodus 15:25; 24:15; 32:30; 33:8; Numbers 11:1,11;
12:13, 14:13–19). No wonder he was so successful in God's
work. The work of God in our lives and our churches is dependent upon prayer much more than our modern prayerless
churches realize. Churches have many new and innovative programs today that are praised as solutions to church growth and
progress. But we note that these programs give little emphasis to
prayer. None of these new programs instruct folk in how to pray
better and how to be more effective in their praying. Prayerless
programs are powerless programs when it comes to spiritual
matters. But most modern churchmen seem unaware of that fact.

Moses did not pray in vain, for God answered Moses'
request with some specific instructions as to what he was to do
to solve the crisis in the camp. We will examine those instructions in detail in our next major point. But here we want to note
a great principle in God's answer to Moses. The principle is in
the first two words God spoke to Moses about what to do. These
words are "Go on" (v. 5). Frankly, that is the answer God will
give to each of us in the midst of our troubles. Moses was to
keep going on in his following the Lord in leading Israel. He
may have felt like quitting and going back to being a shepherd—and our sympathies would have been with him. But that
was not God's plan for Moses, and it is not God's plan for us.
We must keep going on in our God-given duties if we want victory in trials and difficulties. It is such a simple thing to do to
just keep going on. But though simple, it is still very important.
Many, in the face of their troubles, lay down and quit. They
throw in the towel and give up. But that only compounds their
troubles. It does nothing to solve their problems. If you want to
solve the troublous situations of your life, you need to keep
going on—not quit. "Go on" may involve different duties in
each individual case—in Moses' case it involved the unique
duty of smiting a rock for water—but regardless of the particular duty of each person, the overall principle is simply "Go on."

C. THE OVERCOMING OF THE SHORTAGE

"Go on before the people, and take with thee of the elders of Israel; and thy rod, wherewith thou smotest the river, take in thine hand, and go. Behold, I will stand before thee there upon the rock in Horeb; and thou shalt smite the rock, and there shall come water out of it, that the people may drink. And Moses did so in the sight of the elders of Israel" (vv. 5,6). In answer to Moses' prayer, God gave Moses a unique plan for overcoming the water shortage. The shortage was to be overcome by a Divine miracle which would bring water out of a rock. This was, of course, a most unlikely place to get water and reminds us again that God can provide for us regardless of the circumstances around us. We may see no means of help, but God is not limited to the usual or normal or logical means. He can make water come out of a rock to supply our need if He so pleases.

To further examine this miracle of supplying water for the Israelites, we will look at the components, the confirming, and the commemorating of the miracle.

1. The Components of the Miracle

There are at least four significant parts to the miracle. They are the specifying of the rock, the standing on the rock, the smiting of the rock, and the stream from the rock. These four components give a good picture of the Gospel of Christ. which we will especially note in this study. They show the *revelation* of the Gospel of Christ, the *incarnation* of Christ, the *crucifixion* of Christ on Calvary, and the *salvation* provided in Christ.

The specifying of the rock. "Behold, I will stand before thee there upon the rock in Horeb; and thou shalt smite the rock, and there shall come water out of it" (v. 6). Divine *revelation* informed Moses where the saving rock was and what he was to do in order to get water. Like the Gospel, this plan would never have been invented by man. It had to be revealed by God to man. The term "the rock of Horeb" indicates that in the mountain range area of the southern portion of the Sinai peninsula

441

was a rock known as "the rock of Horeb." But simply knowing that the rock existed would do nothing to save the Israelites if Divine revelation did not inform Moses how the rock could solve the water problem. Likewise, if Christ is to save us, we need more knowledge about Christ than that Christ existed. We need Divine revelation to tell us that Christ can save us and how He can save us. Today, that revelation comes to us through the Holy Scriptures.

The standing on the rock. "Behold, I will stand before thee there upon the rock" (v. 6). Jehovah God came down to earth and stood on the rock in Horeb. How obviously that speaks of the *incarnation* of Jesus Christ. He came to earth to be our Savior. He dwelt among the sons of men as a man in a place that spiritually is represented by the meaning of the word "Horeb," the place where the rock was located. The Hebrew word translated "Horeb" means "dry, desert, barren" (Stevens) and "desolate" (Strong). Those words certainly describe the spiritual situation on this globe. Men are like a desert spiritually in that they are as barren of righteousness as the desert is barren of vegetation. Men are desolate of any good thing. They are dry in ability to produce spiritual life, and unless they have spiritual water there will be no life. But thanks be to God, Christ came to this very spot in the universe to bring us the water of life.

If there is any question about the fact that the rock speaks of Christ and that the Gospel is pictured in this miracle scene, it is forever cleared up in a statement made by the Apostle Paul. He said, "Moreover, brethren, I would not that ye should be ignorant, how that all our fathers were under the cloud, and all passed through the sea . . . And did all eat the same spiritual meat [manna]; And did all drink the same spiritual drink; for they drank of that spiritual Rock that followed them; and *that Rock was Christ*" (I Corinthians 10:1–4).

The smiting of the rock. "And thou shalt smite the rock, and there shall come water out of it" (v. 6). The smiting of the rock

442

by the rod of Moses speaks of the *crucifixion* of Christ. It was both judgmental and essential.

First, it was *judgmental*. "Smiting" certainly represents an act of judgment. And Calvary was a place of judgment. On the cross Christ was smitten—"smitten of God" (Isaiah 53:4)—for the sins of the world. He was being judged by God for us, for He was "made a curse for us; for it is written, Cursed is every one that hangeth on a tree" (Galatians 3:13). God does not save us by winking at our sins. He is holy and must judge all sin. But Calvary provided judgment for us so we could escape it by receiving Christ as our Savior. This is all seen in the smiting of the rock. Israel had grievously sinned in their outrage against Moses. Before the water that saved them came, judgment had to come because of their sin. It came in the form of the smiting of the rock—a substitute for Israel just as The Rock Christ Jesus is a substitute to bear the judgment of our sins.

Second, it was *essential*. The smiting of the rock was absolutely necessary if Israel was to have water and thereby have their lives saved. Until the rock was smitten, there were no streams of lifegiving water. In like manner Calvary is also necessary. Without it we have no salvation. Christ "must" (John 3:14) be lifted up on the cross if men are to be saved. Apostates do not want to view Calvary as a necessity, but only as an unfortunate event. But unless Christ dies for our sins, we will have no blessed Gospel to preach.

The stream from the rock. "Thou shalt smite the rock, and there shall come water out of it, that the people may drink" (v. 6). The stream of water from the rock saved the people's lives. And this saving is a marvelous picture of the *salvation* we have in Jesus Christ Who said, "If any man thirst, let him come unto me, and drink" (John 7:37). The water from the rock speaks in a number of ways about the salvation from The Rock, Jesus Christ. We note the grace in it, the gift of it, the greatness of it, the gladness from it, and the gaining of it.

First, the *grace* in it. Israel did not deserve the water. They

443

deserved to die of thirst, for their conduct was so deplorable. They spoke against God and against God's men. They attacked the best. So it is with man. Sin causes him to oppose God and His Word and His workers. It justly condemns him to an eternity in hell fire. He does not merit salvation in the least. But God still provides it, so we must say to all the redeemed, "By grace are ye saved" (Ephesians 2:8). Both the water for Israel and salvation for the soul are a result of God's matchless grace.

Second, the *gift* of it. This water from the rock did not come with a water bill! It was free. It was a gift from God. The Israelites could help themselves freely to all they wanted. Salvation is also "the gift of God" (Ephesians 2:8). The Old Testament message is "Ho, every one that thirsteth, come ye to the waters, and he that hath no money; come ye, buy, and eat; yea, come, buy wine and milk without money and without price" (Isaiah 55:1). Jesus spoke in the same symbolic way when He told the woman at the well in Samaria, "If thou knewest the *gift* of God, and who it is that saith to thee, Give me to drink; thou wouldest have asked of him, and he would have *given* thee living water" (John 4:10).

Third, the *greatness* of it. The water that came from the rock was abundant. Psalm 105:41 said the waters "gushed out" and "ran . . . like a river." The water from the rock was sufficient to meet every need of water for the entire Israelite camp—some two million or more souls plus all the livestock. What a great supply of water that was. Millions of gallons would be required daily to meet the need, but "the rock of Horeb" did the job.

Jesus Christ likewise provides mankind with "so great salvation" (Hebrews 2:3). It will meet the soul need of every person. "Whosoever drinketh of the water that I shall give him shall never thirst; but the water that I shall give him shall be in him a well of water springing up into everlasting life" (John 4:14). He alone can save anyone and completely. As the rock of Horeb did not need other water help to support Israel at Rephidim, neither do we need anything or anyone else to help us be saved. Christ can do the job all by Himself.

444

Fourth, the *gladness* from it. The gladness that swept over the camp of the Israelites when they saw the water had to be tremendous. Being in great thirst and having their livestock making much noise plus the small children crying and fussing, the water would bring unmitigated joy to the Israelites. And what great joy salvation brings and will yet bring in all eternity. It brings the greatest of joys.

Fifth, the *gaining* of it. Though the water was given in grace, was free, would fully satisfy their thirst, would gladden the heart, and save lives; yet it would do absolutely no good if the people did not drink the water. The water had to be received by the body if the person was going to be saved. In like manner, though soul salvation be so wonderful, it will do no good if a person does not receive Christ as Savior. We may look at Christ, admire Him, remark at what great things He can do in salvation and yet die in our sins if we do not receive Him as Savior.

2. The Confirming of the Miracle

This smiting of the rock of Horeb to obtain water was not done in the sight of the entire congregation as it would be done some thirty-eight years later (Numbers 20:9–11) in a similar situation. Here Moses was instructed by God to "Go on before the people" (v. 5) to smite the rock. That is, Moses was to go a ways beyond the camp to smite the rock for water. However, Moses was not to be entirely alone; for Moses was instructed to "take with thee of the elders of Israel" (Ibid.). And when Moses smote the rock and water gushed forth, "Moses did so in the sight of the elders of Israel" (v. 6).

We can see at least two good reasons why God instructed Moses to take the elders of Israel (there were at least seventy elders—heads of the people—in the camp according to Exodus 24:1 and 9) with him: it would confirm both the details of the miracle and the doer of the miracle.

The details of the miracle. God wanted good witnesses of His work. Since the congregation would not see the actual miracle themselves (though they would see the result of the miracle, namely, the water), God wanted them to have excellent testimony regarding the miracle and how it occurred so they would know how the water was provided for them. The seventy elders would provide that excellent, trustworthy testimony.

Unlike fraud, truth has nothing to cover up but instead seeks to be examined in order that the evidences may be seen to substantiate truth. Therefore, we can expect that the evidences of a Divine work will be many and excellent. The resurrection, as an example, has this kind of evidence—"To whom also he showed himself alive after his passion [crucifixion] by many infallible proofs" (Acts 1:3). The Apostle John speaks of the abundance of evidences when he says, "And there are also many other things which Jesus did, the which, if they should be written every one, I suppose that even the world itself could not contain the books that should be written" (John 21:25). Peter likewise speaks of the evidences when he says, "For we have not followed cunningly devised fables, when we made known unto you the power and coming of our Lord Jesus Christ, but were eyewitnesses of his majesty" (II Peter 1:16). Yes, if it is truly a work of God, the evidences will be present, prominent, and plentiful. This will mean among other things that a great many folk who profess to be Christian are not Christian. They do not give forth the evidences. "Ye shall know them by their fruits" (Matthew 7:16), and the fruits do not say Christian!

The doer of the miracle. The presence of the elders at the miracle would also attest to the Divine call of Moses as well as to the details of the miracle. The people wanted to kill Moses, but they would learn from the witness of the elders that it was Moses who smote the rock with his rod and then the water came out. God takes care of His servants and provides them with the necessary honors they need. We who serve God do not need to be concerned about the honors, however, but need to be concerned about obeying God. If we take care of our duties, God will take care of the honors.

3. The Commemorating of the Miracle

"And he [Moses] called the name of the place Massah, and Meribah, because of the chiding of the children of Israel, and because they tempted the LORD, saying, Is the LORD among us, or not?" (v. 7). These names are different than the usual names we give to places where great blessings have occurred. Massah means "temptation," and Meribah means "strife." These names were a continual reminder to Israel of their poor behavior. "The unbelief of the people was not to be lost in the glory of the Divine action, as if it were a thing of no consequence" (Young). The habitual poor behavior of Israel needed to be forcefully rebuked, and it needed to be labeled for what it really was. Israel needed this constant reminder of the sinfulness of their reaction to trial in order to prompt them to better conduct in future trials.

God forgives our sins, but He does not remove all the scars in this life. That is not meanness, but it is mercy to help us remember the evil of our past ways and thereby be prompted to act better in the future. Sin leaves many scars on people, and many of the redeemed have very conspicuous scars. Let all the scars, whether they be ours or that of another, exhort us to faithful obedience.

C. A. Goodhart in *The Pulpit Commentary* made a worthy comment when he said, "Churches are called 'Eben-ezer' and the like; they might often as truly be called 'Meribah.'" We do give our churches some quite attractive names, such as, Grace, Faith, Berean, Sunnyside, Missionary, and Victory. But, unfortunately, the character of the church often does not reflect the name of the church. What would Moses name your church?

XIX.

STRIFE WITH AMALEK

EXODUS 17:8–16

ONCE AGAIN MOSES and Israel encounter a trial. No sooner is one trial (the shortage of water) over than another trial (strife with Amalek) presents itself. But one trial following on the heels of another has been the continual experience of Moses and the Israelites ever since they left Egypt. The trials have varied in their nature (from the cul-de-sac situation at the Red Sea to the shortages of food and water and now the strife with Amalek); but until this trial with Amalek, Israel's response to the trials has not varied. They have reacted very poorly in each of their previous trials. In those trials they murmured vehemently against Moses which was actually murmuring against God. But in this trial, there is a blessed and welcomed difference—there is no murmuring recorded. They meet the trial without a whimper and perform courageously.

To experience trials one right after another, as Moses and the Israelites did in their wilderness journeys, is not unique. As we have noted in previous chapters, trials are part and parcel of life, for "man is born unto trouble, as the sparks fly upward" (Job 5:7). Therefore, we need to earnestly study these trials which the Israelites had and also the many other trials we read about in Scripture; for in them we can find much help in how to deal well with our own trials. Trials, while they may not seem like it at the time, are opportunities for blessings; and the better we respond to the trials the greater the blessing will be. Hence, the more we can learn about how to deal successfully with trials, the better it is for us.

To study Israel's trial of strife with Amalek, we will consider the making of the strife (v. 8), the mastering of the strife (vv. 9–13), and the memorials of the strife (vv. 14–16).

A. THE MAKING OF THE STRIFE

"Then came Amalek, and fought with Israel in Rephidim" (v. 8). The Amalekites started the conflict. Israel was drawn into the strife not because they wanted to make war but because they were forced into war. While war is terrible, it is not necessarily terrible to be in a war as some seem to always think. Rather, it is criminal for a nation to offer no strong opposition to evil powers who would attack and kill and oppress its people. To oppose all war is the same senseless attitude that opposes executing a murderer even though it saves the lives of many innocent people.

To examine the making of this strife by the Amalekites, we will look at the men, the method, and the moment of the attack.

1. The Men of the Attack

Here we take a look at who the Amalekites were. This will help us to understand why they behaved as they did. The Amalekites were descendants of Esau. In fact, Amalek, the father of the Amalekites, was a grandson of Esau. "And Timna was a concubine to Eliphaz Esau's son; and she bare to Eliphaz Amalek" (Genesis 36:12). Later we learn that Amalek had the title of "duke" (Genesis 36:16). But titles do not a character make! Many bad characters have had high sounding titles.

Amalek descended from the man (Esau) who gave such great priority to the appetites of the flesh that he "despised his birthright" (Genesis 25:34). This meant he despised Jesus Christ, for Christ was involved in Esau's birthright (you will never fully understand the seriousness of Esau's evil in the despising of his birthright until you understand that Christ was involved in it). Those given to the appetites of the flesh will not be devoted to Christ. The Amalekites' conduct as recorded in Scripture reflects the attitude of Esau and what it involved; for they were ever opposed to the Israelites—from whom Jesus

Christ was born. Therefore, it is not surprising to read that in their attack upon the Israelites in the wilderness, they "feared not God" (Deuteronomy 25:18). Lacking the fear of God is why we have a lot of wars in this world of ours.

In noting who the men were that made the attack upon Israel at Rephidim, we can also see in the attack the conflict of the flesh and the spirit. The flesh is ever fighting the spirit be it in the individual or otherwise. Amalek's attack upon Israel is typical of this conflict that confronts all the saints of God.

2. The Method of the Attack

There is nothing honorable in the way the Amalekites attacked the Israelites at Rephidim. Their method of attack is recorded not in our Exodus text but in Deuteronomy. "Remember what Amalek did unto thee by the way, when ye were come forth out of Egypt; He met thee by the way, and smote the hindmost of thee, even all that were feeble behind thee, when thou wast faint and weary" (Deuteronomy 25:17,18). Two things can be said about the method of their attack—they attacked the hindmost and the helpless. The method of attack by these evil Amalekites tells us much about the way evil attacks good and how the way the flesh wars against the spirit.

The hindmost. The first thing Scripture says about the attack by the Amalekites is that they attacked those in the rear of the camp. They "smote the hindmost of thee" (Deuteronomy 25:18). It was a characterless approach in fighting, but evil will never be known for character. This sort of attack shows up at church, too. Dissidents often will not come to the pastor and state their problem. Rather, they circulate among the members when the pastor is some distance away and stir up these members with their endless gripping and grumbling.

There is a lesson here concerning the peril of walking at a distance from Jesus Christ. While it is not necessarily wrong to be in the rear of the march (someone has to be the last one in the march), the lesson we do see here, however, is the vulnerability of those who lag behind the leader. Peter on eve of the crucifixion "followed him [Christ] afar off" (Mark 14:54), and soon was denying Christ. A good many church members like to be far back in the pack. This kind usually sits as far back in the church as possible so when the service is over, they can scoot out in a hurry. That, of course, is not a mark of spirituality. In our many years of pastoring, we have learned that those sitting in the rear of the church generally reflect a spiritual attitude that lags behind and walks far from Jesus Christ. This, of course, does not condemn every person who sits in the back, especially parents with small children who do not want their children to distract the rest of the congregation. But a good many folk who sit in the back do so because that is about all the enthusiasm they have for the Lord. So it is not surprising that they do not do well in the battle against sin. Lagging behind is a good way to get picked off by the devil.

The helpless. In attacking the Israelites, the Amalekites also took advantage of the "feeble" and the "faint and weary." They did not attack the strength of Israel, but attacked Israel where they were weak. The devil likewise takes advantage of our weaknesses. As an example, when he made his great attack against Christ in the wilderness, it was after Christ "had fasted forty days and forty nights . . . [and] was afterward an hungered" (Matthew 4:2). The devil attacks us when we are sick, when we have suffered the loss of a loved one or the loss of a job or some other painful loss, when we are discouraged, when we are weary in our work, and he especially attacks us when we are weak spiritually as we noted above in his attacking those in the rear of the camp—this exhorts us to always be "strong in the Lord, and in the power of his might" (Ephesians 6:10).

3. The Moment of the Attack

"Then" (v. 8) tells us the moment of the attack. We note four aspects of this moment. They are a moving time, a murmuring time, a miracle time, and a military time.

Moving time. The Amalekites roamed the Sinai peninsula; and at this time of the year, they would be moving their flocks to different pasture land in the Mount Horeb area where the Israelites were headed. "The attack upon the Israelites was made under circumstances at a time and place fully explained by what is known of the Peninsula. It occurred about two months after the Exodus, towards the end of May or early June, when the Bedouins leave the lower plains in order to find pasture for their flocks on the cooler heights. The approach of the Israelites to Sinai [Mount Horeb area] would, of course, attract notice; and no cause of warfare is more common than a dispute for the right of pasturage" (F. C. Cook). That good pastures were in this area is attested by the fact that Moses was shepherding his flock in this area when God called him at the burning bush.

Every forward movement by the church will conflict with the movements and program of the devil. Therefore, we can expect conflict with evil when we are progressing on the path of God's leading. Some might try to justify the Amalekites' attack on the basis that it was their pasture land. But that thinking ignores three important facts—first, it was not their pasture land anymore than it was the Midianites and others in the area; second, there was pasture land enough in the area for both Israel and the Amalekites; and, third, it was God's will that Israel be where they were. The Amalekites' attitude towards God, which we noted above, and their cruel method of attack cancels out any sympathy for the Amalekites. But many today still sympathize with the criminal in a willful ignoring of the facts.

Murmuring time. This attack by the Amalekites came shortly after the Israelites had murmured against Moses and God. Murmuring is never a good thing for God's people to be doing. It always gives much advantage to the enemy. Matthew Henry said, "They had been quarreling with Moses, and now God sends the Amalekites to quarrel with them; wars abroad are the just punishment of strifes and discontents at home." This murmuring, of course, was not the only factor in the strife with

Amalek, but don't leave it out as part of the picture; for it teaches a much needed lesson about the peril of the fussing and fighting that goes on in the church. We have so much contention in our churches today, and it only helps the enemy in his attack upon the church. We cannot be doing our best against the opposition outside the church when we are fighting with those battles inside the church. This does not mean that when someone causes trouble in the church, we should ignore it in the interest of peace. Rather, this is an indictment upon those who cause trouble in the church. If the pastor, as an example, did not have to spend so much time dealing with the dissidents in the church, he could be doing more work in reaching folk outside the church with the Gospel.

Miracle time. Another aspect of the time which "then" speaks of is that Israel fought the Amalekites right after a miracle had just been performed by God for Israel in bringing them water from the rock. This is also a time when the enemy attacks. God's blessings bother the enemy, and so he attacks the one who is blessed. Just as thieves would steal from the rich, so the devil attacks those who have been enriched with blessings. Trials will follow triumphs because of this fact. And when a person becomes saved—takes of the miracle water of life which is Christ Jesus—he soon encounters the Amalekites of opposition.

The devil, however, often outwits himself; for God's blessings strengthen us for the battles ahead. The miracle of the water from the rock provided water for the thirsty Israelites and it also strengthened their faith. All in all, they became a much stronger people because of the blessing. When the order was given for Israel to "fight" the Amalekites, the miracle concerning the water provided them the strength to do it.

Military time. "Then" also instructs us that Israel was now ready for a military encounter. When they first came out of Egypt, they were not ready for warfare. Therefore, "God led them not through the way of the land of the Philistines, although

453

that was near; for God said, Lest peradventure the people repent when they see war, and they return to Egypt" (Exodus 13:17). But during those first few months of traveling from Egypt, Israel was not just walking and talking, they were obviously getting some military training among other things. Therefore, when the Amalekites attacked, Israel was now ready for warfare. The Israelites did not go to war against Amalek with soldiers undisciplined, ill-armed, etc. as some writers say. It is true they were inexperienced in actual battle, but they were not untrained.

One reason the Israelites were duly trained was that Moses was a man who unquestionably believed in training. He had himself been well trained in Pharaoh's palace in his early days and, as a result, became a man "mighty in words and in deeds" (Acts 7:22). When Israel came out of Egypt, we noted that the way they grouped together and marched evidenced they had been trained in advance by Moses on how they were to travel as a group. And in the first few months of the wilderness journey, Moses obviously gave some military training to the Israelites. The need for the training was evident in the fact that God did not lead them by the Philistine way when they first left Egypt. But they are now trained enough to battle. And they also have a great captain in Joshua, which we shall see more about later.

God graciously adjusts our trials to our strength. We have seen this truth before and will see it again. It is an encouraging truth, but it must not be used as an excuse for postponing or procrastinating in spiritual training.

B. THE MASTERING OF THE STRIFE

Moses' response to the Amalek problem certainly demonstrated the greatness of his character and ability. It was a cool-headed response that evidenced much wisdom in plan and procedure and showed much faith in God. No wonder Israel mastered the strife with Amalek. Oh, that we had leaders at the head of our government who had the character of life, the sagacity in leadership, and the faith in God that Moses continually manifested in leading the Israelites in the wilderness.

To examine the mastering of the strife, we will note the deputizing of Joshua, the drafting of soldiers, the decree to fight, the duty of Moses, and the discomforting of Amalek.

1. The Deputizing of Joshua

"And Moses said unto Joshua, Choose us out men, and go out, fight with Amalek . . . So Joshua did as Moses had said to him" (vv. 9,10). The first thing Moses did in regards to getting Israel ready to fight Amalek was to deputize a man to lead the troops. Like leaders of nations in every age, Moses appointed a general to oversee the military. No leader ever made a better appointment! Joshua was a general supreme, and the more we read of him in Scripture the more evidence we see of his great military skill, excellent character, and steadfast faith in God.

This is the first mention of Joshua in Scripture. Heretofore, we have not been told about this gallant man in Israel's camp. But while he was in obscurity, he was not sitting around twiddling his thumbs. He was obviously being trained and prepared for his post by Moses. The capable way in which Joshua responded to Moses' call and commands to him indicates he had learned his lessons well, for he became one of the greatest military generals in the history of mankind.

The name "Joshua" is significant. It means "Jehovah is salvation [or saves or is the Savior]". In the New Testament, the name Jesus (in the Greek) "is a transliteration of the Hebrew Joshua" (Vine). The translators of the King James Version, in fact, called Joshua by the name Jesus in Acts 7:45 and Hebrews 4:8. It would have been better, in our judgment, to have translated the name as Joshua in those verses to distinguish it from Jesus Christ. But the point we are illustrating with those verses is that the names are the same. Only the context will determine which person is referred to in the text. That Joshua had the same name as our Redeemer is most fitting because of the work that Joshua did in regards to Israel. His actions as the general of the army and later as the leader of Israel truly speak often of the greater Joshua to come, namely, Jesus Christ.

455

2. The Drafting of Soldiers

"Choose us out men, and go out, fight with Amalek" (v. 9). Israel's first war after leaving Egypt was fought by draftees. Joshua was in charge of the drafting, and his orders were to draft "men." The word "men" means more than a contrast to female. It involves manliness. It is men in the sense of courage and soldiership. The military is no place for the timid or the weak. It needs the brave and the strong. Joshua obviously knew about the men of Israel and would be able to wisely pick the right persons to go to war with Amalek. If you were drafted by Joshua, it was a compliment.

The greater Joshua, Jesus Christ, is also choosing men (and women, too) to serve Him and go to battle for His cause. And like Joshua of old, He does not choose just anyone; for though "many are called . . . few are chosen" (Matthew 22:14, cp. Matthew 20:16). Many saints show up for God's army, but after they have been examined, they are refused—as it also is with our military selection process today. Sometimes folk are refused for God's service because of the sinful way they been living. Sometimes they are refused for lack of knowledge of the Word of God. Sometimes they are refused because their dedication to the Lord is very poor—as an example, many church members are not chosen for service in the church because they are so unfaithful in attendance. We need to take care that our life is in good spiritual health and readiness so when God calls, we will be ready and qualified to be chosen for service in His army. You may be obscure and unknown by most people, but God knows where you are, and He also knows what you are. You take care of the "what you are" and the day will come when God will choose you for His service.

3. The Decree to Fight

"Go out, and fight" (v. 9). This command is in contrast to the command given Israel at the Red Sea. There they were told to "stand still, and see the salvation of the LORD" (Exodus 14:13). Here, however, they are told to fight. God does not work miracles unless they are necessary. At the Red Sea, the Israelites were in no shape to fight against the Egyptians; and God's plan was to part the sea, something the Israelites could not do. Here, we have a different situation, and Israel is ready to fight and are ordered to fight.

Many folk reject this command to fight. They say it is unchristian to fight. In the early part of this chapter, we mentioned that though war is terrible, it is not necessarily terrible to be in a war. Rather, it is often the proper and necessary thing to do. Here we look again at this truth. God's people should not be of a contentious spirit and always fussing and feuding. But this command to "fight" is not in that category. There is an evil (Amalek) to be opposed, and to not oppose it is an admission of being soft on sin. God's people are not to be soft on sin, or God will get upset. This is demonstrated in the career of King Saul, Israel's first king. He was instructed to go to war against these same Amalekites and "smite Amalek, and utterly destroy all that they have, and spare them not" (I Samuel 15:3). Saul did not obey this command but spared some of that which he was to destroy. As a result, Samuel the prophet announced to Saul that "Because thou hast rejected the word of the LORD [regarding destroying the Amalekites], he hath also rejected thee from being king" (I Samuel 15:23). So we had better fight evil when God tells us to fight evil. We need to fight it in our own lives, we need to fight it in the church, and we need to fight it in society by taking a strong stand against it. Let the pastor preach vigorously against sin. Let not the church tolerate sin in the midst of the congregation. We are to "Fight the good fight of faith" (I Timothy 6:12) or sin will defile and defeat us.

4. The Duty of Moses

After Moses gave Joshua his orders, he then told Joshua what he, Moses, would do in regards to the fighting of the Amalekites. His duty would be to "stand on the top of the hill with the rod of God in mine hand" (v. 9) and hold it up in the air (v. 11). To further examine this duty of Moses, we will look at the strangeness, the significance, the symbolism, and the supporters of his duty.

The strangeness of Moses' duty. Human reasoning will view Moses' duty as very strange indeed. His duty does not make sense to natural thinking. It would ask, "How can Moses by holding a rod up in the air on the top of a hill have any effect whatever upon the battle?" Swords and spears and chariots and horses and bows and arrows on the battlefield are what effect a battle reasons the natural mind. But natural reasoning leaves out God. Therefore, it will view a lot of God's orders as strange.

The strangeness of Moses' duty would test his faith to see if he would obey God regardless of the command. Moses has experienced this test before. Smiting the Nile River to make it blood, leading Israel down the west side of the Red Sea rather than the east side, lifting up his rod by the Red Sea to effect the parting of the Red Sea, and smiting a rock to obtain water were all strange things to do as far as human reasoning thinks. But Moses did not let that bother him, he obeyed God anyway.

Christians face this same test. The world, which can only reason with the natural mind, thinks believing the Bible is strange, thinks creationism is strange, thinks a holy moral life is strange, and looks at the God-ordered lifestyle of Christians as a strange way to live. But God's people must not let the attitudes of mere human reasoning deter them from believing God and living as God decrees. Never mind if the human reasoning of the world thinks God's way is strange—if God orders it, it is the wisest thing to do.

The significance of Moses' duty. We do not all have the same duty in God's army. Some are generals, some are foot soldiers, and some have tasks away from the battlefield. The tasks away from the battle field, such as Moses' task, are, however, often played down and even ridiculed by folk who foolishly think that the only action is where the spotlight is. But all jobs are important, all have significance, even those away from the battlefield. David, who was a great battlefield warrior, had great appreciation for those duties away from the battlefield and made the famous decree that said, "As his part is that goeth down to the battle, so shall his part be that tarrieth by the stuff" (I Samuel 30:24). You may not be up front doing the preaching or even holding an office or teaching a class at church. But you can do much to help the Lord's work anyway. Moses was on the hill holding up his rod while Joshua was out directing the battle. Moses' duty was just as important as Joshua's. In fact, as if to emphasize the importance of the duty away from the battlefield, more is written about Moses' duty in this battle against Amalek than that of the duty of Joshua or of the other soldiers.

The symbolism of Moses' duty. Holding the rod up in the air on the hill overlooking the battlefield is symbolic of at least two things—prayer and power.

First, Moses' action is symbolic of *prayer*. The symbolism of prayer comes from the fact that sometimes in Scripture the uplifted hand is associated with prayer. We cite two verses as examples of this fact. "Hear the voice of my supplications, when I cry unto Thee, when I *lift up my hands* toward thy holy oracle" (Psalm 28:2) and "I will therefore that men pray everywhere, *lifting up holy hands*, without wrath and doubting" (I Timothy 2:8). Several important truths about prayer are seen in Moses' action here. They are the effort in prayer, the enlightenment for prayer, and the essentialness of prayer.

The *effort* in prayer. True praying is hard work. Moses' hands got tired and he had to have help to keep them up all the time on behalf of the troops on the field (vv. 11,12). "Prayer is labor! . . . Without doubt prayer of the right kind means strenuous and exhausting labor. It is the most exhausting exercise that the soul can possible sustain" (F. B. Meyer). Matthew Henry spoke likewise when he said, "We do not find that Joshua's hands were heavy in fighting, but Moses' hands were heavy in praying. The more spiritual any service is, the more apt we are to fail and flag in it. Praying work, if done with due intenseness of mind and vigor of affection, will be found hard work, and though the spirit be willing, the flesh will be weak."

The *enlightenment* for prayer. J. Orr in *The Pulpit Commentary* makes a good observation of Moses' situation in regards to wise praying when he said, "Note, also, it was *in view of* the battle that this intercession of Moses was carried on. Prayer needs to be fed by knowledge, by watchful interest in events as they shape themselves around us, by study of the special needs of circumstances of the times . . . [how much better] would it be in the warfare of the Church were praying men and women to act more on this principle—seeking, as far as possible, to keep themselves informed of the progress and vicissitudes of the Lord's work at home and abroad, and endeavoring to order their prayers with constant reference to the fluctuations in the battle!" Missionary prayer letters are an example of that which can enlighten us so we are able to pray more effectively. Knowledge of any ministry or of an individual's specific needs is needed if we are going to pray well in these areas. We need to be "on the top of the hill" (v. 9) in knowing about that which we pray for if our praying is going to be effective.

The *essentialness* of prayer. "And it came to pass, when Moses held up his hand, that Israel prevailed: and when he let down his hand, Amalek prevailed" (v. 11). With Moses' action speaking symbolically of prayer, we have a great illustration here of the need of prayer for the work of the Lord. When prayer goes forth, we have victory. When we slack off in prayer, we can be defeated. "Prayer makes all the difference in our fight against principalities and powers" (F. B. Meyer).

Second, Moses' action is symbolic of *power*. While the viewing of Moses' action as a symbol of prayer will be valued because it teaches us some good lessons about prayer, the viewing of Moses' action as a symbol of Divine power may be more correct. We have not done Scripture injustice by looking at Moses' action as a symbol of prayer, but we may do Scripture injustice if we do not also see it as a symbol of Divine power. The lifting up of Moses' rod has heretofore never been a symbol of prayer, but it has *always* been a symbol of Divine power. The need of Divine power in this strife against Amalek was very evident. Though Israel was trained for battle, the Amalekites, from a human standpoint, still had a great advantage in terms of fighting a battle; for they were a war-like tribe that was much experienced in warfare. Furthermore, the "Amalekites were at that time the most powerful race in the Peninsula" (F. C. Cook). The Israelites were going up against a strong military force. They really needed God's help.

We must train diligently for our duty, but that will not take away our need of God's power. We are never sufficient in ourselves, "But our sufficiency is of God" (II Corinthians 3:5). No matter who we are or how much we have been trained or how great have been our past accomplishments, we still need Divine power to accomplish our Divinely-ordered tasks. Moses recognized that fact and held up the rod as he had done on other occasions when God acted in a powerful way on Israel's behalf. When the rod was let down, Amalekites prevailed; for without God's power Israel will not win the battle.

The supporters of Moses' duty. Moses had two men who gave great support to him in this battle with Amalek. They were Aaron and Hur (this is the first time we see Hur in Scripture— he was of the tribe of Judah, the grandfather of Bezaleel the artificer of the tabernacle [Exodus 31:2], and tradition says he was Miriam's husband or son, but neither is likely). They accompanied Moses to the hill and when "Moses' hands were heavy . . . they took a stone, and put it under him, and he sat thereon; and Aaron and Hur stayed up his hands, the one on the one side, and the other on the other side; and his hands were steady until the going down of the sun" (v. 12).

Aaron and Hur helped Moses to accomplish his God-given duty. They are a rare breed. So many folk hinder others from doing their duty. The ungodly encourage folk to live sinfully— which is disobedience to our moral duty given us by God. And many in the church do not lift a finger to help those in the

461

church who have rolled up their sleeves to do the work of the Lord. But we all need to be like Aaron and Hur. We need to help others do their duty. A word of encouragement or some other helpful kind of assistance can all be a big help to keeping some in their work for God and some from going astray.

5. The Discomforting of Amalek

"And Joshua discomfited Amalek and his people with the edge of the sword" (v. 13). Israel gained the victory over Amalek at Rephidim. Rephidim will be a bright spot on the map for Israel, for they experienced two great blessings there—they obtained water from the rock and defeated Amalek there.

This was a decisive victory, for the "expression ['with the edge of the sword'] always denotes a great slaughter of the enemy" (F. C. Cook). Though it was a decisive victory, it was not the final one. They will fight Amalek again—not in the wilderness travels but when Israel gets into the promised land. Amalek is like the passions of the flesh, like temptation, and like the arch enemy of our soul; for he will not give up quickly. Though defeated soundly, he will one day come back again to cause trouble. Therefore, a victory over evil must not cause us to sit on our laurels and let down our guard; for evil will sooner or later come back to cause us more trouble. We see this warning in Christ's experience, too; for after Christ went through the temptation scene following His baptism, Scripture says, "And when the devil had ended all the temptation, he departed from him for a season" (Luke 4:13). Yes, the devil departed after Christ's great victory—but it was only for a season. The enemy will be back. But decisive victories in previous encounters gives us much advantage for future encounters.

C. THE MEMORIALS OF THE STRIFE

This strife with Amalek was a most notable event and victory in Israel's history, and much was done to help remember the experience. We note four things that were done after the battle that would help remember it. They are the recording of the strife, the rehearsing of the strife, the retribution for the strife, and the revelation from the strife.

1. The Recording of the Strife

"And the LORD said unto Moses, Write this for a memorial in a book" (v. 14). This is the first mention of writing in the Scripture, and it is a significant one. "The original has, 'Write this in *the* book.' It is clear that a book already existed in which Moses entered events of interest, and that now he was divinely commanded to record in it the great victory over Amalek" (Rawlinson). We have both a doctrinal lesson and a devotional lesson in this recording order from God.

The doctrinal lesson. This "book" which Moses was to record the encounter with Amalek in was either a journal that Moses referred to and copied from in writing the Pentateuch or it was, in fact, the part of the Pentateuch which speaks of Israel's experiences in Egypt and the wilderness. Either way the incident speaks of the doctrine of Divine inspiration and shows how Divine inspiration effects the compilation of the Scripture.

Divine inspiration controls what is put in the Bible. Some Scripture is a result of revelation—that is, God communicates to the writer of the Scripture truths which the writer would not have otherwise known. But other Scripture is a result of common knowledge—that is, the writer knows about the events or truths and writes about them as the Spirit of God moves him. This is what Moses was doing here. But all Scripture, whether a product of revelation or common knowledge, is Divinely inspired. That is, God superintends, controls, and guides the recording of it so that what is said is exactly what He wants said and how He wants it said, so much so, that it can truly be said to be God's Word. Only the Bible is thusly inspired.

The devotional lesson. Keeping a record of our special blessings is a good idea in any age. This is not necessarily an exhortation to keep diaries—some folk may not have the aptitude to keep such things—but it is an exhortation for us to do something of some sort to keep from forgetting God's blessings. The remembering of God's blessings will help promote our faith in God and increase our gratitude to God—both of which are mighty healthy things to occur in our lives.

2. The Rehearsing of the Strife

"And rehearse it in the ears of Joshua" (v. 14). Moses was to be Joshua's history teacher. History is important. Yes, I am acquainted with the saying that goes something like this, "The only thing that we learn from history is that we do not learn from history." That is a clever saying, and it is true that we often do not learn well from history. However, we can, and many do, learn valuable lessons from history. Moses was to especially instruct Joshua because Joshua was to be Israel's leader when Moses died. Joshua needed to be trained in significant history to lead Israel aright.

The word "rehearse" literally means to "put." You can translate verse 14 as "*put* it in the ears of Joshua." It is a graphic way of saying Joshua needed to have *put* in his mind and memory the great truths learned from the striving with Amalek. Joshua was a good listener obviously; for when he took over from Moses, he was a most capable leader. But there are many folk today whose ears are so full of the dirt of the world that you cannot put anything worthwhile in them. God help us to have ears that will receive important truth that God wants us to hear.

3. The Retribution for the Strife

"I will utterly put out the remembrance of Amalek from under heaven" (v. 14). This battle with Amalek upset God with the Amalekites! As a result, God promised an annihilating retribution upon the Amalekites. Amalek would eventually be "put out" of the remembrance of mankind. That is, the Amalekites would one day be no more. Today, we still have the Jews. Israel is a nation that one day will be the greatest nation on the earth. But the Amalekites are no more. There is no nation named

Amalek, and there is no race of people who are named Amalekites. God keeps His Word.

Later, this retribution of God was stated again and as an order. We read it in Deuteronomy 25:19: "When the LORD thy God hath given thee rest from all thine enemies round about, in the land which the LORD thy God giveth thee for an inheritance to possess it, that thou shalt blot out the remembrance of Amalek from under heaven; thou shalt not forget it." Attacks upon the Amalekites did indeed occur later when Israel was settled in the land. King Saul was ordered by God to destroy the Amalekites (I Samuel 15:2,3); but, as we have already noted, Saul did not do a very good job. As a result, God told him through Samuel that this would cost him the throne—which says something about how upset God was with the Amalekites as well as with Saul (I Samuel 15:23). David, Saul's successor, successfully combated the Amalekites (I Samuel 27:8 and 30:1–18, cp. II Samuel 8:12). The finish came during the days of Hezekiah when the Simeonites "smote the rest of the Amalekites that were escaped, and dwelt there unto this day" (I Chronicles 4:43). The end of the Amalekites pictures the end of evil. It may thrive at times, but eventually God will destroy it.

4. The Revelation From the Strife

To also help commemorate this strife with the wicked Amalekite people, "Moses built an altar, and called the name of it Jehovah-nissi; For he said, Because the LORD hath sworn that the LORD will have war with Amalek from generation to generation" (vv. 15,16).

What made the altar especially significant was the name given the altar. It was a new combination name for Jehovah—Jehovah-nissi. The new name means, "Jehovah is our banner." The strife with Amalek had revealed to Moses that Jehovah was Israel's banner (just as the miracle at Marah revealed Jehovah as Jehovah-rapha which is Jehovah the healer). Jehovah-nissi is an inspiring name for Israel especially during battle. When people go to war, they generally carry a banner with them. Banners are different today than in Moses' day. But they still have the same meaning. "When we speak of a banner, we think of a flag, a piece of drapery which is attached to the banner-pole. But the ancients had only a pole with a bright metal ornament at the top." (F. B. Meyer). These banners were very important in warfare. Be it a just a pole or a pole with a flag on it as we have today, the banner inspired, identified, and instructed.

The banner inspired. Francis Scott Key demonstrated how much a banner inspires when he wrote "The Star Spangled Banner." After a night of battle, Key could still see in the early morning light the American flag flying, and what a thrill and inspiration it was to him. However, there is no banner that inspires like God's banner. God's banner inspires men to the noblest of deeds, to the best of thoughts and philosophies. We need this inspiration today, for too much of mankind is being inspired by a host of banners that do not inspire nobly.

The banner identified. The flag you serve under tells us who you are and what you believe and where your loyalties are. The Stars and Stripes represented freedom, the best democracy in the world, and it represents opposition to tyranny.

But how much better is the banner of God, Jehovah-nissi. Oh, what great truths it represents. It represents God, Jesus Christ, the Word of God, truth, purity, the Gospel, etc. It represents what we ought always to be identified with. But so many are ashamed to serve under that flag, to acknowledge their allegiance to that flag, to salute it, and revere it. In the 1960s and 1970s we watched with disgust as flag burning became the "in" thing for the hippies and yippies and other scum of society to do. Not only was burning the Stars and Stripes popular, but so was walking on it and in general giving it as much disgrace as possible. But an even worse demonstration is going on in our land today. It is the disgracing of Jehovah-nissi. His Word is kicked out of schools. Praying to Him in some places, such as our schools, has been stopped by the courts. Loyalty to Him by people calling themselves Christian is deplorably bad. Yes, if God were indeed a literal flag, it would be a terrible sight to see the way society would treat it today. And that only spells trouble for the disgracers.

The banner instructed. The banner tells the troops where they are to be. The banner leads the way. It goes before the troops. A story is told that during one of our wars, the flag bearer got quite a ways ahead of the troops. One of the soldiers hollered at the officer in charge and told him to tell the flag bearer to come back where the troops were. The officer in charge wisely replied that the troops needed to catch up to the flag instead. Many need to catch up to the Jehovah-nissi banner, too. Professing Christendom today seems to be going in a far different direction than Jehovah-nissi. But that direction is wrong, for Jehovah-nissi tells us the right direction to go and the right place to be.

XX.

Sojourn of Jethro

Exodus 18

WHEN ISRAEL WAS "encamped at the mount of God" (v. 5), Moses was visited by Jethro, a Midianite in-law of Moses. Jethro's visit is especially known for his advising Moses on how to deal with Israel's problems. But it is also remembered for his bringing with him Moses' wife and two boys, so they could be reunited with Moses.

Before we get into the details of Jethro's visit, we want to again note his identity problem which we noted earlier in our study of Exodus 3. Jethro is always identified as Moses' "father in law" (v. 2) in our English translations of the Scripture. But this creates some problems; for in Exodus 2 and Numbers 10, Moses' father-in-law is said to be Reuel ("Raguel" in Numbers 10:29 in the King James Version though it is the same word in the Hebrew); and in Judges 4:11, "Hobab" is said to be Moses' father-in-law. To confuse things even more, Numbers 10:29 says that Hobab is the son of Reuel. The critics use this problem to say the Bible contradicts itself and is full of mistakes. However, the critics are not standing on such solid ground as they think; for the solution to the problem is quite simple. It is found in the Hebrew word which is translated "father in law" in our text. This word means "any relation by affinity or marriage" (Wilson). Thus the word is not limited to "father in law," but is also translated into such relationships as "son in law" (Genesis 19:12), and even "husband" (Exodus 4:25, 26). That which determines what the translation should be is, of course, the context in which the word appears.

From the context of these passages, we believe that Reuel is the father-in-law, Jethro is the eldest son of Reuel and a brother-in-law of Moses, and Hobab is a brother of Jethro and another brother-in-law of Moses. "This combination seems to meet all the conditions of the narrative, which would otherwise present serious, if not insuperable, difficulties" (F. C. Cook). The eldest son identity of Jethro is seen in that in Bible times when a father died or became infirm, the eldest son took over the estate. Hence, Reuel's flocks would become Jethro's flocks (Exodus 3:1) and Reuel's position as "priest of Midian" (Exodus 2:16) would become Jethro's (18:1). Furthermore, Jethro taking care of Moses' wife and two sons when they came back to Midian while Moses was in Egypt would also be his logical task as the inheritor of his father's estate. Some believe Jethro was Hobab. But Exodus 18:27 records Jethro's departure from Moses, whereas in Numbers 10:29–32 Hobab appeared to stay, though he at first said he would not. Judges 4:11 indicates Hobab obviously stayed. That Moses should be visited by several of his in-laws (at least by both Jethro and Hobab) at Horeb would not be unusual. In fact, it is only logical. After all, Moses lived for forty years in their home. His in-laws, especially his brothers-in-law, would be glad to see him again; and Mount Horeb was in their vicinity (for Moses kept Jethro's flocks there). So making a visit with Moses was most convenient and expected.

While all do not agree on the identity of Jethro, the consolation is that regardless of whether he is a father-in-law or brother-in-law or is the same as Hobab or not, the lessons of Exodus 18 and Numbers 10:29–32 are the same. We will not, however, be dealing with Numbers 10:29–32 in this chapter; for we do not believe it is an extension of Exodus 18—which it would be if Jethro was the same as Hobab.

With the identity of Jethro addressed, we now turn to our study of Exodus 18 and the details of Jethro's most interesting and instructive visit to Moses. We will divide this study into two main points: the reunion of the family (vv. 1–12) and the remonstrating about the work (vv. 13–27).

A. THE REUNION WITH THE FAMILY

Jethro's visit to Moses provided Moses with a reunion with his in-laws and also with his wife and two sons who had come to stay now with Moses the rest of the journey. To further examine this reunion, we will note the moment of the reunion, the marriage and the reunion, the manners in the reunion, and the message for the reunion.

1. The Moment of the Reunion

We will note five things about the moment of the reunion. It was a publicized, prestigious, peaceful, popular, and parenthetical moment.

A publicized moment. "When Jethro . . . heard of all that God had done for Moses, and for Israel his people, and that the LORD had brought Israel out of Egypt" (v. 1), then Jethro came to visit Moses. The news of Israel's experiences was traveling far and wide. Two million people leaving Egypt, crossing the Red Sea in a marvelous miracle, moving southward in the Sinai peninsula, and defeating the strong Amalekites was news that could not be contained and kept secret. Plenty of people, such as travelers, herdsmen and other dwellers in the area, and even spies of various nations would have "heard" about the movement. They would tell others who would tell others etc., and the news would spread quickly and far. Jethro, therefore, would have no trouble learning about Israel's success and location. Jethro could even have learned of Moses' arrival at Horeb from his shepherds who, like Moses in previous years (Exodus 3:1), might have had Jethro's flocks in the area when Israel came to Mount Horeb. So Jethro's visit occurred when the achievements of Moses and Israel were well publicized.

A prestigious moment. When Moses left his in-laws to go to Egypt, he was the lowly shepherd of Jethro's flock (Exodus 3:1). But when he returned to Mount Horeb, where he had been called by God a year or so earlier, he was the famous shepherd of Jehovah's flock. He was the great emancipator and leader of a nation plus a great miracle worker. Thus Moses prestige had risen tremendously. This great rise in prestige was doubtless very surprising to Moses' in-laws. After forty years of service as a shepherd for his Midianite in-laws, Moses would not be viewed by them as a man who could lead several million people out of bondage and in the process bring about the destruction of the land of Egypt and the army of Egypt. What tremendous achievements Moses had accomplished since he quietly left Jethro (Exodus 4:18) a year or so earlier. But though his leaving of Jethro was unpretentious to the human eye, it was not that way in God's eye; for when a man moves according to the will of God, great things can occur that will amaze man's thinking.

A peaceful moment. Jethro would want a time of peace and safety before he would be encouraged to take Moses' wife and two sons with him to reunite Moses with them. After the battle of Amalek, Israel settled down at Mount Horeb for about a year (cp. Exodus 19:1 with Numbers 10:11,12) in which time they were under no threat from any other people. This would be a good time for Jethro to travel and to enter the camp of Israel. It would also be a good time for Moses to be reunited with his family. Turbulent times could easily have hurt the reunion.

A popular moment. Unlike when they were in Egypt, Moses and Israel would be popular at this time. Such a time is when the undedicated would jump on the band wagon. While we cannot with certainty accuse Jethro of being this way, our text does illustrate the situation. "When" (v. 1) the undedicated "heard" (Ibid.) of great victory, then they decided it was time to identify with the winners. They are like Zipporah, Moses's wife, who waited till Moses was successful before rejoining him. Many will not join with Christ today because He is not popular in the world. They have their finger in the air to see who is winning and then join that side. Such folk have little character and even less faith when they act this way towards Jesus Christ.

471

A parenthetical moment. Because of the mention of the "statues of God, and his laws" (v. 16) which Israel was not given until after our text, and especially because of the mention that Israel was "encamped at the mount of God" (v. 5) a move not reported until later, it makes this narrative "a parenthesis, interrupting the chronological order of the book" (Pink). Writers periodically insert parenthetical material, and for good reasons. Jamieson cites a significant reason why Moses inserted the parenthetical material here. "How, then, did this episode come to be inserted out of its proper chronological place in the history? Just in conformity with the usual manner of the writer [Moses] when about to enter upon a continuous narrative, to dispose of collateral matters of interest, as in giving the genealogy of Judah's family (Gen. 38) before commencing the story of Joseph's life and policy in Egypt; so he adverts to this visit of Jethro, important both on private and public grounds, before commencing the lengthened details of the Sinaitic legislation [including the tabernacle]." All of this emphasizes the excellency of the Bible. The critics say the Bible was tossed together at random. But one cannot study the Bible earnestly and come up with any other conclusion than that the Bible was put together masterfully with great literary skill under Divine supervision.

2. The Marriage and the Reunion

"Jethro . . . came with his [Moses'] sons and his wife unto Moses" (v. 5). Moses' sometimes troublous marriage again comes into focus in the visit of Jethro to Moses. We note two things about the marriage—the separation and the sons.

The separation. Moses' marriage to Zipporah went all right until Moses started on his return to Egypt to be Israel's emancipator. On the way, the neglect of circumcision of the youngest son was brought to Moses' attention by God in a very severe fashion. Moses had neglected this important sign of the very covenant which, among its significant features, promised Israel's release from Egypt. The circumcision was very upsetting to Zipporah (Exodus 4:25,26). While we are not told in Exodus 4 that Moses sent her and his two sons back to her home while he went on to Egypt, that fact is apparent by their return with Jethro in our text.

The temporary separation was a result of a spiritual problem. We pointed out in chapter 7 of our book that Zipporah was not very compatible to Moses spiritually. She disdained circumcision (Exodus 4:25), which no woman would do who appreciated the covenant God had with His people. Because of her spiritual condition, she was not ready to go through the strong testings of faith that Moses would experience in the dealings with Pharaoh before Israel was freed from Egypt. So she was sent back home and only joined up with Moses when Israel had arrived triumphant at Mount Horeb.

The situation here gives us lessons on partners, passion, and peacemaking. First, *partners*. We should not marry one who is not compatible spiritually. Especially should servants of God be careful in this matter. Nothing is more important than spiritual things. Yet, many folk pay little attention to spiritual compatibility when it comes to marriage and, as a result, experience many marriage heartaches. Second, *passion*. We should have such a passion for God and His work that we will not lose heart in battle and have to be sent back to the rear, as Zipporah was, when the battle gets tough. Some complain of not being used much in God's service. Often the reason for this is that they lack devotion to the things of the Lord and will be no good under the pressure and perils of spiritual warfare. Third, *peacemaking*. In bringing Zipporah back to Moses, Jethro is a "great illustration of those noble souls who strive to unit what sin divides . . . Blessed are the peacemakers; and surely of all peacemaking, that is not the lest fruitful of good which reunites and reconstitutes a separated family" (D. Young). We have so many in the world and even in Christendom today who are most quick to suggest and justify divorce when things get a bit rough in a marriage. But that was not the case here. Jethro knew where Zipporah belonged, and Moses received her back without hesitation.

The sons. Moses had two sons. Our text takes the time to tell us about their names. The two names speak of Moses' faith. People back then gave meaningful names to their children; and followers of Jehovah God often expressed their faith, as did Moses, in the names they gave their children. This reminds us we do not have to do some great exploit in life in order to show our faith. We can show it well in the simple and small matters, too. Moses showed his faith in the naming of his boys as well as in such great events as the parting of the Red Sea. Let us so live our faith that it will show in everything we do.

The first born of Moses was named "Gershom; for he [Moses] said, I have been an alien in a strange land" (v. 3). The name Gershom means stranger. Speaking of himself as a stranger in Midian said Moses knew that Midian was not his land but Canaan was. The Israelite who had faith in God's promises, knew that to be any place but Canaan was to be a stranger. Likewise we who profess to be a Christian should acknowledge that we are strangers in this world. This is not our home, we are only abiding here temporarily. Peter understood this truth when he addressed the believers in his first epistles as "strangers and pilgrims" (I Peter 2:11). Don't put your roots down too deeply in this world, for it will not help you to get ready for the next world.

The second son was named "Eliezer; for the God of my father, said he [Moses], was mine help, and delivered me from the sword of Pharaoh" (v. 4). The name "Eliezer" means God is my help. It spoke of Moses' deliverance from the sword of Pharaoh when he fled Egypt and came to Midian. The name is also prophetic, for God delivered Moses from the sword of Pharaoh when Moses dealt with Pharaoh about letting Israel leave Egypt. When the name was given, it was a name of gratitude. Faith is not very good faith that does not show gratitude to God for His deliverances.

3. The Manners in the Reunion

"And Moses went out to meet [Jethro] . . . and did obeisance, and kissed him; and they asked each other of their wel-fare; and they came into the tent" (v. 7). Moses demonstrated excellent manners in his treatment of Jethro. He did not wait for Jethro to come to the tent, but when he saw him he went to meet him and greeted him with the mannerly "obeisance" and the affectionate "kiss" and the asking of his welfare. Moses had left Jethro when he (Moses) was a lowly shepherd but had come back as the head of a nation. This great elevation in position did not, however, puff him up and make him haughty and arrogant around his in-laws. He still had good manners and humble grace.

In referring to this situation, Matthew Henry said, "Religion does not destroy good manners." That statement needs empha-sizing today. Good manners ought to be conspicuous in those professing faith in Christ. But, unfortunately, we see much lack in this area. This makes it all the more refreshing that some of our Christian colleges have insisted on the students exhibiting good manners, such as the boys opening the doors for the girls, the students speaking to their teachers in "Yes sir," "No sir," "Yes ma'am," and "No ma'am" terminology. Good manners ought to be demonstrated at church, too. Especially should visi-tors experience this sort of treatment. It is not a mark of weak-ness to have good manners. As we noted about Moses, he was a great man now; but he still had the best of manners and could exhibit humble grace with the best of them.

It is instructive to note where Moses exhibited his good manners. It was in the home. Good manners in the home are especially important—more important even than good manners anywhere else. Good manners are needed in the home to make a better home, a better marriage, and to assure consistent good manners in public. Some people seem nice at times in public; but when they get home they are inconsiderate, rude, and unkind.

4. The Message for the Reunion

After Moses and Jethro had exchanged their initial greet-ings, "they asked each other of their welfare" (v. 7). We do not have Jethro's report as to how he was doing, but we have

Moses' report, and it was a good one. We note the contents of the message and the consequences of the message.

The contents of the message. "And Moses told [Jethro] . . . all that the LORD had done unto Pharaoh and to the Egyptians for Israel's sake, and all the travail that had come upon them by the way, and how the LORD delivered them" (v. 8). Would that all our friends and relatives were like Moses. He did not talk just about his troubles, but he also talked about his triumphs. He talked about how God gave the victory in all the troubles, how God delivered the Israelites from Pharaoh and from the various trials. Most people you talk with only talk about their troubles and generally in a very negative way. They never talk about them with any kind of heavenly perspective. They drone on and on about this trouble and that trouble, and you listen in vain to hear how they triumphed in them through the help of God. We can understand why the world would talk that way, but Christians ought to talk better or keep their mouth shut. It gives no honor to God when we talk about nothing but troubles and do so in a pessimistic, despairing way. After listening to some Christians talk, I want to ask them, "Where's God?" By the way they talk, you would think God did not exist or had died or was without power to help them.

The consequences of the message. The effect of Moses' message upon Jethro was excellent. Moses gave a great testimony of God, and the response from Jethro was a good one. Sometimes, of course, the best testimony in the world will be rejected. But Jethro would never have acted the way he did had not Moses given such a sterling testimony about God. Let us as individuals and churches give the kind of testimony that if received, it will produce a wonderful response in the hearer.

Jethro's response to Moses' message was fivefold—rejoicing in God, honoring of God, learning about God, worshipping of God, and fellowshipping with God's people.

First, *rejoicing in God.* "And Jethro rejoiced for all the

476

goodness which the LORD had done to Israel" (v. 9). Moses' message made Jethro glad. The Apostle Paul said, "Rejoice in the Lord always; and again I say, Rejoice" (Philippians 4:4). Moses did. God's people ought to be a rejoicing people, not pessimists singing the blues all the time. Moses was a rejoicing saint, because he focused on God. This affected others in a positive way. When he got done speaking, Jethro was glad. Would that more of our talk caused people to be glad rather than down in the dumps, discouraged, and despairing of hope.

Second, *honoring of God*. "And Jethro said, Blessed be the LORD, who hath delivered you out of the hand of the Egyptians, and out of the hand of Pharaoh, who hath delivered the people from under the hand of the Egyptians" (v. 10). Moses' message caused Jethro to honor God. Many messages heard in this world today do just the opposite. Unfortunately, much talk by Christians today does not cause anyone to honor God either. If you cannot honor God by what you are going to say, you should not say it.

Third, *learning about God*. Moses' message caused Jethro to conclude, "that the LORD is greater than all gods; for in the thing wherein they dealt proudly he was above them" (v. 11). Here is more evidence of the excellence of Moses' message—it taught important truths about God. "It would seem that Jethro, like the generality of the heathen, believed in a plurality of gods, and had hitherto regarded the God of the Israelites as merely one among many equals. Now, he renounces this creed, and emphatically declares his belief that Jehovah is above all other gods, greater, higher, and more powerful" (Rawlinson). One of the purposes of the plagues upon Egypt and the deliverances of Israel from their wilderness trials was to instruct about the greatness of God. Moses conveyed that message well to Jethro. May all our messages instruct well about God.

Fourth, *worshipping of God*. "And Jethro . . . took a burnt offering and sacrifices for God" (v. 12). When we learn the truth about God, we will want to worship God. Moses' message encouraged the worship of God. Our testimonies ought to be such that it will encourage people to want to worship the Lord. Some, of course, will despise our testimony though it be the best, but our testimony should be such that if a person is really concerned about his soul, that person will want to attend our church when they hear us talk. But too many Christians by their talk only drive people away from their church.

Fifth, *fellowshipping with God's people*. "And Aaron came, and all the elders of Israel, to eat bread with [Jethro] . . . before God" (v. 12). When you rejoice in God, honor God, learn about God, and worship God, you will generally find good fellowship with God's people. Some folk in our churches complain that they do not have any Christian friends and that no Christian ever gives them the time of day. The reason for this problem is not difficult to discover. The complainer generally does not attend church regularly; and when he comes, he will come late to the service, sit in the back of the auditorium, and then hurry out of church before the benediction is hardly finished. It is pretty difficult to have much fellowship with God's people that way.

B. THE REMONSTRATING ABOUT THE WORK

"And it came to pass on the morrow, that Moses sat to judge the people: and the people stood by Moses from the morning unto evening. And when [Jethro] saw all that he did to the people, he said, What is this thing that thou doest to the people? why sittest thou thyself alone, and all the people stand by thee from morning unto even? . . . The thing that thou doest is not good . . . Hearken now unto my voice" (vv. 13,14,17,19). The second day of Jethro's visit, he gave Moses some unwise and unasked for counsel. Jethro's counsel to Moses concerned the way in which Moses was dealing with the Israelites' problems. The counsel was more than some kindly suggestions and advice, it was an earnest and outspoken protest about Moses' administration and how he should correct it. It was indeed a real remonstrating by Jethro. To remonstrate means to plead and protest, to give a reproof about some action, and to urge a change in the action.

Though Jethro's remonstrating about Moses' conduct was

bad counsel, it is not readily perceived as such. Most commentators, in fact, think it is pretty good counsel. On the surface, some of what Jethro said does sound good, for it seems to embrace time honored truths. But this only helps to make the bad counsel unsuspecting of evil. Evil likes to have an "unsuspecting" character. Then it does not readily appear as evil. It will often be mixed with enough truth that it will beguile the undiscerning. Jethro's counsel was indeed unsuspecting, for it spoke of some good things. This, we believe, has beguiled many good people into thinking that all which Jethro said was good.

In all fairness to Jethro, he, of course, did not think he was giving evil counsel. He was not intentionally trying to sabotage Moses. He thought he was looking out for Moses and trying to help him. But Jethro was filled with the thinking of the world, and so his counsel was indeed faulty counsel.

To further examine Jethro's remonstrating, we will look at the virtue and the vice in the remonstrating.

1. The Virtue in the Remonstrating

Jethro's counselling of Moses said some good things. However, as we just noted, that is what made his counsel so beguiling. We note five aspects of Jethro's counsel that made it quite unsuspecting of being evil. They are the peril of overworking, the precepts for teaching, the prerequisite for judging, the pitying of Moses, and the promoting of laborers. These aspects of Jethro's counsel are spoken of much by the commentators, so much so that Moses is often severely criticized. One writer in *The Pulpit Commentary* went so far as to speak of "a blunder in Moses' system of administration." But after we have examined Jethro's entire counsel, we will conclude that it was Jethro who was blundering, not Moses.

Peril of overworking. Jethro seems to be telling Moses not to overwork ("this thing is too heavy for thee" [v. 18]) and to reduce his work load so he would not "wear away" (Ibid.). It is true "there may be overdoing in well-doing" (Matthew Henry), and that at times we need to "come ye yourselves apart into a desert place, and rest a while" (Mark 6:31). There is no virtue to overworking and thus wearing yourself out unnecessarily. But there was no evidence of that being done here. Furthermore, Jethro indirectly was criticizing God. God had given Moses his assignment, but Jethro does not like the job's description. Beware of people telling you not to do this or that when, in fact, that is what God ordered you to do.

Jethro was concerned that "this people" (v. 18) would also "wear away" (Ibid.) because they would have to stand around too long for counsel. Jethro would have Moses be more considerate of the people—that was a low blow for Moses—little did Jethro understand how very gracious and considerate Moses had been of the people in all their murmuring. The problem wasn't Moses needing to be more considerate of the people, but the people needing to be more considerate of Moses!

Precepts for teaching. "And thou shalt teach them ordinances and laws, and shalt show them the way wherein they must walk, and the work that they must do" (v. 20). Now that bit of counsel sounds very wise, and it is. We cannot fault the advised practice of teaching people the commands of God and showing them God's way and will for their life. But lacing this statement in with error really makes error seductive, of course.

Jethro was rather arrogant here, for Moses did not need that advice. If anyone knew what he was to teach, Moses certainly did. And he had already told Jethro that "I do make them know the statutes of God, and his laws" (v. 16). But Jethro sounds good here with his teaching advice; and when the innocent see the statement about teaching God's laws and lifestyle, they think all of Jethro's counsel must be good.

Prerequisite for judging. "Moreover thou shalt provide out of all the people able men, such as fear God, men of truth, hating covetousness; and place such over them" (v. 21). Jethro certainly stated some good requirements for those that were to help

Moses judge the people. If we had judges with these qualifications today, we would still be praying in our public schools, our streets would not be filled with crime, and justice would be the rule in court. Three great prerequisites are stated here for judges. They were to be men of ability, piety, and integrity. First, they were to be men of *ability*. That stands to reason. If a man lacks the abilities, he certainly should not be placed in the job. But, of course, governments, schools, and even churches do this all the time because they appoint people to position for reasons of friendship or prejudice or government minority quota laws or for personal self-advantage. Second, they were to be men of *piety*. They were to "fear God." If we had judges like that, anti-religious judgments would never come from our courts. And when a judge is God-fearing, he knows he must answer to God about his decision. That attitude will stop bad decisions en mass. Third, they must be men of *integrity*. This is emphasized twice—it is emphasized in the "men of truth" and in the "hating covetousness" phrases. To be a good judge, a man must be honest. He must seek for the truth, and he must not decide his judgments on the basis of bribes rather than truth. Covetousness sees money as more important that truth, however. And courts too often make decisions on that basis.

Jethro's prerequisites for the judges for Israel were excellent. But he left out a very important one—they must be called of God. Moses was called of God to do what he was doing, but those Jethro wanted appointed judges were not. Never assume a calling. Without the calling, all the other qualifications will be null and void though they may reflect good character.

Pitying of Moses. "If thou shalt do this . . . then thou shalt be able to endure" (v. 23). Jethro was not talking about stoning Moses as the Israelites once did. He was not proposing that Moses be whipped or run out of town. Jethro had Moses' welfare as his main concern. This, of course, is a subtle tactic of evil. It wants to appear that it has your best interests in mind when it counsels you to some action. But be careful that you are not deceived. Though Jethro thought he had Moses' welfare in mind, he was actually taking Moses away from some of his calling, from some of his work. That was not good for Moses welfare! The most subtle counsel is that which appears to be for your good when actually it is for your destruction. The devil appeared to be concerned that Adam and Eve got all the benefits of the Garden of Eden, too. But his nice talk was only to bring evil upon them. Jethro, of course, was not purposely trying to destroy as was the devil in the Garden of Eden. But in operating in the flesh, he was unwittingly a tool of the devil here.

Promoting of laborers. Jethro counseled Moses to appoint "rulers [judges] of thousands, and rulers of hundreds, rulers of fifties, and rulers of tens" (v. 21). This meant that for the 600,000 men (Exodus 12:37), it would take 78,600 judges. If all the people were counted in Jethro's proposal, which would bring the total to at least two million, it would take 262,000 judges. That would not only be a lot of judges for the Israelites, but it would take nearly half of the men (44% of 600,000) to be judges, and that would be impractical and unwise. Even some of the commentaries who approve of Jethro's counsel question having so many judges; for they feel, as we do, that there would not be that many qualified men in Israel. However, putting many people to work is praised by most commentaries; for it is generally good to put people to work. Matthew Henry said, "Great men should not only study to be useful themselves, but contrive how to make others useful." Yes, it is good when we can, as an example, get as many people involved in church work as possible. But we must not forget that it is not good to put people to work who do not belong in the job! Jethro's advice would put too many wrong people on the job.

2. The Vice in the Remonstrating

The bits of virtue in Jethro's counsel do not eliminate the considerable vice that is in his counsel. We note five significant aspects concerning his counsel that make it most unacceptable.

His counsel was unqualified, unscriptural, unnecessary, undedicated, and unsatisfactory.

Unqualified counsel. "It came to pass on the morrow, that
Moses sat to judge the people; and the people stood by Moses
from the morning unto the evening. And when [Jethro] . . . saw
all that he did to the people, he said, What is this thing that thou
doest to the people? why sittest thou thyself alone, and all the
people stand by thee from morning unto even? . . . The thing
that thou doest is not good . . . Hearken now unto my voice"
(vv. 13,14,17,19). One of the first questions we need to ask
regarding this counselling is: "Is Jethro qualified to counsel
Moses in this area?" The answer to that question is an obvious
and emphatic "No!" Jethro was very presumptuous in telling
Moses how he should govern Israel. That was definitely not his
job! What did Jethro know about God's orders to Moses? What
did he know about the goal, aim, and mission of Israel? He certainly did not know or understand Divine callings and the
Divine enablement that accompanied them. Furthermore, it
seems very strange that all of a sudden God would start speaking to Moses through Jethro where as heretofore He has always
spoken directly to Moses. Moses is to take orders from God, not
from some worldly man who has only come to the conclusion in
the last twenty-four hours that Jehovah God is superior to all
gods. A new convert of twenty-four hours is not qualified to
walk into the office of a great man of God and tell him how to
run the church!

When weighing advice, always consider the qualifications
of the adviser. Especially must we do this in the area of spiritual
matters that concern our callings and convictions and conduct.
An unsaved high school counsellor is unqualified here. The psychologists and psychiatrists who have been indoctrinated with
the twisted thinking of ungodly men are unqualified here. And
as Pink says, "One thing that this passage does is to warn God's
servants against following the advice of their relatives according
to the flesh." They are often prone to give freely of their advice

on how you should conduct your Divine calling, but unless they are veteran servants of God, beware of their counsel. If you want wise counsel in regards to your calling, convictions, and conduct, study the Word of God and seek the counsel of the godliest of men. Forget the Jethros. They may say some good things at times, as Jethro did, but that does not make their over-all counsel acceptable. It only makes it deceitful.

Unscriptural counsel. Jethro said, "Hearken now unto my voice" (v. 19). Yes, we know the Bible had not been written at this time; but the use of the word "unscriptural" refers to the fact that Jethro's counsel had no support from the God's Word. Moses had no word from God to validate this counsel. We look in vain in Jethro's counsel to see a "thus saith the LORD." We see the word of Jethro but not the word of Jehovah. It is counsel that is, therefore, based solely upon the natural reasoning of man, not upon the Word of God.

We wonder what sort of advice Jethro would have given Moses when Moses faced the angry and continued rejection by Pharaoh of Moses' request to let Israel go? What would Jethro have told Moses when after making the initial request to Pharaoh, Pharaoh responded by adding to the workload of the Israelites (Exodus 5:5–9)? From Jethro's counsel here, we have to believe he would have scolded Moses and told him he was only making matters worse and should, therefore, tone down his request so Pharaoh would not get so upset. Furthermore, what would Jethro have said at the Red Sea when Egypt's army was bearing down on the Israelites? What would he have told Moses at Marah where the water was bitter? Also what would he have counselled Moses when the Israelites had a food shortage in the wilderness and the water shortage at Rephidim? We can be sure of one thing, he would never have told Moses what God told him! Jethro would have laughed at the counsel God gave Moses. He would never have counseled Moses to part the Red Sea or to strike a rock for water! If Jethro thinks Moses is under too much pressure now, what would he have thought in those situations.

In all of those situations, God's Word provided excellent counsel, and it is not time for Moses to depart from the counsel of God's Word now. Jethro is no substitute for God's Word. Worldly counsel may sound good on the surface, but check it out with God's Word.

Unnecessary counsel. "The thing that thou doest is not good. Thou shalt surely wear away . . . this thing is too heavy for thee; thou art not able to perform it thyself alone" (vv. 17,18). The problem Jethro saw was not a problem. If something works, don't fix it. Moses was handling things just fine. In fact, he had been handling things in a superb manner ever since he went back to Egypt. But now Jethro thinks Moses cannot handle things and needs help. Oh, how foolish and arrogant of Jethro to think that he could counsel Moses. Moses had for the last year or so dealt with Israel's problems with great sagacity and great success. Jethro, however, would advise Moses that he is not dealing well with Israel's problems. How stupidly presumptuous! It is like a person who cannot tell the difference between a piano and a tuba giving advice to a concert pianist on how to play a Beethoven piano concerto. It is totally unnecessary.

Jethro, instead of solving a problem, only created one with his advice. We learn this in Numbers 11. After Jethro had visited Moses, Moses started complaining about the load upon him. "I am not able to bear all this people alone, because it is too heavy for me" (Numbers 11:14). Ah, the words sound very familiar. Jethro had been the first to say that about Moses' work—"This thing is too heavy for thee, thou art not able to perform it thyself alone" (v. 18). Moses nearly quotes him verbatim with the "too heavy" and "alone" complaint. Jethro's counsel had only agitated things. Let someone come around and bemoan your situation—even though at the time you are not bemoaning it—and sooner or later you will start complaining if you are not careful. Advertisers use this method with skill. They tell you that your car needs replacing or you can't get along without their product, etc., etc., and in this way they create a dissatisfaction within a person with their situation until that person goes out and buys the advertised product. The devil works this way all the time. He stirs up the people against God's arrangements. Adam and Eve were doing just fine until the devil deceitfully got them to be dissatisfied with their arrangements. We know the rest of the story, and it was not a good one! Neither was the story after Jethro's counsel.

Undedicated counsel. Jethro's advice did not encourage dedication. "This thing is too heavy for thee; thou art not able to perform it thyself alone . . . so shall it be easier for thyself" (vv. 18,22) is not the language of dedication. But it is the language of disobedience, of rebellion, and of lack of devotion. It is the language of wicked King Jeroboam who told the Israelites of the Northern Kingdom, "It is too much for you to go up to Jerusalem [to worship]" (I Kings 12:28). It is also the language of Peter who argued against Christ having to "suffer many things of the elders and chief priests and scribes, and be killed" (Matthew 16:21). Peter said, "Be it far from thee, Lord; this shall not be unto thee" (Matthew 16:22). Christ's response to that counsel was, "Get thee behind me, Satan" (Matthew 16:23)—a fitting response for Jethro's counsel, too. Jethro's counsel was also like the comments of those who when Christ was so busy in His ministry that he missed a meal, said He was "beside himself" (Mark 3:21).

Look out for any counsel that would cool your efforts and limit your commitment to God and His work. No worldly counsellor will ever counsel you to sacrifice for the Lord's work. If you make some sacrificial gifts to the church, they will protest and say such giving is not necessary. Of course, they will not criticize zeal and sacrifice for the things of the world. But the counsel of the world will never encourage great sacrifice and dedication for the Lord's work. It will never accept the effort and sacrifice Moses gave to lead the children of Israel for forty years in the desert. That is a career no worldly counsellor would ever recommend or commend. And Jethro and all the worldly counsellors would reject the way Apostle Paul gave himself so totally to the spreading of the Gospel.

We would never have any great churches or missionary works if we followed Jethro's counsel. You will never accomplish great things for God if you are concerned about wearing away, about things being too heavy for you, and about making things easier for yourself. In fact, that attitude will not accomplish great things in the world either. Great things are just not done on a forty hour week, eight hour day, and a five day work week schedule! The great achievers in life, be it in the world or in spiritual matters have never worried about "burn out." This does not mean we are not to stop and sharpen our scythe. But the problem today is not overworking but underworking. The problem in the church is not too much dedication but too little dedication. If we are being burdened down with our work, it is probably because we are doing too many things that do not pertain to our calling. Stick to your calling, and you will be sustained. Get outside of it, and trouble will occur. But don't look for the easy way or the small-effort career.

Unsatisfactory counsel. "So Moses hearkened to the voice of [Jethro] . . . and did all that he had said to do. And Moses chose able men out of all Israel, and made them heads over the people, rulers of thousands, rulers of hundreds, rulers of fifties, and rulers of tens. And they judged the people at all seasons; the hard causes they brought unto Moses, but every small matter they judged themselves" (vv. 24–26). This sounds good on the surface. But when we compare Scripture with Scripture, we discover that Jethro's counsel, though followed by Moses, was unsatisfactory. It did not do the job. We see this lack of satisfaction in the complaint of Moses and the command of God and the calling of God.

First, the *complaint of Moses.* We noted earlier that not long after Jethro counselled Moses, and Moses implemented the counsel, Moses complained to God and said, "I am not able to bear all this people alone, because it is too heavy for me" (Numbers 11:14). Moses' complaint sure made Jethro's counsel look unsatisfactory. He did what Jethro told him to do, but it did not work! What really happened was that Jethro's counsel only encouraged the problem he claimed to be solving. As we noted earlier, if you tell someone that his situation is bad, if that person is not alert to your negative talk, he will end up complaining about his situation even though it is not a bad situation at all.

Second, the *command of God*. When Moses complained about the problem (which Jethro had exaggerated and gotten Moses unnecessarily all upset about), God's solution was not Jethro's solution! God said, "Gather unto me seventy men of the elders of Israel, whom thou knowest to be the elders of the people, and officers over them; and bring them unto the tabernacle of the congregation, that they may stand there with thee. And I will come down and talk with thee there; and I will take of the spirit which is upon thee, and will put it upon them; and they shall bear the burden of the people with thee, that thou bear it not thyself alone" (Numbers 11:16,17). God completely ignored Jethro's plan. If nothing else reveals Jethro's counsel as bad, this surely does. God met the same problem that Jethro talked about, but much differently—and, we might add, with a lot less bureaucracy, too!

Third, the *calling of God*. Jethro's counsel was mere human reasoning. And, as we have noted before, mere human reasoning does not understand a Divine calling. For one thing, it leaves out the Spirit of God which represents Divine enabling, Divine gifts, and Divine miracles. In God's solution for the overwork problem Moses complained about and which Jethro talked about, God included the Spirit of God. When God calls, God enables—it is expressed in Old Testament times by saying the Spirit of God comes upon a person (cp. Judges 13:25, 14:6, 14:19, 15:14 in regards to Samson's supernatural strength). Therefore, when God called the seventy, God "took of the spirit that was upon him [Moses], and gave it unto the seventy elders" (Numbers 11:25). In order for them to do the job, they needed Divine gifts and Divine enabling. Without the Spirit of God, thousands cannot do the work of one. But with the Spirit of God, one can do the work of thousands. Jethro did not understand how Moses could judge all the people without wearing away because he did not understand the work of the Spirit of God upon Moses. "God had given him great strength both of body and mind, which enabled him to go through a great deal of work with ease and pleasure" (Matthew Henry). When God calls a person to a task that boggles the mind, God will supply the needed means, power, and ability to accomplish the task. Jethro's counsel, however, does not take that into consideration. It is counsel only as the world thinks, only as the natural eye can perceive. The world leaves out the power of God; and when we leave out the power of God, none of us can do the least of the tasks assigned us by God.

The enabling aspect of a calling ought to be a great warning to those who presume a calling. Trying to take up the reins of a calling that is not yours is a great mistake, and it is a good way to make a great mess of things. You will "wear away" (v. 18) with the least of tasks. Jethro's counsel won't even be enough to make you "able to endure" (v. 23). Never attempt a work without a Divine calling, but never back away from a work, no matter how impossible it seems to human reasoning, if you have the calling from God. "Has God imposed that responsibility? If so, He will assuredly be with me in sustaining it; and having Him with me, I can sustain anything" (Mackintosh).

XXI.

STATUTES FOR ISRAEL

EXODUS 19,20

WHEN MOSES WAS called by God at the burning bush to be Israel's emancipator, God promised Moses that "when thou hast brought forth the people out of Egypt, ye shall serve God upon this mountain" (Exodus 3:12). "This mountain" was "the mountain of God, even . . . Horeb" (Exodus 3:1). Our text records the fulfillment of this promise to Moses: "In the third month, when the children of Israel were gone forth out of the land of Egypt, the same day came they into the wilderness of Sinai. For they were departed from Rephidim, and were come to the desert [same Hebrew word as 'wilderness' in these verses] of Sinai, and had pitched in the wilderness; and there Israel camped before the mount" (19:1,2). We noted in earlier chapters that Mount Horeb ("the mount" of 19:2) is also referred to as Mount Sinai. In the text for this chapter this will especially be seen in 19:11,18,20,23.

This mount is a very practical and significant location. It is practical in that with the mountain range and plain in the area, it provided a great natural amphitheater situation which was ideal for the Israelites to gather as a group for Moses to address them. It is significant because of the events that have happened there. It is where Moses saw the burning bush and received his call from God to be Israel's emancipator. It is where Israel spent nearly a year (cp. Exodus 19:1 with Numbers 10:11) in their wilderness journeys and were given the law and also the Tabernacle. Also, it is where Elijah came when he fled from Jezebel and had the moving experience with the strong wind, earthquake, fire, and still small voice after which he was given orders to continue his ministry (I Kings 19:8–18).

Of the significant events that occurred at this location, we will, in this chapter of our book, especially focus on the giving of the law. Here at Mount Sinai, God gave to the Israelites many statutes to govern every facet of their life as individuals and as a nation. There are three classes or categories into which these statutes fall. They are the moral, civil, and religious laws. These laws are often interwoven, for the moral law is the basis of all the statutes given Israel. We must be careful that we distinguish these laws so that when we say with Apostle Paul that we are not under the law but under grace (Romans 6:14,15), we do not throw out the Divine moral standards for conduct. The moral law does not save us; but it is the rule, the standard by which conduct is judged and regulated by God. We are just as obligated to keep the moral law in this day of grace as Israel was in the day of the law. Not being under the law but under grace means we are under no obligation to keep the multitude of Israel's religious laws which in one way or another all portrayed Christ and His redemptive work.

This study about Israel's statutes will certainly not be an exhaustive study, for to engage in such a study of Israel's laws would necessitate studying much of Exodus, Leviticus, Numbers, and Deuteronomy. This would amount to studying something like one-twelfth of the Bible, for that is how much of the Bible is taken up by the giving of the law to Israel at Sinai. That, of course, conflicts with the purpose of our book which is a biography of Moses, not an exhaustive study of the law. But since Moses is inseparately associated with the law and is often spoken of as the great lawgiver, we do want to spend at least one chapter of this book looking at the law which God gave Moses for the Israelites. To do this, we will consider the preparation for the statutes (19:3–25; 20:18–26) and the proclaiming of the statutes (20:1–17). This last point will be a study of the ten commandments, the principal and primary statutes which laid the foundation for all the other statutes given Israel at Sinai.

491

A. THE PREPARATION FOR THE STATUTES

Before God gave the Israelites the many statutes that were to guide every facet of their lives, He prepared them for the receiving of the statutes. This largely consisted of a report from Moses (19:3–7) and a revelation of God (19:9–24; 20:18–26).

1. A Report From Moses

"And Moses went up unto God, and the LORD called unto him out of the mountain, saying, Thus shalt thou say to the house of Jacob, and tell the children of Israel" (19:3). After arriving at Sinai, Moses soon headed for a meeting with God in the mount. This began the work of the giving of the law to the Israelites. In this first meeting of God and Moses in the mount after Israel's arrival in the area, God instructed Moses to make a report to the people regarding the giving of the law. We note three things about the report: the reminder in it, the reward in it, and the response to it.

The reminder. "Ye have seen what I did unto the Egyptians, and how I bare you on eagles' wings, and brought you unto myself" (19:4). It is most appropriate that the giving of the law begin with a reminder of what God had done for the people. This would show Israel's obligation to obey Him! God redeemed Israel ("brought you unto myself"); therefore, they belonged to Him and are obligated to Him. This does not change in the New Testament; for in regards to the redeemed we read, "Ye are not your own . . . For ye are bought with a price; therefore glorify God in your body, and in your spirit, which are God's" (I Corinthians 6:19, 20). God's orders for His own are not optional but obligatory. The only right thing to do is obey Him; for as the chorus says, "After all He's done for me, how can I do less then give Him my best and live for Him completely."

This reminder is appropriately repeated (20:2) when God gives the ten commandments. We need to be reminded repeatedly about what God has done for us so we will be more earnest in obedience to Him.

The reward. "If ye will obey my voice indeed, and keep my covenant, then ye shall be a peculiar [not odd, strange; but special, precious] treasure unto me above all people . . . And ye shall be unto me a kingdom of priests, and an holy nation" (19:5,6). Before the statutes were given, God informed the Israelites of the great benefits of obeying them. He does not want Israel to view the laws as a curse or a bane to enjoyable life. But the devil certainly likes to skip over this promise of reward. He wants to make us think that God's commands are a burden and will take away much pleasure in life. But not so! The greatest blessings come from obedience to God. We do not lose anything that is good for us when we obey His commands. To complain about God's commands is to confess your rebellion to them or your blindness about their benefits or both. "His commandments are not grievous" (I John 5:3) but are for our good. When you try to wiggle out of your obligation to obey some command by inventing some clever excuse or interpretation, you simply reduce your blessings.

The response. "And all the people answered together, and said, All that the LORD hath spoken we will do" (19:8). What the people said in response to the report was excellent. God Himself said so. "And the LORD heard the voice of your words, when ye spake unto me; and the LORD said unto me, I have heard the voice of the words of this people, which they have spoken unto thee; they have well said all that they have spoken" (Deuteronomy 5:28). But what the people said and what they did were two different things. We will learn about the people's shameful behavior in later chapters of our book. Suffice it here to say that their behavior reeked of great sin. It exposed their response here as being very superficial. What they said was not wrong—the wrong was in their insincerity.

Insincerity plagues Christendom in our day. We see it in a number of ways. We see it in church regarding volunteers. At a church service when an appeal for help is given, often many people enthusiastically volunteer to help. Their exuberance in

493

volunteering is most encouraging. But some of the volunteers cannot even follow through long enough to put their name on the "sign-up" list on the bulletin board at the end of the service. We see it in missions. Many young people come forward at mission conferences and other like meetings to dedicate their life to missions. But only a small percentage of those who come forward ever make it to the field; and of those who make it to the field, many are only there for one or two terms and then quit. We see it in people's profession of faith. Many are often most outspoken as to their commitment to the faith; but we notice that when a trial enters their life, that commitment disappears for a good number. We also see this insincerity in marriage. Marriage vows say the couple pledges to be faithful "for better or for worse"; but when "for worse" comes, there are many even among professing Christians who break their vow. And what does not help this situation at all is that there are a host of preachers and books which will find some way to justify a person breaking the marriage vow. Insincerity is indeed a big problem in Christendom. But determine to be different. Make your dedication to be from the heart.

2. A Revelation of God

"And the LORD said unto Moses, Lo, I come unto thee in a thick cloud, that the people may hear when I speak with thee, and believe thee for ever" (19:9). Preceding the giving of the statutes will be a special revelation of God—He "will come down in the sight of all the people upon mount Sinai" (19:11). It is very important that God reveal Himself before He gives the law to the Israelites, for a revelation of God will show the authority and character of the lawgiver. The greater the authority of the lawmaker, the more important are the statutes. As an example, laws made by our congress are more important and weighty than laws made by some grade school committee. Also the better the character of the lawmaker, the better the statutes. When we elect bad men to be our legislators, we can count on them making bad laws; for bad men make bad laws just as good men make good laws. The revelation God gives Israel will inform them they will have laws of the finest character.

To examine this revelation given the Israelites at Mount Sinai, we will look at the readying for the revelation, the record of the revelation, and the reaction to the revelation.

The readying for the revelation. "And the LORD said unto Moses, Go unto the people, and sanctify them today and tomorrow . . . be ready against the third day; for the third day the LORD will come down in the sight of all the people upon mount Sinai" (vv. 10,11). The message here is "prepare to meet thy God, O Israel" (Amos 4:12). God is coming into their camp in a visible manifestation. If they are prepared for the visit, they will be blessed of God. If they are not prepared, it will be judgment. The lesson is the same in every age, be it at Mount Sinai when Israel was there in their wilderness journeys or be it with us in our day. We all are headed for an encounter with God, and we had better be prepared for it. In fact, no preparation is more important than the preparation to meet God.

Preparation for Israel's meeting with God at Sinai involved cleansing, curtailing, and congregating.

First, the *cleansing.* "Sanctify them . . . let them wash their clothes" (19:10). The Israelites must clean up for this meeting with God. Both salvation and fellowship are seen in this requirement. *Salvation* is seen in the fact that we must be clothed with clean clothes if we are going to meet God successfully. But Isaiah said, "All our righteousnesses are as filthy rags" (Isaiah 64:6), and that condition will never pass with God. We cannot wash our clothes as the Israelites could at Sinai, but we can obtain clean clothes through Christ. "I will greatly rejoice in the LORD . . . for he hath clothed me with the garments of salvation, he hath covered me with the robe of righteousness" (Isaiah 61:10). *Fellowship* is seen in the fact that God will only draw nigh to a people that are clean. When we allow sin to rule in our life, it will make our fellowship with God very poor.

Second, the *curtailing.* Two actions of the people were curtailed to help prepare them for the Divine revelation. They were curtailed in where they could go and in what they could do. The order that limited *where they could go* said, "Thou shalt set bounds unto the people round about, saying, Take heed to yourselves, that ye go not up into the mount, or touch the border of it; whosoever toucheth the mount shall be surely put to death" (Exodus 19:12). The order that limited *what they could do* said, "Come not at your wives" (19:15). Many will not like these curtailments. They want freedom to do whatever they want to do wherever and whenever they want to do it. But that will not foster a good meeting with God. Rebelling against the first curtailment will bring *death*. Rebelling against the second curtailment will bring *distraction*. Either one destroys a good meeting with God. Men have trouble with both curtailments. Some rebel against the plain commands of God that warn about conduct that will bring destruction. Others do not get their priorities right and so they are distracted by legitimate pleasures. These pleasures become more important than meeting with God. As an example, many miss church not because they are pursuing some vile evil but because they are pursuing some innocent pleasure.

Third, the *congregating*. "Moses brought forth the people out of the camp to meet with God; and they stood at the nether part [lower part, the base] of the mount" (19:17). When God came to Mount Sinai to reveal Himself, the people needed to be gathered at the mount to see the revelation. So Moses gathered them in the plain at the foot of the mount. Leading them "out of the camp" indicates that the main encampment of the Israelites was somewhat removed from Mount Sinai. But they were not church members who took in church by radio or TV. They went to the place where the revelation was to occur. We need to congregate for worship if we expect to have a meeting with God. Yes, God can meet with us separately, and He does, and this is a vital relationship we must cultivate. But private meetings do not cancel out public meetings. Public meetings are part of God's plan, too! They honor Him, give testimony of Him, instruct and edify the saints, and promote fellowship of the finest sort.

The record of the revelation. "And it came to pass on the third day in the morning, that there were thunders and lightnings, and a thick cloud upon the mount, and the voice of the trumpet exceeding loud . . . And mount Sinai was altogether on a smoke, because the LORD descended upon it in fire; and the smoke thereof ascended as the smoke of a furnace, and the whole mount quaked greatly" (19:16,18). The record given in Scripture of the revelation of God at Mount Sinai certainly conveys a dramatic event. What a mighty and moving manifestation Israel heard and saw at Sinai. No one went to sleep in church that day!

What was the fundamental message in such a revelation? What did it especially say about God? It was that God is a holy God. The thunders, lightnings, thick cloud, fire, smoke, and quaking all speak of Divine judgment. And Divine judgment is rooted and grounded in God's holiness. While other attributes of God can be perceived here, such as His power, the chief revelation of God given here was the holiness of God. Holiness is the fundamental attribute of God. When you learn about God, you must start there; for holiness affects everything about God. The emphasis on God's holiness will tell us the character of the laws that God will give Israel. God's holiness will make His laws holy, a character not seen in many laws man makes.

Even before this dramatic revelation of God, holiness was being emphasized in the bounds that were to be set around Mount Sinai so the people would not touch the mount lest they die. After God came down to Mount Sinai in the tremendous display of thunder, lightning, fire, smoke, and earthquake, He again emphasized the boundary (19:21–25). The message in the boundary is that holiness keeps us away from God. This message is especially fitting here because the law is emphasized here. The law does not save us but only shows how unholy we are and, therefore, how unworthy we are of being near God. Thus it shows the need of the Gospel of Christ, for it is the remedy to this distance problem. We who because of our sin "were far off are made nigh by the blood of Christ" (Ephesians 2:13).

The reaction to the revelation. "All the people that was in the camp trembled" (19:16); and "when the people saw it, they removed, and stood afar off. And they said unto Moses, Speak thou with us, and we will hear; but let not God speak with us, lest we die" (20:18,19). The reaction of the people to the revelation of God is seen in three ways—in their trepidation, location, and supplication.

First, their *trepidation.* "All the people that was in the camp trembled" (19:16). We do not blame them for trembling. In fact, if they did not tremble, we would be critical of them. If the display of Divine power on Mount Sinai did not move them, they have spiritual problems. This is the problem with our world today. We can have great displays of God's power occurring, yet we do not tremble before God. We explain it away as chance or as bad weather caused by capricious jet streams or as some other natural cause, but it seems never to occur to many people that God is behind it all. However, if we do not tremble before God in this life, we will certainly tremble for all eternity.

Second, their *location.* "They removed, and stood afar off" (20:18). The location of the people demonstrates their reverence for God and also their own sinfulness. It is the same attitude exhibited by Peter when he told Christ, "Depart from me; for I am a sinful man, O Lord" (Luke 5:8). Peter's statement must not be misunderstood. Though he told Christ to depart from him, it is not the language of the unbeliever who wants nothing to do with Christ. Rather, it is the exaggerated language of a humbled soul, who, though he loves Christ and desires His companionship greatly, sees himself wholly unworthy of fellowship with Divinity. The sense of unworthiness and self-loathing is the effect of a manifestation of Divinity before the attentive soul.

Third, their *supplication.* "They said unto Moses, Speak thou with us, and we will hear; but let not God speak with us, lest we die" (20:19). The Israelites pleaded for a mediator. The Israelites had gotten an awesome view of the holiness of God and it convicted them of their sin (as was also seen in their moving away from the mount). Now to be saved from death, they plead for a mediator. This gives us a great lesson on the presentation of the Gospel. If you want men to cry out for a Savior in Jesus Christ, you must first convict them that they are sinners worthy of Divine judgment. We have some today who want to leave judgment out of the Gospel message. They want to talk only about the love of God, not the holiness of God. But when you do that, you will not convict men of their sins; and unconvicted sinners see no need of a Savior.

More Gospel is seen here by observing the responses of Moses and God to the supplication. *Moses' response* to the people was "Fear not" (20:20), and "Moses drew near unto the thick darkness where God was" (20:21). "Fear not" is the message for those who seek salvation through their Emancipator. As Moses, Israel's emancipator, spoke it to them, so Christ, the sinner's Emancipator speaks it to us (Luke 12:32). And as Moses drew near to God to mediate for Israel, so Christ draws near to God for us, for He is the "one mediator between God and men" (I Timothy 2:5). *God's response* to the Israelites' supplication was to instruct Moses about an altar where sacrifices were to be made (20:24–26). The altar, of course, speaks of Calvary. Christ can be our Mediator and Savior because of Calvary. Leave out Calvary, and you have no way of salvation; for a holy God must judge sin. Sin is judged either in Jesus Christ Who bore our sins on Calvary, or it is judged in the unrepentant sinner.

B. THE PROCLAIMING OF THE STATUTES

In our study of Israel's statutes in this chapter, we will limit the study to the ten commandments. These were the first and foremost statutes given Israel by God and are the basis for the many statutes which followed. "The ten commandments form a summary of our main duties towards God and towards men" (Rawlinson). Therefore, in a limited study of Israel's statutes, the ten commandments certainly are the statutes that should be studied.

Interestingly, only twice in the Bible is the number "ten" used in regards to this first set of statutes (Exodus 34:28 and Deuteronomy 10:4). That the Scriptures do give a definite number to these commandments is a good thing, for it helps in emphasizing the commandments. And they need to be emphasized. No, they will not save a soul; but they certainly are a great standard of conduct. Men have never devised a better one.

The ten commandments can be divided into two categories which is symbolically suggested by the fact that they were written on "two" tables of stone (Exodus 34:1). The first four commandments speak of man's relationship with God; the last six speak of man's relationship with man. Christ divides all commandments into these two categories. He said the first commandment was "Thou shalt love the Lord thy God with all thy heart, and with all thy soul, and with all thy mind" (Matthew 22:37). That compares to the first four commandments of the ten commandments. Christ said the second commandment is, "Thou shalt love thy neighbor as thyself" (Matthew 22:39). That compares to the last six commandments of the ten. Another fact we need to note in categorizing the commandments is that all the commands are negative except the fourth and fifth commands which are the last one Godward (sabbath) and the first one manward (honoring parents). Some people do not like negatives in the message. But God puts plenty of them in the message, for they are very necessary.

The ten commandments were proclaimed to Israel directly by God's voice (Exodus 20:22, Deuteronomy 5:4,22) during the time God revealed Himself in thunder, lightning, fire, smoke etc. on Mount Sinai. All the other statutes were given to Israel through Moses. That God proclaimed the ten commandments to the Israelites Himself and in such dramatic fashion emphasizes the primary position of the ten commandments among all the statutes given Israel.

The primary position of the ten commandments is also emphasized in that they were later inscribed by the finger of God upon two stone tablets (Exodus 31:18; 32:15,16). But God had to give Moses a second copy; for when Moses came down from the mount and saw the sin going on in the camp, "Moses' anger waxed hot, and he cast the tables out of his hands, and brake them beneath the mount" (32:19). We will study more about that incident in a later chapter. The second set of stone tablets with the ten commandments on them (Exodus 34:1; Deuteronomy 10:4) was eventually placed in the Ark in the Tabernacle (Exodus 40:20; Deuteronomy 10:5).

1. The First Commandment

"Thou shalt have no other gods before me" (20:3). We will look at the prohibitings of the command, the place of the command, and the priority in the command.

The prohibitings of the command. Paganism with its many gods obviously violates the first commandment. But we Americans, in a country of luxury compared to other nations of the world, are not any better than the pagans. We may not actually bow down to idol gods, but we revere many other types of gods. We give so much devotion to pleasure, money, physical appetites, and popularity that we virtually make these things gods in our life. Sunday morning reveals that many professing Christians violate the first commandment by where they are instead of being in church. They are giving devotion to pleasure, physical appetites, etc. that they ought to be giving to God.

The place of the command. This command is properly the first commandment of all commandments. If we do not have God in the proper position in our heart, all the statutes will not be viewed properly. Furthermore, to have good laws, God must be the basis and the foundation upon which the laws are made. Men lose their bearings when God is not the basis of their thinking. As an example, "In the beginning God" (Genesis 1:1) is a fundamental truth which is absolutely essential to understand the origin of the world. Evolution leaves out God, and so they have a ridiculous explanation for our origin.

The priority in the command. This commandment states that God is to have no rivals in our heart. It is Jehovah God first and foremost in our worship and in our devotion. This means it excludes such things as heathen gods and the Masonic Lodge's office of "most worshipful grand master" (what a blasphemous title for any man to assume, but masons do it all the time), and it means we are to put Him first in our lives. "Seek ye first the kingdom of God, and his righteousness" (Matthew 6:33) expresses well this practical application of the first of the ten commandments.

2. The Second Commandment

"Thou shalt not make unto thee any graven image, or any likeness of any thing that is in heaven above, or that is in the earth beneath, or that is in the water under the earth. Thou shalt not bow down thyself to them, nor serve them; for I the LORD thy God am a jealous God, visiting the iniquity of the fathers upon the children unto the third and fourth generation of them that hate me; And showing mercy unto thousands of them that love me, and keep my commandments" (20:4–6). We note the restrictions in the command, the relationship of the command, the rejection of the command, the retribution in the command, and the recompense in the command.

The restrictions in the command. The command puts a threefold restriction upon man. First, it forbids making any graven image; second, it forbids bowing down to them; and third, it forbids serving them. The second and third restrictions remind us that worship ("bow down . . . to them") and service ("serve . . . them") go together. Jesus addressed this truth about worship and service when He was tempted by Satan. He said, "Thou shalt *worship* the Lord thy God, and him only shalt thou *serve*" (Matthew 4:10). We serve that which we worship. If our worship is faulty, our service will also be faulty. Those who are not faithful in worship at church are not faithful in serving.

The relationship of the command. This command is insepa-rably related to the first command. The first command tells us

Who to worship; this second command tells us *how to worship*. Jesus said, "God is a Spirit [hence, not a graven image]; and they that worship him must worship him in spirit and in truth" (John 4:24). Satan is clever; if he does not stop you from worshipping the true God (first commandment), he will endeavor to defile your worship methods (second commandment). Methods are important, and some of our churches who do not have a problem with graven images nevertheless have problems with guileful inducements. Their promotional programs smack of the world, not the Word.

The rejection of the command. Athens, in Paul's day, certainly rejected this command; for Paul found Athens to be a city wholly given over to idolatry. The city was full of idols. The Roman Catholic Church also rejects this command. They do it in their churches and in their counting. They do it in their *churches* in that their churches are filled with all sorts of graven images (we are seeing more and more of this in Protestant churches, too). But crucifixes and other similar things are not necessary for worship and are forbidden in worship by this second commandment. The Roman Catholics also reject this commandment by their *counting*. They count the ten commandments differently than the rest of us do. They combine the first and second commandment into one and divide the last commandment (coveting) into two. In this way they take away the emphasis on the no graven image command, for they only emphasize the no other god part of their first commandment (the combined first and second commandments). So like all false religions, they twist the Scripture to promote their corrupt creed.

The retribution in the command. This second command comes with a note of Divine retribution for those who break God's laws. We note both the extent and explanation of it.

First, the *extent of the retribution* is seen in "God, visiting the iniquity of the fathers upon the children unto the third and fourth generation of them that hate me" (20:5). Many folk get all upset about this. They accuse God of lack of love, etc. But the lack of love in this verse is in man, not God. People ignore the "hate me" problem. What a terrible sin to "hate" God. Hating God leaves scars on any family. But man seems to only get upset if they suspect God is not treating them right.

Second, the *explanation of this retribution* is that when we sin, it affects succeeding generations. As an example, a drug addict produces deformed children who will produce deformed children who will also produce deformed children. Is that God's fault? Not at all. The drug addict disobeyed God and brought on the problem himself. Don't blame God for your troubles or judgments! Rather, thank God for the warnings and heed them.

The recompense in the command. "And showing mercy unto thousands of them that love me, and keep my commandments" (20:6). Retribution is not all there is in this command though for the rebellious soul who hates God, that is all he will experience in eternity. But there is another side, there is the recompense for those that love and obey the Lord. Yes, it pays to love and obey God. We may not seem to experience much of the pay in this life, but eternity is another story. What glory, what blessing will be for God's own.

Note that love comes before obey in this recompense statement. The key to obedience is love. Those who evidence obedience problems are evidencing love problems. Some talk much about their love for God, but we note they do not show much love for God by their walk, for they live in almost a constant state of disobedience to His commands.

3. The Third Commandment

"Thou shalt not take the name of the LORD thy God in vain; for the LORD will not hold him guiltless that taketh his name in vain" (20:7). The third commandment forbids profanity. It speaks of the misuse of the name of God. It means we must not use His name irreverently. We think of people cursing when we think of profanity, and that certainly is a logical application. But profanity also applies to using the name hypocritically and flippantly. To further study this command, we note the popularity of profanity, the prayer opposing profanity, and the punishment for profanity.

The popularity of profanity. Go into any public place today, and you will hear profanity coming from men, women, and children. Some of us can remember when only men used God's name in their cursing. But it spills as easily from the mouths of women and children today. Commonness of profanity predicts commonness of judgment.

The prayer opposing profanity. Not many folk think about it or recognize the fact, but the first petition of what is commonly known as the "Lord's prayer" is a prayer opposing profanity. "Hallowed be thy name" (Matthew 6:9) is the first request of the Lord's prayer. How often those words have been spoken and sung without meaning. But we need to be earnest in praying that we will always use the name of God in utmost respect. That respect, however, does not include the habits of the Jews in refusing to pronounce the name Jehovah but saying Adonai (Lord) instead. That, in fact, is irreverence for the name.

The punishment for profanity. "The LORD will not hold him guiltless that taketh his name in vain" (v. 7). Judgment is certain for profanity. Men may excuse profanity—and some do. Some, as example, explain it as a needed venting of anger and as therapeutic for distraught spirits. But this is nothing but the twisted thinking of sinful minds. God, however, is more holy in His thinking; and, therefore, the sin of profanity will result in judgment. Men need to clean up their mouth, or they will experience Divine wrath.

4. The Fourth Commandment

"Remember the sabbath day, to keep it holy. Six days shalt thou labor, and do all thy work; But the seventh day is the sab-

505

bath of the LORD thy God; in it thou shalt not do any work . . . the LORD blessed the sabbath day, and hallowed it" (20:8–11). This is the last of the four commandments which involve man's relationship with God. Herschel Ford, in noting how each of these first four commandments speak of worship, said, "The first commandment told us to worship God and none other. The second told us to worship Him directly and to have no idols. The third told us to worship Him sincerely and not falsely. The fourth tells us of a special time set aside for worship." To study this command, we note the design of the Sabbath, the day of the Sabbath, the duties before the Sabbath, and the desecration of the Sabbath.

The design of the Sabbath. The design of the Sabbath was rest. We need rest both physically and spiritually. Physical rest results from cessation of work on this day. After six days of work, we need to rest. Furthermore, after six days in the world we need spiritual rest, too. Spiritual rest comes from worship which invigorates and refreshes the soul. "Man is a seven-day clock. He must be wound up with regular accuracy" (F. B. Meyer). The way God made us, it requires the Sabbath rest if we are to function at our best.

The design included all men, not just the Jews; for the Sabbath was already in place before the law was incorporated into the ten commandments. Our Exodus text emphasizes the inclusiveness of the command by including "thy son . . . daughter, thy manservant . . . thy maidservant . . . [and] thy stranger that is within thy gates" (20:10). Also the "cattle" (Ibid.) are included. Experience has proven that animals do much better with a day of rest each week than being worked seven days.

The day of the Sabbath. In the Old Testament, the Sabbath was the last day of the week. It was based on fact that "six days the LORD made the heaven and earth, the sea, and all that in them is, and rested the seventh day" (20:11). But the second creation, soul salvation (II Corinthians 5:17), has changed the day to the first day of the week. This is seen in a number of ways: Christ rose from the grave the first day of the week, Christ's first few post-resurrection appearances were on the first day of the week, Pentecost and the coming of the Holy Spirit was on the first day of the week, Peter's first sermon was preached on the first day of the week, Paul preached in Troas on the first day of the week—he abode seven days in Troas, but it was on the first day of week that the believers gathered for worship (Acts 20:6,7), and Paul instructed the believers to make their gifts on the first day of the week (I Corinthians 16:2). Church history will show that the church's primary meeting day was the first day of the week, and that practice continues right into our day which helps confirm the fact that the day of rest is now Sunday and not Saturday.

The duties before the Sabbath. Part of the fourth commandment speaks of work. "Six days shalt thou labor" (20:9). In examining the fourth commandment, we must not overlook this fact. God intended that we work. Even Adam and Eve were given chores to do in the Garden of Eden before the fall (Genesis 2:15). Work is of such importance that Paul said, "If any would not work, neither should he eat" (II Thessalonians 3:10). But some folk seem more interested in having a day of rest every week then in working the other six days.

The desecration of the Sabbath. Like the other commandments, the Sabbath commandment is broken frequently. Desecration comes in many forms, such as farmers working in their fields, factories operating on a full schedule, folks doing their yard and garden work, and shopping malls and sports stadiums busy selling and entertaining. The Sabbath is also desecrated by those who add many unscriptural rules about keeping it. If the devil cannot keep you from observing the Sabbath, he will encourage you to add to the conditions of observing it. The Jews got so carried away in adding to the restrictions that you could not swat a bug that was stinging you without it being considered

breaking the Sabbath. The Seventh Day Adventists also dese-
crate the Sabbath in the excessive and unscriptural honors they
give to it. One of their early leaders, Ellen White, claimed to
have a vision about the fourth commandment in which "Jesus
raised the cover of the ark, and she beheld the tables of stone on
which the ten commandments were written. She was amazed as
she saw the fourth commandment in the very center of the ten
precepts, with a soft halo of light encircling it" (William Irvine).
Such perverted babbling guides Adventists' thinking.

5. The Fifth Commandment

"Honor thy father and thy mother; that thy days may be
long upon the land which the LORD thy God giveth thee"
(20:12). In examining this command, we will consider the place
of the home, the position of parents, the promise of life, and the
performing of the command.

The place of the home. This command begins the second of
two divisions of the ten commandments. The first four commandments speak of man's relationship with God; the final six
speak of man's relationship with man. It is significant and
instructive that the first commandment regarding man's relationship with man deals with the home. This shows the place of the
home in society. It is the most important institution of society. It
was created by God before human government and before the
church. If the home is right, society, the government, and the
church will be right. But if the home decays, then society, the
government, and the church will also decay.

The position of parents. This command makes it plain that
parents are the authority in the home. Sinful man, however,
wants to undermine that authority. Our day certainly is doing
much to undermine the authority of the parents. As an example,
we hear today about children's rights which means children do
not have to be in subjection to the parents. But God is not dumb
like the so-called experts of society. To let children rule will

bring chaos and will break down authority in society.

We need to emphasize here that position creates responsibility. Parents are to be honored, but they are to conduct themselves in a way that will justify their being honored. In the Old Testament, the Jewish parents were given much responsibility in teaching their children and especially in teaching them about God's Word (Deuteronomy 6:7; Proverbs 22:6). We have many parents in our society who are a despicable lot without a shred of conduct that could be honored. Obviously, the command does not insist children honor corrupt characters.

The promise of life. This command comes with a special promise: "thy days may be long upon the land which the LORD thy God giveth thee" (20:12). Paul refers to this promise when he said, "Honor thy father and mother; which is the first commandment with promise" (Ephesians 6:2). It is true that obedience to any of the commands promises blessings. But this is the first command in which a blessing was specifically stated. The Jews were promised to live a long time in the promised land if they gave honor to their parents. The promise is still present today in principle. In principle, obedience to parents promotes a better life than disobedience. Obedient children will enjoy life a lot more than the disobedient. Of course, this does not necessarily mean that when a saint dies young, he was disobedient to his parents. Some of God's people die young because they stood true to God. But these exceptions do not cancel out the general principle in the promise. It is healthy to be an obedient child. It will bless all your days.

The performing of the command. To give honor to one's parents means to obey them when a child and to give them due love and care and attention in all of your life. Performing the command does not mean, however, that a saved person must obey his unsaved parents in going against the call of God for his life. God is higher in authority than parents; and when orders clash, God's orders come first.

509

6. The Sixth Commandment

"Thou shalt not kill" (20:13). In the English, this is the shortest of the ten commandments. But in the Hebrew, both this and the eighth command are the same length and so share the shortest characteristic. To study this sixth command, we will look at the explanation of the command, the application of the command, and the condemnation in the command.

The explanation. This command has been misused by many to push philosophies wholly opposed to what the Bible teaches. But the meaning of the word "kill" in the command will expose the error of those who misuse it. The word "kill" is a translation of a Hebrew word which means to murder. Therefore, this command does not forbid some things some folks think it does. As an example, this command does not forbid the killing of animals; for God does not forbid the killing of animals for food and clothing but, in fact, sanctions it. Also, this command does not forbid capital punishment. Capital punishment is plainly exhorted by Scriptures as we will see later. Those who would use this command to forbid capital punishment simply ignore the plain commands of Scripture. Furthermore, this command does not forbid killing in war. War is terrible but sometimes necessary. God is sometimes recorded in Scripture as instructing various nations to fight in war.

The application. Murder not only includes a man violently killing someone, but it also includes such acts as abortion and suicide. Abortion is the taking of the life of the unborn. An unborn person is protected by God. In later statutes given Israel, men were punished with death if they hurt a mother with child and death resulted for the unborn child (Exodus 21:22,23). God recognizes what the wicked world does not want to recognize, namely, that the unborn has life and to kill that life is murder. Suicide is also murder. It is murdering of one's self. Life is life whether it is yours or another. You do not have the right to murder another or yourself. Assisted suicides are also murder.

In the New Testament, the application of the command goes beyond the outward act to "Whosoever hateth his brother is a murderer" (I John 3:15). The New Testament also applies other commands to thoughts as well as deeds. It always raises the standard. Some, however, pervert the standard in their wrongful broadening of the command, such as the animal rights people and those against capital punishment which we noted above.

The condemnation. Scripture says the punishment for breaking this command is death. "Whoso sheddeth man's blood, by man shall his blood be shed; for in the image of God made he man" (Genesis 9:6). "He that killeth [murders] any man shall surely be put to death" (Leviticus 24:17, cp. 24:21). "The murderer shall surely be put to death" (Numbers 35:16,17,18, cp. Numbers 35:31,33). If we practiced capital punishment as demanded by the Word of God (capital punishment was mandated long before Israel was given the order to kill the murderer), we would decrease the number of murders dramatically in the land. The FBI has over the years given out figures which say that as many as two-thirds of all murders were committed by repeaters—such as repeaters who had been given short prison sentences or escaped from prison. Executing all murderers would stop many others from becoming murderers, too!

7. The Seventh Commandment
"Thou shalt not commit adultery" (20:14). To examine this command, we will note the acceptance, the attack, the application, the anathema, and the avoidance of adultery.

The acceptance of adultery. Though it is a heinous sin, it is quite accepted in our society. In fact, laws have legalized it through legalized prostitution. But though governments legalize adultery, it is still sin; for the laws of men do not nullify or cancel or make void the laws of God. Man's laws which are contrary to God's laws only encourage men to break God's laws. And woe be anyone who encourages disobedience to God.

511

The attack of adultery. Adultery attacks the most sacred relationship a man and woman can have, namely, marriage. This relationship is so sacred and so important that God decrees it must continue till death ends it. But adultery assaults marriage and the home. It only hurts marriage and the home. It certainly does not help! When you hurt marriage and the home, you strike a most injurious blow upon a land.

The application of adultery. This command is wide sweeping in its application. Some become technical and say this command only applies to married people. Then they go on a great discussion on how it is different than fornication. While there is indeed some differences in the word meanings, any thought that this commandment does not forbid all immoral sexual contact between a man and woman will not hold water. Sex between a man and woman is only sanctioned when the man and woman are properly married—which excludes marriage after divorce. Marriage after divorce leads to adultery; for Christ said, "Whosoever shall put away his wife, and marry another, committeth adultery against her. And if a woman shall put away her husband, and be married to another, she committeth adultery" (Mark 10:11,12). We have many who look for texts of Scripture they can twist to justify divorce, but it is still ends up adultery in God's sight. Christ even warns, "That whosoever looketh on a woman to lust after her hath committed adultery with her already in his heart" (Matthew 5:28). How very high are Christ's standards. Obviously, adultery in the heart does not produce the ramifications of adultery in actual deed. But the heart is where deeds begin. You allow adultery in the heart and you will soon be doing it in deed.

The anathema of adultery. The curse of adultery is great. It has filled society with troubles and tragedies. Adultery does not help any good thing. It only curses. It curses those who commit the act and it curses countless others also—such as the child who is a result of adultery, and the friends and parents and relatives of those whose lives are shamed and shattered by adultery. The writer of the book of Proverbs said, "Can a man [or woman] take fire in his bosom, and his clothes not be burned? Can one go upon hot coals, and his feet not be burned? So he that goeth in to his neighbor's wife; whosoever toucheth her shall not be innocent. . . . whoso committeth adultery . . . destroyeth his own soul" (Proverbs 6:27–29,32).

The avoidance of adultery. The sex passions of man are second only to the passion of self-preservation. Therefore, mankind must be wise and control this passion or it will control and curse him. Adultery does not happen overnight. It is a product of corrupt behavior over a period of time. Adultery (and we include here all immoral acts between man and woman) can be avoided when we avoid those things that would suggest and stimulate illicit sex. What we look at, what we say, the company we keep, the clothes we wear, and the activities we engage in all can encourage or discourage adultery. Sin is best defeated in the embryo stage. Therefore, start opposing adultery when it tempts in the smallest of ways, and you will defeat it.

8. The Eighth Commandment

"Thou shalt not steal" (20:15). Along with the sixth command (do not kill), this is the shortest of the ten commandments. This commandment confirms the right of ownership of property and commands mankind to respect that ownership. To examine the problem of stealing which this commandment condemns, we note the motivation for stealing and the methods of stealing.

The motivation. Coveting is the big motivator in breaking this commandment. Thus this eighth commandment is very closely related to the tenth commandment (the commandment against coveting), for stealing is a result of coveting to possess something that is not yours.

The methods. There are many ways to steal. Robbing a

513

bank, shop-lifting, and pick-pocketing are not the only ways one can steal. An employer can steal from an employee by giving him an inferior wage or forcing him to work extra hours without pay. An employee can steal from an employer by loafing on the job and not putting in his full time on the job. In this way he is paid for more hours than he has worked. One can steal by concealing the defects in a product he is selling. Using false weights (inaccurate scales in our day) is also a means of stealing. Declaring bankruptcy is another means of stealing from others. What makes bankruptcy so guileful is that it obtains the help of the law to steal from one's creditors. In our day of coupons, many have learned how to steal by giving their name in a variety of ways in order to obtain more than their limit in special coupon sales. One can steal from God by not giving to Him what he ought. "Will a man rob God? Yet ye have robbed me. But ye say, Wherein have we robbed thee? In tithes and offerings" (Malachi 3:8). Many steal in the way they fill out their income tax reports, and the government steals from its citizens by unfair and unnecessary taxes. There are many ways to steal, and it seems man has found them all. But God will judge!

9. The Ninth Commandment

"Thou shalt not bear false witness against thy neighbor" (19:16). While this commandment speaks of a court room situation, it by no means is limited to the court room. In future statutes given Israel, the false witness principle is applied to any "false report" (Exodus 23:1). Like stealing, false witnessing can be done in a variety of ways—but though some of the ways may not bother a hardened conscience, it is still false witness. You can lie by telling a boldface untruth. This is what we normally think of in this matter of speaking untruthfully. We usually think of the liar as one who goes around telling things which just are not so. And that is indeed lying, but it is only one way to lie. You can also lie by what you do not say as well as by what you do say. Leaving out pertinent facts about some situation or person can grossly misrepresent things. In this manner of lying, all that you say can actually be the truth. Yet, because you purposely leave out pertinent facts, you are lying. On the other hand, it is possible to not be speaking the truth and yet not be a liar. You may believe that what you are saying is the truth, but it may, in fact, be inaccurate or incorrect.

The liberal news media has some of the worst liars in the land. They lie by exaggeration, by implication, by leaving out pertinent facts, and by telling boldface lies. The news media is very untrustworthy because of this, and they have done much damage to the cause of righteousness.

10. The Tenth Commandment

"Thou shall not covet thy neighbor's house, thou shalt not covet thy neighbor's wife, nor his manservant, nor his maidservant, nor his ox, nor his ass, nor anything that is thy neighbor's" (20:17). To examine this command, we note the contents, comparison, and character of the command.

The contents of the command. This commandment, as recorded in our text, states the principle then gives applications. The principle is "Thou shalt not covet." Applications given here include not coveting a neighbor's house, or a neighbor's wife, or a neighbor's servant, or livestock, or anything else that is your neighbor's. Like the other commandments, it is wide spreading in its application. God's laws are always more wide spreading in application than man is generally inclined to admit. Whenever you see a command of God in the Word, be careful to discern principle from application. If you make an application a principle, you will limit the application of the command.

The comparison of the command. When we compare this tenth commandment with the other nine, we see a strong relationship between it and two other commandments. This tenth commandment is related to the seventh commandment (the commandment against adultery); for adultery is a result of coveting your neighbor's wife. Also, as we noted earlier, this tenth commandment is related to this ninth commandment (the commandment against stealing); for coveting is a great motivation for stealing.

The character of the command. As we noted in our introduction of the ten commandments, this commandment focuses on an inward attitude. The other commandments are primary outward actions, but this is solely an inward attitude. All the other commandments can be enforced by mankind, and laws can be put on human law books corresponding to the other commandments. But this tenth commandment is not an enforceable law in terms of human government. If a government had the law against coveting on the books, if would be impossible to prosecute; for they cannot see the heart of the person where coveting exists. But God, of course, can arrest and prosecute one for coveting; for God sees the heart. The Apostle Paul recognized that this tenth commandment forbids all those evil desires of the heart. He said, "I had not known lust, except the law had said, Thou shalt not covet" (Romans 7:7).

Though coveting is a sin within the heart, it will, of course, produce outward actions if not stopped. The reason coveting is so bad is that it causes men to do some very wicked deeds. Therefore, if we want to live a holy life, we must not only see to it that we do not do overt acts of wickedness; but we must also see to it that we do not let evil thoughts control our life. Sin must be fought in the thought life if it is going to be fought successfully, for thoughts are the foundation of deeds.

XXII.

SANCTUARY OF GOD

EXODUS 25 – 31; 35 – 40

THE FIRST MAJOR revelation Moses received from God at Sinai concerned the statutes for Israel. Now in this chapter we will study the second major revelation Moses received at Sinai. This second revelation concerned the Tabernacle. God instructed Moses to "make me a sanctuary; that I may dwell among them" (25:8). The Tabernacle, the Sanctuary of God, was to be the center of worship and revelation for the Israelites in the wilderness.

The main record in Scripture regarding the Tabernacle takes up nearly a third of the book of Exodus. Chapter 25 through chapter 40 (with the exception of chapters 32, 33 and 34) records the details of the Tabernacle. With this amount of material, the Tabernacle can be, of course, a great and extensive study in itself. But as with the statutes given Israel, we will only give one chapter to it; for the purpose of our book is a biography of Moses, not a detailed study of the Tabernacle.

The Tabernacle was called by various names in Scripture. The best known name is "tabernacle" (Exodus 25:9). Other names by which it was called include "tent" (Exodus 39:33), "tent of the congregation" (Exodus 39:40), "tabernacle of the congregation" (Exodus 27:21), "tabernacle of testimony" (Exodus 38:21), "tabernacle of the LORD" (I Kings 2:28), "tabernacle of witness" (Numbers 17:8), "sanctuary" (Exodus 25:8; 36:1), and "sanctuary of the LORD" (Numbers 19:20).

In a brief description, the Tabernacle consisted of a tent which was 45 feet long by 15 feet wide by 15 feet high (feet measurements are based on the assumption that the "cubit" in

Scripture is approximately 18 inches) divided into two rooms. Surrounding the Tabernacle was a fence which was 7½ feet high and made of white linen. The fence was 150 feet long and 75 feet wide making a sizeable court around the Tabernacle. Six pieces of furniture were made for the Tabernacle. They were the brasen altar, the laver, the table of showbread, the altar of incense, the lampstand, and the ark. The furniture was a very integral part of the Tabernacle's ritual. Priests from the tribe of Levi were consecrated to be the administrators and caretakers of the Tabernacle and its furniture.

To study the Tabernacle in more detail, we will consider the plan for the Tabernacle, the provisions for the Tabernacle, the parts of the Tabernacle, and the priests for the Tabernacle.

A. THE PLAN FOR THE TABERNACLE

"And the LORD spake unto Moses, saying . . . let them make me a sanctuary; that I may dwell among them. According to all that I show thee . . . even so shall ye make it" (Exodus 25:1,8,9). To further examine the plan for the Tabernacle, we will note its purpose, pattern, and place.

1. The Purpose

"That I may dwell among them" (25:8) is the stated purpose of the Tabernacle. "The Tabernacle was God's first dwelling-place on earth. He *walked* in the company of Adam in Eden. He *visited* Abraham at Mamre . . . Here He comes down to *dwell* with His redeemed, and from then till now, He has had a dwelling-place on earth. After the Tabernacle, the Temple in the land (II Chronicles 6:3–6); and when its day was past, the Son from the Father's bosom came . . . 'The Word became flesh, and *tabernacled* among us' (John 1:14 RV) . . . . Next came the Church . . . built of living stones. This is the present dwelling-place of God on earth" (John Ritchie).

F. B. Meyer said, "If the people had only seen the devouring fire on the top of Sinai, the pavilion of God's presence, they would never have dared to think that there was any community of interest between Him and them. To their minds, He would always have seemed distant and unapproachable. So God said, 'Let them make me a sanctuary, that I may dwell among them' (Exodus 25:8) . . . Thus is was ordained that this larger tent should be pitched among them, only differing from their own in its proportions and materials; but standing on the same level sand, struck and pitched at the same hour with theirs, and enduring the same vicissitudes of weather and travel. Did not this say, as plainly as words could, that the tabernacle of God was with men, and that He was willing to dwell with them and become their God? Did it not teach that Jehovah had become a pilgrim with the pilgrim host; no longer a God afar off, but a sharer in their national fortunes? And is not this the very lessons of the Incarnation?"

The purpose of the Tabernacle (that God might dwell with men) expresses the eternal desire and compassion of God for men. God is ever seeking to dwell with His created ones. But men, unfortunately, do just the opposite with God. They try to avoid God, but much to their great loss. When Adam and Eve sinned, God went after them to find them; but Adam and Eve "hid themselves from the presence of the LORD God" (Genesis 3:8). The actions of Adam and Eve are typical of most men in every age. But wise men will seek the presence of God. Moses so valued the presence of God that he did not want to go anywhere without Him (Exodus 33:14,15). We should be the same about the Lord. The great blessing of the second coming is "so shall we ever be with the Lord" (I Thessalonians 4:17). We show our desire to be with God by our attention to our personal prayer and Bible study times and by our attendance and worship at church with God's people. If you do not do well in these things, you evidence a lack of desire to be with God.

2. The Pattern

Moses was not left to his own ideas about building a Tabernacle. God made it plain that He would give the blueprint, the plans, and the pattern for the Tabernacle. "Make me a sanctuary;

519

that I may dwell among them. According to all that I show thee, after the pattern of the tabernacle, and the pattern of all the instruments thereof, even so shall ye make it . . . And look that thou make them after their pattern, which was showed thee in the mount" (25:8,9,40). The emphasis on making the Tabernacle after God's pattern is seen in Exodus 39 and 40 where it is recorded some eighteen times that Moses had the Tabernacle made as the LORD commanded (39:1,5,7,21,26,29,31,32, 42,43; 40:16,19,21,23,25,27,29,32).

One very important reason why Moses needed to follow God's plan for the Tabernacle was that it portrayed Jesus Christ in a multitude of ways. The Tabernacle "was a figure [of Christ] for the time then present, in which were offered both gifts and sacrifices, that could not make him that did the service perfect, as pertaining to the conscience . . . But Christ being come an high priest of good things to come, by a greater and more perfect tabernacle" (Hebrews 9:9,11). When Christ came to earth, the "greater and more perfect tabernacle" came to earth in person. This is what John spoke of when he said, "And the Word was made flesh, and dwelt among us" (John 1:14). Bible students are well aware of the fact that the word translated "dwelt" can be translated "tabernacled." Christ tabernacled among mankind as the Tabernacle in the wilderness dwelt with the Israelites. To portray Christ accurately in the Tabernacle and its furniture meant that Moses must follow the pattern God laid out for him.

There is a much needed practical lesson here about our personal portrayal (witness) of Christ to this world. If we want to witness well for Christ, we need to follow the pattern God has laid out for our lives. In short, we must do the will of God in every facet of our lives. The more obedient we are to the will of God, the better will be our witness. Our witnessing for Christ is not as dependent on clever methods of presentation of the Gospel as it is on the faithful obedience of our lives to His will. Some methods of witnessing do indeed have much merit to them, but the obedient life is the real key to witnessing. It is a constant witness of Christ. Therefore, see to it that you, as Moses did with the Tabernacle, make your life according to "pattern" which God shows you.

3. The Place

The arrangement of the camp of the Israelites is detailed in Numbers 2. The Tabernacle was to sit "in the midst of the camp" (Numbers 2:17) with the Tabernacle entrance facing east (Exodus 27:13–16). Three tribes were located on each of the four sides of the Tabernacle—Judah, Issachar, and Zebulun on the east; Reuben, Simeon, and Gad on the south; Ephraim, Manasseh, and Benjamin on the west; and Dan, Asher, and Naphtali on the north. The Levites (except for Moses, Aaron and his sons) pitched their tents nearer the Tabernacle on the west, south, and north sides of the Tabernacle. Moses, Aaron and his sons pitched their tents near to the Tabernacle on the east side.

The place of the Tabernacle in the camp of Israel teaches us the much needed lesson that Christ is to be in the center of our lives. He is not to be pushed off to a corner of the camp in disrespect or to the rear of the camp in disinterest. As the location of Tabernacle determined the location of all the people of Israel, so our lives should be ordered in reference to where Christ is and to what He is doing. When we adjust our lives to Christ, we will lead organized and productive lives that will honor Him in a great way. Oh, let us make Christ, our Tabernacle, the very center of our lives.

B. THE PROVISIONS FOR THE TABERNACLE

The provisions for making the Tabernacle involved the wealth of the people and workers from the people.

1. Wealth

"Speak unto the children of Israel, that they bring me an offering: of every man that giveth it willingly with his heart ye shall take my offering" (25:2). The provisions for the Tabernacle were to come from the people. The people were to give of their substance to provide the material to make the Tabernacle. To further examine this providing of the material for the Tabernacle, we will note the attitude, ability, and abundance in the giving by the Israelites.

The attitude in giving. God specified the attitude that was to be present in those who gave for the Tabernacle. They were to give "willingly with his heart" (25:2, cp. 35:5). The Israelites did just that; for "they came, every one whose heart stirred him up, and every one whom his spirit made willing, and they brought the LORD's offering to the work of the tabernacle of the congregation, and for all his service, and for the holy garments. And they came, both men and women, as many as were willing-hearted . . . The children of Israel brought a willing offering unto the LORD, every man and woman, whose heart made them willing" (35:21,22,29). Giving willingly from the heart is the only way to give acceptably unto God. God is very interested in our motivation. In fact, God is more interested in our motivation in giving than in the amount we give. Motivation more than the amount is what determines our heavenly reward. If we are serving to impress man, our heavenly reward will be small if any at all, even though we may have given much. But if we are serving God because we love Him, our reward will be great even though we may not be able to give much.

With God desiring noble motivation for the giving, God's plan for giving was very different than the usual plan man uses. God did not tell Moses to use gimmicks to obtain the gifts for the Tabernacle. There were no door prizes, no bingo or raffles or bazaars, no church suppers, no promise of plaques with your name on them hanging up in a conspicuous place in the Tabernacle, and no promise of names engraved on various pieces of furniture in the Tabernacle. No, none of those carnal gimmicks were used to raise an offering for the making of the Tabernacle. Rather, the need was simply laid before the people, and their hearts responded.

The nearly universal use of these gimmicks today in building church buildings, Christian schools, and raising money for other religious endeavors is evident that there is a heart problem among God's people. When a person will not give unless he is induced by some carnal reward, he can forget about heavenly rewards. If you will not give unless your name is put on a plaque or on a stained glassed window or unless you receive some plaque or framed certificate or other souvenir, you will get no reward from God for giving; for you are not giving to Him, but you are giving for your own vain glory.

The ability in giving. God never asks us to do something we cannot do. If we do not have the ability at the time of the asking, He will give it to us when we need it so we can obey. Often, however, God gives us the ability before He asks. Such was the case in regards to the gifts for the Tabernacle. We noted in earlier chapters of this book about Israel spoiling the Egyptians when they left Egypt and that these gifts would in part be used for the Tabernacle. Here we see the actual giving of some of the spoils from Egypt for the Tabernacle. God had amply endowed the Israelites with great riches from the Egyptians, now they are to give some of that back for the Tabernacle.

As we noted in earlier chapters, let us remember from this experience of the Israelites that when God blesses us, it is not for our personal pleasures alone but for our service for God. Let us be good stewards of our blessings and seek to know how we can use them to the fullest in His service. How wicked of men to only see their blessings in terms of personal gain and pleasure. Should considerable riches come into your hands, immediately seek God as to the use of those riches. Do not be so quick to buy an abundance of things for yourself. Rather, look around and see where God is leading you to help His work.

The abundance in giving. "And they [those in charge of building the Tabernacle] spake unto Moses, saying, The people bring much more than enough for the service of the work, which the LORD commanded to make. And Moses gave commandment, and they caused it to be proclaimed throughout the camp, saying, Let neither man nor woman make any more work for the offering of the sanctuary. So the people were restrained from bringing. For the stuff they had was sufficient for all the work to make it, and too much" (36:5–7). What an extremely unusual situation! The people actually gave "too much." This certainly does not happen in our churches today! One simply cannot imagine any pastor having to stand before his congregation to order them to stop giving because they had given too much for the work of the Lord.

The reason that the people gave so much for the Tabernacle was, of course, that they gave from their hearts, as we noted above. When people's hearts are right, the offering will be right. If the offering is not sufficient, there is obviously a heart problem with the people. And heart problems abound in our churches as is evident by the fact that few churches have the finances they need to do the work of the Lord right. Anyone who has ever looked at the giving records of the church people knows that not many church people give as they could. There are some who give from the heart, but not many. Most of them could give a whole lot more, but they do not. And generally, they are the ones who complain the most about the church's deficient financial situation.

2. Workers

In order to make all the things that had to be made regarding the Tabernacle, specially skilled workers were needed. God informed Moses who the workers were who would make all these things. God said, "See, I have called by name Bezaleel the son of Uri, the son of Hur, of the tribe of Judah; And I have filled him with the spirit of God, in wisdom, and in understanding, and in knowledge, and in all manner of workmanship, To devise cunning [artistic] works, to work in gold, and in silver, and in brass, And in cutting of stones, to set them, and in carving of timber, to work in all manner of workmanship. And I, behold, I have given with him Aholiab, the son of Ahisamach, of the tribe of Dan; and in the hearts of all that are wise hearted I have put wisdom, that they may make all that I have commanded thee" (31:2–6, cp. 35:30,31,34,35). This providing of workers to make the Tabernacle is a wonderful lesson on serving God. It instructs in the call, the capacity, and the consecration to serve.

The call to serve. The call of the workers to make the Tabernacle was a Divine call and a distinct call. This will be true with all those called into God's service.

First, *Divine call.* "The LORD hath called . . . Bezaleel" (35:30). Our callings are decided by God. This means God has a plan for us. He has a will for our lives. The problem with mankind, however, is that they are seldom concerned about what God wants them to do. They are more concerned about what others think they ought to do and what they themselves want to do than they are about what God wants them to do. But wisdom recognizes that it is God Who is the One we need to obey in regards to our life's work.

Second, *distinct call.* "I have called . . . Bezaleel . . . to devise cunning [artistic] works" (31:2,4). Bezaleel's calling was spelled out by God. He was given a distinct task to do. It was "to devise cunning [artistic] works." When God calls, He will make plain in due time what your specific task is. So many saints, however, are always so vague about what that task is. They never seem to know for sure what they are to do. The problem in this case is not God, but it is the saints. They do not live close enough to God or pay enough attention to what God is saying to learn their specific calling.

The capacity to serve. As we noted regarding the people giving of their wealth for the Tabernacle, when God calls, He endows the called one with the skills to do the task. So it also was with Bezaleel the Tabernacle builder. "I have filled him with the spirit of God, in wisdom, and in understanding, and in knowledge, and in all manner of workmanship, to devise cunning works" (31:3,4). The capacity to serve provided skills that were appropriate, adequate, and apparent.

First, *appropriate*. To build the Tabernacle required particular skills in working in such things as "gold, and in silver, and in brass, and in cutting stones . . . in carving of timber" (31:4,5). And these skills were the ones Bezaleel possessed. When God needed an artificer to build the Tabernacle, He called an artificer (Bezaleel). When God needs a piano player, He calls a piano player. When God needs a truck driver, He calls a truck driver. If you find yourself in a task for which you do not have the skills, you are either out of your calling or have been delinquent in preparing for your calling. God will not call you to a task you cannot do.

Second, *adequate*. The adequacy of Bezaleel's capacity to serve is emphasized by the word "filled" (31:3). Bezaleel had a great task in building the Tabernacle, but God gave him all the talent and ability he needed. He "filled" him for the job. God will not only give you the right skills for the task but will also give you adequate skills for the job. You will be able to perform well enough to do the task most adequately.

Third, *apparent*. "And Moses did look upon all the work, and, behold, they had done it as the LORD had commanded, even so had they done it; and Moses blessed them" (39:43). When the Tabernacle was finished, there was no question as to the skills of Bezaleel! He and his helpers did a magnificent job. They made the Tabernacle just as God commanded. The phrase, "Moses blessed them," is another way of saying, "Well done." When you obey God's calling for your life, you will not have to argue with people to convince them that you can do the task for which you say you are called. It will be very apparent and evident that you have the gift and, hence, the calling. Those who intrude into callings they do not have betray their presumption by their inability to do the task they have assumed.

The consecration to serve. A Divine calling will never be done unless there is dedication in doing it. Even though men are greatly endowed for the task, they will not do well if they lack dedication. Bezaleel and those who helped him had this consecration. This dedication is described in "Every one whose heart stirred him up to come unto the work to do it" (36:2). This dedication was not only seen in Bezaleel and his helpers in making the Tabernacle, but it also abounded throughout the camp in the giving of the goods for the Tabernacle (35:21,22) which we noted earlier.

How very short we are today in our churches of heart dedication. People come to church when it is convenient, they give if they can do so without sacrifice, they will serve in some position if it does not interfere with their other interests in life, and they get restless and upset if the preacher preaches over thirty minutes. Such dedication will do little in God's work. It explains why so many churches plod along year after year never doing much of anything. People need to have their heart in their professed faith and be "stirred up" by their heart, then dedication will be great, and much will be done for the glory of God.

C. THE PARTS OF THE TABERNACLE

Here we will look at some details concerning the various parts of the Tabernacle. We have already mentioned in our introduction the basic parts of the Tabernacle. Here we examine them in more detail. We will divide the parts into three categories: the fence, the framework, and the furniture.

1. The Fence

In examining the parts of the Tabernacle, we will start from the outside and work our way in. Hence, we start with the fence which surrounds the Tabernacle, for it is the first part one sees from the outside. We will look at the description, design, and door of the fence.

Description. "And thou shalt make the court of the tabernacle; for the south side southward there shall be hangings for the court of fine twined linen of an hundred cubits long for one side;

527

And twenty pillars thereof and their twenty sockets shall be of brass; the hooks of the pillars and their fillets shall be of silver. And likewise for the north side . . . And for the breadth of the court on the west side shall be hangings of fifty cubits; their pillars ten, and their sockets ten. And the breadth of the court of the east side eastward shall be fifty cubits . . . The length of the court shall be an hundred cubits, and the breadth fifty every where, and the height five cubits" (27:9–13,18). This fence went completely around the Tabernacle and was 150 feet long by 75 feet wide by 7½ feet high. It was a very unique fence and a very beautiful fence. It was not a wire or wooden or stone fence that we are so familiar with in our day. Rather, it was a fence made of white linen hangings. The linen was hung by silver hooks to silver bars which were supported by brass posts ("pillars"). There were a total of 60 pillars for the fence, and they were approximately 7½ feet apart thus making each section between the pillars a square inasmuch as the fence was 7½ feet high. The pillars were not driven into the ground like we drive the posts of a fence into ground, but they were set in a foundation of blocks ("sockets") of brass. This would give the pillars both stability and portability.

Design. The purpose of the fence was twofold. It was to debar people, and it was to direct people.

First, it would *debar* the people from unauthorized entrance into the court and Tabernacle. This has important symbolic teaching. Man is prohibited from fellowship with God unless He comes to God by the right way. The whiteness of the linen speaks of the holiness of God which bars men from God. The brass pillars of the fence emphasize this holiness that bars men from God, for the brass speaks of judgment in Scripture. But the hooks and bars of silver offer promise through the atonement, for silver speaks of atonement in Scripture.

Second, the fence would *direct* the people to the gate or opening where you could enter. The fence shut out one from entering into the court and Tabernacle any way but by the one gate in the fence. This reminds us that the law cannot save; it can only condemn. But in condemning, it can direct us to Jesus Christ for salvation (Galatians 3:24).

Door. "And for the gate of the court shall be an hanging of twenty cubits, of blue, and purple, and scarlet, and fine twined linen, wrought with needlework; and their pillars shall be four, and their sockets four" (27:16). The door ("gate") in the fence was located at the eastern side of the fence. To examine this door, we will note the singularity of it, the inclusiveness of it, the view from it, and the hangings of it.

First, the *singularity* of it. There was only one gate. Only one side of the four sided fence had an entrance in it. Thus, the gate reminds us of Jesus Christ. He is the only way of salvation. Jesus said, "I am the door; by me if any man enter in, he shall be saved" (John 10:9). He also said, "I am the way, the truth, and the life; no man cometh unto the Father, but by me" (John 14:6). Christ being the only way to our salvation is also empha-sized by Peter who said, "Neither is there salvation in any other; for there is none other name under heaven given among men, whereby we must be saved" (Acts 4:12), and by Paul who said, "For there is one God, and one mediator between God and men, the man Christ Jesus" (I Timothy 2:5).

Second, the *inclusiveness* of it. While the fence had only one gate, the gate was open to all. Any Israelite was permitted to come through that gate. So it is with Christ. Though He is the only way of salvation, yet anyone can come to Him for salva-tion and be saved. "Whosoever shall call upon the name of the Lord shall be saved" (Acts 2:21).

Third, the *view* from it. When one came to the gate, the first thing he would see when looking through the gate would be the brasen altar. This, as we will note later in this study, was where all the offerings were made. These offerings spoke of Calvary. Thus the gate, which pictured Christ, points to Calvary where Christ was crucified for our sins.

Fourth, the *hangings* of it. The width of the gate took up

four pillars of the fence with the hangings being "blue, and purple, and scarlet, and fine twined linen [white], wrought with needlework" (27:16). Symbolically the repeated emphasis on the number four in the gate hangings is often compared to the four Gospels which speak of Christ. The four Gospels (Matthew, Mark, Luke, and John) have some very distinct characteristics about them, some of which this gate emphasizes in its four different colors. The purple color speaks of royalty—Matthew is the Gospel of the King. Red can speak of servitude—Mark is the Gospel of the servant. White speaks of purity—Luke is the Gospel of the perfect man. And blue is the heavenly color—John's Gospel speaks of the Deity of Christ.

2. The Framework

In looking at the framework, we are looking at the Tabernacle itself. The Tabernacle was basically a tent—and a very elaborate one. It consisted of walls, coverings, and veils.

Walls. The walls were sturdy in function and spectacular in appearance. They consisted of boards 15 feet long and 27 inches wide overlaid with gold. The boards were connected together by five connecting bars of wood overlaid with gold, and then they were stood on end in a foundation of silver blocks (26:15–30). The walls covered just three sides of the Tabernacle as the east end of the tent consisted of a veil.

Service for Christ can be seen from these boards which served the Tabernacle so well. *Humiliation* is needed for service, and it is seen in the cutting down of the trees to provide the wood for the boards. *Preparation* is needed for service, and it is seen in the wood being cut and shaped to the exact dimensions. *Cooperation* is needed for service, and the boards demonstrate this by standing side by side and being connected together by the bars so they could work together. *Exaltation* is the result of faithful service. The glory of the gleaming gold veneer on the boards certainly emphasizes the exaltation. The *foundation* of service is salvation, and that is seen in the boards being set on a foundation of silver blocks ("sockets"). As noted earlier, silver in Scripture often speaks of atonement which speaks of Calvary and, hence, salvation.

Coverings. Four coverings, each of different material, were draped over the walls to provide a ceiling and protective covering for the entire Tabernacle. These curtains would drape completely to the ground so that from the outside you did not see the gold veneered walls. The four different coverings were linen (26:1–6), goats' hair (26:7–13), rams' skin died red (26:14), and badgers' skin—better understood as porpoise or similar sea animal skin—(Ibid.). The linen covering was of four different colors (white, blue, purple, and scarlet) with cherubims woven into the curtain. The linen covering was the covering of the ceiling which could be seen inside the Tabernacle. This meant that inside of the Tabernacle one saw gleaming gold walls and a beautifully woven ceiling—a most beautiful and spectacular sight indeed. Truly this pictures the beauty of Christ. But this sight was only seen by those inside the Tabernacle. From the outside there would be no beauty in the Tabernacle, for it was covered with gray porpoise (or other sea animal) skin. The function of this skin was to protect the Tabernacle from the elements of the weather, but it would be a drab gray in appearance. This drab appearance illustrates that to the natural eye, Christ is not attractive. "There is no beauty that we should desire him" (Isaiah 53:2) is the conclusion of the natural man. But to the spiritual eye, the eye which beholds the inside of the Tabernacle, Christ is absolutely all glorious! The world may despise our Savior, but we who have come to Christ for salvation have seen Him in His beauty. The Apostle John spoke of this when he said, "The Word was made flesh, and dwelt among us, (and we [those who followed and believed Christ] beheld his glory, the glory as of the only begotten of the Father) full of grace and truth" (John 1:14). John and the true followers of Jesus Christ see His beauty, but most of the world does not.

Veils. There were two veils in the Tabernacle. They were the outer veil and the inner veil.

First, the *outer veil*. "And thou shalt make an hanging [veil] for the door of the tent, of blue, and purple, and scarlet, and fine twined linen, wrought with needlework" (26:36). Across the east end of the Tabernacle was the opening of the tent. This opened into the first of two rooms in the Tabernacle. This first room was 30 feet long by 15 feet wide and was called the holy place. The veil that covered the opening was the outer veil and was hung on gold pillars set in brass blocks with gold hooks (26:37).

Second, the *inner veil*. "And thou shalt make a vail [veil] of blue, and purple, and scarlet, and fine twined linen of cunning work: with cherubims shall it be made. And thou shalt hang it upon four pillars of shittim [acacia] wood overlaid with gold: their hooks shall be of gold, and upon four sockets [blocks] of silver . . . the vail shall divide unto you between the holy place and the most holy" (26:31–33). The inner veil was the divider of the two rooms in the Tabernacle—the holy place and the holy of holies. The holy of holies was a cube, for it was 15 feet long and wide and high. This veil was more ornate than the outer veil.

The inner veil is the most famous of the veils as well as the most ornate. Its great fame comes in it being torn in two when Christ was on the cross. The veil that was torn in two was in the Temple then, not the Tabernacle. But that veil did the same thing, for it was that which closed the view of the holy of holies. The rending in twain of the veil would be some scene in the Temple; for at the time of the rending, the priests would be going about their work with the Passover lamb. But to their great surprise and shock, suddenly the way into the holy of holies was no longer barred. Christ had on the cross opened the way for all sinners to come to God through Him, and the rent veil pictured it symbolically. Later in Acts 6:7, we are told that a great number of priests came to Christ. The rending of the veil could have had a lot to do with that. History tells us that attempts were made to sew the veil together again, but all attempts failed.

3. The Furniture

Six pieces of furniture were made for the Tabernacle. Five pieces were placed inside the Tabernacle and two were located in the court. The two in the court were the brasen altar and the laver. The four pieces in the Tabernacle were the table of show-bread, the altar of incense, the lampstand, and the ark.

The brasen altar. This altar had two different names. One was the "brasen altar" (38:30) which spoke of its appearance and material. The other name was the "altar of burnt offering" (30:28) which spoke of its use. The word "brasen" in the King James Version (today we spell it with a "z" not an "s") is trans-lated from a Hebrew word which means a metal made of bronze (or brass).

To further examine the altar and its lessons, we note the par-ticulars, purpose, and place of the altar.

First, the *particulars* of the altar. Exodus 27:1–8 gives us the particulars of this piece of furniture. This was the largest piece of furniture associated with the Tabernacle. It was a hol-low $7\frac{1}{2}$ feet square which stood $4\frac{1}{2}$ feet high. In the middle (from top to bottom) of the altar was a ledge where grating was placed. Upon this the sacrifices were laid. At the top were four horns—one located in each of the four corners. Sacrifices were often bound to the horns (Psalms 118:27) and the blood of the sacrifices was often sprinkled there. The altar was made of wood which was covered with bronze. Also, a number of bronze accessories were made for this altar such as pans, shovels, basins, fleshhooks, and firepans (27:3) to help in handling the sacrifices and the ashes and the clean-up.

Second, the *purpose* of the altar. This was the altar upon which all the sacrifices were to be made. It was the place where the Israelites brought their sacrifices to be killed. The first part of the book of Leviticus details many of these offerings. It is not difficult to see then that this piece of furniture spoke of Calvary. The sacrifices and the shedding of the blood involved in the sac-rifices pointed forward to the death of Christ on the cross as the sacrifice for the sins of man.

Third, the *place* of the altar. It was located inside the gate before the door of the Tabernacle (40:6,33). There was some distance between it and the Tabernacle door, however, as the laver, which we will learn about next, was located between the brasen altar and the Tabernacle door (40:7).

The location of the brasen altar shows the importance and priority of a blood sacrifice before we can enter into fellowship with God. It shows that the first and foremost need we have if we want to dwell with God is to have our sins forgiven. Many religions in the world leave out what the altar speaks of, for they leave out the essentialness of Calvary and Christ's shed blood for fellowship with God.

The laver. The laver was a large bowl (dimensions are not given in Scripture) in which water was placed. The laver, as we noted above, was located between the brasen altar and the entrance (outer veil) to the Tabernacle. To further examine the laver and its lessons, we will note the purpose of the laver and the providing for the laver.

First, the *purpose* of the laver. The laver provided a place for the priests to wash both their hands and feet before they ministered at the brasen altar or before they went into the Tabernacle to minister there (30:18–21). The laver served a very necessary and practical purpose. It was to help the priests become clean for service. Especially can we see this need in regards to the priests going into the Tabernacle after ministering at the brasen altar. After they had been working around the brasen altar with the blood, fire, ashes, etc. both their hands and feet would be soiled. To go into the Tabernacle in that condition would quickly soil the veils and anything they touched in the tent. They needed, therefore, to clean up before they went into the Tabernacle to do service.

What an obvious lesson is here in the purpose of the laver. It is the lesson spoken of in Isaiah: "Be ye clean, that bear the vessels of the LORD" (Isaiah 52:11). The brasen altar speaks of salvation, but the laver speaks of sanctification. We must be clean if we are going to serve God and have fellowship with Him. With water often speaking of the Word, we can see the application of keeping ourselves clean by a faithful pursuit of the Word of God. "Ye are clean though the word which I have spoken unto you" (John 15:3), and "That he might sanctify and cleanse it with the washing of water by the word" (Ephesians 5:26) underscore the purifying work of the Word of God. The importance of being clean is emphasized by the double warning of death (30:20,21) if they are not clean. Uncleanness disqualifies from God's service.

Second, the *providing* for the laver. An interesting and instructive note is made in Scripture about the providing of the material to make the laver. Scripture says, "And he made the laver . . . of the looking glasses [mirrors] of the women" (38:8). We have glass mirrors today. In Moses' day they had polished brass for mirrors. A mirror is mighty important especially to a woman. But the women willingly gave up their mirrors for the construction of the laver.

The giving of the women's mirrors to make the laver is a most helpful lesson on service. The lesson is not that we must look ugly, unkempt, and our hair in a mess in order to be used by God. No, the lesson is that we must be willing to sacrifice our personal glory (which the mirrors speak of) in order to serve God. Too many enter the service of God in order to obtain personal honor, applause, and esteem. But that is not the right motivation for service. Christ gives the right example. He humbled Himself—and no one ever gave up more glory—to provide our salvation (Philippians 2:7,8). We ought to be willing to sacrifice the honor and applause and accolades of men in order to serve Christ. If you cannot sacrifice these things, you will not do well in His service. You will quit when men do not honor you as you think they ought.

The table of showbread. One of the three pieces of furniture to be located in the holy place, the first room of the Tabernacle, was the table of showbread. We note the specifics of the table and the symbolism of the table.

First, the *specifics*. "Thou shalt also make a table of shittim [acacia] wood: two cubits shall be the length thereof, and a cubit the breadth thereof, and a cubit and a half the height thereof . . . And thou shalt set upon the table [the loaves of] showbread before me always" (Exodus 25:23,30). The table was made of wood covered with gold. It measured 3 feet long by 18 inches wide by 18 inches high. In Leviticus 24:5–9 we are told that on this table was placed twelve loaves of bread in two rows of six each. The bread was replaced every week. It was to be eaten by Aaron and his sons who were the priests that ministered in the Tabernacle who we will learn more about later.

Second, the *symbolism*. There are some instructive symbolic details in regards to the table of showbread. Christ is represented here as the bread of life. In the bread, the Word of God is also represented which provides nourishment for service for Christ. The twelve loaves of bread speak of the twelve tribes of Israel which tells us that God was ever identifying Himself with His people. Oh, that we were as willing to identify ourselves with God as He is to identify with us. But too often we keep silent about belonging to Him.

The altar of incense. Another piece of furniture placed in the holy place was the altar of incense. "And thou shalt make an altar to burn incense upon . . . A cubit shall be the length thereof, and a cubit the breadth therefore; foursquare shall it be: and two cubits shall be the height thereof . . . And thou shalt put it before the vail that is by the ark of the testimony, before the mercy seat that is over the testimony, where I will meet with thee. And Aaron shall burn thereon sweet incense every morning: when he dresseth the lamps, he shall burn incense upon it. And when Aaron lighteth the lamps at even, he shall burn incense upon it, a perpetual incense before the LORD throughout your generations" (30:1,2,6–8). The altar of incense was 18 inches square and 2 feet high and was made of wood covered with gold. It was located right in front of the veil that separated the holy place from the holy of holies. To further examine the altar of incense, we note the work of the altar and the warnings concerning the altar.

First, the *work* of the altar. Incense was to be burned on this altar. This was accomplished by bringing coals from the brasen altar and placing them on this altar and then pouring incense on the coals (see Leviticus 16:12,13). Incense speaks of prayer here (Psalm 141:2). Therefore, we can perceive in this piece of furniture the intercessory work of Christ. Christ is our Great Intercessor and Mediator (Hebrew 9:24, I Timothy 2:5). Hebrews 7:25 states that Christ "ever liveth to make intercession for them." This continual intercession of Christ is portrayed in the altar in that Aaron (and succeeding high priests) "shall burn incense upon it, a *perpetual* incense before the LORD throughout your generations" (30:8).

Second, the *warnings* concerning the altar. God gave some special warnings for this piece of furniture of the Tabernacle. The warnings were threefold. (1) There was to be no strange incense put on the altar (30:9). This first warning was against putting anyone in the place of Christ as our Intercessor. Roman Catholics have Mary interceding for the saints and that is nothing but strange incense which produces a foul aroma theologically in gross dishonor of Jesus Christ. (2) There was to be no sacrificial offerings put on the altar (Ibid.). This second warning prohibited replacing the brasen altar with the altar of incense. The brasen altar represents Calvary. We are not to replace Calvary with anything else. (3) There was to be no sacrilegious use made of the incense (30:34–38). This third warning forbids the misuse and perversion of sacred things. They are to be used for worship, not for fleshly pleasure. When men depart from the truth in worship, however, they inevitably reduce worship to sensual excitement. The use of so-called "Christian Rock" and the dance in church worship services illustrates this fact.

The lampstand. A third piece of furniture in the holy place was the lampstand. "And thou shalt make a candlestick of pure gold: of beaten work shall the candlestick be made: his shaft, and his branches, his bowls, his knops, and his flowers, shall be of the same. And six branches shall come out of the sides of it; three branches of the candlestick out of the one side, and three branches of the candlestick out of the other side . . . And thou shalt make the seven lamps thereof; and they shall light the lamps thereof, that they may give light over against it" (25:31,32,37). To examine the lampstand, we note the details and the duty of it.

First, the *details*. The lampstand was a seven bowl lamp—the main trunk with three branches on each side. The "candlestick" rendering in the King James Version is very misleading for our day, for there were no candles involved. This was a lampstand with seven bowls for oil with wicks to burn the oil as lamps. Regarding its location of the lampstand in the holy place "on the side of the tabernacle southward" (40:24), Pink said, "It is most significant . . . that the Lampstand was placed on the south side of the Tabernacle, the more so when we discover that the Hebrew word for 'south' means 'bright, radiant.'"

Second, the *duties*. The duty of the lampstand was, of course, to give light. It was to give light in the holy place. In this the lampstand does not represent Christ as the "light of the world" (John 8:12) as some think; for this lampstand is not visible to the outside world but is visible only to the priests who represent believers. What the light does represent is the work of Christ through the Holy Spirit (the Holy Spirit is sometimes referred to as the "Spirit of Christ" [Romans 8:9, I Peter 1:11]). The lampstand provided light for the priests to do their service with the table of showbread and the altar of incense (Leviticus 24:2–4). One can quickly see the application here. It is the Spirit of Christ, the Holy Spirit, Who helps us in the study of the Word (Table of Showbread) and in prayer (Altar of Incense). The Holy Spirit "will guide you into all truth" (John 16:13); and He will help us pray. His help in our prayer life is explained by Paul when he said, "Likewise the Spirit also helpeth our infirmities: for we know not what we should pray for as we ought: but the Spirit itself maketh intercession for us with groanings which cannot be uttered" (Romans 8:26).

The ark. In the holy of holies part of the Tabernacle was just one piece of furniture. It was the ark. "They shall make an ark of shittim [acacia] wood: two cubits and a half shall be the length thereof, and a cubit and a half the breadth thereof, and a cubit and a half the height thereof. And thou shalt overlay it with pure gold, within and without shalt thou overlay it, and shalt make upon it a crown of gold round about . . . And thou shalt make a mercy seat of pure gold . . . And thou shalt make two cherubims of gold . . . in the two ends of the mercy seat . . . And the cherubims shall stretch forth their wings on high, covering the mercy seat with their wings, and their faces shall look one to another; toward the mercy seat shall the faces of the cherubims be . . . and in the ark thou shalt put the testimony that I shall give thee. And there I will meet with thee, and I will commune with thee from above the mercy seat" (25:10,11, 17,18,20,21,22) To examine the ark, we will note the construction of the ark, the contents of the ark, and the communion at the ark.

First, the *construction.* According to our text the ark was a box 45 inches long by 27 inches wide by 27 inches high. The lid on the box was called the mercy seat. Attached to the lid was two cherubim figures facing each other and covering the lid with their wings. The faces of the cherubims looked down at the mercy seat. The box was made of wood covered with gold. The cherubims were solid gold.

Second, the *contents.* In the ark was placed the "testimony" which was the two stones containing the ten commandments. Later the container of manna and Aaron's rod that budded were also placed in the ark (Hebrews 9:4). Each of the three items speak of Jesus Christ. The tables of the law speak of the obedience of Christ. Christ's obedience was expressed well by the Psalmist when he said, "I delight to do thy will, O my God; yea, thy law is within my heart [typified by the inside of the ark]" (Psalm 40:8). The manna speaks of Christ the bread of life (John 6:32–35). Aaron's rod which budded (Numbers 17) speaks of the resurrection of Christ.

Third, the *communion*. "There I will meet with thee, and I will commune with thee from above the mercy seat, from between the two cherubims" (25:22). The location of God in the Tabernacle was specifically stated as being above the mercy seat of the ark where the cherubims were. Hence, the Psalmist says of God, "Thou that dwellest between the cherubims" (Psalm 80:1) and "he sitteth between the cherubims" (Psalm 99:1). With God being located there, the ark was logically the designated place where God would commune with man.

With the ark representing Jesus Christ, the lesson here is that God will meet with man only through Christ. No other place would God meet man. And note that mercy and blood are involved in this communion. The mercy seat was sprinkled with blood from the sacrifice on the brasen altar on the day of atonement (Leviticus 16:12–14). All of this pictures well that mercy, Christ, and the blood of Christ are most essential factors in meeting with God. Leave out any of these—Christ, His shed blood for the sins of man, and God's grace—and you will never enjoy communion with God but will only experience Divine condemnation instead.

D. THE PRIESTS FOR THE TABERNACLE

To conclude our study of the Tabernacle, we will look briefly at priests who were to keep "the charge of the whole congregation before the tabernacle of the congregation, to do the service of the tabernacle" (Numbers 3:7). We will note the designation, division, dress, and duties of the priests.

1. The Designation of the Priests

The Levites were the ones who were the administrators and caretakers of the Tabernacle. God took the entire tribe of Levi for the priests instead of taking the firstborn from each family.

Setting the tribe of Levi aside for the priesthood is how Joseph's two sons became part of the twelve tribes. Without Levi, there would only be eleven tribes. But Joseph was divided into two tribes—one named after his son Ephraim and the other after his son Manasseh. This fulfilled the prophecy of Jacob recorded in Genesis 48:5. At the beginning of the Tabernacle's existence, Aaron and his sons were the first ones from the tribe of Levi to be set apart for the priesthood in the service of the Tabernacle. Later more of the Levites were set apart for the priesthood.

The holy calling of the Levites was a great spiritual privilege. But as is the case with many who are called into high service for God, they often abused their privilege and used their position for their own personal gain and glory rather than for the glory of God. This abuse of their calling commenced in the wilderness journeys of Israel with Nadab and Abihu, two sons of Aaron. Their sin was to offer "strange fire before the LORD, which he commanded them not" (Leviticus 10:1). Their judgment was to be killed by God right on the spot (Leviticus 10:2). Some may think that such judgment was too severe, but high holy privilege begats high responsibility.

2. The Division of the Priests

There was a twofold division in the priesthood. This consisted of the High Priest and then the regular priests. Aaron was the first High Priest and his sons were the first regular priests. The division is representative of Christ and the believers. Christ is the great High Priest (Hebrews 7:25,26; 8:1; 9:11) and we believers are the other priests (I Peter 2:5,9).

Today we do not need human priests in order to commune with God (Hebrews 10:19). The Tabernacle and the priesthood of Aaron and the Levites were simply types of Christ and the believers. When Christ came, there was no need for maintaining the types. Roman Catholicism has not caught on here, however. Their priesthood, which is a combination of Judaism and paganism with some language of the New Testament mixed in, is absolutely not valid. We do not need to go to a priest to confess our sins or have him pray for us. The veil has been rent in twain giving access to God for all who will come to Him through Jesus Christ.

3. The Dress of the Priests

The priests wore special clothes designed by God. The High Priest's clothes were especially ornate and beautiful (28:2–39). This was to distinguish him from the other priests. Besides the beautiful robes, he wore on his outer robe a breastplate (a separate and special piece of cloth) to which twelve different precious stones were attached. The name of one tribe was written on each stone. On each shoulder he wore another precious stone. Six names of the tribes of Israel were written on each stone on the shoulders. Also the High Priest carried on his clothes (some think in a pocket behind the breastplate) the urim and the thummim which were used to discern the will of God.

The regular priests wore plainer garments (28:40–43). As the divisions of the priests portrayed the differences between Christ and the believers, so do the different designs in the dress of the priests. Christ is all supreme. Believers are to be subordinate to Christ and not take His glory. The pompous display of some preachers in churches today, both apostate and fundamental, certainly does not demonstrate much giving of the glory to Christ.

4. The Duties of the Priests

The duties of the priests regarding the Tabernacle included such things as officiating at the sacrifices, keeping the lamp in the holy place lit, partaking of the bread from the table of showbread, putting incense on the altar of incense, and sprinkling blood on the mercy seat of the ark once a year.

The priests were also to carry the Tabernacle when it was moved. Numbers 3 and 4 detail the assignment of the moving of the Tabernacle. Various groups were to move various parts of the Tabernacle. The instructions for moving the Tabernacle reflects great care and also great efficiency in this work. The various pieces of furniture were covered with the curtains from the Tabernacle to protect them from sight (to preserve sacredness) and from physical damage. All the pieces of furniture were built with rings (normally on the four corners of the piece of furniture) in order that long, gold covered rods (called "staves" in the King James Version) could be inserted through the rings and then priests could carry the piece of furniture by the rods instead of holding onto the furniture itself. This made the hauling of the furniture much safer and easier to move than to carry it by hand. The ark was especially top heavy with the cherubims on top. But carrying it by the staves made the task easy and prevented the top-heavy ark from tipping over. Some centuries later when Israel was in the land, an attempt to move the ark on a cart met with disaster because of it being top-heavy (II Samuel 6:1–11). Oxen were pulling the cart and they shook the cart. This made the top-heavy ark wobble. A man by the name of Uzzah put his hand on the ark to steady the ark and was immediately killed by God. The orders for moving the ark as given in Numbers would have prevented this tragedy. God's way is always the best way. It may not seem as modern or impressive. But it is the best way.

The priests had many duties besides their Tabernacle duties. They were also to be the spiritual leaders of Israel. They were to "teach the children of Israel all the statutes which the LORD hath spoken unto them by the hand of Moses" (Leviticus 10:11), and they were to declare the "difference between the holy and unholy, and between the unclean and clean" (Leviticus 10:10). As spiritual leaders of the people, these are the duties of preachers also. But many of them, like the Levites in Bible times, did not do a good job of fulfilling these important duties.

XXIII.

SIN OF IDOLATRY

EXODUS 32

THE BIBLICAL RECORD of Israel's nearly one year sojourn at Sinai can be divided into three parts—the statutes for Israel, the sanctuary of God, and the sin of idolatry. In the last two chapters of our book, we dealt with the first two parts, namely, the statutes for Israel and the sanctuary of God. Here in this chapter we will look at the third major event of the sojourn at Sinai, the sin of idolatry. The Israelites engaged in gross idolatry while Moses was in Mount Sinai speaking with God. This sin of idolatry by the Israelites was another very severe trial for Moses in his leading Israel from Egypt to Canaan. But in this trial, Moses' noble character shines forth with an even greater brightness than it has already done—even though it has already shown forth with a brightness that exceeds most other men of history.

Some teach that man has a spark of Divinity in him. However, the Bible teaches that man has something like a five-alarm fire of depravity in him instead. Israel's sin at Sinai illustrates the five-alarm fire of depravity. They gave themselves fully to idolatry and wallowed in the pig pen of moral filth as a result. The scene is an ugly one, but sin never paints anything pretty.

To examine Israel's sin of idolatry at Sinai, we will consider the character of the sin, the condemnation of the sin, and the compassion for the sinner.

A. THE CHARACTER OF THE SIN

To examine the character of the sin of idolatry by the Israelites, we will look at its disquietude of spirit, its disrespect for God's

544

man, its disobedience of God's Word, its degradation of worship, its defilement of conduct, its dedication in pursuit, and its dimension in size.

1. Its Disquietude of Spirit

"And when the people saw that Moses delayed to come down out of the mount, the people gathered themselves together unto Aaron, and said unto him, Up, make us gods, which shall go before us" (v. 1). The first problem we see which was involved in the sin of idolatry was a disquietude of spirit. Twice "Moses was in the mount forty days and forty nights" (24:18; 34:28) with God. But before he completed his first forty-day stay in Sinai, Israel became impatient and wanted to move on towards Canaan. This disquietude of spirit caused them to demand of Aaron that he make them gods that would lead them on their way to Canaan. The number forty in Scripture is the number of testing. This forty-day absence of Moses was a test for Israel regarding their trust in God, and they failed the test miserably. Moses had instructed them to "tarry ye here for us, until we come again unto you" (24:14); but their patience was short; for they were walking according to the flesh, not by faith. Sin is impatient and restless. It cannot wait for God's time.

Israel's attitude about Moses coming back is not unlike the attitude of many scoffers regarding the return of Jesus Christ to the earth. Peter mentioned this attitude when he wrote, "Knowing this first, that there shall come in the last days scoffers, walking after their own lusts, And saying, Where is the promise of his coming?" (II Peter 3:3,4). Notice that the scoffers were characterized as "walking after their own lusts." How well that characterizes Israel in our text. And faith and the lust of the flesh do not walk together. Lust will not wait upon God. Beware of the spirit of disquietude that will not wait upon the Lord. If you do not fight it, it will make a mess of you.

2. Its Disrespect for God's Man

"As for this Moses . . . we wot not [know not] what is

become of him" (v. 1). Another deficiency in the people that was involved in the sin of idolatry was disrespect for God's man. The above statement in our text reflects very poorly on the people's respect of Moses. Especially do the two words "this Moses" evidence a tone of scorn. Their complaint that they did not know what had become of Moses was inexcusable as well as scornful. They most certainly did know where he was, for Moses had duly instructed the elders where he was going and what to do in his absence when problems arose (24:14).

The spiritual health of any people will be quickly revealed by their attitude towards God's man. When Israel was in poor spiritual health, they always evidenced poor respect of God's prophets. They not only disrespected Moses, but later in their history they also showed poor respect for such great men of God as Elijah, Micaiah, Jeremiah, and many others. Anyone who is not right with God will sooner or later reveal it by their disrespect of God's man. But where people are right with God, they will honor God's man. We have never been in a thriving church but that one quickly hears people speaking well of their pastor. On the other hand, no church will thrive if the pastor, God's man, is treated poorly. The reason the attitude towards God's man reveals the people's spiritual condition is that he represents God's way. When men despise God's way, God's man will be despised. Preachers who faithfully proclaim the Word of God will not be appreciated by church members who do not want to walk in God's way.

3. Its Disobedience of God's Word

"Make us gods, which shall go before us" (v. 1). Israel's sin was disobedience of the revealed Word of God. We note the inexcuseablness of the disobedience, the increase of the disobedience, and the insincerity of the disobeyers.

The inexcusableness of the disobedience. Just a few weeks earlier, Israel had been told plainly by God Himself in a dramatic declaration of the Decalogue that "Thou shalt not make unto thee any graven image, or any likeness of anything that is in heaven above, or that is in the earth beneath, or that is in the water under the earth; Thou shalt not bow down thyself to them, nor serve them" (20:4,5). But in spite of the plainness of this command and the dramatic way in which it was given, the Israelites unashamedly did exactly what they were commanded not to do. This was inexcusable. So is all sin. Man, of course, invents many excuses for sinning, but they are all sham.

The increase in the disobedience. Verses 6 and 25 indicate that as a result of Israel's worship of the calf idol, they engaged in licentious orgies which would break the seventh command (adultery) repeatedly. Sin breeds sin. One sin leads to another sin. When people break one command, it leads to breaking other commands. Once the Israelites started disobeying, their disobedience increased at an alarming rate. Let this warn all of us. Tolerate a sin and you will soon tolerate more sin.

The insincerity of the disobeyers. In breaking God's Word, the Israelites also broke their own word. They had earlier said, "All that the LORD hath spoken we will do" (19:8). But their sin betrayed their insincerity. This action of Israel in breaking their own word as they broke God's Word instructs us in an important truth about people's character. That truth is that the more willing people are to break the Word of God, the more likely they are to break their own word. People who despise the Word of God are not people whose word can readily be trusted.

4. Its Degradation of Worship

The Israelites' idolatry was an awful degradation of the worship of God. We look at two details regarding this degradation. They are the degraded concept of God and the degrading compromise about God.

Concept of God. Aaron made a calf (v. 4) from the gold earrings given him by the people. Thus in concept, God was degraded to being a cow. What a blasphemous thing to do. Paul spoke of this problem when he wrote the Romans. He said, "When they knew God, they glorified him not as God, neither were thankful; but became vain in their imaginations . . . And changed the glory of the uncorruptible God into an image made like to corruptible man, and to birds, and fourfooted beasts, and creeping things" (Romans 1:21,23). How well this passage in Romans described Israel's action at Sinai. They refused to glorify God as they ought, and they were extremely unthankful for all that God had done for them in delivering them from Egypt. This soon led to bowing down before a calf as their god. Orr said, "Sin bestializes, and the bestial nature seeks a god in bestial form." How true. In turning from God's way, men will act like beasts in their morals (which we will see shortly) and cruelty; and they will degrade God to bestial form.

Though we may not degrade the concept of God by reducing Him to a cow or horse or other animal, we can still do it by speaking dishonorably of God. Saying that He is stupid, weak, effeminate, and immoral greatly degrades Him (the Mormons say Christ had several wives; some Hollywood films say Christ had affairs with women and was homosexual). Rejecting God's Word leads to degraded concepts of God which will cure no problems and heal no heartaches but only infect with deadly spiritual viruses that ruin lives and send souls to hell.

Compromise about God. Aaron did what so many religious leaders do in every age. He attempted to compromise truth with error. He went along with the idol and graven image, but he still tried to keep Jehovah in the picture. He made the golden calf; but then "Aaron made [a] proclamation, and said, Tomorrow is a feast to the LORD [Jehovah]" (v. 5). Aaron's compromise would mix calf worship with Jehovah—which is a terrible degrading of the worship of God. Compromisers always want to mix good and evil. They would mix the hands of Esau with the voice of Jacob (Genesis 27:22). In music they would mix the beat of hell with the words of heaven. In marriage, they want to wed the saved to the unsaved. In religion they want to promote the ecumenical philosophy that would mix apostates with fundamentalists. But beware of the unholy mixture! When you mix truth with error, you will only have error. The calf worship corrupted the people (v. 7) though the feast was "to the LORD." Mixers are, of course, popular with the people while separatists are despised. But separatists will not degrade worship or defile the people and bring the curse of God upon the people.

5. Its Defilement of Conduct

"The people sat down to eat and to drink, and rose up to play . . . dancing . . . [and] were naked; for Aaron had made them naked unto their shame among their enemies" (vv. 6,19,25). Theology affects our manner of life. Our creed will determine our conduct. Our beliefs will be seen in our behavior. Doctrine manifests itself in one's deeds. A corrupt message will promote corrupt morals. Israel gave themselves up to idolatry, so it is no surprise that they "corrupted themselves" (v. 7), for an idolatrous creed produces iniquitous conduct.

What Israel did after they worshipped the golden calf was extremely defiling. While the eating and drinking may have been innocent parts of a feast (although we certainly doubt it was all innocent), the "play" (v. 6) part certainly was not innocent. "This play was scarcely of a harmless kind. The sensualism of idol-worship constantly led on to sensuality; and the feasts upon idol-sacrifices terminated in profligate orgies" (Rawlinson). The befouling "play" included much "dancing" (v. 19) and resulted in the people becoming "naked" (v. 25). Dancing and nakedness always go hand in hand (immodest dress has always been a trademark of the dance), and the dance has destroyed the morals of multitudes. True religion cleans up a person's conduct, but false religion defiles it.

In our day we are hearing more and more of the association of dancing with worship. As unthinkable and repugnant as it is to some of us, yet some mainline denomination churches have had professional dancers come for a service to do their thing (which includes gross immodesty) on the rostrum. All this will do is defile people and bring Divine judgment upon people.

6. Its Dedication in Pursuit

The Israelites pursued their sin with great dedication. They did not dabble in sin, they enthusiastically jumped in over their heads. They sinned with abandon. In three ways we see this dedication to evil: in their quickness, liberalness, and earliness.

Quickness. "They have turned aside quickly out of the way which I commanded them" (v. 8). It had only been a few months since Israel had been miraculously delivered from Egypt, had escaped through the Red Sea, had experienced miracles regarding their water supply at Marah and Rephidim, and had been given the manna which now came six days a week. And it had only been a few weeks since God manifested Himself in dramatic fashion on Mount Sinai and gave the people the great Decalogue, and the people had said they would do all that God commanded them. Yet, in spite of the short time since all these moving events had occurred in which God had worked marvelously for them, the people went deep into sin. How true it is that "The heart is deceitful above all things, and desperately wicked" (Jeremiah 17:9). There is a dedication in the depraved heart to sin that too often exceeds our dedication to about anything else. And one way Israel demonstrated this dedication to do evil was in the quickness in which they pursued their sin.

Liberalness. "Aaron said unto them, Break off [take off] the golden earrings, which are in the ears of your wives, of your sons, and of your daughters, and bring them unto me. And all the people brake off the golden earrings which were in their ears, and brought them unto Aaron" (vv. 2,3). The response of the people to Aaron's request also revealed a dedication to doing evil—they liberally departed with their valuable golden earrings which they had obtained from the Egyptians. "People, as a rule, spend freely on their vices. [But] They are not so ready to part with their valuables for the service of Jehovah" (Rawlinson). Folk will throw thousands of dollars into beer, tobacco, and adult toys and then fuss when asked to give a few dollars to charity. It is a rare exception to see people giving to the Lord's work with abandon as they give to their vices. But, as we noted in our last chapter, Israel later did give so well to the Lord's work (the Tabernacle) that it was "too much" (Exodus 36:7). But generally, men only give liberally to do evil.

We mentioned in a previous chapter a lesson we would mention here again. It is the fact that the devil tries to gain our resources so God cannot have them for His service. The Tabernacle would require much wealth from the people, but the people gave liberally for the golden calf before they actually gave for the Tabernacle. When we are endowed by God, the devil will soon pay a visit and endeavor to get us to spend that money so the Lord cannot have it.

Earliness. "They rose up early on the morrow, and offered burnt offerings, and brought peace offerings; and the people sat down to eat and to drink, and rose up to play" (v. 6). Another way in which the people's dedication to evil is demonstrated is in their getting up "early" in the morning to pursue their evil ways. They were very enthused and excited about their evil. They were very anxious to begin their defiled activities. Oh, that professing saints had this enthusiasm to get up early to read the Word and pray everyday and then on Sunday to get up early so they would not be late to church. The world gets up early to pursue their activities. Yet, so many folk who claim to be Christian show none of this enthusiasm for God. To get up a few minutes early so they could spend some time in the Word and prayer is just too much for them.

7. Its Dimension in Size

To conclude our look at the character of Israel's sin at Sinai, we note that three times we are told in Scripture that the sin of the Israelites at Sinai was "great" (vv. 21, 30, 31). Noting the overall dimension of the sin of the Israelites is a fitting way to conclude our look at the character of Israel's sin. If one is so blind that he has not already seen how great Israel's sin was, this surely should open the eyes; for Scripture plainly and repeatedly states it was a "great" sin.

We need to pay attention to that description of the dimension of Israel's sin, for the world is always playing down the dimension of sin. What is a great sin they call a trivial sin—if they even call it sin. But we must never play down the dimension of sin. We must speak of sin as it is spoken of in Scripture. As an example, adultery is spoken of in Scripture as "great wickedness" (Genesis 39:9), and we must always call it "great wickedness" regardless of how Hollywood or our society or legislatures view it.

B. THE CONDEMNATION OF THE SIN

The sin of Israel was quickly and repeatedly condemned. We note four ways in which the sin was condemned. It was condemned by the announcement of God, by the anger of Moses, by the action of the Levites, and by the anathema of God.

1. The Announcement of God

At the end of Moses' forty days and nights in the mount with God, God announced to Moses that Israel was corrupting themselves in the camp. God's announcement was not complimentary about Israel. What He said condemned Israel. To further examine the announcement we will note the omniscience, observations, order, and outrage of God.

Omniscience of God. While Moses was meeting with God for forty days and nights, he knew nothing of what was going on down in the camp of the Israelites. But God knew! God is omniscient. Nothing is hid from His eyes. And if God knows, others can know, too, if God chooses to inform them. And He chose to inform Moses.

A proper respect for the omniscience of God would clean up

our lives. When we realize that God knows everything about us, we will stop thinking that we can do evil and no one will find out. God knows about all our deeds, he even knows about our thoughts. The Psalmist said, "Thou knowest my downsitting and mine uprising, thou understandest my thought afar off" (Psalm 139:2). You will never conceal anything from God. You may be able to hide things from men, but never from God. God could describe to Moses in detail what Israel was doing, for God saw everything, for He is omniscient.

Observations of God. Verses 7 through 10 tell us of God's observations of Israel's conduct which He reported to Moses. We note four of these observations which certainly condemn Israel. They repeat some of what we have already noted about the character of Israel's sin, but they give us some additional lessons, so we do not hesitate to do some repeating here. The four observations of Israel's conduct are their defilement before God, their departure from God, their dishonoring of God, and their defiance of God.

First, *defilement before God.* "And the LORD said unto Moses, Go, get thee down; for thy people, which thou broughtest out of the land of Egypt, have corrupted themselves" (v. 7). We have already noted that Israel's conduct was defiling. Here we emphasize that it was defiling before God. In God's sight this conduct was corrupt. Many men would not call this conduct defiling, but God does. God calls a lot of things evil that man refuses to call evil. But calling evil by nice names does not stop evil from corrupting mankind. It only causes more people to be corrupted.

Second, *departure from God.* "They have turned aside quickly out of the way which I commanded them" (v. 8). In spite of all their worship, sacrifices, and festivities, Israel was departing from God. We may be very religious and still be far from God. Churches may have more meetings, be growing in number, and be building great edifices, and yet at the same time be departing from God. People may spend more time in prayer

553

and religious meditation and still be departing from God. The key to whether or not we are drawing closer to God or departing from God is how we are obeying the Word of God. Israel was not obeying God's Word, thus they were departing from God.

Third, *dishonoring of God*. "They have made them a molten calf, and have worshipped it, and have sacrificed thereunto, and said, These be thy gods, O Israel, which have brought thee up out of the land of Egypt" (v. 8). Israel greatly dishonored God by attributing to the calf idol their great deliverance from Egypt. God had done so much for them; yet they in a gross, ungrateful act attribute all this great work to a calf idol which they ordered Aaron to make. How stupid is idolatry. If men build a great building or bridge and some other men build a small image and acclaim the image as the one who built the building or bridge, we would call the image people crazy. But when one does this regarding God, mankind simply calls it religion. However, you do not have to be an idol worshipper to attribute your blessings to someone or something other than God. Mankind thanks lady luck, chance, their own strength, etc. for their blessings instead of thanking God; and this dishonors God as much as attributing to an idol Israel's deliverance from Egypt.

Fourth, *defiance of God*. "And the LORD said unto Moses, I have seen this people, and, behold, it is a stiffnecked people" (v. 9). This stiff-neck problem was not a physical problem. It was a spiritual problem. The stiff-neck represents an attitude that will not bow before God. It is representative of defiance. Israel's sin was willful, not accidental. They willfully refused to bow down to God's way. They openly defied God. It is a terrible attitude that will only curse the possessor of it.

Order of God. "And the LORD said unto Moses, Go, get thee down; for thy people, which thou broughtest out of the land of Egypt, have corrupted themselves" (v. 7). The condemnation of Israel's conduct is evident in God sternly ordering Moses to "Go, get thee down" to the people. Their wicked conduct needed to be stopped, and Moses was the one to stop it.

Every man of God is given in principle this assignment. He is to oppose the work of evil. He is to lift up the standard of conduct. His life is to be a constant protest to evil. But, alas, preachers have become more like Aaron than like Moses. Rather than lift the standard, they lower it to the people's wishes. So today preachers go along with the congregation's wish for unholy music. They go along with those in the congregation who want to marry apart from God's holy standards against marrying the divorced and the unsaved. They refuse to say anything derogatory about cocktails. And they become involved with ecumenical movements. Moses, however, was not ordered down to the camp to go along with the crowd but to take strong actions against the evil in the crowd. Let every preacher remember this is his calling, too.

Outrage of God. "Now therefore let me alone, that my wrath may wax [become] hot against them, and that I may consume them" (v. 10). The entire announcement that God made to Moses was made in anger. But the conclusion of the announcement really shows God's outrage over Israel's conduct. It left no doubt that God condemned their conduct and very severely.

This report of God's outrage is not a passage of Scripture a number of people want to read or even admit it is in Scripture. They prefer to view God as a God of love, Who would never get upset with anyone but in kindly benevolence would forgive all. This bunch cannot tolerate sermons on God's judgment or on hell. All they want are nice soothing sermons about God's love and care. However, if God is not outraged with sin, then He is not a just God. But God is holy. And that means He will be outraged with unholiness, especially the gross unholiness that went on in Israel's camp. We suspect that if these folk, who do not like the subject of God's wrath, were treated as badly as God was at Sinai, they would be upset, too!

Woe be the person who outrages God. God was so outraged with the Israelites that He wanted to "consume" them because of their sin. He wanted to destroy them completely and start over with Moses. The mercy of God prevailed here for Israel. But that was not always the case for them in their wilderness journey, for mercy rejected will one day be mercy withheld.

2. The Anger of Moses

When Moses came down the Mount with his helper Joshua, they both heard the evil going on before he saw it. Joshua thought it was the "noise of war" (v. 17), but Moses had inside information from God and properly discerned it as the "noise of them that sing" (v. 18). However, the singing would not rejoice his heart; and when he saw what Israel was doing, he became very angry as God had done earlier. His anger plainly said Moses condemned their conduct, too.

His anger was an illustration of righteous indignation which we need to see a lot more of in people. So many folk can look at evil deeds and hardly get upset. Sin does not bother them as it ought. It ought to really enrage mankind, but it does not. One reason it does not upset folk very much is that they do not spend much time with God. Moses had just spent forty days and nights with God. No wonder he was upset with sin. If you spend much time in the Word of God and in prayer to God, you will not be very tolerant of sin either. Many of our churches have a problem dealing with sin in the church because only a few people live close enough to God to get upset about sin. Most of the congregation is not bothered about the evil in the church, and they will oppose doing anything about it.

Moses' anger is demonstrated in three ways: the destruction of the tablets of law, the dusting of the drinking water, and the denouncing of Aaron.

Destruction of the tablets. "And it came to pass, as soon as he came nigh unto the camp, that he saw the calf, and the dancing: and Moses' anger waxed hot, and he cast the tables out of his hands, and brake them beneath the mount" (v. 19). Moses' action in casting down the tablets of stone upon which God had written the law was both symbolic and sanctified.

556

First, it was *symbolic*. It represents what Israel had been doing. They had been breaking God's law. Breaking both of the tablets reminds us that "Whosoever shall keep the whole law, and yet offend in one point, he is guilty of all" (James 2:10). Israel had broken the second commandment and obviously the seventh also. But, as James said, that made them guilty of breaking the whole law; for the law is a unit.

Second, it was *sanctified*. God never rebuked Moses for breaking the tablets of the law; and later, without any reprimand, God wrote on new tablets all the words that were on the first tablets (34:1). God does not rebuke us when we get upset with sin. God was also angry with sin and spoke of destroying the Israelites. God would be pleased if more folk got as upset about sin as Moses did. Church congregations that are critical of the pastor because of his outspoken opposition to sin need to ponder the action of Moses and remember that God approved!

Dusting of the drinking water. "And he took the calf which they had made, and burnt it in the fire, and ground it to powder, and strawed [dusted] it upon the water, and made the children of Israel drink of it" (v. 20). In the account of this action given in Deuteronomy we read, "I took your sin, the calf which ye had made, and burnt it with fire, and stamped it, and ground it very small, even until it was as small as dust: and I cast the dust thereof into the brook that descended out of the mount" (Deuteronomy 9:21). Charles Simeon said of this action of Moses, "We need not look for any recondite [hidden] mystery in this, because the obvious effect of the act itself was sufficiently instructive. No greater indignity could be offered to this worthless idol, than that which he devised; nor any more humiliating punishment be inflicted upon the people, than to compel them to swallow their god, and to cast him out into the draught with their common food."

Another lesson here is that Israel's sin resulted in a polluted water supply. Their sin polluted the water that came from the rock ("descended out of the mount," cp. Exodus 17:6). Sin affects our environment more than we think. This problem began in the Garden of Eden. Paul speaks of the problem when he says, "For we know that the whole creation groaneth and travaileth in pain together until now" (Romans 8:22). Environmental problems are rooted in sin problems, but you will not find the environmentalists embracing that truth.

Denouncing of Aaron. Though Aaron had been a leader with Moses in the emancipation of the Israelites, Scripture makes no attempt to conceal or water down Aaron's evil. "It tells the story with perfect impartiality. The Bible, like its author, is without respect of persons . . . This is not the way of ordinary biographies, but it is the way of Scripture. It is one mark of its inspiration. It is a guarantee of its historic truthfulness" (J. Orr). To examine this denouncing of Aaron by Moses, we will note the accusation by Moses and the answer of Aaron.

First, the *accusation* by Moses. "And Moses said unto Aaron, What did this people unto thee, that thou hast brought so great a sin upon them?" (v. 21). The accusation is twofold. It attacks Aaron's failure and his foulness. His *failure* was in letting the people lead him rather than the other way around. Aaron, along with Hur, was put in charge of the people (24:14). But he was a poor leader. When the people complained, he did what the people wanted instead of doing what was right. He did not heed the statute which said, "Thou shalt not follow a multitude to do evil" (23:2). He wanted to be popular more than to be pure. Aaron was a people pleaser, not a God pleaser. Furthermore, his faith was not strong in himself; for without Moses, he was very weak. Our faith needs to be personal, and not that which requires some human prop. His *foulness* is emphasized by Moses accusing him of bringing upon the people "so great a sin." What a poor influence Aaron was. Instead of improving the faith of the people, he infected it with idolatry. Instead of lifting the moral standard, he lowered it; for "Aaron had made them naked" (v. 25). We have preachers like that in our day, too. Some would lead us to join hand with the apostates in compromise of doctrine. Others would lower morals by condoning divorce and insisting that when you get a divorce and remarry you have not sinned. But such conduct upsets God. "And the LORD was very angry with Aaron to have destroyed him" (Deuteronomy 9:20). The only reason he was not destroyed is that Moses "prayed for Aaron" (Ibid.).

Second, the *answer* of Aaron. Aaron's answer to Moses was pathetic. We note three things about the answer: it protested Moses' anger, passed the blame to others, and proclaimed a ludicrous explanation.

The first thing Aaron said after Moses' accusation of Aaron was "Let not the anger of my lord wax hot" (v. 22). Aaron *protested Moses' anger* before he said anything else. That certainly condemns Aaron. Rather than focus on his own sin, he first focused on Moses' disposition as though that was the first thing that needed adjustment. This is ever the way of the unrepentant. When accused, they try to reverse things and accuse the accuser. So the policeman who makes the arrest is attacked, the school teacher who writes up a misbehaving student is attacked, and the preacher who denounces sin is attacked.

Aaron's second statement in his answer *passed the blame* to others. "Thou knowest the people, that they are set on mischief. For they said . . . Make us gods" (vv. 22,23). Aaron did what man began to do in the Garden of Eden—blame others for your failures. Our society is full of this. We blame everybody but ourselves. We have gotten so far out in this attitude that if thief breaks into a house and falls and breaks his leg in the process, the owner of the house will be sued and lose at court while the thief who broke into the house will collect a big settlement.

Aaron's last statement *proclaimed a ludicrous explanation* for how the calf came about. "I cast it [the gold] into the fire, and there came out this calf" (v. 24). Aaron would have Moses believe that the calf just happened, that there was no molding and forming and engraving. How stupid are man's excuses for his sin. They are nothing but lies. Aaron lied unashamedly. So do excuse makers.

3. The Action of the Levites

"Then Moses stood in the gate of the camp, and said, Who is on the LORD'S side? let him come unto me. And all the sons of Levi gathered themselves together unto him" (v. 26). The action of the Levites was another condemnation of Israel's sin of idolatry. The action of the Levites was prompted by a great challenge by Moses. "Who is on the Lord's side?" was the challenge. The context tells us some things involved in being on the Lord's side. They are separation, declaration, occupation, and compensation.

Separation. "Who is on the LORD'S side? let him come unto me" (v. 26). To be on God's side required that folk separate from the crowd and stand with Moses. This would not be easy, of course; for it could mean separation from family and friends. Furthermore, it would not be easy because it has never been popular to separate from evil. When you do, many folk will heap scorn on you and criticize you for being "holier than thou." Also, in various ways, they will make it very hard for you. But if you are going to be on the Lord's side, you will have to separate from people, practices, philosophies, and places which are opposed to Him.

Declaration. Being on the Lord's side also means a public declaration of your position. Those on the Lord's side had to go to Moses. This would be in view of all the people. They could not do this secretly. You cannot be on the Lord's side and be a secret disciple. If you are on God's side, you must show it. Not surprisingly, many people do not like this public declaration business. They do not want to take stands publically; for when you take a public stand, you will be attacked. But if you cannot take a public stand for the One Who died publically on the cross for your sins, you are of very poor character.

Occupation. Being on the Lord's side is not an attractive retirement program. It involves much service. Those who were on the Lord's side at Mount Sinai were told to "Put every man his sword by his side, and go in and out from gate to gate throughout the camp, and slay . . . there fell of the people that day about three thousand men" (v. 27). Those who want to be on the Lord's side had better be prepared to do service for the Lord, and that service may not always be enjoyable work. But if you are on God's side, you will do the task regardless.

Moses and the Levites have suffered much criticism for the slaying of some three thousand people. Critics will say that this is not an act of love and does not display God's love and mercy at all. But the critics are not willing to look at the other side of the coin. They ignore the fact that people had degraded God to a cow and that they had engaged in licentious immoral acts. These things destroy people's character and eventually their life. If this sin is not stopped, it will destroy countless more. Also, if the three thousand wicked are not slain, many godly will be slain— persecution tells us that fact. Let apostasy and other evils go unchecked and they will turn on the godly in vicious killing. If murderers are not slain, they will murder more people and inspire others to murder. If homosexuals are not stopped, they will slay mankind. AIDS is already showing us this truth. So this slaying by the Levites was not unjust or unkind. It was an act of love and mercy, for it spared many innocents from destruction later on.

We may not always have to take up a steel sword to slay, for there are other swords by which we can slay evil. We especially need to take up the Sword of the Spirit which is the Word of God (Ephesians 6:17) and use it to slay evil ideas, thoughts, activities, associations, friendships, plans, and habits.

Compensation. "For Moses had said, Consecrate yourselves today to the LORD, even every man upon his son, and upon his brother; that he may bestow upon you a blessing this day" (v. 29). Standing on the Lord's side is rewarding. It may not, however, appear to the flesh to be rewarding. But in due time it will prove to be very rewarding. Deuteronomy tells us about the

561

reward the Levites received because they stood against even their own relatives in the matter of this sin. The reward was the priesthood (Deuteronomy 33:8–10), a great spiritual privilege. Of course, many folk only want material rewards and, therefore, do not perceive spiritual privileges as much of a reward. But wise men know that the greatest rewards are spiritual rewards. Covet them above all other rewards.

4. The Anathema of God
"And the LORD plagued the people, because they made the calf, which Aaron made" (v. 35). God began the condemnation of Israel's sin in His announcement to Moses, and here He finishes it in plaguing the people. God was merciful to Israel and did not slay them all, but He did send judgment upon the people. This judgment caused many more of the Israelites to die which emphasizes that "the wages of sin is death" (Romans 6:23). It is a terrible thing when God plagues people. Egypt found that out. So did Israel at Sinai, and so will multitudes when they enter eternal hell—if they have not discovered this fact sooner. As we noted above, God cannot be faulted here. Man was shown the right way to live, but man rebelled against that way. So the blame is not on God for acting unjustly but on man for acting unholily.

C. THE COMPASSION FOR THE SINNER
In spite of all the judgment from heaven, God's mercy was still displayed in a wonderful way at Sinai. Compassion for the sinner was very prominent in this experience. We especially see this compassion in the two times that Moses made intercession on behalf of the people. These intercessions by Moses were some of his finest performances in life. How noble and gallant and godly was his compassion upon the Israelites.

What we especially want to look at in this demonstration of compassion for the sinner is the basis on which compassion was sought. Moses did not ask God to look the other way or simply to give the people another chance. Moses did not play down the seriousness of the sin in hopes God would be more lenient towards the people, but he called it a "great sin" (v. 31). Moses did not seek mercy through these worthless ways which the world, however, tries to seek mercy from God. No, Moses based his plea for sparing the people on three very important matters—the glory of God, the Word of God, and the atonement for God. This is always the proper basis for mercy with God. This makes God's mercy of much higher character than man's mercy.

1. The Glory of God

When God announced to Moses what Israel was doing and that He, God, wanted to "consume them; and . . . make of thee a great nation [instead] (v. 10), Moses protested. He said, "Wherefore should the Egyptians speak, and say, For mischief did he bring them out, to slay them in the mountains, and to consume them from the face of the earth? Turn from thy fierce wrath, and repent of this evil against thy people" (v. 12). This first plea for compassion was based on the glory of God. Moses was concerned what the Egyptians would think about God if God destroyed the Israelites. How noble of Moses to be chiefly concerned about God's glory. Israel in their wicked idolatry had greatly dishonored God. They had no interest in the honor of God. But Moses was just the opposite.

This concern for the glory of God was so sincere; for in pleading as he did, Moses rejected absolutely the idea that God should raise up from Moses a nation. Moses rejected the honor of being the father of the nation. Moses was tested by this offer, but he passed the test with flying colors. And the reason he passed the test so well was that he was greatly interested in the glory of God. If we were more interested in the glory of God, we would make better decisions, overcome temptation much better, and serve God better.

2. The Word of God

The second basis for pleading for compassion for the people was the Word of God. Moses said, "Remember Abraham, Isaac, and Israel, thy servants, to whom thou swarest by thine own self, and saidst unto them, I will multiply your seed as the stars of heaven, and all this land that I have spoken of will I give unto your seed, and they shall inherit it for ever" (v. 13). Moses argued that God's Word had promised a covenant with Abraham, Isaac, and Jacob and that to destroy the Israelites would go against the Word of God.

Again Moses pleads on good ground; for compassion for the sinner must be based on what the Scriptures say, not on the mere sentiments of mankind. But there have been many folk in every age who ignore God's Word and want people to be saved whether they have gained eternal life in the way the Word of God specifies or not. But when you reject the Word of God, you reject the mercy of God; for the Word of God tells us how to obtain the mercy of God.

Moses' intercession in the mount for the Israelites was effective; for Scripture says, "And the LORD repented of the evil which he thought to do unto his people" (v. 14); and "Therefore he said that he would destroy them, had not Moses his chosen stood before him in the breach, to turn away his wrath, lest he should destroy them" (Psalm 106:23). Oh, for more men like Moses who can so effectively plead to God for the salvation of mankind.

Some may have trouble with the report that God "repented" (v. 14). The word "repented" makes it look like God is sinful. But nothing is farther from the truth. "The expression is an anthropomorphic one" (Rawlinson). It is language which is accommodated to human modes of speech and conception. To repent basically means to change the course you are on. We generally use it in regards to sinning. But repenting does not necessarily involve changing from sin to righteousness. It can involve any change. What is involved here is that God in mercy did not annihilate the Israelites as He had threatened to do.

3. The Atonement for God

After Moses had gone down to the camp, broken the tablets

of the law, burnt the golden calf, put the dust in the drinking water, indicted Aaron, and enlisted the Levites to be on God's side, he spoke to the people and said, "Ye have sinned a great sin: and now I will go up unto the LORD; peradventure I shall make an atonement for your sin" (v. 30). Moses then went up the mount and pleaded with God, offering himself as the atonement for the people's sin. "If thou wilt forgive their sin—; and if not, blot me, I pray thee, out of thy book which thou hast written" (v. 32). This was a magnanimous offer. Moses' compassion for his people was tremendous. He would offer himself in place of the people. This spirit was seen in the Apostle Paul in the New Testament when he said, "I could wish that myself were accursed from Christ for my brethren, my kinsmen according to the flesh" (Romans 9:3).

This is a marvelous picture of the work of Christ. Christ offered Himself to God as the atonement for our sin. In the case of Christ, His offer was accepted. But in the case of Moses, it was not accepted. "And the LORD said unto Moses, Whosoever hath sinned against me, him will I blot out of my book" (v. 33). Moses could not be an atonement for the people because he was not without sin. But Christ could be an atonement because, unlike Moses, He had no sin.

But in spite of the fact that Moses' offer as the atoning sacrifice was rejected, the nobility of his deed is not diminished. Nor is the lesson about the basis of compassion diminished either. The lesson is that compassion for the sinner can be gained through the atonement. We cannot be saved from the curse of our sins through our own works, but we can be saved through Calvary where an acceptable atonement occurred. To leave out Calvary is to forsake the mercy of God. There is no compassion for the sinner who rejects Calvary. It is vain to plead the mercy of God when the work of Christ on the cross is ignored.

XXIV.

SPEAKING WITH GOD

EXODUS 33

WHEN TROUBLE COMES into our lives, we need to spend much time speaking with God. This speaking with God is not a one way street. Rather, it involves both our speaking with Him in prayer and His speaking to us through His Word. This was Moses' experience after Israel's great sin of idolatry at Sinai. Faced with this great problem in the camp, Moses wisely and repeatedly went to the Lord to speak with Him—to bring his cares and concerns to the Lord and to hear words of instruction and encouragement from the Lord. We saw some of this speaking with God by Moses in the text of our last chapter. But the subject dominates the text for this chapter; therefore, we will focus entirely upon it for this chapter's study.

Moses' experience of speaking with God is summed up in our text for this study in "The LORD talked with Moses . . . the LORD spake unto Moses face to face, as a man speaketh unto his friend" (vv. 9,11). What a blessed relationship Moses had with God to be on such good speaking terms with God and to be spoken of as a "friend" of God. It was certainly a contrast to most of the other Israelites. They were definitely not on good speaking terms with God at all; and instead of being friends with God, they so aggravated Him that He talked of consuming them (Exodus 32:10).

As we will see plainly in this study, speaking with God was a very profitable and blessed experience for Moses. Speaking with God can be a way of blessing for anyone. But, unfortunately, not many folk are very interested in speaking with God.

Their interests are carnal not spiritual. They are more interested in talking with just about anyone else than God. Thus they lose countless blessings.

To study the experiences in our text Moses had in speaking with God after Israel's sin of idolatry, we will note the pronouncement in the speaking (vv. 1–6), the place for the speaking (vv. 7–11), and the petitions in the speaking (vv. 12–23).

A. THE PRONOUNCEMENT IN THE SPEAKING

"And the LORD said unto Moses, Depart, and go up hence, thou and the people which thou hast brought up out of the land of Egypt, unto the land which I sware unto Abraham, to Isaac, and to Jacob . . . I will send an angel before thee; and I will drive out the Canaanite, the Amorite, and the Hittite, and the Perizzite, the Hivite, and the Jebusite . . . I will not go up in the midst of thee; for thou art a stiffnecked people: lest I consume thee in the way" (vv. 1–3). The record of Moses speaking with God in our text begins with a pronouncement by God to Moses which he in turn gave to the Israelites. It brought both good news and bad news. The bad news was so bad, however, that it eclipsed the good news and stopped any rejoicing in the good news.

1. The Good News

"Depart, and go up hence . . . unto the land which I sware unto Abraham, to Isaac, and to Jacob . . . I will drive out the Canaanite, the Amorite, and the Hittite, and the Perizzite, the Hivite, and the Jebusite" (vv. 1,2) The first part of the pronouncement was twofold. It directed Moses to leave Sinai and head for Canaan, and it promised Israel that God would drive out the inhabitants of Canaan so Israel could have the land to themselves. Both of these statements would be good news to the Israelites. It would be good news that departure was near at hand (though some forty days would still go by before departure in order to allow for Moses' second forty-day session on Sinai); for, as we noted in our previous chapter, Israel had evidenced it was quite anxious to leave Sinai and be on their way to Canaan (cp. 32:1). It would also be good news to know that God would drive out the inhabitants of the promised land.

The good news in this pronouncement from God indicated that God was keeping His promise which He had made to Abraham, Isaac, and Jacob. And He was keeping His promise in spite of Israel's sin of idolatry. Thus the keeping of this promise emphasized both the infallibleness of the Word of God and the greatness of the grace of God. The Word of God does not fail. When God makes a promise, God keeps the promise. God's Word can always be trusted. The grace of God is beyond all human comprehension or duplication. Apart from it, no one would escape from the judgment of their sins.

2. The Bad News

"I will send an angel before thee . . . for I will not go up in the midst of thee; for thou art a stiffnecked people: lest I consume thee in the way" (vv. 2,3). The bad news was that God would no longer go with Israel in their midst, but an angel would go in His place. This bad news was a pronouncement of judgment upon Israel for their sin. Israel had sinned a great sin, and they are now learning more about the judgment that was coming upon them for their sin.

Moses is to be commended for telling Israel the bad news as well as the good news. Many preachers would not do that. As an example, many only speak of the love of God but never of the judgment of God. Such faithlessness in preaching greatly condemns the preachers and greatly imperils their congregations.

This part of the pronouncement of God and Israel's reaction to it spoke not only of Israel's loss of God but also of Israel's loss of gladness and glory. These are losses that sin always brings to mankind. We will examine them in more detail here.

The loss of God. "I will not go up in the midst of thee" (v. 3). Because of Israel's sin, God said His presence would no longer go with Israel. Losing God's presence is a terrible loss. It is the greatest loss anyone can experience. But sin is in the habit of extracting great losses from sinners. We will learn later that through the grace of God and through the earnest intercessory praying of Moses, God's presence was restored to Israel.

To further study this great loss caused by Israel's sin, we will note the reason for this loss, the replacement for this loss, and the retainment in this loss.

First, the *reason* for this loss. The primary reason for the loss of God's presence was, of course, the sin of idolatry. By their sin, "the people had shown themselves unfit for His near presence, and He would withdraw Himself" (Rawlinson). But God adds an additional and significant reason for this loss which we want to note here. God stated it was necessary to remove His presence from them "lest I consume thee in the way" (v. 3). Because they were "a stiffnecked people" (Ibid.), which means they were habitually rebellious and thus likely to sin again, their future sin would be worse with God in their midst than if He were at a distance. So, because of their propensity to sin, it would be best for them that God remove Himself from their midst lest their future sin lead to their entire destruction.

The principle here is that the greater our spiritual privilege, the greater the adverse consequences when we fail. With God in their midst, Israel would be experiencing a great spiritual privilege which would make their sinning much worse in consequence than if God was not with them. This principle is why God decrees that some cannot be in high position in His service. As an example, those who have failed in marriage are excluded from the ministry (I Timothy 3). This moral failure makes future moral failure more likely. Thus those with this moral failure must not be put in the ministry, for the evil consequences of their sin when in the ministry is far greater than if they are in some other lesser job.

Second, the *replacement* for this loss. "I will send an angel before thee" (v. 2). Instead of the presence of God, an angel would be sent to accompany the people and lead them on their way. It certainly seems a blessing to have an angel accompany us on our ways. But an angel is no substitute for God. An angel may be a great improvement on a man, but it is God that the angel is replacing. It is a case of second best. And second best in the spiritual realm is something we ought to avoid at all costs. It matters little in comparison if we experience second best in the material and physical realm, for they are only temporal situations. But spiritual things are forever. Never live in a way that an angel replaces God in your life. It will be no consolation for what you lose when God departs.

Third, the *retainment* in this loss. "I will drive out the Canaanite, the Amorite, and the Hittite, and the Perizzite, the Hivite, and the Jebusite: Unto a land flowing with milk and honey . . . when the people heard these evil tidings, they mourned" (vv. 2–4). The pronouncement in our text indicated that Israel retained Canaan in spite of their sin. They were still going to live in a land flowing with milk and honey, and they would still be victorious over the inhabitants of the land. But, as our text notes, that news did not keep them from mourning, for you can have many things in this life and still be shorn of the greatest and most important blessing of all—God's presence. We have already seen that an angel was no compensation for the loss of God's presence; but now in this text we also see that great material blessings are no compensation either, for the Israelites mourned greatly here even though the pronouncement indicated that their material blessings were great and still in tact.

This is the same message Christ gave us when He said, "What shall it profit a man, if he shall gain the whole world, and lose his own soul?" (Mark 8:36). For Israel, it was like losing their soul to have God depart from them. They may gain Canaan and all its richness and comforts and be a powerful military country, but it is no consolation for the loss of God's presence. Would that our land would realize this truth. We are loaded with material possessions and boast of great military might. But that is no compensation for the fact that God left us years ago. Most citizens in our land, however, do not care about God's presence. And our laws make even the mention of God in some places to be illegal. How desolate our land is of wisdom.

The loss of gladness. "And when the people heard these evil tidings [that God would no longer be in their midst], they mourned" (v. 4). In mourning here, the people evidence they are finally waking up to the curse of their sin. The results are beginning to be felt very painfully. We have noted this mourning earlier. Here, in noting the mourning again, we want to emphasize the fact that sin brings mourning, not joy. The Israelites are discovering that their sin of idolatry with all its play and indulgence in the lusts of the flesh did not bring as much joy as they thought. Rather, the joy was very short. Any happiness and pleasure sin gives is only short term at its best ("for a season" [Hebrews 11:25]). Sorrow soon sets in, and it will last much longer than any joy sin gives. Furthermore, it will destroy all the happiness of a person. Sorrow ever stalks the sinner with great tenacity. That is why the world is not a happy world. Mourning is one of the main trademarks of the world because the world lives in so much sin. Holiness is the key to happiness. If we want to have gladness in our heart, we must not have guile in our heart. Obeying God may look to be unpleasant at times, but it eventually brings much joy which will more than compensate for any unpleasantness we experienced in obedience. Sin is just the opposite. When sin tempts us by offering delights, do not be deceived. Remember the delights will be very short compared to the sorrow that will follow.

The loss of glory. "And no man did put on him his ornaments. For the LORD had said unto Moses . . . put off thy ornaments from thee . . . and the children of Israel stripped themselves of their ornaments by the mount Horeb [also called Sinai]" (vv. 4–6). Ornaments (jewelry) glorify mankind. People put on jewelry in order to look more glorious. Therefore, when the jewelry is removed, the glory is removed. So the lesson here has to do with the loss of glory that accompanies sin. Holiness dignifies mankind. But unholiness degrades him. Adam and Eve lost much glory when they sinned. Man has been losing glory ever since. Paul summed it up when he said, "All have sinned, and come short of the glory of God" (Romans 3:23).

This truth concerning the loss of glory because of sin is also seen in other applications in Scripture. When Israel departed from God during the time that Eli was the priest, they lost much glory. The culmination of the loss of glory came in a battle against the Philistines when the Philistines captured the ark (where God's glory rested). When Eli heard the news (which included the deaths of his sons Hophni and Phinehas who were in charge of the ark), he dropped dead. When the wife of Phinehas, who was expecting, heard the news, the shock caused her to go into travail and she gave birth to a son. She died as a result of the birth; but before she died, "she named the child Ichabod, saying, The glory is departed from Israel" (I Samuel 4:21). "Ichabod" means "no glory." Many countries, many churches, and many colleges and other organizations and individuals have Ichabod written over them because of their sin. Also in Ezekiel's day, the sin of the people caused the glory of God to depart from them. It did so in stages. It began when "the glory of the God of Israel was gone up from the cherub [cherubims of the ark], whereupon he was, to the threshold of the house [Temple] (Ezekiel 9:3, cp. 10:4). "Then the glory of the LORD departed from off the threshold of the house" (Ezekiel 10:18) and "mounted up from the earth" (Ezekiel 10:19). After that "the glory of the LORD went up from the midst of the city, and stood upon the mountain which is on the east side of the city" (Ezekiel 11:23). These are sad words concerning the loss of glory, but sin causes it to happen all the time.

With the Israelites at Sinai losing their glory and the glory of God's presence, no wonder Moses later pleaded for God to "Show me thy glory" (v. 18). We will note more of that shortly. Suffice it to say here that to the lose the glory that comes from holiness is to lose that which we cannot afford to lose.

B. THE PLACE FOR THE SPEAKING

"And Moses took the tabernacle, and pitched it without the camp, afar off from the camp, and called it the Tabernacle of the congregation . . . Moses went out unto the tabernacle . . . Moses entered into the tabernacle . . . and the LORD talked with Moses" (vv. 7–9). This tabernacle which Moses moved outside the camp is not to be confused with the Tabernacle which God ordered Moses to construct from the gifts of the people. Moses received these instructions for that Tabernacle when he was in the mount the first forty days and nights. But when that stay ended, Moses was informed of Israel's sin of idolatry; and that sin guided his activities before he went into the mount the second time for forty days and night. So the great Tabernacle had not been constructed yet. This tabernacle (the word is a translation of the Hebrew word that simply means "tent") was a special and temporary place set up for Moses to have a private place to speak with God. It was also a place where folk could go and assemble to worship God. It obviously had been in use before this time.

To further study about this place for speaking with God, we will note the position of the tent, the pursuit of the tent, the pillar by the tent, and the pausing in the tent.

1. The Position of the Tent

"And Moses took the tabernacle, and pitched it without the camp, afar off from the camp" (v. 7). The significance of Moses moving the tent "afar off from the camp" in order to speak with God is that since God is no longer in the camp, Moses is going to have to leave the camp to speak with God. Of course, God could hear Moses anywhere, but the position of the tent now being outside the camp symbolically emphasized the judgment that had come upon Israel. So the moving of the tent reminds Israel of what God has just told them about His presence no longer going with them.

This positioning of the tent outside of the camp is an example of the continual reminders given sinners of the loss they have suffered because of their sin. Everywhere sinners turn, they will be reminded in some way of the consequences of their sin. But this continual reminding is not cruelty on the part of God.

Rather, it can be a blessing in disguise. If the sinner pays attention (most of them do not, however) to the constant reminders of the loss caused by their sin, the reminders will be a good restrainer to future sin. Sinners may not like having the evil consequences of their sin brought to their attention so often. But if it keeps them from future sin, the frequent reminders are very profitable even if they are very painful.

2. The Pursuit of the Tent

"Every one which sought the LORD went out unto the tabernacle of the congregation, which was without the camp." (v. 7). The moving of the tent outside the camp did not prohibit men from seeking God. It only required that they must also go outside the camp if they wanted to seek God. This going outside the camp to seek God provides a good lesson on what is involved in the true worship of God. From this incident, we note four things that are involved: a public stand, a passionate spirit, a personal separation, and a painful scorn.

A public stand. For an Israelite to seek God here would definitely mean a public stand. Going outside the camp to the tent would be visible to all in the camp. This could simply not be done in secret. It could only be done openly. And it would be an open break from the idolatry that so many had given themselves to earlier.

We saw this lesson on the public stand earlier when Moses, after seeing the awful condition the Israelites were in from the idolatry, said, "Who is on the LORD'S side? let him come unto me" (Exodus 32:26). To show that you were on God's side there meant a public declaration, and to worship God here requires the same. Secret discipleship is always condemned. There is no merit in it. It dishonors God. Jesus died for our sins in view and earshot of a mocking, godless mob. We should, therefore, not be ashamed to stand for Christ in public.

A passionate spirit. Only those who "sought the LORD"

went outside the camp to the Tabernacle. To worship God there would require considerable desire. It would be harder to worship now that God's presence was removed from the camp. So greater desire would be necessary if one was to go out to the tent to seek the Lord.

Worship always requires desire. "They that worship him must worship him in spirit" (John 4:24) as well as "in truth" (Ibid.). The reason Israel went into the wilderness was to worship Jehovah, to offer sacrifices to Him (Exodus 3:18). But the sin of idolatry revealed that many Israelites did not want to worship Jehovah. They did not have much zeal for Jehovah. Their passion for God was lacking.

They are not alone in this condition. Our churches, let alone the world, is filled with people who have little passion for the worship of God. Their lack of passion is demonstrated by the fact that they will not worship if any inconvenience is involved. To have to go outside the camp will be much too much for them. With all the comforts we have in our church buildings today, the frequent absenteeism of many members really reveals a great lack of passion for God. They have a passion for doing many other things, but not for worship. We need to pray to God that He will give us a great desire for Him. If we lack the desire, it will become a great curse to us.

A personal separation. To go to the tent outside the camp required that the Israelite separate himself from the camp which was so corrupted by idolatry. True worship requires that we separate from unholy conduct and unholy creed both of which the camp of Israel represented at that time. Some, of course, do not appreciate this separation requirement in worship and often call it a "holier than thou" attitude; which it certainly is not. And there are others today who refuse to leave an apostate church because they have so many friends and relatives in the church. But God has left the church; and if they would truly seek and worship God acceptably, they must get out of that unholy place.

We worship a holy God, and to condone unholiness makes a

mockery of our worship. But we need to be careful, however, that we are not guilty of being unnecessarily picky in our separation. No church is perfect, and we cannot leave for every little suspect of sin. If we did this, we would never worship anywhere. But where cardinal doctrines of the faith are denied, we need to leave. Where homosexuality and other forms of unholy conduct are tolerated, we need to leave. Where hellish rock music is accepted, we need to leave. Also, where play and games and parties and suppers are the big emphasis, we need to leave; for we will not find much spiritual food in that church.

A painful scorn. The writer of Hebrews speaks of this scene when he says, "Let us go forth therefore unto him without the camp, bearing his reproach" (Hebrews 13:13). Here we learn of the scorn and reproach that will often accompany going outside the camp to worship. The unholy are not very tolerant with those who leave their midst to worship elsewhere. Leaving is a rebuke to them, for it says their lives and their worship are unacceptable. When you break with the crowd, you invite reproach. But as the writer of Hebrews said, "Jesus also, that he might sanctify the people with his own blood, suffered without the gate" (Hebrews 13:12). Men may heap much scorn upon us, but our compensation is that Christ is with us. It is far better to have the reproach of man than the reproach of God. Those who refuse to go outside the camp to worship God will experience the reproach of God. But those who go outside the camp to worship God will experience only the reproach of man.

3. The Pillar by the Tent

"And it came to pass, as Moses entered into the tabernacle, the cloudy pillar descended, and stood at the door of the tabernacle, and the LORD talked with Moses. And all the people saw the cloudy pillar stand at the tabernacle door: and all the people rose up and worshipped, every man in his tent door" (vv. 9,10). We note two things about the pillar here: the meaning of the pillar and the motivation from the pillar.

The meaning of the pillar. The significance of the pillar here in our text is that it represents the presence of God. This is seen in the first time we were told about the pillar: "The LORD went before them by day in a pillar of a cloud, to lead them the way; and by night in a pillar of fire, to give them light" (Exodus 13:21). Also, in our text here, it is evident the pillar represented the presence of God; for when the "pillar descended, and stood at the door of the tabernacle . . . the LORD talked with Moses" (v. 9). You will note in your Bible that the words "the LORD" are in italics which means they are not in the Hebrew text but were inserted by the translators to make the reading smoother. Without the italicized words, we read, "the pillar . . . talked with Moses" (Ibid.) which really drives home that the pillar represented the presence of God. And it tells us that God's presence is indeed removed from the camp, for the pillar comes only outside the camp where Moses pitched the tent to seek Him.

The coming of the pillar to the tent certainly says volumes about Moses. God would favor Moses with His presence, for Moses was walking with God. Oh, that we would all live such a life that the presence of God would be manifested in our lives, that we might sense His closeness and hear His voice speak to us through His Word. But this will never happen unless you go without the camp to seek Him.

The motivation from the pillar. "And all the people saw the cloudy pillar stand at the tabernacle door: and all the people rose up and worshipped, every man in his tent door" (v. 10). The people knew when the pillar came down to the tent that God's presence was come again, and in gratefulness and gladness they worshipped God. Worshipping God evidenced some repentance on the part of the Israelites. If we are truly repentant for our sin, we will worship. Some who have fallen into sin who later tell us they have repented, betray the insincerity of their repentance by failing to show up regularly for worship at church.

We need to note that though the worshipping here by the Israelites did show some welcomed change in their attitude, it was tainted; for they worshipped from their own tent doors rather than going outside the camp to the special tent to worship. We noted earlier that those who sought the Lord went outside the camp to this tent. But these folks were satisfied to worship from their own tent doors. They did not have the passion to go all out for God. This kind fills many of our churches.

4. The Pausing in the Tent

"But his servant Joshua, the son of Nun, a young man, departed not out of the tabernacle" (v. 11). This almost incidental statement says much about the great devotion of Joshua to God. Before Joshua takes Moses' place as Israel's leader, we learn enough about Joshua in a few references here and there in Scripture to learn of his excellent qualifications to be Moses' successor. In Exodus 17 we learn of the military expertise of Joshua; in Exodus 24 we learn of the humbleness of Joshua in that he was a servant to Moses; in Exodus 32 we learn of the separation of Joshua from all the defilement of the camp of Israel; in Exodus 33, our text for this study, we learn of his devotion to Jehovah. His devotion is seen in his abiding in the tabernacle after Moses left.

Matthew Poole thinks that Joshua abode at the tabernacle "either to keep it from injury . . . or to assist and direct those who resorted thither to seek God in Moses' absence." These services would all be honorable, but we have no Scripture to verify that Joshua stayed in the tabernacle for these reasons. But the fact that he stayed there, whether for these reasons or not, demonstrated an earnest devotion to God which was not the usual case throughout the camp of Israel. He was not like so many at church who complain about the service or sermon being too long. Joshua could not get too much of God. He did not tire of God. One's devotion is seen in one's stamina in worship and in service. Joshua demonstrated great devotion here which qualified him well for his leadership of Israel in the future. If you would desire to serve God well in the future, you need to demonstrate great devotion to Him in the present.

C. THE PETITIONS IN THE SPEAKING

Some of the most noble praying by man recorded in Scripture is found in the record given of Moses' petitions to God in our text. Motivated by the grace of God and also by his love for Israel, Moses presents some earnest petitions to God for himself and for Israel. We are going to note three of those petitions here. They are the seeking of God's path, the securing of God's presence, and the seeing of God's person.

1. The Seeking of God's Path

"Now therefore, I pray thee, if I have found grace in thy sight, show me now thy way" (v. 13). This first petition that we will examine involves more for Moses than being shown the way to Canaan and the way to lead Israel and even the way to live his own life. It also involves learning about God Himself. Moses petition is "Show me thy way, *that* I may know thee" (Ibid.). When we learn God's way, we will learn about God. And if we want to know God's way, we must learn about God.

We note three things about this request: the matter of knowing God's way, the manner of asking God's way, and the means of learning God's way.

The matter of knowing God's way. To petition God to know "thy way" is a most needed request. If there is one thing in life we need to know, it is God's way. Learn many things if you wish, but never neglect the greatest learning of all, namely, the learning of God's way. We need most of all to know God's way of salvation. Then we need to know God's way for our daily lives—how we ought to live and what service He wants us to perform. Neglecting to know God's way, as so many do, can make for an eternal tragedy as well as a wasted life. Much of the world is ignorant of God's way, and that explains why the world has so much trouble. If the world lived God's way, what a different world this would be. But few in the world care to know about God's way, and so the world will not solve its problems but instead will languish in misery.

579

The manner of asking God's way. "If I have found grace in thy sight" (v. 13) is how Moses prefaced his request to know God's way. How we approach God is so vital in regards to whether or not our petitions will be answered. Moses came to God in a very humble way here. Cognizant of Israel's sin and God's wrath against it, and also recognizing his own lowliness before God, Moses approached God by humbly seeking for grace. That is the only way to approach God for anything, and the Psalmist indicates it as the way to obtain direction from God—something Moses was seeking: "The meek will he guide in judgment; and the meek will he teach his way" (Psalm 25:9). That Moses was a meek man cannot be questioned, for Scripture states he was the meekest man on the face of the earth. "Now the man Moses was very meek, above all the men which were upon the face of the earth" (Numbers 12:3).

The means of learning God's way. Moses went to the right place to learn God's way. If we want to know God's way, we need to ask God to show us His way; for we cannot learn God's way apart from Divine revelation. The Psalmist says, "Thou wilt show me the path of life" (Psalm 16:11). If He does not show us the way, we will not know the way. Therefore, how earnest we ought to be in the study of His Word; for it is in God's Word that we will discover God's way. When we study the Scriptures, we need to ask God to "Open thou mine eyes" (Psalmist 119:18) so we can learn and understand the way of God. Then we need to pray that God would help us to live according to His way which He has revealed to us. It will not do us any good to learn the way of God if we do not live the way of God.

2. The Securing of God's Presence

In the pronouncement from God, which we studied at the beginning of this chapter, God said that because of Israel's "stiffnecked" (vv. 3,5) condition, He would no longer dwell in their midst but an angel would be sent in His place to be with them. That, as we noted earlier, was really bad news for Israel.

Losing God's presence was a terrible loss, and an angel was no compensation for the loss of God's presence. Moses, however, in this second petition we are examining in our text, seeks and gains back the presence of God.

In this matter of Moses gaining back the presence of God, we will note the pleading for God's presence, the promise of the God's presence, the priority for God's presence, and the products of God's presence.

The pleading for God's presence. "See, thou sayest unto me, Bring up this people: and thou hast not let me know whom thou wilt send with me" (v. 12). This statement by Moses is not a contradiction of what God said about an angel going with the people. Rather, it is Moses asking for specifics as to who this angel is. However, there was more in the petition than the seeking of the identity of the angel and what appears on the surface of the request. God's response to the petition indicates that what Moses really wanted was God's presence to go with them, not some angel. There was a sanctified dissatisfaction implied in this petition by Moses to know who was going with him. God knows the heart of men when they pray, and He knows what the heart wants even though the words may not make it clear. Oh, to have a heart like Moses that reflects such holy desires as his did. Too many, in contrast to Moses, say nice words but the desires of their heart are not as nice as their words. God knows that, too! And it is reflected in how God answers their prayers.

The promise of God's presence. "And he said, My presence shall go with thee . . . And the LORD said unto Moses, I will do this thing also that thou hast spoken: for thou hast found grace in my sight" (vv. 14,17). We note two things about God's promise of His presence with Israel. They are the gaining of it and the grace in it.

First, the *gaining* of it. Through prayer Moses succeeded in gaining back the presence of God! This was a tremendous achievement for Moses. Through his intercessory prayer, Moses obtained for Israel the greatest blessing they could possibly have. How it inspires us to pray. Moses' great achievement in prayer reminds us of what God said through the prophet Jeremiah: "Call unto me, and I will answer thee, and show thee great and mighty things, which thou knowest not" (Jeremiah 33:3). Paul spoke likewise about God answering our prayers when he said, "Now unto him that is able to do exceeding abundantly above all that we ask or think" (Ephesians 3:20).

Second, the *grace* in it. Scripture makes it plain that this gaining back of God's presence was a result of God's grace. When God told Moses His presence would go with them, He added, "For thou hast found grace in my sight" (v. 17). Israel did not deserve God's presence because of their sin. So it was only through grace that they gained it back. Grace is so prominent in this section. Five times from verses 12 to 17 the word "grace" appears. Then in verse 19 the word "gracious" appears twice and the word "mercy" also appears twice. All of this underscores the essentialness of God's grace if we are to obtain and enjoy His blessings.

The priority for God's presence. "If thy presence go not with me, carry us not up hence" (v. 15). After God promised that His presence would now once more go with Israel, Moses informs God that if His presence does not go with him, he does not want to move. This statement is Moses' way of telling God what a high priority he puts on God's presence and, therefore, how much he values it. It is a priority we need to practice in our lives. If we had this priority for God's presence, we would eliminate a host of problems. Let us not go anywhere that God would not be pleased to go. Let us not keep company with anyone that God does not want to be with. Let us not do those things that would cause God to leave us. Let us so direct our lives that we will always be in His presence.

This priority of Moses is certainly not the priority of the world. Instead of desiring the presence of God, they disdain it. They do not want God with them at all. Instead of being like

Moses and pleading for the presence of God, they are like Adam and Eve who "hid themselves from the presence of the LORD God" (Genesis 3:8). On Sundays we see men hiding from God in sports stadiums, behind cash registers, and in places of recreation instead of being in church where God is. In legislatures, the lawmakers hide from God in the making of laws that forbid praying to Him and reading His Word in various places. All of this distaste about the presence of God, however, is only an admission of wickedness. Adam and Eve hid after they had sinned, not before. The more men hide from God's presence, the more sin is in their lives. The greatest illustration of men disdaining the presence of God was in the crucifixion of Christ. Men so hated His presence that they wanted to do away with Him. Those who despise God's presence will get their wish when they go to hell for all eternity.

The products of God's presence. God's presence provides many great blessings for mankind. We will note a few of the great blessings of God's presence here. They are confirmation, identification, preservation, illumination, delectation, inspiration, and relaxation.

First, *confirmation.* "For wherein shall it be known here that I and thy people have found grace in thy sight? is it not in that thou goest with us . . . I will do this thing also that thou hast spoken: for thou hast found grace in my sight" (vv. 16,17). God's presence confirmed that Israel had found grace from God regarding their sin of idolatry and had been forgiven and accepted by God. This certainly reflects the Gospel. Assurance of salvation by grace is found in God's presence with us which comes about through the indwelling of God's Spirit in us. "Ye are not of the flesh, but in the Spirit [that is, you are saved], if so be that the Spirit of God dwell in you" (Romans 8:9, cp. 8:11). Assurance is very important in life. If you do not think so, just ask a person who has experienced times in his life when he was not certain of his salvation. If you lack assurance of your salvation, it could very well be that you do not practice the presence

583

of God in your life as you should.

Second, *identification.* Because God's presence would go with Israel, Moses said, "So shall we be separated, I and thy people, from all the people that are upon the face of the earth" (v. 16). The word "separated" here can be translated "distinguished" (Wilson). God's presence abiding with Israel would distinguish the Israelites from all the other people of the world. It would distinguish them as God's people. So not only does God's presence assure us *personally* that we are God's people, as we just noted; but our text tells us it also identifies us *publicly* to others that we are God's people. We need that identity if we are going to have any kind of witness for God. Do you live your life in such a way that it is evident that God's presence abides with you? If you do not, your testimony will suffer greatly. Peter and John had a good testimony, for it was evident to the world "that they had been with Jesus" (Acts 4:13).

Third, *preservation.* "Thou shalt hide them in the secret of thy presence" (Psalm 31:20). The Psalmist instructs us that God's presence provides protection. Moses knew Israel needed Divine protection. It was already very evident that God's presence had protected them thus far in marvelous ways on their journey. Without it they would have perished at the Red Sea and in their other troubles, too. The great protection a nation needs is to have God's presence in the land. The way our nation disdains the presence of God forecasts the destruction of our land.

Fourth, *illumination.* The pillar of cloud which represented God's presence was Israel's guide. It illuminated them as to the path they were to travel. Without that pillar, Israel would be in a confused mess in the trackless desert. God was the guide Who knew exactly where they should go. They desperately needed His presence in order to be guided on their journey.

Without God's presence anyone will wander in a confused way. After Cain sinned, he "went out from the presence of the LORD and dwelt in the land of Nod" (Genesis 4:16). The word "Nod" means "vagrant" or "wanderer." How accurately that describes those who leave the presence of God. Without His presence they will indeed wanderer aimlessly in life.

Fifth, *delectation*. The Psalmist said, "In thy presence is fulness of joy" (Psalm 16:11). When God through Moses informed the Israelites that He was not going with them, "they mourned" (v. 4). No wonder they mourned; for if in the presence of God is "fulness of joy," then His leaving them will take away their joy. To hear some talk, however, you would think having God around was the end of joy and that joy is only found in dens of iniquities which practice the absence of God. But wise men know that true joy, the greatest joy, and the most lasting joy comes from God's presence—and there are no bad after effects from God's presence. Such is not the case with many temporal joys of the world, however. If you want real joy, healthy joy, and lasting joy spend much time with God.

Sixth, *inspiration*. "If thy presence go not with me, carry us not up hence" (v. 15). Moses had no desire for service for God as Israel's leader if God's presence was not going with them. God's presence is an inspirer service; therefore, the lack of God's presence discourages service. This is why when Christ gave the great commission to the disciples, He closed it with the promise, "Lo, I am with you always, even unto the end of the world" (Matthew 28:20). The promise of His presence would inspire the disciples, as nothing else would, to go into the world to proclaim the Gospel of Jesus Christ.

Seventh, *relaxation*. "My presence shall go with thee, and I will give thee rest" (v. 14). The "rest" spoken of here refers to Canaan. "This [the word 'rest'] was the common expression for the possession of the promised land [Deuteronomy 3:20]" (F. C. Cook). Canaan was a "rest" for Israel from the toil of their wilderness journeys. When they got to Canaan, there would be relaxation because their laborious travels were over and they could now settle down in their own land. Hebrews 4 shows us that this speaks of a greater rest, namely, the rest which salvation gives us in heaven. Christ also spoke of this rest in "Come unto me, all ye that labor and are heavy laden, and I will give you rest" (Matthew 11:28). When we come to Christ for salvation, the Holy Spirit—the presence of God—comes to dwell in us (Romans 8:9). That assures us that the day is coming when we shall come to the end of our toilsome pilgrim journey on this earth and will enter into heaven's rest. "There remaineth therefore a rest to the people of God" (Hebrews 4:9), the people who through salvation experience His presence.

3. The Seeing of God's Person

"And he said, I beseech thee, show me thy glory" (v. 18). The third petition of Moses which we are examining concerns Moses' desire to see the glory of God which involves seeing the person of God. We note the plea to see God's glory, the plan for seeing God's glory, the prohibitive in seeing God's glory, the protection in seeing God's glory, and the prerequisite for seeing God's glory.

The plea to see God's glory. Moses' plea to see God's glory proclaimed Moses' spirituality and promoted God's honor.

First, the plea *proclaimed Moses' spirituality.* This request is so spiritual that it is totally foreign to the average Christian. It is unlike most of our requests, for our requests are mostly in the material and physical realm. Seldom do we pray for much that is in the spiritual realm. But Moses did. His request expressed a great longing to know more about God, a longing very few have. God was speaking "unto Moses face to face, as a man speaketh unto his friend" (v. 11), and this inspired Moses to know more about God.

The more spiritual we are, the more we will want to know about God. The lowly gossip only wants to know about the scandals of men, but the dedicated godly person wants to know about the splendors of the Almighty. The desire of Moses is like that of Paul who said, "That I may know him, and the power of his resurrection" (Philippians 3:10). It is like Jacob who in wrestling with the angel of God said, "Tell me, I pray thee, thy name" (Genesis 32:29). It is also like the Psalmist who said, "As the hart panteth after the water brooks, so panteth my soul after thee, O God. My soul thirsteth for God" (Psalm 42:1,2). We need to pray that we will all have an earnest desire to know more about God.

Second, the plea *promoted God's honor*. This request by Moses really honored God. It honored God in the specifics of the request and in the size of the request.

The *specifics* of the request honored God in that Moses specifically asked that God be glorified in His manifestation to him. If we were to ask someone to show us the honors, the trophies, medals, etc. they have obtained in this life, it would be a great honor for them to show them to us. This is the nature of Moses' request. His request says He believes God is glorious, and he wants God to display that glory. For God to show Moses His glory is for God to be greatly honored before Moses. The Israelites had greatly dishonored God by their sin of idolatry, but Moses in sharp contrast would seek to honor God by requesting to see His great glory.

How little we pray for the glory of God to be seen. We are too feverish about seeking our own personal honor to have much concern for the honor of God. We are mostly concerned that people see us as glorious and have little, if any, concern that they see God as glorious. But Moses was just the opposite. He was earnest ("beseech" [v. 18]) about God's glory, not about his own. No wonder he was such a great man of God.

The *size* of the request honored God in that it was a very great request. Moses had just been granted a great request in obtaining God's presence for Israel again. That encouraged Moses to ask another big request—the request to see God's glory. It honors God when we ask great things of Him as long as those requests are not selfish—and Moses' request certainly was not selfish. We dishonor God oftentimes by the smallness of our requests, for sometimes our little requests (when we could ask bigger ones) indicate we think we have a weak God.

The plan for seeing God's glory. "And he [God] said, I will make all my goodness pass before thee, and I will proclaim the name of the LORD before thee; and will be gracious to whom I will be gracious, and will show mercy on whom I will show mercy" (v. 19). In granting Moses' request to see His glory, God revealed to Moses the plan for the displaying of His glory. It was basically a threefold plan—Moses would see God's glory in God's goodness, greatness, and grace. The "goodness" of God would "pass" before Moses, the greatness of God would be proclaimed to Moses in the proclaiming of God's name ("I will proclaim the name of the LORD"), and the grace of God would be provided ("I will be gracious") for Moses. This threefold plan, which we will examine in more detail in our next paragraphs, indicated that not only would Moses see the glory of God in God's countenance, but he would also see it in God's character. Usually when we think of Moses seeing God's glory, we only think of the countenance part. But the character of God will display God's glory in a great way, too. We make a great mistake to think that only the countenance of God will display His glory. Instructively, the emphasis in our text in the revealing of God's glory for Moses is upon God's character not God's countenance.

First, the *goodness* of God. "And he [God] said, I will make all my goodness pass before thee" (v. 19). The world is not so sure God is good, for they oppose much of what God commands. The devil's first attack on mankind included an attack upon the goodness of God (Genesis 3:5). But in spite of what man thinks and what the devil wants us to think, God is good. In fact, God is "abundant in goodness" (Exodus 34:6). And this goodness was wonderfully exhibited in Jesus Christ, for "He hath done all things well" (Mark 7:37).

Second, the *greatness* of God. "I will proclaim the name of the LORD before thee" (v. 19). This statement sends us back to Exodus 3 where Moses was told that God's name is "I AM THAT I AM" (Exodus 3:14). We noted there that this name was the meaning of the name Jehovah ("LORD" in our text here). So Jehovah is a tremendous name. It describes God as the greatest of all; for only one can say, "I AM THAT I AM." The name cannot be given to more than one, for the name in itself demands utter exclusiveness. It greatly honors and glorifies the One Who has the name. So for God to "proclaim the name of the LORD before thee [Moses]" was to greatly honor God.

Third, the *grace* of God. "I . . . will be gracious to whom I will be gracious, and will show mercy on whom I will show mercy" (v. 19). Grace is unmerited by man. It is favor which is solely determined and granted by God. In granting grace to man, God is greatly glorified. In this truth we can easily see an evangelical message. The Gospel message, which is of grace, reveals much glory about God that would never otherwise be displayed. Take away Calvary and the Gospel message, and you take away much glory from God. Despise Calvary and you dishonor God!

The prohibitive in seeing God's glory. "Thou canst not see my face: for there shall no man see me, and live . . . thou shalt see my back parts: but my face shall not be seen" (vv. 20,23). Here God speaks specifically of the glory of His countenance. This aspect of the revelation of God's glory would be especially limited. Moses would not see all of this glory. There are at least two lessons in this prohibitive regarding the seeing of God's glory. They are a dispensation and an illumination lesson.

First, the *dispensation lesson*. Moses represents the law and the Old Testament. The law and the Old Testament saw things only in shadow, not in substance—"For the law having a shadow of good things to come" (Hebrews 10:1). But the New Testament gives us the substance (Christ). We no longer see just shadows of the Savior, we see the Savior Himself. "For God, who commanded the light to shine out of darkness, hath shined in our hearts, to give the light of the knowledge of the glory of God in the *face* of Jesus Christ" (II Corinthians 4:6). In using the language of our text here, we can say that the Old Testament shows only the back parts, not the face. But in Jesus Christ, the New Testament shows the face of God. And as Paul said to the Corinthians in contrasting the Old and New Testament dispensations, "If the ministration of death, written and engraven in stones, was glorious, so that the children of Israel could not stedfastly behold the face of Moses [after he had seen God's glory] for the glory of his countenance . . . How shall not the ministration of the spirit be rather glorious? For if the ministration of condemnation be glory, much more doth the ministration of righteousness exceed in glory . . . For if that which is done away was glorious, much more that which remaineth is glorious" (II Corinthians 3:7,8,9,11). Moses could not see in his dispensation the glory which we can see in our dispensation; for we have Christ in person, not in type and shadow.

Second, the *illumination lesson*. Moses on earth saw only a partial view of God's glory. But in heaven, he will see it all. In this life we do not see it all, but we will see it all in eternity. We are given the privilege of seeing some of His glory here in this life. And some see more than others, for many do not care to see much—and that kind will not see much. But in heaven, we shall behold God in all His glory. This principle is spoken of by John who said, "Beloved, now are we the sons of God, and it doth not yet appear what we shall be; but we know that, when he shall appear, we shall be like him; for we shall see him as he is" (I John 3:2). Spiritual illumination comes in steps. Faith will accept that and faithfully pursue the steps, but the flesh will not.

This revealing of God's glory is certainly a contrast to sin. Sin reveals all its glory in a moment in this life—like the flash of fireworks at a fourth of July celebration. But after that fleeting moment, it has nothing left but judgment. On the other hand, God, Christ, righteousness, and salvation reveal some glory now; but oh what a display is waiting for us in eternity. Words fail to describe the greatness of what is yet to come. We only at best see the "back parts" (v. 23) in this life so to speak. In eternity we will see it all.

The protection in seeing God's glory. "And the LORD said, Behold, there is a place by me, and thou shalt stand upon a rock: And it shall come to pass, while my glory passeth by, that I will put thee in a cleft of the rock, and will cover thee with my hand while I pass by" (vv. 21,22). Moses in the flesh could not endure a full sight of the glory of God's countenance. Paul gives us an illustration of this truth when he tells us about the destruction of the antichrist. He said the Lord "shall destroy [the antichrist] with the brightness of His coming" (II Thessalonians 2:8). God is too holy for man in the flesh to behold Him and survive. Therefore, God provided protection for Moses so that the holy glory of God would not slay him. This protection is a beautiful picture of some significant aspects of the Gospel. We see this in the place of the protection, the precept in the protection, and the power in the protection.

First, the *place* of the protection. "And the LORD said, Behold, there is a place by me . . . stand upon a rock . . . I will put thee in a cleft of the rock, and will cover thee" (vv. 21,22). The place of protection speaks of Christ in a fourfold way.

(1) It speaks of Christ in "a place by me." Jesus Christ is nearer to God the Father than anyone else. And after His earthly ministry, Scripture said He has "gone into heaven, and is on the right hand of God" (I Peter 3:22).

(2) It speaks of Christ in the "rock." In the Scriptures, Christ is sometimes called a Rock (cp. I Corinthians 10:4 "that Rock was Christ," Psalm 118:22, and Acts 4:11).

(3) It speaks of Christ in the command to "stand" upon the rock. Standing on the rock emphasizes that Christ is the foundation of our salvation. "For other foundation can no man lay than that is laid, which is Jesus Christ" (I Corinthians 3:11). "Therefore being justified by faith, we have peace with God through our Lord Jesus Christ: By whom also we have access by faith into this grace wherein we *stand*" (Romans 5:1,2). We must "stand" on Christ or we will perish (cp. Matthew 7:24–27).

(4) It speaks of Christ in the "cleft." The "cleft" speaks of the wounded side of Christ obtained at Calvary where He shed His blood and died for our sins. If we want protection from the holiness of God which would send us to hell because of our sins, we must be hidden in Christ (Colossians 3:3).

Second, the *precept* in the protection. God ordered Moses to "stand upon a rock" (v. 21). This command addressed the subject of human responsibility in the matter of salvation. God provides for our protection, but mankind must accept the protection and avail himself of the protection, or he will be doomed. Had Moses refused to stand on the rock, he would have perished when the glory of God's countenance passed by.

We need to note that Moses' standing on the rock is not a meritorious work that contradicts grace anymore than a person obeying God by receiving Christ as his Savior contradicts grace. God "commandeth all men every where to repent" (Acts 17:30). When we do, it does not constitute works in contrast to grace. Rather, the act demonstrates faith in God's Word regarding salvation. So it was with Moses.

Third, the *power* in the protection. "I will put thee in a cleft of the rock, and will cover thee with my hand while I pass by" (v. 22). Moses did not have to put himself in the cleft in the rock. God Himself put him there. This speaks of the power of salvation. God can put anyone in that cleft. He has the power to save any sinner.

This verse which speaks of the cleft of the rock inspired the hymn writer Augustus Toplady to write the beautiful and every popular hymn "Rock of Ages." In that first verse, the hymn says, "Rock of Ages cleft for me, Let me hide myself in Thee." Arthur Pink changes the second line in a way we much prefer. Instead of "Let me hide myself in Thee," Pink says, "Grace hath hid me safe in Thee."

The prerequisite for seeing God's glory. It is instructive to note here that it was only when the flesh of Moses was covered that the glory of God could be fully revealed. The reason God is not glorified in our churches like He ought to be is because too much flesh is showing. We are too prone to exalt ourselves. We would also add that too much flesh is showing in the way some folk dress when they go to church. That, for sure, stops the glory of God from being seen in our churches!

XXV.

SECOND SINAI SESSION

EXODUS 34

TWICE MOSES HAD a forty-day session on Mount Sinai with God. In several earlier chapters of our book we covered the first session. In that session Moses was given the instructions for the Tabernacle and also the "two tables of testimony, tables of stone, written with the finger of God" (Exodus 31:18). During that first forty-day session, Israel committed their great sin of idolatry. When Moses came down from the mount and saw what was going on in the camp because of this idolatry, in holy rage he threw down the two tables of stone and broke them (Exodus 32:19). This necessitated Moses having to spend a second forty days and nights on mount Sinai (v. 28) so God could write on a second set of stones what He had written on the first set.

The second forty-day session was also needed to test Israel regarding the sincerity of their repentance. They failed to wait patiently during the first forty-day stay of Moses on the mount and so committed their sin of idolatry. Now they will be given a second forty days to prove their loyalty to God. When we fail to live as God wants us to live and then beg God for His forgiveness, He grants that forgiveness; but to see how sincere we were in repenting, He often repeats the test we failed. It is true that God knows our hearts and does not need the test to know if we are sincere or not. But we need the test to give opportunity to strengthen our faith and to reveal to others that it is real.

Both of these forty-day sessions on Mount Sinai were times when Moses "did neither eat bread, nor drink water" (v. 28—the second session, Deuteronomy 9:9—the first session). But it will be nigh unto impossible for the average church member to comprehend how one can be so taken up with the things of God that the appetites of the flesh are given so little attention. Those who can hardly stand for a worship service at church to go beyond one hour or for the preacher to go longer than twenty or thirty minutes are light years away from the spirituality of Moses here. Moses was like Christ when He said, "I have meat to eat that ye know not of . . . My meat is to do the will of him that sent me, and to finish his work" (John 4:32,34). But you will be hard pressed to find many professing Christians who are that devoted to the things of the Lord.

In this chapter we will focus on the second forty-day session Moses had on Mount Sinai with God. To do this, we will consider the readying of Moses (vv. 1–4), the revelation for Moses (vv. 5–9), the repeating for Moses (vv. 10–28), and the radiance of Moses (vv. 29–35).

A. THE READYING OF MOSES

The command God gave Moses for the second forty-day session on Sinai was "present thyself there to me" (v. 2). To ready Moses to properly present himself to God on Sinai, God gave him instructions concerning the hewing of the tables, the hour of the presentation, and the hallowing of the mount.

This arresting command "present thyself to me" is a forceful reminder that one day all of us will have to present ourselves to God. That time will be either a time of terror or a time of blessing depending on how we have readied ourselves for the meeting. As God gave Moses instructions to ready him to meet God, so God has given to all men specific instructions (the Gospel) on how to be ready for their meeting with God. Have you heeded the instructions?

1. The Hewing of the Tables

"And the LORD said unto Moses, Hew thee two tables of stone like unto the first: and I will write upon these tables the words that were in the first tables, which thou brakest" (v. 1). In

594

this command by God, we have a recopying of the law and a responsibility for Moses.

A recopying of the law. This provision for the recopying of the law sent an important message to Moses and Israel. It told them that though Israel has been forgiven, the law had not been abrogated. It said that the recovered blessing of the presence of God (which spoke of God's grace for and forgiveness of Israel) was not apart from the precepts of God. "Moses had not asked for a renewal of the tables. He had requested the return of God's favor . . . [but God] will not divorce favor from obedience, privilege from the keeping of his law" (Rawlinson). Carnal man, however, is only interested in the privileges, not the precepts. He is interested in restoration but not regulations. "Man desires the rewards that God has to bestow, but is not anxious to have the rewards tied to a certain course of action. [But] God insists on the combination" (Ibid.).

Like the Israelites at Sinai, those who are redeemed by God's grace in the work of the Gospel are also not freed from the law. "God's redeemed are still under law: not as a condition of salvation, but as the Divine rule for their walk" (Pink). When Apostle Paul said, "Ye are not under the law, but under grace" (Romans 6:14), he was speaking about our salvation, not our walk as a Christian. This law that the redeemed are still obligated to obey does not, of course, include the religious ritual Israel was obligated to keep which was a foreshadowing of Christ and which was done away at Calvary. The law the redeemed are under is the moral law. God has never done away with it. It is the Divine standard of right and wrong.

A responsibility for Moses. In contrast to the first tables of stone upon which God wrote His laws, this second set of stone tables was to be hewed out by Moses. God made the first stone tables (Exodus 32:16), but Moses will make the second set. Since Moses had broken the first set, it would seem fitting that he would have to make the second set. God, however, is never recorded as rebuking Moses for breaking the first set. Moses' action in breaking the first set reflected holy wrath, something God is not going to rebuke; for it is something we need more of in this wicked world. But whether Moses having to hew them this time reflected a bit of chastisement or not, it at least showed the Israelites "that something is always forfeited by sin, even when forgiven, the new tables were made to lose one glory of the first—they were not shaped by God, as the first . . . but by Moses" (Rawlinson). Sin can be forgiven, as Israel's sin was, but one still loses something anyway through sin. Forgiveness, therefore, will never encourage repeated sin as though you can sin without impunity as long as you get it forgiven in time.

2. The Hour of the Presentation

"Be ready in the morning, and come up in the morning unto mount Sinai, and present thyself there to me in the top of the mount" (v. 2). Hewing the tables of stone evidently was not a task that would take a great deal of time, for God ordered Moses to appear on the mount the next morning. To present himself at the top of the mount in the morning required that Moses give ample time for climbing the mount. Therefore, "Moses rose up early in the morning" (v. 4) in order to arrive at the mount at the appointed time. Matthew Henry said, "Moses . . . rose up early to go to the place appointed to show how forward he was to present himself before God and loath to lose time." If we are going to obey God and serve Him successfully, we will have to be prompt in doing our duty. And unless you are on the night shift, that will mean early rising in the morning. Lounging slothfully in bed and procrastinating in doing your duty is not the mark of an obedient saint of God.

3. The Hallowing of the Mount

"And no man shall come up with thee, neither let any man be seen throughout all the mount; neither let the flocks nor herds feed before that mount" (v. 3). Once again Mount Sinai was to be off limits for the people (cp. Exodus 19:12,13). But this time additional restrictions are imposed, for Moses is not to bring anyone with him. He brought Joshua with him on the first stay in Sinai, but this time he must go alone.

All these restrictions regarding the mount underscore the holiness of God. God is so holy that He cannot be approached by sinful man without death being the result for man. A good comprehending of this truth will help us really appreciate the Gospel of Jesus Christ which opens the door for sinful man to have fellowship with a holy God. Through the blood of Christ, man's sins are washed away. This removes all barriers to God for the man who has come to Christ for salvation. He can then come into God's presence without fear or harm.

B. THE REVELATION FOR MOSES

As soon as Moses had arrived at the appointed place on Mount Sinai, "the LORD descended in the cloud, and stood with him there" (v. 5) and then manifested Himself to Moses as He had promised the day before (Exodus 33:18–23). Moses had been punctual in coming to the meeting, and God would be no less punctual. If God seems tardy to us, it is probably because we have been tardy with God.

To study this revelation of God to Moses, we will note the presence of God, the passing by of God, the proclamation about God, and the prostrating before God.

1. The Presence of God

"And the LORD descended in the cloud, and stood with him there" (v. 5). While these words are introductory to the second forty-day meeting of God and Moses on Mount Sinai, they give us a good practical message. The message concerns God standing with us to support us. It comes from the fact that our text describes God presence as that which "stood with him [Moses]." From the message of that statement we have three lessons about God supporting us: the preferment of His support, the place of His support, and the pattern from His support.

First, the *preferment* of His support. Moses could ask for no one as good or better to stand with him than God. We like to have others standing with us in our cause. But it makes a big difference who the others are that stand with us. Good people wisely prefer those of the finest character to stand with them. Some have such bad character that we do not want them standing with us on any matter. However, we can never be upset if God stands with us; for He is the best one to stand with us. Men often will not stand with us when we are loyal to God and His Word as Moses was. But God will stand with us. And if no one else stands with us other than God, it is still better than having all the world stand with us but not having God stand with us. Therefore, we should live in such a manner that God will always be standing with us, not against us.

Second, the *place* of His support. Note that this verse says God stood with Moses "there." God does not stand with us just anywhere. We must be in the appointed place of His will. Moses was indeed in the place where God told him to be, so it is no surprise that God "stood with him there." We need to know where the "there" is in our life and get "there" if we want God's support. We cannot fulfill our tasks without His support, so it is very important that we be in the "there" of His will.

Third, the *pattern* from His support. Here we focus on our standing with God. If God stands with us, we ought to reciprocate. In standing with Moses, God gives a good pattern for us to follow in how to stand for Him. Particularly we note the faithfulness and humbleness demonstrated here in the stand.

The *faithfulness* is demonstrated in that God met Moses in the mount as He said He would do. We noted that fact above. If we are going to stand for God with any kind of success, we must be faithful in standing for God. Lack of faithfulness is to let down God and not stand for Him. Those in our churches who cannot be counted on to be faithful in their tasks are those who are not standing for God.

The *humbleness* is demonstrated in that God "descended" from above to stand with Moses. This humbleness reminds us of Christ "Who, being in the form of God, thought it not robbery to be equal with God: But made himself of no reputation, and . . . humbled himself, and became obedient unto death, even the death of the cross" (Philippians 2:6–8). We may have to do some descending and give up some reputation and popularity with the world in order to stand with God. But we had better stand with God regardless of the cost, for standing against God is always a no-win situation.

2. The Passing by of God

"And the LORD passed by before him" (v. 6). This action by God specifically fulfills the promise God made to Moses the day before about Moses seeing the glory of God's countenance. The description given here is an abbreviated description of the event described in much more detail in Exodus 33:20–23 which we studied in our last chapter. But though the description is abbreviated, it shows well the fulfillment of the Divine promise.

This great experience of Moses was a vision that was so bright and so radiant that the effects were seen for some time upon Moses' face. We will note at the end of this chapter that when Moses came down to the camp of Israel after his forty days in the mount, his face glowed. This resulted in his having to wear a veil over his face when he was talking to the Israelites.

We can learn an important lesson here in noting that the great display of the glory of God's countenance on the mount was not the whole program of the meeting God had with Moses. Much more was to come; for after the brief passing by of God's glory, there was much teaching and instructing to be done as God went over the law again with Moses. If Moses had been like a lot of church members, he would have left the mount after the display of glory, however. These members do not appreciate and are not interested in being faithful to the less spectacular instructions, to the less spectacular common but needed daily round of duties. Unless a church service has something special scheduled, these folk will not come. To listen week after week to the Word of God being taught is not for them. They want some dazzling show for every service.

3. The Proclamation About God

God "proclaimed the name of the LORD" (v. 5). As God promised the previous day, He now proclaims His name to Moses. The proclamation of His name gave forth a great message. As we have noted before, to proclaim the name of God is to proclaim the character of God. So in this proclaiming of the name of God, Moses is instructed in some important truths about God. How much we need instruction about God. Few preachers instruct much in this important knowledge, and few people are interested in this knowledge. But if we do not learn about God, we will be ignorant in the most important areas of life.

The proclaiming of God's name to Moses here on Mount Sinai declared three basic and very important truths about the character of God. They concern the power of God, the mercy of God, and the judgment of God.

The power of God. The power of God was declared in the stating of the proper name, "The LORD, The LORD God" (v. 6), which is Jehovah, Jehovah Elohim. This name spoke of the self-existence and self-sufficiency of God which we have noted in previous chapters in the "I AM THAT I AM" name. It said God can do anything He wants, whenever He wants, wherever He wants. This indicates tremendous power. In fact, there is no power equal to this power. This superiority of God's power, as we noted during the plagues upon Egypt, shows Jehovah as superior to all gods. He is the God of gods, just as we learn in the New Testament that He, in the person of Christ, is the King of kings, and Lord of lords (Revelation 19:16). To know God rightly, we need to know that God is powerful. It will do much to determine the character of our faith in and adoration for God.

The mercy of God. God proclaims Himself as "merciful and gracious, longsuffering, and abundant in goodness and truth, Keeping mercy for thousands, forgiving iniquity and transgression and sin" (vv. 6,7). This is a magnificent piling up of words to describe the greatness of God's mercy. "Many words are here heaped up, to acquaint us with, and convince us of, God's good-ness" (Matthew Henry). These words are an "accumulation of terms that are nearly synonymous . . . an accumulation for the purpose of emphasis—to assure Moses, and through him mankind at large, of the reality of this attribute [of mercy], on which the possibility of our salvation depends, and which had never hitherto been set forth with anything like such fullness" (Rawlinson). Though the words listed here are similar, it will help us to note the particular emphasis of each one.

First, *"merciful"* (v. 6). The word means to be tender and pitiful. It is significant that at Sinai, which is associated so strongly with law and judgment, that we should have such an emphasis and revelation on God's mercy and grace there. But God is so anxious to show mercy to man, that even in the midst of law and judgment, He gives a great revelation of His mercy in order to encourage sinners to repent.

Second, *"gracious"* (v. 6). God's bestowal of mercy upon us is a result of His grace. It is grace that is the ground, the basis, and the foundation for disbursing mercy. Mercy does not come by our merit, but only by His grace.

Third, *"longsuffering"* (v. 6). God's mercy involves God's patience. If God was not longsuffering, none of us would be saved. However, in spite of our continued rebellion, He gave us repeated opportunities to be saved. How merciful that is.

Fourth, *"abundant in goodness"* (v. 6). "The Hebrew word for goodness is more frequently translated 'kindness'" (Pink) in the King James Version. And note it is "abundant" goodness. Matthew Henry, in speaking of this "abundant" aspect of God's goodness said, "The springs of mercy are always full, the streams of mercy always flowing; there is mercy enough in God, enough for all, enough for each, enough forever."

Fifth, *"abundant in . . . truth"* (v. 6). The Hebrew word translated "truth" here also means "trustworthiness" (Strong). Why is this statement about truth stuck in the paragraph about mercy? For several reasons. For one reason, it is often hard for sinful man to believe that God will be merciful to the sinner.

But if God is true then what He says about His mercy is true. The other reason is that in the next verse, which is related to this verse, God speaks of "keeping" (v. 7) mercy. The character of His keeping depends on the character of His truthfulness. If He is abundant in trustworthiness (meaning of "truth), then God is very faithful, He is always dependable, and "The truth of the LORD endureth forever" (Psalm 117:2). This means we can trust His keeping mercy to last forever.

Sixth, *"keeping mercy for thousands"* (v. 7). These words describe a wonderful aspect of God's mercy. Nowhere is this aspect of God's mercy more prominent and seen better than in the fact of the security of the believer. The statement by Christ which says, "I give unto them eternal life; and they shall never perish, neither shall any man pluck them out of my hand" (John 10:28) describes this aspect of God's mercy in a wonderful way.

Seventh, *"forgiving"* (v. 7). To emphasize the great aspect of mercy, our text says God forgives "iniquity and transgression and sin" (Ibid.). Though we could put all three words (iniquity, transgression, and sin) under the heading of "sin," the use of the three different, but similar, words is a piling up of words to effectively emphasize the greatness of God's forgiveness. The Psalmist says that God is "ready to forgive" (Psalm 86:5). That ought to be great news to any sinner. Those who think they are beyond God's forgiveness and that God would not want to forgive them need to ponder this verse. God is often more ready to forgive us than we are to forgive ourselves. But note that this verse in Psalms has a clause to it which we must never ignore. It says God is ready to forgive "all them that call upon thee." If you do not call upon Christ to be your Savior, you will never experience the forgiveness of God.

The judgment of God. God said to Moses that He "will by no means clear the guilty; visiting the iniquity of the fathers upon the children, and upon the children's children, unto the third and to the fourth generation" (v. 7). After God proclaimed His mercy, He then proclaimed His judgment. "While setting forth his attribute of mercy in all its fullness, God will not have his attribute of justice [judgment] forgotten" (Rawlinson). To look further into the judgment of God, we note the essentialness of God's judgment and the extent of God's judgment.

First, the *essentialness* of God's judgment. God is not only a God of love, but He is also a God of holiness. Therefore, God not only shows mercy to sinners, but He also brings judgment upon sinners. Many folk would have preferred that God had stopped after the proclaiming of His mercy to Moses. These folks do not like the judgment of God. They only want a God of love and mercy, but not a God of judgment. Their messages never speak of the judgment of God, but only of the love of God. However, without judgment upon sin, God would not be just, He would not be righteous, and He would not be loving. We would not want a God that was only love and not holy. This would corrupt His love and produce inequity and cruelty. Thus it would kill true love. We must have a God of judgment in order to have a righteous God. "Without it [judgment], God would not be God. Says the poet, 'A God all mercy is a God unjust.' We go further and affirm that without justice [judgment], there would be no mercy left to exercise" (J. Orr). Therefore, the judgment of God is essential if we are to have a God of true and holy love and mercy.

Second, the *extent* of God's judgment. Our text says God will visit the iniquity of the fathers "unto the third and to the fourth generation" (v. 7). That speaks about the extent of His judgment—and it upsets many people. They view this act of God as terrible injustice. "How can God punish the children for the sins of their fathers?" they ask. It is not fair at all, they conclude. But the answer is that the blame for any evil here is not on God's part but on man's part. It is not a capricious acting God Who loves to punish people whether they deserve it or not. This judgment is simply the natural results of sin.

As an example, a man in disobedience to God's warnings in Scripture about taking care of his body, fills his body full of booze and drugs. Then he lives an immoral life which adds

venereal disease to his physical problems. After this the man
fathers some children. Because this man's sins have damaged
his genes, his children are not normal. They are deformed both
physically and mentally. This deformity is part of the judgment
of God upon the sins of the man. Now whose fault is this? Is it a
cruel God punishing innocent people, or is it a wicked man who
disobeys God and reaps what he sows? The answer is obvious;
the man is to blame, not God. The statement in our text is simply the way God states the effect of sin upon man. God has so
made man that wicked living will curse the sinner which will
affect his offspring oftentimes. Hence, the judgment of God will
be felt to the third and fourth generation. In fact, it often goes
farther than that. This statement is not a technical statement but
a general statement about the extended curse of sin which goes
on for generations. Israel today, as an example, is suffering
because of the sins of its ancestors many centuries and generations ago. Furthermore, we all are suffering because of the sin of
Adam and Eve. And how many will suffer after us because of
our sins? It is not a pleasant thought to the conscientious soul.
But the judgment of God is just, and the judgment of God is a
great warning to people to stop disobeying God.

4. The Prostrating Before God

Here we observe the reaction of Moses to this revelation
which God has given him. It was a very noble reaction. Unlike
so much of the world, Moses was not unmoved by Divine manifestations. His heart was greatly stirred in noble ways. This was
evident in his veneration of God and in his supplication to God.

Veneration of God. "And Moses made haste, and bowed his
head toward the earth, and worshipped" (v. 8). Moses' worship
of God was predictable and prompt.

First, *predictable.* We are not surprised at Moses' reaction to
this revelation of God. We have learned enough about Moses in
Scripture to know that when God manifests Himself, Moses will
give due honor. We could use some of this reverence today, for

there is so much disrespect for God in our world. Instead of worship is wickedness. Instead of praise for God is blasphemy and scorn for God. It would cure a lot of problems in our society if multitudes began to bow low before God. We may pass a host of laws to try to improve our society, but until man bows low in humble veneration of God, the problems of our society will become worse and worse.

Second, *prompt.* After the revelation, Moses "made haste" to worship. This promptness revealed the great earnestness of Moses for worshipping God. He was not going through the motions in a disinterested way. But the "made haste" said Moses worshipped God enthusiastically. There are a number of ways to detect how spiritual a person is. One of the ways is to check a person's enthusiasm about worship. The more spiritual a person is, the more earnest he will be in worship. On the other hand, the more carnal a person is, the less enthusiasm he will show for worshipping God. This fact certainly reveals that our churches today are in bad shape spiritually, for so many of the members are lacking in enthusiasm for worship. This lack of enthusiasm is most evident in their absenteeism from the worship services. It does not take much to cause them to miss church.

Supplication to God. "And he said, If now I have found grace in thy sight, O Lord, let my Lord, I pray thee, go among us; for it is a stiffnecked people; and pardon our iniquity and our sin, and take us for thine inheritance" (v. 9). There are four parts to this short but great prayer: reassurance, repentance, remission, and reception.

First, *reassurance.* "If now I have found grace in thy sight, O Lord, let my Lord, I pray thee, go among us." After this revelation of God, Moses wanted reassurance that he (all Israel is included) had found grace with God. That reassurance would come in the form of God's presence abiding with him. God had already told Moses the day before that he and Israel had found grace and that God would go with them. And the revelation of God's mercy here on the mount would encourage Moses to believe God is a God of grace. But the revelation of God's holy judgment would cause any conscientious and devout soul to again recognize his sinfulness before God and his great need of grace. Thus, Moses asks for reassurance of God's grace. Today we can obtain that assurance and reassurance from the Word. Be much in the Word and you will know much about assurance.

Second, *repentance*. "It is a stiffnecked people." We do not get anywhere with God when we refuse to acknowledge our sinfulness to Him. If we want mercy, then we must confess our sins—and that confession must not be watered down. God had earlier called Israel a "stiffnecked people" (Exodus 33:3,5). Now Moses agrees with God. That is true repentance.

Third, *remission*. "Pardon our iniquity and our sin." In the revelation God had just given Moses, He said He was a "forgiving" (v. 7) God. Hence, Moses seeks for forgiveness. Some may feel they are too bad to be forgiven. But as we noted earlier, Scripture says God is "ready to forgive" (Psalm 86:5) All we have to do is ask for this forgiveness as Moses did.

Fourth, *reception*. "Take us for thine inheritance." Moses had the order right. He does not start by asking God to accept the people. Rather, he starts by seeking grace, confessing sin, and asking for forgiveness—then he sought acceptance by God. We must be cleansed of our sins before we can expect God to receive us in heaven. A lot of theology in our churches today ignores that fact.

C. THE REPEATING FOR MOSES

After the special revelation of God to Moses, the remainder of this second session on Sinai was taken up with the repeating of various matters by God to Moses. To examine this repeating by God, we will look at the repeating of the promises, the repeating of the precepts, and the repeating of the printing.

1. The Repeating of the Promises

As God had done before in the first giving of the law, so He does here in the repeating of the law, namely, He intersperses promises with precepts. This is ever the habit of God. It greatly encourages the obedience to His precepts. God is not a harsh taskmaster. He is not all precepts, orders, and commands; but He is also promises, blessings, and rewards.

In our text concerning the second Sinai session for Moses, there are at least four promises stated. They are about the doing of marvels, the dislodging of inhabitants, the distending of borders, and the defending of possessions.

The doing of marvels. "I will do marvels, such as have not been done in all the earth, nor in any nation: and all the people among which thou art shall see the work of the LORD: for it is a terrible [awesome] thing that I will do with thee" (v. 10). This is quite a promise. God had already done tremendous marvels for the Israelites with the plagues in Egypt, the Red Sea deliverance, the miracles involving water and the manna, and the defeating of Amalek. But yet to come were further miracles in the wilderness, then the drying up of the Jordan to help Israel cross to Canaan, the falling down of the walls of Jericho, and the miracles in the battles against the Canaanites such as the lengthening of one of the days to give the Israelites more time to destroy the enemy. God had promised previously to work powerfully for Israel; here in repeating the promise, He indicates great marvels to come.

This promise instructs us that the previous wonders done by God did not exhaust His power. God's power is limitless. We must not limit God in anyway in His power. His wisdom and His will may limit the use of His power, but not the extent of His power. God is omnipotent, and Israel and the world will yet see more and more marvels done by the power of God.

The dislodging of inhabitants. "I drive out before thee the Amorite, and the Canaanite, and the Hittite, and the Perizzite, and the Hivite, and the Jebusite" (v. 11). God promised the Israelites the land of Canaan, and He promised He would drive out the inhabitants of Canaan so Israel could possess the land. In

607

the first giving of this promise, God told Moses some of the details as to how He would drive out the inhabitants. God said, "I will send my fear before thee . . . I will make all thine enemies turn their backs unto thee. I will send hornets before thee, which shall drive out the Hivite, the Canaanite, and the Hittite, from before thee. And I will not drive them out from before thee in one year; lest the land become desolate, and the beast of the field multiply against thee. By little and little I will drive them out from before thee" (Exodus 23:27–30). Three methods of driving out the inhabitants are listed in these verses, and it will benefit us to examine them here.

First, the dislodging was done by *scaring*. "I will send my fear before thee . . . I will make all thine enemies turn their backs unto thee" (23:27). Sinners scare easy. "The wicked flee when no man pursueth: but the righteous are bold as a lion" (Proverbs 28:1). A guilty conscience does not promote genuine courage, but righteousness does. The Canaanites had plenty of sins by which to be frightened into fleeing.

Second, the dislodging was done by *stinging*. "I will send hornets before thee, which shall drive out the Hivite, the Canaanite, and the Hittite" (23:28). God often uses the most insignificant means to accomplish His work. "God hath chosen the foolish things of the world to confound the wise; and God hath chosen the weak things of the world to confound the things which are mighty; and base things of the world, and things which are despised, hath God chosen, yea, and things which are not, to bring to nought things that are" (I Corinthians 1:27, 28). And why does God use the insignificant to defeat the proud and the small to defeat the big? "That no flesh should glory in his presence" (I Corinthians 1:29).

Third, the dislodging was done by *steps*. "By little and little I will drive them out from before thee" (23:30). God's program for conquering Canaan was a step at a time. That is the best way. You climb a ladder best by a step at a time. You progress in life best by a step at a time. Too quick a rise or success is perilous to character. God told Moses that He would "not drive them [the inhabitants of Canaan] out from before thee in one year; lest the land become desolate, and the beast of the field multiply against thee" (23:29). There are a number of beasts, and not necessarily the four-legged kind, that will multiply against us if we gain things too fast. Pride is one of the beasts— if success comes too fast, we will boast about how great we are. Irreverence is another of those beasts—too fast a rise, and we forget God. Laziness is also one of those beasts—give a man a fortune too quickly, and he tends to become lazy. Other of these beasts include poor values—when we get things too easy and too fast we will not value them well; and impatience—patience is never learned by getting things too fast. Step by step is a Divine way of life, and it is the best way of life.

The distending of borders. "I will . . . enlarge thy borders" (v. 24). In the account of the first giving of the law, God said He would "set thy bounds from the Red sea even unto the sea of the Philistines, and from the desert unto the river [Euphrates]" (Exodus 23:31). This promise has not been completely fulfilled yet. David and Solomon gained much ground for Israel, but the day is coming when Israel will have the land from the Nile to the Euphrates—that means some of today's Egypt, Jordan, Syria, Lebanon, and Iraq will belong to the Jews. This is not the plans of the enemies of the Jews today, but their plans are not the final plans—God's plans are.

The defending of possessions. "Neither shall any man desire thy land, when thou shalt go up to appear before the LORD thy God thrice in the year" (v. 24). This promise belongs to a specific command which we will note more about later. The command ordered that "Thrice in the year shall all your menchildren appear before the Lord God, the God of Israel" (v. 23) in attendance to the three feasts mentioned in Exodus 34. With all the men gone to Jerusalem to worship, it would leave the land, the women and the children without protection. The enemy could take advantage of this and easily invade the land and take much

609

from the Israelites. But God will take care of this situation. When He orders the men to all come together, He will guard the land they have left. The principle is that when we obey God, He will take care of us. The flesh gives a lot of excuses for not obeying God. It looks at circumstances and worries about adverse things that could happen if we obey God. But God silences all such protesting with this promise. Some may argue that God's people have, however, lost much in the world by being faithful to God. Yes, that is true. But if we do not see the promise fulfilled in temporal things in this world, then it will be fulfilled even more gloriously in eternity; for God is a debtor to no man. Obedience will always be duly compensated by God. When it is all said and done, the obedient soul will never be a loser, but always a great winner.

2. The Repeating of the Precepts

Chapters 21, 22, and 23 of Exodus list a number of precepts covering many areas of life. Some of these precepts are repeated here in our text. It is significant that a good portion of the precepts mentioned here speak of worship. There is a good reason for that. The reason is that Israel had just committed the terrible sin of idolatry. They had sinned greatly in the area of worship. Hence, the needed emphasis on the worship precepts in this repeating of the precepts during the second forty-day session on Sinai.

For the sake of our study, we have organized the precepts into five groups. We have labeled the groups friendship, fidelity, feasts, firstfruits, and fatigue.

Friendship. Israel was to "Take heed to thyself, lest thou make a covenant with the inhabitants of the land whither thou goest, lest it be for a snare in the midst of thee . . . and they go a whoring after their gods . . . And thou take of their daughters unto thy sons, and their daughters go a whoring after their gods, and make thy sons go a whoring after their gods" (vv. 12,15,16). These statements emphasize the great principle of separation.

They exhort us to be very careful about whom we choose as friends. Bad friends lead to bad faults and to bad faith. Israel was exhorted to make no friendship ("covenants") with the Canaanites for it would eventually lead to apostasy spiritually. Special mention is put on the peril of intermarriage with the Canaanites (v. 16). When we marry, we must especially be careful that we do marry someone that would cause us to compromise our faith. Matthew Henry said regarding this injunction for Israel about marriage, "If they espoused their children [to the Canaanites], they would be in danger of espousing their gods." Many folk have turned from the faith because of an unsanctified marriage.

Fidelity. Often in Scriptures, the relationship of God with His people is pictured as that of a husband and wife. This is the case here, for in our text God describes departure from Him as "a whoring" (vv. 15,16). To guard against spiritual "a whoring," God gave Israel some strong precepts here to promote spiritual fidelity. They concern the protesting in the faith, the praising of the faith, and the prohibiting for the faith.

First, the *protesting.* "But ye shall destroy their altars, break their images, and cut down their groves" (v. 13). Fidelity of worship not only includes worshipping correctly, but it also includes opposing incorrect worship. Israel was to take strong action in removing from the land the altars, images, and groves (female idols) of the wicked Canaanites. If evil is not opposed strongly, it will eventually corrupt. The preacher that preaches against sin is often disliked by many in the congregation; but he is doing the much needed work of destroying the altars, breaking down the images, and cutting down the groves of sin.

Second, the *praising.* "For thou shalt worship no other god: for the LORD, whose name is Jealous, is a jealous God" (v. 14). Here we are told Whom to worship and Whom to praise. It is Jehovah. He is said to be a jealous God. Jealousy in man is wicked, but not in God. God said, "I will not give my glory to another" (Isaiah 48:11, cp. Isaiah 42:8), and this is absolutely proper, for He deserve the glory. We must give our praise to Him in worship, not to others.

Third, the *prohibiting*. "Thou shalt make thee no molten gods" (v. 17). This precept is part of the Decalogue. Israel especially needed it repeated, for this is one of the commandments of the Decalogue they broke so blatantly in their sin of idolatry. People sometimes get upset when the preacher preaches about their sins, but they need this preaching to keep them from repeating their sin. It is either a repeating of the duties or a repeating of the disobedience.

Feasts. In our text, Israel is commanded by God to keep three feasts. They are the "feast of unleavened bread [the Passover]" (v. 18), the "feast of weeks [Pentecost]" (v. 22), and the feast of ingathering [Tabernacles]" (Ibid.). Some special commands regarding these feasts are recorded here. We note three of them. They concern the leaven in meals, the legion of men, and the leftovers of meat.

First, the *leaven* in meals. In two verses the leaven subject is mentioned. The Passover was called "The feast of unleavened bread" (v. 18) and the Israelites were commanded to eat unleavened bread "seven days" (Ibid.) at this feast. Later God warned that "Thou shall not offer the blood of my sacrifice with leaven" (v. 25). Leaven symbolizes sin. Prohibiting of leaven in these feasts emphasizes that sin will take away from our spiritual joys and corrupt our worship. Furthermore, not allowing leaven with the sacrifices is to keep the type accurate. Christ is pictured in the sacrifices and Christ is sinless. Leaven in the sacrifices would destroy this type.

Second, the *legion* of men. "Thrice in a year shall all your menchildren appear before the Lord God" (v. 23). It would require much effort by the men to assembly together for these major feasts. But the effort was needed to maintain faithfulness to the faith and experience needed fellowship with the saints. We noted earlier that this precept came with the promise of protection for the land when the men were at the feasts. Promises are always given to encourage obedience to His precepts.

Third, the *leftovers* of meat. "Neither shall the sacrifice of the feast of the passover be left unto the morning" (v. 25). We examined this command in our study of Exodus 12. There we noted that leaving any parts of the meat of the lamb till the next morning risked putrefaction of the meat. The putrefying of the meat would bring revulsion of it. Since the lamb represented Christ, God was making sure that in type nothing was done that would create revulsion for the Christ. Unfortunately, many in our land do not have that concern. Rather, they seem to delight in degrading the character of Christ.

Firstfruits. The repeating for Moses included some precepts concerning the firstfruits. Basically this had to do with giving to God. In examining these precepts we note the priority, persons, possessions, place, and portrayal in giving.

First, the *priority* in giving. "The first of the firstfruits of thy land thou shalt bring unto the house of the LORD thy God" (v. 26). God is to come "first." Before we start paying any bills, and before we spend on personal needs and wants, God comes first. That is the priority that should govern our giving.

Second, the *persons* in giving. "None shall appear before me empty" (v. 20). This precept says all persons are to give to God. How dare any of us come without a gift for God. After all He has done for us, we need to be most liberal in giving to Him. But many come to church empty-handed. Giving is a major problem in our churches. Yes, there are some who are dedicated and give well. But that number is few; for most give poorly. If folk do tithe, they figure their tithe to the penny seemingly afraid they might give too much. Few have gotten beyond the tithe to where they give with great devotion to the Lord. Many churches struggle year after year because the people in the church refuse to give substantially. God takes note of this selfish attitude; and when we come to God empty handed, we will be empty handed when it comes to rewards from Him.

Third, the *possessions* in giving. "All that openeth the ma-

613

trix (womb) is mine" (v. 19). This informs us that God owns all. Giving to God is only giving back to Him what He has given to us. Not giving to God is to steal from God. So the prophet Malachi said, "Will a man rob God? Yet ye have robbed me . . . in tithes and offerings" (Malachi 3:8).

Fourth, the *place* in giving. Regarding where to bring the gifts, God said, "thou shalt bring [them] unto the house of the LORD thy God" (v. 26). Giving to the United Fund or some other charity of the world will not pass for giving to God. You are to give where the worship of God is promoted in truth.

Fifth, the *portrayal* in giving. "The firstling of an ass thou shalt redeem with a lamb: and if thou redeem him not, then shalt thou break his neck" (v. 20). This giving precept portrays the Gospel. One is either redeemed by the blood of the Lamb of God or he meets with judgment (neck broken). Israel was portrayed as being "stiffnecked" (v. 9) which relates to the broken neck language. All sinners are in the "stiffnecked" category and need Christ to save them from eternal judgment (the broken neck of the soul).

Fatigue. "Six days thou shalt work, but on the seventh day thou shalt rest: in earing time and in harvest thou shalt rest" (v. 21). Again God speaks of the need for rest. Man has a built in fatigue factor that requires periodic rest. Ignore that truth and you hurt yourself. We gain nothing by going full speed ahead seven days a week. To emphasize the importance of the Sabbath rest, God commands man to rest on the Sabbath even though it be "earing" (old English word for plowing) time or "harvest" time. These two times are times when men would have a tendency to skip the Sabbath rest with the excuse they must get their work done before the weather changes. However, the philosophy of "Make hay while the sun is shining" is no excuse for ignoring rest. Rather, our busy times need rest more than other times. Men invent clever excuses to circumvent God's commands, but they will never pass with God.

3. The Repeating of the Printing

"And the LORD said unto Moses, Write thou these words: for after the tenor of these words I have made a covenant with thee and with Israel . . . And he [God] wrote upon the tables the words of the covenant, the ten commandments" (vv. 27,28). Not only were the promises and precepts repeated, but it was necessary to repeat the printing of them. The printing here involved writing the Decalogue upon a second set of stone tables and producing a written record of the other precepts which God gave Moses on the mount.

In our day we do not appreciate the difficulty involved in writing in Moses' day. With our typewriters, word processors, computers, and printing presses, it is very easy for us to print voluminous records quickly, neatly, and accurately. And if we must write by hand, we have a multitude of pens and pencils and writing material upon which to write. But in Moses' day, recording anything in written form was laborious and difficult; for the instruments by which they could write and the material upon which they wrote were very crude compared to our day. However, they still recorded in print many things. And some of those writings are of extreme value. Of greatest value, of course, is the writing of the Word of God which our text speaks about.

While the writing of the Word of God was done in various ways, as it was done here, it was always done under such control of God that it can always be said that what is written is indeed the Word of God. Whether God did the actual writing or man did the writing, the results are the same; namely, we have the Word of God in written form. In the two verses we have just quoted, we have both God and man doing the writing. In verse 27, Moses was instructed to write what God had just spoken to him on the mount. But in verse 28 the "he" in "he wrote" refers to God. It appears that Moses is the "he" in that verse, but in comparing that verse with other verses, we must conclude that the "he" of verse 28 refers to God. Rawlinson says of this identity problem, "It has been argued from this expression that Moses wrote the words on the second tables; and it would be natural so to understand the passage, had nothing else been said on the subject. But in verse 1 we are told that 'God said, I will write upon these tables'; and the same is repeated in Deut. 10:2. Moreover in Deut. 10:4, it is distinctly declared 'He [i.e. God] wrote on the tables according to the first writing.' We must therefore regard 'he' in this passage as meaning 'the Lord,' which is quite possible according to the Hebrew idiom."

How grateful we can be for the written Word of God. It is a blessing exceeded only by our personal salvation. No writing of any kind equals or exceeds in value the writing of the Scriptures. The written Word of God conveys to us the most important knowledge that can engage the mind of man. The written Word of God reveals to us the knowledge of God and the way to eternal life. Every man will sooner or later realize the Bible is the most important book ever placed in the hands of man. Some will not realize it until it is too late, however; for in this life they despise and scorn the Word. But eternity will change their view drastically and dramatically and also to their damnation.

D. THE RADIANCE OF MOSES

When Moses came down from Mount Sinai after his second forty-day session with God, "the skin of his face shone" (v. 29). Moses' face was luminous. The word "shone" means to "emit rays" (Wilson). It is "literally, shot out rays . . . irradiated, became radiant" (C. A. Goodhart). We note the reason for the radiance, the reaction to the radiance, and the reference to the radiance.

1. The Reason for the Radiance

Moses' face shone because he had a revelation of the glory of God's countenance when he was with God on Mount Sinai. So the reason for the radiance is at least twofold: the countenance of God and the consecration of Moses.

The countenance of God. Moses's radiance came as a result of his being allowed by God to see some of the glory of God's countenance. That glory, as we noted earlier, was so great that God had to put Moses in a cleft in a rock and cover him with His hand to shield Moses from a full view of it lest Moses be consumed (Exodus 33:20–22). But while the seeing of only part of the glory of God's countenance did not destroy him, it did leave a radiance on Moses that lasted for some time. Since he saw the revelation at the beginning of his forty days in the mount, and it continued after he came down out of the mount, this luminous condition must have lasted at least six weeks or more. It was a great testimony to the gloriousness of God's countenance. How glorious is God's countenance to do that to Moses and to be so great that man in the flesh cannot take a full view of it without being killed. And as we noted earlier, God is not only glorious in His countenance but also in His character. Thus He is "glorious in power" (Exodus 15:6), "glorious in holiness" (Exodus 15:11), He has a "glorious name" (I Chronicles 29:13), "His work is . . . glorious" (Psalm 111:3), and He has a "glorious voice" (Isaiah 30:30) to name some of the glorious things about God's character.

The consecration of Moses. Had Moses not spent time with God, he would, of course, not have had the revelation of God's countenance which he experienced. Being with God will affect a person. "No soul can enjoy real fellowship with the all-glorious God without being affected thereby, and that to a marked degree" (Pink). The effect may not be a luminous face, but it will be an effect of some sort that will manifest that one has indeed been with God. The best effect of being with God is a character that radiates holiness. Peter and John had spent much time with Jesus and people could tell (Acts 4:13). "The man who is thoroughly devoted to the Lord needeth not to wear some badge or button in his coat lapel, nor proclaim with his lips that he is 'living a life of victory.' It is still true that actions speak louder than words" (Pink). If we would shine in the valley, we need to stay on the mount long enough to get charged up. This requires great consecration to God.

While spending time with God will mark a person, so will spending time away from God. People who spend time in a den of iniquity show where they have been by the smell of their clothes, the smell of their breath, and over a period of time by the marks on their bodies. What sort of evidence are you giving in your life? Are you giving evidence that you have been *with* God or that you have been *away* from God.

2. The Reaction to the Radiance

The shining of Moses' face was bound to produce a pronounced reaction and it did. We note the reaction of Moses and the reaction of the multitude to this phenomena.

The reaction of Moses. "Moses wist not [knew not] that the skin of his face shone . . . he put a veil on his face" (vv. 29, 33). Not having a mirror to look at to view himself, Moses would not be aware of his shining face. Furthermore, being with God during those forty days would not draw his attention to any glory he had when a glorious God was speaking with him. But when Moses came down from the mount to the people, they saw his luminous face and told him. And when Moses found out from the people that his face shone, he did not strut the fact; but he covered his face with a veil. Moses did not try to use this unusual honor to exalt himself.

In this reaction by Moses, we see a most commendable modesty in Moses. Unlike so much of mankind in every age, Moses was not concerned about his own glory, but about the glory of God. One can easily imagine what some of the religious hucksters of our day would do with this glory. They would parade it ostentatiously before the people, and the phenomenon would be the main theme of their ministries. Even without the glory, these frauds are forever going around pointing to themselves and saying, "Look at me," instead of pointing to Christ. Moses' modesty in this radiance is a great contrast to these religious frauds and is more evidence of his great character.

The reaction of the multitude. "They were afraid to come nigh him" (v. 30). One can understand why the multitude felt this way. "Being conscious of guilt, they feared the worst, especially remembering the posture Moses found them in when he last came down the mount. Holiness will command reverence; but the sense of sin makes men afraid of their friends, and even of that which really is a favor to them" (Matthew Henry).

The multitude's fear of Moses because of the radiance provides us with one of the reasons why God permitted this radiance to be on the face of Moses. The reason is that it gave respect to Moses as Israel's leader. It would help to strengthen Moses' authority before the people. The Israelites had frequently not given good respect to Moses. If the sun shone, then Moses was a hero; but if clouds came over their circumstances, then Moses was to blame. So the people needed to improve in their respect for Moses, and the radiance surely helped. But the effect did not last permanently. For later on "they murmured against him; for the most sensible proofs will not of themselves conquer an obstinate infidelity" (Henry).

3. The Reference to the Radiance

The Apostle Paul refers to this experience in one of his letters to the church at Corinth. From that passage (II Corinthians 3:7–16) we note two lessons about the veil: the contrasting of law and grace, and the condemning of Israel.

The contrasting of law and grace. "If the ministration of death, written and engraven in stones, was glorious, so that the children of Israel could not stedfastly behold the face of Moses for the glory of his countenance; which glory was to be done away: How shall not the ministration of the spirit be rather [more] glorious? For if the ministration of condemnation be glory, much more doth the ministration of righteousness exceed in glory . . . For if that which is done away was glorious, much more that which remaineth is glorious" (II Corinthians 3:7–9,11). Moses' veiling himself speaks of the veiling of the

619

Gospel in the Old Testament whereas in the New Testament we see the Gospel unveiled. The Old Testament is just shadows of the Gospel and Christ, but the New Testament brings us the substance. The Old Testament is like luminous dials on clocks which absorbed and then radiated the light from another source. But the New Testament shows us the source. And the source was much more glorious than the shadow.

The condemning of Israel. This passage in Second Corinthians is also used to condemn Israel for their unbelief. "But their minds were blinded: for until this day remaineth the same veil untaken away in the reading of the old testament; which veil is done away in Christ. But even unto this day, when Moses is read, the veil is upon their heart" (II Corinthians 3:14,15). Paul uses the veil experience to show how Israel's heart is veiled so it cannot perceive the message God gave them in the Old Testament. It is another way of saying they have closed their mind to the truth. They refuse to understand the Word of God. They do not want to see what God has to say to them about Christ.

It is a terrible thing to intentionally and willfully cover the eyes and stop the ears so you cannot see or hear God's message. But Israel is guilty of that conduct. They are not alone, however. The world is filled with multitudes, both Jew and Gentile, who will not accept the Word of God, who will not bow down before Christ as their Savior. They have put a veil over their heart to keep from seeing the glory of the Gospel of Christ. "Nevertheless when it [the heart] shall turn to the Lord, the veil shall be taken away" (II Corinthians 3:16). When we come to Christ, we come out of darkness and into light.

XXVI.

SERIES OF COMPLAINTS

NUMBERS 11

ISRAEL SPENT NEARLY eleven months camped before Mount Sinai (also called Horeb). They had arrived there in "the third month" (Exodus 19:1) after they had left Egypt. Then on the "twentieth day of the second month, in the second year [after they had left Egypt] . . . the children of Israel took their journeys out of the wilderness of Sinai" (Numbers 10:11,12).

The Israelites' sin of idolatry delayed their leaving from Horeb by six weeks or more; for as a result of their sin, Moses had to have a second forty-day session in Mount Sinai to receive the law again from God. Sin always impedes progress. But finally God ordered them to move. "The LORD our God spake unto us in Horeb, saying, Ye have dwelt long enough in this mount. Turn you, and take your journey" (Deuteronomy 1:6).

As the Israelites made ready to leave Sinai, Moses invited "Hobab, the son of Raguel the Midianite, Moses' father in law" (Numbers 10:29) to journey with them that "thou mayest be to us instead of eyes" (Numbers 10:31). Hobab was evidently familiar with the Paran wilderness where Israel went after leaving Horeb (Numbers 10:12). But the invitation was a questionable act by Moses, for Israel did not need the help of an outsider to guide them when they had God as their guide. Hobab's response to the invitation was "I will not go" (Numbers 10:30) which showed his lack of enthusiasm for the work of God. However, later Scripture (Judges 4:11) indicates Hobab must have had a change of mind and went with Moses. But there is no record of his being helpful "eyes" for Israel. God was all the

621

guidance Moses needed. Moses did not need Hobab. But Hobab needed Moses if he wanted to experience some of the blessing God was going to give Israel.

After Israel had left Horeb and journeyed for some "three days" (Numbers 10:33), the problem of complaining became prominent in the camp. This complaining was not a single incident but a series of complaints. From our text we will note three of these complaining problems: the complaining by the laggards (vv. 1–3), the complaining by the lusters (vv. 4–9,18–23, 31–34), and the complaining by the leader (vv. 10–17,24–30).

A. THE COMPLAINING BY THE LAGGARDS
The first complaining problem of the Israelites after they left Horeb was not a complaining about some particular thing but a general attitude of complaint that can complain about any thing. This complaining was chiefly among the laggards; for in analyzing Scripture later, we will see that "the discontent seems to have been confined to the extremities of the camp" (Jamieson). To study this complaining problem, we will note the perpetualness of the complaining, the place of the complaining, the punishment for the complaining, and the praying for the complainers.

1. The Perpetualness of the Complaining
It is instructive to note that Israel's complaining here was not the first time they had complained on their journey from Egypt. Rather, they were perpetual complainers. They had complained at the Red Sea, at Marah, after leaving Elim, at Rephidim, and also at Sinai. Now shortly after leaving Horeb and heading for Canaan, they are once again in complaining mode.

This perpetual practice of complaining is not unique with the Israelites; for, unfortunately, we all are too well acquainted with such an attitude. We have all had the problem, and we all know others who have the problem. It is an attitude that can always find something to complain about regardless of the circumstances. Blessings can abound on every hand, yet the person with this attitude can still find something to complain about. It is either too hot or too cold, too wet or too dry, too early or too late, too much or too little, too fast or too slow, too easy or too hard. Nothing is ever right and nothing satisfies. It is a sick attitude, and we need to pray it will not be part of our attitude. No one will serve God well who is an habitual complainer.

2. The Place of the Complaining

This complaining occurred in the proximity of Horeb, on the pathway of Paran, and on the periphery of the camp.

The proximity of Horeb. Israel was only three days from Horeb (Numbers 10:33) when this complaining took place. Thus it did not take long for Israel to start complaining again. They were so addicted to complaining, that like one addicted to smoking, they could not go very long without engaging in their evil habit. Being only three days removed from Horeb increased the sinfulness of their complaining. The great experiences of Horeb should have kept them from complaining for a long time. But Israel proved in the past that they could praise God one day and profane Him the next. We are not much better. As an example, before we arrive home from a great service at church, we will often in some way demonstrate more flesh than faith. Hence, we must always guard against the work of the flesh in our lives.

The pathway of Paran. The complaining occurred on the southern edge of the Paran wilderness (Numbers 10:12). The three days' journey from Horeb was time enough for Israel to cross the great sand belt that separates the wilderness of Sinai (where Horeb was) from the wilderness of Paran. Paran was the roughest of the wilderness areas of the Sinai peninsula. Called "that great and terrible wilderness" (Deuteronomy 1:19; 8:15), it had mountains, gorges, desert lands, and also such discomforting things as "fiery serpents, and scorpions" (Deuteronomy 8:15). A complaining spirit would have no difficulty complaining in this place especially after a three-day trip across hot sands. "The fatigue and anxiety of the march . . . the frightful nature of the country into which they were marching, and the unknown terrors of the way which lay before them . . . were quite enough to shake their nerves and upset their minds. Such things could only be borne and faced in a spirit of faith and trustful dependence upon God and their appointed leaders . . . [but of] that spirit they knew nothing." (Winterbotham).

The periphery of the camp. The location of the judgment for this complaining supports the belief that the complaining came from the laggards. "The fire of the LORD burnt among them, and consumed them that were in the uttermost parts [periphery or outskirts] of the camp" (v. 1). While some have to march on the outside ranks (we noted this in a previous study), yet the outer ranks of the camp often represent those who lag behind and do not have the dedication of those farther into the camp. We have many of this kind at church. They never get very involved; they sit at the back of the church and come late and leave early. But they are the first ones to complain. Do not be part of this group. It is not a safe place to be.

3. The Punishment for the Complaining

"And when the people complained, it displeased the LORD; and the LORD heard it; and his anger was kindled; and the fire of the LORD burnt among them, and consumed them that were in the uttermost parts of the camp" (v. 1). We note the source, starting, severity, specialness, and site of the punishment.

The source of the punishment. God was the punisher. Four things are said in verse 1 about God which relate to Him as the source of punishment—God was "displeased" with the complaining, He "heard" the complaining, His "anger was kindled" by the complaining, and "the fire of the LORD burnt among them" as a result of the complaining. We list these four things under four words: evil, ears, enraged, and execution.

First, *evil.* The word "displeased" means "to be evil" (Wilson). The meaning of the statement here is that this complaining was evil in God's thinking. The Israelites may not have viewed their complaining as evil. But God certainly did. And God punishes what He deems as evil.

Second, *ears*. "The LORD heard it [the complaining]." God always hears what we say. Men often ignore the fact that God hears everything we say. But if we pondered more the fact that God hears all, we would be much more careful about what we say; for when God hears us speak evil, judgment can be our lot.

Third, *enraged*. Because of this complaining, God's "anger was kindled." He was really upset with the Israelites' complaining. And well He should be, for He had wonderfully blessed them—He had delivered them from Egypt, provided for their daily needs in the wilderness, and was most gracious in forgiving them for their terrible sin of idolatry. Some do not want to get upset about sin; but if God gets upset about sin, we had better get upset about it, too—and upset enough to forsake it.

Fourth, *execution*. "The fire of the LORD burnt among them, and consumed them." When something is evil in God's thinking and He hears it with His ears and gets really angry because of it—there will be judgment! Some, of course, do not want a God of judgment in their theology. But as we noted in the last chapter, it is a good thing God judges evil. He would not be a very nice God if He didn't. The judgment of hell fire may be unacceptable to some, but it honors God's character.

The starting of the punishment. This is the first time that God punished the Israelites for complaining. Though they complained a number of times before on their journey from Egypt, God never punished them for it. But things have changed in Israel's situation which now mandate judgment. These changes involve the probation of Israel, the patience with Israel, the pledge of Israel, and the privileges for Israel.

First, the *probation* of Israel. Because of the sin of idolatry, God had warned that if His presence continued with them, He would now "consume" them (Exodus 33:3) when they sinned again. Moses was able through his intercessory prayer to regain the presence of God for the people. But while God's presence is a great blessing, Israel's sin of idolatry now made their sinning more serious because it put them in a probation situation. And a small misdeed will receive much more judgment for one on probation than for one who is not.

Second, the *patience* with Israel. God's spirit does not strive with men forever (Genesis 6:3). There is a limit to which God will go. Israel had complained again and again and had finally reached that limit. Now they will be punished for complaining. Beware of causing God to lose His patience with you.

Third, the *pledge* of Israel. When Israel was given the law at Horeb, they vowed to keep the law. "All the people answered together, and said, All that the LORD hath spoken we will do" (Exodus 19:8). But they did not keep their word. Therefore, they must be punished. We get upset and rightly so when others do not keep their word with us. God also gets upset when men are unfaithful to Him. God always keeps His Word. It is a hallmark of His character; and it should be the same with us, too.

Fourth, the *privileges* for Israel. The punishment also reflects the fact that they were walking in more light than before. They had seen some great revelations of God while at Horeb. Therefore, they should be acting better. Privilege brings responsibility. Spiritual privilege demands improved behavior. The more light we walk in, the greater will be our judgment; for our judgment depends on the amount of light in which we walk.

The severity of the punishment. "The fire of the LORD burnt among them, and consumed them that were in the uttermost parts of the camp" (v. 1). God warned Israel earlier that His presence would "consume" (Exodus 33:3) them if they sinned. His warning comes to pass here as some Israelites are "consumed" by Divine fire. This was a very severe judgment and the severity of it underscored the great seriousness of the sin. We have just noted above that some changed situations of the Israelites would intensify judgment for their sin. Here we note that the seriousness of their sin will also intensify their judgment and make it very severe. This punishment of fire says complaining is not a trivial sin! It is a lot worse sin than most realize. This judgment should help us perceive this fact more clearly, and it should also really discourage our complaining.

The specialness of the punishment. Being described as "the fire of the LORD" says this judgment was a special act of God and not just a natural act such as lightening. God could have used some natural act to punish Israel, but He did not do so here. Judgment here was a special act from God. Similar judgments occurred with Nadab and Abihu, when "there went out fire from the Lord, and devoured them" (Leviticus 10:2) because of their misdeeds in the priesthood and when Elijah called down fire from heaven to slay several groups of soldiers who were threatening his life (II Kings 1:10,12). Sinners think if they can protect themselves from natural laws, they are safe, but not so; for God is not limited by natural laws.

The site of the punishment. The punishment occurred "in the uttermost parts [outskirts] of the camp" (v. 1). We saw earlier that where the punishment occurred indicated where the complaining occurred. God sent the fire where the failure was. Sending the fire to the outskirts of the camp also reflected grace. God did not consume the whole camp even though later verses show that many others in the camp were infected by the complaining. God warned future complainers with this judgment, but they paid little attention.

4. The Praying for the Complainers

"And the people cried unto Moses; and when Moses prayed unto the LORD, the fire was quenched" (v. 2). We note the seeking of Moses and the success of Moses in this praying for the complainers.

The seeking of Moses. "And the people cried unto Moses." Going to Moses for help reflects a change of heart about Moses

627

on the part of the people. While Scripture does not specifically say that any of the complaining here was about Moses, precedence says he was the number one human complained about; for when Israel previously got in trying circumstances, they always complained much about Moses. So Moses would doubtless be complained about here. But when trouble came, these folk did an about-face and headed to Moses for help. It was a wise move on their part, and it was a gracious response on Moses' part that he prayed for them. Sometimes one would like to tell the complainers to go find a fellow complainer to pray for them instead. But grace prays for the offenders.

The seeking of Moses by the Israelites reminds one of the time when Abraham was sought out by a resident of Sodom after Sodom was sacked by Chedorlaomer and his allies. Sodom had nothing to do with Abraham up on the hill in Hebron away from Sodom but would criticize and scorn him for his holy ways. However, when trouble came, Abraham suddenly looked a whole lot different to the folks in Sodom. So it is with sinners and their attitude about believers many times. Therefore, let believers be faithful in their conduct so when the ungodly see the peril of their ways, they will seek the believer out for help. Let churches keep themselves holy so when the world around them recognizes their need for spiritual help, they will seek out the church for help.

The success of Moses. "And when Moses prayed unto the LORD, the fire was quenched" (v. 2). The success of Moses in praying here was not an accident. He, in contrast to most of the Israelites, had lived an holy and upright life before God. One of the biggest helps we can have in our prayer life is a pure life. "If I regard iniquity in my heart, the Lord will not hear me" (Psalm 66:18) underscores that truth. Moses could accomplish more in a few minutes of praying than about all of Israel put together could accomplish in many hours of praying because Moses was obedient before the Lord, but Israel was not. Be pure if you want power in prayer with God.

B. THE COMPLAINING BY THE LUSTERS

The second complaining problem of the Israelites which we will examine that occurred soon after they had left Horeb was the complaint about their food. To examine this complaint, we will note the desire for meat, the deficiency of memory, the despising of manna, the display of mourning, and the death of many.

1. The Desire for Meat

"And the mixed multitude that was among them fell a lusting; and the children of Israel also wept again, and said, Who shall give us flesh to eat?" (v. 4). We will note the problem of lust and the people who lusted in this desire for meat.

The problem of lust. Lust was the cause of this particular complaining by the Israelites. Lusting does not bring contentment; it only fosters discontent. We will never be content when we allow our lives to be governed by our fleshly lusts. The world honors the "lust of the flesh" (I John 2:16), but that does not change the character and results of lusting.

The lusting here was for meat. The Israelites had been on a diet of manna for nearly a year now. The manna was most sufficient to supply all their need for food (we will see more about this shortly), but they still had a strong appetite for meat. Though they had cattle and sheep which they could butcher for meat, they did not do that; for the animals would not last long for meat, and they needed these animals for milk and wool and other essential products which the flocks and herds provided them. So the cattle and sheep and other animals which they had did not provide an adequate or practical source of meat for the camp. Hence, the cry for flesh.

The desire for flesh was not evil in itself. The Israelites were permitted under their law to eat many types of animals. But in the wilderness they were denied that diet. And when God denies something, it is evil for us to desire it. Paul confirms this in his comment on this incident. He said, "But with many of them God was not well pleased: for they were overthrown in the wilderness. Now these things were our examples, to the intent we should not lust after evil things, as they also lusted" (I Corinthians 10:5,6). "What is lawful of itself becomes evil to us when it is what God does not allot to us and yet we eagerly desire it" (Matthew Henry). It takes spiritual wisdom to distinguish between that which is evil at all times and that which is evil only for a time. Many professing Christians try to justify their evil conduct because it is not forbidden conduct in itself. They refuse to see, however, that it is at times denied conduct; and when it is denied, it is then evil for them to do. Therefore, boating may not be evil in itself; but when you should be in church on Sunday, boating is evil. Yet some carnal saints will say that when they missed church to go boating, they were not doing anything evil. Such is the rationale of the "lust of the flesh."

The people who lusted. There were three groups of people who lusted and, hence, complained about the food. They were the instigators, the influenced, and the inattentive. These groups overlap, but it is helpful to note the three groups in order to better see the lessons in our text.

First, the *instigators.* The "mixed multitude" instigated the complaining. This is not surprising, for they were a corrupt group. They were corrupt in *race* (this group included some who had intermarried with the Egyptians, which means they had intermarried with the ungodly, cp. Nehemiah 13:3), corrupt in *reason* (their reason for joining the exodus from Egypt was one of the flesh, not of faith), and corrupt in *reputation* (their conduct here forever marks them as poor in character). This group represents the unsaved and worldly-minded church members who conduct themselves not according to faith in the Word of God but according to the ways of the world. They are trouble in any church. They want the church to appeal to the flesh and be like the world. And it only takes a few of them to get the whole church in an uproar. If the church wants peace in its midst, it needs to turn a deaf ear to their complaining and keep these folk off the membership.

Second, the *influenced*. The children of Israel "also" became complainers. They were influenced by the mixed multitude to complain about the food. As we noted above, it only takes a few to get something started, then it spreads like wild fire throughout the congregation. Complaining is especially contagious. Therefore, we need to be on our guard when we are around folk prone to complain. Especially do we need to be on our guard when the complainers are gripping about things at church. When this complaining is heard, give due attention to the character of the complainers and note just how spiritual they are or aren't. It is not a mark of spirituality to let a backslidden, carnal church member influence you to start criticizing at church.

Third, the *inattentive*. This complaining was done in spite of the fact that complaining had just been punished severely by God. A fire from God had consumed some of the people on the outskirts of the camp for complaining. This should have caused those who escaped the punishment to walk softly and to avoid complaining at all costs. But those who escaped the punishment were inattentive to the warning. They did not take this warning seriously. They were obstinate in their heart.

Many are like these inattentive folk in Israel's camp. In spite of the fact that there are warnings abundant in our society about the curse of evil living, these people continue to live an evil life. Though warnings are plain and plentiful about such things as drinking, smoking, gambling, and abortion, these people still go right ahead and do these things anyway. They shut their eyes to the truth and rush to destruction. God help us to be of a different sort than that.

2. The Deficiency of Memory

"We remember the fish, which we did eat in Egypt freely; the cucumbers, and the melons, and the leeks, and the onions, and the garlick" (v. 5). Lusting not only encourages complaining, but it also fosters a deficient memory. The Israelites remembered their diet in Egypt, but they did not remember their despair in Egypt. "They remember the cucumbers, and the melons, and the leeks, and the onions, and the garlick . . . but they do not remember the brick-kilns and the taskmasters, the voice of the oppressor and the smart of the whip" (Matthew Henry). The Israelites forgot the cost of the food in Egypt, for they talked about eating fish "freely" in Egypt. That, however, was far from the truth. None of their food in Egypt was free—it all cost the terrific price of cruel slavery. They paid dearly with hard service for all their food.

Lust has a very faulty memory. Lusting cannot remember the curse of evil. Listen to your lusts and you will never be reminded of all the trouble that sin brings. We need to remind ourselves frequently of the poor memory of lust lest we become ensnared by its deceptive solicitations.

It is worthy to note here that the mention the Israelites' diet in Egypt is significant proof of the accuracy of the Scripture. Winterbotham says, "If we look at these different articles of food together, so naturally and inartificially mentioned in this verse, we find a strong argument for the genuineness of the narrative. [For] They are exactly the luxuries which an Egyptian laborer of that day would have cried out for if deprived of them; they are not the luxuries which a Jew of Palestine would covet or would even think of."

3. The Despising of Manna

"Now our soul is dried away, there is nothing at all, beside this manna, before our eyes" (v. 6). This was a despicable complaint by the lusters. It was most ungrateful of them to complain about the food that God provided daily for them. To emphasize the unjustified nature of this complaint, a description of the manna is given in verses 7 through 9. This description said the manna was good for food, pleasant to the eye, agreeable to the palate, capable of being made into a variety of dishes, completely free of cost, most adequate in supply, and requiring little labor to obtain it. If anything could be called free, it was certainly the manna—not the fish or other foods in Egypt. The Psalmist also spoke of the excellent character of manna, he called it "corn of heaven" (Psalm 78:24) and "angels' food" (Psalm 78:25). But the lusters were sick spiritually; and like those sick physically, even good food did not appeal to them.

We noted in an earlier chapter in this book that manna pictures both the Word of God and the Son of God. Therefore, this complaint about the manna will also reflect the complaint by many people about the Scriptures and the Savior.

The complaint about the Scriptures. Many folk in our churches do not like a steady diet of the Word of God for the services. They want the entertainment of the world to be part of the services. Cut down on the sermons but give us more entertainment is their cry. The sermons are too boring and tasteless for their carnal appetites. They frequently complain that the church does not have enough socials, suppers, and recreation. They badger the church to have more of these things especially for the young people. According to these folk, giving the young people the Word of God is not enough, but you must entertain them as well. These folk never complain if they do not get enough of the Word (if they did they would have much to legitimately complain about in most of our churches today). Their complaints only center on the things of the flesh.

The complaint about the Savior. A number of folk do not like the exclusiveness of Christ as the Bread of life (John 6:35). They do not want Him as the only Savior. They want to be ecumenical and include other ways in their creed. But all that we need for salvation is Christ just as all that Israel needed for nourishment was the manna. They did not need any fish, melons, leeks, onions, and garlick saviors!

An illustration of complaining about the heavenly manna is found in John 6. The people followed Christ because He fed their stomachs. But when He went to feeding their souls, He soon lost His crowd. He then asked His disciples if they were going to leave, too. But Peter indicated that he still had a great appetite for heavenly manna—both the Word of God and the

Son of God—when he said, "Lord, to whom shall we go? thou hast the words of eternal life. And we believe and are sure that thou art the Christ, the Son of the living God" (John 6:68,69).

4. The Display of Mourning

"Then Moses heard the people weep throughout their families, every man in the door of his tent" (v. 10). This outward display of mourning by the Israelites reminds us that lusting leads to unbecoming conduct and unhappy conduct.

Unbecoming conduct. Typical of complainers, these folk made sure they got plenty of publicity in their complaining. When they mourned, they did it in the tent door where they could be easily seen and heard by Moses. This public mourning was an obnoxious bit of ostentatious complaining. Winterbotham said, "So public and obtrusive a demonstration of grief must, of course, have been prearranged. They doubtless acted thus under the impression that if they made themselves sufficiently troublesome and disagreeable, they would get all they wanted; in this, as in much else, they behaved exactly like ill-trained children." Lusting certainly does not help us behave becomingly. It destroys our manners, promotes selfishness, and acts despicably. We either control our passions and behave properly, or we let our passions control us and behave improperly.

Unhappy conduct. This public weeping also shows how lusting makes one unhappy. Lusting promotes discontent and discontent is not happiness. The Apostle Paul had the right attitude when he said, "I have learned, in whatsoever state I am, therewith to be content" (Philippians 4:11). If we rejoice in the blessings we do have rather than lust for that which we do not have, we will find our blessings to be great and our happiness to be likewise. Focus on (lust for) what you do not have and do not need, and you will make life miserable for yourself and for those around you.

5. The Death of Many

"The anger of the LORD was kindled greatly" (v. 10) as a result of this complaining in the camp of Israel. And, as we saw in the previous complaining problem, when God gets angry, judgment will fall! To examine this judgment, we will note the plan for the judgment, the preparation for the judgment, the power in the judgment, the possessing before the judgment, the plague in the judgment, the people for the judgment, and the persuasion of the judgment.

The plan for the judgment. "For ye have wept in the ears of the LORD, saying, Who shall give us flesh to eat? . . . therefore the LORD will give you flesh, and ye shall eat . . . until it come out at your nostrils, and it be loathsome unto you" (vv. 18, 20). God's plan for punishing the complainers was to give them what they wanted. God oftentimes punishes mankind in this way. "God punishes our greed by letting us have as much as we want of the coveted thing. The covetous person is punished by ample wealth, the slothful by abundance of ease, the proud by success and flattery, the vain by large admiration, the sensual by unstinted gratification." (Winterbotham). This form of punishment teaches us several important truths about God's dealings with man. It shows us why God forbids certain things and why He favors the wicked at times.

First, why God *forbids* certain things. When God forbids some things in our lives, He does not forbid them to make us unhappy but to make us happy. An abundance of the forbidden will drive that fact home most readily. Israel would be given all the flesh they wanted, but it would become "loathsome" (v. 20) unto them. It would not make them happy but would bring much sorrow to them. And it would impoverish their soul which also makes one unhappy. "He gave them their request, but sent leanness into their soul" (Psalm 106:15). You cannot pamper your fleshly appetites without impoverishing your soul. Giving higher priority to your physical desires than to your spiritual needs will ruin you spiritually. Like Esau, you can have that bowl of pottage; but it will cost you your birthright which speaks of the most valuable things which you possess. And this loss produces unhappiness, not happiness (Genesis 27:38, cp. Hebrews 12:17).

Second, why God *favors* the wicked at times. It is often a frustration to the godly to see the wicked prosper. But our text explains the prosperity. It is to fatten up the wicked for slaughter. Hence, let us not envy the wicked who seem to do so well in this world. God may allow them to have an abundance of the things of the world for which they so inordinately lusted. But that abundance will only destroy them as it did the Israelites.

The preparation for the judgment. Moses was ordered to tell the people to "Sanctify yourselves against tomorrow, and ye shall eat flesh" (v. 18). This seems like a strange order. But God does not give strange orders. He was simply ordering Israel to get ready for their appearance in court to receive their sentence and judgment. "By certain ablutions, and by avoidance of legal pollution . . . The people were to prepare themselves as for some revelation of God's holiness and majesty. In truth it was for a revelation of His wrath, and of the bitter consequences of sin. There is about the words, as interpreted by the result, a depth of very terrible meaning; it was as though a traitor, unknowing of his doom, was bidden to a grand ceremony on the morrow, which ceremony should be his own execution" (Winterbotham). God gave a touch of formality to it all, but the people did not realize it was for their doom. Obstinate sinners never do, for sin so blinds their eyes they cannot recognize peril.

The power in the judgment. "There went forth a wind from the LORD, and brought quails from the sea, and let them fall by the camp, as it were a day's journey on this side, and as it were a day's journey on the other side, round about the camp, and as it were two cubits high upon the face of the earth" (v. 31). In giving the complainers what they lusted for, God provided a tremendous supply of quail. This great supply of meat demonstrated that God had power to supply the flesh if He wanted to. The people's complaint implied that God could not supply so much food. This questioning of God's power was also seen in an earlier complaint about a lack of food. "Can God furnish a table in the wilderness?" was the dishonoring question about God's power (Psalm 78:19) before the manna was supplied. So again the power of God is questioned. But God will show them His power. However, it will not be for their blessing but for their judgment.

The possessing before the judgment. "And the people stood up all that day, and all that night, and all the next day, and they gathered the quails: he that gathered least gathered ten homers: and they spread them all abroad [laid the quail out on the ground to dry] for themselves round about the camp" (v. 32). When the quails became available, the insatiable lust of the people was manifested in their zealous collecting of the quail. They worked straight through two days and a night in order to possess as much quail as possible. And the amount they accumulated was great! Some scholars estimate the ten homers as being enough to fill a 450 gallon container (or approximately sixty bushels). And this amount was gathered for each person!

Working all day and all night and then all day again is a good example of what happens to a life that is obsessed with getting all of this world's goods that he can get. We can see examples of this all around us. Greedy for wealth, men sacrifice their lives to gain as much of this world's goods as possible. They will go all day and all night and give little time to worship or family or other important and sanctifying interests. But then when they have it all gathered, they, like the Israelites with their quail, do not enjoy it very long.

If a person is going to give himself all day and all night to anything, let him, as Paul did, do it in serving the Lord instead (Acts 20:31; I Thessalonians 2:9, 3:10; II Timothy 1:3). Paul's reward will be great and eternal for such laboring. But laboring day and night simply to accumulate that which is to satisfy the lust of the flesh will be a venture doomed to great disappointment and loss.

The plague in the judgment. "And while the flesh was yet between their teeth, ere it was chewed, the wrath of the LORD was kindled against the people, and the LORD smote the people with a very great plague . . . they buried the people that lusted" (vv. 33,34). The plague upon the Israelite complainers said their judgment for lusting was sure, swift, and severe.

First, *sure.* James said that "when lust hath conceived, it bringeth forth sin: and sin, when it is finished, bringeth forth death" (James 1:15). Unbridled lust (which characterized the complainers) will for sure bring judgment. Control your fleshly appetites, or you will encounter the wrath of God. Israel found this out in this lusting in the wilderness; and you will find it out, too, if you do not heed the Word of God about lusting.

Second, *swift.* "While the flesh was yet between their teeth, ere it was chewed . . . the LORD smote the people" (v. 33). Hardened sinners will be struck down at times with rapidity. "He, that being often reproved hardeneth his neck, shall suddenly be destroyed, and that without remedy [without mercy]" (Proverbs 29:1). Swift judgment means the sinner will not have time to reconsider and change his ways. When sinners use up all their opportunities to repent, judgment will come without opportunity to escape.

Earlier God had said, "Ye shall not eat one day, nor two days, nor five days, neither ten days, nor twenty days; But even a whole month" (vv. 19,20). But judgment was obviously moved up to the first day of the eating. This swiftness of judgment did not contradict God's first prediction, for God did supply enough flesh for them to eat for a month or more, but Israel's great inordinate lust (demonstrated by their going straight through two days and a night in collecting the quail) obviously hastened their destruction. Their obstinacy in evil increased rapidly and, therefore, made their judgment swifter.

Third, *severe.* As with the earlier complainers, the judgment here was also death. The severity of the punishment said the sin was great. Uncontrolled passions will slay us. Being lenient with men's passions, as child psychologists tell us to do with children, invites death. The world is filled with spiritual and moral carcasses of those that had uncontrolled passions.

The people for the judgment. "The wrath of God came upon them, and slew the fattest of them, and smote down the chosen men of Israel" (Psalm 78:31). The Psalmist informs us that this plague caused Israel to lose some of their finest people in terms of strength and prospect. "By 'the fattest of them,' we understand the strongest and the healthiest" (Rawlinson). The word "chosen" refers to "the young men" (Ibid.), that is, the youth in the prime of life. The emphasis in noting who was destroyed shows us the terrible toll lust can take on anyone. We have personally seen healthy, vigorous, young men in the military destroy their bodies in a matter of months through giving themselves to the lusts of the flesh in drink and dames. Youth and physical strength are no match for the destructive forces of lust.

The persuasion of the judgment. "For all this they sinned still" (Psalm 78:32). The Psalmist says this judgment (as was the judgment upon the earlier complainers) was ignored by a great portion of the people. The Israelites did not take to heart the judgment of God upon the lusting complainers. Rather, Israel kept right on complaining as we will see in our next chapters. Thus many more of them were slain by Divine judgment.

Those who ignore God's judgments are an obstinate bunch who will not listen to any counsel or pay attention to any chastisement. They can explain away any judgment of God as some mere happenstance. But the Israelites demonstrated here that to ignore judgment and not let it affect your conduct is to play the fool. It will hasten your destruction. Such is the way the world acts today, but let us not be like those who ignore God's hand of judgment. "Despise not thou the chastening of the Lord" (Hebrews 12:5). You will lose big if you do.

C. THE COMPLAINING BY THE LEADER

The complaining of the people got Moses, their leader, to complaining. When the people complained about the food, "the anger of the LORD was kindled greatly; [and] Moses also was displeased" (v. 10). Moses' displeasure about the people's complaining is commendable, but how he expressed his displeasure is another story, for Moses exhibited his displeasure by complaining to God. We need to be upset with sin, but it makes a big difference how that displeasure with sin is exhibited.

The complaining by Moses can be divided into three parts: his duty, his dilemma, and his death. In looking at each of these three parts, we will note what Moses had to say and then observe how God responded to it.

1. His Duty

"Moses said unto the LORD, Wherefore hast thou afflicted thy servant? and wherefore have I not found favor in thy sight, that thou layest the burden of all this people upon me? Have I conceived all this people? have I begotten them, that thou shouldest say unto me, Carry them in thy bosom, as a nursing father beareth the sucking child, unto the land which thou swarest unto their fathers? . . . I am not able to bear all this people alone, because it is too heavy for me" (vv. 11,12,14). To examine this complaint by Moses about his God-given duty, we note the substance of the complaint and the seventy because of the complaint.

The substance of the complaint. Moses did not complain about the same thing the Israelites complained about. He was not lusting for meat and complaining about the manna. Rather, Moses complained about his job. He complained that his duty was more than he could do—"it is too heavy for me" (v. 14). This complaining reflected Moses at the bush when God called him, not Moses at Sinai when he was praying earnestly for God's help, presence, and mercy.

To emphasize the fact that the job was too heavy for him,

Moses piled up some self-pitying descriptions of his job that did not speak well of God. He accused God of being mean to him ("afflicted" [v. 11]), of not loving him ("not found favor" [Ibid.]), and of being unfair to him ("Have I conceived all this people?" [v. 12]) in giving him this heavy duty. None of what Moses said was true, of course. It was simply the complaint of the despondent soul who, when faced with difficulty, wilts under the problem and seeks to blame God for the problem.

Moses' complaint that his duty was too heavy for him shows the influence of Jethro which we noted in an earlier chapter of this book. Jethro did not like the way Moses was doing things (though things were going well) and told Moses his job was "too heavy for thee" (Exodus 18:18). The world never understands that when God calls, God enables. Without Him the easiest task is too much, but with Him the most difficult task can be done. In complaining to God here, Moses almost quoted Jethro word for word. Jethro had implanted in Moses' mind some unsanctified thoughts. All worldly counselors do that. Their counsel frequently causes people to argue with the will of God and to speak dishonorably of the character of God. Therefore, we need to always be on the alert lest we be influenced by the clever but corrupt counsel of the world.

The seventy because of the complaint. God's response to Moses' complaint about the work being too much for Moses was to give Moses seventy men to help him in the work. We note three things about the seventy: the selecting of the seventy, the spirit for the seventy, and the speaking of the seventy.

First, the *selecting* of the seventy. "And the LORD said unto Moses, Gather unto me seventy men of the elders of Israel, whom thou knowest to be the elders of the people, and officers over them [the people]; and bring them unto the tabernacle of the congregation, that they may stand there with thee" (v. 16). In our last chapter, we saw that God "stood with" Moses (Exodus 34:5). Here we will see seventy choice men of the congregation "stand . . . with" Moses (v. 16). These seventy were to be the best men of the congregation. They were to be "elders" (wise and experienced men) and "officers" (the word means an over-seer who was a writer or scribe—the New Testament "scribe" comes from this office). "No one was appointed who was not in public office already . . . Only those were eligible who had given proof of ability and faithfulness in public service . . . This rule was a good one. No man should be raised at one bound to high office, either in Church or State" (W. Binnie).

Second, the *spirit* for the seventy. "And the LORD came down in a cloud, and spoke unto him, and took of the spirit that was upon him, and gave it unto the seventy elders" (v. 25). The "spirit" here refers to the enabling ability which God gave to the seventy. If they were going to help Moses, they needed ability to help him. Some seem to think that when God took of the spirit that was upon Moses and gave it to the seventy, that Moses was reduced in ability to the level of the seventy. We cannot agree with that at all. Moses was still unequalled (Deuteronomy 34:10, Numbers 12:6-8, we will note this more in our next chapter). God's taking of the spirit upon Moses and putting it upon the seventy was like taking a lighted candle and lighting other candles. Doing this does not diminish the light of the lighting candle but only multiplies the lighted candles. Moses was still the biggest and best candle.

Third, the *speaking* of the seventy. "And it came to pass, that, when the spirit rested upon them, they prophesied, and did not cease" (v. 25). The word "prophesied" is not limited in meaning to the predicting of the future. The meaning also in-volves Holy Spirit inspired exhortations regarding godly living, adoration for God, and explanations of God's Word. This, and not predicting, is obviously what is involved here.

There are two things to especially note about the speaking of the seventy: the proof and the problem in the speaking.

The *proof* in the speaking involved the elders' calling. Their prophesying gave proof to the congregation that they were indeed Divinely called to a special position. They needed some sort of credentials to make it evident that they had been given a new office of authority in the camp, and the prophesying provided the credentials and the proof. When God calls a person, there will be evidence of the calling. When evidence is not present, the calling is not real even though a person may profess he has the calling. Some folk, for reasons of prestige, glamour, power, or other personal gain, claim to have a calling they do not in truth have. But you can expose their false claim by checking for evidence—they will not have good evidence.

The *problem* in the speaking was caused by two of the seventy deputies, Eldad and Medad. They did their prophesying in the camp, not by the tabernacle as the other sixty-eight had done. These two for some reason or other were not at the tabernacle for the special service with the other sixty-eight. But they were still officially and properly selected (they were "of them that were written" [v. 26]) by Moses and so the spirit came upon them, too. Because of the location of their prophesying, some of the Israelites got quite upset and thought it infringed upon Moses' authority. When Joshua found out about Eldad and Medad, he told Moses, "My lord Moses, forbid them" (v. 28). One cannot be very critical of Joshua for being so loyal to Moses. But he obviously did not understand all that was going on. Moses did, however, and responded, "Enviest thou for my sake? would God that all the LORD's people were prophets, and that the LORD would put his spirit upon them!" (v. 29).

Moses certainly demonstrated an exemplary God-honoring spirit here in his response to the prophesying of Eldad and Medad. He was not jealous of others in the ministry. He did not covet to monopolize power, honor, and wisdom. His main concern was the glory of God. In contrast, "A spirit of self-aggrandizement is set on retaining its exclusive position as the sole depository of the Divine blessing" (F. B. Meyer). But Moses rejoiced that others were speaking forth the praise of God even if the speaking appeared to take away some glory from Moses. Few will find this easy to do, however. "There is no test more searching than this. Am I as eager for God's kingdom to come through others as through myself? In my private intercessions can I pray as heartily and earnestly for the success of my competitors as for my own? Can I see with equanimity other and younger men coming to the front, and showing themselves possessed of gifts which I always considered to be my special province?" (Ibid.). Much petty criticism today by preachers of other preachers is nothing more than jealousy. The criticizers cannot stand for an Eldad or Medad to do as well or better than they are doing; for they, unlike Moses, want to monopolize the spotlight and receive all the accolades.

2. His Dilemma

Moses was in a dilemma about how to provide the meat for the Israelites. So he complained to God: "Whence [from where] should I have flesh to give unto all this people? . . . Shall the flocks and the herds be slain for them, to suffice them? or shall all the fish of the sea be gathered together for them, to suffice them?" (vv. 13,22). We will note the reasoning, the remembering, and the rebuking involved in this complaint.

The reasoning. Moses reasoned as natural man reasons. "Moses said, The people, among whom I am, are six hundred thousand footmen; and thou hast said, I will give them flesh, that they may eat a whole month. Shall the flocks and the herds be slain for them, to suffice them? or shall all the fish of the sea be gathered together for them, to suffice them?" (vv. 21,22). This bit of reasoning sounded like the reasoning of the disciples of Christ many years later. When Christ spoke of feeding a great multitude, "his disciples answered him, From whence can a man satisfy these men with bread here in the wilderness?" (Mark 8:4). Both Moses and the disciples were looking only at human sources for the supply of food. No wonder they were troubled about how to supply the food.

All of us are prone to look only at human sources when our needs are great. If the human sources do not appear sufficient, we conclude it is impossible to have our need met. How that exposes the smallness of our faith. It also greatly dishonors

God, for it limits God to the circumstances, and a God limited by our circumstances is not much of a God.

The remembering. The remembering here by Moses was conspicuously deficient. We noted earlier that the congregation of the Israelites had a problem with deficient memory in regards to the conditions in Egypt and the food supply there. Now Moses is also manifesting a memory problem. Like the other Israelites, Moses' memory was not biological but spiritual. Moses seems to have forgotten all about the wonderful ways in which God had supplied Israel's needs in the last year—such as the dividing of the Red Sea, the sweetening of the bitter water at Marah, the manna miracle that was still occurring six days a week, the water from the rock at Rephidim, and the defeating of the Amalekites. "They soon forgat his works" (Psalm 106:13) certainly characterized Israel and Moses here in the wilderness. And it also characterizes many of us oftentimes. How easy it is to forget that God has in His power delivered us many times from trouble and with timeliness has supplied us many urgent needs. When new troubles and needs present themselves, we often act as though God never solved any problems for us before. Let us pray for a better memory regarding God's blessings so we will have better faith when future difficulties arise.

The rebuking. "The LORD said unto Moses, Is the LORD's hand waxed [become] short? thou shalt see now whether my word shall come to pass unto thee or not" (v. 23). In a much deserved rebuke, Moses got his answer about how the flesh would be provided. God would provide the flesh through His power. In the question God asked Moses ("Is the LORD's hand waxed short?"), God indirectly declared that His power is never diminished nor does He ever run out of power. He is as powerful as He ever was. He does not get tired or faint and lose His strength. Therefore, God can supply the flesh just as He provided the manna and just as He provided all the other great needs for Israel. And so He informed Moses, "Thou shalt see now whether my word shall come to pass unto thee or not." And Moses really saw God's Word come to pass in a wonderful way; for as we have already noted, God's supply of the meat was abundant. Moses had spoken poorly of God's power, but God did not act poorly in the display of His power.

3. His Death

"And if thou deal thus with me, kill me, I pray thee, out of hand, if I have found favor in thy sight; and let me not see my wretchedness" (v. 15). In his complaining, Moses asked God to kill him. This means Moses wanted to quit. Complainers are prone to quitting. Complaining does not help your stamina in doing your duty.

Even though Moses' attitude was wrong here, I do not think any of us are going to be puzzled why Moses wanted to quit. Trying to shepherd the sort of flock he had would cause all of us to eventually want to resign. In fact, we would have turned in our resignation long before Moses wanted to quit. However, quitting, regardless of the circumstances, is always wrong if God has not terminated our assignment. But the best of God's men have trouble sometimes with this quitting business. As an example, both Elijah (I Kings 19:4) and Jonah (Jonah 4:8,9) also got discouraged enough to want to die. And you will note that both Elijah and Jonah, like Moses, were complaining before they said (by their request to die) that they were quitting.

God did not answer Moses' request to die. God responded to Moses' complaint about the burden being too heavy, and He responded to Moses' complaint about the problem of supplying the meat, but He never responded to Moses' complaint-inspired request to die. He did not answer that prayer request. And how glad Moses can be that God did not answer that request. And how glad we all can be that God does not answer some of our prayer requests. It is safe to say that God's refusal to answer some of our requests results in some of our biggest blessings. What a tragedy had it been for Moses had God killed him then in the wilderness as Moses requested. What tremendous blessings Moses would have missed. How much gallant service for God he would have been unable to perform. We would have no Pentateuch if he had died then. Elijah also would have missed so very much had God shorted his life as Elijah desired. And if Jonah had died outside of Nineveh as he wished, he would never have been able to write the book after his name which is the greatest and most far-reaching work he ever did. Before we get too upset about some of our prayers not being answered as we would like, we need to earnestly ponder the blessing of God's denials.

XXVII.

SHUTTING OUT MIRIAM

NUMBERS 12

MORE TROUBLE AWAITED Moses when the Israelites stopped at Hazeroth (Numbers 11:35)—the first stop after they had left Kibroth-hattaavah where many died from lusting for meat. The continuous uprising of trouble in Israel's camp on their journey from Egypt to Canaan should not be surprising, for there are two good reasons for this constant troubling of the camp. First, the *depravity* of man assures us of constant troubles. Because "The heart is deceitful above all things, and desperately wicked" (Jeremiah 17:9), we can always expect trouble to be near at hand. Second, the *devil* also assures us of constant trouble. Whenever a work of God is taking place (as it was in Israel's deliverance from Egypt and their journey to Canaan), the devil will oppose it continuously. But these troubles need not overcome us. God can give us victory over them, for "God is our refuge and strength, a very present help in trouble" (Psalm 46:1).

The trouble we will consider in this chapter concerns a verbal attack against Moses by Miriam and Aaron. It resulted in Miriam being shut out of the camp for a week. To examine this trouble, we will look at the criticism of Moses (vv. 1–3), the counsel from God (vv. 4–8), and the curse on sin (vv. 9–16).

A. THE CRITICISM OF MOSES

No Israelite performed so excellently as Moses did on the journey from Egypt to Canaan. Yet, no one was so criticized as Moses. But excellence is no immunity from criticism, especially spiritual excellence. Spiritual excellence is more likely to provoke criticism than to inspire commendation. To study this criticism of Moses, we will note the source of the criticism, the subject of the criticism, and the saintliness of the criticized.

1. The Source of the Criticism
"Miriam and Aaron spake against Moses" (v. 1). We note the leader of the source and the painfulness of the source.

The leader of the source. Both Miriam and Aaron criticized Moses, but Miriam was the leader in this criticizing. This is evident in at least five ways. First, she is mentioned first in this criticism. Second, the verb "spake" in verse 1 is a feminine verb. Third, she was the one who was punished most for the criticizing, as we will note later. Fourth, Aaron by nature was not a leader but was easily influenced as was seen in the sin of idolatry. Miriam, however, was a leader as is seen in her leading the women in singing after the Red Sea crossing. Fifth, the first criticism was "a peculiarly feminine one" (Winterbotham). We need leaders, but not leaders in criticism like Miriam. We need leaders in piety, not in poison tongues.

The painfulness of the source. The source of the criticism would intensify the pain of it. It is always painful to be criticized; but when strangers criticize us, it is not as painful as when those close to us criticize. Especially is it painful to be criticized by one's own family as was Moses here. It was his own sister and brother who criticized him. That had to really hurt him. Heretofore, he could always count on their sympathy when attacked. In fact, in some of the earlier criticism, Aaron particularly was criticized right along with Moses. But here Moses is being attacked by those closest to him. Such an attack can only be handled well by those with much character and faith.

2. The Subject of the Criticism
This criticism of Moses by Miriam and Aaron was twofold. They criticized the mate of Moses and the ministry of Moses.

The mate of Moses. "And Miriam and Aaron spake against Moses because of the Ethiopian woman whom he had married: for he had married an Ethiopian woman" (v. 1). To look into this criticism, we will examine the identity of the woman and her irritation to the critics.

First, her *identity*. Questions regarding the identity of Moses' wife here have forever puzzled Bible students. Was this woman Zipporah whom he had married some forty years earlier and who was just recently reunited with him (Exodus 18:2) at Mount Sinai (she had been left behind when Moses went to Egypt to deliver the Israelites)? Or was this a second wife whom Moses had just recently married? If it was a second marriage, does it mean that Zipporah had died or that Moses now had two wives? If this was a second marriage, it seems very strange that there is no other information given in Scripture as to why Moses married again and under what circumstances.

The main fact which keeps us from being very confident that the woman mentioned in our text was Zipporah is the emphasis on the woman being an Ethiopian. Zipporah was a Midianite (Numbers 10:29). However, it is possible that she could be an Ethiopian and still be from Midian; for "The descendants of Cush [the Ethiopians] were distributed both in Africa (the Ethiopians proper) and in Asia" (Winterbotham). And "There was a part of Arabia called Cush and that land of the Cushites included a part of the territory occupied by the Midianites" (B. H. Carroll). If she was a recent bride from Ethiopia, it raises a big question about how Moses met her since he was not in Ethiopia but in Sinai. Our position is that the woman was Zipporah. But the important lessons about the criticism will be the same regardless of who the woman was.

Second, her *irritation*. Moses' wife, whoever she was, obviously caused some envy (though no fault of hers) especially in Miriam. Up until just recently, Moses did not have a wife with him. Thus Miriam, being his sister, enjoyed a priority among women, for she would be the closest woman acquaintance of Moses in the camp. But with a wife coming on the scene (either

650

by the reuniting of Zipporah or by a new marriage) and thereby becoming a more important woman in Moses' life than Miriam, Miriam had to play second fiddle. That would not go over well with Miriam as is easy to understand. So the real problem was not Moses' wife per se; it was envy over position. Miriam (and Aaron, too) wanted more recognition and position in the camp. The next criticism will confirm that this was the real problem; and so will the fact that in dealing with the criticism of Moses, God never mentioned the criticism of Moses' wife.

The ministry of Moses. "And they said, Hath the LORD indeed spoken only by Moses? hath he not spoken also by us? And the LORD heard it" (v. 2). In this statement the real concern of Miriam and Aaron is now voiced without any disguise. It was not the woman who was the wife of Moses that upset them so much, but what really upset them and caused them to criticize was the fact of her position with Moses. The real problem with Miriam and Aaron was the matter of position and rank. They (especially Miriam in this case) not only did not like the fact that Moses' wife had higher position than they did, but they also did not even like the fact that Moses himself had a higher position than they did. They wanted to be at least equal with him.

That which doubtless affected the timing of this criticism about position—and it even may have been the main cause of it—was the recent elevation of seventy men to help Moses. This was a significant event in the camp, and it evidenced Divine power when the seventy "prophesied" (Numbers 11:25). But Miriam and Aaron were left out of this. With the kind of attitude they evidence in the criticism, being left out in the glory of this event would rankle their small souls and start them on a campaign to belittle those above them in rank, such as Moses' wife and particularly Moses himself. It is ever the habit of people controlled by envy to belittle those above them. With their attitude of envy, Miriam and Aaron would also find that "It is hard for them both to forget that Moses was only their younger brother: for Miriam that she had saved his life as an infant; for

Aaron that he had been as prominent as Moses in the original commission from God to the people" (Winterbotham).

Their criticism is not unlike some heard in society and in churches in our day. In society, the spirit of this criticism is heard in the "equal rights" movement. Under the guise of correcting wrongs, the "equal rights" movement too often smacks of an effort by the unqualified to gain positions of prestige and honor which they do not merit and cannot manage. In church it is not uncommon to hear dissidents belittling the pastor's position and exalting themselves until they are equal in authority, honor, and worth. But it is all inspired from the attitude of envy and pride that is more interested in one's own personal honor than in the honor of God and in the prosperity of His work.

3. The Saintliness of the Criticized

"Now the man Moses was very meek, above all the men which were upon the face of the earth" (v. 3). This verse defines meekness, defends Moses, and denounces the critics.

Defining meekness. With our verse saying Moses was the meekest man in the world, we learn much about meekness that is not the common view of the world about meekness. Meekness is often viewed as weakness, shyness, passiveness, backwardness, femininity, a lack of courage, and as someone who would never lift up his voice in protest of anything. But meekness as seen here is far different. It is strength to hold your tongue when you are being attacked by unjust criticism; it is humbleness that does not arrogantly strut your calling and position; and it is faith that trusts God to take care of your vindication needs. Meekness did not stop Moses from being a firm, strong, and outspoken leader for God. "When God's honor was concerned, as in the case of the golden calf, no man [was] more zealous than Moses; but, when his own honor was touched, no man [was] more meek: [he was] as bold as a lion in the cause of God, but as mild as a lamb in his own cause" (Matthew Henry). Meekness, as seen in Moses, is submission to the will and way of God.

Defending Moses. The claim by Miriam and Aaron that they were equal with Moses indirectly accused Moses of assuming authority that he should not have. This charge will be heard again in a later incident when others tell Moses, "Ye take too much upon you, seeing all the congregation are holy . . . wherefore then lift ye up yourselves above the congregation of the LORD?" (Numbers 16:3). But all these charges will be cancelled out by Moses' meekness. His meekness would rule out any pursuits of self-aggrandizement, any seeking after position that did not belong to him, and any arrogance with the people. Moses was what he was and of the rank he was because God had called him and elevated him above the people. Any charge of Moses promoting himself wrongly is completely cancelled out by his superior meekness. His great meekness would prevent him from any usurping of position or power.

Denouncing the critics. This verse also shows how deficient Miriam and Aaron were in character. They did not even begin to possess the noble attribute of meekness. If they had, they would never have criticized Moses as they did. Rather, they would have humbly submitted to their position of inferior rank without a whimper, and they would have served in their position with zeal and excellence. But they lacked that noble character. They were just the opposite of meekness and were not interested in meekness. They were not interested in Moses' meekness but in Moses' ministry. They sought superiority in position not superiority in piety. They wanted to excel in rank, not righteousness. This kind is all too frequently found among the members of our churches. They are the ones who will fuss the most about elections and will unhesitantly push themselves into consideration for positions they are not qualified for, and they will complain much if they do not get those positions.

B. THE COUNSEL FROM GOD

The criticism of Miriam and Aaron was answered quickly by God, for "the LORD spake suddenly unto Moses, and unto

Aaron, and unto Miriam, Come out ye three unto the tabernacle of the congregation . . . And the LORD came down in the pillar of the cloud, and stood in the door of the tabernacle, and called Aaron and Miriam" (vv. 4,5). Moses did not have to answer the charges of the critics, for God was going to do that. "Moses had often shown himself jealous for God's honor, and now God showed himself jealous for his [Moses] reputation; for those that honor God he will honor" (Matthew Henry). God's vindication of Moses in this counselling of Miriam and Aaron can be a great encouragement to those who faithfully serve God, especially to godly pastors whose pastorates and calling are often challenged by church dissidents.

We will note four things which God spoke about to Miriam and Aaron in vindicating Moses and in rebuking Miriam and Aaron. They are the sovereignty of callings, the supremacy of Moses, the steadfastness of Moses, and the sin of disrespect.

1. The Sovereignty of Callings

"He said, Hear now my words: If there be a prophet among you, I the LORD will make myself known unto him" (v. 6). In criticizing Moses and in trying to claim equality with him, Miriam and Aaron ignored a very basic and important truth about Divine callings—they are determined solely by God Himself. They are not determined by man. Paul spoke the same truth when he spoke of his own calling. He said, "Paul, an apostle, not of men, neither by man, but by Jesus Christ, and God the Father, who raised him from the dead" (Galatians 1:1). Men may recognize a call through ordination and various other services which indeed have their place. But these services do not determine a call, they only recognize a call. God alone determines a call. Other things that do not determine a call and position in the Lord's service—though men oftentimes think they do—are family ties, family wishes, talent, church councils, seniority, charter membership, schools, fame, and fortune. Preachers are not called by their fathers or mothers. Missionaries are not called by seminary professors. God does the calling!

Miriam and Aaron obviously felt their relationship with Moses made them equal in calling if not superior. After all, Moses was their younger brother. But God's counsel indicated that family relationship had absolutely nothing to do with God's call.

The sovereignty of a call to service ought to cause men to fear to tread in presumption into a calling not given them. To presume a calling is dangerous business. Rebelling against a call brings Divine judgment. But so does presuming a call as Miriam and Aaron did, for we will shortly see that Miriam paid a big price for her disregard of Divine callings. Know your calling and do it. Do not try to be something God never called you to be, and do not rebel against what God called you to be though that calling may be a task which men do not especially honor or esteem. It is not position in the eyes of men that is important; it is obedience in the eyes of God that is important.

2. The Supremacy of Moses

"My servant Moses is not so . . . With him will I speak mouth to mouth, even apparently, and not in dark speeches; and the similitude of the LORD shall he behold" (vv. 7,8). When Miriam and Aaron criticized Moses' position, they particularly addressed the matter of prophesying. "Hath he [God] not spoken also by us?" (v. 2) was their statement which said they thought they were equal to Moses in prophesying. With the seventy doing some prophesying, Miriam and Aaron did not want to be left out. Furthermore, they wanted to be equal with Moses and not with the seventy. But God made it plain in His counselling that Moses was supreme in his position as a prophet—which means he is supreme in his position in the camp.

God said the difference between Moses and all the other prophets was in how Moses received his message from God. Other prophets received their message from God through visions and dreams. "I the LORD will make myself known unto him [other prophets] in a vision, and will speak unto him in a dream" (v. 6). But Moses was different. "My servant Moses is not so [not the same as the others in how he receives his message] . . . With him will I speak mouth to mouth . . . not in dark speeches; and the similitude of the LORD shall he behold" (vv. 7,8). Moses did not receive his message from God through dreams and visions. Rather, God spoke to him "mouth to mouth" (or "face to face" as in Exodus 33:11). Furthermore, Moses was superior in his calling in that in a special way he saw the glory of God ("similitude of the LORD shall he behold").

We learn later in Scripture that this supremeness of Moses' ministry foreshadows Jesus Christ. "The LORD thy God will raise up unto thee a Prophet from the midst of thee, of thy brethren, like unto me; unto him ye shall hearken . . . and [I] will put my words in his mouth; and he shall speak unto them all that I shall command him" (Deuteronomy 18:15,18).

3. The Steadfastness of Moses

"Who is faithful in all mine house" (v. 7). God not only made it clear to Miriam and Aaron what Moses' calling was, but He also made it clear to them what sort of character Moses had. And what a great testimony God gave of Moses' character. God said Moses was "faithful." We may be talented, popular, and impressive to men; but none of that will matter with God if we are not faithful to Him. Faithfulness is the chief qualification. Other qualifications may have their place, but faithfulness comes first. "It is required in stewards, that a man be found faithful" (I Corinthians 4:2).

Moses' faithfulness emphasizes the fact that he was not only superior in his calling, but he was also superior in his character. We saw this in regards to his meekness, too. And, as we noted regarding Moses' meekness, Miriam and Aaron should have been more interested in being Moses' equal in character rather than in calling. That would have brought blessing to the camp instead of trouble.

The mention of Moses' faithfulness should have brought great shame to Aaron especially, for he had been so grossly unfaithful in the matter of the sin of idolatry. Moses' faithfulness was a great contrast to Aaron. So how foolish of Aaron to think he is equal to Moses. How easily God can silence the critics.

Faithfulness needs to be stressed more in our churches today. And not only do we need to stress faithfulness in the matter of our ministries but also in the matter of our morals and marriages. Some, however, seem quite taken up with the justification of unfaithfulness in the area of morals and marriage. Books and sermons can be found almost everywhere to justify divorce. But we do not need those books and sermons! We need books and sermons that stress faithfulness instead. God does not commend unfaithfulness; He only commends faithfulness.

4. The Sin of Disrespect

"Wherefore then were ye not afraid to speak against my servant Moses?" (v. 8). The disrespecting of Moses by Miriam and Aaron was totally unjustified. God had cleared Moses of every charge by Miriam and Aaron. "Wherefore" means that in view of the sovereignty of Moses' calling, the supremacy of Moses' position, and the steadfastness of Moses' performance, why were they (Miriam and Aaron) not afraid to criticize Moses? The answer is that depravity can criticize anyone; it can criticize perfection. It can even criticize God. Therefore, the cause of this criticism is not the faults of the one who is criticized but the faults of the those who do the criticizing. Jesus Christ is often severely criticized by mankind though He is the personification of perfection. Hence, the criticism of Christ only reveals the wickedness of the hearts of those who criticize Him. Sin cannot tolerate righteousness and will soon criticize it.

We need to remember these truths when God's faithful servants are being maligned by the critics. Do not chime in with the critics. Rather, turn away from the critics; for their criticism only hurts God's work. Churches have made great mistakes in listening to the dissidents criticize God's man in the church. Evil needs to be put out of the church, not honored. Listening to the dissidents criticize a pastor is to give honor to evil. A multitude of churches have not grown, and some have even dissolved because the criticism of God's man has been given much respect while the criticized pastor has been treated disrespectfully. In some churches, the criticized pastor is more likely to be voted out than any dissident. That surely shows the poor spiritual condition of those churches.

C. THE CURSE ON SIN

As a result of the sinful criticism by Miriam and Aaron against Moses, "the anger of the LORD was kindled against them [Miriam and Aaron]" (v. 9). Sin makes God angry. And when God gets angry, there will be judgment! Sin may look appealing to man, but it is appalling to God, and it comes with a Divine curse that no one will like. To examine the curse on the sin of Miriam and Aaron, we will note the retribution upon Miriam, the repentance about Miriam, the request for Miriam, the restriction of Miriam, and the remembering of Miriam.

1. The Retribution Upon Miriam

"Behold, Miriam became leprous, white as snow: and Aaron looked upon Miriam, and, behold, she was leprous" (v. 10). In the Bible, God is sometimes recorded as judging disobedience by inflicting the disobedient person with leprosy. He did this with Gehazi the lying servant of Elisha (II Kings 5:27); He did this with King Uzziah when Uzziah intruded into the priests' office—his attitude, like that of Miriam and Aaron, did not recognize Divine callings (II Chronicles 26:19); and God did this with Miriam.

Regarding Miriam's leprosy, we note the degree, the display, the discrimination, and the disgrace of her leprosy.

First, the *degree* of her leprosy. Her leprosy is described as "white as snow." That description says her leprosy was "the most virulent and incurable of all" (Poole). Leprosy was "nothing short of a living death" (F. C. Cook) especially her kind. All of this indicates the seriousness of her sin. Attacking God's man is risky business. "Touch not mine anointed, and do my prophets no harm" (Psalm 105:15) is a command you do not violate without serious consequences. People in church who attack their godly minister are asking for big trouble from God. Far worse is to speak against Christ. As Matthew Henry said, "If she was thus chastised for speaking against Moses, what will become of those that sin against Christ?"

Second, the *display* of her leprosy. "Aaron looked upon Miriam, and, behold, she was leprous." Because of the way women dressed then, about the only skin of Miriam that Aaron could see would be the skin of her face and hands. The words "looked upon" certainly implies that her face especially was affected quite pronouncedly. Matthew Henry said, "Her foul tongue . . . is justly punished with a foul face." How different was the face of Miriam than the face of Moses. Earlier Moses had to veil his face because of the glory of it; now Miriam would veil her face because of the gruesomeness of it. Sin destroys one's glory.

Third, the *discrimination* of her leprosy. God was discriminate in whom He cursed with leprosy. It was Miriam, not Aaron. "Miriam was struck with a leprosy, but not Aaron, because she was first in the transgression, and God would put a difference between those that mislead and those that are misled" (Henry). There is justice in God's judgment. Aaron is not exonerated by the judgment here, but the judgment points out who was the leader of the attack on Moses.

Fourth, the *disgrace* of her leprosy. Leprosy is a great dishonor to the person that has it. It shuts them out from society, and they are filled with shame as their body becomes loathsome with the disease. Thus it was a very appropriate judgment for Miriam. "Miriam was very anxious about honor for herself, not for God. So she was stripped of her honor and humiliated by this judgment" (F. C. Cook). When we do not give honor where honor is due, we will lose our own honor.

2. The Repentance About Miriam

"And Aaron said unto Moses, Alas, my lord, I beseech thee, lay not the sin upon us, wherein we have done foolishly, and wherein we have sinned. Let her not be as one dead, of whom the flesh is half consumed when he cometh out of his mother's womb" (vv. 11,12). When God punishes us, its intent is that we will be brought to our senses about our sin and confess it. Commendably, Aaron got the message very quickly. He was not like many folk who can be chastened again and again and still go on their stubborn way unrepentant of their sin.

Aaron not only repented of his sin, but he forsook his sin in that instead of trying to make himself equal with Moses, as he and Miriam had tried to do earlier (v. 2), he now calls Moses "my lord" which is a distinctly different attitude. In that term he recognizes Moses as his superior. Too bad he and Miriam had not done that sooner, for it would have eliminated the leprosy.

3. The Request for Miriam

"And Moses cried unto the LORD, saying, Heal her now, O God, I beseech thee" (v. 13). Once again we behold the noble character of Moses. How magnanimous of Moses to so quickly and so earnestly pray for one who had so unjustly and unkindly attacked him. Again and again we have seen this most commendable trait of Moses illustrated in Scripture. He was ever praying for those who treated him poorly. Christ commanded us to do the same when He said, "Pray for them which despitefully use you, and persecute you" (Matthew 5:44). But that is not easy to do! We want those who mistreat us to be duly punished. However, had God done to us what we want done to our enemies, we would never have tasted of the cup of salvation.

There is a special blessing in praying for those who do not treat you well. This truth is especially seen in Job's life. Scripture says, "The LORD turned the captivity of Job, when he prayed for his friends [whose unjust criticism of Job made them more like enemies than friends]" (Job 42:10). Praying for your enemies helps to remove bitterness, frustration and other problems from your heart. It also greatly helps your fellowship with God. Make a list of those who have especially given you a difficult time in life and then pray for them regularly. It will calm your heart and provide you with some choice blessings.

4. The Restriction of Miriam

"And the LORD said unto Moses, If her father had but spit in her face, should she not be ashamed seven days? let her be shut out from the camp seven days, and after that let her be received in again. And Miriam was shut out from the camp seven days: and the people journeyed not till Miriam was brought in again" (vv. 14,15). We note two lessons in this restriction of Miriam. They involve the discipline of Miriam and the delay of the multitude.

The discipline. While God answered Moses' prayer and healed Miriam of her leprosy, she was still shut out of camp for seven days; for mercy was not exercised apart from discipline. That does not diminish the character of mercy but only enhances it. The Psalmist stated this practice of exercising both mercy and discipline when he said, "Thou wast a God that forgavest them, though thou tookest vengeance of their inventions [evil deeds]" (Psalm 99:8). Forgiveness is not apart from discipline. We can be mighty thankful for that fact, for discipline is to correct us so we will not go back to our sin again. Miriam was healed of her leprosy which she got for criticizing Moses, but being shut out a week from the camp would help repress any future urges she might have to criticize Moses.

God used the stigma of a parent spitting in the face of a child (v. 14) to show the necessity of the discipline of shutting out Miriam for seven days. "The Jews, in common with all people in the East, seem to have had an intense abhorrence of spitting; and for a parent to express his displeasure by doing so on the person of one of his children, or even on the ground in his presence, separated that child as unclean from society for seven days" (Jamieson). So if separation occurred for the spitting, then how much more for leprosy even though the leprosy was healed. The stigma, the discipline, and the chastisement must be felt to be effective.

We need to emphasize this discipline truth in our churches a lot more, for so many church members have a poor concept of forgiveness. This is especially seen in regards to church discipline. When some church member commits a flagrant act of sin, the church members talk about forgiveness but seldom about church disciplinary action. In the thinking of many church members, disciplinary action is equated with a lack of forgiveness. However, nothing could be farther from the truth. Disciplinary action is to strengthen the fallen ones so they will not sin again in that area in which they fell so badly. Of course, there are always some who will protest any discipline by saying it will discourage the forgiven one. That protest, however, is simply a bit of rebellion against God's way that tries to mask itself as pity and kindness. The discipline will not discourage the fallen in the way the dissidents claim, but it will discourage the fallen from sinning again. We need that kind of discouragement in great abundance in our churches!

This understanding of discipline is also needed in society in the matter of punishing criminals and in the home in the matter of punishing children. Slacking off on discipline does not help either the wrongdoer or anyone else.

The delay. Because of Miriam's sin, the "people journeyed not till Miriam was brought in again" (v. 15). Miriam's seven days of being shut out of the camp had to expire before the Israelites could renew their journey. The lesson is twofold: sin hinders progress and sin hurts others.

First, *sin hinders progress.* "Outbreaks of sin always entail disaster and delay. Neither we nor others can be where we might have been had they not occurred" (F. B. Meyer). We can be forgiven of our sin, but the sin will still cost us. Sin leaves many scars in our lives even though it is forgiven. Never take a light view of sin, for it will always hurt you even though forgiven.

Second, *sin hurts others.* Because of her sin, Miriam caused the whole camp of Israel to be delayed a week in their journey. Thus we learn here what we often learn in Scripture, namely, that "none of us liveth to himself" (Romans 14:7). Everything we do influences others—and a lot more than we think. And our sin adversely influences others. Some, especially sinning people, would deny this truth. They tell us it is none of our business how they want to live—but it is too our business; for how they live affects us. If someone wants to drink or gamble or steal or lie or commit adultery or do some other sin, we will be adversely affected by it in many ways. As an example, we pay much money in taxes because many in our country are immoral, booze up their money or gamble it away, and end up on welfare rolls—which our tax money supports. May we not be like those who have such an irresponsible attitude, but may we each live a life that will be a blessing and not a curse to others.

5. The Remembering of Miriam

The judgment of God upon Miriam was an incident God did not want the Israelites to forget. Therefore, we read in Scripture, "Remember what the LORD thy God did unto Miriam by the way" (Deuteronomy 24:9). All of God's judgments upon mankind are intended to be instructive. But sometimes in Scripture, He singles out some of His judgments to be especially remembered. When He does that, we need to be especially attentive to the incident. Another illustration of a judgment God specifically said He wanted us to remember was the judgment upon Lot's wife; for Christ said, "Remember Lot's wife" (Luke 17:32).

What can we particularly remember about Miriam's judgment? We can particularly remember the peril of pride and envy, the peril of ignoring Divine callings, the peril of presuming a calling, the peril of being more interested in earthly rank than in personal righteousness, and the peril of speaking against God's servant. We can also remember from her judgment the value of discipline. There are surely many other lessons to remember from her judgment, too. But if we will simply remember the ones we have listed here, we will save ourselves from much trouble in life, be a blessing instead of a burden to others, and bring much honor to our God.

XXVIII.

SPYING OF CANAAN

NUMBERS 13,14

THE MOST HURTFUL rebellion of the Israelites on their journey from Egypt to Canaan occurred at Kadesh (also called Kadesh-barnea) which is located on the northern border of the Paran wilderness. This rebellion came in the summer of the second year after the exodus from Egypt, and it came just as Israel was ordered to go into and possess Canaan. The rebellion was associated with the spying of the land of Canaan by twelve men appointed by Moses for the spying task. After the spies gave their report of the forty-day spying mission, the people became adamant in their refusal to believe God or obey God about Canaan. This led to the great rebellion which delayed Israel's entrance into Canaan by over thirty-eight years.

This tragic delay in Israel's journey to Canaan had to be a crushing disappointment for Moses. Just when it looked like his gallant work of leading Israel from Egypt to Canaan was about to come to a most triumphant conclusion, the rebellion occurred and the long delay of many years was announced by God. Only by great faith could Moses overcome this extreme disappointment. But Moses had that great faith in God, and it gave him great hope in God's promises and great steadfastness in obedience of God's precepts in spite of the extreme disappointment which he would experience in this delay.

To study this rebellion of the Israelites which is associated with the spying of the land of Canaan, we will note the record of the spying (13:1–25), the report of the spies (13:26–33), the response of the people (14:1–10), the reconciliation with God

(14:11–20), the retribution from God (14:21–39), and the revolt of the people (14:40–45).

A. THE RECORD OF THE SPYING

At Kadesh, near the southern border of Canaan, Moses sent spies into Canaan—the promised land—to examine it. We will note the injunction for the spying, the identity of the spies, the instructions for the spies, and the investigating by the spies.

1. The Injunction for the Spying

"And the LORD spake unto Moses, saying, Send thou men, that they may search the land of Canaan, which I give unto the children of Israel" (13:1,2). To examine this injunction for the spying, we will note the instigators of the injunction and the infliction in the injunction.

The instigators of the injunction. Bible students know that comparing Scripture with Scripture helps one to understand Scripture much better. Hence, when we compare the injunction in our text in Numbers with the record of the spying initiative as given in Deuteronomy, we discover not some inconsistencies in Scripture, as critics want us think, but the instigators of the command for Israel to spy out Canaan. The instigators of the command were the Israelites. Their desire for spies was declared right after Moses told the Israelites the time had come to enter Canaan. Moses said, "Ye are come unto the mountain of the Amorites, which the LORD our God doth give unto us. Behold, the LORD thy God hath set the land before thee: go up and possess it, as the LORD God of thy fathers hath said unto thee; fear not, neither be discouraged" (Deuteronomy 1:20,21). One would think the Israelites would have been overjoyed at this announcement and have begun immediately to go about moving into Canaan. But that was not the case at all. Instead, they "came near unto me [Moses] every one of you [them], and said, We will send men before us, and they shall search us out the land, and bring us word again by what way we must go up, and into what cities we shall come" (Deuteronomy 1:22).

This desire for spies may have sounded very prudent, but it was totally unnecessary. The Israelites did not need the spies to show them the way or to tell them about the land. They had the pillar above them to show them the way, and they had been repeatedly informed by God that the land was a good land, one that was "flowing with milk and honey" (Exodus 3:8). So why did they want to spy out the land? Obviously, the desire for spies "was the fruit of their unbelief . . . [which] would not take God's word that it was a good land, and that he would, without fail, put them in possession of it. They could not trust the pillar of cloud and fire to show them the way to it, but had a better opinion of their own politics [means wisdom, shrewdness here] than of God's wisdom. How absurd was it for them to send to spy out a land which God himself had spied out for them, to enquire the way into it when God himself had undertaken to show them the way" (Matthew Henry).

God saw the unbelief behind the Israelites' desire to spy out the land. He was not fooled by their attempt to hide unbelief under the guise of prudence. But Moses evidently did not see the unbelief in the desire for the spies, for when they spoke about spying the land, it "pleased me [Moses] well" (Deuteronomy 1:23). But the fact that Moses was pleased does not approve the spying. Furthermore, though Moses was pleased, he obviously took this request to God for His counsel which then resulted in God giving the injunction to spy.

The infliction in the injunction. If the spying out of the land was unnecessary and reflected unbelief, why then did God command Moses to send out spies? The answer is that God gave the command in order to punish Israel. Israel did not believe God about the promised land, so God in judgment let the Israelites have their unbelieving way, for the spying would only encourage their unbelief. This increased unbelief would result in a great rebellion in the camp which would keep Israel out of the promised land for many years. The Israelites got their way about the spying, but it kept them out of Canaan, for God would not allow unbelief to enter Canaan—"So we see that they could not enter in because of unbelief" (Hebrews 3:19).

As we have noted before, when rebellion insists on its own way, God in judgment sometimes grants the rebellious folk their way as a form of punishment. God did this to Israel when He granted them their desire for flesh shortly before the Kadesh spying incident (Numbers 11:18–20). God also did this when He granted Israel their desire for a king (I Samuel 8:4–7). And God did it here in regards to Israel's refusal to enter the land. So once again we are warned forcefully of the peril of insisting on our own way. The worst thing that can happen to us at times is to get our own way.

2. The Identity of the Spies

Twelve spies were selected to do the spying of Canaan. One was selected from each tribe except from the tribe of Levi. The Levites were excluded because they were the priests. Their place was taken by making Joseph two tribes through his sons Manasseh and Ephraim. The names of the twelve spies (the tribe each represents is in parenthesis) as given in Numbers 13:4–16 are Shammua (Reuben), Shaphat (Simeon), Caleb (Judah), Igal (Issachar), Oshea who was Joshua (Ephraim), Palti (Benjamin), Gadielel (Zebulun), Gaddi (Manasseh), Ammiel (Dan), Sethur (Asher), Nahbi (Naphtali), and Geuel (Gad). "All those men were heads of the children of Israel" (13:3); but as ten of these men evidence, being a head of a tribe does not guarantee faith! Position among men is not synonymous with faith and character. In fact, most people in high positions of the world are just like the ten spies; for they are filled with unbelief.

Only the names of the two men with faith, Caleb and Joshua, are recognizable today. The other ten names have gone into oblivion because of their unbelief. Mention their names and no one knows who you are talking about. But mention Joshua and Caleb, and it is a different story. It will be the same in eternity and even more so.

In the listing of the twelve spies, an instructive notation is made about the name change of Joshua. Scripture says, "Moses called Oshea, the son of Nun, Jehoshua [elsewhere shortened to Joshua]" (13:16). Oshea (or Hoshea or Hosea) is also the name of an Old Testament prophet who wrote a book in the Bible named after him, and it is the name of the last king of Israel (the Northern Kingdom). The name Joshua is a most significant name, for it the same as Jesus (the Hebrew "Yeshua" [Joshua] is "Iesous" in the Greek, "Jesu" in Latin, and "Jesus" in the English), and it means "Jehovah saves" (some render it "Jehovah is our salvation" or "Jehovah is deliverance" which means the same). By both his name and leadership, Joshua pictures Jesus Christ. Winterbotham says about the name of Joshua, "The fact that our Savior received the same name because he was our Savior throws a halo of glory about it [the name Joshua] which we cannot ignore. In the Divine providence Hoshea became Joshua because he was destined to be the temporal savior of his people, and to lead them into their promised rest." If we were named for our service for God, would the name honor God?

3. The Instructions for the Spies

"And Moses sent them to spy out the land of Canaan, and said unto them, Get you up this way southward, and go up into the mountain: And see the land, what it is; and the people that dwelleth therein, whether they be strong or weak, few or many; And what the land is that they dwell in, whether it be good or bad; and what cities they be that they dwell in, whether in tents, or in strong holds; And what the land is, whether it be fat or lean, whether there be wood therein, or not. And be ye of good courage, and bring of the fruit of the land" (13:17–20). The instructions were fourfold and concerned the people of the land, the protection of the land, the products of the land, and the pluckiness in the land.

First, the *people* of the land. The spies were to see "whether they [the people of the land] be strong or weak, few or many" (v. 18). Israel did not need to know how many people were in the land or how strong or weak they were in order to possess the land. God was able to give them the land whether He must drive out many or few or whether they were weak or strong. But because the Israelites chose to walk in unbelief, God decreed that they know this information; for such information feeds the hearts of unbelief with great fear. The increased fear and alarm is a form of Divine judgment upon the Israelites for not trusting in God's Word.

Second, the *protection* of the land. The spies were told to see if the people "dwell in . . . tents, or in strong holds" (v. 19). Again this was information the Israelites did not need to know in order to possess the land. God was able to deliver the land to the Israelites whether the inhabitants of the land were in nothing but defenseless tents or were barricaded behind strong fortresses. But this information obtained by the spies would encourage their unbelief and increase their fears. When we choose to walk by sight rather than by faith, we have no one to blame for our fears but ourselves.

Third, the *products* of the land. The spies were to see if the land was "fat or lean, whether there be wood therein or not . . . and bring of the fruit of the land" (v. 20). They did not need to know this information before they began to possess the land either. God had repeatedly told them it was a great land. But they doubted. Here the spies would, however, bring home great proof of the veracity of God's Word. But unbelief can look evidence right in the face and still be uninspired to believe.

Fourth, the *pluckiness* in the land. Moses exhorted the spies to "be ye of good courage" (v. 20). They would need some courage to go through the land where to be discovered could mean their death. But the command to have a plucky attitude in spying out the land cannot be limited to just the time of spying but also to the whole business of possessing Canaan. Only two of the twelve had that continuation of the courage in their lives. "The wicked flee when no man pursueth: but the righteous are bold as a lion" (Proverbs 28:1). Faith brings courage; unbelief does just the opposite in regards to obeying God.

4. The Investigating by the Spies

"They went up, and searched the land from the wilderness of Zin unto Rehob . . . And they came unto the brook of Eshcol, and cut down from thence a branch with one cluster of grapes, and they bare it between two upon a staff; and they brought of the pomegranates, and of the figs . . . And they returned from searching of the land after forty days" (vv. 21,23,25). We note the distance, the days, and the displays of the investigation.

The distance. The spying mission went all the way from the camp in Kadesh through the wilderness of Zin (on the south of Canaan) all the way up to Rehob (northern border area of Canaan) and then back south through Hebron and to the Israelites' camp again. The spies could, therefore, see that the land was indeed "large" as God had promised (Exodus 3:8). This was part of the abundant evidence the spies would see that God's promises regarding the land were indeed true. But except for Joshua and Caleb, the spies rejected the evidence. So the spy trip only increased the condemnation of unbelief.

The days. The spies took forty days for the spying mission. The forty days gave them ample time to discover that what God had said about the land was true. The spies could not complain that God did not give them enough time to discover whether His promises were true or not. Significantly, the number forty is often associated with testing in the Scripture. The forty days certainly did test the spies' faith, and ten of them failed the test badly. God always gives us enough time to decide for Him. When God brings judgment upon mankind, they can never complain that He did not give them opportunity to repent.

The displays. The spies brought back some great displays of the productiveness of the land of Canaan. The cluster of grapes from Eshcol was so large that it took two men to carry it. Pomegranates and figs were also brought back by the spies. In all of this we are again impressed with the great evidence of the truth of God's promises. God had said He would bring them "unto a good land and a large, unto a land flowing with milk and honey" (Exodus 3:8, cp. Exodus 3:17, 13:5, 33:3, Leviticus 20:24). "Milk and honey" represent more than just those products but speak symbolically of a fruitful land. The spies verified all of this abundantly. However, they (except Caleb and Joshua) also verified that unbelief pays no attention to evidences as we have been noting repeatedly. Unbelief is a matter of the will, not a matter of lack of evidences. Though the evidence was tremendous, as the cluster of grapes illustrates, unbelief refused to obey. Unbelief did the same with Christ. When Christ "showed himself alive after his passion by many infallible proofs" (Acts 1:3), multitudes still rejected Him. Let us all pray that every particle of unbelief will be driven out of our hearts.

B. THE REPORT OF THE SPIES

After spying out the land of Canaan for forty days, the twelve spies returned "to Moses, and to Aaron, and to all the congregation of the children of Israel, unto the wilderness of Paran, to Kadesh; and brought back word unto them, and unto all the congregation, and showed them the fruit of the land" (13:26). The report was a divided report. There was the majority report of the ten spies and the minority report of two spies (Caleb and Joshua). The majority report reached a far different conclusion than the minority report. The majority report was a bad report, but the minority report was a good report.

1. The Majority Report

To examine the majority report, we will note seven features of the report. They are the duration of the report, the dishonesty of the report, the dismalness of the report, the deduction of the report, the disagreement in the report, the disbelief in the report, and the despising in the report.

First, the *duration* of the report. Of the seven verses given for the initial report of the spies, six of them (13:27–29, 31–33) concern the majority report. In this world evil often gets to say much more than goodness does. Turn on the radio or TV or read the newspaper and it is the same, for most of what you hear and see and read is error, not truth. But the length of the report does not sanctify it. Hence, do not be deceived into accepting error just because it takes up the most space in the newspaper or on the library shelves or has the most time on radio or TV.

Second, the *dishonesty* of the report. The majority report was not truthful. The overall character of the report is stated in verse 32 where it is called an "evil report." The word "evil" in that verse means "slander, calumny" (Gesenius). Hence, the report was dishonest. It did not represent the situation in the land of Canaan truthfully. It would have the Israelites believe the land "eateth up the inhabitants thereof" (v. 32) which was not true. It also stated that "all the people that we saw in it [the land] are men of great stature" (Ibid.) which, of course, was not true. Some were of tall stature, but definitely not "all." Then they exaggerated (which is a form of lying) when they said they (the spies) were "grasshoppers . . . in their sight" (v. 33).

Some Christians are like the spies, in that the way they live, they give a dishonest report about the faith. "If . . . we are gloomy and desponding in our spirit, and complaining in our language—then is it not evident that we give an evil report of the land, for we give a false impression of the promises and of the nature of the Christian life" (Wagner).

Third, the *dismalness* of the report. After the initial statement that the land "floweth with milk and honey" (v. 27) and after showing the people "the fruit of the land [the big cluster of grapes plus the pomegranates and figs]" (v. 26), those making the majority report then spent the rest of their time emphasizing the negative aspects of the land. We still have people like that today. They view everything from a dismal point of view. They only emphasize the negatives in their life. They look mostly at the blessings, not the burdens. They give little consideration to possibilities but much consideration to problems. This kind will never get in the promised land but will live forever in the wilderness. They will oppose every advancement by the church, discourage people on every hand from pursuing any difficult endeavor, and accomplish very little in their own life.

Fourth, the *deduction* of the report. "We be not able to go up against the people; for they are stronger than we" (v. 31). Those making the majority report insisted Israel could not conquer the land. The reason they came to this conclusion is that they left out God. God had promised to give the land to the Israelites. But these spies did not consider God; they only considered the circumstances which they could see when they made their conclusion. If you leave out God, then, of course, nothing is possible. Israel would never have gotten out of Egypt or as far on the journey as they then were without the great power of God. Measure difficulties by human strength and you will be overwhelmed by the slightest of difficulties.

Fifth, the *disagreement* in the report. People who do not tell the truth often contradict themselves. The majority report manifested this problem. Initially it said the land "floweth with milk and honey" (v. 27) which meant the land was a good land to live in. But later it said the "land eateth up the inhabitants thereof" (v. 32). Beware of those whose talk is contradictory. It is an indication that all is not right. Politicians are notorious for having this habit. They talk out of both sides of their mouth. Those with character speak otherwise.

Sixth, the *disbelief* in the report. The Psalmist says of the spies and Israel here, "They believed not his word" (Psalm 106:24). That, of course, accounts for all the bad features of the report. We should not be surprised about all the unbelief in the report, for the request to Moses for spies was motivated by unbelief as we have already noted. And, as we have noted earlier, their unbelief will bring the judgment of God upon them. No one does well where it counts the most who does not believe God's Word. He may advance clever arguments to cast doubt on the veracity of the Word of God, but the cleverness of the arguments will not change the character of the Word of God but only increase the severity of the judgment upon unbelief.

Seventh, the *despising* in the report. The ten spies' unbelief so fouled up their thinking that they "despised the pleasant land" (Psalm 106:24) and so gave a bad report of it. This caused the other unbelieving Israelites to also despise the land. Unbelief always despises the good things of God. It despises morality, honesty, decency, the preaching of the Word of God, prayer, church, and other choice blessings. Beware of unbelief. It can ruin discernment and understanding in the most important areas of life. It can cause you to chose hell instead of heaven.

2. The Minority Report

How differently do people who live by faith in God react to facts than do those who live in unbelief and rebellion of God. The minority report was very different than the majority report even though it was given by men who saw exactly the same things that those giving the majority report saw.

We noted seven features of the majority report, here we will note seven features of the minority report. They are the speaker of the report, the sincerity of the report, the shortness of the report, the stilling in the report, the service in the report, the stoutheartedness in the report, and the sureness in the report.

First, the *speaker* of the report. Scripture informs us that Caleb (13:30) gave the minority report (we are not told who or how many gave the majority report). Caleb spoke most nobly in this report; but he was not just a man of words, he was also a man of deeds. His talk matched his walk as one will see in the book of Joshua and Judges. Some folk are fine speakers; but unlike Caleb, they do not practice what they preach.

Second, the *sincerity* of the report. Unlike the majority report, the minority report was not given deceitfully. It was a truthful and factual report. It did not pervert the facts, exaggerate, give undo emphasis to difficulties, contradict itself, or dishonor the Word of God. It was not a clever manipulation of the facts to mislead the multitude. The report was spoken with godly sincerity.

Third, the *shortness* of the report. As we noted when examining the majority report, the minority report was the shortest of the two reports. It takes up but one verse (13:30) compared to the six it takes to report the majority report. The shortness is, however, no call for short sermons as the carnal would like us to think; but it represents what is oftentimes the case in the world, namely, lies get the most time and attention but truth gets little time and attention. And you will note that truth did not get to speak first either. Lies seems to always get the first say.

Fourth, the *stilling* in the report. "Caleb stilled the people" (13:30). Much noise was connected with the majority report, and so Caleb had to still the people before he could make the minority report. Stilling the people has some good lessons. For one thing it underscores the wisdom of stilling the audience before one speaks. Paul stilled the people before he spoke (Acts 21:40), and today a preacher sometimes has to still bawling babies (who ought to be in the nursery) and talkative congregation members before he can preach. Some get upset when he stills the crowd; but if they valued the message properly, they would not get upset about removing distractions to the message. Another lesson in the stilling matter is that the truth stills and calms the heart. The majority report caused a great commotion among the people, but truth will bring calmness if received.

Fifth, the *service* in the report. The minority report, given by Caleb, said, "Let us go up at once, and possess it [the land of Canaan]" (13:30). The majority did not want to serve God as commanded, but the minority did. And note the promptness of this service. Caleb said they should go up "at once" to possess the land. True faith and obedience will be prompt in obeying. Unbelief delays and procrastinates (one of the reasons for wanting the spying mission). But delay in obedience and in serving God is a good way to lose your blessings. All of the Israelites (except two) who were twenty years and over at that time of the spying mission never possessed the land at all because they would not go up "at once" to possess the land of Canaan. Procrastination in God's service is a loser all the way.

Sixth, the *stoutheartedness* in the report. "Let us go up at once, and possess it" (13:30). In view of the strength of the

675

enemy, it would take courage to obey the command of God to possess the land. But faith has courage to obey God. Unbelief does not. Often people view Christians as weaklings who lack courage and are afraid of their own shadow. Thus Christians are sometimes called sissies and other like names by these caustic critics of Christianity. But the truth of the matter is that it takes great courage to live by faith in God. The cowards were those of the majority who wilted at the thought of going against the opposition in the promised land. Faith does not wilt, however; it has courage to obey God regardless of the circumstances.

Seventh, the *sureness* in the report. "We are well able to overcome it" (13:30). The minority report was one of faith, not unbelief. It was sure of success. Their "well able" statement was not, however, just some whistling in the dark; for it did not disregard realities ("overcome" indicated they recognized there was opposition to fight), and neither did it disregard potentialities (for later Caleb amplified on the fact that the "LORD . . . will bring us into this land, and give it us" [14:8]). The minority report had confidence in God to give them the land. It saw the problems, but it also saw God. The majority report, however, did not take God into the situation. They were too busy looking at themselves and their problems (13:33).

C. THE RESPONSE OF THE PEOPLE
The response of the Israelites to the two reports was a disastrous response. To examine their response, we will note the crying of the people, the criticism by the people, the conspiracy of the people, the counsel for the people, and the cruelty of the people.

1. The Crying of the People
"And all the congregation lifted up their voice, and cried; and the people wept that night" (14:1). The first response which Scripture records of the Israelites to the two reports was their crying. This indicated Israel's acceptance of the majority report and their rejection of the minority report. It said they chose to go the way of unbelief in God and not the way of faith.

676

Sorrow is always the eventual result of unbelief in God. Unbelief does not fill the world with joy! The devil, however, advertises unbelief as the way of fun and games and describes Christianity as a killjoy lifestyle and says Christians will never have any fun in life if they are going to adhere to Biblical teaching. But experience will always end up showing that the saint of God is the one with real joy and the unbeliever is the one with great sorrow. "Weeping and gnashing of teeth" (Luke 13:28) will be the eternal experience of unbelievers. But in heaven, "God shall wipe away all tears" (Revelation 21:4). Both faith and unbelief beckon to us in life. Unbelief, like the majority report, is generally more popular and louder and gets more attention; but it is the way of sorrow. "The pleasures of sin [are only] for a season" (Hebrews 11:25); and that season, which is extremely short at its best, is only in this life, not in eternity.

2. The Criticism by the People

The crying was followed by criticizing. This indicated that the response of the Israelites to the reports was getting worse. They criticized their leaders, their living, and their Lord.

They criticized their leaders. "And all the children of Israel murmured against Moses and against Aaron" (14:2). Moses is again under attack. Unbelief always attacks those who represent faith. Those who would lead the people to faith in God will not be unacquainted with this constant criticism. Hence, if you are going to make it in the ministry, you had better have thick skin or you will soon throw in the towel. Note that Aaron is also included in this criticism. He has been included before; but the last time Moses was criticized, Aaron was one of the criticizers. He discovered in the judgment upon Miriam that criticizing God's man was not a smart thing to do. Here he must have been humbled by the unjust criticism when it reminded him of the unjust criticism he had made of Moses earlier.

They criticized their living. "Would God that we had died in the land of Egypt! or would God we had died in this wilderness!" (14:2). Unbelief certainly is foolish and fatalistic. These Israelites were critical of the fact that they were alive! How dumb! The unbelief of these Israelites caused them to wish they had already died either in Egypt or in the wilderness rather than try to conquer Canaan. What these complaining Israelites did not know at the time of their complaining was that they will get their wish to die in the wilderness as we will see later. God punished them by granting them their wish. Matthew Henry diagnoses their attitude well. He said, "How base were the spirits of these degenerate Israelites, who, rather than die . . . like soldiers on the bed of honor with their swords in their hands, desire to die like rotten sheep in the wilderness." Nothing is noble at all about their attitude here. But unbelief does not produce noble attitudes about life and death.

They criticized their Lord. "And wherefore hath the LORD brought us unto this land, to fall by the sword, that our wives and our children should be a prey?" (14:3). In criticizing God, the Israelites now plainly state the real problem in their hearts. Criticizing Moses and Aaron and then criticizing the fact they were still alive had simply been a disguised criticism of God. These folks do not like God's way for their life. Here they try hard to make it sound like God's way is cruel and uncaring.

When troubles come to unbelieving men, they like to blame God for it all. They may start out by blaming their fellow man; but eventually, if their criticism is not checked, it will go after God. So folk blame God for sickness, accidents, lack of employment, wars, poverty, crime, and anything else they can think of. Such criticism not only reflects unbelief in God, but it also reflects irresponsibility, rebellion, and stupidity. And it will solve no problems, but it will only aggravate them.

3. The Conspiracy of the People

"Were it not better for us to return into Egypt? . . . Let us make a captain, and let us return into Egypt" (14:3,4). The response of the people to the reports now progresses to a conspiracy. The conspiracy involved a ridiculous conclusion by the people and a replacement captain for the people.

Ridiculous conclusion. "Were it not better for us to return into Egypt" is an utterly ridiculous conclusion. Matthew Poole described it well when he said of this conclusion, "Stupendous madness! Whence should they have protection against the many hazards and provision against all the wants of the wilderness? Could they expect either God's cloud to cover and guide them, or manna from heaven to feed them? Who should conduct them over the Red Sea? or, if they went another way, who should defend them against those nations whose borders they were to pass? What entertainment could they expect from the Egyptians, whom they had deserted and brought to so much ruin?" Unbelief thinks so stupidly. It will criticize God's will as impractical (entering Canaan in Israel's case), but then propose a plan that is ridiculously impractical. It will criticize the Biblical explanations of history and origins as foolish, but its alternative explanations are so stupid that they insult everyone's intelligence. Unbelief is no improvement of faith; it only worsens situations.

Replacement captain. "Let us make a captain, and let us return to Egypt." Nehemiah 9:17 says they did indeed appoint a new captain. "In their rebellion [they] appointed a captain to return to their bondage." The Israelites, like many churches, wanted a leader who would lead them as they wanted to go, not as God wanted them to go. And, unfortunately, there are many men in every age who will be more than glad to be the appointed captain (or pastor) for this kind; for they are not interested in pleasing God but in pleasing man. Such men are only hirelings and not true shepherds in character. Thus, they will be a curse to every group they lead.

"This proposal to depose him [Moses], and choose another in his place, marked the extremity of the despair, the unbelief, and the ingratitude of the people" (Wagner). This conspiracy to replace Moses was also the worst revolt against Moses thus far in Israel's journey from Egypt to Canaan. And it would cost them dearly, too; for instead of saving their lives, this conspiracy caused them to lose their lives. The effort to replace Moses was, however, a great compliment for Moses; for it said Moses was no compromiser. He would only lead Israel as God wanted them led. If they wanted to go another direction they would have to get another leader. Oh, for more pastors like that today.

4. The Counsel for the People

Moses, Aaron, Joshua, and Caleb all gave counsel to the Israelites to attempt to get them to respond better to the reports. But the people did not heed the counsel. "The friends of Israel here interpose to save them if possible from ruining themselves, but in vain. The physicians of their state would have healed them, but they would not be healed; their watchmen gave them warning, but they would not take warning" (Henry). The counsel of these men was given in two ways. It was given in their actions and in their arguments.

Their actions. "Then Moses and Aaron fell on their faces before all the assembly . . . And Joshua . . . and Caleb . . . rent their clothes" (14:5,6). These actions were pronounced outward reactions to the Israelites' unbelieving, rebellious, and insurrectionist conduct. Some will criticize and say that Moses, Aaron, Joshua, and Caleb should have been more restrained in their reactions. Sinners get upset at any reaction against their sin— that is generally why policemen are attacked at times for the way they arrest a criminal. But we need to evidence a strong reaction to sin to show how sinful it is. We do not need to act stupid and strange, but we need to act in a forceful enough way that a clear message of protest is sent to the sinners. The actions of Moses, Aaron, Joshua, and Caleb were proper and noble ways in their days for showing their great disapproval of evil. Today, Christians need to show a lot more forceful reaction to evil than they do. Rather than being passive when dirty stories are told, we need to walk out of the room. Some will laugh and mock, but the message of protest will be plain and and pungent, and that is important. When unholy music occurs in church, God's people need to get up and walk out rather than sit there and listen and compromise. If those who oppose such music would be more pronounced in their protesting actions, we might not have so much of the wretched music in our churches. Also, Christians need to stop giving money to churches and schools that have changed their policies to conform and appeal to the world. We counsel people by our actions, and too often our actions against sin are so mild that folk think we approve.

Their arguments. Moses, Joshua, and Caleb presented good arguments to the Israelites to encourage them to go into Canaan to possess the land. The arguments of Moses are recorded in Deuteronomy 1:29–31, that of Joshua and Caleb in Numbers 14:7–9. The arguments of these men addressed four areas: the capability of the Lord, the character of the land, the condition of the inhabitants, and the commands for the people.

First, the *capability of the Lord*. Moses especially stressed this point. He said, "The LORD your God which goeth before you, he shall fight for you, according to all that he did for you in Egypt before our eyes; And in the wilderness, where thou hast seen how that the LORD thy God bare thee, as a man doth bear his son, in all the way that ye went, until ye came into this place" (Deuteronomy 1:30,31). This certainly was wise counsel. Moses pointed to all the tremendous work God had done in the past on behalf of Israel. If God could do all of that, surely He can defeat the people in the land of Canaan. To buoy up our faith in difficult times, we will do well to look back at what God has already done for us. And we also need to look at Scripture to see what God has done in the past for others. "For whatsoever things were written aforetime were written for our learning, that we through patience and comfort of the scriptures might have hope" (Romans 15:4).

Second, the *character of the land*. Joshua and Caleb had

seen the land, and so their arguments put great emphasis upon the excellence of the land. "And they spake unto all the company of the children of Israel, saying, The land, which we passed through to search it, is an exceeding good land . . . a land which floweth with milk and honey" (14:7,8). The Israelites had "despised" the land (Psalm 106:24), but Joshua and Caleb told them they have no reason to despise it, rather they ought to greatly desire it. The fact that the land is "exceeding good" ought to motivate them to try to possess it at the least. But the Israelites, like so many in the world, had listened to the wrong people about the blessings of God and, therefore, despised them. Likewise, if you listen to ungodly professors, apostate ministers, and the liberal news media talk about Christ, the Bible, and good morals, you certainly will not think well of Christ, the Bible, and good morals.

Third, the *condition of the inhabitants*. Joshua and Caleb could speak on this subject, too; for as spies, they had seen the condition of the inhabitants of Canaan. The inhabitants of Canaan had been described by the majority report as too strong to overcome, but Joshua and Caleb describe them much differently—"They are bread for us: their defence is departed from them, and the LORD is with us" (14:9). To help understand the forcefulness of this description of the inhabitants of the land, we need to know that the phrase "their defence is departed" literally says "their shadow is departed." This indicates that what shielded them, such as a cloud shadows us from the hot rays of the sun, is departed from them. This phrase was a figure of speech used by Orientals then; and "The departing of the shadow was regarded as an indication of some evil . . . So that the meaning of the phrase, 'their defence is departed' from them, is, that the favor of God was now lost to those [the inhabitants] whose iniquities were full . . . and transferred to the Israelites ['the LORD is with us']" (Jamieson). The inhabitants of the land may be strong; but when God has departed from them and has come to help the Israelites, the inhabitants will indeed be "bread for us." This argument does not deny the reality of difficulties, but it puts the difficulties in proper perspective. The Israelites should have listened. When God is with us, no force can overcome us.

Fourth, the *commands for the people*. The commands were twofold—do not dread and do not disobey.

(1) *Do not dread*. Moses said, "Dread not, neither be afraid of them" (Deuteronomy 1:29), and Joshua and Caleb said the same when they exhorted the people, "Neither fear ye the people of the land . . . fear them not" (14:9). The majority report created much fear and no faith. The minority report would encourage faith and remove fear if it was heeded. Unbelief does not remove fear but encourages it. Faith does just the opposite.

(2) *Do not disobey*. Joshua and Caleb exhorted, "Only rebel not ye against the LORD" (14:9). Disobedience will remove Divine help. God's help was conditioned on "If the LORD delight in us" (14:8). He will not delight in them if they disobey Him. Israel was not very concerned, however, about whether God was delighted with them or not. Neither are most mankind. Men seemed concerned about delighting many others, but delighting the Lord does not interest many. This failure will cost them dearly as we will note shortly.

5. The Cruelty of the People

"But all the congregation bade stone them with stones. And the glory of the LORD appeared in the tabernacle of the congregation before all the children of Israel" (14:10). Here we examine the response of the people to the noble counsel of the four men. The response was a very cruel response. We note this in the plan for the cruelty and the prohibiting of the cruelty.

The plan for the cruelty. After the four men had pleaded with the Israelites to reconsider and go in and possess the land of Canaan, "all the congregation bade stone them with stones." The Israelites had their minds absolutely closed to the truth and would not tolerate those who spoke the truth. They wanted to stone them to death. When men's hearts are set on doing evil, they will attack with cruelty anything that represents opposition to their evil. That explains why some pastors are treated so poorly. It is also why Christians are persecuted. When one dares to proclaim or live God's way, he is exposing himself to the potential of cruel treatment.

The prohibiting of the cruelty. The "glory of the LORD" suddenly appeared on the scene to save the four men. The great cruelty of the evil of the people is underscored by the fact that such dramatic Divine intervention was necessary to save the four men. God does not forsake His faithful servants. God delivers them from hostilities in due time. But that deliverance may not always be the saving of His servants' earthly lives, though that is what it did here. Matthew Henry expressed the right prospective about this when he said, "Those who faithfully expose themselves for God are sure to be taken under his special protection, and shall be hidden from the rage of men, either under heaven or in heaven." The martyrs of Christ are hidden from the rage of men "in heaven."

D. THE RECONCILIATION WITH GOD
Israel's rebellion against God about going into Canaan put them in great need of reconciliation if they were going to experience anything but annihilation. That reconciliation came through the mediation of Moses. To further examine this reconciling with God, we will note the provocations for reconciliation, the praying for reconciliation, and the providing of reconciliation.

1. The Provocations for Reconciliation
"And the LORD said unto Moses, How long will this people provoke me? and how long will it be ere they believe me, for all the signs which I have showed among them? I will smite them with the pestilence, and disinherit them, and will make of thee a greater nation and mightier than they" (14:11,12). Moses stood between God and Israel. "What passed between God and Israel went through the hands of Moses: when they were displeased

with God they told Moses of it (14:2); when God was displeased with them he told Moses, too [14:11,12]" (Henry). To examine the provocations which made reconciliation with God imperative, we will note the determinant of the sin, the duration of the sin, the defenselessness of the sin, and the damnation for the sin.

Determinant of the sin. "How long will it be ere they believe me?" (v. 11). Israel's unbelief was the primary cause of God being provoked with Israel. Unbelief was the root cause of all of Israel's poor conduct at Kadesh. Unbelief is always the main determinant of sin. Faith purifies, but unbelief defiles. We live in a nation and a world that is submerged in unbelief—one reason we know this fact is because our nation and world are so defiled. In our churches we also have a great amount of unbelief. Even though many church members insist they believe, their foul lifestyles tell us they do not.

Duration of the sin. Twice in verse 11 God asked "How long?" the people would continue to sin against Him. He asked, "How long will this people provoke me? and "how long will it be ere they believe me?" Let us remember that "The God of heaven keeps an account [of] how long sinners persist in their provocations; and the longer they persist the more he is displeased" (Henry). The sooner we stop and forsake our sin, the better it will be for us. Israel had provoked God and manifested unbelief on the entire journey from Egypt until now. The "How long?" question implies that God's grace has a limit, and it does; for "My spirit shall not always strive with man" (Genesis 6:3).

Defenselessness of the sin. Israel had no excuse for their sin. "All the signs which I have showed among them" (v. 11) emphasized that fact. These signs included the great plagues in Egypt, the parting of the Red Sea, sweetening the bitter waters at Marah, providing manna six days every week for the last year, the water from the rock at Horeb, the marvelous manifestations of God at Mount Horeb, the tremendous supply of quail,

685

and the constant presence of the pillar of cloud by day and fire by night. Israel's unbelief could not be justified in the slightest, for they had so many signs to encourage their faith. We are in a similar situation today. We have the written Word of God in our possession plus many other spiritual opportunities which gives us far greater advantage for faith than any people before us. We have no excuse whatsoever for unbelief.

Damnation for the sin. "I will smite them with the pestilence, and disinherit them, and will make of thee a greater nation and mightier than they" (v. 12). The judgment which God declared here upon Israel for their great sin at Kadesh was twofold: death and disinheritance. God would kill all the current Israelites, and He would start a new nation with Moses. This was severe judgment, but it was just. And it underscored Israel's urgent need for reconciliation with God if they were going to experience any kind of survival. Sinners today likewise stand in great need of reconciliation because of the damnation on their sin; for without being reconciled to God through the blood of Jesus Christ, they will end up in hell fire for all eternity.

2. The Praying for Reconciliation

As Moses did at Sinai after the great sin of idolatry, so here he again becomes Israel's intercessor. How much Israel owed to this godly man. His great intercessory work saved them from destruction. "Therefore he [God] said that he would destroy them, had not Moses his chosen stood before him in the breach, to turn away his wrath, lest he should destroy them" (Psalm 106:23). Charles Simeon in commenting on the intercessory work of Moses and applying it to the blessing saints are to the world said, "Little does the world think how much they are indebted to the saints. They are the cluster for the sake of which the vineyard of the Lord is spared, the elect, for whose sake the days of vengeance have been often shortened; the little remnant, without which the whole world would long since have been made as Sodom and Gomorrah."

To study Moses' great intercessory prayer, we will note the seeking in his prayer, the support for his prayer, the saintliness of his prayer, and the sagacity of his prayer.

The seeking in his prayer. Moses sought blessing for Israel. In examining his request for blessing, we will note what blessing he sought and how he sought the blessing.

First, *what blessing he sought.* Moses was seeking forgiveness for the Israelites. His desire for Israel is summed up in "Pardon, I beseech thee, the iniquity of this people according unto the greatness of thy mercy" (14:19). Moses sought for Israel what they most needed. They did not need money, food, clothes, jobs, or other things of this world. Those may be legitimate needs of men, but let us never forget that mankind's most important need is forgiveness of his sins. Churches too often get carried away with the other needs of mankind and ignore the greatest need of all. Those who emphasize salvation as the primary need of men are often criticized for neglecting the other needs. But far better to be poor and without many things of this world and yet go to heaven when you die than to have all these other things but go to hell when you die.

Second, *how he sought for the blessing.* Moses sought the blessing of forgiveness on the basis of mercy. It was "according unto the greatness of thy mercy" (14:19) that Moses asked for pardon for the people. He did not foolishly pray that God would forgive them because of their merit. But we have many today who think that is the way to get to heaven. To ask for pardon because of Israel's merit here in the wilderness is ridiculous, but no more so than to ask for soul salvation on the basis of merit. We are sinners like Israel and merit judgment, not salvation! Plead for mercy if you want to be saved from Divine judgment.

The support for his prayer. When we pray, we need to have some good support for our requests. Moses had two great pillars to support his request for pardon for Israel. They were the glory of God and the Word of God.

First, the *glory of God*. Moses began his prayer for Israel's pardon by emphasizing that the glory of God was involved in pardoning Israel. If God brought death and disinheritance to the Israelites (14:12), "Then the Egyptians shall hear it . . . And they will tell it" (14:13,14). And what Egypt would tell is that "The LORD was not able to bring this people into the land which he sware unto them" (14:16) and that would dishonor God. So Moses pleads the honor of God as a reason for granting pardon. This gave Moses excellent support for the answering of his prayer. Many of our prayers are not answered because they reflect a desire for personal glory, not God's glory.

Second, the *Word of God*. "I beseech thee, let the power of my LORD be great, according as thou hast spoken" (14:17). Moses also based his prayer upon God's Word ("according as thou hast spoken"). This, too, is wise praying. Too often we base our prayers on our fleshly wants and desires, but not on God's Word. If you want to make headway in your prayer life, make sure your prayers are in conformity with the Word of God.

The saintliness of his prayer. The saintliness of Moses' prayer is seen in its kindness and its unselfishness.

First, *kindness*. The people were being cruel to Moses, but in his praying Moses was being kind to them. While the people were plotting to replace him, he was praying that God would not replace them. When the people were ready to hurl stones at him to kill him, he was hurling supplications at God to keep the people alive. As he did when he prayed for Miriam, so Moses did here—he prayed "for them which despitefully use you, and persecute you" (Matthew 5:44). It takes great faith to be so kind. Our lack of kindness reflects our lack of faith.

Second, *unselfishness*. God had offered to start a new nation with Moses (14:12). This would have been a great personal honor for Moses, but his prayer indicated that he was not interested in personal honor especially when it was at the expense of God's honor and at the expense of the welfare of the Israelites. How great was Moses' unselfishness! How much better would be our prayers if we were as unselfish in our praying. "Let us ponder the lesson; and when next a dear delight is within our reach, and it will be more for the glory of God and the good of others to turn from it, let us ask grace to take the rugged path of the wilderness, though it mean a lonely life for forty years, and a death on Pisgah" (F. B. Meyer).

The sagacity of his prayer. "The Lord . . . by no means clearing the guilty" (14:18). Moses wisely included justice in his prayer as is seen by the "by no means clearing the guilty" statement of his prayer. Mercy is not apart from justice. God does not forgive sinners apart from Calvary (justice). Moses, while seeking pardon, did not seek escape from the chastening hand of God. He did not want God to disinherit the people, but he realized that some form of judgment must come in order for the people to realize the great sinfulness of their sin. So when we note next the pardoning by God of Israel, it will not be apart from retribution upon Israel for their sin. This is a lesson not recognized well today in society. We think forgiveness cancels out every form of punishment. But it does not. We can forgive the criminal, but he still must be punished properly. We can forgive our children, but they still must be chastened for their wrongs. We can forgive sinning church members, but they still must be disciplined by the church in the interest of holiness.

3. The Providing of Reconciliation

"And the LORD said, I have pardoned according to thy word" (v. 20). The reconciliation illustrates the plenitude of the mercy of God and the potential of prayer to God.

The plenitude of mercy. The Psalmist says, "For thou, Lord, art good, and ready to forgive; and plenteous in mercy" (Psalm 86:5). The pardoning of Israel here certainly demonstrates the truth of that verse in Psalms. Israel did not deserve any pardon at all. They had sinned against God repeatedly and never seemed to learn any lessons from God's chastening hand. Yet,

God pardoned them anyway. Truly His mercy is plenteous beyond human comprehension. And it is His great mercy that makes Him "ready to forgive" men of their sins.

The potential of prayer. Moses prayed and a nation was saved! One man can certainly accomplish much in prayer! That should really encourage us to pray. We are so taken up with fleshly methods and programs today that we forget about the potential of prayer. Many folk think they cannot do much because they lack talent, position, wealth, and other things the flesh thinks so important. But all can pray. And if you can pray, you can do much for God. How much more the church could do in the work of the Lord if it had members who knew how to pray effectively. Also, much needed blessings could be obtained for our nation if we had citizens who could pray effectively.

E. THE RETRIBUTION FROM GOD

Moses was successful in obtaining reconciliation with God for Israel: but, as we have noted above, the reconciliation did not completely eliminate all judgment for Israel. The judgment Moses prevented was the disinheriting of Israel. God would not start over with Moses or someone else. However, though disinheritance will not now take place, the retribution upon Israel for their evil will still be great. To examine this revised judgment upon Israel, we will note the causes of the retribution, the crowd for the retribution, and the character of the retribution.

1. The Causes of the Retribution

We note three causes God gave for the revised retribution for the Israelites. They, of course, are the same problems which God cited earlier to Moses concerning what provoked God about Israel's behavior. Though we have already examined these causes, we will do so again here because of some added details about them in our text. The three causes we cite here for the retribution upon Israel are the character of their evil, the continuation of their evil, and the compounding of their evil.

The character of their evil. God said the Israelites "have not hearkened to my voice" (14:22). Earlier God cited Israel's unbelief as a problem. But disobedience is not a different charge, for it is simply the fruit of unbelief. Israel's disobedience had to do with the command to possess the land. Israel did not like God's commandment. They thought it too hard to do and that they would be losers for obeying. But God never commands us to do something we cannot do; and His commands are for our blessings, not our curse. Israel missed great blessing because they disobeyed God's commands. The next time you take a dim view of God's commands and are tempted to disobey, remember the great loss Israel suffered through disobedience at Kadesh.

The continuation of their evil. Again this aspect of the sin is brought up by God. God said Israel had "tempted me now these ten times . . . [and] How long shall I bear with this evil congregation, which murmur against me?" (14:22,27). Twice before God had asked "How long?" (14:11) and now He asks it again (14:27). The question emphasizes the sinful continuation of their sin. The sinful continuation was also emphasized in a new way here in God stating that Israel had now rebelled "ten times" (14:22). The words "ten times" are sometimes used as a figure of speech in Scripture. In negative usage, "It is the language of indignation, meaning that the full measure of provocation has been received [cp. Genesis 31:7, Job 19:3]" (Winterbotham). Some have counted up "ten times" from the Red Sea to the present. To do so, however, they have had to count three murmuring problems in the manna episode in Exodus 16 (one in 16:2, one in 16:20, and one in 16:27). But whether it was exactly ten times or not does not matter as far as the message is concerned. The message is that Israel had been persistent in their sin, and that condemned them greatly. God keeps a record of the number of our sins, and unless we get them under the blood, He will bring them against us in eternity. The more we sin, the worse our judgment will be. In our courts, habitual offenders receive stiffer sentences. It is no different with God.

691

The compounding of their evil. What compounded Israel's evil was that they sinned against God in spite of the fact they "have seen my glory, and my miracles, which I did in Egypt and in the wilderness" (14:22). God had previously indicted Israel for their failure to pay attention to "all the signs which I have showed among them" (14:11). Here He elaborates on that charge. They were a very privileged people to see the glory of God and the miracles of God. Their spiritual privileges should have caused them to act better. Hence, Israel's sin was aggravated by the fact that it was done in spite of all the privileges they had. Spiritual privileges do bring solemn responsibilities.

2. The Crowd for the Retribution

God specified who would be included in the judgment and who would be excluded.

The included. "Your carcases shall fall in this wilderness; and all that were numbered of you, according to your whole number, from twenty years old and upward, which have murmured against me" (14:29). This meant that over six hundred thousand men (besides women) were included in the judgment. At the beginning of the book of Numbers, a census was taken of the male Israelites twenty years and older, and the number totaled 603,500. When a census was taken some forty years later just prior to entrance in Canaan, the new census totaled 601,730. And "among these there was not a man of them whom Moses and Aaron the priest numbered, when they numbered the children of Israel in the wilderness of Sinai" (Numbers 26:64). So those included in the retribution were indeed many. It is still so today, for "broad is the way, that leadeth to destruction, and many there be which go in thereat" (Matthew 7:13).

The excluded. "Ye shall not come into the land, concerning which I sware to make you dwell therein, save Caleb the son of Jephunneh, and Joshua the son of Nun" (Numbers 14:30). Two in this group of age twenty and above escaped the retribution of

God. Only two in over six hundred thousand! Sin may be popular, but that does not diminish its punishment.

Scripture makes two observations about Caleb's character which we note here. Caleb is especially cited here because he was the spokesman of the two in giving the minority report. We have already learned some excellent things about Joshua, and Scripture will tell us many more good things about Joshua later. But here the focus is on Caleb. The two observations about Caleb concern his spirit and his submission.

First, his *spirit*. "Caleb . . . had another spirit" (14:24) than the ten spies who supported the majority report. They were inspired by an evil spirit, Caleb by the Holy Spirit. Which spirit moves you?

Second, his *submission*. Caleb also "hath followed me fully" (14:24, said also of Joshua here). This great submission is because he had "another spirit" in him. This is a great commendation of Caleb. It said he obeyed completely. He did not pick and choose what commands he would obey or disregard. Where God led, he would follow. Doing that will keep you out of a lot of trouble in life. It may put you at odds with men, for Caleb faced a mob that wanted to stone him (14:10), but that is a small problem compared to being in trouble with God.

3. The Character of the Retribution

We note six aspects of the Divine retribution upon Israel for their refusing to go into Canaan. They are the reciprocation, refusal, rerouting, ruin, reprisal, and remorse in the retribution.

The reciprocation. "As ye have spoken in mine ears, so will I do to you"(14:28). The Israelites had said they wished they had died in the wilderness. As we noted earlier, they will get their wish. God will reciprocate! He will speak in their ears what they spoke in His ears. This reciprocation warns us again about the peril of insisting on our own will. When we insist on our will over God's will, God in judgment sometimes grants us our will—but always to our sorrow. Also this reciprocation warns us that we reap what we have sowed. Young people especially need to be reminded of this truth; for if you sow wild oats in your youth, you will reap wild oats in your older years.

The refusal. Part of the judgment was that the people twenty and over "shall not see the land which I sware unto their fathers, neither shall any of them that provoked me see it" (14:23). This land was described in glowing terms by both the majority and minority reports. But the rebellers will not set eyes on it. Likewise, there are many folk today who have heard glowing things about heaven. But they have despised this information and so will not see heaven. If you would see the blessings of God you must submit to the commands of God.

The rerouting. "Tomorrow turn you, and get you into the wilderness by the way of the Red sea . . . and your children shall wander in the wilderness forty years" (14:25,33). Because of Israel's sin, God rerouted them. We note the direction of the rerouting and the duration of the rerouting.

First, the *direction* of the rerouting. God's original route for Israel at Kadesh was to go north into Canaan. But the Israelites refused to go on that route, so God changed their course to go south "unto the wilderness by the way of the Red Sea"—which was the opposite way of the promised land (the Red Sea spoken of here is the eastern inlet of the Red Sea, not the western inlet where they had crossed earlier). Instead of the land flowing with milk and honey, it was a barren desert that was to be their lot. How tragic to be rerouted by God in life because you rejected His will for your life. But many have experienced this rerouting. We have known some who refused the call to the ministry and, as a result, had the rest of their life rerouted into a wilderness of disappointment, frustration, despair, and regret.

Second, the *duration* of the rerouting. "Your children shall wander in the wilderness for forty years." The selection of forty years for the duration of the wandering in the wilderness was done according to the number of days taken for the spying trip.

"After the number of the days in which ye searched the land, even forty days, each day for a year, shall ye bear your iniquities, even forty years" (14:34). As we learn later in Scripture, the forty years included the time already spent in the wilderness. The forty years began not from the time of spying but from the time they left Egypt. In judgment God simply extended their journey to forty years. One whole generation had to pass away before Israel would be allowed to enter Canaan.

Some churches have had or are presently in this experience. They came to a Kadesh where a building program or mission program or a relocation was needed; but the congregation only saw the difficulties and wanted no change from status quo. So the church sits in a wilderness and never grows, wandering around for a generation until new blood takes over which allows the church to move forward. In a number of churches, there are members who need to die before the church will ever progress.

The ruin. "Your carcases shall fall in this wilderness . . . they shall be consumed, and there they shall die" (14:29, 35). As we noted above, the death penalty is given to all those twenty years of age and over. "The wages of sin is death" (Romans 6:23). What an awful thing it was for thousands of Israelites to march around the wilderness knowing that this was the end of their course and they were just waiting to die because of their sin. Sin does not give one a bright future. It ruins all of one's hopes. Sin may look attractive when it is trying to solicit people, but it will eventually make life a boring existence with no hope for the future. What does a sinner have to look forward to? The believer can anticipate heaven and all the blessings that go with it. But the unbeliever has nothing to lift his hopes.

The reprisal. "Those men that did bring up the evil report upon the land, died by the plague before the LORD" (14:37). Special judgment came upon the ten spies who gave the majority report. And rightly so, for they were ringleaders in this sinful rebellion. These spies had not only sinned against God themselves by their unbelief, but they had also led others to sin. Their quick and severe judgment would in a pronounced way condemn them. It would also vindicate and commend Caleb and Joshua. Righteousness may be greatly outnumbered; but when God gets done with it all, it will be vindicated and honored.

The remorse. "And the people mourned greatly" (14:39). The mourning here is not noble mourning. These people were only mourning the fact of their judgment; they were not mourning over their rebellion against God. Proof of that will be seen shortly as we watch them try to enter Canaan against God's orders. Christ said in the Sermon on the Mount, "Blessed are they that mourn" (Matthew 5:4); but that mourning has to do with mourning over our sin and, therefore, forsaking of our wicked ways. Mourning over our judgment and not over our sin says we are sorry we got caught, not we are sorry we sinned.

These Israelites brought a lot of sorrow upon themselves that was totally unnecessary. First they sorrowed (14:1) because they disbelieved God; now they sorrow because they disobeyed God. Again we observe that though the world mocks Christianity as that which is a killjoy, it is the world and their sin that kills real joy. You will not bring happiness in your life by going contrary to God's ways. You may have to suffer in order to obey God, but it will eventually bring you eternal joy. Sin, however, leads to eternal sorrow.

F. THE REVOLT OF THE PEOPLE

Because of the people's disobedience about Canaan, God had ordered that "Tomorrow turn you, and get you into the wilderness by the way of the Red sea" (14:25). But when "tomorrow" came the people revolted. "They rose up early in the morning, and gat them up into the top of the mountain, saying, Lo, we be here, and will go up unto the place [Canaan] which the LORD hath promised: for we have sinned" (14:40). To examine this revolt, we will note the delinquency in the revolt, the divulging in the revolt, the doom of the revolt, the deadliness of the revolt, the disassociation from the revolt, the disrespect in the revolt, the dislocation from the revolt, and the dismay from the revolt.

1. The Delinquency in the Revolt

The revolt was a delinquent attempt to obey God. Israel had refused earlier to obey God and enter Canaan, but they now attempt to do so. However, it is too late to enter now. Their refusal to obey earlier had caused God to change His orders. The new orders forbid their entering Canaan. Delay in doing the will of God can take away opportunity for doing it in the future. Opportunity is not forever. Some seem to think they can wait around about doing God's will until they feel like doing it. But waiting will remove the opportunity. Instead of getting God's first best, you will end up with second or third best or even worse. And these substitutes will never satisfy like first best! The time to be earnest about obeying God is when He gives His commands. "O, if men would be as earnest for heaven while their day of grace lasts as they will be when it is over" (Henry).

2. The Divulging in the Revolt

The revolt revealed that the repentance of the Israelites ("for we have sinned") was not real. It also revealed that their mourning all night about the judgment was not repentance. Since they were now forbidden to enter Canaan, attempting to do so was contrary to the will of God. If they had really repented of their sin, they would have been submissive to God's will and not have tried to enter Canaan. They may acknowledge their sin of not going into Canaan all they want, but it will not be repentance if they keep rebelling. The rebellious unbelief of the Israelites simply went from unbelief in the command to enter Canaan to unbelief in the command not to enter Canaan. Either way it was rebellion, not repentance.

3. The Doom of the Revolt

Moses told the Israelites they would fail in their attempt to go into Canaan. "It [their plan for entering Canaan] shall not prosper" (14:41). Sin may look very promising, noble, and gallant; but it is always doomed to fail. Some think they have gotten ahead through sinful acts, and they may be successful in the eyes of the world for awhile. But success in the eyes of the world will not change failure into success. The world is very poor at judging what is successful and what is a failure. They generally have things all backward in this matter. If you want to know what is successful and what is not, you will need to check with God's Word.

4. The Deadliness of the Revolt

Moses warned the revolters that death would stalk their revolt. "Go not up . . . that ye be not smitten before your enemies" (14:42). The warning said it would be suicide to attempt to go up against the enemy now. If they had done it earlier, it would have been a different outcome. But as usual the Israelites paid no attention to Moses' warning; so when they tried to invade Canaan, death pursued them. It was a real bloodbath. "The Amalekites came down, and the Canaanites which dwelt in that hill, and smote them" (14:45). The account in Deuteronomy adds, "And destroyed you" (Deuteronomy 1:44). Sin always leads to death. "The wages of sin is death" (Romans 6:23).

5. The Disassociation From the Revolt

God would have no part of the revolt. "Go not up, for the LORD is not among you . . . the LORD will not be with you" (14:42,43). Only fools will pursue an endeavor without God. But the revolting Israelites played the fool and did not count the presence of God as necessary. People are still that way today. Few value the presence of God. Most live in a way that says they do not want God around.

Besides the disassociation of God from the revolt, Moses and the ark of the covenant were also dissociated from it. When the revolters tried to go into Canaan, "the ark of the covenant of the LORD, and Moses, departed not out of the camp" (14:44). Sin separates us from the best things in life.

6. The Disrespect in the Revolt

"They presumed to go up unto the hill top [to go into Canaan]" (14:44), and they "went presumptuously up into the hill [to enter Canaan]" (Deuteronomy 1:43). The two presumption words in these texts are not from the same Hebrew word though they are similar in meaning. Both words involve the idea of pride and arrogance. The word in Deuteronomy also involves insolence. All of this says the Israelites gave no respect to the authority of God and His Word. Nor did they give due respect to the authority of Moses. Even though God had ordered them to head south instead of north, and even though Moses (their only legitimate leader) did not go with them to lead them into Canaan, they went anyway.

Presumptuous people are very disrespectful of authority. Hence, beware of listening to and going along with folk who show disrespect for legitimate authority. These folk "Despise government [authority]. Presumptuous are they, self-willed, they are not afraid to speak evil of dignities" (II Peter 2:10); and they get in big trouble with God. We need to note that Peter is not saying here in this verse that we must not expose or speak out against evil and evil people in high places. He is condemning speaking against God-approved authority—authority that represents what we should be submissive to and respect.

7. The Dislocation From the Revolt

The invasion soon turned into a retreat, and the revolters retreated "even unto Hormah" (14:45). The Deuteronomy account describes the retreat in more detail. "And the Amorites, which dwelt in that mountain, came out against you, and chased you, as bees do, and destroyed you in Seir, even unto Hormah" (Deuteronomy 1:44). Describing the chasing of the Israelites by the Amorites "as bees do" indicates the panic and pace of the retreat. When bees come after you, you turn and run with dispatch and are not very concerned about where you are running just so long as you get away from those bees. So the retreating Israelites ended up "in Seir, even unto Hormah" which would put them over into the neighborhood of the Edomites. Trudging back to Kadesh from there would be a humbling and unhappy trek. People often get themselves into strange and unhappy places because of their sin.

8. The Dismay From the Revolt

"And ye returned and wept before the LORD; but the LORD would not hearken to your voice, nor give ear unto you" (Deuteronomy 1:45). This is the third time sorrow has come upon the Israelites because of their disobedience at Kadesh about entering the land (see Numbers 14:1 and 39 for the other two times). What an accurate picture of sin. It fills one's life with sorrow; and, as we have been noting in this chapter, that sorrow will follow many into eternity.

There is a finality about the sorrow in this passage seen in the words "But the LORD would not hearken to your voice, nor give ear unto you." This reaction of God to their sorrow is like that recorded in Proverbs 1:30,31: "They would none of my counsel: they despised all my reproof. Therefore shall they eat of the fruit of their own way, and be filled with their own devices," and like that recorded in Hebrews 12:17 regarding Esau who "found no place of repentance, though he sought it carefully with tears." Sin and misery are inseparable. Sin may look so adventuresome, exciting, and pleasure-promising while holiness looks dull, drab, and joyless. But get into the Word of God so you can discern the truth about sin and holiness lest you fill your life with sorrow.

XXIX.

SEDITION OF KORAH

NUMBERS 16,17

ONCE MORE MOSES has his position of leadership challenged. Korah, a proud and contemptuous Levite, led a revolt to replace the leadership of Israel. This sedition, as our text shows, really pained Moses. Not only was it painful in itself, but this sedition would also aggravate the extremely painful wound which Moses incurred by being ordered by God to lead Israel back into the wilderness rather than into the land of Canaan. This rebellion of Korah was so notorious that the New Testament, in condemning apostasy, compares it to Korah's rebellion by saying, "Woe unto them [the apostates] for they have . . . perished in the gainsaying [means rebellion] of Core [Korah]" (Jude 1:11).

"The sedition of Korah . . . is the only important occurrence recorded in connection with the thirty-seven years' wandering in the wilderness" (Keil). Exactly when it occurred during those years in the wilderness is difficult to ascertain. But it being the main incident recorded about the wilderness stay after the Kadesh rebellion emphasizes the ingrained rebellious nature of the Israelite generation which caused the extended stay in the wilderness until all that generation should die off.

This rebellion of Korah is similar to what many pastors and churches have experienced and will continue to experience until Christ comes for the church. Dissidents in the church frequently rise up against rightful authority in the church, especially the pastor, and attempt to either remove that authority or usurp it. To help understand this uprising of the dissidents in the church and how to deal with it, we are wise to turn to this portion of

Scripture about Korah and examine it thoroughly. When we do, we will be surprised at how accurately it describes many of the problems and people in our churches. Sin does not change—the actors often change, but the acts are the same.

In our study of this sedition of Korah, we will consider the confronting of Moses—Korah's assault on the leadership of Israel (16:1–14), the consuming by God—the judgment of God on the sedition (16:15–50), and the confirming with the rods—God's vindication of His appointed leaders (17:1–13).

A. THE CONFRONTING OF MOSES

Korah's sedition came to light in a public confrontation with Moses. There were no private meetings with Moses where grievances could be aired in respectable ways and responded to in a non-inflammatory climate. But the sedition arrogantly and shamelessly confronted Moses in a most despicable way. To examine this confronting of Moses by Korah and his followers, we will note the crowd of the rebels, the contention of the rebels, the counsel for the rebels, and the contempt by the rebels.

1. The Crowd of the Rebels

The crowd that confronted Moses can be divided into three groups: the leaders, the associates, and the followers—the followers becoming a very large group before the rebellion ended.

Leaders. "Korah, the son of Izhar, the son of Kohath, the son of Levi, and Dathan and Abiram, the sons of Eliab, and On, the son of Peleth, sons of Reuben . . . rose up before [against] Moses" (16:1,2). Four men are listed here as the primary leaders of the rebellion. They are Korah, Dathan, Abiram, and On. Korah was the chief leader as our text for this study plainly shows. Dathan and Abiram were next in prominence in leadership, but On faded from the picture. He is never mentioned again. He may have quit the rebellion, or had a lesser post of responsibility, or had a falling out with his fellow rebellers—it is not unusual for conspirators to fight among themselves.

The situation of these leaders included some factors which would upset small hearts and encourage them to rebel. Korah, who was a cousin of Moses (his father and the father of Moses were brothers, see Exodus 6:18) had been passed over in the appointment of chief for the Levite family of the Kohathites (to which he belonged). Elizaphan, who was less senior than Korah (because his father was a younger brother of Korah's father), was given that prestigious post (Numbers 3:30). Also Korah (as well as other Levites) was excluded from the priesthood when it was given to Aaron and his family. As for Dathan, Abiram, and On, though they were of the tribe of Reuben, the firstborn, they did not enjoy the privileges of the firstborn tribe, for Reuben was denied the birthright (I Chronicles 5:1,2). So like Korah, Dathan, Abiram, and On (and the other Reubenites) had been passed over for some prestigious positions of leadership in Israel. Small, pride-filled hearts do not handle this well. So these four men were ripe to lead a rebellion against Israel's leadership.

Desire for position destroys many men and their service for God. Here it destroyed Korah, Dathan, Abiram, and On. In the New Testament it was the scribes and Pharisees who were condemned and destroyed because they "love the uppermost rooms [places, positions] at feasts, and the chief seats in the synagogues" (Matthew 23:6). Humility is imperative if we are to serve the Lord faithfully. Christ set the example, for "he humbled himself" (Philippians 2:8) to be our Savior. "The One Who now occupies the very highest place in heaven is the One who voluntarily took the very lowest place on earth" (Mackintosh).

Associates. "They [Korah, Dathan, Abiram, and On] rose up before Moses, with certain of the children of Israel, two hundred and fifty princes of the assembly, famous in the congregation, men of renown" (16:2). The rebellion spread from the leaders (Korah, Dathan, Abiram, and On) to include 250 princes of Israel—those who were "heads of the thousands of Israel" (Numbers 10:4). Being the heads of people, they were, of course, "famous" and "men of renown" as our text says. High

703

position begets fame and prestige. It also can beget pride. And it was the pride in these 250 leaders that led to their undoing as it does to many in high places. It takes a man of great character to survive high position. Moses was one of few who could hold a high position without being destroyed by pride. Do not covet and push and shove, as many do, to gain a high position in the world. It can be your undoing. If you gain high position, let it be because God put you there. Then pray earnestly everyday that the place of fame and prestige will not destroy your character.

Followers. "Korah gathered all the congregation against them [Moses and Aaron]" (16:19). Korah was a very persuasive person and pushed his cause with great energy until he had gained most of the congregation for his supporters. We have had many wicked men down through the ages who have had the persuasiveness and aggressiveness of Korah for evil causes. In our day we have seen Hitler, Mussolini, Mao of China, Arafat of the PLO, and other wicked men (including a good number of American politicians) who have influenced multitudes and even great nations to become their supporters and followers in causes that were evil from start to finish. One is often amazed how these wicked men can influence so many folk to adopt evil philosophies and programs. But we should not be amazed when we remember that the Bible says, "The heart is deceitful above all things, and desperately wicked" (Jeremiah 17:9). Wicked hearts will follow wicked men. Our nation is becoming more wicked everyday which helps explain why vile men are elected to lead our nation and why gambling and abortion and homosexualism and other evils are so acceptable and defended in our land.

But all the people have not gone to the dogs yet. Even in Korah's day, there were some who did not follow him. A notable exception is recorded in Numbers 27. He was Zelophehad from the tribe of Manasseh. Scripture notes that "he was not in the company of them that gathered themselves together against the LORD in the company of Korah" (Numbers 27:3). God observes us; and though we may be a small, obscure, and despised minority, God sees us and will in due time honor our faithfulness to Him. So when evil sweeps the land as it swept the camp in Moses' day, let us be faithful and stand true, as did Zelophehad, even though we have to stand alone.

2. The Contention of the Rebels

"And they gathered themselves together against Moses and against Aaron, and said unto them, Ye take too much upon you, seeing all the congregation are holy, every one of them, and the LORD is among them: wherefore then lift ye up yourselves above the congregation of the LORD?" (16:3). We note the specifics of the contention and the support for the contention.

The specifics of the contention. As we have already noted, the contention of Korah and his followers was over leadership. It was a twofold problem. First, they did not like Moses being the chief prince of the people (which would especially upset Dathan, Abiram, and On; for they were Reubenites). Second, they did not like the fact that the Levitical priesthood was given exclusively to Aaron and his family (which would especially upset Korah, a Levite; and which was the main contention of his sedition). The rebels charged Moses and Aaron with taking too much power for themselves and exalting themselves above the people. The charge was absurd, of course; for Moses and Aaron were only doing what God called them to do. "It would be quite as reasonable to charge the sun, moon, and stars with taking too much upon them when they shine in their appointed spheres, as to charge any gifted servant of Christ therewith when he seeks to discharge the responsibility which his gift most surely imposes upon him. These luminaries serve in the place assigned them by the hand of the almighty Creator, and so long as Christ's servants do the same, it is charging them falsely to say that they take too much upon them" (Mackintosh).

Especially is this charge ridiculous in regards to Moses when we remember Moses' attitude about taking his job. "Surely, the most cursory glance back at the history of that dear

705

and honored servant would have been sufficient to convince any impartial person that, so far from taking dignity and responsibility upon him, he had shown himself only too ready to shrink from them when presented, and sink under them when imposed. Hence . . . any one who could think of accusing Moses of taking upon him [too much authority], only proved himself totally ignorant of the man's real spirit and character" (Mackintosh). Furthermore, Aaron did not seek the position of the high priest; but Moses bestowed it upon him by Divine order (Hebrews 5:4). Those who fuss the most about wanting prestigious positions are generally the ones who are least qualified for it. The qualified, like Moses, are more likely to be hesitant about taking position. But it seems the more unqualified a person is, the more likely he is to pursue a position in which he does not belong, and to fuss much when he is rejected and passed over for the position.

The support for the contention. The argument Korah gave to support his contention that Moses and Aaron were exalting themselves wrongfully above the congregation was that "all the congregation are holy, everyone of them, and the LORD is among them" (16:3). This is a common argument heard everywhere today. It is an argument that would level all the people and make everyone qualified for any position. It is the argument that lowers important standards and qualifications. It is an argument which fails to recognize skills and abilities, and especially Divine callings. It is an argument that is akin to the rights movement of our day. The rights movement looks innocent on the surface, but underneath it too often is an effort to advance the unqualified. So today we have the quota system which results in the unqualified being given high positions while the qualified are shunted aside and given lessor positions. This has produced great problems in business and government and wherever else it is practiced, but the rights people close their eyes to the fact. In church Korah's argument is used by women to campaign for their right to hold any church office; and Korah's argument is used by others, such as the divorced, who insist they are just as qualified, yea just as holy as other men to be a deacon or pastor.

Korah's argument was, of course, wholly unfactual. All the congregation were not holy, and they were not in God's favor either (the rebels' had claimed God's favor with the statement "the LORD is among them"). "Small reason they [Korah and his cohorts] had to boast of the people's purity, or of God's favor, as the people had been so frequently and so lately polluted with sin, and were now under the marks of God's displeasure" (Henry). Israel had been rebelling in unholy ways ever since they left Egypt. But Korah ignored that fact just as his kind in every generation ignore their lack of qualification for positions they seek presumptuously.

3. The Counsel for the Rebels

Here we look at the counsel Moses gave Korah and his company when they first came up against Moses. Moses' counsel here was mostly directed at "ye sons of Levi" (16:8) inasmuch as Korah was a Levite and the priesthood (which had to do with the Levites) was the main issue of the sedition. Moses' counsel was excellent. He counselled by deed as well as by word. To examine the counselling, we will note the conduct of humility, the contest for high priest, and the condemning of evil.

The conduct of humility. "And when Moses heard it, he fell upon his face" (16:4). The accusation that Moses and Aaron were assuming positions of authority which they should not have assumed was met by humble action on the part of Moses. That should have shamed Korah and his company. Moses was no arrogant, self-seeking, misbehaving man who coveted high position so he could lord it over the people. Such a man would not fall on his face in humility after being charged with such evil. But it was Korah and his company who lacked humility, who in pride sought high position that did not belong to them, and who behaved unbecomingly.

It has been our experience that in church troubles the dissidents are the ones who lack good behavior, good manners, and common courtesies; but those in the right are the ones who usually demonstrate the best behavior. When you are right, you can afford to act civil. You do not have to rail on people and interrupt others in a business meeting to yell out a bunch of twisted accusations across the auditorium at another member. But those in the wrong act that way. They will not demonstrate good conduct—especially not the humility of Moses

The contest for high priest. "And he spake unto Korah and unto all his company, saying, Even tomorrow the LORD will show who are his, and who is holy; and will cause him to come near unto him: even him whom he hath chosen will he cause to come near unto him. This do; Take you censers, Korah, and all his company; And put fire therein, and put incense in them before the LORD tomorrow: and it shall be that the man whom the LORD doth choose, he shall be holy" (16:5–7). Moses leaves the choice of the high priest (and, therefore, of all the priesthood) up to God. The choice would be manifested in the offering of incense with the censers. It would not only reveal which Levites were or were not in the priesthood but also if only the Levities were to be in the priesthood, for all the 250 princes were included in this test, and many of them were not Levites. Of course, as we will see later, God did not choose any of the 250 men. He rejected their offering of incense by destroying them, but God accepted Aaron's offering which confirmed Aaron as high priest and his sons as the other priests.

Those in the right in God's work are glad to go to God and His Word to see what God says about who should be in place of leadership, for it will vindicate them. One area where we need to get back to the Word of God today is in the area of the women's place in church. The women's movement in the world today, which has greatly affected (better to say infected) the church, is most definitely not in accord with God's Word. Rather, it is a Korah movement which would put women and men on the same level for all tasks. But God does not call women to be preachers or pastors!

The condemning of evil. In a noble fashion, Moses condemned Korah and his company for their rebellion. In pointing out the evil of their actions, Moses spoke of the duplication of their charge, the disrespect of their privileges, the desire of their ambition, and the direction of their opposition.

First, the *duplication* of their charge. "Ye take too much upon you, ye sons of Levi" (16:7). Moses set the situation straight. Korah and his company had earlier charged Moses and Aaron with the same charge: "Ye take too much upon you" (16:3). They charged Moses and Aaron with taking upon themselves more position and authority than they ought. But in truth it was Korah and his gang that were guilty of this charge. They were presumptuously and arrogantly trying to command Israel's secular and religious government. But that was not their job. So they were doing the very thing they accused Moses and Aaron of doing. They were like hypocritical church members who speak out of place with inflammatory language at a business meeting to accuse others, particularly church leaders, of behaving poorly.

Second, the *disrespect* of their privileges. "Hear, I pray you, ye sons of Levi: Seemeth it but a small thing unto you, that the God of Israel hath separated you from the congregation of Israel, to bring you near to himself to do the service of the tabernacle of the LORD, and to stand before the congregation to minister unto them?" (16:8,9). We note several lessons about spiritual privileges which the rebels possessed but did not respect well.

One lesson is that *privileges should deter from evil.* The Levites had been given special privileges not accorded the other tribes. Some of the Levites (Aaron and his family) were made priests (Leviticus 8), and the other Levites (which would include Korah) were given other duties (Numbers 3,4) which, though they were not priesthood duties, also constituted special religious privilege. These privileges should have caused Korah and his fellow rebelling Levites to in gratefulness act better. Hence, their rebellion increases in sinfulness because it was done in spite of their spiritual privileges. Privileges aggravate sin.

Another lesson is that *privileges will destroy the proud.* Proud people (which the rebels were) cannot handle privilege well. It goes to their head, and they expect more privileges. Promotion to high position only puffs up proud people into thinking they ought to be given even higher position (this was Satan's problem, see Isaiah 14:12–15). Rather than being concerned about the important responsibilities their privilege gave them, the proud rebellers before Moses only coveted more honor. This often happens in church. As an example, some folk who are put on the church board do not have the character to handle that position. So once they get on the board, they begin to covet more power. Soon they are taking it upon themselves to order the pastor around. When you are given privilege, do not let it go to your head; rather concentrate on the responsibilities that go with the privilege.

Third, the *desire* of their ambition. "Seek ye the priesthood also?" (16:10). Moses saw right through Korah (and the other Levites, too). He knew what Korah wanted and said so. As we noted above, God limited the priesthood to Aaron's family. This did not go over well with Korah. He wanted in the priesthood, too. He tried to disguise this desire, of course, under the guise of the rights of the people. "This is always the way with promoters of sedition or disaffection. Their real object is to make themselves somebody. They talk loudly and very plausibly about the common rights and privileges of God's people; but in reality, they themselves are aiming at a position for which they are in no way qualified, and at privileges to which they have no right" (Mackintosh). In our society, some groups have been asking for equal rights who in fact do not want equal rights but want special privileges. Some laws passed to supposedly help equal rights have, in fact, only given special privileges to the complaining group. And what do some of these complaining groups do when they get special privileges—fuss for more privileges under the guise of equal rights. Korah's devious practice is not out of date.

Fourth, the *direction* of their opposition. "All thy company are gathered together against the LORD: and what is Aaron, that ye murmur against him?" (16:11). Moses takes off another mask of Korah's argument. Korah and his gang were not primarily upset with Moses or Aaron ("what is Aaron, that ye murmur against him?"), but the primary problem was that Korah and his followers were "against the LORD." It was God's order they were rebelling against. Moses did not set himself up as prince over Israel, neither did he decide in himself to give the priesthood to Aaron and Aaron's sons. This was all ordered of God. So if folk do not like this set-up, they are arguing against God.

Dissidents in God's work are those who have problems submitting to God's will in their lives. They are "against the LORD" because His will is not acceptable to them. So the church must be changed to fit their disobedient, unsubmissive ways or they will cause all kinds of commotion in the church. Such folk court disaster, however; for though God is a most merciful God, yet His mercy does not trample on His holiness. Therefore, judgment will sooner or later come upon these dissidents as it did with the rebelling Israelites in Moses' day. You cannot be continually against the Lord and come out a winner.

4. The Contempt by the Rebels

Moses' wise counsel for the rebels was followed by great contempt for him. The contempt came from Dathan and Abiram, co-leaders of the rebellion with Korah. Their contempt consisted of despising Moses' authority and defaming Moses' actions.

Despising Moses' authority. "And Moses sent to call Dathan and Abiram, the sons of Eliab: which said, We will not come up" (16:12). For some reason, Dathan and Abiram were not at the Tabernacle after Moses had finished speaking with Korah and his company about the contention. Keil thinks that Dathan and Abiram "as is tacitly assumed, had gone back to their tents during the warning given to Korah." But for whatever reason they had left, Moses had to send for them so he could also speak to them. Their answer to Moses' call was filled with insolence

711

and rebellion: "We will not come up." To emphasize their despising of Moses' authority, they repeated this scornful answer (v. 14) after they had attacked Moses' actions (which we will note next). This most disrespectful answer so much as said, "Who do you think you are to order us around." It forcefully indicated that they were not supporting Moses as Israel's leader.

Those who are unwilling to submit to the will of God, as these men were, will show it in their disrespect for proper authority be it at work or at school or at home or at church. This accounts for the rebellion we see on every hand in society. This disrespect of authority is especially distressing in the church and in the home, for if these two institutions have trouble with disrespect for authority, the rest of society is in big trouble. Society will not function well unless authority is given its proper respect. Without this respect, chaos will eventually reign.

Defaming Moses' actions. It was not enough for Dathan and Abiram to despise Moses' authority, but they also spoke in a very untruthful and derogatory way regarding Moses' actions as the leader of Israel. They accused him of doing five evil things. The five actions dealt with deprivation, death, dignity, deficiency, and deception.

First, *deprivation.* "Is it a small thing that thou hast brought us up out of a land that floweth with milk and honey" (16:13). These rebels had the audacity to accuse Moses of depriving them of good things when he brought them out of Egypt. How utterly ridiculous is this charge. Egypt was no land of milk and honey! In fact, when Israel left Egypt, Egypt had been stripped bare of crops and livestock and wealth. The rebels' charge was totally false. But these type of people do not need facts to accuse. They simply make false accusations and twist situations to suit their evil purpose. When you hear people like that talk in church, check the facts before you get excited about their accusations of church leaders and other church members.

Second, *death.* "Thou hast brought us up out of [Egypt] . . . to kill us in the wilderness" (16:13). Once again Moses is accused of bringing the Israelites into the wilderness to kill them (cp. Exodus 14:11; 16:3; 17:3). Yes, many had died in the wilderness of late, but whose fault was that? It was not the fault of Moses; it was the fault of the people's sins. The truth of the matter is that more people would have died if Moses had not interceded with God and gained the lives of the people.

God's faithful servants will often find that rebellious people will accuse them of evil in the very area in which they are doing so much good. Moses was keeping people from death, and yet they accused him of killing people. Pastors are often accused of lack of love and patience when with their long hours of service and meager pay they demonstrate more love and patience than anyone else in the church.

Third, *dignity*. "Thou make thyself altogether a prince over us" (16:13). Dathan and Abiram repeat the charge that Moses is exalting himself above others by presumptuously taking unto himself the position of prince of the congregation. As noted before, Dathan and Abiram were more upset about the prince position than the priesthood position, for they were Reubenites who lost the prince position because of Reuben's sin. Dathan and Abiram make it plain what position they are interested in. They want authority over the people and will despise anyone who has a position of power they covet. They will insist that those in the positions they covet are usurpers. Such is always the way of the proud. They will not hesitate to accuse anyone over them of exceeding their limits of authority. But, of course, this kind thinks any authority over them exceeds its limits.

Fourth, *deficiency*. "Moreover thou hast not brought us into a land that floweth with milk and honey, or given us inheritance of fields and vineyards" (16:14). Another very false accusation is the accusation which charges Moses with failure to lead Israel into Canaan—implying that this failure should disqualify him from his office of leadership. But it was not Moses' fault Israel was not in Canaan; it was the rebels' fault. However, those who rebel against God will blame everyone and everything but the real problem which is themselves. So if the church declines in attendance, it has to be the pastor's fault every time; even though the dissidents by their conduct have driven people away from the church and have given the church such a poor testimony in the community that it keeps others in the community from wanting to attend the church.

Fifth, *deception*. "Wilt thou put out the eyes of these men?" (16:14). The final accusation in this tirade accuses Moses of being deceitful, of blinding the people's eyes so that they do not know what is going on. However, those who were doing the deceiving were the ones making the accusation. They were deceiving others by false accusations and trying to make it look like Moses was part of the problem and not part of the solution.

These were sharp and painful barbs for Moses to experience. And they are barbs which many pastors and other church leaders will feel frequently. "In the history of all workers for God there will come crises, when wrong motives will be imputed and unkind suggestions passed from mouth to mouth, even by those whose spiritual life has been due to their prayers and tears" (F. B. Meyer). These attacks, however, must not stop us from serving. We need to remember that others far greater than ourselves have also experienced these attacks. Also we must console ourselves with the fact that God will see us through these difficult times as He did Moses and Aaron.

B. THE CONSUMING BY GOD

The sedition inspired by Korah did not, of course, go over well with God. Hence, God brought judgment on the rebels. He "consumed" (16:26, 35) many of the Israelites because of this rebellion. To further examine this consuming judgment by God upon the rebellers, we will note the call for judgment, the compassion in judgment, and the character of the judgment.

1. The Call for Judgment

The first sign of judgment coming upon the rebels was the call for judgment by Moses. We note in the call the enragement of Moses, the entreaty by Moses, and the exoneration of Moses.

Enragement. "Moses was very wroth" (16:15). We have no difficulty understanding why Moses was upset. He had been accused of taking too much authority upon himself, of depriving the people of good things, of bringing the people into the wilderness to kill them, of failing to bring the people into Canaan, and of being deceitful. Furthermore, he had just had his orders insultingly rejected by Dathan and Abiram.

As is evident by his conduct, Moses' anger was not of the flesh but of the spirit. It was a holy indignation against evil. "Moses was very wroth, not so much for his own sake, for he had learnt to bear indignities . . . as for God's sake, who was highly dishonored, blasphemed, and provoked by these speeches and carriages, in which case he ought to be angry, as Christ was, Mark 3:5" (Matthew Poole). There is a holy anger that is found in people who respect godliness and abhor evil. A holy anger will call for just judgment upon the offenders. It will honor godliness and punish evil. We have little holy anger in our land today which is why we are so lenient with criminals, with disobedient children, with problem students in school, and with dissidents in church.

Entreaty. Moses "said unto the LORD, Respect not thou their offering" (16:15). The rebels' offering was represented by the incense offered up by the 250 men (16:16–18). This prayer was sure to be answered, for Moses was praying within the will of God. The incense offering, as we noted earlier, was to determine who were the appointed priests in Israel. God will not respect and accept the offering of those who offer outside the will of God. We learned this early in the Bible. "But unto Cain and to his offering he had not respect" (Genesis 4:5).

One can see an important Gospel truth here. It is that God respects only one offering when it comes to soul salvation. That offering is the offering offered up by Christ at Calvary. All other offerings man offers up for his salvation will not be accepted. Only the offering of Christ will provide salvation for the sinner. Aaron's high priest position is at issue with Korah. Aaron repre-

715

sented Christ, but the 250 men with their censers did not. Hence they will be rejected as we will see later. As it is with sinners who reject Christ, they will experience a fiery judgment.

Exoneration. "I have not taken one ass from them, neither have I hurt one of them" (16:15). Moses gives a brief declaration of his innocence of misconduct towards the Israelites. Saying he had not taken one "ass" from them indicates he had not taken even things of little value, for "The ass was the least valuable of the ordinary live stock of those days" (Winterbotham). Moses could say what he did because his conduct towards the Israelites had been so exemplary throughout his leading of them from Egypt to their present location in the wilderness. It was the rebels who were faulty in conduct. But being innocent of the charges did not keep Moses from being viciously accused of misconduct. Holiness does not keep us from accusations before men, but it will keep us from accusations before God. The best of men, yea, even Jesus Christ Himself, have been vilely condemned as great transgressors before men. But God is the one with the final say, and it is in His court that we want to be exonerated as was Moses here.

2. The Compassion in Judgment

Divine judgment is not without Divine mercy. Even though judgment was set for the rebels, mercy was still exercised at the last minute to give some a chance to escape the judgment. The compassion in this judgment is seen in Moses and Aaron as well as in God. Two actions show this compassion in our text: supplicating for mercy and separating the multitude.

Supplicating for mercy. When God announced that He was going to consume the people "in a moment" (16:21), Moses and Aaron "fell upon their faces, and said, O God . . . shall one man sin, and wilt thou be wroth with the all the congregation?" (16:22). How magnanimous of Moses and Aaron to plead for Divine mercy for the Israelite congregation here. These two men had been under special attack by the rebels who had influenced nearly the entire congregation of Israel to take sides against Moses and Aaron. Yet, Moses and Aaron beg God for clemency for the congregation in judgment.

How much Israel owed to Moses. They literally owed their lives to him, yet they treated him with utter disdain. God's servants can expect this sort of treatment; but when they do, they need to do as Moses did and have compassion for one's enemies. The greatest example in having compassion for one's enemies is Christ. Though He was without sin and though He was the greatest blessing to come to man, yet mankind crucified Him. However, on the cross He prayed, "Father, forgive them; for they know not what they do" (Luke 23:34). The spirit of forgiveness is seldom easy to exercise. But it will come when we walk close to the One Who has forgiven us of our sins.

Note that Moses and Aaron did not ask God to wink at sin and be lenient with criminals. They entreated God to be merciful to the people of the congregation who were only being led astray—not doing the leading astray. God was ready to consume the entire congregation, but Moses and Aaron intercede so that in judgment God will not destroy all the congregation.

Separating the multitude. "Speak unto the congregation, saying, Get you up from about the tabernacle of Korah, Dathan, and Abiram. And Moses rose up and went unto Dathan and Abiram; and the elders of Israel followed him. And he spake unto the congregation, saying, Depart, I pray you, from the tents of these wicked men, and touch nothing of theirs, lest ye be consumed in all their sins" (16:24–26). God accepted the intercessory work of Moses and Aaron. Therefore, judgment will not fall upon the whole congregation. However, the congregation must separate from the rebel leaders as God ordered or they will not experience His mercy. Thus mercy came with responsibility. It is the same with the Gospel. Christ provides a way to escape from Divine judgment, but the sinner must receive Christ as Savior, or he will perish in his sin though mercy has been offered

717

to him. We must use the means of mercy or we will perish.

We have a great lesson on separation in this warning (as we also had in a similar warning God gave Moses and Aaron earlier in 16:21). The lesson is that separation is vital if we want to stay out of trouble. There are people, places, practices, and philosophies that we must separate from if we are going to keep from destroying our lives. But though separation is so important, it is not well received in our day. Mixing is the accepted practice instead. Separatists are called legalists and accused of being "holier than thou" in their separatist attitudes and actions. But separation is most profitable as many Israelites learned. They "gat up from the tabernacle of Korah, Dathan, and Abiram, on every side" (16:27)—and, as a result, escaped judgment. We see the ruined lives of many professing Christians on every hand today because they refused to separate from the world. Mixing is popular with the world, but it eventually brings ruin to the life of the mixer.

3. The Character of the Judgment

The judgment upon the Israelites because of Korah's sedition was threefold. It came by fissure, fire, and fever.

Fissure. Moses said about the rebels that if "the earth open her mouth, and swallow them up, with all that appertains unto them, and they go down quick into the pit; then ye shall understand that these men have provoked the LORD" (16:30). And since the rebels had provoked God, "it came to pass . . . that the ground clave [split] asunder that was under them [the rebels]: And the earth opened her mouth, and swallowed them up, and their houses, and all the men that appertained unto Korah, and all their goods. They, and all that appertained to them, went down alive into the pit, and the earth closed upon them: and they perished from among the congregation" (16:31–33).

The first judgment to come upon the rebels was a fissure opening in the earth with many rebels falling into it and perishing. It was more than just a large hole opening in the ground into which people fell to their death. Rather, it was a fissure that opened up all the way to sheol. The word "pit" (16:33) tells us that fact, for the word "pit" is the word "sheol" in the Hebrew and means the place of the dead—not just the grave. This is the place described in Luke 16 which is divided into two parts—the place of tormenting fire for the unrighteous and the place of rest for the righteous. After Christ died, the righteous part was taken to be with Him. But the unrighteous sector still exists and will continue to do so until it is emptied one day so the wicked in it can appear before God in judgment. After this judgment, the wicked will be sent to the lake of fire for all eternity (Revelation 20:13,14). Some folk reserve the word "hell" for the final abode of the wicked which is the lake of fire. Others use the word "hell" to describe both the temporary abode of the wicked and the final abode, for both places are a place of torment and fire ("hell" should definitely not be used, however, to translate "sheol" or the New Testament equivalent "hades" unless it refers only to the wicked sector of "sheol," for the righteous do not go to hell!). The first abode of the wicked compared to the second abode is like a criminal being held in the county jail until his trial and then after the trial being taken to the state prison for the final abode for his crime. Either place is a place of punishment. So it is with the wicked sector of sheol and the lake of fire.

Fire. "And there came out a fire from the LORD, and consumed the two hundred and fifty men that offered incense" (16:35). This is the second form of judgment upon the rebellion. We noted earlier that Moses had instructed "Korah, and all his company [250 men in this case]" (16:6) to each bring a censer with incense in it and to burn it before God at the Tabernacle along with Aaron (16:17). From this action would come the Divine indication as to who was and who was not to be the priests and burn incense before God (which Aaron and his sons were then doing under God's orders). The result, of course, was going to be disaster for the rebels; for God would not accept

719

their burning of incense before the Tabernacle. Irregularities in this type of offering were met with a fiery death in the past (see Leviticus 10:1,2 where Nadab and Abihu were devoured with Divine fire for offering strange fire before God). So when they offered their incense, they experienced what Nadab and Abihu did—Divine fire consumed them. It is a dangerous thing to argue with Divine callings. Uzziah is another case where great punishment came upon this sin (II Chronicles 26:16–21).

A memorial of this fire judgment was ordered by God. "Speak unto Eleazar the son of Aaron the priest, that he take up the censers out of the burning . . . let them make them broad plates for a covering of the altar . . . and they shall be a sign [and] . . . a memorial unto the children of Israel, that no stranger, which is not of the seed of Aaron, come near to offer incense before the LORD" (16:37,38,40). It is human nature to forget Divine warnings quickly. Therefore, God often puts up landmarks, memorials, or gives us scars to remind us of the peril of our evil ways. Too often, however, we ignore these reminders and go on our sinful way to experience more judgment and more humbling and painful reminders.

Fever. To examine this final judgment for the Israelites that came because of the sedition of Korah, we will note the murmuring before the judgment, the manner of the judgment, the magnitude of the judgment, the momentum of the judgment, the mercy in the judgment, and the manifestation in the judgment.

First, the *murmuring* before the judgment. "But on the morrow all the congregation of the children of Israel murmured against Moses and against Aaron, saying, Ye have killed the people of the LORD" (16:41). This murmuring was both stupid and speedy.

The murmuring was *stupid* about cause and effect. The Israelites never seemed to learn. They could experience judgment repeatedly and yet never catch on as to what it meant. Though the fissure and fire judgment made it very plain that God was upset with the rebels, Moses and Aaron still are blamed by the murmurers for the deaths of the people. This kind of perverted cause and effect understanding is still part of the world. As an example, men with bloody cruelty abort babies and then accuse the anti-abortionists of being cruel. Men who rebel against God simply cannot reason well in the matter of right and wrong. It is a tragic situation to be in, for it only brings more judgment upon us as it did here in Israel's case. Their murmuring kept the judgment from stopping sooner.

The murmuring was *speedy* because it occurred "on the morrow" (16:41) after the two judgments. If the Israelites had murmured a year or even a month or so from the time of the two terrible judgments (fissure and fire), we could understand it better though it would still be totally inexcusable. But "on the morrow" shows how hard their evil hearts were. Judgment could shake the camp, but these folks were so dense spiritually that the effects did not last for even as little as twenty-four hours. Reminds us of folk who can sit in a church service where God's spirit is moving in hearts, yet in a matter of minutes after the service is over these folks are frolicking around as though they had never been in the service. Their hearts are so hard that nothing spiritual can penetrate them. Their hearts are like "the way side" soil (Matthew 13:4) upon which the sown seed never penetrated but bounced off and in quick order "fowls came and devoured" it (Ibid.).

Second, the *manner* of the judgment. The judgment is called a "plague" (16:46). The word "plague" is a translation of a Hebrew word which means "an infliction" (Strong) and is "especially used of a fatal disease sent from God" (Gesenius). We have called it a fever, for a fever is usually involved with such diseases. God had warned Israel at Marah on the way to Sinai that, "If thou wilt diligently hearken to the voice of the LORD thy God, and wilt do that which is right in his sight, and wilt give ear to his commandments, and keep all his statues, I will put none of these diseases upon thee, which I have brought upon the Egyptians" (Exodus 15:26). Israel did not heed the warning. Sin is the great disease carrier of the human race.

721

Third, the *magnitude* of the judgment. The total killed in this judgment was "fourteen thousand and seven hundred" (16:49). This number made it the worst judgment of the three in the amount of people killed. In fact, it killed more than the other two judgments put together. The magnitude of the judgment emphasizes the fact that the more we rebel against God, the worse will be the judgment. If suffering small losses does not correct your ways, you will suffer bigger and bigger losses.

Fourth, the *momentum* of the judgment. The judgment came quickly and killed quickly. The judgment coming upon the people quickly was doubtless done in part to protect Moses and Aaron who were facing a vicious crowd that could bring death to Moses and Aaron with dispatch. But also sudden judgment is often the experience of those who have been repeatedly warned, as were these Israelites, yet continue to ignore the warnings (Proverbs 29:1). The Israelites had been fast in ignoring judgment and in castigating Moses and Aaron, so now God in return is fast in bringing judgment upon this obstinate bunch.

Fifth, the *mercy* in the judgment. Once again mercy was associated with Divine judgment. "And Moses said unto Aaron, Take a censer, and put fire therein from off the altar, and put on incense, and go quickly unto the congregation, and make an atonement for them: for there is wrath gone out from the LORD; the plague is begun . . . And he stood between the dead and the living; and the plague was stayed" (16:46,48). Despite being accused of killing the rebels, Moses and Aaron still act in mercy towards the people. This reminds us of God's mercy towards sinful men which ever gives men opportunity to repent. If a man perishes, he has no one to blame but himself; for he has had to climb over many barriers of God's mercy in order to perish.

If Christians demonstrated this sort of holy mercy towards others in church, many church fights would cease. Also many marriages would not end up in the divorce court if this kind of mercy was exercised between husband and wife.

Sixth, the *manifestation* in the judgment. A great contrast is seen here between Aaron and the 250 regarding burning of incense in the censers. The 250 tried it and were devoured by Divine fire. Aaron did it and not only survived, but he stopped the plague. The contrast manifested who was and who was not called to the priesthood. God had called Aaron to his post (Hebrews 4:5) but had not called the 250 to be priests.

C. THE CONFIRMING WITH THE RODS

Though God had confirmed in three ways (the three judgments) for the Israelites that the priesthood belonged to Aaron, the people still murmured and complained. So in grace, God gave them one more confirmation of the Aaronic priesthood. Unbelief can never complain about lack of evidence. God does not have to give all the evidence that He does, but in grace He provides an abundance of evidence for our faith so that no man can ever rightfully complain of lack of evidence.

To study this final confirmation of the Aaronic priesthood, we note the plan, proof, panic, and portrayal in the confirmation.

1. The Plan

God gave Moses a unique plan for confirming the Aaronic priesthood. We note the particulars and the purposes of the plan.

The particulars of the plan. "Take of every one of them a rod according to the house of their fathers, of all their princes according to the house of their fathers twelve rods: write thou every man's name upon his rod. And thou shalt write Aaron's name upon the rod of Levi . . . And thou shalt lay them up in the tabernacle of the congregation before the testimony, where I will meet with you. And it shall come to pass, that the man's rod, whom I shall choose, shall blossom: and I will make to cease from me the murmurings of the children of Israel, whereby they murmur against you . . . that they die not (17:2–5,10). To confirm the Aaronic priesthood a final time, God ordered Moses to take a rod from each tribe with the name of the chief ruler of that tribe to be written on each rod. On the tribe of Levi was written Aaron's name. The rods were to be left in the Tabernacle's holy of holies before the ark overnight. The rod that blossomed that night would be the confirming factor.

This was a good plan because it left the decision up to God. Moses did not make the decision, God did. Moses could have presented many good arguments for the Aaronic priesthood—and there is nothing wrong with doing that—but this Divine confirmation will be more effective. There are times when we need to reason with opposition by showing them good arguments for a cause or creed. But at other times, God must step in and vindicate His servants because of the belligerency of the opposers. Those who are right can count on Divine vindication.

The purposes of the plan. There was a threefold purpose in this confirmation plan. The blossoming rod would indicate "whom I shall choose . . . take away their murmurings . . . that they die not" (17:5–10). First, it was to *specify the mediator*; that is, it was to indicate ("choose") who was the high priest and, thus, who was the priestly family. That was the main purpose of the plan, and it was the main issue of Korah's rebellion. Second, it was to *stop the murmuring* of the people. Judgment had not stopped it, although it certainly should have. However, God said this sign would stop the murmuring. Third, it was to *save the multitude*. If the murmuring is stopped, then, of course, the judgment will stop and the people will not die. You stop judgment by stopping the sin that causes the judgment.

With the rod speaking of the resurrection of Christ (we will note more of this later), this threefold purpose demonstrates the work of Christ's resurrection. It indicated who is the mediator—it is Christ. It stopped the murmuring—the resurrection will stop all challenges to Christ's position. It saved the people—Christ "was raised again for our justification" (Romans 4:25).

2. The Proof

After receiving the rods, "Moses laid up the rods before the LORD in the tabernacle" (17:7) to await the verdict which would be evident on the next day. When the next day came, the proof was there for the Aaronic priesthood. We note the plentifulness, the publicness, and the preservation of the proof.

The plentifulness of the proof. "And it came to pass, that on the morrow Moses went into the tabernacle of witness; and, behold, the rod of Aaron for the house of Levi was budded, and brought forth buds, and bloomed blossoms, and yielded almonds" (17:8). Moses had stated early that the rod which would "blossom" (17:5) would indicate who had the priesthood. When he examined the rods the next morning, not only did blossoms show up on Aaron s rod, but so did buds (which precede blossoms), and even almonds (the fruit which follows blossoms). Thus the proof was overwhelming! God made it extremely evident that Aaron and his family were indeed the chosen priests. This is typical of God's evidence. The resurrection of Christ (which is foreshadowed in this miracle of Aaron's rod) likewise came with an abundance of evidence. "To whom also he showed himself alive after his passion by many infallible proofs" (Acts 1:3). The "many infallible proofs" certainly applied to Aaron's rod as it did to the resurrection of Christ. Our faith is not built on a few flimsy pillars of supposition and speculation. But it is built on an abundance of solid pillars of self-evident facts.

The publicness of the proof. "And Moses brought out all the rods from before the LORD unto all the children of Israel: and they looked, and took every man his rod" (17:9). Nothing was done under the table here. Everything was done up front and out in public. Moses brought out all the rods for all to see and then gave the rods to their owners so they could examine them at length. Openness is characteristic of the truth but not of error. False religions are always hiding, concealing, manipulating, covering up, and double-talking. The church at Rome with all its artifices, pieces of the cross, etc. that it has tried to pass off on the people over the years has been most reluctant to have its relics examined for veracity. Healing campaigns are the same. But when God is at work, proof of His work is made public so mankind can scrutinize it. May we who claim to be followers of Christ live so godly that those around us will see great proof of our faith when they scrutinize our conduct.

The preservation of the proof. "And the LORD said unto Moses, Bring Aaron's rod again before the testimony, to be kept for a token against the rebels" (17:10). This was a wise move. Had the rod been given back to Aaron and then stripped of its buds, blossoms, and almonds; soon the skeptics would again contest the results. Unbelief intentionally has a very short memory regarding evidences. But God preserves much proof for the skeptics. As an example, archeologists have found an abundance of proof of the claims of our faith in many parts of the world.

It is instructive to note that this rod that budded was eventually not found in the ark (we noted this fact in an earlier chapter of this book but will repeat it here because it is so applicable to our text). We know that the rod that budded was at one time in the ark, for "Moses did so [put the rod in the ark]: as the LORD commanded him, so did he" (17:11); and the New Testament verifies this when it says regarding the ark, "Wherein was the golden pot that had manna, and Aaron's rod that budded, and the tables of the covenant" (Hebrews 9:4). But when Solomon dedicated the Temple, "there was nothing in the ark save the two tables of stone, which Moses put there at Horeb, when the LORD made a covenant with the children of Israel, when they came out of the land of Egypt" (I Kings 8:9). The significance of the absence of the rod is found in the fact that the Temple in some ways pictures apostasy (as an example, there were small windows in the holy of holies for outside light whereas in the Tabernacle the holy of holies was lighted only by the glory of God). The absence of the rod, which represents the resurrection of Christ, is also indicative of apostasy; for apostasy leaves out the resurrection of Christ in their message.

3. The Panic

"And the children of Israel spake unto Moses, saying,

Behold, we die, we perish, we all perish. Whosoever cometh any thing near unto the tabernacle of the LORD shall die: shall we be consumed with dying?" (17:12,13). With the overwhelming evidence as to whom God had chosen for the priesthood, the people panicked and concluded they were all dead people. The panic of the people said two things about the people. One was good and the other was bad.

The good part said they *now recognize their sin*. That was something they had not been willing to do earlier even though judgment had come in three dramatic and pronounced ways upon the rebellion. The peoples' hearts were hard, like that of Pharaoh of Egypt, and so each judgment seemed to only harden them more. However, the latest proof—the confirmation in the rods—convinced them.

The bad part said they did *not recognize their salvation*. They saw they were wrong but refused to see that they could be saved by God's mercy. If the devil cannot keep us from admitting we are a sinner, he will next try to convince us that we are too great a sinner to be saved. If he cannot keep us from believing in Divine judgment then he will try to keep us from believing we can escape Divine judgment.

4. The Portrayal

The rod confirmation gives us a portrayal of Christ and also a portrayal of conversion. We will examine each separately.

The portrayal of Christ. The rod pictures Christ in its association, deprecation, restoration, and location.

First, *association*. The rod with Aaron's name on it was numbered with the rods of the rebellers, those who were guilty of much transgression in their seditious behavior. Likewise, Christ "was numbered with the transgressors" (Isaiah 53:12) in His death.

Second, *deprecation*. The rod of Aaron, because it had Aaron's name on it, was despised by the rebels; for it represented that which they hated. They had vented their dislike of

727

the Aaronic priesthood in very strong terms and had made some gross accusations concerning Aaron's conduct. Christ also was "despised and rejected of men" (Isaiah 53:3); and some terrible accusations were made of Him, too, such as, He was accused of being demon possessed (John 8:48).

Third, *restoration*. Aaron's rod was restored to life (as was evidenced by the buds, blossoms, and fruit). Christ also was restored to life and raised from the grave. And as the evidence was abundant that Aaron's rod was alive and that, therefore, Aaron was the chosen priest; so the evidence is abundant regarding Christ's resurrection (Acts 1:3) and that, therefore, He is the Great High Priest (Hebrews 9:25, 26).

Fourth, *location*. After Aaron's rod budded, blossomed, and bore fruit, it was kept in the ark of the Tabernacle where the presence of God dwelt. Shortly after His resurrection, Christ, too, was located in the presence of God (Mark 16:19). And as Aaron's rod in God's presence in the Tabernacle protected the Israelites from death (17:10), so Christ intercedes for His own in heaven before God's presence to keep them from eternal death (Romans 8:34, Hebrews 7:25).

The portrayal of conversion. As Aaron's rod pictured Christ in four ways, so we will note how it also pictures conversion in four ways. The four ways are mortification, regeneration, transformation, and glorification.

First, *mortification*. The rod of Aaron was dead at the beginning. Though it had participated in doing some great works, it was still a dead stick until it was restored to life by a Divine miracle. Likewise the sinner is also dead before salvation. He is "dead in trespasses and sins" (Ephesians 2:1). He may have done some great works in this world, as did Aaron's rod, but he is still dead spiritually. Do not confuse great works in this world with spiritual life.

Second, *regeneration*. The rod of Aaron was regenerated and given new life because it had the name of the high priest on it. The difference in the rods was not in the wood or their shape or size or past. The significant difference in the rods which made the difference between life and death was the name on the rod. The sinner is regenerated in the name of Jesus Christ. It makes no difference what his race, past, size, or age may be. What brings salvation is Jesus Christ. "Neither is there salvation in any other: for there is none other *name* under heaven given among men, whereby we must be saved" (Acts 4:12).

Third, *transformation*. The regeneration of Aaron's rod brought a tremendous transformation to it. A dead stick was changed to one that had buds, blossoms, and bore fruit. It was a dramatic change indeed. This pictures the great change that takes place in a person when he gets saved. "If any man be in Christ, he is a new creature: old things are passed away; behold, all things are become new" (II Corinthians 5:17). The redeemed soul is transformed from spiritual deadness to a producer of good works. "For we are his workmanship, created in Christ Jesus unto good works" (Ephesians 2:10). The redeemed evidence life. They bud, they blossom, and they produce fruit for God. "The fruit of the Spirit is love, joy, peace, longsuffering, gentleness, goodness, faith, meekness, temperance" (Galatians 5:22,23). Some folk who claim to be saved are not like Aaron's rod that budded, blossomed, and bore fruit. They still act and look like nothing but a dead stick which indicates their profession of faith is false. But if we are really saved, it will show.

Fourth, *glorification*. After Aaron's rod budded, blossomed, and bore fruit, and was shown to the people, it was placed in the ark where the presence of God was. It was thus given a very glorified position. So when a person is saved, his future will be one of glory. "Whom he justified, them he also glorified" (Romans 8:30). The redeemed will one day go to heaven where they will be in the presence of God, and that will be a glorified situation indeed. It is the greatest glory man can ever have.

XXX.

STRIKING THE ROCK

NUMBERS 20

THE MOST TRAGIC event in the life of Moses occurred when the wilderness wanderings were about over. The event involved a water problem in which Moses disobeyed God by striking a rock with a rod for water instead of speaking to it. Moses' sin "blighted the fair flower of a noble life, and shut the one soul, whose faith had sustained the responsibilities of the Exodus with unflinching fortitude, from the reward [of entering Canaan] which seemed so nearly within its grasp" (F. B. Meyer). Commenting on the gravity of this experience in Moses' life, Charles Simeon said, "Scarcely shall we find any portion of sacred history that is more calculated to affect a pious mind, than this."

Numbers 20, the chapter which records this tragic event in Moses' life, is a most solemn chapter. It begins with the death of Moses' sister Miriam (v. 1), ends with the death of Moses' brother Aaron (vv. 23–29), and in the middle tells of the sin that determined the death of Moses. The events of Numbers 20 took place in the last year of the forty years it took Israel to get from Egypt to Canaan. After wandering in the wilderness of Paran for some thirty-eight years in punishment for their rebellion at Kadesh, Israel finally returned to Kadesh in the "first month" (v. 1) of the fortieth year (cp. Numbers 33:38) of their trip from Egypt to Canaan. Then Miriam died, and this was followed by the rock striking incident that so adversely affected Moses.

We noted in our last chapter that not much was reported of the thirty-eight years Israel spent in the wilderness as a punishment for their rebellion at Kadesh. The sedition of Korah was

730

the main experience recorded. A few other minor events were also recorded, but for the most part, the thirty-eight years were a blank in Israel's history—in fact a total blank of good reports. This blank of good reports is typical of sin, for sin does that to our lives. It leaves them blank in terms of good things.

After the thirty-eight years were expired, action did pick up again, however; and much was recorded about the movements of the Israelites towards their goal of reaching Canaan. The first major event recorded is the event in which Moses struck the rock for water instead of speaking to it.

To examine this most tragic event in Moses' life which occurred the second time Israel got water from a rock, we will consider the shortage of water (vv. 2–6), the supplying of water (vv. 7,8,11,13), and the sin about water (vv. 9–12,23–29).

A. THE SHORTAGE OF WATER
The rock-striking incident was brought on by a shortage of water. To look more into this water shortage in Israel's camp, we will note the seriousness of the shortage, the snarling because of the shortage, and the supplication about the shortage.

1. The Seriousness of the Shortage
"And there was no water for the congregation" (v. 2). Water shortage problems in the Sinai peninsula should not surprise us. What should surprise us is the fact Israel did not have more of these shortages. Of course, the reason they did not have more of them was that at times God worked miracles to provide water for them. But here when they return to Kadesh, they experienced a water shortage, a shortage which led to the tragic rock-striking incident in Moses' life. This would not be Israel's last water problem before entering Canaan; for as they journeyed from Kadesh on their way to Canaan, Numbers 21 reports they soon experienced more water problems.

Water problems are major problems as we have noted in earlier studies. "It is a great mercy to have plenty of water, a mercy which if we found the want of we should own the worth of" (Henry). The value of water is emphasized a bit later in the book of Numbers when we learn of Israel singing a song because a well had been successfully dug to bring the people water (21:16–18). We can get along without just about anything easier and longer than we can get along without water. This makes water a good symbol of soul salvation, a symbol Jesus used at Jacob's well when speaking to the woman of Samaria. He spoke of salvation as "living water" (John 4:10) which is given by Him. Without this water, you have the greatest, most perilous shortage you could possibly have in life. Soul salvation is the most important need of anyone's life. One may have other needs which are legitimate, but they are not as important as the need of salvation, for you can meet all those other needs and still go to hell when you die.

2. The Snarling Because of the Shortage

During that thirty-eight year period of wandering in the wilderness for punishment for the rebellion at Kadesh, the old generation died off and the new generation grew up. But when the new generation moved back to Kadesh from where they would begin to move northward to go into Canaan, they evidenced here the same old rebellious attitudes of the old generation. When this crisis came in the camp, they snarled at Moses just like their fathers had done. In this water crisis, we see their snarling in their animosity, attitude, and accusations.

Animosity. "And they gathered themselves together against Moses and against Aaron. And the people chode with Moses" (vv. 2,3). The water shortage in the camp turned the Israelites against Moses and also Aaron. This is nothing new for the leaders of Israel. Every time a problem came up, their popularity ratings went down. Those who want so much to be in high places need to remember that this is one of the things that comes with the position. You can be cheered today but "chode" tomorrow depending on how the sun shines. Popular approval is very fickle and seldom has anything to do with logical thinking. It often dims much of glory of high position. Too many folk who want high position only see the glory of high places, they never see the groaning involved—but there is plenty of groaning. In fact, there is generally a lot more groaning than glory. People in high position are not to be envied.

Attitude. "Would God that we had died when our brethren died before the LORD!" (v. 3). In their snarling at Moses, the Israelites revealed a terrible attitude about life, but an attitude that is not uncommon either with the Israelites or with people in every age. We note several ways in which this attitude is bad. First, it was an *unprofitable* attitude. Wishing you were dead is hardly a profitable way to deal with a problem. This attitude helps nothing. It is the quitters' attitude which only intensifies your problem instead of helping to solve it. Second, it was an *uncomplimentary* attitude. It criticized God's dealings with them. The Israelites, as others do in every age, were stupidly second guessing God. But instead of second guessing God, they ought to have been submitting to God. That would have helped them solve their problems, but second guessing does not. Third, it was an *unthankful* attitude. God had protected and provided for them for all these years in the wilderness and all God gets in return from them is their complaint and criticism, not their thanks. This, too, only makes their problems harder to bear. Unthankfulness never makes life easier.

Accusations. The Israelites in their snarling made two very serious and uncalled-for accusations of Moses. They accused him of being injurious and incompetent.

First, they accused him of being *injurious* when they said, "Why have ye brought up the congregation of the LORD into this wilderness, that we and our cattle should die there?" (v. 4). Moses has to be tired of hearing this same old accusation. Again and again, as we noted in our last chapter, the Israelites accused Moses of bringing them into the wilderness to kill them. This is a pretty vicious accusation. Pastors can learn from this. They

733

will also be viciously accused of preposterous purposes. Let the pastor propose a larger mission program, and he will be accused viciously by some dissidents of not caring for the church's own community (of course if you check the dissidents' offering, you will understand that they do not care about anyone's souls—but hypocrites that they are, they ignore that fact in accusing the pastor). Let the board propose a building program and the dissidents will viciously accuse the board of not caring for the needs of the poor but wasting money on buildings instead (it never seems to occur to the dissidents that a building program will help reach many more people with their greatest need of all—their spiritual need). The unholy can perversely interpret any work of God as wasteful, useless, and even as evil and injurious. The devil, of course, is behind all such accusations.

Second, they accused him of being *incompetent* when they said, "Wherefore have ye made us to come up out of Egypt, to bring us unto this evil place? it is no place of seed, or of figs, or of vines, or of pomegranates; neither is there any water to drink" (v. 5). The blame is again laid on Moses for the Israelites not being in Canaan yet. This accusation was very prominent in the sedition of Korah. The accusers ignore the true reason why the Israelites were still in the wilderness (which was the rebellion at Kadesh against Moses about going into Canaan). They ignore the fact that had they followed Moses, they would have been in Canaan. Dissidents are gifted at twisting the facts so that black is white and white is black. But when men rebel against God, their minds simply do not reason well at all in areas of right and wrong (cp. Romans 1:21–32).

3. The Supplication About the Shortage

"And Moses and Aaron went from the presence of the assembly unto the door of the tabernacle of the congregation, and they fell upon their faces: and the glory of the LORD appeared unto them" (v. 6). Again we witness a noble reaction of Moses to problems in his life (Aaron did the same as Moses; but Aaron's actions, though commendable here, was that of a follower, not a leader. Moses is the one to get the most praise for this reaction). When trouble came, Moses went to God for help. There is no wiser action than this.

But though this is a most wise reaction to problems, few practice it. Instead of seeking God in their problems, many often do a lot of other things which puts them into a nervous stew and makes them unable to do their work well. In their problems, some will call a few of their friends on the phone and pour out their troubles, often exaggerating them in order to gain more sympathy. Others seek the advice of psychologists and psychiatrists whose advice indicates they have not solved major problems in their own lives and do not know how to truly solve the problems of others either (although they know how to take your money via counselling fees). Still others react to their problems by going off the deep end and getting drunk or taking drugs or even committing suicide. But none of these reactions to problems do anything to help solve problems; they only worsen problems. God is the great problem solver. Go to Him in prayer and seek His Word if you want real wisdom to meet your problems successfully. Of course, you must heed His Word about your problems. Failure to heed it will aggravate your problem as it did Moses which we will see more about later.

B. THE SUPPLYING OF WATER
God had a solution for the water problem. God is never out of solutions. And His solutions are always the best solutions. To examine God's solution for the supplying of water, we will note the command for the supply, the copiousness of the supply, and the commemoration of the supply.

1. The Command for the Supply
"And the LORD spake unto Moses, saying, Take the rod, and gather thou the assembly together . . . and speak ye unto the rock before their eyes; and it shall give forth his water, and thou shalt bring forth to them water out of the rock: so thou shalt give the congregation and their beasts drink" (vv. 7,8). God's

solution for the water supply came via a command. We note the place of the command and the particulars of the command.

The place of the command. With this solution coming via a command, we once again see the association of miracles with commands and of blessing with duty. God does not work miracles in a way that would hinder character. God does not supply our needs in a way that would discourage industry and hard work. Salvation comes full and free without works attached, but it will not come if we do not repent and call upon the name of Christ—so even salvation is not apart from responsibility. Israel needed water, and God will supply water. But the supply will not be apart from some sort of duty for them all.

This is a simple principle but a very important one in life. However, many have not caught on yet to its value. As an example, governments have made the tragic mistake of doling out welfare in a way that fosters immorality, promotes sloth, and kills responsibility. In the home the same thing often happens. Children are given many things by their parents except duties and responsibilities—such as chores around the house. Churches even fall into this trap, too. They give out charity carelessly which only encourages professional tramps to keep begging. Many rescue missions are wise to make those they help at least attend a preaching service before they are fed.

The particulars of the command. "And the LORD spake unto Moses, saying, Take the rod . . . gather thou the assembly together . . . speak ye unto the rock before their eyes; and it shall give forth his water, and thou shalt bring forth to them water out of the rock" (vv. 7,8). This command involved three things—wand, witnesses, and words.

First, the *wand.* "Take the rod . . . And Moses took the rod from before the LORD" (vv. 8,9). With the rod being taken "from before the LORD," it means it had to be Aaron's rod which had budded, for it was only one rod that was "before the LORD." This term "before the LORD" is used to describe anything that was in the holy of holies of the Tabernacle where the ark and the presence of God was. A container of manna was to be laid up "before the LORD" (Exodus 16:33), and we know from Hebrews 9:3 and 4 that this meant it was put in the ark in the holy of holies in the Tabernacle. Another term used to express the same location was "before the Testimony" (Exodus 16:34, Numbers 17:4,10). That some argue that this rod was not Aaron's rod but another rod amazes us, for Scripture does not speak of any other rod but Aaron's as being "before the LORD." We do not see what the problem is in using this rod that causes some commentaries to insist this was not the rod that budded. But on the contrary, we can see the wisdom of using this rod here; for the rod had been used earlier in the budding experience to stop the murmuring of the Israelites against Moses and Aaron (Numbers 17:5); and its appearance here was to do the same. The rod confirmed the authority of Moses and Aaron. God was wisely sending forth His servants with valid credentials. If you lack the needed credentials, you may be presuming a calling.

Second, the *witnesses*. "And gather thou the assembly together . . . and speak ye unto the rock before their eyes" (v. 8). The whole congregation was to see this miracle. In the first miracle in which water was obtained from a rock, Moses was told by God to take only "the elders of Israel" (Exodus 17:5) with him when he smote the rock to obtain water from it. But here the whole congregation is to see the miracle. Either way, however, the lesson is the same—God wants His work attested. He wants His work to be scrutinized to see how excellent it is and that it is not fraudulent or unreal. Truth wants examination. Error, of course, does not. When a person is accused of a crime, he will be glad to be examined thoroughly if he is innocent. But if he is guilty, he will try every legal loophole possible to keep from being examined. An accused person only evidences his guilt when he shuns inspection.

Third, the *words*. "Speak ye unto the rock . . . and it shall give forth his water" (v. 8). All that Moses is required to do to obtain water from the rock here is just speak to it. The speaking gives us two lessons. One on diversity of methods and the other on disobedience of man.

The first lesson in the speaking concerns the *diversity of methods* used in God's work. In the former miracle of water from the rock, God ordered Moses to strike the rock. Here is it different; he is to only speak to the rock. Moses, of course, resorted to striking the rock again (which we will note more about shortly) which was a very great mistake. F. B. Meyer said about the different methods, "But how much there is of this reliance on the rod in all Christian endeavor! Some special method has been owned of God in times past, in the conversion of the unsaved, or in the edification of God's people, and we instantly regard it as a kind of fetish. We try to meet new conditions by bringing out the rod and using it as of yore. It is a profound mistake . . . It is for us to consult Him, and to abide by his decision; doing precisely as He tells us, and when, and where." Some always approach a lost person with "The Romans' road" technique. Others always use "The four spiritual laws." These methods are certainly not condemned here, but neither are they the only ways by which to approach a sinner. Jesus used different approaches with Nicodemus, Zacchaeus, the woman at the well, and others. We need to know Scripture well enough so we can meet any sinner where he is and lead him to Christ. Philip used the "Understandest thou what thou readest?" approach with the Ethiopian eunuch. Such a method would not work with many others, however. But Philip was following the leading of the Holy Spirit, something we need to be doing in our methods.

The second lesson in the speaking concerns the *disobedience of man*. God said that when Moses spoke to the rock, it would give forth water. This rebukes man, for the rock would thus obey God better than the Israelites were obeying God. We need that lesson as well as Israel did. If nature was as rebellious as we humans are, what a mess creation would be. If the sun, moon, and stars did not stay in their commanded courses, it would be chaos and destruction for all of us. If the earth did not revolve around the sun at the speed it does, and if it did not tilt back and forth on its axis as it does, what chaos would result. It is always a rebuke to mankind to behold nature obeying God better than we do. Would that man would recognize that when he disobeys God, he is creating chaos in God's creation.

2. The Copiousness of the Supply

"And the water came out abundantly, and the congregation drank, and their beasts also" (v. 11). From the rock came enough water to satisfy the thirst of several million people plus a host of livestock. No small supply was this to provide the water needs of a multitude of people that was large enough to compare to a great city of our day. This was a tremendous supply of water from just one source. Sometimes artists paint this situation so poorly. They show a small stream of water coming from a rock with a small group of people and a few animals drinking from the stream. That does not represent the situation at all, and it does not help us see the greatness of God's miracle power.

It is marvelous how God supplies the needs of His people. Here again God supplies water from a most illogical place—out of rock. This should instruct and strengthen our faith. None of us goes long in life without some need pressing greatly upon us and in a situation in which we see no circumstantial means of supplying the need. We look for wells or rivers or lakes to meet the need of water, but none are near. This really tests our faith, and it causes us to look vertically instead of horizontally for help. But how often we doubt that God can supply our need when we see no help in our circumstances for supplying that need. If the horizontal is barren, we often times think the vertical is barren, too. If all we have are rocks in our circumstances, we cannot possibly see how God can supply water for us. But God can supply water from rocks! His supplies often come from strange and unexpected places so that we will keep our eyes focused on Him rather than on the means of the supply. Looking only at circumstances can be very disheartening. But God is greater than our circumstances. He can make the rocks in our circumstances supply in a copious way all our pressing needs.

3. The Commemoration of the Supply

"This is the water of Meribah, because the children of Israel strove with the LORD, and he was sanctified in them" (v. 13). After the first miracle of water from the rock which occurred at Rephidim, the place was named Meribah (Exodus 17:7). The word means strife. Here the name is given again as circumstances are the same. The lesson in this name commemoration is that God often leaves reminders in our life of our sin in order to help us live better and to avoid the repeating of our sin. The reminders may be physical scars or they may be daily burdens which we must carry because of our disobedience. These reminders do not mean God has not forgiven us, but that He is only giving us some pungent reminders of the peril of disobedience in order to hinder our repetition of the sin. If you do not pay attention to these reminders, you will be given more. One "Meribah" should be enough; but when we repeat our sin, we ask for more humiliating and painful scars.

C. THE SIN ABOUT THE WATER

Moses' response to God's solution for the water problem was a disaster for Moses though it provided water for the people. Moses' response was that which brought his exclusion from the promised land (Aaron was also excluded for he sinned here, too). To further study some of the details about this sin of Moses and its consequences, we will note the deportment of Moses, the declaration by God, and the death of Aaron.

1. The Deportment of Moses

When we think of Moses' sin here, we generally think only of his striking of the rock instead of speaking to it. That was indeed part of his sin and the most pronounced part. But that was not all the sin involved in Moses' actions in this incident. There were more sin problems involved. Scripture speaks of at least five sin problems in the deportment of Moses which excluded him from Canaan. They are disobedience, denunciation, dishonor, disbelief, and distemper.

Disobedience. "And Moses lifted up his hand, and with his rod he smote the rock twice" (v. 11). God had instructed Moses to "speak ye unto the rock" (v. 8) as we have noted a bit earlier. But instead of speaking to the rock, he smote the rock twice. He had smitten the rock the first time water was obtained from the rock (Exodus 17:6) which gave Moses a precedence for such action. But precedence must not usurp precept in God's work. It makes no difference how you did it before if God tells you to do it differently the next time. Precedence has its place, but it is not above precept. You can ignore precedence and not get in trouble with God, but you can never ignore God's precepts without getting into big trouble. In Christ's days on earth, the religious leaders exhibited Moses' problem here when they gave more honor to tradition than to God's commandments.

Denunciation. Scripture makes it plain that Moses also sinned with his lips regarding this water problem, for the Psalmist says, "He spake unadvisedly with his lips" (Psalm 106:33). We have no difficulty knowing what he said that was "unadvisedly" spoken. It was his denunciation of the Israelites. He said, "Hear now, ye rebels; must we fetch you water out of this rock?" (v. 10). It is the "Hear now, ye rebels" of this speech that we especially focus on for this particular sin of Moses. What Moses said was true—they were rebels of the first order! But it was the manner in which he spoke this rebuke to them that was wrong. His manner of speaking is found in the meaning of the word "unadvisedly" in the above text from Psalms. The word "unadvisedly" is translated from a Hebrew word which means "to vociferate angrily" (Wilson). Moses lashed out at the people in an uncharacteristic angry way for him, and that was wrong. We must not, however, use this condemnation of Moses' speech to put velvet on preachers' tongues and to water down the message of judgment. Rather, we must use it to show the importance of having the right spirit when we speak.

Dishonor. When Moses said, "Must we fetch water out of

741

this rock?" (v. 10), he dishonored God in that Moses assumed some honor that did not belong to him. The "we" takes upon himself and Aaron the honor that was due to God. It was God's power that brought forth water from the rock, but Moses' speech puts the honor upon himself and Aaron instead. Hence, when rebuking Moses, God said Moses and Aaron did not "sanctify me in the eyes of the children of Israel" (v. 12) which means "they did not give him that glory of this miracle which was due unto his name" (Henry). We always foul up our service for God when self-glorying gets in the way as it does so often with many men. To hear some preachers and evangelists talk and write about themselves, you would think they are the greatest answer to the world's problems and that God is fortunate they are serving Him. But pride cancels out much of their worth for service.

Disbelief. Lack of faith was the foundation of Moses' poor deportment here. "Because ye believed me not" (v. 12) is the root of the problem. It is hard to accept the fact that Moses, after serving so gallantly for many years and demonstrating such great faith when hardly anyone else demonstrated any faith, should now be guilty of unbelief himself. But Scripture does not lie. Lack of faith was indeed a big problem with Moses here. He did not believe what God said about the manner in which he was to get the water. It was not so much a lack of faith in the power of God as it was in the plan of God. But lack of faith is condemned no matter how it manifests itself.

This lack of faith coming late in Moses' life is a strong warning to every child of God to stay faithful to the end. We cannot let up near the finish line or we will not finish as victoriously as we could. A runner who lets up near the finish line is liable to be passed and thus lose a great victory.

Distemper. In Moses' words and actions, we have already seen a man acting in uncontrolled passion. But we mention it here separately, for the Bible mentions it separately. "They *angered* him also at the waters of strife, so that it went ill with

Moses . . . they *provoked* his spirit, so that he spake unadvisedly with his lips" (Psalm 106:32,33). Though Moses should not have gotten so angry, we can easily understand why he did. Most of us would have blown our cool long before Moses did in dealing with the ever provoking Israelites. Our amazement is how he dealt so patiently with them for so long.

In losing his temper, Moses sinned in his strongest area, for he was the meekest man on the earth (Numbers 12:3). "What a warning is here, admonishing us that we sometimes fail in our strongest point . . . Let us watch and pray lest beneath a fair exterior we yield our jewel of faith to the solicitation of some unholy passion. Let us especially set a watch at our strongest point. Just because we are so confident of being strong, there, we are liable to leave it unguarded and unwatched, and therefore open to the foe" (F. B. Meyer).

2. The Declaration by God

Moses' poor deportment was soon met by a very unwelcomed message from God. It was a declaration of Divine judgment. "And the LORD spake unto Moses and Aaron, Because ye believed me not, to sanctify me in the eyes of the children of Israel, therefore ye shall not bring this congregation into the land which I have given them" (v. 12). Moses got results when he struck the rock, but results do not guarantee reward, nor do they exempt one from punishment for disobedience. What does guarantee reward and exemption is obedience. Results reflect the grace of God; they do not necessarily sanction a method.

This exclusion from Canaan was certainly a very severe sentence for the crime committed. One has to really admire Moses in being faithful to record his wrong actions and the sentence they received. To examine this sentence more, we will look at the arguments for the sentence, the appealing of the sentence, and the alleviation of the sentence.

Arguments for the sentence. The usual reaction by the reader to this sentence is one of shock. The sentence seems so extreme, much too severe, not reflective of justice at all, and just down-right cruel. The reader wants to ask what is wrong with God. How can he do this to Moses, a man who has been so gallant for so long? Aaron being excluded from the promised land is not hard to accept, for he was a rascal at times anyway. But not Moses. It seems so unfair to the average reader that Moses should be excluded from Canaan for just this one failure. But God's judgments can never be faulted. They are all executed with Divine wisdom. Though the human mind may recoil at Moses' sentence, yet the punishment was fair and holy; for it came from Almighty God who always does right. Hence, it behooves us to do some examining of Scripture to find the justi-fication for this judgment. And justification can be found, and it will underscore how merciful God is to all of us.

We note four arguments that justify the severity of the Divine judgment upon Moses. They are the privileges of Moses, the publicness of the sin, the portrayal of Christ, and the peril for the rod.

First, the *privileges of Moses*. We noted in our last chapter that privilege aggravates our sin. This was seen when Moses rebuked the Levites for their sin by referring to their privileges as that which should have discouraged their rebellion. When we sin in spite of our privileges, the judgment will be greater. And the greater our privilege, the greater our judgment. Moses walked in tremendous privilege. He had spoken with God as no other man in Israel's camp. He had been permitted to see the glory of God in a special revelation at Sinai. He had been the means through which tremendous miracles had been worked in Egypt and in the wilderness. To do what he did at Meribah after these privileges really makes his sin most serious. The prophet Amos reminded Israel that the reason God often dealt with them more harshly than other nations was that "You only have I known of all the families of the earth; therefore I will punish you for all your iniquities" (Amos 3:2). Spiritual privileges bring responsibilities. When we walk in great light, we have less excuse for stumbling and more rebuke for falling.

Second, the *publicness of the sin*. Another thing that aggravated Moses' sin was that it was done in public. It was done before the entire congregation. Everyone saw him lose his temper. While the congregation may not have known of all the things Moses was doing wrong, they saw his bad temper and heard him exalt himself instead of God about the miracle power of fetching water. It was before the "eyes of the children of Israel [the whole congregation]" (v. 12) that Moses did not "sanctify me [God]" (Ibid.). Private sins are not to be minimized and played down; but while they are bad, they generally do not cause the problem that public sins do. Public sins multiply the evil influence of the deed. Therefore, with the sin being worse in its effect upon people because it was public, it requires more severity in judgment.

Third, the *portrayal of Christ*. A third reason why Moses was severely punished is that he destroyed the message of Christ. The smiting of the rock the first time was a great picture of Christ being smitten at Calvary. We noted this in detail in chapter 18 of this book. To smite the rock a second time ruined the picture of Christ, for Christ was only smitten once. "So Christ was once offered to bear the sins of many" (Hebrews 9:28), "For Christ also hath once suffered for sins" (I Peter 3:18), and "He died unto sin once" (Romans 6:10). "These texts prove how important it was to keep clear and defined the fact of the death of Christ being a finished act, once for all. It is evident that for the completeness of the likeness between substance and shadow, the rock should have been stricken but once. Instead of that, it was smitten at the beginning and at the close of the desert march. But this was a misrepresentation of an eternal fact" (F. B. Meyer). After Christ has been smitten once, we only need to speak to Him for the water of life. But reject this message and you will not go to heaven. Since Moses in type rejected this message of salvation by perverting it, he in type shows what happens to those who reject the Gospel—they are kept out of the place of soul rest (cp. Hebrews 3:18,19).

Fourth, the *peril for the rod*. The rod Moses was using was the one that had buds, blossoms, and fruit on it. This came about when the rod was placed in the Tabernacle in the contest with the Levites during the sedition of Korah. We studied this in detail in the last chapter of this book. Smiting the rock twice as he did was a great "endangering [of] the blossoms of the rod" (Jamieson) as well as the buds and fruit. This rod was a very valuable rod with the buds, blossoms, and fruit on it; for it gave great proof concerning the Aaronic priesthood which is a type of Jesus Christ. God, therefore, is not going to have Moses use this rod for smiting anything, for it could the damage the buds, blossoms, and fruit and thus destroy the proof in the rod. But Moses used the rod to smite the rock anyway. Again we can understand why the judgment was so severe. Damaging the rod could challenge the priesthood. In type, it means that the message of Christ was again being handled poorly. And God does not look lightly upon corrupting the message of Jesus Christ.

Appealing of the sentence. Moses later vainly appealed to have the sentence removed. "I pray thee, let me go over, and see the good land that is beyond Jordan, that goodly mountain, and Lebanon"(Deuteronomy 3:25). It was an earnest but sad appeal for clemency which received a harsh rebuke from God. "But the LORD was wroth with me for your sakes, and would not hear me: and the LORD said unto me, Let it suffice thee; speak no more unto me of this matter" (Deuteronomy 3:26). No pious person can read this appeal and its rejection without much solemn soul searching. It causes us to want to be more careful in our obedience to God. "It is a solemn question for us all whether we are sufficiently accurate in our obedience" (F. B. Meyer).

The rejection of the appeal reminds us that though God forgives, He still often brings much chastening to us. Some view the mercy and forgiveness of God as an encouragement to sin. They think that they can sin with impunity as long as they run to God for forgiveness after they sin. But such thoughts will lead to disaster. God forgives the sinner but not in a way that will ever encourage more sinning. We have seen this lesson repeatedly in the study of Moses' life. Generally the lesson has been seen in the suffering Israel experienced for their sin after it was forgiven. But here it is the suffering Moses must experience.

Alleviation of the sentence. God's mercy did allow, however, that Moses would many centuries later set foot on the promised land. It occurred doing the days of Christ's earthly ministry when Christ was transfigured. During the transfiguration "there talked with him two men, which were Moses and Elijah" (Luke 9:30). Moses' entrance into Canaan was delayed some fifteen hundred years. While this was a glorious experience for Moses to be at Christ's transfiguration, it does not take away from the fact that Moses could have earlier had some more glorious experiences had he not failed at Meribah.

3. The Death of Aaron

Numbers 20 ends with an account of the death of Aaron which occurred on the first day of the fifth month "in the fortieth year after the children of Israel were come out of the land of Egypt" (Numbers 33:38). Aaron was 123 years old when he died (Numbers 33:39). Aaron's death was the first fulfilling of the sentence God gave to Moses and Aaron for their sin at Meribah, for Aaron was also included in the sentence. Aaron did not have the lead in the sin as did Moses, but neither did he do anything to hinder Moses' sin. Aaron was a willing accomplice in it all. Men may not accuse Aaron of much sin in the incident, but God sees the hearts and that makes His judgments accurate.

The details of the death of Aaron gain significance when we look at them from the standpoint of typology. As High Priest, Aaron was a type of Christ, and in his death he is fittingly also a wonderful type of the death of Christ in a number of points. We will note twelve of these points.

First, the *announcement* of his death. "The LORD spake unto Moses . . . Take Aaron and Eleazar his son, and bring them up unto mount Hor . . . and [he] shall die there" (vv. 23,25,26). The details of Aaron's death were stated by God to men before

Aaron died. Likewise, God informed men about the death of Christ before Christ died. Isaiah 53 of the Old Testament is an example of this informing of men about Christ's death before He died. In the New Testament numerous statements predicting and detailing Christ's coming death were made before His death—most of them coming from Christ Himself.

Second, the *awareness* of his death. Aaron knew well about the plans for his death. Christ likewise was very cognizant of the plans for His death. When speaking with Moses and Elijah during the transfiguration, He talked with them concerning His death (Luke 9:31). And as we noted in the previous point, He repeatedly spoke of His death to the people during His earthly ministry.

Third, the *accusation* at his death. His death was a result of the fact that he was accused of sin (v. 24). But for sin, Aaron would not have died. So it was with Christ. Christ died as an accused sinner and for our sin. He was sinless, of course, but vicariously He died as a sinner.

Fourth, the *audience* on his way to death. "They went up into mount Hor in the sight of all the congregation" (v. 27). A great crowd of people saw Aaron go to the place of his death. And a great crowd of people saw Christ go to Calvary, for "there followed him a great company of people" (Luke 23:27) as He was led to Calvary. Aaron's crowd did not follow him up the mount, but the type is that a great crowd of people saw both Aaron and Christ go to their place of death.

Fifth, the *area* of his death. Aaron died on a hill. It was Mount Hor in his case. Israel was beginning their northward journey towards the east side of Jordan when they came to Mount Hor. Christ also died on a hill. It was Calvary in His case. No hill is so famous. Still ranked as one of the most favorite hymns of our time is the hymn that begins, "On a hill far away, stood an old rugged cross."

Sixth, the *abasing* at his death. God told Moses to "strip Aaron of his garments . . . And Moses stripped Aaron of his garments" (vv. 26,28). Aaron wore the beautiful garments of the high priest. But in death he was abased by being stripped of this glory. Christ was also abased in His death by being stripped both in position and physically. In position Christ "humbled himself, and became obedient unto death, even the death of the cross" (Philippians 2:8). Physically, soldiers "stripped him" (Matthew 27:28) during His trial, and at Calvary soldiers stripped Christ again of His garments when they "took his [Christ's] garments" (John 19:23) and divided them up among themselves (Ibid.). Much humility was involved for both Aaron and Christ in their deaths.

Seventh, the *acquiescing* to his death. Scripture does not record anywhere that Aaron protested his death in anyway. He was taken up the mountain without any fighting or rebelling. Christ did not protest His death either. Calm and quiet at His trial, He went willingly and without protest to Calvary. Isaiah describes it well when he said, "He was oppressed, and he was afflicted, yet he opened not his mouth: he is brought as a lamb to the slaughter, and as a sheep before her shearers is dumb, so he openeth not his mouth" (Isaiah 53:7).

Eighth, the *abruptness* of his death. Aaron died suddenly. There was no sickness, no lengthy lingering. He simply died quickly at the hand of God. Likewise Christ died quickly on the cross. Dying on a cross was a excruciating way to die and often took days for the one on the cross to finally succumb unless measures were taken to hasten the death such as the breaking of one's legs (John 19:31,32). But when the soldiers came to break the legs of Christ, they discovered that "he was dead already" (John 19:33), and as a result, "Pilate marvelled if [that] he were already dead" (Mark 15:44).

Ninth, the *abyss* after his death. Aaron was "gathered unto his people" (v. 24) after he died. That means that he went to sheol, the place of the spirits of the departed dead. This was also Christ's experience, but Scripture stresses it was only a temporary experience for Christ, for Christ rose from the grave—"Because thou wilt not leave my soul in hell" (Acts 2:27). The word translated "hell" here is from the Greek word "hades" ("sheol" is the equivalent Hebrew word) which does not always mean a place of torment. Therefore, "hell" is a poor translation in this text in Acts. Hades (or sheol) was divided into two compartment (Luke 16:26). One part was for the damned and was a place of fire and torment as is seen in Luke 16:23–25. "Hell" is a good description and a permissible translation for this part. But the other part, which was sometimes called "Abraham's bosom" (Luke 16:22), was where the souls of the righteous were until after the crucifixion when the souls of the righteous were then taken to be with the Lord. Christ went to this part. "Hell" is definitely not a good description or permissible translation for it.

Tenth, the *associates* in his death. Two men were with Aaron when he died. They were Aaron's son Eleazar and Aaron's brother Moses. When Christ died on Calvary, there were two with Him also. "They crucified him, and two others with him, on either side one, and Jesus in the midst" (John 19:18).

Eleventh, the *anguish* over his death. "And when all the congregation saw that Aaron was dead, they mourned for Aaron thirty days, even all the house of Israel" (v. 29). The Israelites will also mourn for Christ. That day is yet to come, but it will come, and it will be a day of great mourning. "And they shall look upon me whom they have pierced, and they shall mourn for him, as one mourneth for his only son, and shall be in bitterness for him, as one that is in bitterness for his firstborn. In that day shall there be a great mourning in Jerusalem" (Zechariah 12:10,11). The mourning which Scripture records for Aaron and also for Christ demonstrates a failure of mankind. It is only after men lose their blessings that they seem to finally learn to appreciate them. While Aaron and Christ were alive, most of the Israelites scorned them, not honored them. But send your flowers while the person is alive. Do not wait until they are dead to buy that huge and expensive bouquet. We have no problem with one buying a large bouquet of flowers for a friend or relative who has died, but we see some character problem when that is about the only time the flowers are bought for the person.

Twelfth, the *advancing* of his work after his death. When

Aaron died, his work continued; for his garments were put on his son Eleazar (v. 28) who then continued Aaron's work—in this case as the high priest. When Christ died and left this earth via His ascension, His work of the Gospel was continued on, too. It continued on through His disciples, through those who had received Him as Savior. In Eleazar we see three important truths about serving Christ in this work: the prerequisite of service, the position in service, and the power for service.

(1) The *prerequisite for service*. Eleazar continued Aaron's work by virtue of his birth into Aaron's family. So the believer can serve Christ because he has been born into the family of God through the new birth. This means we cannot serve until we are saved. Salvation is the first prerequisite for service.

(2) The *position in service*. Eleazar was given Aaron's priestly robes (v. 28) to designate his replacement of Aaron as the high priest. The believer does not replace Christ, but in advancing the work of Christ, he, like Eleazar, is given a priestly position. Believers are "an holy priesthood" (I Peter 2:5) and "a royal priesthood" (I Peter 2:9).

(3) The *power for service*. Eleazar's name shows us where we get power or strength to serve. His name means "whom God aids" (Gesenius) or as Strong says, "God is helper." Service cannot be done without God's help. "Except the LORD build the house, they labor in vain that build it; except the LORD keep the city, the watchman waketh but in vain" (Psalm 127:1).

XXXI.

SERPENT OF BRASS

NUMBERS 21:4–9

APART FROM GENESIS 3, we have in our text the most important snake story in the Bible. In terms of numbers, it is the biggest snake story in the Bible (which makes it fitting that the story is in the book of Numbers). The most famous snake in the story is not a real snake but a serpent of brass. Jesus Christ gave this snake story its greatest fame by referring to the serpent of brass (John 3:14) when talking with Nicodemus and informing him (and everyone who reads that text in John) that the serpent of brass spoke of Christ (we will see more on this later). Paul also associated this story with Christ when he said, "Neither let us tempt Christ, as some of them also tempted, and were destroyed of serpents" (I Corinthians 10:9).

This famous snake story occurred shortly after Israel had ended their wilderness wanderings and had started on the path that would eventually lead them into the promised land. The story revolves around some more misbehavior on the part of the Israelites. Though Israel was only a few months from entering Canaan, they still engaged in some nasty fussing because some things were not the way they would like them to be on the journey. This, of course, did not go over well with God; and so God judged the people. The judgment for their poor behavior was snakes with the serpent of brass providing the means of escape from the judgment.

To study this snake story and the famous serpent of brass, we will consider the conduct of the people (vv. 4,5), the curse on the people (vv. 6,7), and the cure for the people (vv. 8,9).

752

A. THE CONDUCT OF THE PEOPLE

Israel's conduct in this snake incident was despicable. We can see that fact in at least five ways. We see it in their attitude about the way, in their alienation from God and Moses, in their accusation of Moses, in their appraisal of the supplies, and in their abhorrence of manna.

1. Their Attitude About the Way

"And they journeyed from mount Hor [where Aaron died] by the way of the Red sea, to compass [go around] the land of Edom: and the soul of the people was much discouraged because of the way" (v. 4). The people did not think much of the way in which they were traveling. The word "discouraged" in our verse is the word that speaks of the Israelites' attitude about the way, but the Hebrew word from which the word "discouraged" is translated means a good deal more than discouragement. In fact, discouragement is really not the dominant attitude. Impatience is. The Hebrew word means to cut off and to shorten. When applied to one's attitude or spirit it means a short spirit—we would say a short temper. Gesenius says of the word as it is used here, "My spirit is short, i.e. I am impatient, my patience is wearied out." Keil says, "As they went along this road the people became impatient." It is evident by the actions of the Israelites here that they were of a bad temper. Discouragement could easily be and was doubtless present with their circumstances, which we will detail shortly; but the Hebrew word and their actions indicate primarily a lack of patience and its attendant shortness of temper. The context basically shows the Israelites throwing a temper tantrum. We note four features of "the way" which could be factors in giving them (and all those who walk in the flesh instead of by faith) an impatient attitude about it. These four features are the detour, the difficulties, the direction, and the deprivations of the way.

Detour. The Israelites were on a detour around Edom when this uprising broke out in camp. Our verse said, "They journeyed from mount Hor by the way of the Red sea, to compass the land of Edom." Earlier at Kadesh, Moses had sent messengers to the king of Edom requesting permission to pass through their land (Numbers 20:14). But "Edom refused to give Israel passage through his border" (Numbers 20:21). This meant that Israel had to detour around Edom. They had to go south to Ezion-Geber (Deuteronomy 2:8) on the northern tip of the eastern inlet of the Red Sea (Gulf of Aqaba) and then up north to go around Edom. This circuitous way to Canaan made for a long trip—too long for Israel's patience.

It requires a lot of patience to follow God's route. We like the short cuts which will get us where we want to go in a hurry. Some shortcuts are permissible and even advisable. But many times in God's way, the long route is the ordered route. Shortcuts, such as trying to go through Edom, often result in much loss. Satan offered Christ a shortcut to "the kingdoms of the world" (Matthew 4:8). But Christ chose the long way of the cross rather than the short cut of worshipping Satan. Had He not made the choice that He did, it would have been chaos for everybody. But He went the long way. He *"endured* the cross" (Hebrew 12:2) and also *"endured* such contradiction of sinners against himself" (Hebrews 12:3) because of going the way of the cross. The word "endured" in these two verses comes from a Greek word rendered "patient" in Romans 12:12 ("patient in tribulation") and "patiently" in I Peter 2:20 ("ye shall take it patiently . . . ye take it patiently"). We need to frequently pray for patience to stick to God's way.

Difficulties. The area through which Israel was passing to make this circuitous trip around Edom was a very rugged area. This way was "a stony, sandy, almost barren plain shut in by mountain walls on either side, and subject to sand storms" (Winterbotham). Also in comparing Numbers 33:38 (the time of Aaron's death) with 20:29 (the mourning time for Aaron's death), we can see that the trip occurred around the sixth or seventh month of the fortieth year which was during some of the hottest times of the year in that area. The heat itself would easily and quickly shorten tempers as well as the difficulty of the terrain. "Portions of our pilgrimage are among the green pastures of peace; but others over hills of difficulty, intricate paths, and rugged mountain passes, and amidst powers of darkness" (E. S. Prout). When we are on these difficult ways, we need patience to continue faithfully on the pathway. It is easy to be patient when we are on a smooth road; but when it gets rough, tempers often shorten and we behave in unsavory ways.

Direction. Another factor that would be upsetting to the Israelites, was the fact that though they had just had a great victory over king Arad and his Canaanites (Numbers 21:1–3) who had attacked them, Israel was not permitted to continue on into Canaan from the south where they had defeated the Canaanite attackers. Though they had "utterly destroyed them [the Canaanites of King Arad] and their cities" (Numbers 21:3), yet the Israelites were ordered to go around Edom which would lead to an eastern entrance into Canaan rather than to go straight ahead and enter Canaan from the south. This change of direction would not sit well with the flesh. Like the detour caused by Edom's refusal to let Israel through their land, this change of direction would really test the patience of Israel's faith. Sometimes God seems to lead us in the opposite direction we think we should be going. But be patient; God knows the way better than we do. Our duty is simply to follow His leading.

Deprivations. Traveling the route the Israelites were traveling meant they would not enjoy the abundance of pasture, watering places, food variety, and comforts. This was not a luxury trip. It was a trip that involved spartan conditions for the people. They had to do some sacrificing and going without. God supplied their needs, of course; but they would not enjoy the extras that came with better territory. We will note shortly that they did some complaining about the lack on this way (which they exaggerated). Here we note that the deprivations during the lengthy journey were another feature of this way which wore out the patience of the Israelites. Many Christian servants can attest to this problem. Having to go without year after year in the ministry can wear one's patience thin especially when you see the miserly way the well-to-do church members give. But it is part of the "way" God sometimes leads us, and we need to learn how to handle this experience well for the honor of God and for the advancing of the work of God. We may have to be deprived of many comforts of life in order that the work of God advance according to God's plan. But if we are truly dedicated to the advancing of His work, we will have the patience to go without as long as necessary. Christ certainly suffered much deprivation in order to perform His ministry and advance the cause of the Gospel. How shameful for us to get upset and complain if we must suffer some deprivations also.

2. Their Alienation From God and Moses

"The people spake against God, and against Moses" (v. 5). One of the things which made the Israelites conduct so despicable here is that they alienated themselves from God and Moses. They literally turned against the best. As we noted in some previous chapters, being against or speaking against Moses when he was leading Israel in God's way was actually also being against and speaking against God. Our text simply repeats that fact when it says Israel spoke against both God and Moses. You cannot separate the two. If the Israelites are going to be against God, they will also be against Moses; for Moses is for God. If they are going to be against Moses, they will also be against God; for Moses is leading them in God's way. When people do not like Moses when he is obeying God, they will not like God. If people do not like God's ways, they will not like Moses; for Moses walked in God's ways. This situation still exists today. Therefore, we who love the Lord should not be surprised if a number of people do not like us, for everyone that does not love the Lord is our potential enemy. Jesus said, "If the world hate you, ye know that it hated me before it hated you. If ye were of the world, the world would love his own: but because ye are not of the world . . . the world hateth you . . . If they have persecuted me, they will also persecute you" (John 15:18–20). If pastors preach the Word faithfully, those who are out of sorts with God will not like the pastor. This explains why many pastors are not liked by a number of church members.

It is significant that in all the Israelites' fussing here, they did not once speak out against the Edomites for any of their troubles, though the Edomites were indeed the reason why the long detour was being taken. How often this blaming exemption occurs. We never seem to blame the devil for our troubles but blame God instead; or at church, we blame the pastor. This must make the devil laugh in glee. He causes so much trouble to happen, but then people blame God or His people instead.

3. Their Accusation of Moses

"Wherefore have ye brought us up out of Egypt to die in the wilderness?" (v. 5). This is at least the eighth time that Moses has been charged by the Israelites with trying to kill the congregation of Israel (see Exodus 5:21; 14:11; 16:3; 17:3; Numbers 14:3; 16:41; and 20:4 for the previous seven times). It must have wearied Moses to repeatedly hear this vicious and cutting accusation which accused him of murderous designs in bringing the Israelites into the wilderness. How backward was this ugly charge. It was, in fact, Moses, who through his gracious intercession with God, kept these people alive. They needed to thank Moses that they were alive instead of accusing him of plotting their death. But as we noted in some previous chapters, the accusers of God's faithful servants do not need facts to accuse; and they often accuse God's servants of deficiency in the very area in which God's servants are performing with excellence.

4. Their Appraisal of the Supplies

The impatient Israelites took stock of their supplies and concluded "there is no bread, neither is there any water" (v. 5). This was not a true appraisal of their supplies. They were not without bread, for they had the manna which provided all the bread they needed. Furthermore, they were not without water, for there was no special providing of water by God here as would have been done if they were without water. Water sources were not plentiful on this route, of course; but they were not without water. However, the Israelites distorted the facts, as complainers do, and said there was no water.

Israel was doing what a lot of people do in times of trial—they only focused on the bad part of their situation, not on any good parts. They only looked on the dark side of things, not on the bright side. If we only look on the dark side, the difficulties, the problems, the privations, and the clouds in life, we will be miserable all the time; for we are never totally free of negatives in life. But if we want to be something other than a sour, critical, and negative person, we will need to focus on what blessings we do have instead. Israel was well supplied with manna, was on its way to entering Canaan regardless of the detour, and their difficult trip was not going to be forever. So they needed to cheer up. But the Israelites only looked at the negatives factors in their life—and exaggerated them at that—and ended up complaining, criticizing, and in general acting very poorly. And that is what usually happens when you focus only on the negatives.

5. Their Abhorrence of Manna

"Our soul loatheth this light bread" (v. 5). This complaint about manna really condemned them. The people "quarreled with God's food. He gave them the best of the best, for 'men did eat angels' food;' but they called the manna by an opprobrious [contemptuous] title ['light'], which in the Hebrew has a sound of ridicule about it, and even in our translation conveys the idea of contempt" (Spurgeon). They accused God in this complaint of providing bread that was deficient bread. They said it was not that which would make them strong and robust and healthy. That was, of course, a lie. Manna was sufficient for their dietary needs. But people are ever complaining about God's provisions and insisting the provisions are not sufficient.

This complaint especially reminds us of how people complain about the Word of God, which the manna typifies. Spurgeon says, "This is another of man's follies; his heart refused to feed upon God's word or believe God's truth. He craves for the flesh-meat of carnal reason, the leeks and garlic of superstitious tradition, and the cucumbers of speculation; he cannot bring his mind down to believe the Word of God, or to accept truth so simple, so fitted to the capacity of a child. Many demand something deeper than the divine, more profound than the infinite, more liberal than free grace." Many folk do not believe the Bible is capable of meeting our needs. They think we need something else at church. To many folk, having only a Bible-preaching and teaching ministry at church is very boring and distasteful. They "loath" the Word instead of love it. But if you truly love God, you will love His Word. One who loathes the Word of God also loathes God. One can easily discern the affection or lack thereof which people have for God by observing the affection or lack thereof which they have for the Word of God. Unfortunately, our churches are filled with people who have very little affection for the Word—which says they have little affection for God though they may be very active at church.

B. THE CURSE ON THE PEOPLE

The despicable performance of the Israelites was, of course, most unacceptable to God; and so God sent judgment upon the people. He cursed them with snakes. We note the infliction of the curse, the influence of the curse, and the intercession because of the curse.

1. The Infliction of the Curse

"And the LORD sent fiery serpents among the people, and they bit the people; and much people of Israel died" (v. 6). Three things can be said about these snakes in their coming upon the Israelites in judgment for their sin. They are the sending of the snakes, the striking by the snakes, and the slaying by the snakes.

759

The sending of the snakes. God "sent" the snakes. We are told in Deuteronomy 8:15 that the wilderness of Paran was a place of "fiery serpents." But the people were protected from them by God. Here, on this journey southward, God ceased to protect the people from the snakes and turned them loose on the people. God controls creation and can make it bless or curse people. When we live in sin, we risk turning creation against us. Sin makes blessings become curses.

The striking by the snakes. "They bit the people." Strong describes the meaning of "bit" as "to strike with a sting." Therefore, the venom not only hurt the people, as we will note next; but obviously the bite also hurt. There are not many things more unsettling than to walk in an area infested with snakes. The congregation of Israel must have been filled with shrieks and screams and great horror as they found their pathway infested with writhing snakes and then began to be attacked by these snakes. Throughout the congregation, which was, of course, traveling on foot, snake after snake would raise its ugly head and strike forward sinking its sharp fangs into the flesh of some Israelite and shooting its poisonous venom into the bitten one. Complain about your situation too much and God will give you something to really complain about.

The slaying by the snakes. "And much people of Israel died." The snakes were poisonous snakes as we have noted above. And the venom of these poisonous snakes appears to have worked very fast in killing the Israelites as snake venom often does. Once an Israelite was bitten, he or she soon became violently sick as the venom worked its way through the body shutting down the vital organs until the bitten one succumbed to the poison. It is a good picture of the way sin works. The problem with sin, however, is that unlike the snakes, people often do not think sin will hurt them. They play with the serpents, pet them, caress them, feed them, and delight in them only to be destroyed by them.

2. The Influence of the Curse

Because of the snake problem, "the people came to Moses, and said, We have sinned, for we have spoken against the LORD, and against thee; pray unto the LORD, that he take away the serpents from us" (v. 7). The judgment by God upon Israel had its intended effect. God chastens us to cause us to turn from our sin. This is exactly what Israel did. They acknowledged and confessed their sin of speaking against both God and Moses.

The response of the Israelites to their snake problem was an excellent response, and the response condemns our world today. People today, unlike the Israelites in this incident, do not associate adversities with their evil deeds. They refuse to see any adversity as judgment for their conduct. We are experiencing many judgments of God upon us because of our sin, yet we do not hear people confessing their evil. We have diseases, earthquakes, floods, extreme weather conditions, and other disasters plaguing our land; but any talk of repentance is laughed at by people. They attribute all these adversities to chance and happenstance. Israel did nothing of the sort, however. They wisely saw the true cause and effect.

3. The Intercession Because of the Curse

When the people confessed their sin and asked Moses to pray for them, "Moses prayed for the people" (v. 7). Again, as before in similar situations, how magnanimous of Moses to intercede for the people. He could have told them they were getting what they deserved and if they want prayer, they can pray for themselves. But Moses was of another spirit, a spirit that Christ has exhorted us to embrace. It is the spirit of forgiveness that we are to have when people genuinely repent. But one cannot exhibit this spirit well without God's help. As we said in an earlier chapter, we must walk close to the One Who demonstrated this spirit the best in order to possess it ourselves. If more marriages reflected this spirit, divorce courts would run out of business. If more Christians acted this way one towards another, the work of the Lord would progress as never before.

761

But Christ's "Father, forgive them; for they know not what they do" (Luke 23:34) and Stephen's "Lord, lay not this sin to their charge" (Acts 7:60) is a great contrast to the spirit of vengeance that rules our day.

We would note here before going on to the next point that this spirit of forgiveness does not, of course, mean we should stop punishing criminals and that hell should be closed for further admittance. This spirit is a spirit that is ready to forgive when there is repentance. But until there is repentance, forgiveness cannot be properly and fully given. But the readiness to forgive must always be present.

C. THE CURE FOR THE PEOPLE

"And the LORD said unto Moses, Make thee a fiery serpent, and set it upon a pole: and it shall come to pass, that every one that is bitten, when he looketh upon it, shall live. And Moses made a serpent of brass, and put it upon a pole, and it came to pass, that if a serpent had bitten any man, when he beheld the serpent of brass, he lived" (vv. 8,9). God graciously provided a cure for this great affliction of snakes that came upon the Israelites for their sin. The cure involved a serpent of brass which Moses was to make and put on a pole so the stricken Israelites could look at it to be healed of their snake bites. To further examine this cure, we note three things about it. They are the plan of salvation in it, the person of the Savior in it, and the perversion by sin over it.

1. The Plan of Salvation

This cure is a great picture of the Gospel. That the Gospel is indeed pictured in this cure is proven by what Christ said to Nicodemus. "And as Moses lifted up the serpent in the wilderness, even so must the Son of man be lifted up; that whosoever believeth in him should not perish, but have eternal life" (John 3:14,15). In at least ten ways this cure pictures the plan of salvation. They are the source, the strangeness, the sufficiency, the singularity, the simplicity, the supernaturalness, the suddenness, the stipulation, the saliency, and the supporting of the cure.

First, the *source* of it. The source of this cure for Israel was God. It was His plan and idea. Men did not think it up. Moses did not sit down with the princes of Israel and work this plan out from a consensus of ideas. The plan of salvation is the same. It was God who devised the plan of salvation, then He revealed it to mankind. Apart from Divine revelation, neither the cure for the snake bites nor the cure for sin would ever have been known by man.

Second, the *strangeness* of it. This was a strange plan for bringing about a cure for snake bites. Medical officials in Moses' day and also in our day would view this plan as the strangest of plans. The Gospel plan also seems strange to the thinking of the world. "We preach Christ crucified, unto the Jews a stumblingblock, and unto the Greeks foolishness" (I Corinthians 1:23). But it makes no difference how the world views the plan if the plan works. And this plan in the wilderness worked and so does the Gospel of Jesus Christ!

Third, the *sufficiency* of it. The cure revealed by God to Moses was sufficient to cure anyone who had been bitten by the snakes. No one who was bitten by a snake would die if they looked at the serpent of brass. Christ likewise is sufficient for every sinner. "Whosoever shall call upon the name of the Lord shall be saved" (Romans 10:13).

Fourth, the *singularity* of it. The serpent of brass was the only means by which the inflicted Israelites could be saved from death. It was the only cure, the only remedy, and the only solution made known to them. Likewise, the Gospel of Christ is the only means of our soul salvation. "Neither is there salvation in any other: for there is none other name under heaven given among men, whereby we must be saved" (Acts 4:12), and "Jesus saith unto him . . . no man cometh unto the Father, but by me" (John 14:6).

Fifth, the *simplicity* of it. The cure was so simple. All a stricken person had to do was look upon the serpent (v. 8) and he was healed. There were no rituals to go through, no money to pay, and no joining of any organization to be done before the sick person could be made well. All the person bitten by a snake had to do was to look at the serpent. Salvation is also very simple. We simply receive Christ as our Savior. We do not have to go through any rituals or pay any money or join any church or turn over a new leaf to be saved. All we must do is receive Christ as our Savior. Many people of the world struggle over the simplicity of the Gospel, and many religions have tried to complicate it. But they cannot change the fact that faith in Christ is all that is needed. Salvation is so simple to obtain, yet it is so tremendous in its effect upon man.

Sixth, the *supernaturalness* of it. The cure was obviously a miracle. The healing was not of natural means. It required the supernatural power of Almighty God to bring it to pass. Salvation also requires the power of God. Paul speaks of that power when he said, "I am not ashamed of the gospel of Christ: for it is the power of God unto salvation" (Romans 1:16). Salvation is the greatest miracle that ever touched the lives of men.

Seventh, the *suddenness* of it. As soon as an Israelite looked upon the serpent of brass, the cure came about. It was a good thing it was sudden; for the venom of the serpent's bite, like that of most poisonous snakes, would work very fast. After looking at the serpent of brass, the Israelite did not have to wait for days before the cure took effect. If that had been the case, none of the Israelites would have survived. Salvation is also sudden in its effect. When a person receives Christ as Savior, immediately that person is saved. If salvation was not immediate in its effect, many would not be saved. Growing may take a lifetime, but birth takes but a moment.

Eighth, the *stipulation* of it. The Israelite who was bitten by a snake was the one who needed to look upon the serpent of brass (v. 8) in order to be saved. Someone else looking at the snake would not bring healing for them. It was a personal matter. You were not healed by proxy. So it is in soul salvation; another person cannot accept Christ for you. You must do that yourself. Your parents, grandparents, brothers, sisters, cousins, aunts, uncles, and friends may be saved; but that does not save you. Their receiving Christ does not bring you into the fold. You must yourself receive Christ if you want salvation.

Ninth, the *saliency* of it. The serpent of brass was to be put on a pole so all in the camp of Israel could see it. Thus the cure was to be accessible to everyone, not just those near the serpent of brass. Likewise the Gospel of Christ is accessible to all; for the offer is "whosoever" (Romans 10:13). The Gospel is offered to all men. No one is excluded from the offer. But one can, of course, exclude himself from salvation by rejecting the Gospel.

Tenth. the *supporting* of it. The serpent of brass was supported by a pole. Apart from the pole, which "lifted up" (John 3:14) the serpent, the serpent of brass would have done very little for the people; for few people could have seen the serpent to look upon it. This pole in its work of supporting the serpent pictures the work God's people should be doing regarding the Gospel message. God's people must make Christ known (seen) to the world. They must support the work of the Gospel so it can be proclaimed to people. Paul told the Philippians they were to "shine as lights in the world; holding forth the word of life" (Philippians 2:15,16). How well are you supporting the Gospel? Are you helping in any way to lift up the message of Christ so it can be heard in your community and the world?

2. The Person of the Savior

Christ is proclaimed in the Old Testament much more than people think. As an example, Christ said the ladder which Jacob dreamed about spoke of Christ (John 1:51). If that spoke of Christ, how many other things in the Old Testament must have spoken about Him. One would like to have been with Christ on the road to Emmaus that first Easter Sunday when He began "at Moses and all the prophets . . . [and] expounded unto them in all the scriptures the things concerning himself" (Luke 24:27). One of the Scripture texts He would have referred to would be this text in Numbers. We know that fact because when speaking with Nicodemus, Christ said it spoke of Himself (John 3:14). We note here three ways in which this serpent of brass spoke of

765

Jesus Christ. They are the character of Christ, the curse on Christ, and the cross of Christ.

The character of Christ. The serpent of brass was made like the fiery serpents whose bite brought death to mankind. But the serpent of brass did not have poison in it. It was like the serpent but not full of poison. In character, Christ "was made in the likeness of men" (Philippians 2:7); but He was not sinful like man. The corrupt part, the poison, was not in Him. This made it possible for Him to be our Savior and die in our place. Had He been sinful, He could only have died for His own sins.

The curse on Christ. In order to save us, Christ had to be made a curse for us. That is, He had to take our place as a sinner. "Christ hath redeemed us from the curse of the law, being made a curse for us" (Galatians 3:13). In two ways the curse on Christ is seen in the serpent of brass. One way is in it being a the serpent. The serpent was cursed by God (Genesis 3:14) in the Garden of Eden after the fall of man. The other way is in the fact that the serpent was raised up on the pole which pictures the cross of Christ. And this constitutes a curse, "for it is written, Cursed is every one that hangeth on a tree" (Galatians 3:13).

The cross of Christ. The serpent was put on a pole then lifted up as the pole was put in the ground. This is what Christ spoke of to Nicodemus. The "lifted up" in John 3:14 spoke of the cross of Calvary on which Christ was nailed and then lifted up on it to die.

3. The Perversion by Sin

Men habitually pervert God's blessings into curses. This was done with the serpent of brass some seven centuries later. During the time Hezekiah reigned as king of Judah, "He . . . brake in pieces the brasen serpent that Moses had made: for unto those days the children of Israel did burn incense to it: and he called it Nehushtan" (II Kings 18:4). The only instructions

God gave regarding the serpent of brass pertained to their wilderness travels and the snake bites. But centuries later, the Israelites ignored these commands of God and perverted things by burning incense to the snake as though it were a god. Hezekiah did the right thing. He named it a fitting name and then destroyed it. The name "Nehushtan" according to Ryrie in his study Bible means "a mere piece of bronze [or copper]"; that is, it is not a god at all, but just a piece of metal. There are several good lessons in this action of Hezekiah. They have to do with praise and pollution.

First, there is a lesson about *praise*. Like the Israelites in Hezekiah's day, we are honoring things God is not honoring. We need to call them what they really are instead. Modern art comes to mind. We are giving it great praise and honor when it is nothing but some blobs of paint on a canvas or some pieces of junk piled together. Sports achievements also need to be put in their place, for they are greatly overrated. The same is true regarding making money and a host of other things we get so excited about to the exclusion of God. We need to stop burning incense of undue honor to them and call them "Nehushtan."

Second, these is the lesson about *pollution*. The perverted use of the serpent polluted the simple and pure Gospel message. The serpent of brass was a simple cure for a sinful curse. But the Israelites were adding a host of unsanctified observances to the serpent of brass which were of a corrupt theology. A corrupt Gospel does not save but curses, just as the misuse of the serpent of brass did not heal of anything but only cursed.

XXXII.

SETTLEMENT OF GILEAD

VARIOUS TEXTS

THE LAST GREAT achievement by Moses in leading Israel from Egypt to Canaan was the settling of some of the Israelites in Gilead. While Moses was not permitted by God to cross the Jordan and go into Canaan where the bulk of the Israelites settled, he was permitted to lead the Israelites in the obtaining of land for two and a half tribes (Reuben, Gad, and half the tribe of Manasseh) who settled on the eastern side of the Jordan in "the land of Gilead" (Numbers 32:29). Moses gave "half mount Gilead, and the cities thereof . . . unto the Reubenites and to the Gadites. And the rest of Gilead . . . unto the half tribe of Manasseh" (Deuteronomy 3:12,13). As we will note later, these two and a half tribes were required to go across Jordan and help conquer the land of Canaan for the Israelites; but after the conquering of Canaan, "the children of Reuben and the children of Gad and the half tribe of Manasseh returned . . . to go unto the country of Gilead, to the land of their possession" (Joshua 22:9).

To study this last great achievement of Moses, we will consider the passing to Gilead, the possessing of Gilead, the protecting of Gilead, and the partitioning of Gilead.

A. THE PASSING TO GILEAD

The trip to Gilead began after the Israelites had defeated King Arad and the Canaanites he ruled (Numbers 21:1–4). This victory came at the end of the thirty-eight years of wandering in the wilderness Israel was sentenced to for their sin at Kadesh. Thus, with the sentence completed, the time had now come to enter

Canaan. The entrance to Canaan was to be from the east side of the Jordan; therefore, Israel headed for Gilead as it was located on the east side of the Jordan. To study the passing to Gilead, we will look at the route, the rules, and the rivers. We could insert one more point here and call it "rebellion," for it was at the beginning of this trip to Gilead that the brazen serpent incident occurred. But because of its significance, we gave the entire preceding chapter to the study of that incident of rebellion.

1. The Route

The trip north to Gilead actually began by going south as we noted in our last chapter. It began at Kadesh and went south seventy-five miles or so to Ezion Geber, a town located near the north end of the Gulf of Aqaba, the eastern inlet of the Red Sea. Going south was necessary in order to go around Edom which had refused to let Israel pass through its land (Numbers 20:21; 21:4). From Ezion Geber, Israel then turned north "through the way of the plain from Elath" (Deuteronomy 2:8) and went around the borders of Edom and Moab to the land of Gilead.

The route was not the easiest route to travel. It would have been much easier if Israel had been able to go directly from Kadesh to Canaan. But that was not the path God directed them to take. We noted in our last chapter that the route south was a very rough path. Here we note that the route north was no improvement. In fact, some of it was even worse than what they had traveled before. Because they had to march around Edom and Moab, they marched "on the very outskirts of the great sandy, shadeless waste, stretching far into the Persian Gulf, which was even more terrible than the desert highway they had just left beyond the mountains . . . In truth, their circumstances at this time were more trying, and even apparently more desperate, than any their ancestors had ever encountered in their marching" (Jamieson). We who live in the luxuries of the western world with our interstate highways, automobiles, fast moving trains, and faster moving planes with all their built-in comforts have little appreciation of the rugged traveling conditions Israel experienced on their trip from Egypt to Canaan. These conditions ought to silence our complaints about difficulties on our way. The next time you think you are experiencing a bit of discomfort or inconvenience to attend church, remind yourself of the traveling conditions Israel experienced in order get to the promised land. Then go to the mourners' bench and repent of your complaining.

2. The Rules

God gave Moses several rules about how the Israelites were to act as they made their way to Gilead. These rules specifically concerned Israel's dealings with the Edomites, Moabites, and Ammonites. These three nations were related to Israel. The Edomites were descendants of Esau, the brother of Jacob. The Moabites and Ammonites were descendants of Moab and Ammon, the sons of Lot by incest with his daughters. Lot was Abraham's nephew and thus related to the Israelites. Israel was to "take ye good heed unto yourselves" (Deuteronomy 2:4) how they treated these nations as they passed by them. We note two specific rules to be followed in regards to the treatment of these nations. The rules concerned peace and payments.

Peace. Five times God warned the Israelites not to aggravate these three nations they were passing by. "Meddle not with them" (Deuteronomy 2:5), "distress [them] not" (Deuteronomy 2:9), "neither contend with them" (Ibid.), "distress them not" (Deuteronomy 2:19), "nor meddle with them" (Ibid.). The words "meddle" and "contend" come from the same Hebrew word and mean to not irritate or anger or stir up or make war against. The word "distress" comes from the Hebrew word meaning to cramp or confine or press upon one in an hostile way. Israel was simply to leave the Edomites, Moabites, and Ammonites alone and do nothing that would provoke any contention.

This rule would be especially hard to obey because of the way two of the three nations (the Edomites and Moabites) had treated Israel. Neither of these two nations would let Israel pass through them but forced Israel to go on a circuitous trip around them. The natural reaction would be to war against these nations. But God said, "No." And when God says, "No," that is final. God often tests our faith to see just how well we will obey Him. And it is especially hard to obey Him when we have been wronged and the flesh cries out for revenge.

This rule says we are not to be unnecessarily contentious. Israel was to war against the Canaanites, but that did not mean they were to war with everyone. Christians are to put up a good fight against evil, but that does not mean we are to be of a contentious spirit with everyone. Paul said, "As much as lieth in you, live peaceably with all men" (Romans 12:18). While there are wars to fight and battles to be won, we do need to primarily be peaceful people. We need to try and get along with others. If greater efforts were made in this matter among God's people, we would have fewer church fights and splits, and we would not see so many marriages break up either.

Payments. Another rule for Israel was that they were to pay for any food or water they got from these nations. "Ye shall buy meat of them for money . . . and ye shall also buy water of them for money" (Deuteronomy 2:6). This rule stated that Israel was not to freeload. Though the rulers of some of these nations were hostile towards Israel, some of the people were not; and they were willing to sell Israel needed supplies. When this occurred, the Israelites were to pay for the supplies.

Christians need this exhortation. It is shameful the way many saints travel through this world in this matter. They freeload as much as they can. They are poor at paying bills, complain if a doctor wants his payment right after he has performed his services, get behind in their payments, and in general evidence a very poor attitude about paying their dues to others. Paul said, "Owe no man any thing" (Romans 13:8). This does not mean one cannot borrow money or other goods. It means we should not get behind in making payments and paying our bills. All our accounts should be up to date.

3. The Rivers

Two rivers stand out rather significantly in Israel's trip to Gilead. They are the Zered River and the Arnon River. The two rivers formed the south border (Zered River) and the north border (Arnon River) of the nation of Moab. One river (Zered) represented the end of the old generation of Israel; the other river (Arnon) represented the beginning of Israel's conquests of land for their possession. One river (Zered) speaks of retribution; the other (Arnon) speaks of responsibility.

Zered River. "Now rise up, said I, and get you over the brook Zered. And we went over the brook Zered. And the space in which we came from Kadesh-barnea, until we were come over the brook Zered, was thirty and eight years; until all the generation of the men of war were wasted out from among the host, as the LORD sware unto them" (Deuteronomy 2:13,14). The Zered River (called "brook" in our text, but it is the same word translated "river" in Deuteronomy 2:24 in "river Arnon") marked the end of the old generation of Israelites. God had decreed their death thirty-eight years earlier at Kadesh when they refused to enter the land of Canaan. Many of them did not die right away after the Kadesh experience but lived on for many years. However, by the time they reached the Zered River, all the old-timers had finally died (except Moses, Joshua, and Caleb).

This mention of judgment at Zered emphasizes the certainty of Divine retribution upon sinful man. Mankind has a habit of mocking God's judgments and insisting they will not come to pass. The critics of God's judgments make a lot of noise when the judgments do not happen right away. They think that since judgment does not come right away, the deed was not bad. But sooner or later there will be a Zered of some kind that will silence the mockers of the certainty of Divine judgment. You may be living a profligate life today without any apparent effects, but Zered is on your pathway, and you will not pass it.

Arnon River. "Rise ye up, take your journey, and pass over the river Arnon: behold, I have given into thine hand Sihon the Amorite, king of Heshbon, and his land: begin to possess it, and contend with him in battle" (Deuteronomy 2:24). Whereas the Zered River marked an ending, the Arnon River marks the beginning. Once Israel passed over the Arnon River, they were now in Gilead territory; and it was land which God wanted Israel to possess. Therefore, God commanded Israel to go ("contend") to battle. The command says if they want the land, they have some responsibilities to fulfill to obtain the land. The word "contend" in verse 24 is translated from the same word as "meddle" in Deuteronomy 2:5 and 19 and "contend" in Deuteronomy 2:9. There are places where we are not to war, as those verses state, but there are other places where we are to war. Some are fighting where it does not matter but not fighting where it does matter. We need heavenly wisdom to know the difference.

B. THE POSSESSING OF GILEAD

For over four hundred years, Israel had been without any land. Most of those years they had lived in exile in Egypt with the last forty years being lived in the Sinai peninsula. Now they are going to begin to get some land of their own where they can settle down and live. The first segment of land to be possessed is land on the east of the Jordan often called Gilead (a city in Gilead was also called Gilead, see Deuteronomy 2:36). The possessing of this land came about through war with the two kings who governed Gilead—Sihon king of Heshbon and Og king of Bashan. These kings were called "the two kings of the Amorites" (Deuteronomy 3:8), for Gilead was the land where the Amorites lived. Sihon's kingdom was the southern half of Gilead, and Og's kingdom was the northern half.

1. The War with Sihon

The first step in possessing Gilead was to go to war with Sihon. To examine this war, we will note the envoy for peace, the exhortation from God, the eradication of the people, the endowment of goods, and the exaltation for victory.

The envoy for peace. "I sent messengers out of the wilderness of Kedemoth unto Sihon king of Heshbon with words of peace, saying, Let me pass through thy land . . . But Sihon king of Heshbon would not let us pass by him" (Deuteronomy 2:26,30, cp. Numbers 21:21,22). Before the war with the Amorites took place, Moses offered them peace. But they rejected it. It was a dastardly attitude of Sihon, and it cost him his life and kingdom. He had nothing to lose in allowing Israel to pass through his land. The Israelites were not going to hurt him at all, and they would pay him for any water or food they procured from them (Deuteronomy 2:27,28). But Sihon would not accept this offer and instead went to battle with Israel.

Sihon is an illustration of every perishing soul in that peace has also been offered to them on very gracious terms, but they have rejected the offer to their doom. Christ has died on Calvary for our sins and has been raised from the grave to be our Mediator. It is God's offer of peace. But multitudes reject this offer and go to war against God trying to drive Him out of their lives. Such a battle is doomed to failure even as Sihon miserably failed when he went against Israel.

We need to note that Sihon's rejection of Israel's peace envoy is associated with the hardening of his heart by God. "The LORD thy God hardened his spirit, and made his heart obstinate, that he might deliver him into thy hand" (Deuteronomy 2:30). This certainly reminds us of Pharaoh of Egypt. Some, of course, when reading this text about Sihon will conclude that God is not fair; for it looks like God hardened Sihon's heart just so He could punish him. But we must remember that God hardens no one's heart without that person first rejecting God. Sihon got what was coming to him just as Pharaoh did. Beware, therefore, of rebelling against God lest God condemns you to a hard heart to your destruction.

The exhortation from God. Here we look at the exhortation God gave Israel to go to war against Sihon. The exhortation was twofold. It had a precept and a promise.

774

First, the *precept*. The exhortation said to "begin to possess it [the land of the Amorites], and contend with him [Sihon, the king of the Amorites] in battle" (Deuteronomy 2:24). God does not give us blessings in a way that will make us lazy or irresponsible. As we noted earlier when looking at the Arnon River, privilege is not apart from responsibility. And responsibility often requires hard work. It certainly did here. The blessing of the possessing the land required considerable effort by the Israelites. God will give it to them, but they must "possess" it and "contend" for it. God may give you talent, but you must practice to develop that talent. God may call you to preach, but you will have to study to preach good sermons.

Second, the *promise*. The promise about going to battle against Sihon was most encouraging. God promised, "This day will I begin to put the dread of thee and the fear of thee upon the nations that are under the whole heaven, who shall hear report of thee, and shall tremble, and be in anguish because of thee" (Deuteronomy 2:25). Any athlete knows that if you enter the game afraid of your opponent, you are not going to play well. It will destroy your spirit. God brought upon Israel's enemies a great fear that caused them to tremble before Israel and thus made them easier prey for Israel. It was simply one way in which God enabled Israel to do their job. Our tasks may be very formidable, but with God working for us, we will accomplish much in spite of our weaknesses. The precept may seem very difficult and discouraging, but the promise will encourage us that we can do it.

The eradication of the people. Rejecting the peace envoy, Sihon "came out against us, he and all his people, to fight at Jahaz" (Deuteronomy 2:32). Israel then contended with them as God had commanded, and Israel "utterly destroyed the men, and women, and little ones, of every city, we left none to remain . . . there was not one city too strong for us, the LORD our God delivered all unto us" (Deuteronomy 2:34, 36). This was a great victory for Israel. The greatness of it is emphasized in "not one city was too strong for us." This is the kind of victory that always comes when we obey God as Israel did here. Israel obeyed the precept and so obtained the promise. When we obey we will not find any difficulty, any temptation, any task "too strong for us." That is one of the great blessings of obedience. Things may look "too strong for us"; but if we do as God said, they will be overcome.

The endowment of goods. "The cattle we took for a prey unto ourselves, and the spoil of the cities" (Deuteronomy 2:35). To the victor goes the spoils. For Israel that meant cattle from the country and other riches from the cities. Spiritually there are spoils for the victors, too. They, however, are not measured so much in material assets (which will disappoint the carnal) as they are in spiritual possessions. But the blessings are worth all the effort and sacrifice we may have to experience in order to gain the victory.

The exaltation for victory. "The LORD our God delivered him before us" (Deuteronomy 2:33). After the victory, Moses gave due credit to God for the victory. Men are so prone to congratulate and exalt themselves after some great achievement. But not Moses. He knew the source of victory and gave proper credit to God. We need to do likewise if we expect to gain victory in the future over other foes.

2. The War with Og

After Sihon was defeated, "Og the king of Bashan came out against us, he and all his people, to battle at Edrei" (Deuteronomy 3:1). The war with Og was similar to the war with Sihon. We see this when we note the message from God, the might of the victory, the merchandise from the victory, and the magnifying for the victory.

The message from God. "The LORD said unto me, Fear him not: for I will deliver him, and all his people, and his land, into thy hand; and thou shalt do unto him as thou didst unto Sihon king of the Amorites, which dwelt at Heshbon" (Deuteronomy 3:2). As with the exhortation before the war with Sihon, so it is here with the message before the war with Bashan—there was both a precept and a promise in it.

First, the *precept*. "Fear not" was the precept this time. With Sihon there was also fear mentioned in the exhortation, but it was the announcement that Sihon's troops would be fearful of Israel. The message here, however, concerns the fear in Israel. The message suited the situation, for Israel could easily fear going against Og because Og was a big man. He was giant whose "bedstead was a bedstead of iron . . . nine cubits was the length thereof, and four cubits the breadth of it" (Deuteronomy 3:11). He was a Goliath in size. Thirty-eight years earlier, the Israelites were greatly distressed by the news that the land of Canaan was a land with giants in it (Numbers 13:31–33) and concluded they could not, therefore, go up into the land to possess it. Now facing Og meant they were going against a giant; and, therefore, God gave them the precept to "fear not."

We will face many giants in the Christian walk. We will face giant needs and giant problems and difficulties which to the flesh are too great to overcome. But God tells us not to fear these giants. And when He says not to fear, we do not need to fear.

Second, the *promise*. "I will deliver him, and all his people, and all his land, into thy hand" (Deuteronomy 3:2). Again God's promise was given to help do the precept. Let us never forget this fact. Promises are not something to just look at. They are to be used to serve God. Promises are given to encourage and inspire service.

The might of the victory. "And we smote him until none was left . . . we took all his cities . . . there was not a city which we took not from them . . . All these cities were fenced with high walls, gates, and bars: beside unwalled towns a great many . . . we utterly destroyed them" (Deuteronomy 3:3–6). As it was in the war with Sihon, so it was in the war with Og—great victory

777

was achieved. Multitudes were slain and all the municipalities were captured. The might of the victory is emphasized by the description of some of the cities. They were "fenced with high walls, gates, and bars" (Deuteronomy 3:5); but they were still conquered. God does not give us many easy assignments. He often gives us hard assignments with "high walls, gates, and bars" to overcome so He can display His great power in helping us to successfully do our assignments.

The merchandise from the victory. Again, as was the case with the war against Sihon, Israel came away with much spoils of victory. "All the cattle, and the spoil of the cities, we took for a prey [prize of war] to ourselves" (Deuteronomy 3:7). When we obey the Lord, the spoils of victory will be ever increasing. We will add the spoils from Og to the spoils from Sihon. Let not God's people walk in spiritual poverty. They may not walk in material affluence, but no saint of God should ever walk in spiritual poverty. Spiritual poverty is a product of disobedience. But spiritual affluence is a produce of obedience.

The magnifying for the victory. "So the LORD our God delivered into our hands Og also, the king of Bashan, and all his people" (Deuteronomy 3:3). Again, as he did after the victory over Sihon, Moses gives the credit for the great victory over Og to God. How proper to give God credit. Once we stop doing that, we will cease to accomplish much for Him. Therefore, see that you give due honor to God for all your victories.

C. THE PROTECTING OF GILEAD

Satan is always trying to take away from God's people the things which God gives them. He did this in regards to Israel and Gilead. Satan tried to dispossess Israel of the land of Gilead shortly after they had won victories over Sihon and Og. In trying to dispossess Israel of Gilead, Satan particularly worked through the Moabites and the Midianites; but Israel's land was successfully protected from this attack. To study the protection of Gilead, we will divide our study into four parts: Balak, Balaam, beauties, and battle.

1. Balak

"And Balak the son of Zippor saw all that Israel had done to the Amorites. And Moab was sore afraid of the people, because they were many: and Moab was distressed because of the children of Israel" (Numbers 22:2,3). Balak was the "king of the Moabites at that time" (Numbers 22:4), and he and the people were very upset and fearful about the great victories Israel and gained over Sihon and Og. Balak's desire about Israel was to "drive them out of the land" (Numbers 22:6) of Gilead. He was the human kingpin in the effort to dispossess Israel of Gilead. To examine Balak's attempt to get Israel out of Gilead, we will note the advantage, attitude, ally, and appeal of Balak.

The advantage of Balak. Satan is clever. In his effort to dispossess Israel of Gilead, he began his attack through a nation that Israel was forbidden to war against (Deuteronomy 2:9). Frequently Satan attacks this way. It is like the Viet Cong soldiers in the Vietnam war who would grab a woman or child and hold the woman or child in front of them as a shield so our troops could not shoot at the Viet Cong soldiers without killing a woman or child. Satan attempts to shield many of his schemes with that which is good. Hence, if we attack ecumenical evangelism, we will look like we are attacking evangelism. Dissidents in church know how to work this advantage to perfection. If we attack them, we are certain to be accused of attacking some good cause under which they have hidden their attack. As an example, they will oppose some proposed new local ministry under the guise that we need to do more for missions. So if you attack them, you are attacking missions. God's people need to be alert to this devious method of Satan.

The attitude of Balak. Balak's attitude towards the Jews was fundamentally wrong. He wanted Israel to be cursed (Numbers

779

22:6,17; 23:7,11,13). He wanted Israel dispossessed from the land God had given Israel. We have had many Balaks in our world over the years. They have cursed Israel and do not want Israel to have the land God gave them. This is a fatal attitude. No nation will prosper whose attitude towards Israel is like Balak's attitude. World War II saw the terrible destruction upon Hitler and Germany because of this attitude. Many nations over the past in both ancient and present history have experienced God's judgment because of Balak's attitude. Today, we witness Balak's attitude towards Jews in our own country and in the United Nations and among the Arabs. Such an attitude, if not checked, will ultimately end in judgment from God. Israel is God's chosen people. God has given them the land of Palestine. Those who oppose Israel oppose God. This does not mean we should sanction the unsavory conduct of the Jews, nor does it mean we must sanction their rejection of Christ. What it means is that we must honor the Word of God regarding Israel, or we risk the anathema of God.

The ally of Balak. Balak and the Moabites had the Midianites as an ally. They were very close allies. This is seen in several ways. It is seen in the fact that when Balak became upset about the Israelites, he and other Moabite officials quickly counselled with the Midianites. "And Moab said unto the elders of Midian, Now shall this company lick up all that are round about us" (Numbers 22:4). It is also seen in the fact that when Balak sent to Balaam to try and obtain his prophetic services to curse Israel, Balak sent both "the elders of Moab and the elders of Midian" (Numbers 22:7) to visit Balaam. The ally arrangement between Moab and Midian was an especially bad arrangement for the Midianites. Because of their involvement in this animosity towards Israel, the Midianites later suffered a terrible slaughter from the Israelites at the command of God—a slaughter we will look at in more detail later in this chapter. The lesson is that the Midianites were allies with the wrong people. Take care, therefore, whom you chose as friends and close companions. A bad friend can be your ruin as it was with the Midianites.

The appeal of Balak. Balak's scheme to dispossess Israel of Gilead was to first get the prophet Balaam to curse Israel for him (Numbers 22:6). Balaam, whose home was in Pethor (Numbers 22:5) by the Euphrates River in Mesopotamia, was a famous prophet in that day (we will see more about him shortly); and Balak felt confident that Balaam could help Moab get rid of the Israelites. So he sent a delegation to Balaam to request his services. The delegation was made up of elders from both Moab and their ally Midian (Numbers 22:7).

Balak's appeal to Balaam is a good picture of how temptation works. Therefore, to examine this appeal, we will view it from the standpoint of temptation. We will note eight similarities between the appeal by Balak and the temptations of sin.

First, the *dignity* of the appeal. Balak sent honorable messengers to Balaam to try and convince him to come and curse Israel. He sent the "elders" of Moab and Midian (Numbers 22:7); and when that failed, "Balak sent yet again princes, more, and more honorable than they" (Numbers 22:15). Temptation also works this way. It likes to solicit from an impressive position in society. Advertisers illustrate this practice; for they use the famous and those in high positions of the land to advertise their product because it gets people to buy the product quicker than if some lowly, unknown person advertised it. So evil uses professors with a string of degrees behind their name to advocate evolution, churches are used to approve of homosexualism, governments are used to approve of gambling and abortion, and fundamental preachers are used to promote divorce. All of this makes temptation effective.

Second, the *flattery* of the appeal. Balak flattered Balaam in trying to obtain his services. He said, "I wot [know] that he whom thou blessest is blessed, and he whom thou cursest is cursed" (Numbers 22:6). The statement told Balaam that he was very esteemed by Balak. The statement was a very high compliment, and it would cause him to give Balak's envoy a more wel-

comed reception. Evil often uses flattery when it wants to seduce you. The writer of Proverbs notes this especially about the
harlot. "With her much fair speech she caused him to yield, with
the flattering of her lips she forced him" (Proverbs 7:21). Since
"a flattering mouth worketh ruin" (Proverbs 26:28), we should
be very cautious when people flatter us and put no stock in their
words.

Third, the *rewards* of the appeal. Balak offered some
impressive rewards. He sent his envoy with "rewards of divina-
tion [fees for prophesying] in their hand" (Numbers 22:7) and
promised to "promote thee unto very great honor" (Numbers
22:17). Temptation likes to work this way, for it often offers
rewards of possessions and positions, and it causes many to
yield to the temptation of sin. An increased salary and higher
position on the job have caused many to decrease their attendance at church. Many are the sports heroes who have ditched
worship on Sundays for games and money. But the rewards of
sin are not lasting and only defile and destroy.

Fourth, the *persistency* of the appeal. Balak was very persistent in appealing to Balaam. The persistency of the appeal is
seen in several ways. It is seen first of all in the *repeating of the
invitation*. Balaam did not at first accept the invitation from
Balak. But Balak did not give up. Instead "Balak sent yet again
princes, more, and more honorable" (Numbers 22:15) to Balaam
to try to get him to accept the invitation to curse Israel. The persistency of the appeal is also seen in the *changing of the views*
Balak gave Balaam of Israel after Balaam had accepted Balak's
invitation to come to Balak. When Balaam came to Balak, he
was taken to Kirjath-huzoth (Numbers 22:39) to view Israel.
When this did not cause Balaam to curse Israel, then Balak took
him to the top of Pisgah (Numbers 23:14). When this did not
work either, Balak then took Balaam to the top of Peor (Numbers 23:28) to view Israel from still another place. To defeat
temptation you will be required to repeatedly say, "No!" If you
are going to walk victoriously against sin, you will have to be as
persistent as sin. Dedication wins the victory, but lack of dedica-

tion will soon lead to defilement.

Fifth, the *rebuke* of the appeal. "And Balak said unto Balaam, What hast thou done unto me? I took thee to curse mine enemies, and, behold, thou hast blessed them altogether" (Numbers 23:11, cp. Numbers 22:37 and 24:10). When Balaam did not perform in the way Balak wanted him to perform, Balak severely rebuked Balaam. No one likes to be rebuked or criticized. Temptation knows that fact and uses it at times to try and coerce the tempted into yielding. If compliments do not seduce, then criticism is tried. Balak tried several times through sharp criticism to cause Balaam to yield to Balak's wishes. Many folk have capitulated to temptation when the barbs of rebuke and criticism have been jabbed at the tempted.

Sixth, the *compromise* of the appeal. "And Balak said unto Balaam, Neither curse them at all, nor bless them at all" (Numbers 23:25). When Balaam kept blessing Israel instead of cursing them, Balak resorted to compromise. If Balaam will not curse Israel, then Balak asks that he not bless Israel, either. It is the practice of sin that says if you will not criticize godliness, don't praise it, either. Of course, if we cease to praise goodness, we will eventually end up criticizing it. But temptation does not tell you that fact.

Seventh, the *ostracizing* of the appeal. When Balaam still refused to do as Balak said, Balak then said to Balaam, "Therefore now flee thou to thy place" (Numbers 24:11). Rejection is often an effective tool of temptation. Many folk have given up the fight against evil in a church when threatened with excommunication. Some have yielded to sin when loss of friendship is threatened. Others have given up the fight against evil when they have been threatened to be kicked out of their home.

Eighth, the *mixing* of the appeal. Balak tried to associate God with his evil in his attempt to get Balaam to curse Israel. This is especially seen in Balak's statement, "I thought to promote thee unto great honor; but, lo, the LORD hath kept thee back from honor" (Numbers 24:11). Because Balaam would not curse Israel, Balak claimed that God would now not honor Balaam. What a wicked mixing of God with evil this was! But this is the habitual practice of sin and temptation. It craftily mixes evil with religion to make evil look acceptable. The German Nazis, as an example, had "God with us" inscribed on their belt buckles in an attempt to mix God with the vileness of the Nazi creed to make it look acceptable. In our churches, mixing is a common method used to seduce churches into corruption. Ecumenical evangelism would mix apostasy with fundamentalism which, of course, will only corrupt fundamentalism. Large and impressive movements rise up periodically under the guise of spiritual renewal which in truth are only movements to mix truth with error, to mix bad doctrine with good doctrine. Many are deceived by this crafty and destructive mixing practice.

2. Balaam

Balaam, the prophet that Balak hired to curse Israel, has a good bit of interesting and instructive material written about him in Scripture. Three chapters of Scripture are written about Balaam in the book of Numbers, and he is spoken of three times in the New Testament in a significant way beside being mentioned in some other places in the Old Testament. Balaam could be a extended study by himself, but our look at him will of necessity be brief. We look at him because of his involvement in the need Moses had for protecting Gilead from the enemy. In our study of Balaam, we will look at his desire, donkey, declarations, doctrine, and death.

The desire of Balaam. Balaam had two strong desires. They had to do with gain and the grave, and they were very opposed to each other.

First, the desire for *gain.* When Balak invited Balaam to come to Moab to curse the Israelites, the Numbers' account hints that Balaam did some squirming. He tried to make it appear that he was not interested in money (Numbers 22:18; 24:12,13), but actually he was very much interested in money. We are plainly informed in II Peter 2:15 of that desire. Peter said Balaam "loved the wages of unrighteousness." Balaam wanted to appear to have high standards; but when you flashed money in front of him, he was moved inside. Many are like that in every age. They have a price, but they do not have principles. They talk principles; but when the price is right, they give priority to price not principles.

Second, the desire for a respectable *grave*. In his first prophecy before Balak, Balaam said, "Let me die the death of the righteous, and let my last end be like his!" (Numbers 23:10). These are noble words indeed. But Balaam had a problem here—though he wanted to die like the righteous, he did not want to live like the righteous. Dying like the righteous, however, is inseparably related to living like the righteous. "A man's death is in keeping with a man's life. You cannot have a tropical sunset in an arctic zone" (D. Davies). You cannot live a life of the vice and expect to die the death of the virtuous. To die in honor, you must live honorably.

Balaam's opposing desires are seen in many folk who come to church. They want to appear pious and gain the blessings of piety, but they do not want to subdue the passions of the flesh. They want get the best of both worlds; they want to play both sides of the street. But it is an impossible act, for "no man can serve two masters: for either he will hate the one, and love the other; or else he will hold to the one, and despise the other" (Matthew 6:24).

The donkey of Balaam. Probably the most famous incident in Balaam's life had to do with his very unusual donkey ride. It occurred after the second invitation from Balak. Balaam had turned down the first invitation from Balak; but when a second envoy was sent to him and they were higher ranked men (Numbers 22:15), Balaam said he would pray about the matter again (Numbers 22:19). His wanting to pray about the matter gave Balaam's heart away. God had already told him in no uncertain terms that what Balak wanted Balaam to do was evil (Numbers 22:12). You do not have to pray again about something that is evil. But the appeal of earthly honor and monetary gain were too much for Balaam to refuse, and so he again went to the Lord—obviously hoping the Lord would change his mind.

God answered Balaam's prayer by giving Balaam permission to go. This answer did not sanction evil but was another case where God in judgment gave a person what they wanted. Then came the incident with the donkey. Shortly after Balaam began his trip, he met up with "the angel of the LORD" (Numbers 22:22) with a sword in his hand; for "God's anger was kindled because he went" (Ibid.). The donkey saw the angel and the sword, but Balaam did not. The donkey refused to continue on the path which caused Balaam to do some smiting of the donkey. The donkey then talked to Balaam. Eventually Balaam got his eyes open to what the donkey was seeing. Peter said, "The dumb ass speaking with man's voice forbad the madness of the prophet" (II Peter 2:16). The donkey had more sense and discernment than did Balaam. But when a man is blinded by a passion for the things of the world, he will lose much discernment and act worse than animals. Jeremiah said that the people of his day were this way. "Yea, the stork in the heaven knoweth her appointed times; and the turtle [dove] and the crane and the swallow observe the time of their coming; but my people know not the judgment of the LORD" (Jeremiah 8:7).

After getting his eyes opened, Balaam acknowledged his sin (Numbers 22:34). But notice the remark Balaam made after his acknowledgement of sin which revealed that his acknowledgement of sin was not a sincere repentance of his sin—"If it displease thee, I will get me back again" (Ibid.). Of course, it displeased the Lord—that was the reason for the angel of the Lord and the sword! Balaam's question was so stupid. But that comes when the heart is set on doing evil. In judgment upon Balaam, God let Balaam go on to Balak. This led to Balaam's ruin. God judges many folk in this way. Beware that you do not get so persistent in your disobedience that God lets you have your way, for it will not be long before you will loath your way, and it will ruin you.

The declarations of Balaam. Scripture records four separate prophetic declarations which Balaam gave to Balak. One declaration was given at Kirjath-huzoth, one from the top of Pisgah, and two from the top of Peor. These declarations are filled with great and wonderful truths which could be a great study in themselves. They spoke of such things as Israel's protection, Israel's great future, and Israel's coming Messiah. "How shall I curse, whom God hath not cursed? or how shall I defy, whom the LORD hath not defied? (Numbers 23:8); "He hath not beheld iniquity in Jacob, neither hath he seen perverseness in Israel: the LORD his God is with him" (Numbers 23:21); "Blessed is he that blesseth thee, and cursed is he that curseth thee" (Numbers 24:9); and "There shall come a Star out of Jacob, and a Scepter shall rise out of Israel . . . Out of Jacob shall come he that shall have dominion" (Numbers 24:17,19) are a few of the great statements in Balaam's declarations.

Yes, Balaam had quite a message. But he is a great warning for us; for while he sounded so wonderful at times, yet his message was not real in his heart. He just mouthed words. We see the truth of this insincerity next as we look at his doctrine.

The doctrine of Balaam. What did Balaam really believe? His real creed was corruption. His high sounding declarations were not his creed at all. After the great prophetic declarations, Balaam gave some advice to Balak on the side. It was terrible advice. It was immoral advice. It was the doctrine of Balaam. "The doctrine of Balaam . . . [which he] taught Balak [was] to cast a stumblingblock before the children of Israel, to eat things sacrificed unto idols, and to commit fornication" (Revelation 2:14). Moses' comment about this doctrine and its great peril was as follows: "These [women] caused the children of Israel, through the counsel of Balaam, to commit trespass against the LORD" (Numbers 31:16). Balaam's doctrine was the doctrine of the lust of the flesh. It was to be the rule of one's life. The stomach and sex were the two appetites of the flesh especially cited in the Revelation text that Balaam stressed.

We have many today even in church circles who embrace the doctrine of Balaam. In apostate circles this doctrine of the flesh advocates acceptance of such perverted fleshly appetites as homosexuality. In fundamental circles, this doctrine advocates acceptance of divorce which is nothing but giving way to the lust of the flesh. And all it does is destroy. Like Balaam, many pulpits of our fundamental churches give forth some wonderful declarations. But when they start counseling, divorce is accepted and unsavory marriages are encouraged.

The death of Balaam. Later we will see Israel going to battle against the Midianites to help protect Gilead. When they did, "Balaam also the son of Beor they slew with the sword" (Numbers 31:8). Though Balaam wanted to die the death of the righteous, he died the death of the reprobate. He died in ignominy. There was nothing honorable about his death. He kept company with the wicked and received wages and honor from them. When judgment came upon the wicked, he was included in it. What a shameful life was the life of Balaam. His life has been held up for some three millenniums ever since as an example of how not to live. In our day, there are a multitude of people just like him. They are the darlings of the world—famous, talented, and the world has paid them big money to perform. But when it is all over, they will be an illustration of shame, not nobility.

3. Beauties
"And Israel abode in Shittim, and the people began to commit whoredom with the daughters of Moab" (Numbers 25:1). The attempt to dispossess Israel of Gilead takes a different approach now. Balak could not get Israel cursed by Balaam's prophetic utterances, but he did get Israel corrupted by following Balaam's advice (Numbers 31:16). It was an indirect method of cursing Israel. To examine this scheme, we will note the seducing by women, the sacrificing to idols, the sentencing for sin, the scorning by sinners, and the spearing of evil.

The seducing by women. After his prophetic utterances in which he failed to curse Israel, Balaam, who had his eye on those rewards of Balak, instructed Balak on how to corrupt Israel, as we noted above. He "taught Balak to cast a stumbling-block before the children of Israel, to eat things sacrificed unto idols, and to commit fornication" (Revelation 2:14). The plan to corrupt Israel was to have Moabite girls seduce the Israelite men into immoral conduct (and to idolatry which we will note next). Unfortunately the plan worked very well. Many Israelite men fell for the trap and "began to commit whoredom with the daughters of Moab" (Numbers 25:1).

This failure of Israel certainly gives a strong warning to God's people about the peril of courting the unsaved. The devil will always see to it that there are plenty of attractive men and women available for God's people if they want them. Christian young people will seldom be without the temptation to go with an unsaved person. But once a Christian starts going with an unsaved, he is walking on very thin ice morally. It has been the ruin of multitudes. Going with the unsaved is to date with defilement, court with corruption, romance with ruin, and flirt with foulness.

The sacrificing to idols. "They called the people unto the sacrifices of their gods; and the people did eat, and bowed down to their gods. And Israel joined himself unto Baal-peor" (Numbers 25:2, 3). As Balaam had taught Balak to counsel his people, the Moabite women not only got the Israelites to commit "whoredom" with them, but they also got the Israelites to worship with them. Bad women lead to bad worship. King Solomon is a notorious example of one being led away from God this way. Solomon had many women who were idol worshippers, and they "turned away his heart after other gods" (I Kings 11:4). But though the illustrations and commands are plain and frequent in Scripture, many of God's people still ignore the warnings and go after the unsaved. The results are tragic both morally and spiritually.

The sentencing for sin. "The anger of the LORD was kindled against Israel" (Numbers 25:3). The anathema of God was upon Israel for their unholy morals and unholy worship. Therefore, "the Lord said unto Moses, Take all the heads of the people, and hang them up before the LORD against the sun, that the fierce anger of the LORD may be turned away from Israel" (Numbers 25:4). We can just hear the compromisers gasp at the severity of the sentence. But holiness will not gasp. It knows how destructive sin is, that hell is the destiny for multitudes because of this sort of evil, and that firm action must be taken to stop it. Moses did not argue with God, for Moses knew God well, and he also knew the work of sin well. Therefore, "Moses said unto the judges of Israel, Slay ye every one his men that were joined unto Baal-peor" (Numbers 25:5). The sentence on the sin was severe, but the sin was very serious and deserved it. Literally slaying people is not always necessary in order to combat these evils earnestly, but earnestness is always necessary if we are going to combat them successfully.

The scorning by sinners. "And, behold, one of the children of Israel came and brought unto his brethren a Midianitish woman in the sight of Moses, and in the sight of all the congregation of the children of Israel, who were weeping before the door of the tabernacle of the congregation" (Numbers 25:6). We never cease to be amazed at the shamelessness of sinners. When many of the Israelites came to the Tabernacle to mourn over the corruption which had come in Israel, one of the offending Israelites brashly brings his unholy woman with him to the area. You would think that sinners would keep their shameful conduct behind closed doors. But that is not the nature of gross evil. This couple in our text and many in our day are like the Israelites in Jeremiah's day of whom Jeremiah said, "Were they ashamed when they had committed abominations? nay, they were not at all ashamed, neither could they blush" (Jeremiah 8:12). Sinners often seem to take pride in how far they can go in strutting their shameful living. Unholy couples often come to church services together in defiance of opposition to their dirty living. In society we witness more and more "gay" parades in which homosexuals in utter shamelessness strut their perverted morals. How terribly sin debases the sinner.

The spearing of evil. "When Phinehas, the son of Eleazar, the son of Aaron the priest, saw it, he rose up from among the congregation, and took a javelin in his hand; And he went after the man of Israel into the tent, and thrust both of them through, the man of Israel, and the woman through her belly. So the plague was stayed from the children of Israel" (Numbers 25:7,8). Phinehas was the hero in stopping evil. His actions were really pronounced, but they were needed. The value of this action by Phinehas, though criticized by the carnal crowd, was that it stopped the plague that had come upon the Israelites for their sin. Twenty-four thousand Israelites had already died in the plague (Numbers 25:9). While people who would go easy on sin stand in horror of Phinehas' actions, they need to be reminded that it stopped the plague that was killing thousands.

We need a lot of spearing in our land today. We are not talking about literal spears, but about spears of laws, punishment of criminals, and discipline in the home and church. If we did some sanctified spearing of such things as homosexualism, we could stop the plague of AIDS. But the powers that be are not about to take any action against homosexualism. Hence, AIDS continues to kill multitudes. If we speared abortion, criminals, juvenile delinquents, the immoral, and other evils through laws, better court decisions, etc., we would stop a lot of evil and stop the plagues that curse our society. Those who oppose strong action against sin simply refuse to recognize that either we spear sin or sin spears others. Either we kill the murderer or he will kill others.

Phinehas was rewarded by God for his strong stand against sin by being given an "everlasting priesthood" (Numbers 25:13). The world may criticize Phinehas, but God will compliment him. The world may abhor, but God will applaud. The world may rebuke, but God will reward. Let our actions be the kind that please God and the kind that God will honor.

4. Battle

"And the LORD spake unto Moses, saying, Vex the Midianites, and smite them; for they vex you with their wiles, wherewith they have beguiled you" (Numbers 25:16–18). This is the battle to protect Gilead for Israel, and it is the last battle that Moses will oversee, for Scripture says, "Avenge the children of Israel of the Midianites: afterward shalt thou be gathered unto thy people" (Numbers 31:2). To examine this battle, we will note the people to battle, the problem in battle, and the prey from the battle.

The people to battle. It is instructive to note that God said to fight the Midianites, not the Moabites, though the Moabites were the main cause of the problem that necessitated the battle. But God had earlier ordered Israel not to fight with Moab and that order still held. The Midianites were so intermingled with the Moabites that at times they seemed to be one people. Being so close to the Moabites caused great trouble for Midian, however. It is a good lesson about the peril of bad friends and associates, a lesson we noted earlier.

This is the first of several significant battles by Israel against the Midianites. The next great battle was during Gideon's time in which Gideon led Israel to a miraculous and mighty victory over the marauding and murderous Midianites. We will discover in our Christian lives that there are many Midianites we must occasionally fight. The Midianites represent a host of different evils. We must fight these evils not only in our personal lives but also in the church. Failure to fight these evils as God instructs us to fight them is a sure way to defilement and defeat.

The problem in battle. "And they warred against the Midianites, as the LORD commanded Moses; and they slew all the males. And they slew the kings of Midian, beside the rest of them that were slain . . . Balaam also the son of Beor they slew with the sword. And the children of Israel took all the women of Midian captives" (Numbers 31:7–9). Israel did a good job for the most part in battling the Midianites, but they were not willing to do a complete job. They killed the evil leaders, and they also killed Balaam who advocated the evil. But they went easy on the women. This upset Moses and justifiably so. He said to the soldiers, "Have ye saved all the women alive? Behold, these caused the children of Israel, through the counsel of Balaam, to commit trespass against the LORD" (Numbers 31:15,16). Moses was probably not the most popular person in camp when he railed against this saving of the Midianite women. The Israelite soldiers liked these women. They did not want to get rid of them in battle. But Moses ordered the soldiers to get rid of these women. He only let the soldiers save the virgins among the women (Numbers 31:18). None of the whores, as an example, who had seduced Israel were permitted to live. It is always difficult for the flesh to give up everything. It cries out to spare some lust, some evil habit, or some pet sin. But victory cannot be complete if we allow some seeds of evil to remain.

The prey from battle. When the battle was finished, Israel had gained much booty. God gave orders to Moses on how to divide it. The prey was divided significantly. We note this in the way it was divided among the people and among the priests.

First, the distribution to the *people.* "And divide the prey into two parts; between them that took the war upon them, who went out to battle, and between all the congregation" (Numbers 31:27). The soldiers did not get all the spoils. They must share with rest of the congregation. This is not unjust. It is the same practice that David exhorted many years later. He said "As his part is that goeth down to the battle, so shall his part be that tarrieth by the stuff: they shall part alike" (I Samuel 30:24). The support crew gets recognition by God just as much as those that go out into the actual battle. Many cannot preach or go to the mission field, but they can provide the means whereby others can. And those who provide the support will be recognized by God as well as those who go to the battlefield.

Second, the distribution to the *priests*. "And levy a tribute unto the LORD" (Numbers 31:28). Both the soldiers (Numbers 31:28,29) and the congregation (Numbers 31:30) were told to give part of their gain to the work of the Lord (in this case it would go to the priests who served the Tabernacle, see Numbers 31:29,30). When God has blessed us, we have an obligation to give to Him. God does not bless us so we can use it just for our own personal interests. He blesses us so we can promote the service of God. And giving to the Lord has a high priority. The priority of the giving to the Lord is emphasized in that this giving to the Lord was mentioned right after the prey was divided. God's part must be taken off the top. Some want to wait until all their expenses and bills are paid and then if anything is left give some of that to the Lord. But that is not God's policy. We first give to Him; then we get along on what is left.

D. THE PARTITIONING OF GILEAD

Now that the land of Gilead has been conquered from its inhabitants and has been protected from the enemy, the land is partitioned by Moses among several of Israel's tribes. To study this partitioning of the land, we will note the request, the remonstrating, the resolve, and the ratifying in the partitioning.

1. The Request

"The children of Gad and the children of Reuben came and spake unto Moses, and to Eleazar the priest, and unto the princes of the congregation, saying . . . if we have found grace in thy sight, let this land be given unto thy servants for a possession" (Numbers 32:2,5). The partitioning of the land was initiated by the request of several tribes. The tribes of Rueben and Gad (half the tribe of Manasseh will later become involved, too) recognized that Gilead was good land for their cattle. This land also included some of "the most picturesque and the most productive" (F. B. Meyer) land of the Holy Land. The tribes desired that this land be given to them rather than land on the other side of Jordan. The request was practical; and, importantly, it was asked in a good manner as "if we have found grace in thy sight" indicates. The character of the request is a pattern for any request we ask God. Our requests should represent legitimate need and should be asked with due respect to God. We have no right to dictate to Almighty God what He should or should not do. Submitting our requests to the will and grace of God does not weaken them in the slightest. Rather, it makes them more acceptable.

2. The Remonstrating

The request did not go over well with Moses at all. He was fearful that it would discourage the other Israelites if these tribes settled on the east side of the Jordan, for it would mean they would probably not be interested in going to battle with the other Israelites on the other side of Jordan. To Moses, this request represented the attitude of those who at Kadesh refused to go into the land of Canaan. (Numbers 32:7–15). He reminded them of the judgment of God upon those who rebelled at Kadesh and said, "Ye are risen up in your fathers' stead, an increase of sinful men, to augment yet the fierce anger of the LORD toward Israel" (Numbers 32:14).

One cannot blame Moses for this remonstrating with the tribes that wanted Gilead for their inheritance. The warning was needed on this occasion, for responsibilities must not be shirked. That the request was not a bad one does not negate the wisdom of Moses' concern. Better to be too cautious than not cautious enough in the matters that concern the Lord. Our problem today is that few see any harm in anything.

3. The Resolve

The tribes wanting Gilead for an inheritance were not upset by Moses' remonstrating, and that showed good character on their part. Instead of being upset, they readily volunteered to go to battle on the other side of Jordan for their fellow tribes and only come back to the land of Gilead when the land of Canaan had been conquered (Numbers 32:16–18). This resolve was noble. It said these tribes were as interested in responsibility as they were in privilege. They wanted the privilege of Gilead, but they would not forsake their responsibility of going to battle on the other side of Jordan.

We certainly could use more of that attitude in every segment of society today. Everyone wants privilege (or "rights" as it is called by many folk). But no one talks much about responsibility. They want Gilead, but do not talk to them about going over the Jordan to fight battles there. They want more pay, but they do not talk about more production. This kind is ever demanding God do more for them while they do less.

4. The Ratifying

Moses accepted this proposal of the tribes who wanted Gilead for their inheritance. But he warned them not to fail to keep the promise about going to battle with the rest of the Israelites on the other side of Jordan. In warning them, Moses made a statement that has become a very well known Scriptural text to every generation. The statement says, "Be sure your sin will find you out" (Numbers 32:23). Moses warned the tribes inheriting Gilead that if they failed to go to battle as they promised, they would not escape the judgment of their evil. The warning is universal. We cannot conceal our sin. Somewhere, sometime, somehow, it will find us out. Men in every age have tried to beat this truth, but all who have tried to beat the truth have fallen victim to it. We cannot sin with impunity.

XXXIII.

SEPULCHER IN MOAB

DEUTERONOMY 34

THE LAST MONTHS of Moses' life were filled with much work. Besides leading Israel into the possession of Gilead and then fighting off the enemies that would dispossess Israel of Gilead, he had many other assignments to fulfill. These assignments included reviewing the law for the new generation (which takes up much of the book of Deuteronomy), copying down the law in writing and giving it to the Levites for safe keeping (Deuteronomy 31:24–26), writing a new song given him by God to give to the people (Deuteronomy 31:19,22,30; 32:1–47), and then pronouncing the tribal blessing upon Israel (Deuteronomy 33). When these tasks were finished, it was then time for Moses to die and be buried in a sepulcher in Moab.

It is most commendable the way Moses finished his life. He finished it by being busy in the Lord's service. He worked full time right to the very end. Not every one has the health to work full time right to the end. But too often retirement from a secular job means no more work of any kind for the retiree, not even in God's service. Hence, many folk stop serving God long before they die. This is a great mistake; for as long as God leaves us in this world, we are to be serving Him. We may not be able to do everything that we used to do when we were younger and stronger. But we must never cease serving God as much as we are able. Let us die in the saddle. Let us not rust or rot away the last years of our life.

To study the finale of Moses' life in this the last chapter of our book, we will consider the showing for Moses (vv. 1–4), the

797

succumbing of Moses (vv. 5–7), the successor for Moses (v. 9), and the superiority of Moses (vv. 10–12).

A. THE SHOWING FOR MOSES

Just before Moses died, "the LORD showed him all the land [of Canaan]" (v. 1). To examine this special viewing of Canaan, we will note the prompting of the showing, the power for the showing, and the prohibiting after the showing of the land.

1. The Prompting of the Showing

After the securing of Gilead for several tribes, Moses "besought the Lord at that time, saying . . . I pray thee, let me go over, and see the good land that is beyond Jordan" (Deuteronomy 3:23,25). God refused this request of Moses to enter Canaan, for God would not remove the punishment given Moses earlier for striking the rock instead of speaking to it. However, this request did prompt the showing of Canaan to Moses by God from a mountain in Moab; for though God refused to let Moses go over the Jordan into Canaan to see the land, He did allow him to see the land from a mountain on the east side of Jordan. God was gracious in permitting Moses this viewing of the land, but it was still second best, and second best is never an acceptable replacement for first best. Therefore, when temptation beckons, remember the cost for yielding is never compensated for by any rewards you may gain from temptation.

2. The Power for the Showing

To view the promised land, God ordered Moses to "get thee up into this mount Abarim, and see the land which I have given unto the children of Israel" (Numbers 27:12). The specific location in the mountain range of Abarim where Moses went was "the top of Pisgah" (v. 1). There Moses had a great panorama of the land. He saw "all the land of Gilead, unto Dan, and all Naphtali, and the land of Ephraim, and Manasseh, and all the land of Judah, unto the utmost sea [Mediterranean], and the south, and the plain of the valley of Jericho, the city of palm trees, unto

Zoar" (vv. 1–3). While his location was advantageous for seeing great distances, "This wide prospect could not be surveyed by any ordinary owner of vision" (Alexander). As an example, Moses saw the Mediterranean Sea; but it is not visible from the mountains where he viewed the land. However, Scripture says, "The LORD showed him all the land" (v. 1) which implies Moses "eyes were strengthened to take in the vision of its goodliness from north to south, from east to west" (Orr). This reminds us that the natural eye is limited as to what it can see of God's goodness and that without Divine help we cannot see all that God has for us. Hence, Paul said, "Eye hath not seen, nor ear heard, neither have entered into the heart of man, the things which God hath prepared for them that love him. But God hath revealed them unto us by his Spirit" (I Corinthians 2:9,10).

3. The Prohibiting After the Showing

After Moses had seen the land, God reaffirmed to Moses that "thou shalt not go over thither" (v. 4). This had to be a bitter pill for Moses to swallow, but he took his medicine without complaint. Good people cannot read of this exclusion of Moses from the land without serious soul-searching. If Moses, the great man that he was, missed out on such a great blessing because of his sin, how much more can we, who are so much less than Moses, miss out on great blessing. Moses' exclusion from Canaan is a solemn reminder of the loss sin causes even though it be forgiven. Therefore, "Let not the ease of pardon ever tempt thee to think light of sin, or to imagine that it leaves no traces on soul or life . . . If one act of mistrustful anger laid Moses, the friend and servant of God, in the desert grave on the frontiers of the Land, what may it not do for thee?" (F. B. Meyer). Moses saw the land but could not enjoy the land. Oh, the frustration which sin can bring to one's life. Let us never look lightly upon sin, or we will experience many such judgments.

B. THE SUCCUMBING OF MOSES

After being shown the promised land, "Moses the servant of the

LORD died there in the land of Moab, according to the word of the LORD" (v. 5, see Numbers 27:13 for the command referred to in "according to the word of the LORD"). Though Moses was a very godly man and a very useful man, yet he was not exempted from dying. No one is exempted from death (unless they experience the rapture when Christ comes back for His own or unless they were Enoch or Elijah), for "it is appointed unto men once to die" (Hebrews 9:27).

Moses' death was different than the death of most people in that he knew when and where he was going to die. However, we need not envy him in that knowledge. If we were to know when and where we were going to die, it most likely would cause us to be in sadness the rest of our life. There are some things God does not tell us, and we can be glad. One of them is the time and situation of our death. We do not need to know when we are going to die, but only that we will one day die and that we need to be ready to die.

To examine Moses' death, we note the condition of Moses, the cemetery of Moses, and the crying over Moses.

1. The Condition of Moses

Two things are said in our text about the condition of Moses when he died. They have to do with his age and his aging.

First, his *age*. "Moses was an hundred and twenty years old when he died" (v. 7). This was not exceptionally old in those days. Moses' father Amram lived to be 137 years of age (Exodus 6:20), his grandfather Kohath lived 133 years (Exodus 6:18), his great-grandfather Levi lived 137 years (Exodus 6:16), and his great-great-grandfather Jacob lived 147 years (Genesis 47:28). What is significant about Moses' 120 years is the way in which his years are divided. They are divided into three distinct forty-year periods as we noted in the early part of our book. The first forty years were spent in Egypt in Pharaoh's house being raised as an adopted son of Pharaoh's daughter. The second forty years were lived in Midian (near Sinai) as a shepherd. The third forty years were spent leading Israel out of Egypt through the wilderness and finally to the land of Gilead. The first eighty years, then, were times of preparation. The first forty years were preparation in the palace; the second forty years were preparation in the pasture. After eighty years of preparation, Moses was ready to emancipate the Israelites. We often fuss over lengthy preparation times, but generally the greater the work, the greater the preparation.

Second, his *aging*. Scripture says that when Moses died, "his eye was not dim, nor his natural force abated" (v. 7). Moses was still in excellent health when he died. He had not greatly aged, and he did not even need glasses even though he was 120! His "natural force" not being "abated" indicates a "vigor [and] freshness" in his health (Gesenius). God had kept him in excellent health so he could endure the rigors of his task of leading the Israelites. The fact that he climbed a high mountain on the last day of his life attests to his good health right up to the day of his death. It is true that on his final birthday Moses said, "I am an hundred and twenty years old this day; I can no more go out and come in" (Deuteronomy 31:2). But though he had aged some, he still was in exceptionally good health for his age.

God does not see fit to bless every saint with vigorous health. Many godly people who have accomplished much for God have done so with bodies plagued with a multitude of problems. While God does not give robust health to everyone, He does, however, provide enough health for us to do the work He wants us to do. But in serving God, what matters more than the condition of our body is the consecration of our heart. We are, of course, to still take good care of our bodies; for "your body is the temple of the Holy Ghost" (I Corinthians 6:19). Many saints do not do well here at all, for they have given themselves up to their physical appetites and have paid a big price for so doing. They hurt and limit their service for God by taking poor care of their bodies.

2. The Cemetery of Moses

"And he buried him in a valley in the land of Moab, over

against Beth-peor: but no man knoweth of his sepulcher unto this day" (v. 6). To examine the interment of Moses' body, we note the covering of the body, the concealing of the body, and the contention over the body.

The covering of the body. Moses had a unique situation in his death in that it was God who buried him. This certainly gave great honor to Moses. God could have had an angel bury Moses, and that would have been very special for Moses. But God did not do that. Rather, He buried Moses Himself. And no ordinary grave digger is Almighty God!

This burying of Moses by God is a significant contrast to God's actions regarding Christ when Christ died. The contrast represents the dispensational differences between the two. Moses, who represents the law, was *buried* by God. But Christ, Who represents grace, was *raised* by God. This reminds us of what Paul said in Galatians: "For I through the law am dead to the law, that I might live unto God" (Galatians 2:19). The law kills, but Christ gives life. Hence, God buried Moses, who represents the law, but raised Christ, Who represents life.

The concealing of the body. "No man knoweth of his sepulcher unto this day" (v. 6). When God buried Moses, He did not place a prominent tombstone at the grave to mark the site. Rather, He kept the site so secret than no one has ever discovered where Moses was buried. The concealment of Moses' grave site is not hard to understand. "Is it not more than likely that, if the Lord had not concealed his grave, the valley of Beth-peor would have become a second Mecca, trodden by the feet of pilgrims from all the world? It was best to make such idolatry impossible." (F. B. Meyer). The greatness of Moses coupled with the proneness of Israel to idolatry, necessitated the concealment of the grave. God keeps some things from us because we would misuse them.

The contention over the body. In the book of Jude, we find an interesting statement concerning the body of Moses. It says, "Michael the archangel, when contending with the devil, he disputed about the body of Moses" (Jude 1:9). Little do we know of the wars that go on in the spirit world which are beyond our knowledge. But they occur. Daniel 10 gives an account of another great battle going on behind the scenes between the forces of righteousness and sin. And here in Jude we learn of a similar battle between evil and good in the spirit world—in Jude the battle had to do with the body of Moses. Details of the battle are not given us. All we know is that there was a dispute of some kind. But that tells us enough to remind us that there are great powers ever fighting truth and righteousness. The will of God will always be opposed by someone somewhere. We must remember that opposition is always certain when we serve God. But this fact must not discourage us, it should only inspire us to stronger and more persistent efforts, for God is the ultimate victor in all of these battles.

3. The Crying Over Moses

"And the children of Israel wept for Moses in the plains of Moab thirty days: so the days of weeping and mourning for Moses were ended" (v. 8). We note two things about this mourning over Moses' death. They are the regret in the mourning and the restraint in the mourning.

The regret in the mourning. It was not until Moses died that some people began to realize how important he was to Israel and how much he had done for them. Though a new generation had risen up in the wilderness to replace the old, cantankerous generation, the new generation was also guilty of not appreciating Moses as they ought and of also complaining against Moses as did the old generation. But when he died, then they mourned. How often it is that we never appreciate our blessings until we lose them. "We often underrate the living, and have to wait until they are removed from us to estimate them truly" (F. B. Meyer). We noted this same truth when Aaron died. To counter this problem, we need to be more thankful for our blessings than we are. The same goes for people whom we should revere. Do not save all the flowers for the funeral!

The restraint in the mourning. The mourning did not last forever. At the end of thirty days, the mourning "ended." That was a good thing, for mourning should not go on indefinitely. Forever standing over a grave and mourning is not productive. It accomplishes no good at all. Too much mourning, in fact, demonstrates a lack of faith in God, yea, even rebellion against God. A period of mourning is proper, but the period of mourning must cease in due time. Even for Moses the time came to stop mourning over his death.

C. THE SUCCESSOR FOR MOSES

"And Joshua the son of Nun was full of the spirit of wisdom; for Moses had laid his hands upon him: and the children of Israel hearkened unto him, and did as the LORD commanded Moses" (v. 9). Joshua was Moses' successor, and he was a great successor of Moses. Few people have had such excellent successors as did Moses. Now with the death of Moses having taken place, Joshua takes over the leadership of Israel. From verse 9, we note four things about Joshua as Moses' successor. They are the calling of Joshua, the capacity of Joshua, the character of Joshua, and the compliance to Joshua (for a more extensive study on Joshua, see author's book on Joshua).

1. The Calling of Joshua

"Moses spoke unto the LORD, saying, Let the LORD, the God of spirits of all flesh, set a man over the congregation . . . that the congregation of the LORD be not as sheep which have no shepherd. And the LORD said unto Moses, Take thee Joshua the son of Nun . . . and lay thine hand upon him" (Numbers 27:15–18). Moses had been very concerned that an able successor be appointed to replace him after he had passed away, and he expressed that concern to God. God responded by telling him to appoint Joshua as his successor.

Moses' recognition of Joshua's calling by laying his hands on Joshua in a formal service is a good pattern and principle for any day regarding Divine callings to the Lord's service. We practice this laying on of the hands at ordination services for preachers and sometimes also for missionaries. If you have a calling from God for Christian service, it will be recognized by the godly. And the godly need to demonstrate their recognition in a formal and solemn way. The public recognition service is not what determines a Divine call, of course; but it is important in declaring the call to others and in giving due honor to the calling. Christian callings are not to be treated casually or shabbily by either the called or others.

2. The Capacity of Joshua

With every calling comes the capacity to fulfill the calling. Therefore, since Joshua was given a Divine call, we are not surprised to read that Joshua is said to be "full of the spirit of wisdom" (v. 9). Matthew Henry wisely observed that Joshua needed to be full of the spirit of wisdom because he "had such a peevish people to rule, and such a politic people to conquer." The skill with which Joshua guided Israel as they crossed the Jordan and then conquered Canaan validates the fact that he was "full of the spirit of wisdom." His performance certainly was noble, and it made him a worthy successor of Moses.

God equips His servants for the task to which they are called. Joshua had a gigantic task given him by God, but God enabled him to perform it with excellence. Do not hesitate to enter your calling though you may in yourself feel most incapable of fulfilling it; for if God has called you, He will enable you. On the other hand, however, never enter a calling to which you are not called; for you will not have the ability to fulfill it. Your work will be of the flesh, not of faith.

3. The Character of Joshua

Joshua's call to replace Moses is no surprise, for Joshua had proven himself already to be a gallant and godly man. When speaking about the selection of some church officers, the Apostle Paul said, "Let these also first be proved" (I Timothy 3:10). That is a good principle in selecting any church officer or anyone for a important position. And it was followed in the selection of Joshua by God. Joshua had proven himself in the past in a number of ways to be qualified for the appointment as Moses' successor. He had proven himself to be excellent military leader in battle against the Amalekites, he had proven his concern about holiness in regards to the sin of idolatry at Sinai, he had proven his loyalty to Moses when he saw others prophesying in the camp and thought this was a revolt against Moses, and he had proven his steadfastness of faith when he was one of the twelve spies. Joshua's life demonstrates that if we want promotion to higher responsibilities, we must be faithful in the lesser responsibilities as Joshua was. If you feel left out in God's service, maybe it is because you have not been faithful in your lesser assignments.

4. The Compliance to Joshua

"The children of Israel hearkened unto him, and did as the LORD commanded Moses" (v. 9). It was good that Israel followed their new leader and complied to his orders. Had they not done that, they would not have conquered Canaan. Designated authority is necessary for society to function properly. The home, the church, the government, and any other organization or institution will never function well without designated authority. In our day we see a number of movements and philosophies which are attacking God-ordained authority in various places. Various women's movements are attacking the authority of the husband in the home. Other movements are for giving the children so much say in the home that they are literally put on the throne in place of their parents. Dissidents in church are ever attacking authority in the church by attacking the pastor. But churches will not truly thrive who do not follow their pastor well. That is why so many churches struggle on year after year and seemingly make little progress in their ministry. They, of course, blame their pastors. But most of the time the problem is that the people will not follow their pastors. In government, police are often an object of attack by those who oppose authority. In the Navy, the first thing we had drilled into us at boot camp was this matter of authority. Rank is very important in the military. You respected that, or you would soon be in big trouble. You will never win any wars if authority is not respected in the military.

D. THE SUPERIORITY OF MOSES

"And there arose not a prophet since in Israel like unto Moses" (v. 10). The book of Deuteronomy ends with a brief but inspiring eulogy of Moses. The eulogy speaks of the superiority of Moses as a prophet, a superiority that also made him "one of the greatest men who have ever lived; perhaps, all things taken together, the greatest next to Christ" (J. Orr). The superiority of Moses spoken of in this eulogy has especially to do with his acquaintance with God and his accomplishments for God.

1. His Acquaintance With God

The first thing cited in this eulogy regarding Moses' superiority is that he was a man "whom the LORD knew face to face" (v. 10). It is fitting that Moses' acquaintance with God is the first thing said about Moses' superiority; for, after all, that is the most important thing in life with any man. Moses walked very close to God as "whom the LORD knew face to face" indicates. In our study of Moses, we repeatedly witnessed him in close conversation with God. This distinguished him above others, and it will always distinguish men above others. Of course, this is not the way the world judges men. Closeness with God will be despised, not honored by the world. But God evaluates things far differently than the way the world evaluates things. In your own life, count your relationship with God as the most important thing in your life. Give great priority and importance to the times when you are alone with God in His Word and prayer.

807

2. His Accomplishments for God

The second thing cited in this eulogy regarding Moses' superiority is that he was superior "in all the signs and wonders, which the LORD sent him to do in the land of Egypt to Pharaoh, and to all his servants, and to all his land, and in all that mighty hand, and in all the great terror which Moses showed in the sight of all Israel" (vv. 10–12). Our study of Moses has been a study of tremendous accomplishments in the service of God. It is most fitting then that we should conclude our book on Moses with mention of the greatness of his work. "Leaving out of view our Lord Jesus Christ, there is no man who has left so deeply the impress of his character upon the world as the Jewish legislator. By no man have so many and such mighty works been achieved. By no man has such wise legislation been devised for the government of human society. By no man has a great national emancipation been so skillfully and successfully executed . . . The history of the Western world would have been very different from what it is, if Moses had found an early grave among the rushes of the Nile" (D. Davies).

The key to his great accomplishments for God was, of course, his acquaintance with God. The two always go together. The better your acquaintance with God, the greater your accomplishments for God. Limitations in service vanish when our acquaintance with God excels. You may bemoan your lack of abilities and opportunities for service and think your lack in these areas is what keeps you from accomplishing much for God, but the truth of the matter is that it is a poor acquaintance with God that stifles your service. Get close to the Lord in prayer and the study of His Word, and you will indeed do much for Him.

Quotation Sources

The person listed is the author of the book which follows his name unless an asterisk (*) appears after the book title. In this case the person is a contributor to the book or is quoted in the book. Our quoting a person does not mean we necessarily endorse all the beliefs, practices, or associations of that person.

Alexander, W. L. *The Pulpit Commentary (Vol. 2).* *

Binnie, W. *The Pulpit Commentary (Vol. 2).* *

Carroll, B. H. *An Interpretation of the English Bible (Vol. 1).*

Cook, F. C. *The Bible Commentary (Vol. 1).*

Davies, D. *The Pulpit Commentary (Vol. 3).* *

Delitzch, F. *Commentary on the Old Testament (Vol. 1).*

Dennett, Edward. Pink's *Gleanings in Exodus.*

Edersheim, Alfred. *The Bible History, Old Testament.*

Epp, Theodore. *Moses (Vol. 1).*

Ford, W. Herschel. *Simple Sermons on the Ten Commandments.*

Gesenius, H. W. F. *Hebrew-Ghaldee Lexicon to the Old Testament.*

Gray, J. C. *The Biblical Illustrator (Vol. 2).* *

Goodhart, C. A. *The Pulpit Commentary (Vol. 1).* *

Henry, Matthew. *Matthew Henry's Commentary on the Whole Bible (Vol. 1).*

Irvine, William C. *Heresies Exposed.*

Jamieson, Robert. *A Commentary (Vol. 1).* *

Keil, C. F. *Commentary on the Old Testament (Vol. 1).*

Luther, Martin. Keil's *Commentary on the Old Testament (Vol. 1).* *

Mackintosh, C. H. *Notes on Exodus.*

Maclaren, Alexander. *Expositions of Holy Scripture (Vol. 1).*

Meyer, F. B. *Moses, The Servant of God.* *Devotional Commentary on Exodus.*

Orr, J. *The Pulpit Commentary (Vols. 1 and 2).* *

Parker, Joseph. *Preaching Through the Bible (Vol. 1).*

Pink, Arthur W. *Gleanings in Exodus.*

Poole, Matthew. *A Commentary on the Whole Bible (Vol. 1).*

Prout, E. S. *The Pulpit Commentary (Vol. 2).**

Rawlinson, George. *The Pulpit Commentary (Vols. 1 and 8).**

Ritchie, John. *The Tabernacle in the Wilderness.*

Simeon, Charles. *Expository Outlines on the Whole Bible (Vol. 2).*

Smith, James. *Handsfuls on Purpose (Vol. 2).*

Spurgeon, Charles. *The Treasury of the Bible, O.T. (Vol. 1).*

Stevens, Charles H. *The Wilderness Journey.*

Strong, James H. *Strong's Exhaustive Concordance.*

Strauss, Lehman. *The First Person.*

Taylor, W. M. *Moses the Lawgiver.*

Thayer, J. A. *Greek-English Lexicon of the New Testament.*

Vine, W. E.` *An Expository Dictionary of Biblical Words.*

Wagner, George. *Practical Truths from Israel's Wanderings.*

Wilson, Williams. *Old Testament Word Studies.*

Winterbotham, R. *The Pulpit Commentary (Vol. 2).**

Young, Robert. *Analytical Concordance to the Bible.*

Young, D. The *Pulpit Commentary (Vol. 1).**